HANDBOOK OF POSTCOLONIAL ARCHAEOLOGY

WORLD ARCHAEOLOGICAL CONGRESS
RESEARCH HANDBOOKS IN ARCHAEOLOGY

Sponsored by the World Archaeological Congress

Series Editors:

George Nicholas (*Simon Fraser University*)
Julie Hollowell (*DePauw University*)

The World Archaeological Congress Research Handbooks in Archaeology series provides comprehensive coverage of a range of areas of contemporary interest to archaeologists. Research handbooks synthesize and benchmark an area of inquiry by providing state-of-the-art summary articles on the key theories, methods, and practical issues in the field. Guided by a vision of an ethically embedded multivocal global archaeology, the edited volumes in this series—organized and written by scholars of high standing worldwide—will provide clear, in-depth information on specific archaeological themes for advanced students, scholars, and professionals in archaeology and related disciplines.
All royalties on these volumes go to the World Archaeological Congress.

Bruno David and Julian Thomas (eds.), *Handbook of Landscape Archaeology*
Soren Blau and Douglas Ubelaker (eds.), *Handbook of Forensic Anthropology and Archaeology*
Jane Lydon and Uzma Z. Rizvi (eds.), *Handbook of Postcolonial Archaeology*

HANDBOOK OF POSTCOLONIAL ARCHAEOLOGY

Jane Lydon and Uzma Z. Rizvi

Editors

Left Coast Press Inc.

Walnut Creek, California

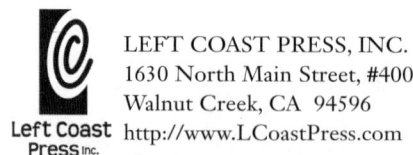

LEFT COAST PRESS, INC.
1630 North Main Street, #400
Walnut Creek, CA 94596
http://www.LCoastPress.com

Copyright © 2010 by Left Coast Press, Inc.

All rights reserved. No part of this publication may be reproduced, stored in a retrieval system, or transmitted in any form or by any means, electronic, mechanical, photocopying, recording, or otherwise, without the prior permission of the publisher.

ISBN 978-1-59874-182-7 hardcover

Library of Congress Cataloguing-in-Publication Data:
Handbook of postcolonial archaeology / Jane Lydon, Uzma Z. Rizvi, editors.
      p. cm. — (World Archaeological Congress research handbooks in archaeology)
   Includes bibliographical references and index.
   ISBN 978-1-59874-182-7 (hardcover : alk. paper)
 1. Archaeology—Social aspects—Handbooks, manuals, etc. 2. Archaeology—Political aspects—Handbooks, manuals, etc. 3. Archaeology—Moral and ethical aspects—Handbooks, manuals, etc. 4. Social archaeology—Handbooks, manuals, etc.
 5. Ethnoarchaeology—Handbooks, manuals, etc. 6. Postcolonialism. 7. Colonization—History. 8. Indigenous peoples. 9. Cultural property—Protection. 10. Archaeology—Philosophy. I. Lydon, Jane, 1965– II. Rizvi, Uzma Z., 1973–
   CC175.H36 2010
   930.1—dc22   2010019810

Printed in the United States of America

∞ The paper used in this publication meets the minimum requirements of American National Standard for Information Sciences—Permanence of Paper for Printed Library Materials, ANSI/NISO Z39.48–1992.

CONTENTS

Figures and Tables 11
Series Editors' Foreword 13
Acknowledgments 15

1: Introduction: Postcolonialism and Archaeology
Jane Lydon and Uzma Z. Rizvi 17

**PART I: The Archaeological Critique of Colonization:
Global Trajectories 35**

2: Colonialism and European Archaeology
Alfredo González-Ruibal 39

3: Near Eastern Archaeology: Imperial Pasts, Postcolonial Presents, and
the Possibilities of a Decolonized Future
Benjamin W. Porter 51

4: "Diba Jimooyung"—Telling Our Story: Colonization and Decolonization
of Archaeological Practice from an Anishinabe Perspective
Sonya Atalay 61

5: The Colonial Legacy in the Archaeology of South Asia
Dilip K. Chakrabarti 73

6: The Colonial Experience of the Uncolonized and Colonized: The Case
of East Asia, Mainly as Seen from Japan
Koji Mizoguchi 81

7: Resurrecting the Ruins of Japan's Mythical Homelands: Colonial
Archaeological Surveys in the Korean Peninsula and Heritage Tourism
Hyung Il Pai 93

8: Archaeology in Colonial and Postcolonial USSR
Pavel Dolukhanov 113

Commentaries

9: Subjectivity and Science in Postcolonial Archaeology
Ania Loomba 125

10: Archaeology Enters the 21st Century
Thomas C. Patterson 133

PART II: Archaeological Narratives of Colonialism 141

11: Writing New Archaeological Narratives: Indigenous North America
Stephen W. Silliman 145

12: The Archaeology of Historical Indigenous Australia
Alistair Paterson 165

13: Liberation, and Emancipation: Constructing a Postcolonial Archaeology of the African Diaspora
Theresa A. Singleton 185

14: Encounters with Postcolonialism in Irish Archaeology
Charles E. Orser, Jr. 199

15: An Africa-Informed View of Postcolonial Archaeologies
Peter R. Schmidt and Karega Munene 215

Commentaries

16: The Archaeological Survey of India and the Science of Postcolonial Archaeology
Ashish Chadha 227

17: Shades of the Colonial
O. Hugo Benavides 235

PART III: Addressing/Redressing the Past: Restitution, Repatriation, and Ethics 241

18: Repatriation in the United States: The Current State of NAGPRA
Jon Daehnke and Amy Lonetree 245

19: Repatriation: Australian Perspectives
Michael Green and Phil Gordon 257

20: Australian and International Perspectives on Native Title, Archaeology, and the Law
    Peter Veth 267

21: Cultural Property: Internationalism, Ethics, and Law
    Alexander A. Bauer 285

22: New Museological Ways of Seeing the World: Decolonizing Archaeology in Lebanese Museums
    Lina G. Tahan 295

   Commentaries

23: The Global Repatriation Debate and the New "Universal Museums"
    Magnus Fiskesjö 303

24: Efficacy of "Emic" and "Etic" in Archaeology and Heritage
    Joost Fontein 311

PART IV: Colonial and Postcolonial Identities **323**

25: Gender and Sexuality
    Louise Ströbeck 327

26: Cultural Identity, and Colonial and Postcolonial Archaeologies
    Sarah Croucher 351

27: Class Identity and Postcolonialism
    Gavin Lucas 365

28: Race and Class
    Paul R. Mullins 375

Commentaries

29: An Archaeologist Finds Her Voice: A Commentary on Colonial and Postcolonial Identities
    Whitney Battle-Baptiste 387

30: Archaeology, Ancestral Bodies, and Native American Identity in the New Millennium: Commentary on Colonial and Postcolonial Identities
    John Norder 393

PART V: Strategies of Practice: Implementing the Postcolonial Critique 401

31: Community Heritage and Partnership in Xcalakdzonot, Yucatán
Fernando Armstrong-Fumero and Julio Hoil Gutierrez 405

32: Partnership Archaeology and Indigenous Ancestral Engagement in Torres Strait, Northeastern Australia
Liam Brady and Joe Crouch 413

33: Archaeological Practice at the Cultural Interface
Martin Nakata and Bruno David 429

34: Ethnographic Interventions
Lynn Meskell 445

35: Colonialism, Conflict, and Connectivity: Public Archaeology's Message in a Bottle
Sandra Scham 459

Commentaries

36: Public Interest Anthropology: A Model for Engaged Research Tied to Action
Peggy Reeves Sanday 471

37: Cultural Resources Management, Public Archaeology and Advocacy
Carol McDavid and Fred McGhee 481

38: Epilogue: Postcolonialism and Archaeology
Uzma Z. Rizvi and Jane Lydon 495

Index 505

About the Contributors 513

For Roy and Dash, both younger than this book.
For Amma and her refusal to speak to me in English.

FIGURES AND TABLES

FIGURES

3.1: The Palestine Exploration Fund's surveyor and local assistant measure distances from a fixed point. 51
3.2: Under the supervision of PACE, Palestinians clean Mar Ubadia, an ancient church located in the Palestinian village of Aboud. 55
4.1: Dioramic scene of two people carving on stone at entrance of the "Diba Jimooyung" exhibit. 61
4.2: Petroglyphs at the Sanilac site depicting an archer. 62
4.3: Stone at Sanilac in the form of a spiral carving. 62
7.1: Professor Sekino Tadashi of Tokyo Imperial University surveying pagodas in Korea (ca. 1932). 98
7.2: Imperial family relatives taking official tourist commemoration portrait in front of Sŏkkuram after reconstruction, October 1935. 102
7.3: Japanese archaeologists assisting Prince Gustaf of Sweden at Sobongch'ong. 102
12.1: Map of Australia with locations mentioned in chapter indicated. 167
12.2: Nineteenth century dark olive flaked glass bottle base, and conjoined baseflakes, Strangways Springs contact site, Central Australia. 173
12.3: Aboriginal historical rock engravings, Inthanoona contact site, Western Australia. 174
20.1: Determinations of Native Title. 270
32.1: Map of Torres Strait showing location of Kibu. 419
32.2: Discovery of the Ikis turtleshell mask on Badu in 2001; Ikis turtleshell mask; piece of decorated turtleshell (probably from a headdress). 420
32.3: Celebration at Goba's father's grave on Mua in 2002; black and white computer tracing of the rock-art panel depicting Goba climbing between two palm trees; traditional dancing at the Goba celebration. 422

TABLE

7.1: Chronology of Heritage Management in Japan and Korea and Tourist Industry. 94

SERIES EDITORS' FOREWORD

George Nicholas and Julie Hollowell

A broad synthesis of ideas and practices related to archaeology's varied encounters with postcolonialism, which this timely volume represents, has been long overdue. The topics central to this discourse—unequal power relations, issues of race, class, and identity, essentialism, scientific colonialism, collaboration, globalization, multivocality, subjectivity, and resistance, among many others—reflect a deep and nuanced history of archaeology's engagement with the colonial project in different parts of the world. The emergence of critical discourse, of community-based initiatives, and of more equitable relations in the production and distribution of knowledge, all signal an acknowledgment that archaeology is not simply about interpreting the past, but is deeply implicated with contemporary people, places, politics, and practices. These stirrings in archaeology also respond to the postcolonial critique coming from anthropology, cultural studies, literary criticism, and, most especially, from those affected by the ideas and actions of archaeology and archaeologists in all places and times.

Archaeology has never been a politically neutral enterprise. In many parts of the world, the history of archaeological practice is inextricably linked to colonialism. Its practitioners (both amateur and professional) have appropriated, possessed, and controlled someone else's cultural heritage, often in the name of colonialism. Yet over the past decade, much has been written about "decolonizing archaeology." The promotion of truly collaborative research practices and benefit sharing, the inclusion of non-Western epistemologies and local community values, exploration of the relationships between tangible and intangible heritage, recognition of the breadth and depth of scientific colonialism, and the continuing explication of culture-based rights are but a few of the topics that figure prominently here.

Today we find archaeology grappling with postcolonialism not only philosophically and theoretically, but at the important level of grounded practice—a perspective that is often missing from other discussions. Indeed, because of the discipline's fundamental involvement with practices and technologies that interpret "the past" in the present, its close relationship with state authority, and the need to come to terms with its own intensely colonialist legacy, archaeology has emerged as one of the most vibrant terrains for actualizing postcolonial theory and working out what postcolonialism means or looks like in practice.

Contributors to this volume demonstrate how and why this is true through their varied explorations of postcolonial thought and practice. From beginning to end, these are thought-provoking contributions that examine the history, theory, epistemology, and practice of postcolonialism from global, multicultural, and sometimes contradictory perspectives.

Postcolonialism itself is a concept that embraces a broad spectrum of meanings. For some authors, the term defines an actual historical moment that represents the end of official colonial rule; for others, it has to do with relationships within political, social, and cultural contexts that in some way move beyond colonialist constructs. Likewise, some contributors wrestle with the explicit elements of the colonial legacy within archaeology (such as issues of repatriation, official histories, or institutionalized heritage management), while others target broader, less concrete aspects of the postcolonial critique, including the very concepts, categories, and ways that make thinking and theorizing about the past appear natural or naturalized.

This volume attests to archaeology's involvement with colonialism as well as its potential to decolonize practice, interpretation, and theory. It is extraordinary and notable in bringing together perspectives from so many places around the world. In doing so, it provides inspiration and impetus for further examining the nature of the relationships between postcolonialism and archaeology. In fact, we believe it is largely by delving deeply into this undercurrent that archaeology will sustain itself as relevant and ethical social theory and practice over the next century. Just as archaeology has been central to the colonial project, so it may have an important role in re-visioning the relations of production of knowledge about the past.

We take this opportunity to express our admiration for volume editors Jane Lydon and Uzma Rizvi, who first envisioned this challenging project more than five years ago and pursued it with passion and grace at every stage. We knew that things were going to go well when they convened an editorial board just for the volume. Due to their perseverance and leadership, this volume, with its multiperspectival and global aspirations, became a reality. We extend thanks and appreciation to each of the authors for contributing to this important topic. We also thank Mitch Allen for his patience and guidance, and for being the one who puts things out there. We are grateful to the members of our editorial board who took the time to review and provide comments on the manuscript at various stages, particularly Robert Paynter and Yannis Hamilakis who reviewed major sections of the volume in the final stretch. Kudos go to Carol Leyba for the meticulous work of final copyediting, and to April Ruttle, who ably assisted with editorial tasks along the way.

All royalties generated by sales of books in this series go directly to the World Archaeological Congress, the sponsor of this series. Since its inception, WAC has challenged the legacy of colonialism around the world, nurtured the growth of grassroots archaeological communities and discussions, and supported participation in meetings by those for whom economic and political conditions make this difficult. One way WAC accomplishes this is through the royalties from WAC-related publications. In addition, Left Coast Press, Inc. donates 50 copies of each volume produced in the Research Handbook Series to WAC's Global Libraries Project, for distribution to libraries around the world.

ACKNOWLEDGMENTS

We thank many who assisted us with a rigorous, even turbulent, peer review process that sometimes challenged contributors to rethink their positions on their work. Like the authors, these reviewers were drawn from around the world, each scholar helping the volume with timely, in-depth comments. In addition to our reviewers, we have had many scholars serve in advisory and supportive capacities, to whom we also owe much gratitude.

Our sincere appreciation to Wendy Ashmore, Tony Bennett, Sari Braithwaite, Heather Burke, Ashish Chadha, Annie Clark, Meg Conkey, Cressida Fforde, Alice Gorman, Joan Gero, Michael Given, Praveena Gullapalli, Yannis Hamilakis, Nelson Hancock, Ann Holder, Julie Hollowell, Audrey Horning, Sian Jones, Philip Kohl, Adria LaViolette, Matthew Liebmann, Mark Leone, Ian Lilley, Ian McNiven, Lynn Meskell, Stephanie Moser, Albert Naccache, Sarah Nelson, George Nicholas, Charles Orser, Jr., Susan Pollock, Gregory L. Possehl, Robert Preucel, Patricia Rubertone, Lynette Russell, Peggy Sanday, Claire Smith, Suzanne Spencer-Wood, Murtaza Vali, Peter van Dommelen, and LouAnn Wurst. Also, we would be remiss if we did not thank Sophia Straker-Babb at Pratt Institute for her support in seeing the volume through to its completion.

Moreover, we are sincerely grateful for the careful editing and support that the series editors, Julie Holloway and George Nicholas, provided us through this entire process. We would also like to thank Carol Leyba for her attention to detail as copyeditor, her patience and good humor while working with us on this large project. And to Asad Pervaiz, our gratitude for being able to articulate our concepts of intervention and change, into topographic lines that make the familiar unfamiliar in such a format and scale. Without the careful guiding discussions with Left Coast Press, Inc., this volume would not have reached completion. For his amazing ability and capacity to support our many different ideas and dreams, we would like to thank Mitch Allen.

If ever we could thank our families enough, we offer our sincere thanks to them for their constant support, encouragement, and belief in our words.

1

INTRODUCTION: POSTCOLONIALISM AND ARCHAEOLOGY

Jane Lydon and Uzma Z. Rizvi

Writing as we do from two settler colonies—Australia and the United States—that continue to struggle with their pasts, we are confronted every day by the legacies of colonialism in the form of persistent structural inequalities within our societies, which determine differing life expectancies, health care, education, and other basic rights for more or less privileged groups. As archaeologists, our professional and intellectual concern with the past makes very clear to us that these inequalities originate from the colonial experiences of our countries. This volume explores the relationship between the postcolonial critique and archaeology, two fields of intellectual endeavor that intersect in a growing body of research concerned with the concrete and pervasive heritage of colonialism and imperialism.

In a research handbook in a series sponsored by the World Archaeological Congress (WAC), it is appropriate to reflect that such a synthesis owes its existence and form to the organization's central goal of addressing present social inequality through a concern with the past. WAC was founded in Southampton in 1986 in response to the call by the Anti-Apartheid Movement to impose sanctions against the South African regime in accordance with United Nations resolutions (Stone 2006; Ucko 1987). Among its objectives, WAC is "committed to diversity and to redressing global inequities in archaeology through conferences, publications, and scholarly programs. It has a special interest in protecting the cultural heritage of Indigenous peoples, minorities and economically disadvantaged countries, and encourages the participation of Indigenous peoples, researchers from economically disadvantaged countries and members of the public."[1] Hence, many of WAC's aims and programs reflect broad global processes of scholarly and political acknowledgment of the inequalities created by colonialism, Indigenous and minority demands for restitution, and the ethical necessity for us all to engage with strategies of decolonization.

This handbook to archaeology's engagement with postcolonialism specifies strategies for decolonizing archaeological research that still bears the marks of the colonial enterprise. Summary articles review the emergence of the discipline of archaeology in step with the colonialist enterprise, critique the colonial legacy evident in continuing archaeological practice around the world, identify current trends, and chart future directions in postcolonial archaeological research. Contributors provide a synthesis of research, thought, and practice on their respective topics. Many of the articles take a regional approach, a perspective that emphasizes the diverse forms of colonial culture that emerged around the globe. There is no one colonialist experience, nor its concrete ramifications in the present; such local perspectives foreground the need to counter totalizing narratives of historical and cultural process. These diverse perspectives regarding colonialism reflect historical loyalties and experiences as well as contemporary geopolitics.

In addition to the review-based chapters, each section includes commentary chapters, which provide short, specialized narratives related to the larger theme. Unusual in such handbooks, these shorter chapters offer space for new ways of thinking and formally challenge the structure of a traditional handbook. In its entirety, this collection provides a companion to archaeologists grappling with postcoloniality through a global survey of key concepts, developments, and directions, contributed by leading practitioners and particularly scholars from traditionally disenfranchised communities such as Indigenous peoples, minorities, or other historically and politically marginalized populations. Archaeological interpretation is widely perceived to play an important role within contemporary articulations of identity in providing a deep foundation for modern assertions of authority, and contributors explore this process. Overall, the handbook provides guidelines to enable practitioners around the globe to understand how these issues are integral to archaeological fieldwork, and to assist archaeologists to better understand and to implement the approaches reviewed.

Definitions: Colonial, Postcolonial

Postcolonial scholarship developed in relation to the expansion of the empires of Western Europe that occupied most of the world from 1492 to 1945. As a body of ideas and methods, it originates in the political activism of post–World War II anti-colonial liberation movements, allied to the intellectual critique of the structures of colonialism—a project often said to have been initiated in 1961 by the publication of Frantz Fanon's *The Wretched of the Earth* (1968 [1961]). Such a critique aims to show that colonialism and European culture are deeply implicated within each other, and to demonstrate the reliance of Western systems of thought upon the colonial "other." Postcolonial scholarship has also revealed the disjunction between the apparent progressivism and benevolence of the universals of the European Enlightenment tradition—concepts such as historicism, reason, and humanism—and their restricted deployment in colonial practice, where they were reduced to the figure of the "White settler male." As historian Dipesh Chakrabarty (2000: 4–5) points out, universal categories such as a "conception of a universal and secular humanism" continue to underpin the human sciences, and they are indispensable because "without them there would be no social science that addresses issues of modern social justice," including the critique of colonialism itself. Hence, Western concepts such as "historicism" and "political modernity" are both necessary to non-Western histories yet are simultaneously inadequate to explain them.

In temporal terms, "post-colonial" therefore pertains to a distinct period in world history—namely, the aftermath of European imperialism post–World War II. The colonialism of this era is distinguished from earlier forms by its global scale, integration, and overlap with the emergence of modernity and capitalism. However, the term does not imply the triumphant transcendence of colonialism: while these great world systems have been dismantled, various disguised forms of colonialism and neocolonialism continue to flourish. In what follows, we use the term primarily to refer to a specific theoretical approach rather than denoting a temporal period; we remain wary of defining our own time as somehow having left colonialism behind (see also Pagán-Jiménez 2004).

It follows that postcolonial scholarship may be distinguished from earlier approaches toward the study of colonialism by its integrally self-reflexive, political dimension: it has been termed a kind of "activist writing," committed to understanding the relations of power that frame colonial interactions and identities, and to resisting imperialism and its legacies. The postcolonial critique, unlike those of poststructuralism and postmodernism with which it intersects, has a fundamental ethical basis in examining oppression and inequality in the present, including those grounded in neocolonialism, race, gender, nationalism, class, and/or ethnicities. Postcolonialism's concern with the past is guided by that past's relationship with the present, foregrounding the links between cultural forms and geopolitics. It is intellectually committed to contributing to political and social transformation, with the goal of countering neocolonialism and facilitating the assertion of diverse forms of identity.

Postcolonial scholarship has therefore reconsidered colonialism from the perspective of colonized peoples and their cultures, as well as revealing its continuing ramifications in the present. Interdisciplinary and transcultural in its theory and effects, postcolonialism has followed diverse historical trajectories, making it difficult to generalize or to satisfactorily theorize the process of colonialism as a coherent project. As

Ania Loomba (1998: xvi) warns, colonialism's historical and geographical heterogeneity means that "we must build our theories with an awareness that such diversity exists, and not expand the local to the status of the universal." While colonialism has often been evoked as a "global and transhistorical logic of denigration," a "coherent imposition" rather than a practically mediated relation (Thomas 1994: 3), here we seek to place these diverse processes in historical and global contexts.

Colonialism centers on the conquest and control of other peoples' lands and goods. In its inescapably material character, it is particularly amenable to archaeological investigation, raising a range of questions that have long been central to the discipline, such as the role of material culture in constituting identities and mediating between cultures. Like Michael Rowlands, we use the term "colonialism" to refer to the modern phenomenon in which the colonizers' relations of domination over the colonized are of primary salience. By contrast, the more specific term "colonization" is restricted to describing the movements and settlements of people with no implication of power relations (Rowlands 1998a).

Colonialism, Culture, and Representation

Crucially, postcolonial scholarship has revealed the importance of representation in securing the West's dominance over the colonized. Drawing on Foucault's arguments for the mutual constitution of knowledge and power through discourse, and for the role of classification in differentiating and governing populations, Edward Said's (1978) *Orientalism* demonstrated how management of the peoples of the Middle East was effected through a Western discourse of orientalism organized through such academic disciplines as anthropology, archaeology, and history. Said showed that Western conceptions of history and culture, and the devices we use to conceive, construct, and convey meaning about other peoples, are profoundly implicated in imperialism and oppression. While Said has in turn been criticized for distinguishing between the "fantasy" of Western imagination and the reality of its political effects (rather than seeing these as belonging to the same system of operation), one of his most important insights was to show the interpenetration of power and knowledge in colonial rule.

Another critique of Enlightenment epistemologies was developed by the Subaltern Studies school of historiography that formed around the historian Ranajit Guha and his followers during the late 1970s (see Lucas, chapter 27, this volume). This collective asked to what extent subaltern groups such as peasants, women, the working class, and other marginalized people had been able to make their own history and constitute an "autonomous realm" (e.g., Guha 1982). Utilizing Antonio Gramsci's notions of the subaltern, this school sought to recover marginal experience through the fissures, silences, and rhetorical strategies of colonial documents, producing a critique of modernity and its master narratives focused on Indian colonial history (e.g., Chatterjee 1998; Spivak 1988).

During the 1980s, these insights were developed within postcolonial scholarship through a central concern with representation and the analysis of colonial discourse—that is, the ways that Western powers wrote about, depicted, and administered the colonized. A chief analytical tactic of postcolonial critique has been to identify and destabilize discursive strategies such as the use of stereotypes and the construction of binary opposites; by demonstrating the radical interdependence of cultural and political formations, it has been possible to challenge oppositions between East/West, center/periphery, us/them, Black/White, and so undermine the basis for colonial inequalities. In an influential approach drawn from semiotics and psychoanalysis, Homi Bhabha has argued for the "ambivalence of colonial rule," suggesting that "the colonial presence is always ambivalent, split between its appearance as original and authoritative and its articulation as repetition and difference" (2004: 153). Confronted by paradoxical colonial demands, the subaltern must assume a stable and essential identity. Yet, as Bhabha notes, simultaneously for the subaltern's transformation, a doubleness in enunciation can emerge—an excess that comes through colonial mimicry and produces a threatening, subversive hybridity in cultural forms. Bhabha advanced the notion of a "liminal" or "interstitial" category that occupies a "space between" competing cultural traditions, historical periods, and critical methodologies. The performative excess of colonial mimicry suggests a capacity for resistance that has proved appealing to many scholars. However, the psychoanalytic dimensions of Bhabha's program have also been criticized for their fixity, imposing a predetermined meaning on cultural processes regardless of their historical or cultural specificity. Postcolonial scholarship's emphasis on discourse and language has been extended by cultural theorists, following Bourdieu, to embrace "a pluralized field of colonial narratives, which are seen less as signs than as practices, or as signifying practices rather than elements of a code" (Thomas 1994: 8). Conceiving colonialism as a series of cultural projects has proved a fruitful avenue for anthropological analysis, while situating colonial images and narratives in a specific time and place reveals how localized subjectivities are constituted.

A key question remains the extent to which Western structures of thought, or epistemologies, permit us to understand subaltern experience—a question first, and powerfully, posed as the title of Spivak's article "Can the subaltern speak?" (1988). The question of subaltern status has been complicated further by feminist scholars. Within these newly negotiated cultural logics, feminist scholars complement the postcolonial critique with an enhanced understanding of subjectivity, exposing the layers of a double colonization (Spivak 1999). This enterprise is no longer solely concerned with the colonial self and colonized other, but rather, considers how gender schemas place the colonized women into categories that must contend with simultaneous gender and racial inequities. Feminist critiques have confronted postcolonial scholarship for its tendency to construct a single category of the colonized, thus erasing the axes of gender, class, and other social categories.

Affecting both subject and object, Third World and postcolonial feminisms both emerged from this history of colonial oppression, critiquing Western forms of feminist philosophy in which the female experience is universalized (see Mohanty 2000 [1986] for critique). Postcolonial feminism pushes beyond the binary of male/female as homogeneous group or category, forcing Western feminists to recognize that they are not the only true "subjects" of feminist practice, and that Third World women should not be viewed only as the "oppressed woman," never rising above their generality and their "object" status (Mohanty 2000 [1986]: 1202).

When the "Third World woman" is displaced, removed, and categorized as "transnational"—or moved into minority status—she is simultaneously given a voice but is also rendered static and "other." Women of color in majority white populations find themselves in what Trinh T. Minh-ha has called the "triple bind," a critique that revolves around the simple fact that these women can never be known just through their professional attributes, but rather must first be viewed through the lens of their race and sex. As Minh-ha argues,

> Neither black/red/yellow nor woman but poet or writer. For many of us, the question of priorities remains a crucial issue. Being merely "a writer" without doubt ensures one a status of far greater weight than being "a woman of color who writes" ever does. Imputing race or sex to the creative act has long been a means by which the literary establishment cheapens and discredits the achievements of non-mainstream women writers. She who "happens to be" a (non-white) Third World member, a woman, and a writer is bound to go through the ordeal of exposing her work to the abuse of praises and criticisms that either ignore, dispense with, or overemphasize her racial and sexual attributes. (1989: 6)

In a similar manner, the confines of heteronormative Western sexuality have a very specific history within colonial frameworks and are structurally bound to the ways in which we understand the past, present, and future of such relations. Continuing to deconstruct these power structures past the first wave of postcolonial critiques has allowed for postfeminist, queer, and masculinist studies to pose new questions (e.g., Chopra et al. 2004; Gopinath 2005; Mohanty 2003; Srivastava 2004). Such questions are particularly relevant for revealing how colonial states affected domestic orders and household power structures: from this standpoint, it becomes untenable to apply the Western heterosexual ideals of passive/femininity and active/masculinity, as these preclude recognition of the colonized as fully human (Sen 2004). This critique finds its roots in Fanon's *Black Skin, White Masks* (1967), which uses psychoanalysis and psychological theories to uncover the desire, realities, and affects of becoming white in order to survive and succeed.

Within the academy, survival depends on citations, publications, and conferences, in particular for those groups that have been traditionally marginalized both within the state and within the discipline of archaeology. The politics of representation are thus significant for scholars in terms of their identity and practice (Rizvi 2008: 111). The recognition that identity, particularly as concerns marginality and alterity, informs and shapes one's standpoint is best illustrated by a question posed by Bhabha: "What changes when you write from the middle of difference, when you inscribe that intermediary area that invites the ambiguous gamble with the historical necessities of race, class, gender, generation, region, religion?" (1997: 435). Such a question is, of course, contingent on having the space, resources, and opportunity to write. We contend that it is important to have these voices heard and valued, despite criticism of postcolonial intellectuals as complicit with the Western academy and global capitalism (e.g., Dirlik 1994). We believe that it is crucial to understand the global place of academics and to deconstruct those power structures.

Postcolonialism and Archaeology

Several major themes have emerged from archaeologists' engagements with postcolonial studies, including the critique of colonial traditions of thought, new accounts of the past that emphasize Indigenous and subaltern experiences, and strategies for restitution and decolonization. Archaeologists have reflected on how their discipline is shaped by colonial forces, tracing the intimate relationship between imperialism and forms of archaeological knowledge. As Chris Gosden (2001: 245) points out, archaeology and anthropology are both outgrowths of liberal philosophy, and their agenda has been to study the "other," an enterprise that has been fundamental in justifying colonial intervention, constituting a colonial tool of governance in charting and knowing subaltern peoples, and dissociating Indigenous descendants from their heritage (see also Gosden 1999; Pels 1997). Such critique has followed Said in tracing the continuation of colonial discourse, structures, and practices into the present, revealing the role of archaeology within current relationships and inequalities. In a classic essay originally published in 1980, Bruce Trigger's "Archaeology and the Image of the American Indian" showed how assumptions that Native American culture was primitive and inherently static were linked to archaeological arguments for the comparatively recent arrival of Native American peoples in North America, and their consequent dissociation from the material remains of social complexity. This important study documented how archaeological interpretation reproduced popular stereotypes of Native American peoples and reinforced the political interests of Euro-American culture.

Since that time, Trigger (1980, 1984, 2003, 2006) and other historians of the discipline (e.g., Díaz-Andreu 2007; Dietler 2005; Gosden 1999; Kehoe 1998; McNiven and Russell 2005; Mulvaney 1981; Murray 1989; Rowlands 1998b; also González-Ruibal and T. Patterson, this volume, chapters 2 and 10, respectively) have systematically reviewed the Enlightenment tradition that framed archaeology's inception and professionalization and its relationship with colonialism. Western ideas of progress, human difference, and "prehistory" were developed through colonial experience, in the Americas and Africa during the 17th and 18th centuries, and in the Pacific and Australia during the 19th century.

Directly emerging from these processes was the idea of social evolution in which human populations move from less complex to more complex societies—with the colonial state sitting on the top rung of the evolutionary ladder of civilization. These models of complexity have continued to affect archaeological interpretation, in assumptions that the progress of civilization inevitably follows from "primitive" hunter-gathers to civilized state-level societies. The resulting nomenclature draws on such texts and scholarship as Lewis Henry Morgan's influential book, *Ancient Society, or Researches in the Lines of Human Progress from Savagery through Barbarism to Civilization* (1877) and, more recently, Elman Service's four classifications of the stages of social evolution/political organizations (1962). Such a linear model of social evolution is complicated by the continued usage of terms such as Stone Age, Chalcolithic, Bronze Age, and the like.

The professionalization of prehistory as a science during the 19th century was stimulated by a wider search for national identity across Europe (for a Soviet example, see Dolukhanov, this volume, chapter 8). In addition, as contributions to this volume show very clearly, the national imagination played a constitutional and fundamental role in creating the discipline of archaeology. Colonialism and nationalism have recently been conceptualized as connected systems of thinking and practice, and archaeology often developed at the intersection of colonialism and nationalism (Hamilakis 2007). The recognition of this process stimulated research concerned with the intersection between archaeology and nationalism from the mid-1990s (e.g., Atkinson et al. 1996; Díaz-Andreu and Champion 1996; Kohl and Fawcett 1995). Yet archaeologists have not always linked this process to the larger imperialist and modernizing ambitions of the major European powers, nor to the ways that these also entailed the creation of particular views of the colonized that justified conquest and domination and appropriated Indigenous or subordinate groups into a national identity. Nonetheless, it is clear that many conceptual categories and techniques of governance were symmetrically applied in order to subjugate external cultural others and to subordinate internal groups (e.g., Cooper and Stoler 1997; Hall 2000; Stoler 1995; also González-Ruibal, this volume, chapter 2). A growing literature traces the intersection of anti-colonial critique and heritage in a variety of locales (e.g., Crawford 2000; Smith 2004; Tsosie 1997; Watkins 2000). In particular, there is a much-needed critique of interpretations that position Indigenous materiality at a lower level of complexity and technology than that of other "civilized" groups (see McGuire 1992; McNiven and Russell 2005; Pikirayi 2001).

Only through contesting those ideologies can the image and trope of Indigenous people as ancient, timeless, and unchanging actually be reimagined.

Postcolonial scholars have revealed the importance of transnational histories in demonstrating the interdependence of social categories, as ideas about race, class, and gender were developed in global counterpoint between the metropolis and the colonies. Such accounts also throw into question the centrality of the nation and Western colonialism as analytic categories, by showing the diversity of movement and exchange "from below." As Chris Gosden has argued (2004: 20), there is a need for transnational archaeologies to develop a broad comparative framework to allow local specificities and differences to become apparent. Recent analysis has also extended postcolonial studies' temporal scope to explore processes of colonization over the millennia—defining what is really new about globalization. For example, Gosden (2004) emphasizes the central role of material consumption and exchange, and the mutually transformative effects of the circulation of people, ideas, and objects within colonialism (see also Stein 2005). Through its longitudinal, comparative perspective, archaeology makes an important contribution to this analysis, allowing us to better historicize these phenomena by showing that global processes of colonialism and exchange have a longer history than has often been understood, and illuminating colonialism by reference to a range of examples from different periods and regions (e.g., Given 2004; Lyons and Papadopoulos 2002; Stein 2005).

The use of the postcolonial critique to inform archaeological interpretation, specifically within a colonial context of exchange, has been instrumental in opening new research directions. Identity has become a significant variable (see also Part IV of this volume), showing how the politics and performance of personhood affect different forms of exchange. Additionally, significant research can be done on the role that scientific paradigms and language have played in dissociating Indigenous people and minority communities from their heritage and appropriating it in order to forward particular discourses of power and knowledge production (see Chadha, this volume, chapter 16).

Certain theoretical notions that emerge from the postcolonial critique may be applied to the materiality of archaeological studies more readily than others. Homi Bhabha's (2004) concept of *hybridity* is one such concept; it is often used to replace older terms such as "cultural intermixing," used to describe time periods such as the Orientalizing period in ancient Greece during the 8th century B.C.E. In a recent paper, Benjamin Porter and Bruce Routledge argue that hybridity can be a "more fruitful concept for archaeological interpretation if used not simply to signify the formation of new cultural forms, but rather to represent the struggle over the production of diverse cultural forms, especially cultural forms that diverge from those linked to dominant forms of political power" (2008: 3). Peter van Dommelen focuses instead on hybrid practices. Investigating colonial networks controlled by the city of Carthage during the 7th to 4th centuries B.C.E., which developed out of an earlier Phoenician colonial presence, van Dommelen demonstrates how colonial interactions relate to subsequent hybrid practices and how the localized effects of colonization might be understood in the context of the colonized (1997).

One of the most significant sites where both localized and global effects of colonization can be located at once as both material and practice is the museum, founded on the colonial impulses to collect, order, and define. As an implicit strategy of colonialism, the museum becomes the site where identities are created and the interpretation of information affects the building of shared imaginaries and national ideals (Barringer and Flynn 1998; Preziosi and Farago 2003). In both the materiality of the often magnificent edifices within which collections are housed or displayed, the public learns about the Other in a very formal manner (Mitchell 1992). Thus, the contemporary Other is placed side by side with prehistoric artifacts assigned to the category of "primitive," establishing rational, scientific patterns of thought by contrast (Bennett 2004; Colwell-Chanthaphonh and Ferguson 2008; Guha-Thakurta 2004). Perpetuating the desire to commemorate ancestors, museums have become Eurocentric regimes of memory, their fixity and permanence an antidote to modernity's sense of instability and anxiety (Butler and Rowlands 2006).

Volume Organization

In response to these major developments within postcolonial archaeology, we have organized the volume into five parts. Where appropriate, these sections are regionally based to reflect distinct historical and intellectual traditions and modern geopolitical formations. These are followed by short commentaries in which scholars engage in an interdisciplinary dialogue or provide a specialized discussion of the theme. Part I, The Archaeological Critique of Colonization: Global Trajectories, examines the emergence of archaeology in conjunction with imperialism, and the ways that European structures of thought have shaped research in colonial situations across the globe. Part II, Archaeological Narratives of Colonialism, presents archaeological accounts that have only become possible with the recognition of the discipline's complicity with colonialism. These narratives foreground Indigenous perspectives and experience. Part III, Addressing/Redressing the Past: Restitution, Repatriation, and Ethics, presents concrete strategies that aim to redress injustice in the present. Part IV, Colonial and Postcolonial Identities, addresses the articulation of identities, one of the central issues raised by new forms of collaboration and interpretation. Finally, in Part V, Strategies of Practice: Implementing the Postcolonial Critique, the volume ends with practical and pragmatic approaches to changes in methodology that allow for a new kind of archaeological practice. Prefacing each of these five sections, we offer brief introductions that reflect on core questions addressed by individual chapters.

In an epilogue to the volume, the editors reflect on forms of alterity, the roles of cosmopolitanism, social change, and ethics in archaeology, and we canvass ideas for new research. In compiling and editing a volume that ranges across many scales, from the local to the global, and in varied histories and cultural contexts, we have found it necessary to embrace multiple voices, case studies, and approaches. We have consciously sought to recognize the utility of comparative work and interdisciplinary approaches to understanding the past. The chapters and commentaries included in this volume offer new ways to engage with the past, present, and the future.

Note

1. World Archaeological Congress, 2009 (accessed 27 October 2009). Available from *www.worldarchaeologicalcongress.org/site/home.php*.

References and Recommended Sources

Appadurai, A. 2002. The globalization of archaeology and heritage. *Journal of Social Archaeology* 1: 35–49.

Asch, M., and Samson, C. 2004. On the Return of the Native. *Current Anthropology* 45 (2): 261.

Asch, M., Samson, C., Dahre, U., and Kuper, A. 2006. More on the Return of the Native/Reply. *Current Anthropology* 47 (1): 145.

Atalay, S. 2006. Decolonizing archaeology. Special Issue. *American Indian Quarterly* 30 (3).

Atkinson, J.A., Banks, I., and O'Sullivan, J. (eds.). 1996. *Nationalism and Archaeology: Scottish Archaeological Forum*. Glasgow: Cruithne.

Barringer, T., and Flynn. T. (eds.). 1998. *Colonialism and the Object: Empire, Material Culture and the Museum*. London: Routledge.

Bennett, T. 2004. *Pasts beyond Memory: Evolution, Museums, Colonialism*. London: Routledge.

Bhabha, H. K. 1997. Editor's introduction: Minority maneuvers and unsettled negotiations. *Critical Inquiry* 23 (3): 431–459.

———. 2004. *The Location of Culture*. New York: Routledge.

Blakey, M. L. 1998. The New York African Burial Ground Project: An examination of enslaved lives, a construction of ancestral ties. *Transforming Anthropology* 7 (1): 53–58.

Butler, B., and Rowlands, M. 2006. The man who would be Moses, in R. Layton, S. Shennan, and P. Stone (eds.), *A Future for Archaeology: The Past in the Present*, pp. 97–105. London: UCL Press.

Chakrabarty, D. 2000. *Provincializing Europe: Postcolonial Thought and Historical Difference*. Princeton, NJ: Princeton University Press.

Chatterjee, P. 1998. Beyond the nation? Or within? *Social Text* (56): 57–69.

Chopra, R., Osella, C., and Osella, F. (eds.). 2004. *South Asian Masculinities: Context of Change, Sites of Continuity*. New Delhi: Kali for Women and Women Unlimited.

Colwell-Chanthaphonh, C., and Ferguson, T. J. 2004. Virtue ethics and the practice of history: Native Americans and archaeologists along the San Pedro Valley of Arizona. *Journal of Social Archaeology* 4 (1): 5–27.

——. 2008. Introduction: The collaborative continuum, in C. Colwell-Chanthaphonh and T. J. Ferguson (eds.), *Collaboration in Archaeological Practice: Engaging Descendant Communities*, pp. 1–32. New York: AltaMira Press.

Conkey, M. W. 2005. Dwelling at the margins, action at the intersection? Feminist and indigenous archaeologies. *Archaeologies* 1 (1): 9–59.

Cooper, F., and Stoler, A. L. (eds.). 1997. *Tensions of Empire: Colonial Cultures in a Bourgeois World*. Berkeley: University of California Press.

Crawford, S. J. 2000. (Re)constructing bodies: Semiotic sovereignty and the debate over Kennewick Man, in D. A. Mihesuah (ed.), *Repatriation Reader: Who Owns American Indian Remains?*, pp. 211–236. Lincoln: University of Nebraska Press.

Díaz-Andreu, M. 2007. *A World History of Nineteenth-Century Archaeology. Nationalism, Colonialism, and the Past*. Oxford: Oxford University Press.

Díaz-Andreu, M., and Champion, T. 1996. *Archaeology and Nationalism in Europe*. Boulder, CO: Westview.

Dietler, M. 2005. The archaeology of colonization and the colonization of archaeology: Theoretical challenges from an ancient Mediterranean colonial encounter, in G. Stein (ed.), *The Archaeology of Colonial Encounters: Comparative Perspectives*, pp. 33–68. Santa Fe: School of American Research Advanced Seminar Series.

Dirlik, A. 1994. The postcolonial aura: Third World criticism in the age of global capitalism. *Critical Inquiry* 20 (2): 328–256.

Epperson, T. W. 2004. Critical race theory and the archaeology of the African diaspora. *Historical Archaeology* 38: 101–108.

Fanon, F. 1967. *Black Skin, White Masks*. New York: Grove Press.

——. 1968 [1961]. *The Wretched of the Earth*. New York: Grove Press.

Franklin, M. 1997. Power to the people: Sociopolitics and the archaeology of Black Americans. *Historical Archaeology* 31 (3): 36–50.

Funari, P. P., Zarankin, A., and Stovel, E. 2005. *Global Archaeological Theory: Contextual Voices and Contemporary Thoughts*. Boston: Kluwer Academic/Plenum Publishers.

Gavin, L. 2004. *An Archaeology of Colonial Identity: Power and Material Culture in the Dwars Valley, South Africa*. New York: Kluwer/Plenum.

Gero, J. M., and Conkey, M. 1991. *Engendering Archaeology: Women and Prehistory*. Oxford: Blackwell.

Given, M. 2004. *The Archaeology of the Colonized*. London and New York: Routledge.

Gopinath, G. 2005. *Impossible Desires: Queer Diasporas and South Asian Public Cultures*. Durham, NC: Duke University Press.

Gosden, C. 1999. *Anthropology and Archaeology: A Changing Relationship*. London: Routledge.

———. 2001. Postcolonial archaeology: Issues of culture, identity, and knowledge, in I. Hodder (ed.), *Archaeological Theory Today*. Cambridge: Polity Press.

———. 2004. *Archaeology and Colonialism: Cultural Contact from 5000 BC to the Present*. Cambridge: Cambridge University Press.

Gosden, C., and Knowles, C. 2001. *Collecting Colonialism: Material Culture and Colonial Change*. Oxford: Berg.

Green, L. Fordred, Green, D. R., and Góes Neves, E. 2003. Indigenous knowledge and archaeological science: The challenges of public archaeology in the reserva Uaça. *Journal of Social Archaeology* 3 (3): 366–398.

Guha, R. 1982. On some aspects of the historiography of colonial India, in R. Guha (ed.), *Subaltern Studies I*, pp. 1–8. Delhi: Oxford University Press.

Guha-Thakurta, T. 2004. *Monuments, Objects, Histories: Institutions of Art in Colonial and Postcolonial India*. New York: Columbia University Press.

Gullapalli, P. 2008. Heterogeneous encounters: Colonial histories and archaeological experiences, in M. Liebmann and U. Z. Rizvi (eds.), *Archaeology and the Postcolonial Critique*. Lanham, MD: AltaMira Press.

Hall, M. 2000. *Archaeology and the Modern World: Colonial Transcripts in South Africa and the Chesapeake*. London: Routledge.

Hamilakis, Y. 2005. Whose world and whose archaeology? The colonial present and the return of the political. *Archaeologies* 1 (2).

———. 2007. *The Nation and Its Ruins: Antiquity, Archaeology, and National Imagination in Greece*. Oxford: Oxford University Press.

Harris, H. 2005. Indigenous worldviews and ways of knowing as theoretical and methodological foundations for archaeological research, in C. Smith and H. M. Wobst (eds.), *Indigenous Archaeologies: Decolonizing Theory and Practice*. London: Routledge.

Harrison, R., and Williamson, C. (eds.). 2002. *After Captain Cook: The Archaeology of the Recent Indigenous Past in Australia*. Sydney: Archaeological Computing Laboratory, University of Sydney.

Hirsch, F. 2005. *Empire of Nations: Ethnographic Knowledge and the Making of the Soviet Union*. Ithaca: Cornell University Press.

Horning, A. J. 2006. Archaeology, conflict and contemporary identity in the north of Ireland: Implications for theory and practice in comparative archaeologies of colonialism. *Archaeological Dialogues* 2006 (13): 183–200.

Kehoe, A. B. 1998. *The Land of Prehistory: A Critical History of American Archaeology*. New York: Routledge.

Kohl, P. L. 1998. Nationalism and archaeology: On the constructions of nations and the reconstructions of the remote past. *Annual Review of Anthropology* 27: 223–246.

Kohl, P. L., and Fawcett, C. (eds.). 1995. *Nationalism, Politics, and the Practice of Archaeology*. Cambridge: Cambridge University Press.

Kuper, A., Omura, K., Plaice, E., and Ramos, A. R. 2003. The return of the native: Comments and reply. *Current Anthropology* 44 (3): 389.

Langford, R. 1983. Our Heritage—Your Playground. *Australian Archaeology* 16: 1–6.

Lawrence, S., and Shepherd, N. 2006. Historical archaeology and colonialism, in D. Hicks and M. C. Beaudry (eds.), *Cambridge Companion to Historical Archaeology*. Cambridge: Cambridge University Press.

Liebmann, M. 2008. Postcolonial cultural affiliation: Essentialism, hybridity, and NAGPRA, in M. Liebmann and U. Z. Rizvi (ed.), *Archaeology and the Postcolonial Critique*. Lanham, MD: AltaMira Press.

Liebmann, M., and Rizvi, U. Z. (eds.). 2008. *Archaeology and the Postcolonial Critique*. Lanham, MD: AltaMira Press.

Loomba, A. 1998. *Colonialism/Postcolonialism*. London: Routledge.

Lydon, J. 2009. *Fantastic Dreaming: The Archaeology of an Australian Aboriginal Mission*. Lanham, MD: AltaMira Press.

Lyons, C. L., and Papadopoulos, J. K. 2002. *The Archaeology of Colonialism*. Los Angeles: The Getty Research Institute.

Marshall, Y. 2002. What is community archaeology? *World Archaeology* 34 (2): 211–219.

McDavid, C. 2004. From "traditional" archaeology to public archaeology to community action, in P. A. Shackel and E. J. Chambers (eds.), *Places in Mind: Public Archaeology as Applied Anthropology*. New York: Routledge.

McGuire R. 1992. Archaeology and the First Americans. *American Anthropologist* 94: 816–836.

McNiven, I., and Russell, L. 2005. *Appropriated Pasts: Indigenous Peoples and the Colonial Culture of Archaeology*. Lanham, MD: AltaMira.

Meskell, L. (ed.). 1998. *Archaeology under Fire: Nationalism, Politics and Heritage in the Eastern Mediterranean and Middle East*. London: Routledge.

——. 2001. Archaeologies of identity, in I. Hodder (ed.), *Archaeological Theory Today*, pp. 187– 213. Malden, MA: Polity Press.

——. 2002. The intersections of identity and politics in archaeology. *Annual Review of Anthropology* 31: 279–301.

Million, T. 2005. Developing an aboriginal archaeology: Receiving gifts from the white buffalo calf woman, in C. Smith and H. M. Wobst (eds.), *Indigenous Archaeologies: Decolonizing Theory and Practice*. London: Routledge.

Minh-ha, T. 1989. *Woman, Native, Other: Writing Postcoloniality and Feminism*. Bloomington: Indiana University Press.

Mitchell, T. 1992. Orientalism and the exhibitionary order, in N. Dirks (ed.), *Colonialism and Culture*, pp. 289–317. Ann Arbor: University of Michigan Press.

Mohanty, C. T. 2000 [1986]. Under Western eyes: Feminist scholarship and colonial discourses, in D. Brydon (ed.), *Postcolonialism: Critical Concepts in Literary and Cultural Studies*, pp. 1183–1209. London: Routledge.

——. 2003. *Feminism without Borders: Decolonizing Theory, Practicing Solidarity*. Durham and London: Duke University Press.

Morgan, L. H. 1877. *Ancient Society or Researches in the Lines of Human Progress from Savagery through Barbarism to Civilization*. London: MacMillan & Company.

Moser, S., Glazier, D., Phillips, J. E., N. el Nemr, L., Saleh Mousa, M., Nasr Aiesh, R., Richardson, S., Conner, A., and Seymour, M. 2002. Transforming archaeology through practice: Strategies for collaborative archaeology and the community archaeology project at Quseir, Egypt. *World Archaeology* 34 (2): 220–248.

Mulvaney, D. J. 1958. The Australian aborigines, 1606–1929. *Historical Studies, Australia and New Zealand* 8 (30): 131–151; 8 (31): 297–314.

——. 1981. Gum leaves on the golden bough: Australia's Palaeolithic survivals discovered, in J. D. Evans, B. Cunliffe, and C. Renfrew (eds.), *Antiquity and Man; Essays in Honour of Glyn Daniel*, pp. 52–64. London: Thames and Hudson.

Murray, T. 1989. The history, philosophy, and sociology of archaeology: The case of the Ancient Monuments Protection Act (1882), in V. Pinsky and A. Wylie (eds.), *Critical Traditions in Contemporary Archaeology: Essays in the Philosophy, History, and Socio-Politics of Archaeology*. Cambridge: Cambridge University Press.

Nicholas, G. P. 2009. *Intellectual Property Issues in Cultural Heritage: Theory, Practice, Policy, Ethics*. Simon Fraser University 2008 (accessed 27 October 2009). Available from *http:// cgi.sfu.ca/ipinch/cgi-bin/*.

Nicholas, G. P., and Andrews, T. D. (eds.). 1997. *At a Crossroads: Archaeology and First Peoples in Canada*. Burnaby: Simon Fraser University Archaeology Press.

Nicholas, G. P., and Bannister, K. P. 2004. "Copyrighting the past?": Emerging intellectual property rights issues in archaeology. *Current Anthropology* 45 (3): 327–350.

Orser, C. E. 1996. *A Historical Archaeology of the Modern World*. New York: Plenum Press.

——. 2004. *Race and Practice in Archaeological Interpretation*. Philadelphia: University of Pennsylvania Press.

Pagán-Jiménez, J. R. 2004. Is all archaeology at present a postcolonial one? Constructive answers from an eccentric point of view. *Journal of Social Archaeology* 4 (2): 200–213.

Pels, P. 1997. The anthropology of colonialism: Culture, history, and the emergence of Western governmentality. *Annual Review of Anthropology* 26: 163–183.

Pikirayi, I. 2001. *The Zimbabwe Culture: Origins and Decline in Southern Zambezian States*. Walnut Creek, CA: AltaMira Press.

Porter, B., and Routledge, B. 2008. Religious heterodoxy and rural hybridity across the Middle Islamic Dhiban Plateau (Jordan), in *Hybridization and Colonization: Old World Perspectives*. 2008 Annual meeting of the Society for American Archaeology, Vancouver, British Columbia.

Preucel, R. W., and Hodder, I. 1996. *Contemporary Archaeology in Theory*. Oxford: Blackwell Publishers.

Preziosi, D., and Farago, C. (eds.). 2003. *Grasping the World: The Idea of the Museum*. Burlington, VT: Ashgate.

Reid, A., and Segobye, A. 1999. The archaeology of the Makgadikgadi pans, Botswana, in *4th World Archaeological Congress*. Cape Town, South Africa.

Rizvi, U. Z. 2006. Accounting for multiple desires: Decolonizing methodologies, archaeology, and the public interest. *India Review* 4 (3–4): 394–416.

———. 2008. Decolonizing methodologies as strategies of practice: Operationalizing the postcolonial critique in the archaeology of Rajasthan, in M. Liebmann and U. Rizvi (eds.), *Archaeology and the Postcolonial Critique*. Archaeology and Society series. Walnut Creek, CA: AltaMira Press.

Rodríguez, I. (ed.). 2001. *The Latin American Subaltern Studies Reader*. Durham, NC: Duke University Press.

Rowlands, M. 1998a. The archaeology of colonialism, in K. Kristiansen and M. Rowlands (eds.), *Social Transformations in Archaeology: Global and Local Perspectives*, pp. 327–333. London: Routledge.

———. 1998b. The archaeology of colonialism and constituting the African peasantry, in K. Kristiansen and M. Rowlands (eds.), *Social Transformations in Archaeology*, pp. 375–396. London: Routledge.

Said, E. W. 1978. *Orientalism*. New York: Vintage.

Scham, S. A., and Yahya, A. 2003. Heritage and reconciliation. *Journal of Social Archaeology* 3 (3): 399–416.

Schmidt, P. R. 2009. *Postcolonial Archaeologies in Africa*. Santa Fe: SAR Press.

Schmidt, P. R., and Patterson, T. C. (eds.). 1995. *Making Alternative Histories: The Practice of Archaeology and History in Non-Western Settings*. Santa Fe: SAR Press.

Sen, S. 2004. Colonial aversions and domestic desires: Blood, race, sex, and the decline of intimacy in early British India, in S. Srivastava (ed.), *Sexual Sites, Seminal Attitudes: Sexualities, Masculinities and Culture in South Asia*, pp. 49–82. New Delhi: Sage.

Service, E. 1962 *Primitive Social Organization*. New York: Random House.

Shepherd, N. 2002. Heading south, looking north: Why we need a post-colonial archaeology. *Archaeological Dialogues* 9: 74–82.

———. 2003. "When the hand that holds the trowel is black...": Disciplinary practices of self-representation and the issue of "native" labour in archaeology. *Journal of Social Archaeology* 3: 334–352.

Smith, C., and Wobst, H. M. 2005. *Indigenous Archaeologies: Decolonizing Theory and Practice*. London: Routledge.

Smith, Laurajane. 2004. *Archaeological Theory and the Politics of Cultural Heritage*. London: Routledge.

Smith, Linda T. 1999. *Decolonizing Methodologies: Research and Indigenous Peoples*. London: Zed Books.

Spivak, G. C. 1988. Can the subaltern speak?, in C. Nelson and L. Grossberg (eds.), *Marxism and the Interpretation of Culture*, pp. 271–313. Urbana: University of Illinois Press.

———. 1999. *A Critique of Postcolonial Reason: Toward a History of the Vanishing Present*. Cambridge: Harvard University Press.

Srivastava, S. (ed.). 2004. *Sexual Sites, Seminal Attitudes: Sexualities, Masculinities and Culture in South Asia*. New Delhi: Sage.

Stein, G. J. (ed.). 2005. *The Archaeology of Colonial Encounters: Comparative Perspectives*. Santa Fe: SAR Press.

Stoler, A. L. 1995. *Race and the Education of Desire: Foucault's History of Sexuality and the Colonial Order of Things*. Durham, NC: Duke University Press.

Stone, P. 2006 "All smoke and mirrors...": The World Archaeological Congress, 1986– 2004, in R. Layton, S. Shennan, and P. Stone (eds.), *A Future for Archaeology: The Past in the Present*, pp. 53–64. London: UCL Press.

Thomas, N. 1994. *Colonialism's Culture: Anthropology, Travel, and Government*. Princeton: Princeton University Press.

Trigger, B. G. 1980. Archaeology and the image of the American Indian. *American Antiquity* 45 (4): 662–676.

———. 1984. Alternative archaeologies: Nationalist, colonialist, imperialist. *Man* 19: 355–370.

———. 2003. *Artifacts and Ideas: Essays in Archaeology*. New Brunswick, NJ: Transaction Publishers.

———. 2006. *A History of Archaeological Thought*. Cambridge: Cambridge University Press.

Tsosie, R. 1997. Indigenous rights and archaeology, in N. Swidler (ed.), *Native Americans and Archaeologists: Stepping Stones to Common Ground*, pp. 64–76. Walnut Creek, CA: AltaMira Press.

Ucko, P. 1987. *Academic Freedom and Apartheid: The Story of the World Archaeological Congress*. London: Duckworth.

van Dommelen, P. 1997. Colonial constructs: Colonialism and archaeology in the Mediterranean. *World Archaeology* 28 (3): 305–323.

Watkins, J. 2000. *Indigenous Archaeology: American Indian Values and Scientific Practice*. Walnut Creek, CA: AltaMira Press.

PART I
THE ARCHAEOLOGICAL CRITIQUE OF COLONIZATION: GLOBAL TRAJECTORIES

This section examines the emergence of the discipline of archaeology in conjunction with imperialism and the ways that European structures of thought shaped research in colonial situations across the globe. Through regional overviews, these chapters map the role of archaeological knowledge within specific historical trajectories of conquest and resistance, as well as charting the diverse traditions of postcolonial critique that have emerged. Ancient Greece, for example, was construed as fundamental ancestral heritage for European modernity, and contemporary Greece offers fertile ground for debating the intersection between colonialism and nationalism, examining the local appropriations and uses of Western ideologies about antiquity, and the deployments of orientalist and occidentalist discourses (e.g., Herzfeld 2002; Hamilakis 2007, 2008; Plantzos and Damaskos 2008). These contributions emphasize historiography, but also identify developing neocolonial archaeologies.

Alfredo González-Ruibal traces a genealogy of Western thought about "the other" from its origins in classical times to its deployment in the development of European archaeology. He identifies two broad orientalizing discourses created from the mid-19th century onward that provided the European middle classes with both a glorious origin and a preeminent position within the modern family of man. The chapter provides a critical analysis of Eurocentric discourses, particularly how they establish histories and create the "prehistoric" and the "primitive" as conceptual categories. Benjamin Porter notes the initiation of archaeological research in the Near East in the aftermath of Napoleon's military conquests of the late eighteenth century and the discipline's subsequent role in colonization of the region. Analysis of this history was inaugurated by

Silberman's (1982) *Digging for God and Country*, and a critical archaeological tradition began to explore how ideas about race and culture informed such research, revealing the dominance of national frameworks in shaping a range of archaeological narratives across the region. Porter suggests that, ironically, the ravages of conflict in the region have simultaneously destroyed archaeological remains but also opened up a space for local initiatives and Indigenous narratives to be crafted.

Indigenous and minority views about the meaning of the past increasingly shape forms of research, methodology, and management of cultural resources, while a growing cohort of Indigenous archaeologists uses Indigenous methods for the analysis of archaeological data. Here, Sonya Atalay reviews the relationship between archaeological thought and Native peoples in North America, from the stance of a woman who is both Ojibwe and an archaeologist. Drawing on concepts of time and history specific to the Anishinabe people of Michigan's Great Lakes region, she contrasts Anishinabe concepts of time that connect past, present, and future, with a Western separation between past and present.

Shifting to Asia, Dilip Chakrabarti discusses the colonial legacy embedded in the archaeology of South Asia, reviewing the history of archaeological research and concluding with contemporary projects in various nation-states. In his critique, he identifies the publication and citation (or lack thereof) of Third World scholars as a form of neocolonialism. From a Japanese perspective, Koji Mizoguchi surveys the development of local traditions of archaeology in response to the history of European and Japanese colonialism in East Asia. Mizoguchi discusses how contemporary Japanese archaeologists struggle with these difficult histories and the reemergence of nationalism, while earlier theoretical frameworks are superseded by postmodern and global archaeological theory derived from the West. Using the example of archaeological surveys in the Korean peninsula sponsored by the Colonial Government-General, Hyung Il Pai's chapter focuses on the imperial promotion of heritage tourism. By highlighting the link between tourism and the development of academic disciplines, Hyung Pai's chapter accentuates the political undertones in the heritage management laws of colonial Korea.

Similar subtext is uncovered in Pavel Dolukhanov's examination of the Soviet Union's use of archaeological data to justify its control of the ethno-administrative units it claimed as a vast Russian empire. Dolukhanov explores how a Marxist framework of increasing "stages" of development displaced earlier culture-historical models, and migrationist and diffusionist interpretations were rejected as racist and imperialist. After the collapse of the Communist regime, the romanticizing nationalist deployment of ethno-cultural paradigms reemerged, and archaeological cultures have been deployed as the basis for ethnic origins and to bolster neocolonial mythologies.

In the final chapters in this section, Ania Loomba and Thomas Patterson reflect on the connections among science, subjectivity, and a postcolonial archaeology, thus allowing for a discussion of future archaeologies. Ania Loomba notes that what is held in common by critics of postcolonialism across disciplines is their (impossible) claim "to impartiality and wholeness," reminding us that Edward Said's contribution was to show that scholarship and political power continue to be deployed in the emergence of a new global order; within this nexus, archaeological knowledge occupies a key place in debates about national pasts and futures. In turn, Patterson honors the revolutionary contributions of Bruce Trigger (1937– 2006), whose research since the 1980s examined the structures of Western thought that have governed archaeological approaches to human origins, development, and difference, and their relationship to political interests.

Trigger's important contribution marks the beginning of a new era of self-reflection and political change, as reviewed by contributors to this section. As events overtake scholarly analysis, many questions remain: for example, to what extent have the collapse of the Soviet Union, the return to an aggressive capitalism, and the initiation of a number of western European and North American projects in this region created a neocolonial archaeology? How have the events of the last decade, including neo-imperialism, the "war on terror," and decolonization processes, especially in the global Southern Hemisphere, shaped disciplinary practice?

References

Hamilakis, Y. 2007. *The Nation and Its Ruins: Antiquity, Archaeology, and National Imagination in Greece*. Oxford: Oxford University Press.

———. 2008. Decolonizing Greek archaeology: Indigenous archaeologies, modernist archaeology and the post-colonial critique, in D. Plantzos and D. Damaskos (eds.), *A Singular Antiquity: Archaeology and Hellenic Identity in Twentieth Century Greece*, pp. 273–284. Athens: The Benaki Museum.

Herzfeld, M. 2002. The absent presence: Discourses of crypto-colonialism. *The South Atlantic Quarterly* 101: 899–926.

Plantzos, D., and Damaskos, D. (eds.). 2008. *A Singular Antiquity: Archaeology and Hellenic Identity in Twentieth Century Greece*. Athens: The Benaki Museum.

Silberman, N. 1982. *Digging for God and Country: Exploration, Archeology, and the Secret Struggle for the Holy Land, 1799–1917*. New York: Random House.

2

COLONIALISM AND EUROPEAN ARCHAEOLOGY

Alfredo González-Ruibal

Modern European colonialism affected the whole world, and its legacy is overwhelming today. From this point of view, we could almost start and finish the book with this chapter; it would be enough to review the works and thoughts of European archaeologists on other continents. However, since Said's *Orientalism* (1979), we know that colonial categories not only constructed an image of the Other, but were also fundamental in shaping European identity, science, and politics. Thus, there is a particular relationship between colonialism and European archaeology that should be explored. This chapter is divided into two parts: the first part deals with colonial times up to the mid-20th century, the second with the postcolonial period.

The Colony: Studying Others, Understanding Ourselves

The first intellectual appropriations of the Other by European states can be traced back at least to classical times, when ancient scholars created the concept of "barbarian" populations in order to build notions of "Greekness" and "Romanness" (Hall 1989; Webster 1996). The Roman historian Cornelius Tacitus, for example, saw in the Germans the long-lost qualities of his own ancestors (Cro 1977: 40–45). With the expansion of Europe from the late 15th century onward, the populations that the conquerors found in their way were increasingly used to understand the remotest European past. This is most clearly exemplified by Antoine de Jussieu (1686–1758) and Father Lafiteau (1681–1746), who resorted to exotic ethnographic analogies in their interpretation of European prehistoric tools (Schnapp 1996: 267–268). This approach pioneered the methodology that would prevail during the second half of the 19th century: a blend of anthropology and archaeology, which, allied to evolutionism, provided key intellectual support to the colonial enterprise and bourgeois ideology (Trigger 1992).

Broadly speaking, two main types of colonialist/imperialist discourses can be described in archaeology for the period between the mid-19th and the mid-20th centuries: the discourse of civilization and the discourse of origins. The discourse of civilization focused on the Mediterranean and the Middle East, while the discourse of origins focused on places like sub-Saharan Africa or Oceania. Countries such as Greece, Rome, Egypt, and Mesopotamia provided Europe with a glorious cradle of civilization. The rest of the world had a double role: it helped interpret through analogies the prehistory of Europe and served to reassure the bourgeois classes of the cultural and moral superiority of Western civilization, which was considered the only civilization that had been capable of progressing from savagery to industrialization (Trigger 1992: 109, 141–143).

It is worth remembering, however, that archaeology furnished colonialism with much more than a discourse. As a field discipline, it was crucial, along with other sciences, in producing practical knowledge of the conquerable lands (Fernández 2001: 176) and in disciplining subjects (Chadha 2002).

The Discourse of Civilization

European powers appropriated the pasts of other formerly "progressive" countries. This is especially obvious in the case of the Hellenic world, including Turkey and the Levant (Bernal 1987; Dietler 2005; Marchand 1996; Morris 1994; Shanks 1996). Here the appropriation was both spiritual and practical. On the one hand, northern Europeans considered themselves the true heirs of the Hellenic miracle (Shanks 1996: 81), as opposed to degenerate modern Greeks or Turks. Some scholars even attributed the creativity of Greek civilization to the work of Aryan invaders (Trigger 1992: 155). On the other hand, foreign institutions (museums, schools, and universities) dictated the agendas of archaeology, philology, and historiography with the utmost disregard for local needs or beliefs. As diplomatic institutions, foreign schools were often politically involved in the larger imperialist enterprise (Krings and Tassignon 2004). This twofold orientalist agenda was crudely put by a German diplomat in 1902, who, referring to Turkey, noted that "the economic will follow the intellectual conquest as a natural result, and then these two diffused phases will be naturally followed by the third stage, that of political exploitation and consolidation of the cultural values we have created" (Marchand 1996: 318).

Classical Greece was fundamental in defining national and class identities in 19th-century Europe, from cultural capital (Dietler 2005; Tsignarida and Kurtz 2002) to bodily behavior (Leoussi 2001). In recent times, Eurocentric views have been contested, most notably by Martin Bernal (1987), who, in his highly controversial *Black Athena*, emphasizes the African and Oriental roots of Greece. In any case, modern Greeks (and Turks) lie as marginal historical subjects in a no-man's-land governed by foreign academic controversies and identity politics.

The case of Rome is somewhat different. Whereas the appropriation of Greece was mostly cultural, in the case of Rome it was obviously political. Rome provided theoretical and practical models of colonization and offered justifications for European colonialism (Díaz-Andreu 2004; Dietler 2005: 43–45; Hingley 2000, 2001, 2006). Just as Roman imperialism had supposedly been advantageous for the conquered, despite the violence of the process, the civilizing mission of modern European powers was equally framed in positive terms. This was clearly stated in scholarly publications: "Rome made a genuine effort to unite Liberty and Empire, and, although she ultimately failed, she offered . . . at least a highly interesting analogy to similar modern experiments. In particular the English historian is irresistibly reminded of the British Empire" (Fiddes 1906: 5). The Roman Empire played another relevant role in colonialism. The presence of ancient monuments in certain lands allowed colonial powers to lay claim over those territories. This was the case with the French in Algeria and Tunis (Cañete 2006; Mattingly 1996) and the Italians in Libya (Munzi 2004).

Egypt and the Middle East have suffered manifold processes of intellectual expropriation, with repercussions in the present day (Bahrani 1998; Marchand 1996; Meskell 2003; Said 1979). They are the homeland of some of the cultural products that the West values most, such as literacy, urbanism, statehood, and Christianity. However, dominant discourse held that the true heirs of the Middle Eastern legacy were not the Arabs, but the Europeans. The ruins of ancient civilizations with no match in the present were held as proof that the modern inhabitants of the Orient had to be controlled and recivilized by the West. The Middle East provided a counter-image of the classical world as well—a land of despots and stagnation. Even a genius like V. Gordon Childe (1944: 23) yielded to those clichés when he asserted, "It is hardly an accident of excavation that the full fruits of iron technology have come to light first in the republics of Greece and Italy and not in the despotic states of the Orient." Far from having vanished, orientalist discourses have been revived during both Iraq wars (Pollock and Lutz 1994; Hamilakis 2005).

The Discourse of Origins

The discourse of origins has had more sinister outcomes, since it denied true humanity to a large proportion of the humankind. The move was inevitable after the 18th century's universal declarations of human rights. Indeed, the only way to reconcile these declarations with colonial exploitation was to locate the Other on a lower stage of the evolutionary ladder—that of the inhumane, prehistoric savage. The discourse of origins created a radical divide between history and prehistory, which, in the last instance, can be attributed to Hegel. Hegel (1975) distinguished between "World-History," a Western history of spiritual progress based on statehood, and "Prehistory," the history of people without history (Guha 2002).

The archaeological invention of the concept of "prehistory" in the mid-19th century

(Trigger 1992: 86) is somewhat independent from philosophy, although the idea is related, as it identifies "*Vorzeit*," "*Vorgeschichte*," or "Prehistory" as time that preceded authentic (state) history. Originally used to describe the period before the appearance of written records in Europe, it was quickly employed by other continents as a way to make sense of not only the past, but also the present (McNiven and Russell 2005). The best example of this can be found in John Lubbock's *Prehistoric Times*, published in 1865, which saw several editions over the next 50 years. Despite its early use of the term "prehistory," the book deals largely with modern "primitives." The underlying idea of this and other books is simple: savage societies are relics from another era. The similarity of their customs and artifacts with those of prehistoric peoples is considered obvious, and they are inevitably condemned to disappear with the expansion of superior white populations, for the betterment of humankind. This notion was rarely camouflaged.

Writing in the 1910s, William Sollas considered the Tasmanians an example of the Early Palaeolithic race, whose ancestors, widely distributed over the Old World, were "displaced almost everywhere by superior races" (Sollas 1924: 125). He regrets their extermination by Europeans, given their scientific interest, but notes that "we can only hope that the replacement of a people with a cranial capacity of only about 1,200 c.c. by one with a capacity nearly one-third greater may prove ultimately of advantage in the evolution of mankind" (Sollas 1924: 127). In this way, Hegelian philosophy, Darwinism, positivism, anthropology, and archaeology came together to produce a powerful discourse that would support colonialism for over a century.

Archaeology was also useful for denying Indigenous peoples their roots and their historical rights to the land. Whenever monuments were discovered in "primitive" lands from sub-Saharan Africa (Hall 1995; Keenan 2002) to Australia (Russell and McNiven 1998), they were automatically linked to superior, white populations that had supposedly occupied the land before the arrival of their current inhabitants. This strategy was buttressed by diffusionist ideas in the early 20th century, which conceived a very restricted number of creative core areas from which cultural products spread all over the world (Harris 1968: 379–383).

Although challenged by scholars for over half a century, the discourses of origins and civilization still prevail in the cultural imagination of the West. It is the task of archaeologists to keep fighting these stereotypes and decolonizing discourses not only in academia, but also at a popular level.

Colonizing the Nation

When we think about the relationship between Europe and colonialism, we invariably consider Europe's aggressions against other regions. However, there has been a very important inner colonialism in Europe, which is linked to the consolidation of the nation-state. For the triumph of the modern nation-state, rural communities and cultural minorities had to be fully incorporated into the common project. Thus, the Bretons, Basques, and Irish were very often the target of colonial cultural policies (Bush 2006: 70–71; Hingley 2006). On the other hand, anthropologists have noted the parallels traced by 19th-century folklorists between the rural populations of Europe and the "primitives" of other continents (Hoyt 2001: 333–336). The state's behavior in relation to minorities was often comparable to that deployed in external colonies, but there was an unsolvable ambiguity: peasants were ridiculed as primitives and subjected to modernizing projects, but at the same time they were considered to be the cultural repositories of the nation's essences (Sánchez Gómez 1997: 311).

Archaeology played a pivotal role in incorporating minorities into the nation-state. Although the intellectual strategies of incorporation have been labeled nationalist (Trigger 1984), the line between nationalism and colonialism is blurred. Algeria, for example, was considered part of France, and Angola and Mozambique were perceived as Portuguese provinces (Cooper 2002: 139). Similarly, General Franco used a colonial language and policy in Catalonia and the Basque country (Díaz-Andreu 1997; Tomlison 1991: 76–77). An example of where nationalism and imperialism were more clearly conflated can be found in the case of Germany in the 1930s and 1940s. The subjugation of the Slavic neighbors of Germany was both an explicit colonial enterprise and part of the Nazi nation-building. Archaeologists tried to demonstrate through material culture that the Germans had settled in most of Eastern Europe before the Slavic expansion (Arnold 1990, 2002; Gasche 2006).

The Postcolonial Paradox

By the 1970s, most countries in the world had gained independence from Western European states. If we leave places like Puerto Rico aside (Pagán-Jiménez 2004), we can say that we live in a postcolonial world today; but is this a world free of empires? We may say that we have new, postmodern empires without colonies (Bush 2006: 187–215; Hardt and Negri 2000), endowed with their own strategies of knowledge-power. Although much attention has been paid to the United States (Chomsky 2003), the European "cosmopolitan empire" should be scrutinized too (Beck and Grande 2007: 61–62). It would be interesting, for example, to study whether different neocolonial strategies in the United States and the European Union are related to different modes of archaeological knowledge. In both cases, it has been noted that postcolonial discourses could be little more than another way of using the Other to define Western identities (Hernando 2006).

"Cooperation" is the crucial word in the European empire (Beck and Grande 2007: 67). As archaeologists, we help communities on other continents to recover their history and presuppose that locals are unable to address their past in a proper way. This echoes colonial ideas that "subject cultures required management and regimes to articulate, map, and control resources, specifically their monumental past" (Meskell 2003: 151). However, people all over the world have been dealing with their history in manifold ways before Western knowledge arrived. The language of cooperation cannot avoid the uncomfortable fact that Euro-American scholars are still the gatekeepers of knowledge about others. This is obvious in mainstream scientific literature (Hamilakis 2005: 98). In a recent study on journal gatekeepers, it was noted that three European countries (United Kingdom, Germany, and France) had 2,555 researchers in that category, whereas Africa and Latin America together had 109 (Braun and Dióspatonyi 2005: table 1).

"Cooperation" is a word used to justify archaeological projects abroad. The neocolonial nature of this cooperation is often revealed in the fact that archaeologists tend to work in their former colonies due to the support granted by former imperial powers, which have all kinds of political and economic stakes in those countries. Thus, British archaeologists control East Africa and French archaeologists their old West African colonies and the Maghreb (McEachern 1996).

The study of current archaeological projects abroad has elicited little interest, despite their relevant implications (Bray and Glover's 1987 text is a rare exception). In fact, current archaeological projects are often portrayed in celebratory nationalistic terms (e.g., Ministère des affaires etrangères 2004), and the self-praise is sometimes extended to colonial times (La Rosa 1986). Especially remarkable is the natural smoothness with which institutions of power-knowledge in the colony have survived, without any conspicuous act of contrition or any hint of self-reflection on their former and current role. Many research institutes still bear the name they had in colonial times, with a very colonialist flair, such as the British School of African and Oriental Studies (SOAS), founded in 1916 in the heyday of colonialism, or the Istituto Italiano per l'Africa e l'Oriente (IsIAO), with roots in the colonial and fascist period.

Neocolonial attitudes have also been denounced in international agencies and institutions that pay lip service to "world heritage" (Meskell 2003), but often seem to be more concerned with facilitating exotic playgrounds for Europeans (Bush 2006: 213). Colonial ideas appear repeatedly in academia as well, especially when it comes to the restitution of cultural property (Boardman 2000) or the categorization of past societies as more or less civilized, implying that those groups that have not developed urbanism, monuments, or writing were, or still are, savages (Hamilakis 2005: 96).

One of the characteristics of modern empires is the neutralization of politics, in keeping with the "end of history" announced after the fall of communism (Fukuyama 1992). Politics are reduced to identity issues (Huntington 1996), a fact that is mirrored in the social sciences. Postprocessual archaeology echoes these neoliberal concerns especially well (Díaz-Andreu et al. 2005; Kane 2003; Meskell 2002). Whereas Americans, in the processual tradition, are still concerned with political economy, power structures, and statehood, Europeans, following postprocessual trends, usually focus on culture and identity. Although both lines are somehow converging (Stein 2005a: 8), the difference is still quite clear. It is illustrative to compare the way in which American archaeologists study pre-Columbian empires (Covey 2006; D'Altroy 1992; Feinman and Nicholas 2004) and how the Roman and Phoenician colonizations are currently understood in Europe (Hingley 2005; Jiménez 2008; Mattingly 1997; van Dommelen 1997; Woolf 1998). It is worth noting that the interests of scholars coincide with the foreign policies of the United States and the European Union as they are performed on the global stage; the former is harder and more interventionist, with a strong concern for state-building, while the latter is softer and cooperative, with an alleged interest in social and cultural issues.

Postcolonial studies have indisputably produced a richer, more complex, and nuanced vision of colonial processes (Gosden 2004; Lyons and Papadopoulos 2002; Stein 2005; van Dommelen 2006). However, despite van Dommelen's reminder (2005: 115) that "cultural hegemony and economic exploitation are not two different or even opposed interpretations of colonial power, but they should rather be seen as two sides of the same coin," the truth is that the political side of colonialism tends to be ignored in current studies of the phenomenon (Gosden 2001: 243). This might be dangerous; by stressing fluid encounters, negotiation, hybridity, consumption, agency, and creative appropriation (Dietler 2005; van Dommelen 2005, 2006; Vives-Ferrándiz 2005; Webster 1996), we neglect the crudest side of colonialism—politics, including political economy (Wolf 1982), asymmetrical power relations, massacres, looting, disease, impoverishment, unequal wars, heavy taxes, and genocide. Surely, these are not always relevant, especially in ancient examples (e.g., Dietler 2005: 55–61; Vives-Ferrándiz 2005). Yet by overlooking politics, we run the risk of depriving the people without history of the history that hurts, the experience of daily humiliation and abuse by foreign masters (Given 2004: 163).

Future Directions

Colonialism and European archaeology have been close allies for a long time. Even today, the colonial sin is far from being washed away. Postcolonial archaeology has to be less self-indulgent and more critical in order to deconstruct the ongoing relationship with neocolonialism. Here are a few suggestions for producing a more radical archaeology. First, it is necessary to get rid of the condescending language of cooperation and progress, which simply transforms the savage of colonialism into the undeveloped native of the postcolony (González-Ruibal 2009). Second, we must take equality seriously (Rancière 1995) and stop dreaming of impossible, idealized partnerships. As Alberto Memmi (2004: 163) reminds us, "Partnership does not make sense except when both partners have a reasonably equal force." It is still Western archaeologists who study Africa's past, not the other way around. Third, it is important to embrace politics beyond identity issues, and recognize that politics is all about conflict (Žižek 2007). We have to be able to accept conflict in postcolonial situations.

From here, we have to consider ruling out concepts that have been deeply tainted by colonial values and Eurocentricity, such as "prehistory" (McNiven and Russell 2005), which situates contemporary Indigenous communities in another time (Fabian 1983), or "historical archaeology," which only considers Western World History as "historical" (Guha 2002). Then, archaeological traditions in Europe must properly address their colonial pasts and neocolonial presents. And finally, a dichotomy has to be broken between conscious postcolonial scholars who focus on deconstructing their discipline and researchers who, without caring much about the history of the discipline, Indigenous communities, or colonialism, tell us how the past truly was (Langebaek 2006: 118).

References

Arnold, B. 1990. The past as propaganda: Totalitarian archaeology in Nazi Germany. *Antiquity* 64 (244): 464–478.

——. 2002. Justifying genocide: The supporting role of archaeology in "ethnic cleansing," in A. Hinton (ed.), *Annihilating Difference: The Anthropology of Genocide*, pp. 95–116. Berkeley: University of California Press.

Bahrani, Z. 1998. Conjuring Mesopotamia: Imaginative geography and a world past, in L. Meskell (ed.), *Archaeology under Fire: Nationalism, Politics and Heritage in the Eastern Mediterranean and Middle East*, pp. 159–174. London: Routledge.

Beck, U., and Grande, E. 2007. *Cosmopolitan Europe*. Cambridge: Polity.

Bernal, M. 1987. *Black Athena: The Afroasiatic Roots of Classical Civilization*, Vol. 1. *The Fabrication of Ancient Greece, 1785–1985*. London: Free Association Books.

Boardman, J. 2000. The Elgin marbles: Matters of fact and opinion. *International Journal of Cultural Property* 9 (2): 233–262.

Braun, T., and Dióspatonyi, I. 2005. The counting of core journal gatekeepers as science indicators really counts: The scientific scope of action and strength of nations. *Current Science* 89 (9): 1548–1551.

Bush, B. 2006. *Imperialism and Postcolonialism*. Harlow: Pearson/Longman.

Bray, W., and Glover, I. C. 1987. Scientific investigation or cultural imperialism: British archaeology in the Third World. *Bulletin of the Institute of Archaeology* 24: 109–125.

Cañete, C. 2006. La Antigüedad en la comisión de exploración científica de Argelia (s. XIX): Variabilidad para un fin común. *Al-Andalus Magreb: Estudios Árabes e Islámicos* 13: 43–68.

Chadha, A. 2002. Visions of discipline: Sir Mortimer Wheeler and the archaeological method in India, 1944–1948. *Journal of Social Archaeology* 2 (3): 378–401.

Childe, V. G. 1944. Archaeological ages as technological stages. *The Journal of the Royal Anthropological Institute of Great Britain and Ireland* 74 (1/2): 7–24.

Chomsky, N. 2003. *Hegemony or Survival: America's Quest for Global Dominance*. London: Hamish Hamilton.

Cooper, F. 2002. *Africa since 1940: The Past of the Present*. Cambridge: Cambridge University Press.

Covey, R. A. 2006. *How the Incas Built Their Heartland: State Formation and the Inno-*

vation of Imperial Strategies in the Sacred Valley, Peru. Ann Arbor: University of Michigan Press.

Cro, S. 1977. Las fuentes clásica de la utopía moderna: El "buen salvaje" y las "Islas Felices" en la historiografía indiana. *Anales de Literatura Hispanoamericana* 6: 39–52.

D'Altroy, T. N. 1992. *Provincial Power in the Inka Empire*. Washington: Smithsonian Institution.

Díaz-Andreu, M. 1997. Prehistoria y franquismo, in G. Mora and M. Díaz-Andreu (eds.), *La Cristalización del pasado: Génesis y desarrollo del Marco Institucional de la Arqueología en España*, pp. 547–552. Málaga: Universidad de Málaga.

——. 2004. Britain and the other: The archaeology of imperialism, in R. Phillips and H. Brocklehurst (eds.), *History, Identity and the Question of Britain*, pp. 227–241. New York: Palgrave.

Díaz-Andreu, M., Lucy, S., Babic, S., and Edwards, D. 2005. *The Archaeology of Identity: Approaches to Gender, Age, Ethnicity, Status and Religion*. London: Routledge.

Dietler, M. 2005. The archaeology of colonization and the colonization of archaeology: Theoretical challenges from an ancient Mediterranean colonial encounter, in G. J. Stein (ed.), *The Archaeology of Colonial Encounters: Comparative Perspectives*, pp. 33–68. Santa Fe: School of American Research Advanced Seminar Series.

Fabian, J. 1983. *Time and the Other: How Anthropology Makes Its Object*. New York: Columbia University Press.

Feinman, G. M., and Nicholas, L. M. 2004. *Archaeological Perspectives on Political Economies*. Salt Lake City: University of Utah Press.

Fernández, V. M. 2001. La idea de África en el origen de la prehistoria española: Una perspectiva postcolonial. *Complutum* 12: 167–184.

Fiddes, E. 1906. Introduction, in E. Fiddes (ed.), *Studies of Roman Imperialism by W. T. Arnold*, pp. 1–7. Manchester: Manchester University Press.

Fukuyama, F. 1992. *The End of History and the Last Man*. New York: Free Press.

Gasche, M. 2006. Zum konzept der "Germanenkunde" im ahnenerbe der SS. *Ethnographisch- Archäeologische Zeitschriftt* 47 (1): 127–135.

Given, M. 2004. *The Archaeology of the Colonized*. London: Routledge.

González-Ruibal, A. 2009. Vernacular cosmopolitanism: An archaeological critique of universalistic reason, in L. Meskell (ed.), *Cosmopolitan Archaeologies*, pp. 113–139. Durham: Duke University Press.

Gosden, C. 2001. Postcolonial archaeology: Issues of culture, identity, and knowledge, in I. Hodder (ed.), *Archaeological Theory Today*, pp. 241–261. Cambridge: Polity.

——. 2004. *Archaeology and Colonialism: Cultural Contact from 5000 B.C. to the Present*. Cambridge: Cambridge University Press.

Guha, R. 2002. *History at the Limit of World-History*. New York: Columbia University Press.

Hall, E. 1989. *Inventing the Barbarian: Greek Self-Identification*. Oxford: Oxford University Press.

Hall, M. 1995. Great Zimbabwe and the lost city: The cultural colonization of the

South African past, in P. J. Ucko (ed.), *Theory in Archaeology: A World Perspective*, pp. 28–45. London: Routledge.

Hamilakis, Y. 2005. Whose world and whose archaeology? The colonial present and the return of the political. *Archaeologies* 1 (2): 94–101.

Hardt, M., and Negri, A. 2000. *Empire*. Cambridge, MA: Harvard University Press.

Harris, M. 1968. *The Rise of Anthropological Theory: A History of Theories of Culture*. New York: Crowell.

Hegel, G. W. F. 1975. *Lectures on the Philosophy of World History. Introduction*, H. B. Nisbet (trans.). Cambridge: Cambridge University Press.

Hernando, A. 2006. Arqueología y globalización: El problema de la definición del "otro" en la postmodernidad. *Complutum* 17: 221–234.

Hingley, R. 2000. *Roman Officers and English Gentlemen: The Imperial Origins of Roman Archaeology*. London: Routledge.

——. 2005. *Globalizing Roman Culture: Unity, Diversity and Empire*. London: Routledge.

——. 2006. Projecting empire. *Journal of Social Archaeology* 6 (3): 328–353.

Hingley, R. (ed.). 2001. *Images of Rome: Perceptions of Ancient Rome in Europe and the U.S. in the Modern Age*. Portsmouth: Journal of Roman Archaeology.

Hoyt, D. L. 2001. The reanimation of the primitive: Fin-de-siècle ethnographic discourse in Western Europe. *History of Science* 39: 331–354.

Huntington, S. 1996. *The Clash of Civilizations and the Remaking of World Order*. New York: Simon and Schuster.

Jiménez, A. 2008. *Imagines hibridae: Una Aproximación postcolonialista al estudio de las necrópolis de la Bética*. Anejos de Archivo Español de Arqueología, 43. Madrid: CSIC.

Kane, S. (ed.). 2003. *The Politics of Archaeology and Identity in a Global Context*. Boston: Archaeological Institute of America.

Keenan, J. 2002. The lesser gods of the Sahara. *Public Archaeology* 2 (3): 131–150.

Krings, V., and Tassignon, I. (eds.). 2004. *Archéologie dans l'Empire Ottoman autour de 1900: Entre politique, économie et science*. Rome: Institut Historique Belge de Rome.

Langebaek, C. H. 2006. Arqueología e izquierda en Colombia, in P. P. A. Funari and A. Zarankin (eds.), *Arqueología de la represión y la resistencia en América Latina 1960–1980*, pp. 103–120. Córdoba: Encuentro.

La Rosa, V. (ed.). 1986. *L'Archeologia italiana nel Mediterraneo fino alla Seconda Guerra Mondiale*. Catania: Centro di Studi per l'archeologia greca del Consiglio Nazionale delle Ricerche.

Leoussi, A. S. 2001. Myths of ancestry. *Nations and Nationalism* 7 (4): 467–486.

Lubbock, J. 1865. *Prehistoric Times, as Illustrated by Ancient Remains and the Manners and Customs of Modern Savages*. London: Williams and Norgate.

Lyons, C. L., and Papadopoulos, J. K. (eds.). 2002. *The Archaeology of Colonialism: Issues and Debates*. Los Angeles: Getty Research Institute.

Marchand, S. 1996. Orientalism as Kulturpolitik: German archaeology and cultural imperialism in Asia Minor, in G. W.

Stocking, Jr. (ed.), *Volksgeist as Method and Ethic: Essays on Boasian Ethnography and the German Anthropological Tradition*, pp. 298–336. History of Anthropology 8. Madison: University of Wisconsin Press.

Mattingly, D. 1996. From one colonialism to another: Imperialism and the Maghreb, in J. Webster and N. Cooper (eds.), *Roman Imperialism: Post-colonial Perspectives*, pp. 49–70. Leicester: Leicester University Press.

———. 1997. Dialogues of power and experience in the Roman Empire, in D. Mattingly (ed.), *Dialogues in Roman Imperialism*, pp. 1–16. Portsmouth: Journal of Roman Archaeology.

McEachern, S. 1996. Foreign countries: The development of ethnoarchaeology in Sub-Saharan Africa. *Journal of World Prehistory* 10 (3): 243–304.

McNiven, I. J., and Russell, L. 2005. *Appropriated Pasts: Indigenous Peoples and the Colonial Culture of Archaeology*. Lanham, MD: AltaMira Press.

Memmi, A. 2004. *Portrait du décolonisé Arabo-Musulman et de quelques autres*. Paris: Gallimard.

Meskell, L. 2002. The intersections of identity and politics in archaeology. *Annual Review of Anthropology* 31: 279–301.

———. 2003. Pharaonic legacies: Postcolonialism, heritage, and hyperreality, in S. Kane (ed.), *The Politics of Archaeology and Identity in a Global Context*, pp. 149–171. Boston: Archaeological Institute of America.

Ministère des affaires étrangères 2004. *Archéologies: Vingt ans de recherches françaises dans le monde*. Ministère des affaires étrangères. Paris: Maisonneuve et Larose.

Morris, I. 1994. Archaeologies of Greece, in I. Morris (ed.), *Classical Greece: Ancient Histories and Modern Archaeologies*, pp. 9–47. Cambridge: Cambridge University Press.

Munzi, M. 2004. Italian archaeology in Libya: From colonial romanità to decolonization of the past, in M. L Galaty and C. Watkinson (eds.), *Archaeology under Dictatorship*, pp. 73–108. New York: Springer.

Pagán-Jiménez, J. R. 2004. Is all archaeology at present a postcolonial one? *Journal of Social Archaeology* 4 (2): 200–213.

Pollock, S., and Lutz, C. 1994. Archaeology deployed for the Gulf War. *Critique of Anthropology* 14 (3): 263–284.

Rancière, J. 1995. *On the Shores of Politics*. London: Verso.

Russell, L. and McNiven, I. J. 1998. Monumental colonialism. *Journal of Material Culture* 3 (3): 283–299.

Said, E. 1979. *Orientalism*. New York: Vintage.

Sánchez Gómez, L. A. 1997. Cien años de antropologías en España y Portugal, 1870–1970. *Etnográfica* 1 (2): 297–317.

Shanks, M. 1996. *Classical Archaeology of Greece*. London: Routledge.

Schnapp, A. 1996. *The Discovery of the Past*. London: Trustees of the British Museum.

Sollas, W. 1924 [1911]. *Ancient Hunters and Their Modern Representatives*. 4th ed. London: McMillan & Co.

Stein, G. J. 2005a. Introduction: The comparative archaeology of colonial encounters, in G. J Stein (ed.), *The Archaeology of Colonial Encounters: Comparative Perspectives*, pp. 3–31. Santa Fe: School of American Research Advanced Seminar Series.

Stein, G. J. (ed.). 2005b. *The Archaeology of Colonial Encounters: Comparative Perspectives*. Santa Fe: School of American Research Advanced Seminar Series.

Tomlison, J. 1991. *Cultural Imperialism: A Critical Introduction*. Baltimore: John Hopkins University Press.

Trigger, B. 1984. Alternative archaeologies: Nationalist, colonialist, imperialist. *Man* 19 (3): 355–370.

——. 1992. *Historia del pensamiento arqueológico*. Barcelona: Crítica.

Tsignarida, A., and Kurtz, D. 2002. *Appropriating Antiquity. Saisir l'Antique: Collections et collectionneurs d'antiques en Belgique et en Grande-Bretagne au XIXe siècle*. Brussels: Livre Timperman.

van Dommelen, P. 1997. Colonial constructs: Colonialism and archaeology in the Mediterranean. *World Archaeology* 28 (3): 305–323.

——. 2005. Colonial interactions and hybrid practices: Phoenician and Carthaginian settlement in the ancient Mediterranean, in G. J. Stein (ed.), *The Archaeology of Colonial Encounters: Comparative Perspectives*, pp. 109–141. Santa Fe: School of American Research Advanced Seminar Series.

——. 2006. Colonial matters: Material culture and postcolonial theory in colonial situations, in C. Tilley et al. (eds.), *Handbook of Material Culture*, pp. 104–124. London: Sage.

Vives-Ferrándiz, J. 2005. *Negociando encuentros: Situaciones coloniales e intercambios en la costa oriental de la península Ibérica (ss. VIII–VI a. C.)*. Cuadernos de Arqueología Mediterránea 12. Barcelona: Universidad Pompeu Fabra.

Webster, J. 1996. Ethnographic barbarity: Colonial discourse and "Celtic warrior societies," in J. Webster and N. Cooper (eds.), *Roman Imperialism: Post-colonial Perspectives*, pp. 111–124. Leicester: Leicester University Press.

Wolf, E. 1982. . *Europe and the People without History*. Berkeley: University of California Press.

Woolf, G. 1998. *Becoming Roman: The Origins of Provincial Civilization in Gaul*. Cambridge: Cambridge University Press.

Žižek, S. 2007. *En defensa de la intolerancia*. Buenos Aires: Sequitur.

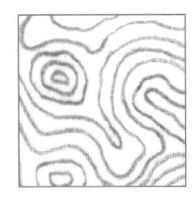

3

NEAR EASTERN ARCHAEOLOGY: IMPERIAL PASTS, POSTCOLONIAL PRESENTS, AND THE POSSIBILITIES OF A DECOLONIZED FUTURE

Benjamin W. Porter

Archaeological research in what is commonly known as the "Near East" or "Middle East" began in the late 18th century, when European explorers fanned out through the region following Napoleon's 1798 Egyptian campaigns. Although made up of an assortment of archaeologists and explorers, historians, and philologists, the collective discipline that emerged over the 19th and 20th centuries now bears the title "Near Eastern Archaeology." Like archaeological practice around the world, Near Eastern archaeology often played a role in European and North American imperial and colonialist enterprises in the region, in part due to Western fascination with the "Land of the Bible." Currently, the region's nation-states manage their own antiquities, often using them to construct narratives that legitimate postcolonial circumstances. However, despite more than a half-century of independent control, decolonization of archaeological practices has only recently begun in this region.

The Near East is not so much a place to be located on a map as a discursive formation consisting of assemblages of ideas, peoples, and things fixed in the minds of scholars. Discovering a collective geographic term for the area under review is therefore a difficult and unsolvable problem.[1] The term "Near East," like related terms "Middle East" and the French-inspired "Levant," have their origins in late 19th- and early 20th-century European military nomenclature for the region (Keddie 1973). Such terms have largely surpassed earlier labels such as the "Orient" and now dominate North American and European discourse. Some archaeologists working in the United Kingdom have adopted perceived neutral categories such as "Western Asia" or "Southwestern Asia" in their research. These terms have overtaken older indigenous designations such as the Arabic *mashriq*, or, "eastern part of the Arab world," and *bilad ash-sham*, or "province of Damascus," and replaced them with translations of the "Middle East" into Arabic *ash-sharq al-'awsat* and Hebrew *ha-mizrakh ha-tikhon*. These earlier and relatively emic terms more accurately account for the area under discussion in this chapter (Naccache 1992: 6–7).

Like the discipline's cartography, its chronologies have often been organized according to external, rather than internal, factors that impacted social life in antiquity. Three distinct chronological taxonomies have tended to dominate. The most general version divides the study of the region's human occupation into prehistory and history. A second taxonomy divides Classical and pre-Classical periods, classifying the latter according to the appearance of technologies such as stone (Palaeolithic), copper (Chalcolithic), bronze, and iron into the region. A third schema segments historical eras into three exclusive periods that rarely overlap in academic discussions: an ancient period from the fourth millennium B.C.E. to Alexander the Great's campaigns in 333 B.C.E.; a Classical period spanning the Hellenistic, Roman, and Byzantine empires' occupation; and an Islamic period beginning with the introduction of Islam in the 7th century and continuing until World War I. In this last taxonomy, smaller time periods are established according to whichever local or foreign imperial power dominated the region: e.g., Akkadian, Hellenistic, or Crusader. Rarely are chronologies defined according to local historical or cultural developments in antiquity, and when they are, scholars often apply blanket ethnic labels such as "Canaanite" and "Israelite" with little critical thought. Although archaeological research in prehistoric and Islamic periods has increased in recent decades, the discipline has traditionally focused on ancient and Classical periods.

Histories and Historiographies of Near Eastern Archaeology

Near Eastern archaeology's vision of itself is apparent in the many disciplinary histories its practitioners have produced. The subjects of these historical projects have ranged from hagiographic biographies (Running and Freedman 1975), to intellectual (Davis 2004; Moorey 1991), excavation (Blakely and Toombs 1980), and institutional histories (King 1983), the last of which organizes actors and their contributions according to nationality such as "American" and "French" (Drinkard et al. 1988) and schools of thought (e.g., "Albright" and "Chicago"). These disciplinary histories, however, have not critically examined how pervasive ideas about race, culture, politics, and language come to inform archaeologists' claims about the region's history and society. Not until Silberman's 1982 publication of *Digging for God and Country* and his 1989 follow-up, *Between Past and Present: Archaeology, Ideology, and Nationalism in the Middle East*, did a more critical period of reflection arise. The last decade has seen the publication of additional studies that investigate, critique, and sometimes counter the extent to which Near Eastern archaeologists participated in 19th- and 20th-century colonialist enterprises. Primary sources for such studies include travelers' accounts, photographs, memoirs, excavation field notes, and interviews both published and archived in universities, foundations, museums, and research centers in the Middle East, Europe, and North America. While some consideration has been paid to Iraq (Abdi 2008; Bernhardsson 2005; Goode 2007; Larsen 1989, 1996), Iran (Abdi 2001; Goode 2007; Majd 2003), Jordan (Corbett 2009), and Turkey (Goode 2007; Shaw 2003), and very little to Syria and Lebanon (but see Naccache 1998), the state of Israel and Palestine have received the most attention (Abu El-Haj 2001; Davies 1992; Kletter 2006; Steen 2002; Whitelam 1995).

These disciplinary histories have drawn attention to three distinct eras when Near Eastern archaeology played an instrumental role in advancing imperial, colonial, or postcolonial objectives. The first period spans the end of the 18th through the early 20th centuries, the final century of Ottoman imperial rule. During these decades, European and North American diplomacy, pilgrimage, and settlement increased in coastal ports like Jaffa and Beirut, and in urban centers such as Aleppo, Damascus, and Jerusalem. Explorers such as Paul-Émile Botta and Austen Henry Layard in Iraq and Edward Robinson in Palestine conducted early excavations, and, in the case of Botta and Layard, brought physical evidence of early "civilizations" back to European museums, in turn stimulating further interest in the region's ancient societies. Layard's discovery of Ashurbanipal's library and, in particular, an account of a catastrophic flood similar to that described in Genesis 6:9 were sensational discoveries widely reported in the European press. No undertaking would be bigger, however, than the Palestine Exploration Fund's Survey of Western Palestine, a multi-year survey of the region's ancient remains, as well as its contemporary peoples and infrastructure (Figure 3.1) (Conder and

Figure 3.1 The Palestine Exploration Fund's Survey of Western Palestine was a multi-year survey of the region's ancient remains as well as its contemporary peoples. Here, a surveyor and local assistant measure distances from a fixed point (1925, courtesy of the Palestine Exploration Fund).

Kitchner 1881; Moscrop 2000; Watson 1915). Not only did these maps and descriptions assist archaeological research for the next several decades, they also were an important resource for the British military during World War I. The end of the 19th and the beginning of the 20th centuries saw the first systematic excavations at sites such as Nippur, Carchemish, and Tell el-Hesi. Excavation projects were often supported by recently established foreign research institutes such as the American Schools of Oriental Research, now the W. F. Albright Institute of Archaeological Research in Jerusalem, and universities such as the Syrian Protestant College, now the American University in Beirut, and the Jesuit-run Université Saint-Joseph. Intellectual trends during this period dwelled on theories of race, oriental despotism, biblical history, and the divergent legacies of Classic and Near Eastern civilizations.

The end of World War I and the collapse of the Ottoman Empire ushered in the second era: a three-decade-long British Mandate of Iraq, Palestine, and Transjordan and the French Mandate of Lebanon and Syria. Now that archaeologists were no longer beholden to Ottoman authorities, the region witnessed a surge in excavations. The exploration of regions that were previously too volatile for foreigners was now possible (Glueck 1940). Colonial powers established government offices to manage this increased activity. Baghdad, Beirut, Damascus, and Jerusalem saw the construction of museums that stored and displayed excavated artifacts. This period also saw interests in chronological foci diverge; while British and North American scholars remained interested in biblical archaeology, the French concentrated on Classical-period remains in Syria and Lebanon. Prehistoric and Mesopotamian archaeology, however, attracted interest from scholars regardless of national affiliation. Despite the social and ethnic unrest that marked this second era, so-called biblical archaeologists consider this time their "golden age" due to the flourishing of excavations in Palestine and the intense intellectual debates over the origins and nature of biblical societies (Moorey 1991: 54–78).

Although notions of Jewish and Arab nationalism and their imagined connections to more historically remote societies began earlier, these sentiments would not see full expression until the third era, with the dismantling of European empires, the withdrawal of colonial powers, and the establishment of the region's modern nation-states. At their inception, these new states inherited the laws, institutions, and museums established previously under colonial rule, and foreign researchers were now required to seek permission from government officials. The need to train indigenous archaeologists to manage these antiquities arose, and undergraduate and graduate curricula were instituted in universities. Excavations at Hazor in Israel and Tall Mazar in Jordan trained indigenous archaeologists in excavation methods, sometimes with the assistance of Western scholars. Departments of antiquities, universities, museums, and research institutions published periodicals in Arabic, Hebrew, and European languages. Besides excavation, archaeology was charged with developing antiquity sites for tourism, an initiative that would grow to become an important revenue generator for these young countries.

Despite this thriving archaeological infrastructure, the intellectual concerns of indigenous archaeologists closely mirror those of their Western counterparts, stressing culture history, subsistence practices, and social evolution. Such similarities can be explained, in part, by the fact that scholars from Arabic-speaking countries are often trained in European, North American, and Australian graduate programs and then return to fill university and high-ranking government posts. However, the situation in Israel is different, as almost all Israeli archaeologists receive training in Israeli graduate programs where, at times, European and North American scholars also seek training.

The role that archaeological evidence has played in national narratives that create justifications for these contemporary states has differed in each country and across time, making generalizations impossible (Meskell 1998; Silberman 1989). In Israel, archaeological evidence associated with the First (ca. 1000–580 B.C.E.) and Second (500 B.C.E.–approximately 200 C.E.) Temple periods has played an active and at times controversial role in national narratives. The dominant paradigm argued that archaeological research provided substantial evidence for an ancient Israelite kingdom closely resembling the Hebrew Bible's description (Yadin 1972). Such affirmations resonate with some Israelis as well as with the Jewish diaspora and North American Christians who support the country. For some, the claim that an ancient antecedent existed not only proves the biblical account, but also lends legitimacy to the State of Israel's existence. But recent reflections on past research as well as new excavations have challenged these assumptions (Davies 1992; Finkelstein and Silberman 2001; Whitelam 1995). The arguments vary in nature, but most suggest that archaeologists have overstated the evidence for an Israelite kingdom, while some challenge the extent to which evidence can be securely dated to a particular century. While this debate has produced heated conversations and at times unprofessional behavior that has spilled out of the ivory tower and into the public square, it has also led scholars to reflect on the methods they use to prove their claims. One consequence has been a movement away from relative ceramic chronologies and toward absolute dating methods such as carbon-14 (Levy and Higham 2005). Despite these shifts toward new dating techniques, the argument over the extent and nature of ancient Israel is far from settled.

The use of archaeology in national narratives has been relatively unsteady elsewhere in the region. For example, limited attempts to base Lebanese nationalism on "Phoenicianism" slowly died out, making archaeology a peripheral concern in national identity. In Iraq, Syria, and Jordan, archaeology was used to provide *qutri* (regional) histories that demonstrated the historical logic of the new national borders largely drawn by colonial administrators. At the same time, these works countered appeals to Arab national unity that were popular in the 1950s and 1960s, which depended more on a shared Islamic history than on any archaeological remains. This relative dearth of local and national writings about the past has created a situation whereby local and national categories and chronologies are informed by Western research.

Decolonizing Near Eastern Archaeology

Despite the dominant role that nation-states play in managing archaeological resources, there are several signs that archaeological practice, frameworks, narratives, sites, and artifacts no longer rest strictly in the hands of nation-states. The enormous challenges that government agencies face in management and funding make it impossible to govern a nation's archaeological resources systematically, especially during periods of conflict and social upheaval in countries such as Iraq and Lebanon. These discrepancies in management open up spaces for individuals and groups to participate in archaeological discourse and practices. At times, this participation can lead to site destruction and subsistence looting, as was seen with the breakdown of the Iraqi government during the 2003 United States invasion (Emberling and Hanson 2008) and the clandestine destruction of archaeological remains during the rebuilding of downtown Beirut by the private construction firm Solidaire (Naccache 1996, 1998).

There are, however, more productive examples where communities and nongovernmental organizations are actively managing cultural properties. One recent and well-documented instance has been the work of the Palestinian Association for Cultural Exchange (PACE), a nonprofit organization located in the West Bank dedicated to preserving Palestinian heritage. One 2004 initiative saw a campaign to raise the public's awareness of the damages that nearby antiquity sites were experiencing due to a lack of management (Yahya 2002). These efforts led to multiple coordinated projects in which communities cleaned and secured archaeological sites (Figure 3.2). Structures in danger of collapse were bulwarked with temporary materials in preparation for more professional conservation measures. While some critics may see such initiatives as symptomatic of neoliberal practices, where fledgling government agencies consequently bring nongovernment groups to perform the role of the state, these moments, at the same time, open up opportunities for indigenous communities to interact with and craft their own narratives about the archaeological resources in their midst. Whether or not these narratives coexist, complement, or conflict with alternative "scientific" and "nationalist" narratives requires scrutiny of local circumstances.

The recognizable differences between state-sponsored and local narratives of the past are a second symptom that decolonization is occurring. The looting of the Baghdad Museum and the illegal sale of artifacts on the antiquities market indicate the extent to which ordinary Iraqis believed themselves unassociated with the nation-state or its projected past. But these alternatives can be subtler as well. In their work in Central Jordan, Jacobs and Porter (2009) have recognized differences between na-

Figure 3.2. Under the supervision of PACE, Palestinians clean Mar Ubadia, an ancient church located in the Palestinian village of Aboud. The German Fund for Palestinian non-governmental organizations provided funding for this project (Courtesy of PACE archives).

tional and local discourse concerning notions of "history" and "heritage." While the kingdom promotes a national heritage that includes more than the last 5,000 years of history, concentrating mainly on Nabataean, Classical, and early Islamic remains, local communities instead dwell on the recent past, beginning in the mid-18th century C.E., as some communities believe that groups before this time share no biological or cultural connections with contemporary Jordanian society. These local sentiments about the past are expressed in language and material culture, as well as in performances in community festivals.

Despite the growing role that the public is playing today in crafting alternative discourses about the past, it is still difficult to identify attempts by scholars based in the region that explore alternative, even subaltern, histories and archaeologies that challenge dominant Western or state-sponsored paradigms. Naccache's writings on ancient Amorites stand as rare examples of an attempt to explore alternative frameworks for understanding ancient Near Eastern societies (Naccache 1992). In fact, scholars working in Western institutions have taken the lead in decolonizing the discipline, emphasizing themes of alterity, gender, communalism, and non-elites in their research (Pollock and Bernbeck 2005). The consequences of this trend are that non-native scholars continue to guide research agendas in the region as they have for the last two centuries.

Today, Near Eastern archaeology finds itself at a critical juncture. Its origins in imperial and colonialist practices need not dictate the future course of the discipline. Having recognized its problematic role in past colonial and imperial enterprises, and at the same time, the power that archaeological research has to shape contemporary identities, some practitioners are grappling with a way forward. Collaborations among archaeologists, government and non-government agencies, and local communities offer one framework for moving ahead that empowers a variety of stakeholders in the process. Whether or not such moves will create a space for alternative narratives that challenge dominant archaeological paradigms is, for now, too early to judge.

Acknowledgments

The author thanks Albert Naccache, Matthew Rutz, and Kevin McGeough for their feedback while writing this essay. The ideas expressed here remain the author's alone.

Note

1. In this discussion, emphasis is placed on research in modern Iraq, Israel, Lebanon, Palestine, Syria, and Turkey. This is not to ignore Iran, Saudi Arabia, Yemen, and the countries lining the Persian Gulf. The history of archaeological research in these countries has received limited attention and calls for further investigation.

References

Abdi, K. 2001. Nationalism, politics, and the development of archaeology in Iran. *American Journal of Archaeology* 105 (1): 51–76.

——. 2008. From Pan-Arabism to Saddam Hussein's cult of personality: Ancient Mesopotamia and Iraqi national ideology. *Journal of Social Archaeology* 8 (1): 3–36.

Abu el-Haj, N. 2001. *Facts on the Ground: Archaeological Practice and Territorial Self-Fashioning in Israeli Society*. Chicago: University of Chicago Press.

Bernhardsson, M. 2005. *Reclaiming a Plundered Past: Archaeology and Nation Building in Modern Iraq*. Austin: University of Texas Press.

Blakely, J., and Toombs, L. 1980. *The Joint Archaeological Expedition to Tell el-Hesi*. Cambridge: American Schools of Oriental Research.

Conder, C., and Kitchner, H. 1881. *The Survey of Western Palestine*. London: Palestine Exploration Fund.

Corbett, E. 2009. *Jordan First: A History of the Intellectual and Political Economy of Jordanian Antiquity*. Ph.D. diss., University of Chicago.

Davies, P. 1992. *In Search of Ancient Israel*. Sheffield: JSOT Press.

Davis, T. 2004. *Shifting Sands: The Rise and Fall of Biblical Archaeology*. Oxford: Oxford University Press.

Drinkard, J., Mattingly, G., Miller, J. M., and Callaway, J. 1988. *Benchmarks in Time and Culture: An Introduction to the History and Methodology of Syro-Palestinian Archaeology*. Atlanta: Scholars Press.

Emberling, G., and Hanson, K. 2008. *Catastrophe! The Looting and Destruction of Iraq's Past*. Chicago: Oriental Institute, University of Chicago.

Finkelstein, I., and Silberman, N. 2001. *The Bible Unearthed: Archaeology's New Vision of Ancient Israel and the Origins of Its Sacred Texts*. New York: Touchstone.

Glueck, N. 1940. *The Other Side of the Jordan*. New Haven: American Schools of Oriental Research.

Goode, J. F. 2007. *Negotiating for the Past: Archaeology, Nationalism, and Diplomacy in the Middle East, 1919–1941*. Austin: University of Texas.

Jacobs, J., and Porter, B. 2009. Excavating *Turaath*: Documenting local and national heritage discourses in Jordan, in L. Mortenson and J. Hollowell (eds.), *Archaeologies and Ethnographies: Iterations of "Heritage" and the Archaeological Past*. Gainesville: University of Florida Press.

Keddie, N. 1973. Is there a Middle East? *International Journal of Middle Eastern Studies* 4: 255–271.

King, P. 1983. *American Archaeology in the Mideast: A History of the American Schools of Oriental Research*. Philadelphia: American Schools of Oriental Research.

Kletter, R. 2006. *Just Past? The Making of Israeli Archaeology*. London: Equinox.

Larsen, M. 1989. Orientalism and Near Eastern archaeology, in D. Miller, M. Rowlands, and C. Tilley (eds.), *Domination and Resistance*, pp. 240–245. London: Unwin Hyman.

———. 1996. *The Conquest of Assyria: Excavations in an Antique Land, 1840–1860*. London: Routledge.

Levy, T., and Higham, T. 2005. *The Bible and Radiocarbon Dating: Archaeology, Text and Science*. London: Equinox Publishing.

Majd, M. G. 2003. *The Great American Plunder of Persia's Antiquities, 1925–1941*. Lanham: University Press of America.

Meskell, L. 1998. *Archaeology under Fire: Nationalism, Politics and Heritage in the Eastern Mediterranean and Middle East*. London: Routledge.

Moorey, P., and Roger, S. 1991. *A Century of Biblical Archaeology*. Louisville: Westminster/John Knox Press.

Moscrop, J. 2000. *Measuring Jerusalem: The Palestine Exploration Fund and British Interests in the Holy Land*. London: Leicester University Press.

Naccache, A. 1992. The empire of the Amorites revisited, in F. Ismail (ed.), *International Symposium on Syria and the Ancient Near East, 3000 to 300 BC*, pp. 29–51. Aleppo: University of Aleppo.

———. 1996. The price of progress: How short-sighted government policies favored development at the expense of archaeology. *Archaeology* 49 (4): 51–54.

———.1998. Beirut's memorycide: Hear no evil, see no evil, in L. Meskell (ed.), *Archaeology under Fire: Nationalism, Politics, and Heritage in the Eastern Mediterranean and Middle East*, pp. 140–158. London: Routledge.

Pollock, S., and Bernbeck, R. 2005. *Archaeologies of the Middle East: Critical Perspectives*. Malden, MA: Blackwell.

Running, L., and Freedman, D. 1975. *William Foxwell Albright: A Twentieth-Century Genius*. New York: Two Continents.

Shaw, W. M. K. 2003. *Possessor and Possessed: Museums, Archaeology, and the Visualization of History in the Late Ottoman Empire*. Berkeley: University of California.

Silberman, N. 1982. *Digging for God and Country: Exploration, Archeology, and the Secret Struggle for the Holy Land, 1799–1917*. New York: Random House.

——. 1989. *Between Past and Present: Archaeology, Ideology, and Nationalism in the Modern Middle East*. New York: Holt.

Steen, D. 2002. Nation building and archaeological narratives in the West Bank. *Stanford Journal of Archaeology* 1. www.stanford.edu/dept/archaeology/journal/newdraft/steen/paper.pdf.

Volk, L. 2008. When memory repeats itself: The politics of heritage in post civil war Lebanon. *International Journal of Middle East Studies* 40: 291–314.

Watson, C. 1915. *Fifty Years' Work in the Holy Land: A Record and a Summary, 1865–1915*. London: Palestine Exploration Fund.

Whitelam, K. 1995. *The Invention of Ancient Israel: The Silencing of Palestinian History*. London: Routledge.

Yadin, Y. 1972. *Hazor*. London: Oxford University Press.

Yahya, A. 2002. A Palestinian organization works to preserve sites in the West Bank in the midst of war. *Near Eastern Archaeology Magazine* 65 (4): 279–281.

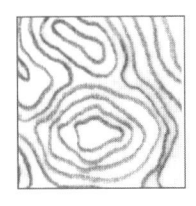

4

"DIBA JIMOOYUNG"—TELLING OUR STORY: COLONIZATION AND DECOLONIZATION OF ARCHAEOLOGICAL PRACTICE FROM AN ANISHINABE PERSPECTIVE

Sonya Atalay

The relationship between archaeologists and Native peoples in North America has been a rocky one. However, there has been greater interaction and marked improvements in some of these relationships since the passage of the Native American Graves and Repatriation Act (NAGPRA) in 1990. But does this signify substantial and sustainable change? If recent discussions over "culturally unidentifiable" human remains are any indication, it's clear much work remains to be done.[1] This chapter aims to provide a glimpse into Native American experiences of colonization in relation to archaeology using the lens of one tribal perspective. It also attempts to suggest a path toward a more sustainable archaeological practice, one that marks a true departure from the uneven power dynamics that remain a part of many relationships between archaeologists and Native Americans.

As both a Native American (Anishinabe-Ojibwe) and an archaeologist, I feel the only way to achieve a postcolonial archaeology is through a decolonizing paradigm that brings Native American systems of knowledge and concepts of stewardship to the center, and works to combine them with standard archaeological approaches in new and creative ways. This process of decolonization necessarily involves a fully participatory, collaborative process in which Native people and archaeologists work as equal partners. It requires ongoing reexamination of the state of the field by both archaeologists and Native communities, and a commitment to working together to develop future directions.

The approach I've taken in this chapter is one step in that process. I have outlined the historical context and current state of the field of archaeology within the United

States, relying on an Indigenous system of knowledge that recounts time and historical understanding according to Anishinabe traditional teachings. This knowledge system and the oral traditions related to it are specific to Anishinabe people of the Great Lakes region of the United States and Canada. One of the important tenets of postcolonial approaches is to give voice to those who were silenced or marginalized through the processes and practices of colonization. Therefore, writing about Native American experiences of colonization is challenging, because when one calls attention to the ways that Native peoples' experiences differ from the master narrative written in popular understandings of early "American" history, one must be careful not to homogenize and compress the diversity of Native American experiences into one shared story. The key is to simultaneously recognize the diversity of experiences, reactions, maintenance of personal and community agency, and solutions forward, and at the same time say something meaningful on a broader level. To address this, I make note, where appropriate, of Anishinabe experiences that share commonalities with other Native American communities, yet recognize and acknowledge that each case is unique in itself.

The Anishinabe historical knowledge and teachings outlined here are powerful, and they offer a meaningful way of framing some of the experiences other Indigenous people have had with archaeology. These teachings are part of an oral tradition that continues to be shared and maintained through ceremonies and contemporary practice. They are also beautifully depicted in the permanent museum exhibit of the Ziibiwing Center of Anishinabe Culture and Lifeways in the Saginaw Chippewa community near Mt. Pleasant, Michigan. Here I have incorporated descriptions of the exhibit, entitled "Diba Jimooyung: Telling Our Story," along with more detailed explanations of these teachings and the way they relate to archaeology. Both the teachings themselves and their depiction in the "Diba Jimooyung" exhibit clearly demonstrate aspects of colonial experiences for Anishinabe people, while providing a positive framework for moving forward in a decolonizing effort that aims to build a sustainable archaeological practice that is truly postcolonial. The exhibit title also appropriately describes this chapter, as it is my goal to provide a glimpse into the important stories of Native peoples' experiences with archaeologists from a Native perspective.

Before Contact—
Knowledge Written on Stone

Entering the "Diba Jimooyung" exhibit, visitors are presented with a dioramic scene of two people carving on stone (Figure 4.1). They are engaged in the act of adding another teaching, engraved in pictographic form, on a large stone outcrop that already holds multiple inscriptions. The place depicted in the exhibit's stone-engraving scene is known today by archaeologists as Sanilac Petroglyph site #20SA01. For Anishinabe people, this place, located in the eastern thumb region of Michigan, holds importance as a traditional cultural prop-

4. "Diba Jimooyung"—Telling Our Story

Figure 4.1 Dioramic scene of two people carving on stone at enterance of the "Diba Jimooyung" exhibit.

the time before contact, the spaces are opened with soft and warm lighting, and the subtle scents of smoke-tanned animal hides, burning cedar, and stewed corn fill the air.

The rock-carving scene at the exhibit entrance is a reminder that, prior to colonization, Native people had the ability to manage our sacred sites and landscapes as we saw fit. We were the sole keepers of knowledge about these places and the teachings they were created to hold. The responsibility that comes with holding this knowledge was securely in our hands, as we maintained sovereignty over the production and reproduction of knowledge about our past, and the way it was best preserved and shared for those in the future. At the time of contact, Native peoples across North America had their own methods of recording history and of preserving that knowledge for current and future generations.

The concern for recording knowledge and preserving it for future generations is attested by the rock art itself. One of the petroglyphs at the Sanilac site depicts an archer (Figure 4.2). As the exhibit text panels explain, and present-day community teachings at the Sanilac Petroglyph site document, oral traditions tell us that this archer depicts our ancestors shooting knowledge into the future to benefit later generations. These images were recorded on stone because our ancestors knew a time would come when our language, traditions, and practices would be threatened by colonization; thus carving knowledge on stone ensured permanence. Caring for this place and for the knowledge held there are both

erty; we call it *ezhibiigaadek asin* ("the place where knowledge is written on stone"). As museum visitors pass this opening scene and continue along the museum pathway, they find dioramas depicting daily life for the Anishinabe people prior to contact. Scenes of cooking, gardening, collecting wild rice, and a lodge housing ceremonial material fill the space. Visitors are also introduced to the Anishinabe system of reckoning time: a series of prophecies passed down from our ancestors, preserved through oral tradition. As museum visitors learn of

Ebmodaakowet
The Archer

Ebmodaakowet shoots an arrow of knowledge and wisdom into the future.

Ebmodaakowet symbolizes our *Anishinabek* ancestors and their promise to teach the next Seven Generations.

The body of *ebmodaakowet* represents the staff of an arrow and the carving above the head represents the arrow's point. Our ancestors knew the body and mind, like an arrow, send prayers upward to the Creator and the Spirit World.

Figure 4.2 Petroglyphs at the Sanilac site depicting an archer.
Photo courtesy of the Ziibiwing Center of Anishinabe Culture and Lifeways.
Photo credit: Jennifer Jones.

Bimaadiziwin
Life and All Its Meaning

The never-ending Circle of Life symbol represents our journey and connection to all of Creation.

Many *Anishinabek* believe that our earthly walk of life is just the beginning of a long journey. Like the Earth and the Universe, we will change form, but our spirit will remain the same as we continue on our journey. On our path, we must walk in a good way with love and respect for every part of Creation.

Figure 4.3 Stone at Sanilac in the form of a spiral carving.
Photo courtesy of the Ziibiwing Center of Anishinabe Culture and Lifeways.
Photo credit: Jennifer Jones.

part of traditional knowledge stewardship practices.

Also depicted in the rock art of Sanilac is the important connection many Native people understand to exist among past, present, and future. This teaching is carved into the stone at Sanilac in the form of a spiral (Figure 4.3). The spiral teaches us of the connection of all things in creation, and of the ongoing and lasting relationship of the past with the present and the future. This connection is shared and understood by other Native American Nations, who describe the unbroken continuum of the past with the present and future. It can be contrasted with an archaeological reckoning of time, which tends to separate and divide the past from the present and the future, utilizing artificial demarcations such as "prehistoric" and "historic."

Places like Sanilac, and others across North America, were places of learning, celebration, and remembering that were cared for through ceremonies involving traditional stewardship methods. The ceremonies held there involved sharing history and knowledge with the community, and also involved caring for the sacred places themselves. In many cases, caring for knowledge and place was often interwoven in traditional forms of stewardship. One example of this at Sanilac is the annual practice of summer solstice ceremonies in which four generations are present to simultaneously cleanse the stone through a cedar bath while learning the teachings the stone holds in our native language of Anishinabemowin. Caring for the sacred place, language, teachings, and community are all interwoven in this traditional practice. The importance of touching the stone and repeatedly bathing the petroglyphs with water and cedar provides one example of the way traditional stewardship practices differ from archaeological ones, where touching the images is thought to damage the petroglyphs. This example of traditional Anishinabe stewardship is only one window into a circumstance that was common throughout North America. Communities had their own methods of preserving sites, investigating and learning about the past, and serving as stewards of the land, and of the knowledge and ancestors held there. Some communities still hold this knowledge or aspects of it, while others may have lost all or part of it through the varied experiences that assimilation, genocide, removal, and relocation brought.

Trees Pulled by White Clouds

Long before the first European set foot on North America, Anishinabe people knew of their imminent arrival. Hundreds of years before contact, Ojibwe prophets foretold what was to happen to us as Anishinabe people in a series of seven prophecies. Each prophecy talks about a period of time referred to as a "fire." These concepts of time and cultural teachings drive the "Diba Jimooyung" exhibit, so that while visiting the museum, one is introduced to and able to experience first contact, the process of colonization, and the view of the future from the Anishinabe perspective.

The first, second, and third prophecies discuss the Anishinabe migrations westward into the Great Lakes region long before European contact. The work of Andrews and Zoe (1997), Denton (1997), Echo-Hawk (2000), Greer (1997), Hanks (1997), Harris (1997), Henderson (1997), and Kritsch and Andre (1997) all demonstrate that oral traditions such as these should be taken as useful and legitimate sources of data by archaeologists studying pre-contact life, as they can add to scientific understandings of settlement and migration patterns and may even aid in locating and identifying sites. Oral traditions are currently recognized by law under NAGPRA as one form of evidence that can be used to determine cultural affiliation. In Anishinabe contexts, and elsewhere in North America, there is a wealth of knowledge to be gained by archaeologists from studying oral traditions such as these.

The fourth prophecy foretold the time of the fourth fire when a "light-skinned people" would come to our land in "trees pulled by white clouds." We now understand these prophets were talking about wooden ships pulled by sails, and were describing the first arrival of Europeans in North America. In the "Diba Jimooyung" exhibit, visitors reach the time of the fourth fire after the diorama scenes illustrating daily life prior to contact. The visitor is introduced to bilingual, written, and audio formats telling of the fourth prophecy, accompanied by a visual representation of the prophecy demonstrated as wooden ship hulls (trees) with billowing white sails overhead (clouds).

The arrival of these ships marked a dramatic change for many Native peoples in terms of self-management of their traditional places and sites, as European visitors began letting their curiosity lead them. The beginnings of archaeology in North America involved curious exploration of mounds, earthworks, and other sites. Exploration led to larger-scale, more systematic excavation, such as the study carried out by Thomas Jefferson near his home in Virginia (Jefferson 1787). With the rise of the profession of archaeology, our ancestors' bodies and resting locations and our sacred and important cultural places became "research data" and "sites" for archaeologists. Responsibility for their care was claimed by archaeologists, as they appointed themselves stewards over the "archaeological record." Some Native communities now point to the important fact that they never relinquished care of these places in treaties or otherwise. For many Anishinabe, traditional management and preservation strategies that were in place during the time depicted in the Sanilac rock-carving scene were no longer possible, as the knowledge system of the newly dominant culture claimed, collected, studied, and stored the bodies, places, and material remains of our ancestors. As a result of colonization, the right to care for and manage important places was taken from Anishinabe people, along with another critical human right: the ability to care for our dead. For a time, the ability to care for ancestral bodies and places—in some cases, even the ability to pass on cultural knowledge—was removed, and the connection of the past with present and future generations was temporarily disrupted. Our ancestors were wise in understanding that our people were going to need the knowledge they left for us on the Sanilac stone.

The fifth and sixth prophets told us that when the time of the fifth and sixth fires arrived, our people would attempt to live in a new way. We were warned about this way of life, that it would lead to the abandonment of traditional ways and would be a time of extreme loss for our communities. We know that the fifth and sixth fires occurred during the late 1800s and early to mid-1900s, when many Native people gave up the "old ways" either through force or choice, and boarding schools were established to "kill the Indian, and save the man" (Pratt 1892: 46). In terms of cultural materials and ceremonial places for both the living and the dead, it was truly as the prophets warned: a time of great loss for many Native Americans. Collections were amassed in museum shelves around the world. While Native communities struggled for survival, their bodies, sacred landscapes, and important cultural materials were avidly excavated, studied, and collected, with the hopes of recording the remnants of a so-called dying race.

Ebmodaakowet—The Archer who Shoots Knowledge into the Future

Although the fifth and sixth fires were a time of great loss for Anishinabe and other Native peoples of North America, there are stories of survival and strength also. Some communities and families were able to maintain cultural knowledge and practices, often holding them secretly. Responses were varied, but, across North America, communities found inventive ways to maintain their traditional knowledge and spiritual practices. In the case of the Anishinabe, this meant burying sacred items in a log to protect them. We are told that this log will be found in the future by a little boy who will dream of where it's buried when the time is right. Knowing that during the fifth and sixth fires the Anishinabe people would become weak, our ancestors took steps to care for this and future generations. With concern for us, they wrote messages and teachings on birchbark and stone, creating rock art sites such as the one in Sanilac. Ebmodaakowet is the archer figure described above from the Sanilac petroglyph site. He is shown in the act of shooting knowledge written on stone into the future. The teachings on the stone can now be passed on during the time when our people come back, looking to care for the knowledge and places left for them.

The final prophet spoke of the time of the seventh fire. He relayed that this would be a time when Anishinabe people would remember the old ways and seek out knowledge from the elders about traditions and ceremonies. *Bipskaabiiwaat* is the time of the seventh fire, a time when "they come back." Our elders tell us that we are now in the time of the seventh fire. This fire started in the 1960s when Native American activists across the country organized protests against human rights violations being perpetrated against Native peoples, including the desecration of Native ancestral remains (see Riding In 2002 for a powerful historical overview) and the large-scale appropriation of Native American cultural materials. Native American activism certainly had an impact on archaeology during the time of the seventh fire. The impact of this activism can be seen in articles, books, and edited volumes that highlight the early efforts made at working together and improving communication and understanding between Native peoples and archaeologists (Lippert 2006; Nicholas and Andrews 1997; Swidler 1997; Watkins 2001).

In Michigan, this activism was reflected in the creation of the Michigan Anishinaabek Cultural Preservation and Repatriation Alliance (MACPRA), an alliance that includes members from each of the federally and state-recognized tribes in Michigan. MACPRA members work together to protect cultural materials and places and to oversee repatriation of Anishinabe ancestral remains. The "Diba Jimooyung" exhibit explains the importance of caring for ancestral remains and sacred places, while highlighting the diligent work of MACPRA to fulfill our responsibility to the ancestors.

Across North America, we see examples of the ways Native people are "coming back" as described in *bipskaabiiwaat*, the time spoken of in the seventh prophecy. Native nations have developed cultural and language preservation programs, and there are numerous tribal historic preservation officers in Native communities across the United States. Native American communities have also developed collaborative research methodologies and tribal archaeology programs for ensuring they have a level of control in deciding issues related to their heritage. The Sanilac site is an excellent example of this process of "coming back."

Just as Sanilac was used in the past for teaching, sharing, and storing knowledge, today it has once again become a place of learning for Anishinabe people. Sanilac is in the traditional territory of the Saginaw Chippewa Indian Tribe. The tribe's Ziibiwing Center hosts regular ceremonies at the site that focus on multiple forms of cultural knowledge education and preservation. Caring for this important cultural place is now partially back in the hands of Anishinabe people, who work collaboratively with the Michigan Department of Natural Resources to ensure that traditional methods of stewardship are followed.

These types of contemporary practices that rebuild and strengthen connections with the past to the present and into the future are taking place across "Indian Country" in North America. Native communities are working with archaeologists to develop creative agreements and productive strategies for managing sites and conducting collaborative research (see Colwell-Chanthaphonh and Ferguson 2007 and Kerber 2006 for excellent examples). New methods of teaching archaeology through collaborative field schools and other education methods are also being developed (Silliman 2008).

Eko Niizwaaching—
The Seventh Story of the Future

The "Diba Jimooyung" exhibit does not end with the time of the seventh fire. There is a second part to the seventh prophecy that asks people from all walks of life to make decisions about our shared future. We are told that during the seventh fire, all people will have to make a choice between two paths. One path is well worn, and is scorched and blackened. The second path is green and lush, with less evidence of wear. We are taught by our elders and spiritual leaders that if we choose the right path, it will lead to peace between ourselves and the light-skinned people, and we will collectively light the eighth and final fire, the eternal fire of peace. This teaching holds important implications for the field of archaeology. Archaeologists and Native peoples have started to develop productive strategies of decolonizing the field of archaeology and moving toward a practice that is truly postcolonial. But a great deal of work remains to restore Native peoples' sovereignty over their cultural materials and ancestral remains. Can we combine our systems of knowledge to develop an archaeological practice that is respectful of Native sovereignty? Is such hybridity possible?

Visitors to the "Diba Jimooyung" exhibit are left thinking about the choice of paths they wish to walk as they exit the exhibit. After learning of the possibility of the eighth fire of peace, they exit the exhibit at *ezhibiigaadek asin*, the Sanilac stone-engraving scene. This time, they are along the opposite side of the stone, with full view of the daily life scenes they first encountered at the start of their tour. Visitors have traveled full circle in the museum space, as they followed the clockwise circling movement of the exhibit. For archaeology, we are also following a similar path of coming full circle. As a discipline, we are at a place in our history where there are important choices we must make about the future of the discipline.

With war, poverty, global climate change, and a host of other important issues facing our global community, we must find ways to make our work relevant to the public that funds our research. Native people and archaeologists share some common goals, and one example is sustainable site management and preservation. There are other more complex areas where there is not a great deal of agreement or common ground between Native American communities and archaeologists, such as in the disposition of culturally unidentifiable human remains. I argue that the only sustainable future for archaeology is through shared collaborative management, with Native people taking the lead. If we hope to find social justice in an archaeology that is truly beyond a colonial paradigm, then we must continue working to create a practice that provides Native people with control over their sacred places, ceremonial materials, and ancestors' bodies. Does this mean the end of a "shared past"? Not at all. It calls for creating a shared past that places stewardship and management in the hands of Native people, recognizing the special and unique relationship that Native people have with much of the archaeological record of North America. Excellent examples already exist, demonstrating that along this path there are many ways we can learn from each other as we move toward building a shared future.

Recognizing Native peoples' special relationship to the archaeological record and reflecting this in both the ethical guidelines we model ourselves on as archaeologists and the practices we follow in planning and carrying out research are critical steps in the right direction. One important yet very complex area that still requires attention is repatriation. There is a great deal of work that remains if we hope to "decolonize NAGPRA" (Riding In 2004: 63). The National NAGPRA program estimates that approximately 125,000 ancestral remains are still kept in museums across the United States, labeled as "culturally unidentifiable." Archaeologists must work to ensure that their home institutions and museums in their states do the important work necessary to repatriate these large collections of ancestral remains. This is not an easy or straightforward task, because there are multiple views on how to appropriately move forward, among both archaeologists and Native Americans. But there are also successful models in place to follow, such as the coalition arrangement in Minnesota involving the Minnesota Indian Affairs Council. This coalition successfully worked with archaeologists to determine the disposition of over 2,000 sets of ancestral remains, including those that were labeled as culturally unidentifiable. It is also important to place pressure on archaeological and anthropological professional associations to explore solutions for repatriating the large collections of culturally unidentifiable ancestral remains. Whatever creative solutions these organizations explore, the critical point is to include a variety of Native voices in the decision-making process from both federally and non-federally recognized tribes.

These are some of the critical issues our generation faces, and this important work can only be accomplished if archaeologists and Native people work together and continue to improve their working relationships. This is only the start of the "to-do" list for an archaeology that wishes to call itself *post*colonial in North America.

Notes

1. See, for example, the NAGPRA & UCB blog that was created in response to changes in the organization of the NAGPRA program at the University of California, Berkeley. The blog includes a resolution by the National Congress of American Indians in support of NANC (Native American NAGPRA Coalition), the group that is fighting UC Berkeley over the NAGPRA reorganization because they did not include Native Americans in the decision-making about the reorganization. *http:// nagpraucb.blogspot. com/*.

2. For another recent example of some of the strongly opposing views between Native Americans and archaeologists on this issue, compare the Society for American Archaeology statement on culturally unidentifiable human remains (Society for American Archaeology 2007) and that from the National Congress of American Indians (NCAI 2008), the nation's largest Indian organization.

References

Andrews, T. D., and Zoe, J. B. 1997. The Idaà trail: Archaeology and the Dogrib cultural landscape, Northern Territories, in G. P. Nicholas and T. D. Andrews (eds.), *At a Crossroads: Archaeology and*

First Peoples in Canada. Burnaby, BC: Archaeology Press.

Colwell-Chanthaphonh, C., and Ferguson, T. J. 2007. *Collaboration in Archaeological Practice: Engaging Descendant Communities*. Lanham, MD: Rowman and Littlefield.

Denton, D. 1997. Frenchman's Island and the Nataawaau bones: Archaeology and Cree tales of culture contact, in G. P. Nicholas and T. D. Andrews (eds.), *At a Crossroads: Archaeology and First Peoples in Canada*, pp. 105–124. Burnaby, BC: Archaeology Press.

Echo-Hawk, R. 2000. Ancient history in the New World: Integrating oral traditions and the archaeological record in deep time. *American Antiquity* 62 (2): 267–290.

Greer, S. C. 1997. Traditional knowledge in site recognition and definition, in G. P. Nicholas and T. D. Andrews (eds.), *At a Crossroads: Archaeology and First Peoples in Canada*, pp. 145–159. Burnaby, BC: Archaeology Press.

Hanks, C. C. 1997. Ancient knowledge of ancient sites: Tracing Dene. Identity from the late Pleistocene and Holocene, in G. P. Nicholas and T. D. Andrews (eds.), *At a Crossroads: Archaeology and First Peoples in Canada*, pp. 178–189. Burnaby, BC: Archaeology Press.

Harris, H. 1997. Remembering 10,000 years of history: The origins and migrations of the Gitksan, in G. P. Nicholas and T. D. Andrews (eds.), *At a Crossroads: Archaeology and First Peoples in Canada*, pp. 190–196. Burnaby, BC: Archaeology Press.

Henderson, L. 1997. The Arviaq and Qikqtaarjuk Oral History Project, in G. P. Nicholas and T. D. Andrews (eds.), *At a Crossroads: Archaeology and First Peoples in Canada*, pp. 197–213. Burnaby, BC: Archaeology Press.

Jefferson, T. 1787 [1954]. *Notes on the State of Virginia*. Edited by W. Peden, pp. 97–100. Chapel Hill: University of North Carolina Press.

Kerber, J. E. (ed.). 2006. *Cross-Cultural Collaboration: Native Peoples and Archaeology in the Northeastern United States*. Lincoln: University of Nebraska Press.

Kritsch, I. D., and Andre, A. M. 1997. Traditional knowledge and heritage studies in the Gwich'in settlement area, in G. P. Nicholas and T. D. Andrews (eds.), *At a Crossroads: Archaeology and First Peoples in Canada*, pp. 125–144. Burnaby, BC: Archaeology Press.

Lippert, D. 2006. Building a bridge to cross a thousand years. *American Indian Quarterly* 30 (3): 431–440.

National Congress of American Indians. 2008. Comments on the proposed rule (43 CFR Part 10), Disposition of culturally unidentifiable human remains. Letter signed by Jacqueline Johnson, Executive Director, National Congress of American Indians.

Nicholas, G. P., and Andrews, T. D. (eds.). 1997. *At a Crossroads: Archaeology and First Peoples in Canada*. Burnaby, BC: Archaeology Press.

Pratt, R. 1892 [1973]. Official report of the nineteenth annual conference of charities and correction, reprinted in R. H. Pratt, "The Advantages of Mingling Indians with Whites," in F. P. Prucha (ed.), *Americanizing the American Indians: Writings by the "Friends of the Indian" 1880–1900*, pp. 260–271. Cambridge: Harvard University Press.

Riding In, J. 2002. Our dead are never forgotten: American Indian struggles for burial rights and protections, in P. Weeks (ed.), *They Made Us Many Promises: The American Indian Experiences, 1524 to the Present*, pp. 291–323. Wheeling: Harlan Davidson.

———.2004. Decolonizing NAGPRA, in W. A. Wilson and M. Yellow Bird (eds.), *For Indigenous Eyes Only: A Decolonization Handbook*, pp. 53–66. Santa Fe: SAR Press.

Society for American Archaeology. 2007. Comments on 2007 Proposed rule relating to culturally unidentifiable human remains under the Native American Graves Protection and Repatriation Act.

Silliman, S. W. (ed.). 2008. *Collaborative Indigenous Archaeology at the Trowel's Edge: Exploring Methodology and Education in North American Archaeology*. Tucson: University of Arizona Press.

Swidler, N. (ed.). 1997. *Native Americans and Archaeologists: Stepping Stones to Common Ground*: Lanham, MD: Rowman and Littlefield.

Watkins, J. 2001. *Indigenous Archaeology: American Indian Values and Scientific Practice*: Lanham, MD: AltaMira Press.

5

THE COLONIAL LEGACY IN THE ARCHAEOLOGY OF SOUTH ASIA

Dilip K. Chakrabarti

Of the eight sovereign countries of South Asia, Afghanistan, Bhutan, and Nepal were never colonies. However, four others were colonies, with India and Pakistan gaining independence in 1947 and Sri Lanka in 1948; Bangladesh seceded from Pakistan in 1971. The Maldives, a chain of small islands in the Indian Ocean, was a British "protectorate" until 1965. North of the Hindu Kush, Afghanistan belongs to Central Asia, as there is no geographical barrier between the windswept Central Asian steppe and northern Afghanistan. South of the mountain range, Afghanistan geographically borders Pakistan and is, in this sense, South Asian, but the story of its archaeological research (Allchin and Hammond 1978) takes in both Iran and Central Asia and falls outside the South Asian orbit. Bhutan is the only South Asian country where archaeological research has not yet taken off, but elsewhere the tradition, either in the form of systematic studies or sporadic discoveries, dates from the 19th century and earlier.

The purpose of this chapter is threefold: (1) to outline the colonial legacy of archaeology in those South Asian countries that were colonies/protectorates, with comments on those that were non-colonial; (2) to specify the current concerns and structure of archaeological research in these colonies; and (3) to examine the extent to which this region is being subjected to the neocolonialism implicit in the present archaeological research tradition of the West. The archaeology of Bangladesh, India, and Pakistan up until 1947 are discussed together, under the rubric of "British India," with brief allusions to the main concerns in each country in the post-Independence period, whereas there are statements on the history of archaeological research in each of the other countries. The final section presents a critique and some remarks on strains of "neocolonialism" in South Asia.

British India: Legacy of the Colonial Period

Numerous Greco-Roman references to the Indian subcontinent indicate that European knowledge of it was old and continuous, augmented still further by the notices of old monuments in the records of European travelers and the Portuguese of Goa in the 16th to 18th centuries. The identification of the old places mentioned in Classical sources was among the earliest concerns of European scholarship regarding ancient India. The beginning of this scholarship can be traced back at least to the mid-18th century (Herbert 1759). Toward the end of this century, the Asiatic Society, which was established in 1784 in Calcutta, became the main institutional focus. Under William Jones, this Society was interested in theoretically linking India to the pre-evolutionary (and thus biblical) framework of the history of the world. India was assigned to Ham, one of the sons of Noah. Jones's dictum that Sanskrit, Greek, and Latin were related languages is rooted in this pre-evolutionary notion (Teignmouth 1804). A specific archaeological orientation for the Society's interest was brought about by James Prinsep, who made an impassioned plea for investigations in the field and himself deciphered the ancient scripts of Brahmi and Kharosthi, throwing open a hitherto unknown world of inscriptions and inscribed coins. Alexander Cunningham, under whom the Archaeological Survey of India was established in 1861, derived his interest in archaeology from the Prinsep era. His interest in historical geography—that is, the mapping and identifications of sites on the ground—was systematically pursued with the help of the account of Zuang-Zang's 7th-century travels in India. This falls in line with the work of M. W. Leake, who, with the help of Pausanias' 2nd century A.D. travels in Greece, had completed the basic identification and mapping of Greek sites by the early 19th century, and also the work of E. W. Robinson who, by the middle of the 19th century, brought about an understanding of the basic ground reality of the biblical lands (Leake 1841; Moorey 1991; Robinson 1841).

The late 19th-century publications on ancient Indian architecture accomplished for Indian architectural remains what Cunningham had accomplished for Indian archaeological sites. Excavations naturally followed the phase of site identification, and, until the 1940s, excavations of historical sites were a recurrent feature of the activities of the Archaeological Survey of India, a tradition laid down under the Director Generalship of John Marshall (1902–1928). The discovery of the Indus civilization was, in a sense, a part of this tradition to excavate large mounds. The mounds of Harappa and Mohenjodaro, excavated in 1921 and 1922, respectively, were long known; when scholars of ancient Mesopotamia noted that seals similar to those found at Harappa and Mohenjodaro were previously reported from the Bronze Age ruins of

Mesopotamian sites, it became clear that a new Bronze Age civilization had been discovered in India. In the late 1940s, then Director General Mortimer Wheeler introduced the principle of stratigraphy in Indian excavations and drew attention to the significance of the study of prehistory, the basis of which was securely laid down as early as the second half of the 19th century.

Despite its tremendous role in the unraveling of the subcontinent's past, archaeology in India was essentially government controlled, with universities showing no interest at all until the 1930s. Moreover, the theoretical basis of the study of ancient India was formulated not by archaeologists but rather by 19th-century Western linguistic, racial, and historical scholarship, which argued that all historical changes in India, as elsewhere, were caused by the successive migrations of groups of people, each with their own physical features, language, and culture. This scholarship, however, went one step further, by arguing that outside the realm of religion and philosophy, Indian civilization had not contributed anything to human culture, nor had it generated any technological innovation. It preached, as in the case of Africa, that all innovations came with the migration of superior groups of people, and nothing original could be ascribed to the Indigenous population.

Trends in Post-1947 Pakistan and India: Effects of a Colonial Past

Independence and Partition in 1947 meant that the colonial Archaeological Survey of India was now shared between these two independent countries, each developing its own archaeological tradition. Depending more on international collaborations than India, Pakistan had significantly elaborated its prehistoric and protohistoric heritage from Baluchistan and the Northwestern Frontier to Sindh and Bahawalpur, focusing on the antiquity of stone tools in the Potwar plateau, the multiple courses of development toward the Indus civilization, and how the civilization had later transformed itself. Among the historical sites, Buddhist ruins were both mapped and excavated in the hill valleys to the northeast of Peshawar and the Lalmai hills of East Pakistan. Today archaeology is pursued on both the federal and provincial levels, and several universities—Peshawar, Khairpur, and Punjab among them—offer courses in the subject, with Peshawar and Khairpur publishing their own archaeology journals, *Ancient Pakistan* and *Ancient Sindh*, respectively.

India too has built up a complete sequence of prehistory and protohistory in relevant areas, continuing in some depth in the historical domain. This is illustrated by a large series of surveys in virtually all parts of the country and the availability of scientific techniques for dating and analyzing archaeological samples. Apart from the federal Archaeological Survey of India (henceforth referred to as the Survey) and the related state-level or provincial government organizations, a limited number of universities practice archaeology. However, there is a keen interest in offering an archaeological history of India vis-à-vis the history obtained from more traditional sources, such as from religious texts.

For at least the first 20 years after Independence, Indian archaeology was lucky to have at its helm people with both commitment and a national perspective. The situation is currently different. Good excavation programs still take place, but the Survey and many state organizations are generally headed by non-archaeologists with varying levels of education and perspective, and the universities are almost invariably full of people who have been appointed solely on the basis of their region, caste, political affiliations, and personal loyalties. Although there is no dearth of money for archaeological research in contemporary India, it seems that most of the archaeological organizations currently suffer from a lack of motivation and leadership. To a great extent, I believe this is rooted in the refusal of the burgeoning Indian middle class to take serious interest in the country's past beyond the domain of philosophy and religion. Archaeology catches media headlines for all the wrong political reasons, and meanwhile, the state of preservation of the major national monuments, such as the painted caves of Ajanta, suffer from a serious lack of constructive concern. The basic charm of classical Indian paintings lies in the glow of their naturally obtained colors. The glow of the Ajanta paintings (ca. 2nd century B.C.–9th century A.D.), which one could observe and experience about 25 years ago, has now been replaced by a dark patina. The 7th- and 8th-century paintings of the cave of Sittanavasal in Tamil Nadu have been completely destroyed while under the care of the Survey. The point is that there is no indication that anybody is bothered by such happenings. Although this has been my experience in India, it seems unlikely that the archaeological situation is significantly better in the other South Asian countries. Based on my experiences in India, I would believe that the subcontinental middle class is hardly interested in such financially unrewarding areas as the study of the past.[1]

Sri Lanka, Nepal, Bangladesh, Bhutan, and the Maldives

Pre-independence Sri Lankan archaeology was based somewhat on the model of archaeology in British India (Bell and Bell 1993; Godakumbura 1969), with a federal Department of Archaeology at the helm of affairs. Although its traditional focus has been on three famous historical sites—Anuradhapura, Polonnurawa, and Sigiriya—emphasis has always been placed on working out the island's earlier archaeological background, best exemplified currently in Siran Deraniyagala's monograph on that theme (Coningham 1999, 2006; Deraniyagala 1992).

In the archaeology of Nepal, Buddhist sites, especially those in the "Tarai" area such as Lumbini, Nigliva, Gotihawa, and Tilaura Kot (Verardi and Acharya 2002), have played a dominant role since the late 19th century. Emphasis on the archaeology of other areas—the ruins associated with the Malla kings of western Nepal, the sites in the Kathmandu valley, the Biratnagar area in the east, the high-altitude zones near Tibet, and later sites such as Simraongarh in the "Tarai" area itself—is essentially a feature of contemporary times (Verardi 1992), which have also witnessed the beginnings of prehistoric archaeology in Nepal (Shaha 1992). Tribhuvan University in Kathmandu offers courses in the ancient history and archaeology of the country.

In Bangladesh, many Buddhist monastic sites have come to be excavated both in Pakistan and post-Pakistan, or post-1971, periods, but preoccupations with prehistory or the major early historic sites such as Mahasthangarh and Wari Bateshwar are comparatively recent. The government department, Archaeology of the People's Republic of Bangladesh, regularly conducts its annual exploration and excavation programs, but there is hardly any way to access the results because of a long-embedded tradition of non-publication. Among the Bangladeshi universities, only Jahangirnagar University runs a separate Department of Archaeology, which publishes its own journal, *Pratnatattva* (Chakrabarti 1992; Sen 2002; Smith 2000).

In the Maldives, archaeological discoveries are primarily of Roman coin finds, which attest to the significance of the Maldives' position in Rome's sea traffic with the East, and later Buddhist remains (Bell 1940; Maniku 1988; Mikkelson 2000; Mohamed 2002; Skjolsvold 1991). In Bhutan, except for the accidental finds of some 8th-century A.D. structural remains reported by the Swiss-Liechtenstein Foundation for Archaeological Research Abroad in 1999–2000, there has been no archaeological research.

There is a general point of similarity among the archaeological publications of all South Asian countries. Except for two Indian nongovernmental journals, *Puratattva* and *Man and Environment*, the former published annually and the latter biannually, all governmental publications are irregular. The annual publication of the Archaeological Survey of India, *Indian Archaeology: A Review*, has a backlog of about six years, which means there is absolutely no way one can know about the general range of archaeological discoveries and excavations in India within the last six years. *Pragdhara*, a journal of the Uttar Pradesh State Department of Archaeology, published annually, is the only scholarly governmental publication in India. More or less the same situation persists in the cases of *Pakistan Archaeology, Bangladesh Archaeology, Ancient Nepal*, and *Ancient Ceylon/Sri Lanka*. The state of publication is equally depressing for detailed excavation reports. Only about 15% of the excavations conducted in India since independence have been published in detail, testifying to an inordinate disinterest on the part of the excavators to publish their results in detail.[2]

Strands of Neocolonialism

There is a whole range of situations that need attention from the Third World point of view. First, as is the case in modern India, there is a continuation of the firm belief in the colonial Indological notion that ancient India was indeed an area where no innovation ever took place (Sankalia 1973), and its prehistory was merely a history of colonization (Misra 2001). There is also the general predilection that developments in India were generally tied to external factors, such as trade with West Asia in the case of the Indus civilization (Dhavalikar 1995). The fact that three leading Indian scholars, all belonging to a reputed Indian institution, should unquestioningly accept an old colonial premise indicates that neocolonialism survives not merely among First World archaeologists in the Third World, but also among the Third World scholars themselves. Of course, neocolonialism is most brazen in the general indifference of First World scholars toward the contributions made by Third World scholars to the archaeology of their respective areas. The citation pattern of First World archaeological literature in relation to the Third World points in this direction. Even if I ignore here the arrogant anonymous comments Third World scholars often receive on their research proposals or manuscript submissions in the First World context, how many references to native scholars can one find in Western archaeological literature from the Nile to the Indus? Even if some names occasionally get listed, careful scrutiny will reveal that such citations of Third World scholars are generally for their empirical studies, and seldom, if at all, for their theoretical contribution. First World scholars writing on South Asian archaeology write only for fellow First World scholars, and that they carry a notion of superior intellect in relation to the "natives" is inescapable.

This situation arises from three distinct features of modern archaeological research. First, the emphasis these days is not on area-specialization, but on pursuing a theoretical model in a given context. This is attempted usually with vast "scientific" input that the natives cannot match. In such enterprises, the existing archaeological framework of the region is rendered largely irrelevant. To get around the possible local difficulties, the recourse is usually to secure patronage money, which First World funding agencies provide as conference grants or fellowships under which Third World persons can be brought over to First World campuses for short periods. Second, it is still an endemic neocolonial feature of Third World scholarship that whatever emanates from the First World in its particular field is unquestioningly accepted, whatever its logic, scientific validity, or implication. And third, there is a serious difference of approach to the study of the past between the First and Third Worlds. In contemporary India, for instance, archaeology is generally nationalistic, whereas First World archaeologists of the American anthropological school tend to be look beyond the nation for research. I have argued elsewhere (Chakrabarti 2008) that the American anthropological school of scholarship has contributed nothing fundamental or new to the study of ancient India. The difference that has already emerged in Indian archaeology between First World archaeologists and their Indian associates (those who have been beneficiaries of their patronage) and the ordinary run of Indian archaeologists is more or less true of the rest of South Asia. The spirit of current First World archaeology in South Asia is regrettably far more colonial and racist than it ever was during the colonial years proper.

Notes

1. The history of archaeology in British India and modern India has been discussed in a number of volumes, e.g., Imam 1966; Chakrabarti 1988, 1997, 2003; Lahiri 2005; and Singh 2005. The primary source of the history of archaeology in Pakistan is the successive volumes of *Pakistan Archaeology*, which began in 1963. This journal and the rather irregular volumes of *Ancient Pakistan*, *Ancient Sindh*, and the more recent *Frontier Archaeology* help us to piece together the post-1947 history of archaeological activities in Pakistan.
2. On Sri Lanka, see Godakumbura 1969; Bell and Bell 1993. On the Maldives, Bell 1940 and Skjolsvold 1991 offer an idea. An idea of the development of archaeology in Nepal can be gleaned from Shaha 1992. For Bangladesh, see Chakrabarti 1992, and for archaeological investigations in Bhutan by the Swiss-Liechtenstein Foundation for Archaeological Research Abroad in 1999–2000, the only source of information seems to be their website, www.slsa.li.

References

Allchin, F. R., and Hammond, N. (eds.). 1978. *Archaeology of Afghanistan: From Earliest Times to the Timurid Period*. London: Academic Press.

Bell, B. N., and Bell, H. M. 1993. *H. C. P. Bell, Archaeologist of Ceylon and the Maldives*. Denbigh: Archetype Publications.

———. 1940. *The Maldive Islands: Monograph on the History, Archaeology and Epigraphy*. Colombo: Government Printing Press.

Chakrabarti, D. K. 1988. *A History of Indian Archaeology from the Beginning to 1947*. Delhi: Munshiram Manoharlal.

———.1992. *Ancient Bangladesh*. Delhi: Oxford University Press.

———.1997. *Colonial Indology: Sociopolitics of the Ancient Indian Past*. Delhi: Munshiram Manoharlal.

———.2003. *Archaeology in the Third World: A History of Indian Archaeology since 1947*. Delhi: DK Printworld.

———.2008. *The Battle for Ancient India: An Essay in the Sociopolitics of Indian Archaeology*. Delhi: Aryan Books.

Coningham, R. 1999. *Anuradhapura: The British-Sri Lankan Excavation at Anuradhapura Salgaha Watta 2*, Vol. 1: *The Site*. Oxford: Archaeopress.

———.2006. *Anuradhapura: The British-Sri Lankan Excavation at Anuradhapura Salgaha Watta 2*, Vol. 2: *The Artefacts*. Oxford: Archaeopress.

Deraniyagala, S. U. 1992. *The Prehistory of Sri Lanka: An Ecological Perspective*, rev. ed. Memoirs of the Archaeological Survey of Ceylon, Vol. 8. Colombo: Archaeological Survey Department of Sri Lanka.

Dhavalikar, M. K. 1995. *Cultural Imperialism: Indus Civilization Sites in Western India*. Delhi: Books and Books.

Godakumbura, C. E. 1969. History of archaeology in Ceylon. *Journal of the Royal Asiatic Society Ceylon Branch*, New series, 13: 1–38.

Herbert, W. 1759. *A Geographical Illustration of the Map of India, translated from the*

French of M. D'Anville, with some explanatory notes and remarks by William Herbert, hydrographer. London: Printed for the author.

Imam, A. 1966. *Alexander Cunningham and the Beginnings of Indian Archaeology*. Dhaka: Asiatic Society.

Lahiri, N. 2005. *Finding Forgotten Cities*. Delhi: Permanent Black.

Leake, M. 1841. *The Topography of Athens: With Some Remarks on Its Antiquities*. London: J. Redwell.

Maniku, H. A. 1988. *Archaeology in Maldives: Thinking on New Lines*. Malé: National Centre for Linguistic and Historical Research.

Mikkelson, E. 2000. *Archaeological Excavations of a Monastery at Kaashidhoo*. Malé: National Centre for Linguistic and Historical Research.

Misra, V. N. 2001. Prehistoric human colonization of India. *Journal of Bioscience* 26: 491–531.

Mohamed, N. 2002. Pre-Islamic Maldives. *Man and Environment Journal of the Indian Society for Prehistoric and Quaternary Studies* 27 (1). http://nclhr.gov.mv/docs/whitepapers/history/Pre-Islamic_Maldives.pdf.

Moorey, R. 1991. *A Century of Biblical Archaeology*. Cambridge: Lutterworth Press.

Robinson, E. 1841. *Biblical Researches in Palestine, Mount Sinai and Arabia Petrae*. London: John Murray.

Sankalia, H. D. 1973. Prehistoric colonization of India. *World Archaeology* 5 (1): 86–91.

Sen, S. 2002. Community boundary, secularized religion and imagined pasts in Bangladesh: Archaeology and historiography of unequal encounter. *World Archaeology* 34 (2): 346–362.

Shaha, R. 1992. *Ancient and Mediaeval Nepal*. Delhi: Manohar.

Singh, U. 2005. *The Discovery of Ancient India*. Delhi: Permanent Black.

Skjolsvold, A. (ed.). 1991. *Archaeological Test Excavations on the Maldive Islands*. Oslo: Kon-Tiki Museum.

Smith, M. L. 2000. Bangladesh: Building national identity through archaeology. *Antiquity* 74 (285): 701–706.

Teignmouth, J. S. Baron 1804. *Memoirs of the Life, Writings, and Correspondence of Sir William Jones*. London: J. Brettell.

Verardi, G. 1992. *Excavations at Harigaon, Kathmandu: Final Report*. Rome: IsMEO.

Verardi, G., and Acharya, K. P. 2002. *Excavation at Gotihawa and a Territorial Survey in Kapilavastu District of Nepal: A Preliminary Report*. Lumbini: Lumbini International Research Institute.

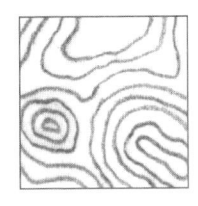

6

THE COLONIAL EXPERIENCE OF THE UNCOLONIZED AND THE COLONIZED: THE CASE OF EAST ASIA, MAINLY AS SEEN FROM JAPAN

Koji Mizoguchi

Colonial and postcolonial experiences vary along with the historical positionality of those who think, remember, imagine, talk, and write about them varies. For those who live in East Asia, this fact is felt with special poignancy. China was subjected to colonial interventions and partial colonization by major Western colonizing nations of the 19th century, such as Britain and France, and later by Japan. Korea was colonized and annexed by Japan; it (then the Korean Empire) became a protectorate of Japan in 1905, and the Japan-Korea annexation treaty (1910), whose legality is still disputed, allowed Japan to incorporate Korea into its sovereign domain (1945). Japan began modernizing itself in reaction to the Western colonial expansion to East Asia. The process was set in motion by the shock of the Opium War in which the Qing (Ch'ing) Dynasty was defeated by Britain (1840–1842). Japan's rapid modernization took the form of abolishing the Edo feudal regime[1] and adopting outright major attributes of the modern nation-state, such as the constitution-based system of governance, conscription, industrialization, mass education, and on the like. The ensuing drive to create a homogeneous and unified nation led Japan to construct a unique ideological concept, the concept of the national-body (see below), and resulted in the forcible assimilation of minority groups such as the Ainu (Mizoguchi 2006: 65–71), who today are still suffering from having no significant say in the way their history is written (though the situation is gradually changing). The different ways in which those countries became incorporated into the colonial world order determined the way modern archaeology was introduced and developed in each country.

In this short essay, I aim to portray commonalities as well as differences among the trajectories that archaeology has taken in both colonized and colonizing nation-states, mainly by examining, albeit briefly, the history of archaeology in Japan. Japan's colonial experience is unique in that it colonized neighboring nations in reaction to Western colonial expansion and threat. That unique positionality has prevented Japan and its majority population from fully grasping and critiquing the damage their colonial activities caused, both to neighboring countries and more broadly. Japan was also protected and supported by the United States as the frontline nation against expanding Soviet communism during the Cold War era, and a range of pre–World War II institutions and ideologies, including those used to legitimize colonial activities, were allowed to survive intact. The end of the Cold War brought with it the demise of Marxist theory in Japan, almost the only critical framework against colonial/nationalistic legacies and discourses that Japanese archaeology has had since the end of World War II; and we Japanese archaeologists are struggling to fully and sincerely confront the negative legacies of the recent past and the resurfacing of nationalistic sentiments. A critique of Japanese colonial/colonizing and postcolonial experiences would allow us to recognize the unique set of postcolonial problems we have to face in East Asia and to consider the way forward in this post–Cold War, postmodern world order.

Regarding the trajectory of modern archaeology's development and its colonial and postcolonial experience in China, Korea, and Japan, we already have a number of concise and excellent reviews in English, including works by von Falkenhausen (1993, 1995), Glover (2006), Nelson (2006), Ikawa-Smith (1982), Fawcett (1986, 1995), and Hudson (2006). Hyung Il Pai's seminal volume (2000) critically examines colonial and postcolonial experiences in Korea. The limitation of space does not allow me to fully incorporate the important findings and insights of Pai into this essay, let alone summarize them briefly. However, I strongly recommend that readers examine Pai's work.

I. Historical Background

On the eve of the Opium War (1839)—which was not only a decisive episode in China's colonization by the West, but was also the beginning of forced modernization of East Asia as a whole—the Qing Empire of China regarded itself, cosmologically as well as politico-ideologically, as the center of the world (Fairbank 1978, 1980; Namiki and Inoue 1977). The China-centered politico-cultural system, mediated as well as supported by tributary and/or economic ties with the countries situated within and on the fringe of its multilayered spheres of governance, control, and influence, was firmly situated in and legitimated by this perception. It was a world system independent from the expanding Euro-centric world system. This partially but significantly explains China's reluctance—in stark contrast with Japan—to modernize itself by emulating Western ways outright.

Korea was a tributary state of China and firmly situated in this system. It remained loyal to China after China's defeat in the Opium War. Japan, separated from the Asian mainland by the sea, was in and out of a tributary relationship with China throughout its premodern history. At the time of the Opium War, Japan, as seen from a China-centric perspective, was a client state on the fringe of the system. The defeat of China sent a shockwave to Japan, which compelled the Japanese to abolish the confederacy of feudal clans and to quickly unify their country as a Western-style nation-state. As its modernization progressed, Japan attempted to set up a defensive buffer zone, which led to the colonization of Taiwan (1895–1945), Korea (1910–1945), and later, Manchuria (1932–1945).

The destruction of the China-centric world system and the modernization of East Asia were two facets of the process through which East Asian countries became forcefully incorporated into the Euro-centric world system. At the beginning of the process, in the China-centric cosmological order, Western colonial powers were categorized as "barbarians" far from the sphere of the enlightening influence of the emperor, who was thought to be entrusted by the heavenly emperor to reign on earth (Namiki and Inoue 1997). When the British government tried to establish treaty-based relations, China naturally rejected them on the grounds that the British government had to, or was expected to, beg the Chinese emperor for enlightenment and for what they needed.[2] The defeat forced China not only to make unequal treaties—first with Britain, and later with France and other Western colonial powers—but also to modernize, by altering its traditional institutions and discarding its cosmology/world view in order to survive. Naturally, the multilayered identities of the Chinese peoples were shaken (the Qing Dynasty was a multi-ethnic empire), as was also the case in Korea and Japan. The reshaping of national and ethno-cultural identities took various paths, depending on such factors as (1) attitudes toward the China-centric cosmology/world system; (2) reactions to the West and its "civilization"; and (3) the emergence of (often reinvented or newly minted) "national" traditions. The trajectory of modern archaeology's development in those countries was also significantly influenced by these factors.

Before the colonial encounter, China's attitude of learning from the past for good governance in the present was nurtured among the intellectual class, and activities that had a number of similarities to modern scientific archaeology were taken up by the elite (von Falkenhausen 1993: 842–843). For instance, the classification of ancient (Shang and Zhou periods, ca. 1600–300 B.C.) bronze vessels, the reading and chronicling of their inscriptions, and their comparison with recorded events were undertaken (cf. Trigger 2006: 74–76). In Japan, the development of commerce and the formation of a bourgeois intellectual class led to the flourishing of antiquarian-like activities, including the collection of unique plants, fossils, and artifacts (Trigger 2006: 76). We can never know if such activities would have eventually developed into something akin to modern scientific archaeology, had there not been Western colonial interventions. The forced modernization-Westernization cut short their development.

In China, the prolonged period of turmoil and struggle against colonial powers resulted in internal power struggles and ideological conflicts, which prompted the fragmentation of discourse about modernization and about regaining independence. This prevented modern scientific archaeology, introduced by Western-educated scholars such as Li Chi (Ji) (cf. Glover 2006:18; Trigger 2006: 265–266), from becoming established and gaining influence on the people's perception of their history.

In Japan, the development of modern scientific archaeology was hindered for quite a different reason. In order to rapidly modernize—and to integrate the confederacy of semi-independent feudal domains into a unified nation—Japan chose to rely heavily on a narrative that gave the imperial family an uninterrupted genealogy from the beginning of the history of the Japanese *ethnie* (e.g., Mizoguchi 2006). As we shall see later, any activity that potentially cast doubt on the authenticity of this notion was severely purged. Referring to the mythological section of the oldest imperial chronicles of *Kojiki* and *Nihon-shoki*, the beginning of the imperial genealogy was believed to coincide with the beginning of rice agriculture, metallurgy, and the construction of gigantic keyhole-shaped tumuli. Therefore, the study of the "Stone Age" (i.e., before the beginning of rice farming, metallurgy, and tumulus [*Kofun*] construction) was relatively free from political interventions, whereas that from the Kofun period onward was severely regulated. This meant that social archaeology as an interpretive framework was not developed before the end of World War II (Asia-Pacific War). The defeat of Japan in that war marked the end of the colonial era in East Asia, which was also the beginning of the new world order, the Cold War. The dispute over the best way to modernize one's own country continued.

In China, with the victory of the Communist Party, the main objective of archaeology became the compartmentalization of archaeological data into the Marxist stages of social development (Glover 2006: 19; Trigger 2006: 267–268). The Communists tended to source the developments of "Chinese civilization" to the Yellow River valley, where improving influences were (interpreted to be) constantly originating (Trigger 2006: 267–268). Naturally, this was the core region of the China-centric ideological cosmology of the imperial eras, and where the capitals of successive imperial dynasties were located. Not only did this fit the Marxist unilinear evolutionary model, but it was also useful for enhancing the sense of national unity and pride evoked by the bygone China-centric world view.

In South Korea (People's Republic of Korea), after the repudiation of Japanese rule, a Korean archaeological tradition was initiated by a denunciation of the theories put forward by Japanese scholars—namely, the *Nissen dōso-ron* theory and the existence of *Mimana-Nihon-fu*. These theories had been politically manipulated to legitimize Japan's annexation of Korea. The former claimed that the myth featured in the oldest imperial chronicles, *Kojiki* and *Nihonshoki*, together with archaeological evidence, showed that the Japanese and Korean nations had descended from a common ancestry (cf. Pai 2000). This thesis was then used to bolster the claim that the annexation brought the two nations back to their original state. The latter theory, derived from entries in the earliest imperial chronicles, asserted that imperial ancestors had already established a colonial outpost in southern Korea as early as sometime in the late 4th century A.D.—an assertion that was used to support Japan's claim of legitimacy for its colonial interventions and subsequent annexation of Korea. The denunciation of these theories was accompanied by a movement to rediscover the authentic and unique nature of the Korean-ness (Pai 2000). The movement was made to fit with the nationalistic and dictatorial nation (re)building; it was also welcomed and tacitly supported by the United States as a stabilization effort of a frontline nation against expanding communism. The consequence was a nationalistic culture-historical archaeology tinged with speculations on Korean origins (Pai 2000).

In Japan, Marxism also functioned as a dominant guiding framework in the critique of the imperial mythology-based ideology of the militaristic regime. However, the effective preservation of many pre–World War II institutions (mentioned above) and the unprecedented economic growth made Marxism-inspired self-critique of the colonial past ineffective (Mizoguchi 2006).

The end of the Cold War and deepening globalization have transformed the global politico-economic order and led to the abandonment of grand narratives of modernity, Marxism being one of the most prominent examples (Mizoguchi 2006). In Japan, the overt application of Marxist-inspired frameworks has been abandoned. In their place are traditional descriptive approaches and various methodologies imported from the West (e.g., processual and postprocessual frameworks; Mizoguchi 1997). In China, the descriptive Marxist-based developmental-stage approach has been gradually replaced by accounts of sequential regional cultural developments (Trigger 2006: 268). Currently, young Chinese, Korean, and Japanese archaeologists, some educated abroad, have begun applying sophisticated processual and postprocessual approaches. In other words, archaeology in East Asian countries currently is in the midst of globalization and postmodern fragmentation.

II. Japanese Views of the Colonial and Postcolonial Trajectory of East Asian Archaeology

"National Body" Concept and Archaeology

Many of the constitutive elements of modernity had not been sufficiently developed in Japan when the "forced" modernization took place. A modern nation-state, for instance, has to be industrialized; its operation rationalized; its contents, human labor, and so on commodified; its organization bureaucratized; and it must also be constituted by the citizens; deconstructed of kinship/local ties; secularized; and institutionally segmented and specialized (Mizoguchi 2006: 19; Waters 1999: xii–xiii). Citizenship is particularly critical for the other factors to be properly implemented, but in Japan citizenship was impossible to establish overnight; manufacturing and commercial sectors had not developed enough to disembed the people from kinship and agrarian tradition-based social ties and to re-embed them in the internally homogeneous nationhood. Instead of striving to establish citizenship, the newly established Meiji government devised a unique conceptual tool to achieve unity: the concept of the "national body," *Koku* (national) *-tai* (body). In this concept, the nation was perceived to be like the human body, and its people were compared to the organs. And, importantly, the emperor was perceived as the "head" of this body as well as the "embodiment" of this conceptualized body. If a part or organ of the body fails, the entire body dies, and if the head dies, the body dies, too. In that way, the concept also managed to establish the relationship between the people and the emperor as one of reciprocity; the people cannot exist without the emperor, and the emperor cannot exist without the people. By imposing this concept on the people's mind and body, the disembedment, re-embedment, and integration of the people as a unified nation were made possible at one go, without the establishment of citizenship (Mizoguchi 2006: 60–71). The invention and integration of nationhood and the rapid imposition of taxation, conscription, and industrialization were made possible by the national body concept.

Because of its artificiality, the national body concept needed various devices to support it. The myths of imperial genealogy as descending from the gods residing in heaven (called *Taka* [high] *-ma* [sky] *-gahara* [field]) and of an uninterrupted imperial lineage up until the present, were derived from the earliest imperial chronicles, the *Kojiki* and *Nihon-shoki*, and were mobilized particularly intensively to help internalize the concept of Japan's nationhood. Equating the origin of the imperial genealogy with the origin of the "Japanese nation" through the mediation of the national body concept made the strategy effective; that way, the national body was perceived as preexistent to everything that was Japan and Japanese, and that perception made the people feel that they owed their very existence to the national body. Therefore, the people had to give back to the national body, even sacrificing their lives, if necessary.

This intellectual discourse was vital for the legitimation of the national body concept, and for that very reason, scholarly activities were placed under constant surveillance and strict regulation (Mizoguchi 2006: 63–65). Any thesis, utterance, or activity that could potentially cast doubt on the authenticity of the mythical origin of the imperial family, the Japanese nation, or the national body was subjected to severe and often violent crackdown. The effect of this "climate of fear" on archaeology, still in its infancy in theoretical and methodological development, was serious. The fear was most acutely felt in the study of the Kofun (mounded tomb) period, because this period was believed/claimed to coincide with the era during which the imperial genealogy and the Japanese nation were founded and established—and also because the imperial ancestors were believed to be buried in the largest examples of the famous keyhole-shaped tumuli. Until the end of World War II (Asian-Pacific War), the study of the Kofun period was confined to the reconstruction of the function of artifacts by comparing them with depictions of the ancient imperial chronicles, *Kojiki* and *Nihon-shoki*, themselves compiled to legitimize the then newly established ancient state of Japan in the late 7th and early 8th centuries A.D.

In contrast, the study of the Jomon period (defined by the use of *Jo* [cord]-*mon* [marked] pottery), then recognized and characterized as the Stone Age, was relatively free from the restrictions that bound the study of the Kofun period. The Stone Age culture is recognized as the culture of the Aboriginal population of the archipelago, which was conquered, colonized, and enculturated by the ancestors of the imperial family. The imperial ancestors were believed to have brought with them (bronze and iron) metallurgy. The study of the Jomon, therefore, was not directly related to the history of the imperial family and the Japanese nation, and in that sense could not cast doubt on the authenticity of the early history of the imperial reign chronicled in the *Kojiki* and *Nihon-shoki*.

As noted earlier, the mythical descent of the imperial family from heaven (*Takama-gahara*), "recorded" in those chronicles, was utilized to ideologically legitimize the annexation of Korea. The so-called thesis of Korean and Japanese populations sharing a single origin (*Nissen-dōso-ron*: see above) was mobilized to claim that the annexation reinstated the original condition of the two nations as one (Nelson 2006: 41; Pai 2000). Ironically, Japanese archaeologists working in the peninsula during the period of the annexation, although covertly/unwittingly supporting the colonial policy and ideology, helped to lay the foundation for Korean archaeology, particularly in terms of methodology and the concept of "cultural property" (Pai 2000).

Post–World War II Reformation and the Erasure of Colonial Memory

The defeat of the Axis in World War II (Asian-Pacific War) and the catastrophe it caused not only to Japan but also to neighboring countries inevitably led to the wide-ranging self-examination of the factors that allowed the war to happen. Expectations placed on archaeology were high. During the war years (1937–1945), the ideological control imposed by the military-led executive reached virtually every corner of social life and rendered democracy dysfunctional; and it was apparent that the image of the emperor as the living god and the one and only embodiment of the history and destiny of Japan had sustained this grotesque state of affairs. It was widely felt that criticism and deconstruction of the very foundation of the national body concept—that is, the origin of the imperial genealogy—was an absolute necessity in order to move forward.

Amid this heated atmosphere, Marxism became an important guiding framework for deconstructing the imperial ideology of the national body (Mizoguchi 2006: 71–79). Marxism had become widespread in Japan under the liberal atmosphere and economic prosperity of the 1920s and quickly established itself as an influential critical theory covering the range of socio-cultural/ economic/political issues that Japan began to face. However, during the 1930s and 1940s, Marxism and Marxist political parties came under severe persecution, as militarism arose and colonial interventions into neighboring regions met with increasingly harsh international criticism. After the war, Marxism was naturally reinstated as the guiding framework of historical disciplines, including archaeology, because its advocates were the only politico-academic group that had continued to criticize the emperor system during World War II (Asia-Pacific War).

A prominent Marxist explanatory model for the Yayoi and Kofun social development goes as follows (Mizoguchi 2006: 75). The introduction of rice paddy field agriculture to the archipelago led to a significant development in the forces of production. Ever-increasing harvests, though at times hampered by bad years, inspired some kin-based communities to become autonomous and independent from the larger corporate organization. The development of the means of production was gradual, which made the occasional cooperation of the larger corporate group necessary. As a result, conflicting interests were generated among individual communities, as well as between them and the larger corporate group of which they were a part. Out of the necessity, then, of mediating the conflicts, mediators were chosen to help ease tensions and to make the larger corporate-group-scale cooperation possible. The mediators carried out this task by organizing communal-agricultural rituals that represented the necessity of communal cooperation and the importance of rice harvests. These two facets of the rituals led to the gradual convergence of images of ancestral and rice spirits. The image of the ancestral figure(s) of the imperial genealogy as the pseudo-communal ritual-conducting mediator-ruler figure(s) was almost identical to the image and symbolic function of the modern emperors, the Meiji (on the throne 1867–1912), the Taisho (1912–1925), and the Showa (1926–1989).

Of course, the closed, insular nature of the model is apparent; the tightly connected, coherent interrelationships within the model made it easy to explain any archaeological data as being material consequences of these coherent, systemic internal processes. This unwittingly veiled the view of Japanese archaeologists in their assessment and criticism of the history of their (unwilling, for some, but willing, for others) cooperation with war efforts or colonial activities and resulted, effectively, in the erasure of colonial memory.

The insularity of the Marxist framework fit the atmosphere of the time very well. A shared sentiment was that Japan, by her own fault, had lost everything that she had strived to achieve, and because of that, mistakes had to be recognized and problems rooted out by Japan—without outside help.[3] This allowed the Japanese to see themselves as victims rather than as responsible agents who caused tremendous harm to the people of Korea, China, and other Asian countries.

This insularity was formed in the early years of the post-war era, and the post-war economic success under the strategic guardianship of the United States hardened it. This has hindered attempts to seriously investigate the consequences of Japan's colonization of and colonial interventions into China and Korea, respectively, and their implications for archaeology.

The end of the Cold War, increasing globalization, and the spread of postmodern fragmentation of socioculturally shared discourses has led to the rise of nihilism and the reemergence of nationalistic sentiments in Japan. In the meantime, Japanese archaeology has lost Marxism, which functioned as a basis for critical theoretical discussions among archaeologists. Under these circumstances, Japanese archaeologists are struggling to recognize, self-examine, and amend colonial legacies and to find ways to confront reemergent nationalistic sentiments (Mizoguchi 2006).

III. Conclusion

What this brief study of East Asian colonial and postcolonial experience has shown is, first, that we are still coming to terms with the reconfiguration of institutions, cosmologies, and identities caused by the colonization-led modernization of East Asia.

Second, Japan, escaping outright colonization, chose to become a colonial power itself to counter colonial pressure. The invention of the national body concept played a significant role in the process of Japan's militarization and colonial interventions into neighboring nations. Ironically, the critique led by Marxist-inspired intellectuals (including archaeologists) of the concept after World War II, the end of which marked the end of the colonial era in the conventional sense, allowed Japanese people and Japanese archaeologists to insulate themselves and to forget their (or Japan's) colonial activities in Korea and China. Globalization and postmodern fragmentation has led to the deconstruction of grand narratives, including Marxism as a dominant critical theoretical framework during and after the colonial era. This has made it extremely difficult to sustain any shared discursive field in which ways to come to terms with colonial legacies and postcolonial difficulties can be discussed.

In summary, both the colonized and the uncolonized in East Asia are still locked up in the structure that originated in the colonial era. We had to react to the Western colonial expansion by Westernizing ourselves. The different conditions under which this came to be implemented defined the subsequent historical trajectories that China, Korea, and Japan have taken. Marxism, originating in the West, had to be adopted as a way to criticize and fight against the home-grown East Asian colonialism of imperial Japan. And now, amid globalization, both the colonized and the uncolonized in East Asia still find it difficult to find our own voices in coming to terms with what we experienced.

Notes

1. The Tokugawa (the name of the paramount feudal clan ruling Japan) shogunate: 1603– 1868.
2. At the beginning of the Opium War, the British imported Chinese tea and exported to China opium grown in India. The British government was aware of the unethical nature of the opium trade, and there were condemnations within and outside the nation on the eve and during the war (Namiki and Inoue 1997).
3. Some intellectuals argued that the militaristic misadventures and colonization of/colonial interventions into the neighboring countries since the Meiji restoration were un-Japanese in character. They claimed that the authentic domain of the national body was confined to the four main islands of the archipelago and surrounding islands, and the loss of the colonially occupied lands led to going back to the original state of the National Body of Japan (Mizoguchi 2006: 71–79).

References

Fairbank, J. K. (ed.). 1978. *Late Ch'ing, 1800–1911*. Cambridge History of China, Vol. 10, Part 1. Cambridge: Cambridge University Press.
——.1980. *Late Ch'ing, 1800–1911*. Cambridge History of China, Vol. 11, Part 2. Cambridge: Cambridge University Press.

Fawcett, C. 1986. Politics of assimilation in Japanese archaeology. *Archaeological Review from Cambridge* 5 (1): 43–57.
——.1995. Nationalism and postwar Japanese archaeology, in P. L. Kohl and C. Fawcett (eds.), *Nationalism and Archaeology: On the Construction of Nations and the Reconstructions of the Remote Past*, pp. 232–246. Cambridge: Cambridge University Press.
Glover, I. C. 2006. Some national, regional, and political uses of archaeology in East and Southeast Asia, in M. Stark (ed.), *Archaeology of Asia*, pp. 17–36. Oxford: Blackwell.
Hudson, M. J. 2006. Pots not people: Ethnicity, culture and identity in postwar Japanese archaeology. *Critique of Anthropology* 26 (4): 411–434.
Ikawa-Smith, F. 1982. Co-traditions in Japanese archaeology. *World Archaeology* 13 (3): 296–309.
Mizoguchi, K. 1997. The reproduction of archaeological discourse: The case of Japan. *Journal of European Archaeology* 5 (2): 149–165.
——.2006. *Archaeology, Society and Identity in Modern Japan*. Cambridge: Cambridge University Press.
Nelson, S. M. 2006. Archaeology in the two Koreas, in M. Stark (ed.), *Archaeology of Asia*, pp. 37–54. Oxford: Blackwell.
Namiki, Y., and Inoue, Y. 1997. *Chūka Teikoku no Kiki* (The crisis of the Chinese Empire). *Sekai no Rekishi* (A history of the world), Vol. 19. Tokyo: Chuokoron.
Pai, Hyung Il 2000. *Constructing "Korean" Origins: A Critical Review of Archaeology, Historiography, and Racial Myth in Korean*

State-Formation Theories. Cambridge: Harvard University Asia Center.

Trigger, B. 2006. *A History of Archaeological Thought*. 2nd ed. Cambridge: Cambridge University Press

von Falkenhausen, L. 1993. On the historiographic orientation of Chinese archaeology. *Antiquity* 67: 839–849.

——. 1995. The regional paradigm in Chinese archaeology, in P. L. Kohl and C. Fawcett (eds.), *Nationalism and Archaeology: On the Construction of Nations and the Reconstructions of the Remote Past*, pp. 198–217. Cambridge: Cambridge University Press.

Waters, M. 1999. General commentary: The meaning of modernity, in M. Waters (ed.), *Modernity: Critical Concepts*, pp. xi–xxiii. London: Routledge.

7

RESURRECTING THE RUINS OF JAPAN'S MYTHICAL HOMELANDS: COLONIAL ARCHAEOLOGICAL SURVEYS IN THE KOREAN PENINSULA AND HERITAGE TOURISM

Hyung Il Pai

The development of Japanese archaeology as a field discipline paralleled territorial expansion and the establishment of modern cultural institutions, such as museums and cultural preservation committees, not only in Japan but also in its colonies. The first modern-era heritage legislation was introduced during the Meiji era (1868–1912) when Japan's newly established Education Ministry and Exposition Office imported classifications systems, museum inventories, and exhibition formats from Europe. Following the Japanese occupation of the Korean Peninsula in 1910, the Colonial Government-General Office in Korea (CGK 1910–1945) sponsored the first systematic archaeological surveys to be carried out in the empire (Table 7.1). The Korean Peninsula was the only Japanese colony where the colonial government and academics spent more than four decades conducting annual surveys and nationwide excavations, building museums, and launching massive tourist restoration projects ranging from burial mounds to Buddhist temples and palaces (Pai 1994, 2000). Here, I have only space enough to introduce the major archaeological discoveries made by the first generation of professionally trained archaeologists, ethnologists, and art historians who were sent to conduct fieldwork in Korea at the turn of the century. Their archaeological discoveries between 1900 and 1915 were critical in the creation of the CGK Committee on Korean Antiquities and the promulgation of the first comprehensive set of archaeological heritage management laws in the peninsula. I then discuss the pivotal role that print media, from picture postcards to travel guidebooks, played in the dissemination of archaeological information targeted toward Japanese tourists as

Table 7.1 Chronology of Heritage Management in Japan and Korea (Fieldwork, Disciplines, Institutions, and Tourist Industry)

1874. 5	Meiji government bans excavations of legendary "burial mounds" and sacred sites.
1884	The Tokyo Anthropological Society is established at Tokyo University (prehistoric archaeology specimens deposited).
1887	Japan's racial origins debate begins: Ainu vs. Prehistoric Koro-pok-guru (Pre-Ainu).
1888	Imperial Office sets up office in charge of preliminary survey of treasures.
1893	Tokyo Imperial University Anthropological Society establishes specimens laboratory under Torii Ryūzō.
1895	Sino-Japanese War. Torii undertakes first survey of Taiwan and Manchuria. Preservation Laws governing Temples and Shrines are promulgated. Government takes over the management and preservation of nationally registered art, artifacts, and documents belonging to temples and shrines (beginning of national treasures system).
1901	Yagi, Sōzaburō sent to conduct first archaeological survey of the Korean Peninsula.
1902	Sekino Tadashi is sent by Tokyo University to survey art and architecture in Korea.
1904	Keifu-sen [Pusan-Seoul] Railways Line is completed.
1906	Imanishi Ryū surveys Keishū (Kyŏngju) Silla capital in southwest Korea.
1907	Excavations of Kimhae Shellmound in Korea are undertaken by Imanishi Ryū.
1908	Yi Royal Museum, zoo, and botanical garden are built in Ch'anggyŏng-wŏn, Keijō [Seoul].
1910	Annexation of Korea.
1911	Colonial Governor-General commissions Torii Ryūzō to conduct first systematic survey of prehistoric archaeological remains and ethnographic surveys. The Shiseki Meisho Tennenkinnenbutsu Hozonkai [Historic Sites, Famous Places, and Natural Monuments Protection Committee] is established in Japan.
1911	Temples Protection Act is promulgated in the Korean Peninsula by the Colonial Governor-General.
1912. 3. 12	Japan Tourist Bureau (JTB) is established at Tokyo Railway Station and is the first bureau to issue a pamphlet printed in English (2,000 copies) and French (3,000 copies).
1912. 11-12	JTB sets up branches in Dalian at South Manchuria Railroad office (SMR), Keijō (Chōsen Railways office), and Taipei office (Taiwan Railways)
1912	Reconstruction of Sŏkkuram funded by the Colonial Governor-General begins.
1913. 6. 10	*Tourist* is published as a bimonthly magazine with bilingual (English/Japanese) articles.
1914. 1	English maps of Keijō, Dalian, and Formosa (3,000 copies) are distributed.
1914. 2	JTB agents/branches are set up in 30 locations around the world.
1914. 10	The Keijō Chōsen Hotel, managed by the Chōsen Railways, is established.
1915.2	JIR "through" pass is offered, linking ship and rail services to Manchuria/Chōsen, sold at Tokyo train station branch (up to 30% discounted tickets valid for six months).

Table 7.1 (continued) Chronology of Heritage Management in Japan and Korea (Fieldwork, Disciplines, Instituions, and Tourist Industry)

1915.8	Kŭmgangsan Station Hotel opens in Onjŏngni in North Korea.
1915.12	The Colonial Governor-General Fine Arts Museum is established in Kyŏngbokkung Palace.
1916	Colonial Governor-General Committee for the Investigations of Ancient Remains and Relics [Chōsen Koseki Chosa ininkai] is established. Regulations on the Preservation of Ancient Sites and Relics are promulgated. These are the first comprehensive preservation laws governing art and archaeological remains, predating Japan by three years. Measurement are taken of Kyŏngju Hwangyongsa temple remains and Sach'ŏnwangsa temple, Chŏlla-namdo Songgwangsa temple. Koguryŏ tombs in Jian are investigated by Sekino Tadashi.
1918	Major reconstruction of Pulguksa begins; Colonial Governor-General Construction department takes eight years.
1918	Kyŏngju Silla tombs excavated (by Kuroita Katsumi and Harada Yoshito).
1921	Kyŏngju Museum is established.
1926	Chōsen Manchuria Office sets up in Tokyo, Shimonoseki, and Shinjuku stations.
1926	Kyŏngju branch museum is established; Keijō tram service begins.
1932	Chōsen Hotel Company is formed to run former Chōsen Railways hotels: Keijō Chōsen, Fusan Station, Shingishu Station, Kumgangsan Onjŏngni, Changanri, Keijō station restaurant, and train restaurants.
1943	JTB shuts down branches due to the expansion of the Pacific War.

well as foreigners. Colonial-era tourist publications featuring Korea's ancient remains (*koseki*) and customs (*fūzoku*) advertising the peninsula as the most "historically scenic" destination transformed the colony into the most popular Japanese tourist destination in the 1920s and 1930s. Since the end of the Pacific War in 1945, many South Korean archaeologists have continued to condemn the prewar-era Japanese archaeologists' activities as "systematic plunder," without understanding why and how ruins and relics were reclaimed as part of "Japanese racial and imperial heritage" in the colonial era.[1]

Empire Building, Heritage Management, and Field Research in Northeast Asia

Cultural nationalism focusing on emperor worship (*tennosei*) and divine imperial sovereignty (*kokutai*) were the two main ideological forces dictating the direction of the prewar Japanese government's legislation of museum antiquities, temples, shrines, and legendary burial mounds (*kofun*). Kofun sites became the earliest targets of government regulations because the Imperial Household Agency (*Kunaichō*) appropriated them as sacred national symbols (*seiseki*) vouching for the unbroken succession of emperors since mythical times *(kami jidai)*. Fabricated monuments and imperial tombs dedicated to successive mythical founding emperors soon became the main political stage upon which the Meiji emperor, as a living deity, performed reenacted ancient rituals.[2] The Meiji government banned unlawful excavations of all "imperial mounds," real or legendary, in 1874 so as to ward off any contentious claims to state ownership of imperial burials, which became indispensable in legitimizing the new imperial order for both domestic consumption and the world media (Fujitani 1996; Suzuki and Takagi 2000; Takagi 1997). The Ministry of Education and the Interior Ministry began sponsoring nationwide art and architectural surveys in the 1880s in order to create a "national" registry (*taichō dōroku*) so they could monitor the circulation of buried properties, antiquities, documents, and buildings to prevent looting and smuggling by antiquity dealers and collectors. University-trained specialists such as art historians, architects, and archaeologists were hired for the first time to identify, authenticate, document, and collect antiquities to be displayed at international expositions and imperial museums as "national treasures" for all to see and learn about (Tokyo Kokuritsu Hakubutsukan 1976). By 1899, the Imperial Household Agency reigned over a trio of state institutions: the Education Ministry; the three imperial museums (*teishitsu hakubutsukan*) in Tokyo, Nara, and Kyoto; and the Tokyo Imperial University–based Anthropological Society Laboratory (Tokyo Jinrui Gakkai 1884–present). They were charged with micromanaging "national properties," from the issuing of excavation permits to registering and monitoring the circulation of antiquities and the preservation of imperial palaces, temples, and shrines. The state monopoly over all aspects of heritage administration and limited access to archaeological sites and research collections resulted in the dearth of stratigraphic excavations, severely impeding the progress of scientific field archaeology in Japan (Teshigawara 1995).

Field opportunities first opened up in Taiwan, Korea, Northeast China, and the Russian Maritime Provinces following Japan's military victories over Qing China and Russia in the Sino-Japanese (1894–1895) and Russo-Japanese Wars (1904–1905). In 1895, the Tokyo University–based Tokyo Anthropological Society (Tokyo Jinrui Gakkai) became the first learned society given permission by the Meiji government and colonial army officials to conduct art/ archaeological surveys and ethnographic expeditions outside their borders (Sakazume 1997).[3] Tsuboi Shōgorō (1863–1913), who was a world traveler, polymath, and charismatic founder of the Anthropological Society (1884–present), supervised the first graduates of the Anthropological Specimens Laboratory (Pai 2004). The young, ambitious students he sent to Korea, China, Taiwan, and inner Asia in the early 1900s, such as Yagi Sōzaburō (1866–1942), Imanishi Ryū (1875–1932), and Torii Ryūzō (1870–1953), represented an entirely new breed of field scholars, trained in the imported disciplines of prehistoric archaeology and biological and physical sciences (Matsumura 1934). Torii Ryūzō's wide-ranging ethnographic surveys all over Asia also resulted in the accumulation of archaeological and ethnographic collections of sherds, stone tools, and weapons, which were required by Meiji buried properties laws to be deposited at the Tokyo University anthropological laboratory, the predecessor to the current University Museum of Tokyo (Akazawa 1991; Akazawa et al. 1993). Torii's vast collection of ethnographic and prehistoric materials, now housed at Tokyo University and the National Museum of Ethnology in Osaka, reflects some 60 years of continuous fieldwork inside and outside of Japan. He was also the first Japanese anthropologist to take a camera into the field in 1896. He recorded thousands of glass plate images of megalithic tombs, stone cist graves, and racial portraits of Indigenous peoples from Siberia, Mongolia, Taiwan, and South China (Pai 2009). By the 1910s, these field collections from the colonies constituted the primary "scientific" evidence for understanding the much debated origins of the Japanese race (*Jinshuron*) and civilization (Hudson 1999; Kudō 1979).

Reclaiming "Imperial Ruins" in Colonial Korea (1900–1945)

In the search for archaeological evidence for the origins of Japanese civilization, the Korean Peninsula became the field of choice even before the official annexation of the Korean Peninsula in 1910 (Mokuyō Club 2003). Sekino Tadashi (1867–1935), a Tokyo Imperial University–trained architect, was sent to Korea in 1902 by Tokyo Imperial University (Figure 7.1). He was at the time the most well-trained and experienced field researcher, since in 1897 he had already conducted field surveys of temples and shrines in Nara (710–784), Japan's oldest recorded imperial capital (Hirose 2003). Though on his first trip he spent only two summer months in the field, he managed to visit, sketch, and photograph all the known ruins located at the former dynastic capitals of Keishū (Kyŏngju), Kaijō (Kaesŏng), Heijō (P'yŏngyang), and Keijō (Seoul). On his return, his prodigious results were published by the Tokyo University Engineering College Research Reports in 1904. This report, entitled *Kangoku Chosa Hokoku*, consisted of 250 pages filled with descriptions, sketches, and photographs of Korean art and architecture, including hundreds of tombs, sculpture, temples, gates, palace buildings, and royal burials (Sekino 1904). Impressed by Sekino's spectacular results, the newly appointed Colonial Resident-General of Korea, Itō Hirobumi (1841–1909), commissioned Sekino and his three assistants to rank 569 heritage remains, sites or artifacts (Sekino 1919), following the same criteria devised for the 1897 preservation laws for Japan's National Treasures *(Kokuhō)* worthy of preservation and protection: (1) *kō*: artwork designated as possessing "superior workmanship" *(seisaku yūshū)*; (2) *ōtsu*: objects reflecting historical origins and legendary accounts *(yūisho)*; and (3) *hei*: remains that can serve as historical evidence (Bunkachō 1997: 197–215).

Korea's archaeological finds were officially registered as Japan's imperial possessions with the 1916 Regulations on the Preservation of Ancient Sites and Relics of

Figure 7.1 Professor Sekino Tadashi of Tokyo Imperial University surveying pagodas in Korea (ca. 1932).

Chōsen (*Koseki oyobi ibutsu hozon kitei*) (CGK 1924). As the first comprehensive archaeological heritage management laws to be promulgated in the empire, they were applied to Korea three years before they were reenacted in Japan.[4] This act was accompanied by the formation of the Committee on the Investigation of Korean Antiquities (*Chōsen Koseki Chosa Ininkai*), which was charged with overseeing the administration of the 1916 laws, ranging from the investigation of archaeological remains to the planning of exhibitions, the preservation and reconstruction of monuments, the registration of national remains, and the publications of their research activities (Pai 2001). The Colonial Governor-General Museum, the first fine arts museum in Korea, opened on December 1, 1915, in a new Western-style building erected on the grounds of the former Yi Dynasty's (1392–1910) royal palace of Kyŏngbokkung, situated in the heart of Seoul (Chŏn 1999).

The 1916 laws were also instrumental in classifying which Korean remains were to be considered for registration, preservation, and research. The first article defined "koseki" (ancient remains) as prehistoric sites containing shell mounds and implements made of stone, bone, and horn; as well as subterranean dwellings, ancient tombs, town fortresses, palaces, barricades, barrier gates, station posts, stages for setting signal fires (beacons), sites of government offices, sites of shrines, mausolea, temples, ruins of ceramic industry (kilns), old battlefields, and other ruins; and also sites associated with historical facts. The category of "ibutsu" (relics) encompassed old pagodas, stele, bells, stone and metal images of Buddha, flagpole supporters, stone lanterns, and other artifacts that may have historical, artistic, and archaeological value (Sekino 1931: 7)

The CGK was heavily involved in publicizing their discoveries of "Korea's thousand-year old ruins," not only for scholars but also for the citizens of the empire at large (CGK 1915: 1). The CGK raised money from a wide variety of public and private sources—including the Imperial Household Agency, CGK Museum, and the Yi Royal Household Agency, to name the most prominent few—to fund excavation budgets, purchase the latest photographic equipment, hire professional photographers and sketch artists, and provide publication subsidies.[5] Consequently, even by today's standards, these CGK-published annual excavations reports (CGK 1918–1937, 1919–1930), museum exhibition catalogs (CGK 1918–1941), and photo album series featuring monumental ruins (CGK 1915–1935), are striking in the number as well as technical quality of photographs, colored maps, and artifact drawings, surpassing any other contemporary publications available for Japan's remains. The CGK's contributions to the field of archaeology were eventually recognized, even among nonspecialists, as superior in methodology, excavation technique, and state-of-the-art equipment and achieved international acclaim (Reischauer 1939).[6]

The main political objective of the CGK in promoting architectural surveys and touting Korea's ancient discoveries to a world audience was clearly articulated in the preface to the first volume of the *Album of Korean Antiquities* (*Chōsen Koseki Zufu*) published in 1915 (CGK 1915–1935). The preface begins with a declaration of how the 1910 annexation of Korea as part of the Japanese Empire became the catalyst for launching the first systematic surveys of the peninsula. It also states that the CGK's assigned mission was the "recovery" of "historical proof" (*rekishi chokyo*) and "artistic models" (*bijutsu no mohan*) "hidden amongst the mysteries of the past" (CGK 1915, Vol. 1: 1). Though it is never mentioned explicitly whose past the CGK editorial team is describing, it is implied that the remains from Korea were reclaimed as empirical evidence for tracing the continental origins of Japanese art and civilization (Pai 2006). This is because, unlike in Japan, where the Imperial Household Agency had imposed censorship by restricting access to protected sites or research collections, the archaeological materials from Korea were excavated stratigraphically and preserved in situ (Yoshii 2006). The published works, biographies, and autobiographies penned by prominent colonial-era archaeologists and art historians—such as Sekino Tadashi (1868–1942), Hamada Kōsaku (1881–1938), Umehara Sueji (1893–1983), Harada Yoshito (1885–1974), and Fujita Ryōsaku (1892–1960—as well as my interview session with the last surviving CGK-employed archaeologist, Arimitsu Kyōichi (1907–present), support the CGK's official stance that the preservation and restoration of Korean remains represented the high point of Japanese cultural administration in Korea (Pai 2000; Mokuyō Club 2003).[7]

Advertising Common Ancestral Terrains: Imperialists' Nostalgia, Archaeological Photography, and Tourism in the Empire

Images of the monumental ruins of pyramids and temples of the ancient civilizations of Egypt, Greece, and India have captured the imagination of colonialists, commercial photographers, scholars, tour operators, and tourists for more than two centuries (Lyons et al. 2005; MacCannell 1976; Pelizarri 2003). Similarly, beginning at the turn of the century, Korea's "picturesque" remains served as the favorite backdrop for commemorative group photos, including official visits by foreign dignitaries, imperial family members, colonial administrators, heads of multinational corporations, missionaries, and organized tour groups. Clearly, for both photographers and paying customers there was an "irresistible" pull of the romance of ruins (Roth 1997). Commercial photographers, as businessmen first and artists second, were keenly aware that visually striking and attractive settings, whether natural or exotic landscapes manufactured in the studio, sold prints and postcards (Ryan 1997). In the case of Korea, the most widely manufactured, collected, and mailed tourist postcards representing "local color" (*fūzoku*) were images of peasant women, cute children, and *kisaeng* (professional dancers/entertainers), who were arranged as "native cultural markers" amid the scenic ruins of pagodas, temples, palace gardens, and fortresses (Kwŏn 2005). By the late 1910s, exotic photographs depicting the "quaint" customs and "backward" images of Koreans were reprinted in business almanacs issued by major colonial enterprises such as the Bank of Chōsen and the South Manchuria Railway Company (Bank of Chōsen 1919); CGK published in-house newsletters, gazetteers, and local daily newspapers and circulated throughout the major colonial cities from Seoul to Taipei and Singapore.

The marketing of Korea's ancient sites as tourist attractions began in earnest in 1912, with the founding of the Keijō (Seoul) branch of the Japan Tourist Bureau (JTB). Japan's oldest travel agency, the JTB (founded in 1912 and still operating today) began working together with Colonial Government Railways of Chōsen (CGR), Taiwan Railways, and South Manchuria Railroad (SMR) to build transportation networks (railways and trams) and accommodations (hotels, spas, and mountain resorts). The main business goal of the JTB, then as now, was to bring in foreign revenue by enticing visitors to travel to remote archaeological sites, famous places, natural monuments, summer resorts, and hot springs (JTB 1982). In order to advertise Korea's archaeological sites to a world audience, local newspapers, the JTB, and travel magazines hired leading specialists, journalists, writers, professional travelers, tour group operators, and educators to write travelogues and guidebooks.[8] Their articles and photos were widely disseminated in CGK monthly newsletters, daily newspapers, guidebooks printed in the colonies, Japan Imperial Railway maps (JIR 1925), and JTB publications such as *Tabi* (Travel) (JTB 1924–present) and *The Tourist* (JTB 1913–1942).

All travelers, be they Japanese, Europeans, or Koreans, raved that the most authentic "Korean" experience could be had by taking a few extra days to visit the oldest historical capitals discovered by archaeologists at Keishū (Kyŏngju), Fuyo (Puyŏ), and Heijō (P'yŏngyang) (Keishū Koseki Hozonkai 1922, 1936). The Tomb of the Gold Crown in the Old Silla Kingdom capital of Keishū (ca. 5th century A.D.) was excavated in 1921. The event was widely promoted in travel magazines, newspapers, and guidebooks as the greatest archaeological discovery of the century. The site was excavated by Professor Hamada Kōsaku (1881–1938) and his student Umehara Sueji (1893–1983), the two most influential Kyoto Imperial University–trained archaeologists working for the CGK Committee on Korean Antiquities. The preservation of Sŏkkuram and Pulguksa temples (ca. 8th century A.D.) took the CGK construction engineers more than a decade to complete. Furthermore, the entire temple grounds were designated as famous scenic places *(meisho)* and promoted in many tourist brochures and travel magazines as equal to Japan's oldest capital of Nara in beauty and historicity (JTB 1934: "Tabi"). By the 1930s, the restored ruins of Keishū and the Keishū Museum (1926–present), built in the center of the concentration of Silla royal burial mounds (ca. 3rd–9th centuries A.D.), became the favorite setting for photo-ops by visiting imperial family members (Figure 7.2) and foreign royalty, including Crown Prince Adolf Gustaf VI of Sweden, an amateur archaeologist and collector (Figure 7.3) who founded the Museum of

Figure 7.2 Imperial family relatives taking official tourist commemoration portrait in front of Sŏkkuram after reconstruction, October 1935, Kyŏngju.

Figure 7.3 Japanese archaeologists assisting Crown Prince Adolf Gustaf VI of Sweden at Sobongch'ong, Kyŏngju, ca. 1926.

Far Eastern Antiquities in Stockholm (Hamada and Andersson 1932). Cities along the northeast railway lines such as P'yŏngyang and Kaesŏng also became popular tourist destinations because of the abundance of ancient tombs. The restored tombs of the Han Dynasty commandery of Rakurō (ca. 2nd century B.C.–2nd century A.D.), situated south of the Taedong River and Koguryŏ painted tombs (ca. 5th–6th centuries A.D.) outside of P'yŏngyang city, were also featured in many guidebooks and tourist maps for their historical importance as the most "scientifically" excavated tombs in Asia (Pai 2000: 127–236). The ancient Paekche (Kudara) capitals of Puyŏ and Kongju (ca. 4th–7th centuries A.D.) were also promoted in tourist brochures as the holiest of Japanese heritage sites because of the kingdom's close diplomatic and cultural relations with emperors in ancient times.

In conclusion, Japanese field researchers spent more than four decades in the Korean Peninsula searching for "imperial treasures and remains," which they were not allowed to excavate in their own country. The "ethnocentric" and aesthetic biases practiced by Tokyo University–based architects and archaeologists have therefore resulted in the preservation and promotion of a select number of royal burial sites, artifacts, and Buddhist architectural monuments most resembling those of Japan. The locations of Korea's archaeological remains, which included shell mounds, bronze mirrors, and burial sites as "key ethnic markers," were plotted and mapped as the conquest route of Japan's mythical emperors whose imperial authority had extended to the southern half of the Korean Peninsula in the protohistoric period (Kuno 1967; Pai 1999a; Umehara 1923).[9] The photographic images and the meanings of Korea's archaeological discoveries were also manipulated by powerful colonial policy makers (Yamamichi 1910) to justify the annexation of Korea as a predestined "return" and reunion between the two races of Japanese and Koreans, who had once shared common ancestors (*Nissen Dōsoron*) (Kita 1921) and thus, a shared cultural patrimony since time immemorial (Pai 2006). The JTB and CGK also propagated a nostalgic image through the "rustic" appeal of Korea's decaying sites and "beautiful" customs in printed postcards and tourist brochures to market their imagined mythical "imperial terrains," luring rich businessmen, as well as foreign and domestic visitors, to invest and settle in the colonies. From the perspective of ordinary Japanese leisure tourists,[10] the conscious act of visiting, absorbing, and experiencing firsthand Korea's customs, peoples, and ancient sites also became part of their search for their own national identity, pride, and belonging as citizens of the growing multiethnic and multicultural Japanese Empire during the 1930s (Weisenfeld 2000).

Epilogue

This recurring theme of imagined "imperialist nostalgia" that romanticized the conquered "other" in time and space, though not unique to the Japanese Empire (Abu El-Haj 2001; Trigger 1984), left a lasting legacy on archaeological heritage management practices not only in Meiji Japan, but a century later in South Korea today (Pai 2001). In the postcolonial era, the contentious topic of "who is to blame for the plunder of Korean remains?" continues to be one of the most controversial debates hindering bilateral diplomatic relations since the end of the Pacific War in 1945 (O 1996).[11] Many prominent archaeologists, historians, and art historians (Kim 1966) over the past five decades have denounced colonial-era archaeologists' activities, and their reports are the "smoking gun" that reveal how systematically the occupation government had utilized knowledgeable scholars' research for the political objective of assimilating Koreans (Nishikawa 1970; H. J. Yi 1964; K.Y. Yi 1996). Thus, Japanese archaeologists as a professional group became the main scapegoats and have been demonized in the press and media for their active role in depriving Koreans of their cultural patrimony and, thus, racial identity (Ch'oe 1997).

Despite such anti-Japanese rhetoric, we have to acknowledge that there are many indelible intellectual, aesthetic, and disciplinary legacies of this "shared" history of colonial-era discoveries. First, we have to acknowledge that the concepts of prehistory, social evolution, unique "indigenous" culture, and periodization schemes based on material culture and artifact typology were all introduced by Japanese archaeologists in the early colonial era. Before the arrival of Japanese collectors and archaeologists in the early 20th century, there was a lively antiquarian tradition practiced by the landed aristocracy, rich merchant classes, and civil officials of high status (*Yangban*).

Objects such as strange-looking stones (*kiseki*), jade, and bronze vessels were dug up and collected mainly for their ritual and symbolic value and/or aesthetic appeal. Rubbings of inscriptions on stone and bronze were made in order to decipher records that would link them to heroes or kings, and not for their "archaeological" value in the modern sense of the word. Furthermore, the *Yangban* scholars believed that stone and jade objects were made by natural forces and/or supernatural elements (e.g., lightning, earthquakes, or the gods), but were definitely not man-made, much like the beliefs of antiquarians in 18th-century England and France. Therefore, it is my opinion that "Koreans were not cheated out of their archaeological heritage by the Japanese looting scholars" as most postcolonial-era nationalistic scholars have asserted (Kim 1966, 1973; Yi 1964); rather, they simply had no knowledge or appreciation of prehistoric objects or ancient sites to be excavated, preserved, and promoted as a body of national heritage. The emergence of a "Korean consciousness" of their own traditions and culture only occurred in the late 1920s and 1930s, when a new generation of Korean-born but Japanese-educated colonial elite started acquiring their own collections. For example, Song Sŏk-ha, now regarded as the "father of Korean ethnology," accumulated his own Korean ceramics collection by emulating the tastes and preferences of sophisticated and urbane Japanese collectors and connoisseurs such as the Asakawa brothers and Yanagi Sōetsu (Brandt 2007; Han 1997).

In August 1945, with Japan's surrender, the U.S. Army Military Government in

Korea (USAMGIK) oversaw the peaceful handover of the CGK Museum collections from the last director, Arimitsu Kyōichi, to the new Korean director of the National Museum of Korea, Kim Chae-wŏn (1909–1992). Arimitsu was asked to stay behind to train the new generation of young Korean graduates of Seoul National University (formerly Keijō Imperial University) so they could return to their excavation sites in Keishū in 1946 (Mokuyō Club 2003). Consequently, my research of colonial-era archives indicates that the most celebrated, reported, documented, and excavated artifacts were inherited mostly intact by the National Museum of Korea leading up to the outbreak of the Korean War (1950–1953), when the museum was evacuated to Pusan in 1951 (Pai 2000: 237–243). However, we still do not have any accurate estimates of the status of the other colonial museum branches located in North Korea (P'yŏngyang, Kaesŏng) or the southern cities of Puyŏ, Kongju, and Kyŏngju during the chaotic period of violence and plunder following the division of the peninsula in 1945. We will probably never know how many artifacts, documents, displays, storage buildings, and sites were destroyed, burned, and/or looted during the chaos of the Korean War years, when the whole peninsula was bombed. Finally, since the 1960s, especially in South Korea, there has been even larger-scale destruction of the landscape in the name of economic and industrial development, with massive infrastructure constructions such as dams, railroads, freeways, factories, airports, and apartment buildings (Pai 1999b). As a result, these early 20th-century-documented photographs, maps, and drawings of archaeological remains preserved in colonial reports, museum catalogs, tourist brochures, and postcards are now consulted as invaluable research and preservation tools as portraits of Korean monuments frozen in time (Pai 2006).

Conventions

The names cited in this work follow the Japanese convention of placing the family names first. Most place-names adhere to their original colonial-era sources, such as Formosa for Taiwan; Japanese pronunciations for colonial cities and addresses such as Keijō, the former name for Seoul, the capital of the Republic of Korea, etc. Their current names are added in parentheses when first appearing in the text. The lesser-known proper nouns, as well as names of archaeological sites, palaces, temples, institutions, customs, etc., are transcribed in Korean. The Korean romanization system here follows the McCune-Reischauer system adopted by scholars in the West, not the current system used by the Republic of Korea. All translations in this paper are the author's own.

Acknowledgments

The research for this article has been made possible by two fellowships: a Japan Foundation Fellowship (2004–2005) and a visiting research professorship at the International Research Center for Japanese Studies (2007–2008). I would like to thank the following professors and staff for their friendship and support during my research trips to archives in Japan: Yoshii Hideo (Kyoto University), Hirase Takao (Tokyo University), Yamada Shōji (International Research Center for Japanese Studies), Yamanashi Emiko (Tokyo National Research Institute of Cultural Properties, Ueno), and Xu Su-bin (Tianjin University Graduate School of Architecture).

Notes

1. The Japanese archaeologists mentioned here also conducted field surveys in northern China, Mongolia, and Taiwan during the 1900s–1930s. However, their archaeological activities were not as systematically organized or sustained over 40 years, as was the case with the Korean Peninsula.
2. The Imperial Household Agency launched the construction of large-scale national mausolea dedicated to mythical founding emperors beginning in the late 1870s. The first to be built was the Tomb of Jimmu (ca. 2,660 B.C.), known as the fifth descendent of the sun goddess, Amaterasu, the legendary founder of Japan (Suzuki and Takagi 2000). However, today there are "nearly 900 locations in Japan that are currently treated as imperial tombs, that is, as mausolea containing the remains of an imperial family member, with 250 being listed as predating the start of written history, in fact their actual connection with the imperial line is still largely open to question" (Edwards 2003: 11). Please consult the Imperial Household Agency website for a complete registry of imperial tombs through the ages (*tennō rekidai ichiran*) and a map of their locations: *http://www.kunaicho.go.jp/ryobo/index.html* (last accessed September 16, 2008).
3. The Meiji government had embarked on foreign military expeditions extending their frontiers into the northern islands bordering on Russia, south to the islands of Taiwan, and into the hinterlands of the Korean Peninsula and northeast China beginning in the late 1870s. The initial goal, as it was with European imperial powers, was to obtain concession rights to natural resources—fisheries, timber, and tropical agricultural products such as tea and camphor. Newly appointed colonial administrators, army officials, and local police, faced with ruling sometimes hostile populations from Siberia to Taiwan, took an active part in supporting anthropologists' surveys. They supported the scholars financially and logistically by providing transportation, equipment, guides, interpreters, and bodyguards. They understood that ethnographic knowledge gathered by experts on local languages and customs (kinship system, class structure, land tenure, religious practices, etc.) had practical applications for controlling, exploiting, and eventually assimilating the natives (Barclay 2001; Ch'oe 1997; Eskildsen 2002; Howell 2004).
4. Kuroita Katsumi (1874–1946), the father of modern Japanese historiography and head of the Meiji Education Ministry historical textbooks compilation committee, was instrumental in drawing up the first

recommendations in 1912 and later adapting them for Korea in 1916. According to the 1912 draft paper he sent to the ministry, his proposed classification and inventory system had been inspired by studying the antiquities laws and national preservation efforts he witnessed during his "fact-finding" trips to France, Germany, and England between 1899 and 1901 (Kuroita 1912).

5. It is important to note here that CGK-sponsored publications, from archaeological reports to magazines and tourist guidebooks, were published only in the Japanese language and sometimes in English, French, or German. There are no Korean-language sources, since the use of written or spoken Korean was not permitted at Japanese schools, officials events, or CGK offices during the colonial period.

6. In 1917, Sekino Tadashi was awarded the prestigious Le Prix Stanislas Julien prize by the Académie des Inscriptions et Belles-Lettres, Institut de France, for his editorial work on the architectural photo albums of Korea. The original drawings, maps, and photographs are now housed at his alma mater, Tokyo University Architecture Department and Museum Archives.

7. The CGK-employed archaeologists did not train Koreans in field excavations. However, my readings of the many memoirs of archaeologists and the hundreds of original archaeological reports and recorded excavation photographs demonstrate that the local population, including peasants, laborers, museum staff, and university students, played an active role as day laborers, museum security guards, and laboratory assistants. However, only Japanese staff members were permitted by 1916 laws to conduct surveys and excavations of sites (Pai 2001). Such racially discriminatory hiring practices were, in fact, a widespread institutionalized phenomenon practiced among the upper echelons of CGK administration and Japanese-owned companies throughout the colonies.

8. Empire guidebooks, postcards, maps, and train and shipping timetables were distributed worldwide by the Japan Tourist Bureau and Japan Imperial Railways Offices at their outlets at ports, train stations, hotels, department stores, and travel agencies (e.g., Thomas Cook and Sons, American Express Co.) from Japan to New York and Paris (see Table 7.1) (Pai forthcoming).

9. Prewar Japanese historians calculated the dates of the conquest genealogy of Japan's imperial lineage based on the legendary records of the 8th-century text of the *Nihon Shoki* (Chronicles of Japan), and inferred that an empress named Jingū established the colony of Mimana in the southern part of Korea around 201 A.D. After more than a century of controversy, it has still not been resolved as to whether the empress and her expedition to Korea are fact or fiction (Kuno 1967: 1–13). The fact remains that the calculations of such a mytho-historical divine lineage was indispensable to the rewriting of the dynastic record, which had to be chronologically brought up in time and spatially plotted so as to overlap with their newly

occupied territories in Manchuria and Korea (Pai 1999a).

10. I have not been able to track down reliable statistics for the number of Japanese tourists who traveled to Korea in the 1920s and 1930s. I suspect this is because by the late colonial period, all citizens who were part of the official empire (Naichi-jin), including Japan, Korea, Taiwan, and Manchuria, could travel throughout the empire without passports and visas. There is one published source by the JTB office in Manchuria that I have located, which gives the following numbers for the year 1940: (1) the total number of organized JTB-led tour groups to Manchuria and Korea: 9,109; (2) total number of group members, including Manchurians, Japanese, and foreigners: 398,299; (3) total number of train schedules distributed: 320,000; and (4) total number of tourist pamphlets distributed: 548,905. A glance at these statistics gives us a sense of the vibrant tourist industry in the late 1930s and early 1940s, before its sudden collapse following the outbreak of the Pacific War in 1943 (Namigata et al. 2004).

11. The-CGK assigned archaeologists were sent to sites that were reported to be under immediate threat of destruction because of infrastructure development during the Taishō period (1915–1925). These archaeologists reported witnessing many tombs belonging to the Three Kingdoms era (ca. 3rd–7th centuries A.D.), including Koguryŏ, Rakurō, and Silla tombs, which showed telltale signs of being raided by looters prior to their arrival. By the 1910s, antiquities from bronze vessels, Koryŏ-era celadon ware (ca. 13th–14th centuries), and Yi Dynasty porcelain (ca. 18th–19th centuries) were much sought-after souvenirs collected by rich Japanese entrepreneurs, colonial administrators, and tourists. To meet the demand, a new occupational class of professional gravediggers started working for antiquities dealers who were engaged in the black market trading at the newly opened ports of Wŏnsan, Pusan, Shinŭiji, and Seoul (Han 1997).

References

Abu El-Haj, N. 2001. *Facts on the Ground: Archaeological Practice and Territorial Self-Fashioning in Israeli Society*. Chicago: University of Chicago Press.

Akazawa, T. 1991. *Kanbanni Kizamaretta Sekai: Torii Ryūzō no mita Ajia* (Lost worlds on a dry plate: Torii Ryūzō's Asia). Tokyo: University of Tokyo Press.

Akazawa, Takeru, Ochiai, K., and Seki, Y. (eds.). 1993. *The "Other" Visualized: Depictions of Mongoloid Peoples*. Tokyo: University of Tokyo Press.

Bank of Chōsen. 1919. *Pictorial Chōsen and Manchuria, compiled in Commemoration of the Decennial of the Bank of Chōsen*. Seoul: Bank of Chōsen.

Barclay, P. D. 2001. An historian among the anthropologist: The Ino Kanori revival and the legacy of Japanese colonial ethnography in Taiwan. *Japanese Studies* 21: 117–136.

Brandt, K. 2007. *Kingdom of Beauty: Mingei and the Politics of Beauty in Imperial Japan*. Durham, NC: Duke University Press.

Bunkachō Bunkazai Hogobu. 1997. Bunkazai hogo kankei hōryo shu Sankō (Reference section of the anthology of preservation laws of cultural properties), in Bunkachō Bunkazai Hogobu (Cultural Properties Division of Japan's Ministry of Culture), *Bunkazai Hogo Kankei Hōrei Shū* (Anthology of cultural properties preservations laws), pp. 195–215. Tokyo: Gyōsei.

Chikazawa Insatsu. 1924. Koseki Oyobi Ibutsu Tōroku Taichō Shōroku (Preliminary records of registration documents of ancient sites and relics). Keijō (Seoul): Chikazawa Insatsu.

Ch'oe, S. Y. 1997. *Ilche ŭi Tonghwa Ideologi ŭi Ch'angch'ul* (The invention of the Japanese imperial ideology of assimilation). Seoul: Sŏgyŏng Munhwa Press.

Chŏn, K. S. 1999. Kankoku hakubutsukanshi ni okeru hyōsho no seiji jinruigaku shokuminchishugi toshide no gurobalizumu (The politics of colonialist anthropology represented in the Korean Museum). *Bulletin of the National Museum of Ethnology* 24 (2): 247–290.

Colonial Governor-General of Korea (Chōsen Sotokufu) (CGK). 1915–1935. *Chōsen Koseki Zufu* (Album of ancient Korean sites and monuments). 15 vols. Keijō (Seoul): CGK.

———. 1918–1941. *Hakubutsukan Shinretsuhin Zukan* (Museum exhibition catalogs). 17 vols. Keijō (Seoul): CGK.

———. 1918–1937. *Koseki Chosa Hokoku* (Ancient sites investigation reports). 16 vols. Keijō (Seoul): CGK.

———. 1919–1930. *Koseki Chosa Tokubetsu Hokoku* (Ancient sites investigation special reports). 6 vols. Tokyo: CGK.

Edwards, W. 2003. Monuments to an unbroken line: The imperial tombs and the emergence of modern Japanese nationalism, in S. Kane (ed.), *The Politics of Archaeology and Identity in a Global Context*, pp. 11–30. Boston: Archaeological Institute of America.

Eskildsen, R. 2002. Of civilization and savages: The mimetic imperialism of Japan's 1874 expedition to Taiwan. *The American Historical Review* 107 (2): 388–418.

Fujitani, T. 1996. *Splendid Monarchy: Power and Pageantry in Modern Japan*. Berkeley: University of California Press.

Hamada, K., and Andersson, J. G. 1932. The Far East. *Museum of Far Eastern Antiquities* 4: 9–14.

Han, Y. D. 1997. *Chosŏn mi ŭi T'amgujadŭl* (Investigators of Korean beauty). Pak Kyŏng-hŭi (trans.). Seoul: Hakkoje.

Hirose, S. 2003. Chōsen no kenchiku, koseki to sono atono "bunkazai" hogo (Japanese investigations into archaeological and architectural sites in the Korean Peninsula and cultural properties management since the 1910s). *Nihon Kōkogashi Kenkyū* 10: 57–106.

Howell, D. 2004. Making "useful citizens" of the Ainu subjects in early twentieth-century Japan. *Journal of Asian Studies* 63 (1): 5–30.

Hudson, M. 1999. *The Ruins of Japanese Identity: Ethnogenesis in the Japanese Islands*. Honolulu: University of Hawaii Press.

Hwang, S. Y. 1973. Ilchegi munhwajae p'ihae charyo (The destruction of cultural relics under Japanese rule). Special issue, *Kogo Misul (Journal of Archaeology and Art)* 22.

Japan Imperial Railways (JIR). 1925. *Travelers' Map of Japan, Chōsen* (Korea), Taiwan (Formosa). Tokyo: JIR.

Japan Tourist Bureau (JTB). 1913–1942. *The Tourist (Tsu-risto)*. Tokyo: JTB.

———. 1924–present. *Tabi* (Travel). Tokyo: JTB.

———. 1982. *Nihon Kotsu Kosha Nanajūnenshi* (Seventy years of the Japan Tourist Bureau). Tokyo: JTB.

Keishū Koseki Hozonkai (Kyŏngju Preservation Society). 1922. *Keishū Koseki Annai* (A guide to ancient remains in Kyŏngju). Keishū (Kyŏngju): Kyŏngju Preservation Society.

———. 1936. *Keishū Koseki Annai* (A guide to ancient remains in Kyŏngju). Keishū (Kyŏngju): Kyŏngju Preservation Society.

Kim, Y. S. 1966. Ilbon Han'guk e issŏsŏui Han'guksa sŏsul (Historical writings about Korea in Korea and Japan). *Yŏksa Hakbo* 31: 128–147.

———. 1973. Ilche kwanhakjadŭrŭi Han'guksagwan (Japanese government-scholars' view of Korean history), in Yŏksa Hakhoe, Historical Society of Korea (ed.), *Han'guksaŭi Pansŏng* (Reflections on Korean history), pp. 29–39. Seoul: Sin'gu Munhwasa.

Kita, S. 1921. Nissen ryōminzoku tōgenron (The common origins of the two races: Japanese and Koreans). *Chōsen* 6: 3–69.

Kudō, M. 1979. *Nihon Jinshuron* (A study on the racial theories of the Japanese). Tokyo: Kichikawa Kobunkan.

Kuno, Y. 1967. *Japanese Expansion on the Asiatic Continent*. 2 vols. Port Washington, NY: Kennikat Press.

Kuroita, K. 1912. Shisekihozonni kansuru ikensho (An opinion paper on the preservations of historical remains). *Shigaku zasshi* 23 (5): 568–611.

Kwŏn, H. H. 2005. *Chosŏnesŏ on Sajin Yŏpsŏ* (Postcards from Korea). Seoul: Minŭmsa.

Lutz, C. A., and Collins, J. L. 1993. *Reading National Geographic*. Chicago: University of Chicago Press.

Lyons, C., Papadopoulos, J. K., and Stewart, L. S. 2005. *Antiquity and Photography: Early Views of Ancient Mediterranean Sites*. Los Angeles: Getty Publications.

Matsumura, R. 1934. Tokyo jinrui gakkai gojūnenshi (The fifty-year history of the Tokyo Anthropological Society). *Tokyo Jinrui Gakkai Zasshi* 49 (11): 419–470.

MacCannell, D. 1999 [1976] . *The Tourist: A New Theory of the Leisure Class*. Berkeley: University of California Press.

Mokuyō Club. 2001. Chōsen kankei bunken mokuroku (Kōkogaku, Jinruigaku, Kenchikushi Mokuroku) (A catalog of Korea-related articles on archaeology, anthropology and architectural history). *Nihon Kōkogakushi Kenkyū* 9: 4–20.

———. 2003. Arimitsu-shi inta-byū (An interview with Professor Arimitsu). *Nihon Kōkogakushi Kenkyū* 10: 3–30.

Namigata, S., Kimura, K., and Sunaga, T. 2004. *Tōaryokōsha Manshū chibu jūnenshi* (Ten years of the Manchuria Branch of the Tōa Travel Agency). *Shashide Miru Nihon Keizaishi Shokuminchi hen* Dai 31 hen (Vol. 31 of *The Economic History of Japan Series: Colonial Era*). Tokyo: Yumani Shobō.

Nishikawa, H. 1970. Nihon teikoku shūgika ni okeru Chōsen kokogaku no keisei (The establishment of Korean archaeology during the era of Japanese imperialism). *Chōsen Gakuhō* 7 (6): 94–114.

O, S. T. 1996. Ilche ŭi munhwajae chŏngch'aek (Japanese policies on cultural properties), in Munhwajae Kwalliguk, Office of Cultural Properties, Republic of Korea (ed.), *Ilche ŭi Munhwajae Chŏngch'aek P'yŏngga Semina* (A seminar report on the re-evaluation of Japanese colonial cultural policies), pp. 15–44. Seoul: Munhwajae Kwalliguk.

Pai, H. I. 1994. The politics of Korea's past: The legacy of Japanese colonial archaeology in the Korean Peninsula. *Shih* (East Asian History) 7: 25–48.

———. 1999a. Japanese anthropology and the discovery of "prehistoric Korea." *Journal of East Asian Archaeology* 1: 353–382.

———. 1999b. Nationalism and preserving Korea's buried past: The Office of Cultural Properties and archaeological heritage management in South Korea. *Antiquity* 73 (281): 619–625.

———. 2000. *Constructing "Korean" Origins: Archaeology, Historiography, and Racial Myth*. Harvard-Hallym Series on Korean Studies. Cambridge: Harvard University Asia Center.

———. 2001. The creation of national treasures and monuments: The 1916 Japanese laws on the preservation of Korean remains and relics and their colonial legacies. *Journal of Korean Studies* 25 (1): 72–95.

———. 2004. Collecting Japan's antiquity in colonial Korea: The Tokyo Anthropological Society and the cultural comparative perspective, in *Moving Objects: Time, Space, and Context*, pp. 87–107. 26th International Symposium on the Preservation of Cultural Property Series. Tokyo: National Research Institute of Cultural Properties.

———. 2006. Shinhwasok koto pokwŏn ŭl wihan yujŏk t'amsaek (Reclaiming the ruins of imagined imperial terrains: Meiji archaeology and art historical surveys in the Korean peninsula [1900–1916]), in Sang-in Yoon and Kyu-tae Park (eds.), *Ilbon ŭi Pallmyŏng kwa Kŭndae* (The discovery of Japan and modernity), pp. 247–284. Seoul: Yeesan Publishing Co.

———. 2009. Capturing visions of Japan's prehistoric past: Torii Ryūzō's field photographs of "primitive" races and lost civilizations (1896–1915), in J. Purtle and H. Bjarne Thomsen (eds.), *Looking Modern: East Asian Visual Culture from Treaty Ports to World War II*, pp. 265–293. Chicago: Art Media Resources.

———. Forthcoming. Guides to the Empire: Travel brochures and the colonial origins of leisure tourism to Korea, in L. Kendall (ed.), *Consuming Korean Tradition in Early and Late Modernity*. Honolulu: University of Hawaii Press.

Pelizarri, M. A. (ed.). 2003. *Traces of India: Photography, Architecture and the Politics of Representation (1850–1900)*. New Haven: Yale University Press.

Reischauer, E. O. 1939. Japanese archaeological work on the Asiatic continent. *Harvard Journal of Asiatic Studies* 4 (1): 87–98.

Roth, M. S., with Lyons, C. and Merewether, C. 1997. *Irresistible Decay: Ruins Reclaimed*. Los Angeles: Getty Research Institute for the History of Art and the Humanities.

Ryan, J. 1997. *Picturing Empire: Photography and the Visualization of the British Empire*. Chicago: University of Chicago Press.

Sakazume, H. 1997. *Taiheiyō Sensō to Kōkogaku* (The Pacific War and archaeology). Tokyo: Kichikawa Kobunkan.

Satō, T. 1999. *Meiji Kindai Kokka to Bijutsu* (Art and the Meiji modern state). Tokyo: Kichikawa Kobunkan.

Sekino, T. 1904. *Kangoku Kenchiku Chosa Hokoku* (Investigations' reports of Korean architecture). Vol. 6 of Tokyo Teikoku Daigaku Kōka Daigaku Gakkujutsu Hokoku. Tokyo: Tokyo Teikoku Daigaku.

———. 1919. *Chōsen Keijutsu no Kenkyū* (A study of Korean art). Keijō: Chōsen Sōtokufu.

———. 1931. Ancient remains and relics in Korea: Efforts toward research and preservation. Paper presented at the fourth biannual conference of the Institute of Pacific Relations, Oct. 21–Nov. 4, 1931, in Hangzhou and Shanghai.

Suzuki, R., and Takagi, H. (eds.). 2000. *Bunkazai to Kindai Nihon* (Cultural properties and modern Japan). Tokyo: Yamagawa Shuppan.

Takagi, H. 1997. *Kindai Tennosei no Bunkashideki Kenkyū* (A study of modern Japanese imperial cultural policies). Tokyo: Kōko Shuppan.

Teshigawara, A. 1995. *Nihon Kōkogaku no Ayumi* (A historical development of Japanese archaeology). Tokyo: Meishō Shuppan.

Tokyo K. H. 1976. *Tokyo Kokuritsu Hakubutsukan Hyakunenshi* (A hundred year history of the Tokyo National Museum). 2 vols. Tokyo: Tokyo Kokuritsu Hakubutsukan.

Trigger, B. 1984. Alternative archaeologists: Nationalist, colonialist, imperialist. *Man* 19 (3): 355–370.

Umehara, S. 1923. Kōkogakujō yori mitaru jōdai Nissen no kankei (The relationship between ancient Korea and Japan from an archaeological perspective). *Chōsen* 8: 138–170.

Weisenfeld, G. 2000. Touring Japan as museums: Nippon and other Japanese imperialist travelogues. *Positions* 8 (3): 747–793.

Yamamichi, J. 1910. *Chōsen Hanto* (The Korean Peninsula). Keijō: Nikkan Shobōzohan.

Yi, H. J. 1964. Chaeil han'guk munhwajae pimangnok (A memo on the tragedy of Korean cultural relics in Japan). *Sahak Yon'gu* 8: 791–808.

Yi, K. Y. 1996. *Han'guk Munhwajae Sunansa* (The tortuous history of Korea's cultural relics). Seoul: Tolbege.

Yi, M. Y. 1976. Ilche kwanhakcha durui singminji sakwan (The colonial historiography of Japanese government scholars), in Yi U-song and Kang Man-gil (eds.), *Han'guk ui Yoksa Insik* (The historical consciousness of Korea), Part 2, pp. 500–521. Seoul: Ch'angjak Kwa Pip'yong.

Yoshii, H. 2006. *Shokuminchu ni okeru kōkogaku chōsa no zaikentō* (A re-analysis of archaeological surveys in colonial Korea). Department of Archaeology research reports. Kyoto: Kyoto University Graduate School.

8

ARCHAEOLOGY IN COLONIAL AND POSTCOLONIAL U.S.S.R.

Pavel Dolukhanov

The aim of this chapter is to examine the history of Soviet archaeological discourse and practice and to provide a discussion of some of the present trends in archaeological narrative in the post-Soviet space. The creation of a new state, the Union of Soviet Socialist Republic, was proclaimed in January 1924, in the wake of the prolonged civil war and shortly before Lenin's death. Originally it included four formally independent republics: the Russian Federation, Ukraine, Byelorussia, and Transcaucasian Federation; soon after, the latter was split up into Georgia, Armenia, and Azerbaijan Soviet Republics. In August 1939, preceding the German invasion of Poland and the beginning of World War II, the Soviet government concluded a "non-aggression" pact with Nazi Germany. By virtue of this agreement (which included a secret "Ribbentrop-Molotov protocol"), the entire area of Eastern Europe was divided into the German and Soviet spheres of influence. Based on this agreement, in June 1940, the Soviet Union occupied three independent Baltic states (Estonia, Latvia, and Lithuania), and later that year annexed the province of Besarabia from Romania. After the mock "elections," all these territories were included into the U.S.S.R. as Estonian, Latvian, Lithuanian, and Moldavian Soviet Socialist Republics. As a result, the area of the U.S.S.R. became nearly equal to that of the Russian Empire. After the war, with the installment of pro-Soviet puppet regimes in Eastern and Central Europe and the communist takeover in China and Vietnam, the Soviet bloc became an empire with a total population approaching 1.5 billion.

History and Politics: The Soviet Period Archaeology

After the revolution, Soviet authorities placed considerable emphasis on the reconstruction of higher education and scholarship, which they considered vital instruments for enhancing the country's military potential and the ideological indoctrination of its subjects. Being a bureaucratic state, the Soviet regime adopted a commanding administrative principle in all spheres of its activities. Consequently, the Russian Academy of Sciences, which had been set up in 1724 by Peter the Great in St. Petersburg, was reorganized along these principles. Originally attached to the People's Commissariat of Education, in 1925 it became a centrally controlled structure comprising a great number of research institutes and laboratories. The changes directly affected Russian archaeology. In 1918, an efficient and well-funded Imperial Archaeological Commission became the Russian State Archaeological Commission. In 1919, it was further transformed into the Russian (later the State) Academy of History of Material Culture. Still later, in 1937, it became known as the Institute for History of Material Culture and was attached to the Academy of Sciences. Since 1943, its head office has been based in Moscow, with a branch in Leningrad (later St. Petersburg).

The instigator and the first director of these institutions was Nicholas (Nikolai Yakovlevich) Marr (1864–1934), a linguist of mixed Georgian-Scottish extraction known as the author of the controversial Japhetic theory, who postulated a common origin of the Caucasian, Semitic-Hamitic, and Basque languages. Further developing this theory, Marr argued that all the languages of the world descended from a single proto-language and passed through common stages, which he equated with the Marxian "modes of production." Since that time, Marxism and "Marrism" have been official ideologies in Soviet archaeology. In the 1920s and 1930s, a young generation of Soviet archaeologists (which included Ravdonikas, Efimenko, Boriskovsky, and Okladnikov) proclaimed the elucidation of "socio-economic pre-capitalist formations" based on studies of material culture as the main priority of archaeology in the U.S.S.R. According to the "synstadial concept," human society passed through several universal stages, which were acknowledgeable in archaeological records. The consequence of this attitude was the total rejection of archaeological typology (deemed as "sterile artifactology"). This approach basically stemmed from the seriation methodology developed in the mid-19th century by Oscar Montelius, a prominent Swedish archaeologist who formulated a technique to date artifacts based on mutual similarities within a certain geographical area. An absolute date was estimated based on the correlation of an artifact with historical references, such as a contemporary written record. This method was widely used in archaeology in the late 19th and early 20th centuries and became particularly popular in Russian and Soviet archaeological schools. Today the validity of typology and seriation is commonly questioned.

Another feature of Soviet archaeology of the 1920s and 1930s was its deep skepticism toward the "cultural-ethnic" concept, which had been popular in pre-revolutionary Russian archaeology. As Klejn (1993) notes, the concept of "archaeological culture" as an equivalent to ethnicity emerged both in Germany and in Russia at about the same time, in the late 19th and early 20th centuries, and stemmed from a "nationalist-romanticist school." In Germany, it is associated with the name of Gustav Kossina (1911). Kossina's method consisted of mapping the distribution of the main types of archaeological artifacts and overlapping them with early maps showing the distribution of "tribes" and "nations" and linguistic reconstructions. Based on these arguments, Kossina derived the surprising conclusion that northern Germany was the homeland of Indo-Europeans (Aryans), the bearers of battle-ax cultures, who eventually conquered primitive indigenous non-Aryan societies and imposed upon them their will, culture, and language. This concept was largely used as Nazi propaganda long after Kossina's death.

In Russia, the cultural-ethnic concept was developed by Gorodtsov (1860–1945) and Spitzyn (1858–1931). Both of these scholars used it as an instrument of classification and distinguished several archaeological cultures on that basis, most of which are recognized to this day. Only in their later works did Gorodtsov and Spitzyn start interpreting archaeological units in ethnic terms. Spitzyn (1899) identified two types of burial sites, known in early medieval northwestern Russia as "long barrows" and "conic mounds" (*sopki*), with two distinct early Slavic tribes. Gorodtsov (1908) distinguished Scythian, Sarmatian, and Gothic sites among the Iron Age antiquities of southern Russia.

Interpretive theories of Soviet archaeology from this era gravitated toward autochthonous development, and both "migrations" and "diffusions" were generally rejected as imperialist and racist. With all its naive exaggerations, early Soviet archaeology was devoid of any nationalist or chauvinist undertones. In many respects, it contained the elements later developed in the postprocessual school.

This situation changed in the aftermath of World War II, with the gradual erosion of the synstadial concept. Its demise was fueled by the sharp criticism of Marr's theories by Stalin (1950) who rejected them as "vulgar Marxism." This coincided with a tacit rehabilitation of the cultural-ethnic paradigm. Soviet archaeologists became much more focused on questions of ethnic origins. Likewise in pre-revolutionary Russia, the normal practice of ethnic reconstruction consisted of the direct identification of "archaeological cultures" (populations of stylistically similar artifacts) with ethnicities. In doing so, they were much more straightforward than their pre-revolutionary predecessors. Bryusov, the leading Soviet archaeologist of the 1950s, wrote: "Archaeological cultures . . . reflect the originality of technology, subsistence, mode of life and other aspects of either ethnic tribes, or, rather, groups of related tribes in their specific historical development" (Bryusov 1956: 20). A similar attitude was shared by archaeologists in the national republic. Braichevsky, a Ukrainian archaeologist, was even more categorical: "We regard archaeological culture as an association of archaeological artifacts which correspond to a certain ethnic identity. We cannot consider as a culture an assemblage which has no ethnic connotations" (Braichevsky 1965: 15).

Remarkably, the 1930s to 1950s saw an unprecedented boom in archaeological fieldwork in the U.S.S.R., largely due to large-scale salvage digs, amply funded by state hydroelectrical projects. In these years, Soviet archaeologists attained extraordinary progress in excavation techniques, exposing large areas of sites with minute fixations of objects and structures in the stratigraphic sequences. This resulted in several outstanding discoveries, particularly that of long-term dwelling structures at Palaeolithic settlements (Yefimenko 1934).

The same years saw the gradual rise of Russian nationalistic undertones in Soviet archaeology. In most cases, this took the form of the glorification of "Old Russia's" achievements. B. A. Rybakov, in a series of articles and notably in the monograph (Rybakov 1948) that won him the Stalin Prize, emphatically demonstrated that in many respects Old Russia's arts and crafts were superior to West European standards. Renewed debates, which arose around the so-called Norman problem (i.e., the presence of Scandinavians in Old Russia and their role in the foundation of Russian statehood) became rapidly politicized (Grekov 1947: 12).

Another controversial issue concerned the ethnic identification of Iron Age sites in Ukraine and southern Byelorussia that had been classified as the Zarubintsy and Chernyakhovian cultures. The burial sites belonging to these cultures were first identified in 1899–1900 on the River Dnieper by Vikenty Chvojka (1850–1914), a Ukrainian archaeologist of Czech origin. Chvojka (1913) hypothesized that both the Zarubintsy and Chernyakhovian antiquities, which he dated, respectively, to the 2nd to 1st centuries B.C. and the 2nd to 4th centuries A.D., were related to the eastern Slavic tribes. This opinion was shared by Spitzyn and many other prominent Russian and Ukrainian scholars. At about the same time, Reinecke, a German archaeologist, advanced an alternative hypothesis, suggesting that these sites belonged to a Germanic group (Reinecke 1906). Since the 1930s. the Zarubintsy and Chernyakhovian cultures were studied intensively, and today several dozen cemeteries and dwelling sites are known. Based on the newly available evidence, discussions about their ethnic allegiance flared up in the 1960s and 1970s, often accompanied by nationalist rhetoric. Many Russian, Ukrainian, and Byelorussian archaeologists shared Chvojka's views about the Slavic affiliation of these cultures. Kukharenko (1965) and several Polish archaeologists argued that the Zarubintsy culture emerged in the Polesye and Volhynia, resulting from the penetration of the Pomeranian cultural group from the Vistula basin. When Tikhanova demonstrated the Gothic (i.e., Germanic) affiliations of certain Zarubintsy and Chernyakhovian antiquities (Tikhanova 1970), she was rebuffed by P. N. Tretyakov (1968), who accused her of a lack of patriotism. In the ensuing debate, B. A. Rybakov branded those who were not ready to accept the Slavic affiliation of the Chernyakhovian culture as "Germanophiles."

Nationalist and racist trends in late Soviet archaeological and historical discourse became particularly apparent in the works of Lev Gumilev (1912–1992), published since the 1960s. These publications, in which fantasies and fiction usually substitute for hard evidence, gained enormous popularity in Russia, particularly in recent years. Gumilev (1980) viewed "ethnos" as part of the biosphere, which passed through the stages of rise, development, climax, inertia, convolution, and memorial. Gumilev argued that under certain conditions, the ethnos undergoes a "genetic mutation," which leads to the emergence of the "passionaries," or individuals of a special temper, who become "creators of new ethnoses, cultures, and states" (Gumilev 1980: 252).

Gumilev's historical views drew largely on the philosophy of the Russian Nationalist School of the late 19th century (for example, figures such as Konstantin Leontiev and Nikolai Danilevsky), on which foundations the Russian émigré philosophers later developed the concept of Eurasianism. Its proponents, Nikolai Savitsky and his followers, invented an idea of a non-Western Christian civilization centered on Russia, and embraced Eurasia as a unique continent, culturally and economically dominated by Russia (Chamberlain 2006). Gumilev regarded the symbiosis of Russian power with Turkic peoples (including the Mongols), who opposed the "destructive influences from Catholic Europe," as a "super-ethnos." Against these he distinguished a "pseudo-ethnos," or "destructive anti-systems," as exemplified by Jews. According to Gumilev, the Jewish culture was mercantile by its nature; it existed outside and in opposition to its environment, aiming to destroy a healthy ethnos from inside. Several writers, notably Tripolsky (1994), qualified Gumilev's views as fascist and anti-Semitic.

A majority of Russian scholars either ignored or sharply criticized Gumilev's theories as unprofessional fantasies (Rybakov 1971). Remarkably, the recently published authoritative monograph on Eurasia's steppe empires, the main subject of Gumilev's studies (Klyashtornyi 2005), failed even to mention Gumilev's name. Yet obviously, under direct political instigation, the popularity of Gumilev and his teachings is currently being "whipped up," particularly in the Turkic-speaking regions. In Kazan, the capital of Tatarstan, an autonomous republic within the Russian Federation, a monument to Gumilev was dedicated in 2005. The university in Astana, the capital of Kazakhstan, bears his name. At the opening ceremony of the university in October 2000, Vladimir Putin stated that "Lev Nikolaevich Gumilev . . . is the greatest Eurasian scholar of our time. . . . His studies not only made a strong contribution to the historical sciences, they also promoted the centuries-old ideas of an inseparable unity and interdependence of peoples inhabiting vast areas of Eurasia, from the Baltic Sea and Carpathians up to the Pacific Ocean."[1]

The Soviet policy toward its national republics vacillated between the encouragement of "national cultures" loyal to "proletarian internationalism" and the ruthless uprooting of drives for independence branded as "bourgeois nationalism." This took the form of establishing the Academies of Sciences with numerous research institutes and laboratories in each Soviet Socialist republic. As a rule, these structures included either institutes of archaeology or departments of archaeology within the institutes of history. In many cases (particularly in the republics of Central Asia), archaeological institutions were initially staffed by Russian archaeologists, mostly from Moscow or Leningrad. But eventually they were replaced by national cadres, who were trained either in the local or Russian universities. Following the annexation of the Baltic states, a considerable number of local archaeologists (including Richard Indreko from Estonia, Eduard Štrums from Latvia, and Marija Gimbutas from Lithuania) emigrated to the West. Yet many others remained in place, and soon after the end of the war, archaeological institutions in these countries were run efficiently by local archaeologists.

Archaeological publications, like all other publications, were subjected to severe censorship. The censors monitored the strictness of Marxist-Leninist ideology, ruthlessly deleting the passages deemed "deviationist." The censors were periodically issued revised instructions, with an index of prohibited topics and names. Thus it was prohibited to make reference to émigré writers or to Western scholars who criticized the Soviet regime.

In the postwar years, archaeologists in the Soviet republics and notably in the Baltic states carried out large-scale ethnogenetic research with use of an ethno-cultural paradigm (Moora 1956). Ligi argued that this had been done in defiance of the official communist ideology, which "maintained that smaller nations were to disappear" (Ligi 1993: 32). This statement is totally unfounded. The Communist policy consisted of encouraging this kind of research to provide proof of the renaissance of smaller nations, safeguarded under Soviet rule from Western capitalist enslavement.

During the 1930s, the wave of arrests that accompanied the Great Terror devastated Soviet archaeology. According to Formozov (2006), in these years no fewer than ten prominent archaeologists were shot, and many others were banished to the gulags and perished there. The majority of those arrested belonged to the older and more experienced generation of Russian archaeologists. The main raison d'être for the mass persecutions of the Russian intelligentsia was the "cleansing" of Soviet society from elements considered hostile to the Communist regime.

Nationalism was the most common and damaging accusation leveled against archaeologists in the union republics. In the 1930s and 1940s, Byelorussia and Ukraine were the preferred grounds for such persecutions. In the late 1930s, nearly the entire staff of the archaeological section of the Byelorussian Academy of Sciences, which was actively involved in the establishment of the Byelorussian national culture, were arrested and accused of bourgeois nationalism. Persecutions of nationalist-minded archaeologists in Byelorussia persist in various forms to this day.

Ironically, in certain cases the censorship was more lenient in the Caucasus and Central Asia, where archaeological publications appeared mostly in national languages. Between the 1950s and 1980s, one can see the first indications of archaeological discussions acquiring hostile nationalist tonalities. It was in this era that a prolonged discussion started between Georgian and Armenian archaeologists, who both claimed their respective nations to be the cultural heirs of the kingdom of Urartu, which existed on the Armenian plateau in the 9th to 7th centuries B.C. and used the cuneiform script of a language quite distant from both Armenian and Georgian. No less ambitious and archaeologically unfounded were the pretensions of Azerbaijani scholars who claimed "in antiquity the forerunners of the Azerbaijani people occupied a vast territory that included both Northern (at that time Soviet) and Southern (Iranian) Azerbaijan" (Kohl and Tsetskhladze 1995). In the 1980s, an intervention by the Academy of Sciences in Moscow was prompted by the publication of controversial histories of Tajikistan and Uzbekistan, which used archaeological arguments to assert territorial claims.

History and Politics: Post-Soviet Period

The collapse of the Communist regime and the formal disbandment of the U.S.S.R. (at the meeting of leaders of Ukraine, Russia, and Belarus at Belovezh Forest in Byelorussia on December 8, 1991) put an end to the existence of the centrally controlled Soviet Academy of Sciences. The academies of the former Soviet republic and their affiliated institutions, including archaeological research centers, acquired an independent status. In various forms they still exist. The acute economic and financial crisis that hit the former U.S.S.R. in the immediate aftermath of the disbandment led to drastic cuts and often total suspension of state funding, which had been the only source of financing for scientific research. Archaeology was most severely crippled, with all major field projects being suspended. For many years, joint projects with foreign participation and foreign sponsorship remained the only way to carry out archaeological excavations in the former U.S.S.R.

In recent years, the recovery of the Russian economy, which has been boosted by high oil and gas prices, has led to a notable increase in state funding of archaeological research. Consequently, many field projects have been reactivated, at least in Russia, and the number of archaeological publications has increased. Remarkably, the role of regional archaeological centers, which often have access to independent sources of funding, was enhanced. Archaeological departments in provincial universities (such as Kazan, Samara, and Rostov) now independently carry out large-scale archaeological projects and publish their own reports. Recent years have also seen a rapid resurgence of salvage archaeology. Numerous private enterprises have provided funds and even hired professional archaeologists for salvage digs in development areas.

Until quite recently, due to the deficit of hard currencies, research institutions in the former U.S.S.R. were unable to buy special literature in sufficient quantities. Although scholars from the former Soviet Union can now freely go abroad, the lack of specialist information has led to their effective isolation from world scholarship, particularly in the area of theoretical archaeology. This, together with the frustration of economic hardship and life inside the ideological vacuum, has led to the enhancement of reactionary nationalist concepts that had started to appear in the later stages of the U.S.S.R. Thus, the change of political decorum has failed to affect the cultural-ethnic paradigm; it remains the leading concept of post-Soviet archaeology. Yet it has been used in a more straightforward manner, with a much more overt political agenda. Ironically, this paradigm is used both by Russian and non-Russian archaeologists, yet obviously with diametrically opposed aims.

Conclusion

The colonial archaeology that came from the U.S.S.R. in the 1920s and 1930s predominantly disseminated Marxist-Leninist ideological dogmas, while ethnic-related issues were largely ignored. Archaeologically perceptible material culture was generally viewed as resulting from autochthonous development; migrations were summarily rejected as reflecting imperialist interventionist ideology and racism. Local archaeological studies and the training of national cadres in the National Soviet republics were encouraged, albeit under strict ideological and political supervision. While paying lip service to proletarian internationalism, national archaeological schools were oriented to stress the progressive nature of Russian colonization. Any deviation from the official line was severely penalized. During the purges of the Great Terror in the 1930s, Soviet archaeology was ruthlessly cleansed of the liberal old-school intelligentsia, who had been deemed nonproletarian and hence potentially hostile to the totalitarian regime. Many of them were either murdered or banished to the gulags. In the Soviet republics, the terror was targeted primarily against national-minded archaeologists.

The situation drastically changed in the years that followed World War II. The importance of socially oriented archaeological schools gradually diminished, and the ethnocultural paradigm, which was popular in pre-revolutionary Russia, was tacitly rehabilitated. This combined with the rising popularity of romanticized nationalist discourse, which glorified Russia's past and its role in European civilization. The foreign impact on Russian history was strongly denied, and those who defended it were branded unpatriotic. Ethnogenetic studies were also encouraged in the national republic and were aimed at stressing the efflorescence of "small" nations under Soviet rule, which protected them from "capitalist slavery." At the same time, manifestations of independent national identities were severely penalized as bourgeois nationalism.

The demise of the U.S.S.R. had a controversial effect on archaeological discourse. On the one hand, the removal of the official Marxist-Leninist ideology and the lifting of taboos were beneficial. Many topics that had been either restricted or prohibited were now openly discussed (Tkachuk 1996). On the other hand, under the conditions of severe economic crises and an ideological vacuum, the ethno-cultural paradigm flourished, as did the romanticist-nationalist discourse and the construction of ethnocentric mythologies. In Russia this led to a series of works in which prehistoric Russian sites were identified with the Aryans' "glorious ancestry." One of the most alarming phenomena in today's Russia is the unprecedented popularity of Gumilev's racist teachings and the ideology of Eurasianism. There are indications that this blatant imperialist and neocolonialist mythology has been officially boosted.

Aryan ancestry as a symbol of cultural supremacy is also being taken up by Ukrainian nationalist writers. In certain cases, the ethno-cultural paradigm has been used by archaeologists in post-Soviet states to disprove the theories, largely accepted by scholarly communities, portraying them as products of Russian colonialist mentality. Certain archaeological texts published in the former Soviet republics acquired abusive anti-Russian tonalities (Chernykh 1995: 144). In some cases, postcolonial discourse draws openly on Western propaganda clichés from the height of the Cold War (Hirsch 2005).

To the credit of Russian, Ukrainian, and other post-Soviet scholars, these extremist views are not shared by mainstream archaeologists. Being increasingly open to the outer world, they have a major task: to demystify the dangerous mythology and to re-create the authentic history of their respective nations, free of both colonial and postcolonial distortions.

Note

1. The full text (in Russian) may be found at *http://www.kulichki.com/~gumilev/matter/Article26.htm* (last accessed April 1, 2010).

References

Anthony, D. W. 1995. Nazi and eco-feminist prehistories: Ideology and empiricism in Indo-European archaeology, in P. L. Kohl and C. P. Fawcett (eds.), *Nationalism, Politics and the Practice of Archaeology*, pp. 82–98. Cambridge: Cambridge University Press.

Bibikov, S. N. 1953. *Rannezemledel'Cheskie (Tripol'skie) Plemna Podnestrov'Ya* (Early farming [Tripol'ye] tribes of the Dniestr area). Materialy I issledovaniya po arheologii. Moscow: Academy of Sciences Publishing House.

Braichevsky, M. Y. 1865. Teoretichni osnovy doslidhen' etnogenezu (Theoretical foundations of ethnogenesis). *Ukrain'sky Istorivhny Zhurnal* 2: 46–56.

Bryusov, A. Y. 1956. Arheologicheskie kul'turyn I etnicheskie obshchnosti (Archaeological cultures and ethnic entities). *Sovetskaya Arheologiya* 26: 5–27.

Callmer, J. 2000. From West to East: The penetration of Scandinavians into Eastern Europe, ca. 500– 900 A.D., in M. Kazanski, A. Nercessian, and C. Zuckermann (eds.), *Les Centres Proto-urbains Russes entre Scandinavie, Byzance et Orient*, pp. 45–94. Paris: Editions P. Lethielleux.

Chamberlain, L. 2006. *The Philosophy Steamer: Lenin and the Exile of the Intelligentsia*. London: Atlantic Books.

Chernykh, E. N. 1995. Postscript: Russian Archaeology after the collapse of the U.S.S.R.: Infrastructural crisis and the resurgence of old and new nationalisms, in P. L. Kohl and C. Fawcett (eds.), *Nationalism, Politics and the Practice of Archaeology*, pp. 139–148. Cambridge: Cambridge University Press.

Chvojka, V. V. 1913. *Drevnie Obitateli Srednego Podneprov'Ya* (Ancient inhabitants of the Middle Dniepr area). Kiev: Sinkevich.

Formozov, A. A. 2006. *Russkie Arheologi V Period Totalitarizma* (Russian archaeologists during the totalitarian period). Moscow: Znak.

Grekov, B. D. 1947. *Kievskaya Rus'* (The Kievan Rus). Moscow: Uchpedgiz.

Gorodtsov, V. A. 1908. *Pervobytnaya Arkhologoya/Prehistoric Archaeology*. Moscow: Imperial Archaeological Commission.

Grigoriev, S. A. 2005. *Ancient Indo-Europeans*. Chelyabinsk: Rifei.

Gumilev, L. N. 1980. *Etnos I Biosfera Zemli* (Ethnos and the biosphere of the earth). Leningrad: Gidrometeoizdat.

Hirsch, F. 2005. *Empire of Nations: Ethnographic Knowledge and the Making of the Soviet Union*. Ithaca: Cornell University Press.

Klejn, L. S. 1993. *Fenomen Sovetskoi Arheologii* (Phenomenon of Soviet archaeology). St. Petersburg: Fan.

Klyashtornyi, S. G. 2005. *Stepnye Imperii: Rozhdenie, Trimpf, Gibel'* (The Steppe empires: Birth, triumph, downfall). St. Petersburg: St. Petersburg University Press.

Kohl, P. L., and Tsetskhladze, G. R. 1995. Nationalism, politics, and the practice of archaeology in the Caucasus, in P. L. Kohl and C. Fawcett (eds.), *Nationalism, Politics and the Practice of Archaeology*, pp. 149–176. Cambridge: Cambridge University Press.

Kossina, G. 1911. *Der Herkunft der Germanen: Zur Methode der Siedlungsarchaeologie*. Mannus-Bibliothek 6. Würzburg: Kabitzsch.

Krichevsky, E. Y. 1940. Tripol'skie ploshchadki (The Tripolye platforms). *Sovetskaya Arheologiya* 6: 20–45.

Kukharenko, Y. V. 1965. *Zarubinetskaya Kul'tura* (The Zarubintsy culture). Moscow: Nauka.

Ligi, P. 1993. National romanticism in archaeology: The paradigm of Slavonic colonisation in North-West Russia. *Fennoscandia Archaeologica* 10: 31–40.

Moora, H. (ed.). 1956. *Eesti Rahava Etniliset Ajakoost*. Tallinn: Eesti Raamat.

Nepomnyashchiy, N. R. 2005. *100 Velikih Tain Drevnego Mira: Tridtsat' sem' Vekov Arkaima* (100 great mysteries of the ancient world: Thirty-seven centuries of Arkaim). Moscow: Veche.

Nosov, E. N. 1981. Nekotorye obshchie voprosy izucheniya pogrebal'nyh pamyatnikov vtoroi poloviny pervogo tysyacheletiya n.e. (Some general problems in the studies of burial sites of the second half of the first millennium A.D.). *Sovetskaya Arheologiya* 1: 42–56.

Platonova, N. I. 2004. "Delo" Sergeya Ivanovicha Rudenko (The "case" of Sergei Ivanovich Rudenko), in *Nevskiy Arheologo-Istoriograficheskii Sbornik*, pp. 126–138. St. Petersburg: Taus.

Rybakov, B. A. (ed.). 1946. *Istoriya SSSR* (The history of the U.S.S.R.), Vol. 1. Moscow: Nauka.

——. 1948. *Remerslo Drevnei Rusi* (The crafts of ancient Russia). Moscow: Academy of Sciences Publishing House.

——. 1971. O preodolenii samoobmana (On overcoming self-deception). *Voprosy Istorii* 3: 153–159.

Reinecke, P. 1906. Aus der russischen archaeologischen literatur. *Meinzer Zeitschrift* 1: 42–50.

Sedov, V. V. 1970. *Novgorodski Sopki* (The Novgorod Sopkas). *Svod Arheologicheskih Istochnikov*, E 1–8. Moscow: Nauka.

——. 1974. *Dlinnye Kurgany Krivichei* (The Krivichi's long barrows). *Svod Arheologicheskih Istochnikov*, E 1–8. Moscow: Nauka.

——. 1982. *Vostochnye Slavyane v VI–XIII Vekah* (Eastern Slavs in the 6th–13th centuries). Arheologiya SSSR. Moscow: Nauka.

Shnirelman, V. A. 1998. Archaeology and ethnic politics: The discovery of Arkaim. *Museum International* 50 (2): 33–39.

——. 1999. Passions about Arkaim: Russian nationalism, the Arians and archaeology. *Inner Asia* 1 (2): 267–282.

Spitzyn, A. A. 1899. Rasselenie drevnerusskih plemen po arheologicheskim dannym (The settlement of early Russian tribes according to archaeological evidence). *Zhurnal Narodnago Prosvyashcheniya* 7: 301–340.

Stalin, J. V. 1950. *Marxism and Problems of Linguistics*. Moscow: Politizdat.

——. 1952. *Marxism and the National Question*. Complete Works, Vol. 2. Moscow: Politizdat.

Tikhanova, M. A. 1970. Esgcge raz k voprosu o proiskhozhdenii chernyakhovskoi kul'tury (Once more on the problem of origin of Chernyakhov culture). *Kratkie Soobshcheniya Instituta Arkheologii AN SSSR* 121: 89–94.

Timofeev, V. I., Zaitseva, G. I., Dolukhanov, P. M., and Shukurov, A. M. 2004. *Radiouglerodnaya Khronologiya Neolita Severnoi Evrazii* (The radiocarbon chronology of the Neolithic of northern Eurasia). St. Petersburg: Teza.

Tishkin, A. A. (ed.). 2004. *Zhiznennyi put', Tvorchstvo i Nauchnoe Naspedie S. I. Rudenko* (Life, works and scholarly legacy of S. I. Rudenko). Barnaul: Altai University Press.

Tkachuk, M. 1996. *Arheologiya Svobody: Opyt Kriticheskoi Teorii* (Archaeology of Liberty: Endeavour at Critical Theory). Chişinau: Stratum.

Tretyakov, P. N. 1968. *Finno-Ugry, Balty I Slavyane na Dnepre i Volge* (The Finno-Ugrians, Balts and Finns on the Dniepr and Volga). Moscow: Nauka.

Tripolsky, M. 1994. Ob izvrashchenii istorii: Khazarskii kaganat, evrei i sud'ba Rossii (On the distortion of history: The Khazar Kaganat, Jews and Russia's destiny). *Novoe Russkoe Slovo*, www.kulichki.com/~gumilev/debate/Article10.htm.

Yefimenko, P. P. 1934. *Dorodovoe Obshchestvo: Ocherki po Istorii Pervobytno-Communisticheskogo Obshchestva* (Pre-clan society: Essays on the History of Pristine Communist Society). Moscow and Leningrad: Socekgiz.

9

COMMENTARY:
SUBJECTIVITY AND SCIENCE IN
POSTCOLONIAL ARCHAEOLOGY

Ania Loomba

In 1988 I returned to India after three years in England writing a doctoral dissertation on Shakespearean and other English Renaissance drama and the ways in which these works were shaped by issues of race and colonialism, both when they were written and performed in the 16th and 17th centuries and subsequently, as they became a central part of British colonial education. I had begun thinking about these issues as a student and teacher of Shakespeare in India, when I became increasingly conscious of the distance between my own interpretation of his plays and the readings offered by dominant Anglo-American critics, which were dutifully echoed by our own teachers and critics in India.[1] Such readings not only distorted Renaissance history by ignoring the colonial and racial dimensions of global contact of the time, but also insisted that Shakespeare and other dramatists were presenting "universal" and "humanist" viewpoints that lay above mere politics. These views, as interpreted by dominant criticism, were conservative, patriarchal, and racist. Thus, it was the task of an alternative literary criticism to both reread the "facts" of Renaissance history and to offer different readings of the literature of the period.

The Renaissance has, since then, been extensively rewritten as the "early modern" period, in which some of the most cherished as well as controversial practices and institutions of our time were set into motion, including colonialism and the slave trade (e.g., Alexander and Wells 2000; Greenblatt 1990, 1991; Hall 1995; Hulme 1986; Loomba 2002; Parker and Hendricks 1994). Not coincidentally, it was the encounter with the non-European world at this time that also initiated certain methods of observing, researching, and recording that later became codified as modern anthropology and archaeology (Hodgen 1998). Just a few years before I started my research, Edward Said published *Orientalism* (1978), a book that greatly helped students like me in questioning some of the established norms of our discipline, because it legitimized a scrutiny into the ways colonialism shaped disciplinary protocols and methods. Luckily, this was also a moment when the attitudes and methods enshrined in the study of English literature were simultaneously being questioned from other perspectives, particularly those made available by feminists, queer critics, and other radicals. These new critics showed the ways in which the history and contemporary practice of English literature was deeply shaped by elitism, patriarchalism, and homophobia, and also how the "universal truths" supposedly enshrined in "great literature" were, at least as interpreted in the work of established critics, highly partisan opinions that explicitly devalued the reality of non-elite subjects (see, e.g., Baldick 1983; Dollimore and Sinfield 1985). So, despite heated debates about the details of Said's methods and conclusions, his work became enormously important to literary critics who wanted to challenge some of the established methods of literary education; colonial history and discourse became a fundamental part of English literary criticism.

When I returned to India, I encountered widespread skepticism about such intellectual developments, most eloquently expressed by people who were not literary critics. Some historians, for example, argued that Said's critique of orientalist practice was not relevant to Indian history because orientalists in India had a deep love for and knowledge of the country.[2] More serious was the critique that an emphasis on colonial discourse attributed too much power to representations and language at the expense of the material processes that constituted colonial rule. An anthropologist friend was scathing in his criticism of Said, arguing that "orientalism" implied that nobody could work on another culture, past or contemporary, objectively. And one of my first encounters was with an archaeologist with whom I had long shared intellectual conversations; this friend suggested that the practice of archaeology was based on an objective assessment of material remains ("stones are just stones," she said) and was therefore less subject to the kind of critiques that I had found so important in the case of literary criticism. She had taken me to the remains of a dig near Delhi, and at that time, as we poked around the dust and the pot sherds, it seemed hard to argue that issues of race and gender mattered in a discipline where the relationship of "fact" to "interpretation" was so differently constituted from what I was used to in literary critique.

I do not want to trivialize the very serious debates about colonialism sparked off by "orientalism," but what interests me is that all of them turn in different ways on the question of the relations between subjectivity and materiality, between the act of individual interpretation and social and historical processes of history, which remain contentious today. In English studies, one scholar had pronounced that the discipline had "lost its innocence" since these fundamental debates began about the ways in which the act of interpretation is deeply implicated in dominant relations of power (Baldick 1983).[3] It seemed to me that some of the critiques I was now encountering wanted to hang onto some notion of this innocence. In the years since then, both the critique of theories of colonial discourse and their application to diverse disciplinary practices have proliferated and become enormously more sophisticated. This volume is a testimony to the changing practice of archaeology, which has had, in several different parts of the world, such an obviously important role to play in challenging colonial legacies. Nevertheless, it seems to me that it has been easier to take on board the question of ideological *interpretation* in those disciplines that are less invested in establishing their own objectivity. Thus, as Jan Vansina writes:

> Historians have too touching a faith in archaeology as a "scientific" discipline, and hence misunderstand some basic realities about it. Mesmerized by the observation that archaeology deals with concrete objective data, they fail to perceive the role played by interpretation—and hence subjectivity—both in the recovery and in the interpretation of its data. Yet when former afficionados discover that archaeologists are after all only human, they . . . tend to be disillusioned and throw out both baby and bathwater. (Vansina 1995: 307)

Whereas in literary debates, political (and postcolonial) criticism is routinely accused of robbing literature of its "emotional" appeal, of being too clinical (politics and emotion are seen as opposing impulses), in subjects such as archaeology, it is accused of "too much" emotion and subjectivity. To deliberately take a highly controversial example, these are the grounds on which David Rosen (2007) attacks Nadia Abu El-Haj's book *Facts on the Ground* (2001), which argues that archaeology in Israel (and in the region more generally) has fabricated the history of Jewish presence in the area in order to legitimize the expulsion of Palestinians from the land, and thus exposes itself as a "colonial science." Rosen contends that the politics of the book

> is profoundly shaped by Edward Said's book Orientalism, which clearly rejects the idea of the objectivity of knowledge. . . . By locating the scientific enterprise within the colonial, it becomes possible for writers like El-Haj to create labels such as "colonial science." . . . [P]ost-colonial studies, cultural studies, and their anthropological progeny. . . construct their analyses with little concern for empirical or logical connectedness. . . . This methodology has no connection to science. Its power lies in its politics and its aesthetics, and not in such boring ideas as validity and reliability. (www.columbia.edu/ cu/current/articles/ fall2007/searching-for-facts-on-the-ground.html)

In this diatribe, a claim to impartiality and wholeness becomes the ground on which to mount a political attack, much the same tactic as that taken by conservative literary critics. But for Rosen, "aesthetics" (usually the high ground such critics claim to be preserving) becomes a dirty word, fused with politics instead of opposed to it.

Tellingly, Rosen's critique also conflates El-Haj's book with all critiques of colonialism, and in attacking it mounts a defense of scientific objectivity. But as Michael Blakey points out, in the context of a debate on how to combine archaeology with social critique,

> science is most materialistic, I would argue, when it is most critical, that is, when it is understood as subjective in meaningful ways and when, therefore, the partial subjectivity of a fact can be explored and stated. This is not encouraged by claims to abstract emancipation or the objective procedures required to produce it. Critical archaeology would be profoundly critical if it came to grips with the meanings and applications of intrinsic subjectivity in scientific knowledge.
> (Leone et al. 1987: 292)

In recent years, archaeology has come to occupy a crucial place in battles about how to interpret and use the past in various once-colonized parts of the world, including the Middle East, Australia, Latin America, and Asia. It is at the heart of debates about colonial plunder of artifacts, colonial perspectives about Indigenous populations, and also about the future of once-colonized populations. Because the highly variable ways in which European colonial rule operated in different places, there can be no uniform template for a global postcolonial archaeology. Whereas a nationalist archaeology can serve anti-imperial ends, it can also become a retrograde operation tied into sectional or communal interests. Thus, in India, the Hindu right-wing has attempted to communalize the discipline and harness it to appropriate the Harappan civilization as Vedic and Hindu (Habib 1997). Here, in the name of an "Indigenous" perspective, one actually gets a highly chauvinist proto-revivalist one.

But today we do not live in a postcolonial world so much as one in which the legacy of earlier empires is being widely invoked to justify a new imperial order—namely, that of U.S. intervention in various parts of the world (Ferguson 2003; Johnson 2003; Kaplan 2003). It is no accident that in this situation, Edward Said and postcolonial critiques are routinely labeled as dangerously subversive influences in U.S. universities. Some years ago, Stanley Kurtz, a fellow at Stanford University's Hoover Institution, urged the U.S. House of Representatives to intervene in a situation where "area studies" centers in U.S. universities have become "anti-American" under the influence of postcolonial scholarship and especially Edward Said's *Orientalism*: "Said equated professors who support American foreign policy with the 19th century European intellectuals who propped up racist colonial empires. The core premise of postcolonial theory is that it is immoral for a scholar to put his knowledge of foreign languages and cultures at the service of American power" (Ganguly and Curthoys 2007: 34).[4] Kurtz got one thing right—one of Edward Said's most valuable achievements in *Orientalism* was not simply to establish the connection between scholarship and state power in the colonial period, but to indicate its afterlife in a postcolonial global formation with the United States at its epicenter. The region Said wrote about is both one of the richest archaeological sites in the world and one of the most politically volatile regions of the world—the nerve center of U.S. global interests. Critics (including Rosen, but also many who write from a very different political perspective) attack Said (and his followers) for his postmodern methods, which are caricatured as incapable of arriving at any stable truth. The fact is that Said did not present a world in which there was no center, or stable truth, but indeed its opposite—one in which a new global order was rapidly consolidating itself and in doing so both utilized old inequities and created new ones. Indeed, it has been fashionable for some time to use the term "Saidian" as synonymous with what is called a "linguistic turn" in the social sciences and to hold both responsible for a wishy-washy culturalist perspective that is politically nebulous and methodologically inconsistent. However, I want to remind us that quite apart from Edward Said, many other literary critics have produced trenchant analyses of social power, colonial history, and neocolonialism by effectively using questions of language, subjectivity, and ideology (Parthasarthy 2003; Sarkar 1994).[5] The real question is not whether we are "scientific" or "literary," but what we do with these methods. To quote Antonio Gramsci (1995):

> Is there any value in the fact of a philosopher's having started off from a scientific experiment or from a "literary" experience? That is to say, which philosophy is more "realistic"—that which starts from the "exact" sciences or that which starts from "literature," i.e. from the observation of man in so far as he is intellectually active and not just a "mechanical part of nature"?

Postcolonial scholarship has pointed to the colonial construction of particular disciplines, including history, literature, and archaeology. With respect to history, Dipesh Chakrabarty (1992, 2000) has wondered whether the discipline can ever "provincialize Europe" or whether it is too deeply shaped by its own history and the protocols of a Eurocentric vision.[6] Similar questions can, of course, be asked of English literary studies and archaeology, but interdisciplinary scholarship has a better chance of arriving at a decolonized perspective by challenging disciplinary chauvinism while utilizing the best methods offered by different scholarly traditions. Thus a postcolonial archaeology would combine the methods of science, history, *and* cultural critique to important effect.

Notes

1. See my book *Race, Gender, Renaissance Drama* (1989), which describes the colonial state of the discipline and this history.
2. Such assertions overlooked Said's argument that the distortion of non-European cultures by orientalists took place despite such knowledge and affection, being an attribute of disciplinary formations rather than individual malice.

3. Patrick Parrinder is quoted by Baldick 1983, p. 6.
4. Quoted from Kurtz's statement reproduced in Ganguly and Curthoys 2007: 34. Kurtz's views can also be accessed at *www.nationalreview.com/kurtz/kurtz061603.asp*.
5. For example, Sarkar 1994 presents a critique from the left; for a trenchant critique of this position, see Parthasarthy 2003.
6. The most pessimistic version of this argument is to be found in Chakrabarty's essay, "Postcoloniality and the artifice of history: Who speaks for 'Indian' pasts?" (1992), pp. 1–26; a revised statement is in *Provincializing Europe: Postcolonial Thought and Historical Difference* (2000), pp. 3–46, 257–268.

References

Abu El-Haj, N. 2001. *Facts on the Ground: Archaeological Practice and Territorial Self-Fashioning in Israeli Society*. Chicago: University of Chicago Press.

Alexander, C. M. S., and Wells, S. (eds.). 2000. *Shakespeare and Race*. Cambridge: Cambridge University Press.

Baldick, C. 1983. *The Social Mission of English Criticism*. Oxford: Clarendon Press.

Chakrabarty, D. 1992. Postcoloniality and the artifice of history: Who speaks for "Indian" pasts? *Representations* 37: 1–26.

——. 2000. *Provincializing Europe: Postcolonial Thought and Historical Difference*. Princeton and Oxford: Princeton University Press.

Dollimore, J., and Sinfield, A. (eds.). 1985. *Political Shakespeare*. Manchester: Manchester University Press.

Ferguson, N. 2003. The Empire Slinks Back. *New York Times Magazine*, April 27.

Ganguly, D., and Curthoys, N. 2007. *Edward Said: Legacy of a Public Intellectual*. Melbourne: Melbourne University Publishing.

Gramsci, A. 1995. *Further Selections from the Prison Notebooks*, Derek Boothman (ed. and trans.). Minneapolis: University of Minnesota Press.

Greenblatt, S. 1990. *Learning to Curse*. New York: Routledge.

——. 1991. *Marvelous Possessions: The Wonder of the New World*. Chicago: University of Chicago Press.

Habib, I. 1997. Unreason and archaeology: The "Painted Grey-Ware" and beyond. *Social Scientist* 25 (1/2): 16–24.

Hall, K. F. 1995. *Things of Darkness: Economies of Race and Gender in Early Modern England*. Ithaca, NY: Cornell University Press.

Hodgen, M. 1998. *Early Anthropology in the Sixteenth and Seventeenth Centuries*. Philadelphia: University of Pennsylvania Press.

Hulme, P. 1986. *Colonial Encounters, Europe and the Native Caribbean 1492–1797*. London: Routledge.

Johnson, P. 2003. Five vital lessons from Iraq. *Forbes*, March 17.

Kaplan, R. D. 2003. Supremacy by stealth. *Atlantic Monthly*, July/August 2003.

Kurtz, S. 2003. Studying Title VI: Criticisms of Middle East studies get a congressional hearing. *National Review*, June 16. *www.nationalreview.com/kurtz/kurtz061603.asp*.

Leone, M. P., Potter, Jr., P. B., and Shackel, P. A. 1987. Toward a critical archaeology. *Current Anthropology* 28 (3): 283–302.

Loomba, A. 1989. *Race, Gender, Renaissance Drama*. Manchester: Manchester University Press.

———. 2002. *Shakespeare, Race and Colonialism*. Oxford: Oxford University Press.

Parker, P., and Hendricks, M. (eds.). 1994. *Women, "Race" and Writing in the Early Modern Period*. London: Routledge.

Parthasarthy, P. 2003. The state of Indian social history—The cultural turn and beyond. *Journal of Social History* 37 (1): 47–53.

Rosen, D. 2007. Searching for "facts" on the ground. *The Current*, Fall. *www.columbia.edu/cu/current/articles/fall2007/searching-for-facts-on-the-ground.html*.

Said, E. 1978. *Orientalism*. London: Routledge.

Sarkar, S. 1994. Orientalism revisited: Saidian frameworks in the writing of modern history. *Oxford Literary Review* 16: 205–224.

Vansina, J. 1995. Historians, are archaeologists your siblings? *History in Africa* 22: 369–408.

10

COMMENTARY:
ARCHAEOLOGY ENTERS THE 21ST CENTURY

Thomas C. Patterson

More than 20 years ago, Bruce Trigger fundamentally changed the direction of inquiries into the origins and development of archaeology—which he broadly saw as bringing the past back to life by understanding its material remains. He was acutely aware that the theory and practice of archaeology varied in important ways from one country to another and that this variation was not random. He suggested that "the nature of archaeological research is shaped to a significant degree by the roles that particular nation-states play, economically, politically, and culturally, as interdependent parts of the modern world-system" (Trigger 2003 [1984]: 68). He proceeded to describe the differences among three alternative archaeologies that were rooted in nationalist, colonialist, and imperialist projects, respectively.

Trigger returned to the problem a few years later. In the first edition of *A History of Archaeological Thought*, he began to explore the complex relations between romantic social thought and archaeology (Trigger 1989: 65–66). He would hone and refine his understanding of romanticism and its linkages over the next decade and a half (Trigger 1995; 1998; 2006: 110–114). Finally, he was among the first to note that the practitioners of archaeology have largely been drawn from the middle classes since the 15th century (Trigger 1989: 14; 2006: 20). Trigger has provided us with a postcolonial framework for thinking about the emergence and development of archaeology within social milieu constituted by the formation of national-states and national minorities, by the rise of capitalism, by colonialism and imperialism, by struggles for political and economic independence, and by the question of modernity. Trigger's ideas are always good to think with, even when one does not necessarily agree with all of their details. My goal in this chapter is to elaborate the themes he framed and to discuss some interconnections with the archaeological critique of colonization.

The Middle Classes, Enlightenment, and Romanticism

It is becoming commonplace to acknowledge today that social class structures are historically constituted; that a social class never exists in isolation; that the totality of a class structure at any given moment is the product of dialectically interrelated cultural, social, and political-economic processes; that particular class positions are often internally differentiated; that individuals in the same class position but of different ages or genders may have experienced the articulations of those processes in different ways and consequently have different understandings of them; and that the distinctions perceived among class positions in one nation-state may be subtly different from those recognized in another (e.g., Resnick and Wolff 1987; Wright 1997). From a structural standpoint, the middle classes are typically composed of wage-workers with some expertise, authority, and cultural capital in the social fields in which they operate (Bourdieu 1984 [1987]). Credentials—increasingly in the form of advanced university degrees—mark the individual as middle class and as someone who possesses both the cultural capital and the skills required to act in the social field (profession); consequently, credentials are important in constituting and reproducing the field as well as its associated class position (Patterson 1989, 1999).

There is, however, another feature associated with middle-class positionality: it is an unstable class location, especially with regard to economic changes which—like those associated with technological innovations, deindustrialization, or globalization—have the capacity to produce a sudden downward social mobility as they dramatically reduce income, alter working conditions, and give new meaning to the vicissitudes of everyday life. As a result, the members of the middle classes hold widely divergent perspectives about the world, running the gamut from conservative to radical (Díaz-Andreu 2007; Trigger 2006: 19–20). Moreover, they often modify their views as their circumstances change. Indeed, it is not uncommon for members of the same household to hold divergent views owing to generational differences, age within the same generation, gender, or how everyday life has been experienced at different developmental stages by the individuals involved.

"Enlightenment" and "romanticism" broadly gloss two world views found among different segments of the middle class—the former with those who hitched their wagons to the state, the aristocracy, or some emerging dominant layer in a new social order, the latter with those whose position and opportunities in life were declining from what they had formerly been. From this standpoint, they are two sides of the same coin, inextricably linked, dialectically interrelated rather than distinct, incommensurable perspectives whose promoters have not fully grasped what the other said but know they disagree with what they heard (Berlin 1999, 2000, 2006; Geras and Wokler 2000; Sherratt 1996; Trigger 1998). The advocates of enlightenment and romantic social thought have been engaged in a dialogue about what it means to be human for more than 2,000 years—among others, the Epicureans and Plato, the Confucians and Taoists, and Kant and Rousseau. They are not necessarily Western or European, or even modern.

Since the mid-1700s, the supporters of enlightenment thought have claimed that human beings are rational; that they are fundamentally the same in all times and places; that local and historical variation is less important than the constant core of humanity; that beliefs should be based on empirical or rational (i.e., scientific) arguments rather than authority or tradition; and that human progress toward modernity (construed as fragmentation or differentiation into separate spheres of everyday life, the capitalization of social life, commercialization, industrialization, the development of instrumental rationality, and the formation of the individual subject) is desirable. The romantics, in contrast, are critics of capitalist civilization and the civilizing process as a whole. They have argued that essential human values were lost in the process of modernity; that these essential values existed in past societies and still exist in societies on the margins; that the individual subject created by capitalist civilization is incapable of developing her/his subjective individuality in that milieu; and that societies, past or present, with "different" ensembles of social relations provide alternative visions for emancipation and future courses of action (Israel 2001; Lee 2005; Löwy and Sayre 2001: 21–25). Needless but perhaps relevant to say, theorists as seemingly diverse as Bruce Trigger, Karl Marx, Sandra Harding, and Jacques Derrida have incorporated and elaborated dimensions of both enlightenment and romantic thought in their own perspectives about what it means to be human.

In a phrase, neither enlightenment nor romantic social thought *per se* is necessarily progressive or reactionary; it depends on how it is being implemented to forge and refine reality. Is it wielded merely as a means to reproduce existing institutions, practices, and circumstances? Is it used to gain a more theoretically informed understanding of those social relations and representations as well as the contradictions inherent in them? Or is this effort to understand human history a prelude, given the contingent particularities of time and place, to exploring the real possibilities that exist for emancipatory change and self-realization for both individuals and communities in the future?

World Archaeologies

Others besides Trigger are now emphasizing the interconnections of archaeological practices in different national states. Chris Gosden (2004: 6) makes this point in slightly different terms when he notes that archaeology developed in a world of shared experiences that were shaped significantly but differentially by colonialism, imperialism, and nationalism during the last 500 years. This means, for example, that the architectural template for the Georgian-style buildings erected in 18th-century Virginia was not imported from England, but rather was forged in the context of the trans-Atlantic relations that linked the two regions.

It is possible for colonialist, nationalist, and imperialist archaeologies to develop simultaneously in the same country. The United States is an example. In the 19th century, the practice of archaeology was imbued with both nationalist and imperialist agendas—as the country expanded westward toward the Pacific, as it sought to establish a heritage in the Mediterranean world, and as its interests were drawn southward toward the Central American republics and later the Yucatan Peninsula. By the early years of the 20th century, archaeologists buttressed the heritage of the settler colonies along the eastern seaboard and constructed new identities in California that both alluded to the Mission Period and sought inspiration from the Spanish Mediterranean (Weinberg 1974). In the wake of the Second World War, the universalizing language of cultural evolutionism, combined with appeals to the power and prestige of science, not only strengthened the imperialist form of archaeology in this country but also exposed fundamental differences between its own presuppositions and those of the historical archaeologists who were concerned not with universals but rather with the historical particularities of 18th- and 19th-century American society (Patterson 1995). This contradiction has only begun to be addressed since the 1980s, when a number of historical archaeologists started to view their object of inquiry not as the settler colonies but instead as the rise of capitalism (e.g., Leone 1995; Leone and Potter 1988, 1999; McGuire and Paynter 1991; Patterson 1993; Schmidt and Patterson 1995). This has helped to create common ground for opening an important dialogue with archaeologists elsewhere who are concerned with the particularities of historical development in other countries and their articulation with capitalist expansion (e.g., Funari et al. 1999; Funari et al. 2005; Schmidt and Patterson 1995).

Because of the uneven development of archaeology and the important roles played by colonial or national states in this development, archaeology's pace and structure in the United States have differed from those found in other countries (e.g., Díaz-Andreu and Champion 1996; Hudson 2006; Kohl and Fawcett 1995). For example, archaeological investigations in Peru have been decidedly nationalist for more than a century; romanticism has successively underpinned claims that Peru's ancient civilization was a consequence of diffusion, and that it developed autochthonously in the mountains. The hegemony of romanticism waned in 1950s and was replaced by evolutionist models rooted in theories of economic growth or unequal exchange; however, contradictions were soon evident between the universalizing conceptual language of these theories and the historical particularist interpretive frameworks involved in producing tourism focused on world heritage sites like Machu Picchu (Flores Ochoa 2004; Silverman

2002). What was immediately apparent in the discourse was the multiplicity of parties—the national state, regional and local governments, professional archaeologists, community members, tourism agencies, and others—all claiming the authority and rights to writing and rewriting the history of those sites and the communities that inhabited them (e.g., Benavides 2004; Mamani Condori 1989).

Archaeology in a Changing World

Globally, by the 1970s, claims of rights and authority by groups who were not professional archaeologists often challenged their hegemonic histories—Australia, Canada, and the United States come immediately to mind (e.g., Bender 1998; Layton 1989; McBryde 1985). These were often linked with wider political and social agendas of Indigenous or descendant communities who were successfully influencing, entering, or participating directly in decision-making circles in ways they had not been able to do earlier. While the social and political bases of the movements, like the American Indian Movement, were typically defined in terms of a particular national state, there were always opportunities for forging alliances with groups in other countries and making their agendas transnational. One of the most successful of these was the Anti-Apartheid Movement, which requested that the British organizing committee of an archaeological congress honor United Nations resolutions calling for academic and cultural sanctions against South Africa and Namibia. The result of these discussions was the creation of the World Archaeological Congress in Southampton in 1986, which brought together scholars from more than 100 countries, including the frontline states in Africa, as well as Indigenous and minority scholars, students, and activists from there and elsewhere (Ucko 1987). Issues of Indigenous rights, oppression, racism, and sexism were on the table for substantive discussion for the first time. More importantly, they continue to be on the table at many archaeological conferences two decades later.

Archaeological Critiques of Colonization

At this moment, it is important to keep at least five things in mind regarding archaeological critiques of colonization. First, however successful organizations like the World Archaeological Congress may be at conveying their message internationally, their members still reside and work in class-stratified, national states that, potentially or in reality, have significant control over how archaeology is done, who does it, who has access to the materials, or whether it is even done at all.

Second, the interests of archaeologists worldwide or even in particular national states have never been monolithic or shaped by a single ethos with regard either to the profession or, perhaps more importantly, to humanity as a whole.

Third, with regard to praxis, questions of short-, middle-, and long-term goals should be considered carefully. Are these goals to increase the multivocality of the dialogue about human history in all its diversity; to enact legislation; to increase the numbers and professional participation of archaeologists from minority and Indigenous communities; to increase the number of truly collaborative ventures between archaeologists and those communities; or to ensure that tradition is maintained?

The fourth thing, keeping in mind that one will usually be tarred with the same brush as one's allies, is to think very clearly and strategically about the political implications of particular standpoints: in other words, whose interests do they serve?

Finally, it is important to realize that a single individual can never resolve all the problems of the world. Devote your energies to two—one global and one local—and be supportive of individuals working on other issues that have the potential to make a difference.

Acknowledgments

I thank Jane Lydon and Uzma Rivzi for the opportunity to contribute to this volume. Over the years, I have profited from the critical comments and sound advice of Bruce Trigger, Karen Brodkin, Carole Crumley, Stanley Diamond, Eddie Boorstein, Christine Gailey, Peter Gran, Phil, Kohl, Bob Paynter, Bob Preucel, Peter Schmidt, Karen Spalding, Kathy Walker, Alison Wylie, and Wendy Ashmore.

References

Bender, B. 1998. *Stonehenge: Making Space.* Oxford: Berg Publishers.

Benavides, O. H. 2004. *Making Ecuadorian Histories: Four Centuries of Defining Power.* Austin: University of Texas Press.

Berlin, I. 1999. *The Roots of Romanticism.* Princeton, NJ: Princeton University Press.

——. 2000. *Three Critics of the Enlightenment: Vico, Hamann, Herder.* Princeton, NJ: Princeton University Press.

——. 2006. *Political Ideas in the Romantic Age: Their Rise and Influence on Modern Thought.* Princeton, NJ: Princeton University Press.

Bourdieu, P. 1984 [1987]. *Distinction: A Social Critique of the Judgement of Taste.* Cambridge, MA: Harvard University Press.

Díaz-Andreu, M. 2007. Internationalism in the invisible college: Political ideologies and friendships in archaeology. *Journal of Social Archaeology* 7 (1): 29–48. London.

Díaz-Andreu, M., and Champion, T. (eds.). 1996. *Nationalism and Archaeology in Europe.* London: UCL Press.

Flores Ochoa, J. A. 2004. Contemporary significance of Machu Picchu, in R. L. Burger and L. C. Salazar (eds.), *Machu Picchu: Unveiling the Mystery of the Incas*, pp. 109–123. New Haven, CT: Yale University Press.

Funari, P. P. A., Hall, M., and Jones, S. (eds.). 1999. *Historical Archaeology: Back from the Edge.* London: Routledge.

Funari, P. P. A., Zarankin, A., and Stovel, E. (eds.). 2005. *Global Archaeological Theory: Contextual Voices and Contemporary Thoughts.* New York: Kluwer Academic/Plenum Publishers.

Geras, N., and Wokler, R. (eds.). 2000. *The Enlightenment and Modernity.* New York: St. Martin's Press.

Gosden, C. 2004. *Archaeology and Colonialism: Culture Contact from 5000 BC to the Present*. Cambridge: Cambridge University Press.

Hudson, M. J. 2006. Pots not people: Ethnicity, culture and identity in postwar Japanese archaeology. *Critique of Anthropology*, 26 (4): 411–434.

Israel, J. I. 2001. *Radical Enlightenment: Philosophy and the Making of Modernity, 1650–1750*. Oxford: Oxford University Press.

Kohl, P. L., and Fawcett, C. (eds.). 1995. *Nationalism, Politics, and the Practice of Archaeology*. Cambridge: Cambridge University Press.

Layton, R. (ed.). 1989. *Conflict in the Archaeology of Living Traditions*. London: Unwin Hyman.

Lee, R. B. 2005. Power and property in twenty-first century foragers: A critical examination, in T. Widlok and W. Gossa Tadesse (eds.), *Property and Equality*, Vol. 2, *Encapsulation, Commericalisation, Discrimination*, pp. 16–31. New York: Berghahn Books.

Leone, M. P. 1995. A historical archaeology of capitalism. *American Anthropologist* 97 (2): 251–268.

Leone, M. P., and P. B. Potter, Jr. (eds). 1988. *The Recovery of Meaning: Historical Archaeology in the Eastern United States*. Washington, DC: Smithsonian Institution Press.

——. 1999. *Historical Archaeologies of Capitalism*. New York: Kluwer Academic/Plenum Publishers [a 1993 SAR Seminar organized in 1991].

Löwy, M., and Sayre, R. 2001. *Romanticism against the Tide of Modernity*. Durham, NC: Duke University Press.

Mamani Condori, C. 1989. History and prehistory in Bolivia: What about the Indians? in R. Layton (ed.), *Conflicts in the Archaeology of Living Traditions*, pp. 46–59. London: Routledge.

McBryde, I. (ed.). 1985. *Who Owns the Past?* Melbourne: Oxford University Press.

McGuire, R. H., and Paynter, R. (eds.). 1991. *The Archaeology of Inequality*. Oxford: Blackwell Publishers.

Patterson, T. C. 1989. Political economy and a discourse called "Peruvian archaeology." *Culture and History* 4: 35–64. Copenhagen.

——. 1993. *Archaeology: The Historical Development of Civilizations*. Englewood Cliffs, NJ: Prentice-Hall.

——. 1995. *Toward a Social History of Archaeology in the United States*. Fort Worth, TX: Harcourt Brace College Publishers.

——. 1999. The political economy of archaeology in the United States. *Annual Review of Anthropology* 28: 155–174.

Resnick, S. A., and Wolff, R. D. 1987 *Knowledge and Class: A Marxian Critique of Political Economy*. Chicago: The University of Chicago Press.

Schmidt, P. R., and Patterson, T. C. (eds.). 1995. *Making Alternative Histories: The Practice of Archaeology in Non-Western Settings*. Santa Fe: SAR Press.

Sherratt, A. 1996. "Settlement patterns" or "landscape studies"? Reconciling reason and romance. *Archaeological Dialogues* 3 (2): 140–159. Amsterdam.

Silverman, H. 2002. Touring ancient times: The present and the presented past in contemporary Peru. *American Anthropologist* 104 (3): 881–902.

Trigger, B. G. 1989. *A History of Archaeological Thought*. Cambridge: Cambridge University Press.

———. 1995. Romanticism, nationalism, and archaeology, in P. L. Kohl and C. Fawcett (eds.), *Nationalism, Politics, and the Practice of Archaeology*, pp. 263–279. Cambridge: Cambridge University Press.

———. 1998. *Sociocultural Evolution*. Oxford: Blackwell Publishers.

———. 2003 [1984]. Alternative archaeologies: Nationalist, colonialist, imperialist, in B. G. Trigger, *Artifacts and Ideas: Essays in Archaeology*, pp. 67–86. New Brunswick, NJ: Transactions Publishers.

———. 2006. *A History of Archaeological Thought*. 2nd ed. Cambridge: Cambridge University Press.

Ucko, P. 1987. *Academic Freedom and Apartheid: The Story of the World Archaeological Congress*. London: Gerald Duckworth.

Weinberg, N. G. 1974. *Historic Preservation and Tradition in California: The Restoration of the Missions and the Spanish-Colonial Revival*. Ph.D. dissertation in Sociology, University of California, Davis (University Microfilms 74–21,639).

Wright, E. O. 1997. *Class Counts: Comparative Studies in Class Analysis*. Cambridge: Cambridge University Press.

PART II
ARCHAEOLOGICAL NARRATIVES OF COLONIALISM: INTRODUCTORY COMMENTS

New archaeological narratives shift our understanding of colonialism by, first, emphasizing the perspective of the colonized and, second, by challenging normative notions of the Native/Other by repositioning forms of alterity within a more complex new world order. While such research has not always been located within an explicitly postcolonial framework, it clearly has been prompted by the same motives, including Indigenous demands, an interest in marginal historical experience, and specifically Indigenous responses to European colonialism. Archaeologists have focused on the subaltern experience of Indigenous populations through studies of "contact" (e.g., Murray 2004) and "cross-cultural" engagement (e.g., Torrence and Clarke 2000), and, for previously colonized populations, by deconstructing colonial narratives of the past (e.g., Liebmann and Rizvi 2008; Reid and Segobye 1999; Schmidt and Patterson 1995; Schmidt 2009).

Complementing these concerns, the Africanist perspective has drawn directly from postcolonial discourses, with a keen interest in decolonizing methodologies specific to an academic culture within Africa and within the African diaspora. These overviews reveal that studies within former colonial domains share several salient elements and, notably, a reluctance (until very recently) to engage with a troublesome colonial past, instead choosing to focus on either prehistory—often entailing a view of Indigenous and local culture as pristine or depleted, and so seemingly divorced from present political struggles—or alternatively constructing a celebratory pioneer past (e.g., Gullapalli 2008).

The contributions to this section document exciting new scholarship that recenters Indigenous and minority experience. These accounts also reveal the diversity of colonialism's cultures—the varied projects, groups, and practices that have comprised this internally differentiated historical process, requiring historically specific analysis that attends to local and temporal manifestations.

Stephen Silliman reviews the historical archaeology of Native Americans and their colonization by British, French, Spanish, Dutch, and Russian invaders, a field that he suggests was initiated by the Columbian Quincentennial in 1992. Recentering history to focus on Indigenous experience lies at the heart of this new scholarship, as exemplified by recent scholarship that addresses changing practices surrounding death, the body, households, and gender relations following colonization. Such symbolic mediations through visual imagery express new identities and serve to negotiate with outsiders.

Alistair Paterson reviews a similar wave of research in Australia, where the 1988 bicentennial of European settlement served as a rallying point for protest and reevaluation. He reviews the major historical processes that have structured this research, including the pastoral industry and institutions such as missions, as well as cultural forms such as exchange, visual representations, and the creation of social landscapes.

Slavery and emancipation were integral aspects of the historical process of colonialism, and, as Theresa Singleton's contribution notes, liberation movements of the 1960s, and specifically the Civil Rights movement in the United States, prompted their archaeological study. Archaeological data provide material evidence of otherwise unrecorded Afro-Atlantic cultures under different colonial regimes throughout the Americas, including the study of "maroon" (runaway slave) settlements and the reorganization of plantation slave quarters and material lives through practices (e.g., hunting, craft, or consumption) that challenged the restrictions of plantation life.

Charles Orser links the historical Irish experience of colonization by England to an emphasis on the archaeology of the period prior to the Middle Ages, which might be considered "truly" Irish. He identifies an empirical, "dispassionate" stream of research that deliberately abstains from political argument, seeming to mask the acceptance of an inevitable Anglicization. However, recent research has explicitly set out to explore aspects of colonialism through study of the multiple identities produced by processes of cultural encounter, key sites such as Gaelic castles appropriated by the English, iconography, and spatial relationships.

Peter Schmidt and Karega-Munene focus on postcolonial archaeologies of Africa, valorizing local histories and subaltern voices and critiquing the silencing of younger, less established voices. They argue that misunderstandings are necessarily part of the decolonization process, and that the resolution "rests in the principle of transparency and open debate, not silence and fear of retribution." Perhaps one of the most distinct aspects of the practice of archaeology in Africa is the issue of disenchantment—in particular, working in communities that continue to be plagued by HIV/AIDS, other serious medical conditions, and issues of livelihood. Schmidt and Karega-Munene tackle this issue head on, providing examples of how archaeologists have worked with communities to establish conditions of ethical and decolonized practice.

Following Schmidt and Karega-Munene's chapter on the tangible reality of working in unchallenged neocolonial structures, Ashish Chadha's commentary discusses similar structural issues within archaeological practice in India. Chadha traces the colonial epistemology of the Archaeological Survey of India and its relatively unchanging stance toward archaeology and science within a bureaucratic postcolonial structure. Chadha uses the Ram Janama Bhoomi/Babri Mosque controversy in Ayodhya to illustrate the complexity and tensions within the postcolonial moment on a very local level. Shifting focus to the New World, yet continuing with the issue of contemporary conditions affecting interpretations of the past, O. Hugo Benavides illustrates how excavation in Latin America is structured by the neocolonial conditions of the present, as Western-inspired national governments deny and erase the past, and simultaneously demand the production of "objective" national histories.

References

Gullapalli, P. 2008. Heterogeneous encounters: Colonial histories and archaeological experiences, in M. Liebmann and U. Z. Rizvi (eds.), *Archaeology and the Postcolonial Critique*. Lanham, MD: AltaMira Press.

Liebmann, M., and Rizvi, U. Z. (eds.). 2008. *Archaeology and the Postcolonial Critique*. Lanham, MD: AltaMira Press.

Murray, T. (ed.). 2004. *The Archaeology of Contact in Settler Societies*. Cambridge: Cambridge University Press.

Reid, A., and Segobye, A. 1999. The archaeology of the Makgadikgadi Pans, Botswana. Paper presented at the Fourth World Archaeological Congress, January 10–14 in Cape Town, South Africa.

Schmidt, P. R. (ed.). 2009. *Postcolonial Archaeologies in Africa*. Santa Fe: SAR Press.

Schmidt, P. R., and Patterson, T. C. (eds.). 1995. *Making Alternative Histories: The Practice of Archaeology and History in Non-Western Settings*. School of American Research Advanced Seminar Series. Santa Fe: SAR Press.

Torrence, R., and Clarke, A. 2000. *The Archaeology of Difference: Negotiating Cross-Cultural Engagements in Oceania*. London: Routledge.

11

WRITING NEW ARCHAEOLOGICAL NARRATIVES: INDIGENOUS NORTH AMERICA

Stephen W. Silliman

Writing new archaeological narratives of Indigenous North America requires revisiting the ways that archaeologists think, write, dig, analyze, interpret, and present their information to colleagues, students, descendant communities, and the general public. As developed throughout this volume, postcolonialism encourages this revisiting, in part as a political project of decolonization and in part as a refinement of our conceptual and practical tools for writing better histories and doing better anthropologies. My goal in this chapter is to relay how archaeologists, both Indigenous and non-Indigenous, have been crafting and will continue to craft new narratives of Native North America thanks to the contributions of postcolonial thinking.

This chapter examines the contributions of postcolonial perspectives to the archaeology of Native North America in the periods frequently labeled, appropriately or not, as "contact," "post-contact," "colonial," "historic," or "post-Columbian."[1] The reason behind my choice of these eras is straightforward: these times and their legacies have become the focus of postcolonial critique; they have also attracted the attention of the majority of archaeologists who have drawn inspiration from postcolonial ideas and politics. As a result, this chapter offers a synthesis of the "historical archaeology of Native Americans" (Rubertone 2000), but it is partial and non-exhaustive, given that my objective is to examine postcoloniality in the practice of archaeologists working on this volatile and important period of Native American history. Inclusion of bibliographic materials has been based primarily on research projects and archaeologists that have adopted postcolonial ideas, have been inspired by them, or can be reframed in a postcolonial light.

General Background

North America is delimited by archaeologists as the contiguous United States, Canada, and northern Mexico, a land area of approximately 20.5 million square kilometers (or about 790,000 square miles) that includes tremendous physiographic, biological, linguistic, and cultural diversity. The sheer numbers of Native American peoples, the length of their tenure on the continent, and their highly differentiated ways of relating to one another, to their physical environments, and to spiritual worlds, preclude any sort of generalized summary. Added to this complexity are the numbers of different European colonial fronts that impinged on these Native territories from the early 1500s to the 1900s, an impact that some argue continues into the 21st century. Obviously, the settler nations of the United States and Canada have controlled most of North America since the late 19th century; however, the development of these nation-states arose from the interplay of various colonial efforts over several centuries. These included the British on the East Coast and in northern Canada, the French along the Mississippi River and around the Great Lakes, the Spanish stretching across the "borderlands" from Florida to Texas to California, the Dutch in New York and along the Connecticut River, and the Russians on the Pacific Coast from Alaska to California (see Deagan 2003; Lightfoot 2003, 2004; Moussette 2003; Rothschild 2003; Thomas 1989, 1990, 1991).

For some time, archaeologists have examined these colonial encounters in Native North America, but not in a sustained way until recently. This is due in part to an earlier focus on the more "glamorous" prehistory of ancient North America and a presumed lack of "pristine"-quality historical or ethnographic cultures which resulted from the influence of Europeans. Similarly, during the first half of the 20th century, most archaeological interest in the so-called historic or ethnographic periods did not serve the goal of studying those periods on their own terms; rather they were used as cultural analogies for the more ancient past. This direct historical approach, pioneered by anthropologists such as Waldo Wedel (1938) and Julian Steward (1942), helped take archaeologists backward in time, but it did not encourage them to look forward, to link the "pre-contact" Native American societies with the ethnographic or even present communities of those descendants. Nor did it cultivate a sustained interest in these colonial periods for the sake of understanding colonialism.

Only with the formal appearance of American historical archaeology in the late 1960s did such "text-aided" periods take on more significance. Even then, Native American sites garnered only minor attention in the burgeoning subfield for the next two decades (for exceptions, see Deagan 1983; Deetz 1963). Not until the buildup to the Columbian Quincentennial in 1992, which marked the 500 years since Columbus's presumed "discovery" of the New World for

Europeans, did a sustained and deepening archaeology of Native Americans in the post-Columbian world take hold (see Thomas 1989, 1990, 1991). The more than 15 years since that time have seen an extensive, pancontinental literature develop that has filled in empirical detail, developed new methodological and theoretical approaches, and begun to synthesize larger issues, particularly during the last decade (e.g., Blanton and King 2004; Carlson 2006; Cobb 2003; Ferris 2003; Jordan 2009; Lightfoot 1995, 2006; Loren 2004, 2008; Rothschild 2003, 2006; Rubertone 2000; Silliman 2004b, 2005; Wesson and Rees 2002).

Postcolonial Perspectives in North American Archaeology

Not all of the burgeoning literature over the last few decades has drawn on or contributed to postcolonial approaches to Native American history. Part of the reason lies in the prevalence of acculturation approaches, particularly up to 1992, that rely on a notion of cultures as having rigid boundaries, exchanging traits upon contact, and tending to change from one into another, usually trending from "Native American" to "European." Admittedly, many of these interpretations took hold before postcolonial approaches began to impact historical studies of colonialism across many fields in the humanities and social sciences. However, the legacies of acculturation remain today in many archaeological notions of culture contact (Loren 2008; Silliman 2005; Wilcox 2002) and in the widespread public belief that Native Americans did "acculturate" and by extension, did become something else—something less—than they had been during initial contacts and interactions with European settlers. This same notion of acculturation is rarely applied to Euro-Americans today, whose authenticity or claim to being cultural descendants of European colonists several centuries ago is never questioned. Even though the legacies of acculturation still permeate our terminologies and assumptions, the acculturation model or paradigm has been mostly laid to rest in colonial and "culture contact" studies (e.g., Carlson 2006; Cusick 1998; Deagan 1998; Lightfoot 1995; Ehrhardt 2005; Rubertone 2000).

Postcolonial approaches seek to examine culture from different angles, ones that avoid perpetuating colonial ideas of difference and essentialisms in their interpretations of the past or in understandings of the present. Rather than culture per se, they tend to emphasize the practices and discourses of identity, gender, labor, race, sexuality, and inequality that colonized and colonizer negotiated in the past and that permeate our understandings today. They emphasize social agency, and as a result, they view cultures, identities, and social relations as contextually malleable, historically situated, frequently hybrid, often ambiguous and discordant compared with simple colonial categories, and constituted, contested, and reproduced in daily practices and, as Thomas (1994) argues, in "projects." For this reason, the dichotomy between colonizer and colonized has less analytical usefulness than a more nuanced view that examines the social, political, economic, racial, and sexual vectors that both solidify and blur those boundaries, depending on the context (e.g., Hall 2000; Loren 2008; Stoler 1989; Thomas 1994; Voss 2005, 2008). Postcolonial approaches also specifically draw out the complexities and realities of Indigenous experiences in an interpretive and historical arena that often has sidelined or filtered such experiences through the words and eyes of those who attempted to dominate. These comprise the focus of this chapter.

Achieving postcolonial outcomes in the archaeology of Native North America during European colonialism and settler nationhood has required, and will continue to require, five components. They are (1) confronting difficult disciplinary histories; (2) rethinking how we practice archaeology today; (3) acknowledging positionality in politics and concepts; (4) recentering history on Native Americans; and (5) exploring cultural creativity and cultural production as strategies of continuity and change for Indigenous people. The rest of this chapter takes up these five aspects to outline the contours of postcolonial archaeologies that focus on Indigenous people in North America. The first three are treated in abbreviated form in one section, as they relate to history, method, theory, and practice. The fourth and, particularly, fifth elements occupy the remainder of the chapter, as a showcase for studies that have helped to develop, refine, and expand the postcolonial agenda in the historical archaeology of Native Americans.

Critical Approaches to History, Practice, and Positionality

For the sake of brevity, I have combined and summarized the first three elements here. The first element, confronting difficult disciplinary histories, involves unpacking the complex historical baggage that encases archaeological, anthropological, and colonial practices in North America, an issue handled by Atalay (this volume, chapter 4), Thomas (2000), and many others. We must come to terms with our own disciplinary and cultural histories and their relationships to colonialism before we can hope to craft new ones. The Native American Graves Protection and Repatriation Act (NAGPRA), passed as federal law in the United States in 1990 to facilitate the inventory and return of human remains and sacred objects to legally eligible Native American nations, reveals these necessary challenges. We also have to move beyond the angst over historical archaeology's rightful place in the study of Native American people, a move well underway thanks to the work of Carlson (2006), Lightfoot (1995, 2006), Rubertone (2000), and others, as well as to the greater presence of Native American studies in historical archaeology graduate programs in North America.

The second element concerns the ways that we produce archaeological and historical narratives. We have to rethink the participants, authorities, and processes, as well as how we deploy each of these to craft rigorous, sound, and helpful histories (Handsman and Lamb Richmond 1995; Silliman

2009a). In many ways, this has taken form in North America through decolonization and indigenous archaeology (Atalay 2006; Watkins 2000) and particularly through collaborative work (Colwell-Chanthaphonh and Ferguson 2007; Dongoske et al. 2000; Ferguson 1996; Ferguson and Colwell-Chanthaphonh 2006; Ferris 2003; Nicholas 1997; Peck et al. 2003; Silliman 2008; Watkins and Ferguson 2005). We also have to rethink how we talk about the historical processes of the post-Columbian era in North America. This requires paying close attention to our terminology, which not only carries our conceptual work but also conveys our research to the public and our various collaborators. For instance, we must be mindful of the dangers and limited usefulness of the term "culture contact" when we refer to the complex colonial relationships formed between Indigenous people and colonists in North America (Silliman 2005), the problems with "acculturation" (Cusick 1998; Deagan 1998; Lightfoot 1995), and uncritical notions of "site abandonment" or "cannibalism" (Watkins 2006). Similarly, others have used postcolonial perspectives to question the ways that archaeologists have talked about disease and demographic collapse in Native North America (Kelton 2004; Wilcox 2002) and have attributed environmental "causes," rather than colonial pressures, to Native American "acceptance" of Spanish missionization in southern California (Dartt-Newton and Erlandson 2006).

A third component emphasizes the positionality of archaeologists today. It is one thing to research the impacts of colonialism on past peoples, but quite another to research it from the perspective of seeking to intervene in the present. This intervention may involve revisiting research ethics, tracing historical legacies that impact contemporary people, questioning neocolonialism, contributing to social justice issues, working with descendant communities for their benefit, exposing dangerous heritage myths, or fostering respect for cultural, social, ethnic, gender, and other diversities. Most postcolonial approaches to North American archaeology have this present intervention as a motivating element, even though their archaeological and historical scholarship may be regarded as impeccable by any "objective" research standards. It is imperative that we cultivate and promulgate both.

Recentering History

As a counter to long-standing historiographic traditions that put colonial—or, more aptly, white—histories as the centerpiece of "real" history or national history, the fourth element of postcolonial approaches to archaeology involves placing Indigenous people in the foreground. For instance, although not with a postcolonial approach per se, Wesson (2001, 2002) has shown that the Creek of the American Southeast changed of their own accord during colonial periods in light of their own cultural and political trajectories. This does not mean making other actors or other processes disappear, but rather articulating histories at different nodes to emphasize Indigenous pasts as equal participants in larger histories. In fact, a postcolonial approach to Native North America during the last millennium *must* return colonialism to the picture so that we can better grapple with large-scale processes, small-scale agencies, contemporary legacies, and misleading terminology (Alexander 1998; Ferris 2003; Jordan 2009; Silliman 2005). In addition, archaeologists need to disabuse their colleagues and the general public of the view of Native history as solely tied to or disappearing in famous colonial battles or so-called Indian Wars. Rather than inaccurate "vanishing points" firmly set within such a perspective, long-term Indigenous histories stretch well before these calamitous events and, usually, well into present-day Indigenous communities (Scheiber and Mitchell 2010).

Recent archaeological and historical anthropological studies in the mid-Atlantic coastal region of North America have demonstrated the value in recentering the colonial past to highlight Native American histories. Studies have reframed the classic case of Jamestown, the first successful British colony on the east coast of North America in 1607 with such heritage icons as Pocahontas and John Smith, to emphasize Native histories, actions, and cultural practices. Hantman (1990) initiated this trend by situating Jamestown not just in British colonial history, but in the history of the Native Americans in the tidewater and piedmont areas of the Chesapeake Bay of Virginia. Through this, he could piece together the broader relationships—political and economic—between the Powhatan and the Monacan. Recent work by Gallivan (2004, 2007) has developed further the understanding of Native landscape and cultural life for 400 years prior to the early 17th-century British colony, a successful move based on recentering history within colonialism and its legacies but away from colonists themselves. In addition, Mallios (2006) has recentered history in the Chesapeake with respect to the Native American responses to the first and last Spanish settlement at Ajacan (1570–1572), the failed English colony at Roanoke (1584–1590), and the initial British occupation of Jamestown (1607–1612). The key element that charted the trajectory of these encounters for Mallios was cultural differences in gift-giving and commodity exchange, transgressions that led to violence, local competition, and tense misunderstandings. Even though these models cannot account for the colonial system that developed afterward, the microhistories analyzed by Mallios, in the tradition of Sahlins (1981, 1985), go a long way toward understanding cultural conflict in these first few years of colonial encounters.

Cultural Creativity and Production

The fifth aspect draws on recentered history in an explicit acknowledgment that colonial contexts produce culture and history as much as they destroy it. This is not an apology for colonialism. Rather, it is a dual recognition: first, that talking about colonialism as a process does not translate perforce into only destruction and victimization; and second, that those communities surviving the European/Euro-American attempts at domination, capitalist penetration, physical and spiritual violence, racism, and dispossession could only continue as a result of cultural production and reproduction in these difficult times. To deny the persistence of history-making and the continuity of cultural trajectories during colonialism is to sever contemporary Native American communities from their rightful pasts, to contribute to public perceptions of inauthenticity and disappearance, and to inscribe colonialism with success and finality.

This component also requires that a postcolonial perspective on Indigenous history in North America foster an appreciation for local scales, microhistories, and nuances in context and action. This does not minimize the importance of macroscale processes, such as looking at colonialism from a comparative perspective (e.g., Gosden 2004; Lightfoot 2005; Stein 2005), but it does require making sure that these larger processes, if not also narratives, are grounded in or at least juxtaposed with a smaller scale—the one that people live through in their daily lives. Herein lies the fundamental ambiguity in past cultural lives and in present attempts to render them through material culture. Sometimes these are accessible through a close reading of archival documents, but often, these Indigenous lives are more visible in the houses, tools, food, trash, images, and stories they left behind, frequently unfiltered through the eyes of literate Europeans and Euro-Americans, although perhaps affected by their presence. These social practices maneuver through the labyrinth that anthropologists try to capture with concepts such as resistance, domination, residence, accommodation, acquiescence, hybridity, creolization, and ethnogenesis, frequently doing so through complex dimensions of gender, age, status, ethnicity, sexuality, and more. As the following cases illustrate, rarely is one of these anthropological terms sufficient to capture the explicitly strategic and implicitly mundane ways that people cope with and make meaning in their social worlds.

Studies of Native American cemeteries from the colonial period—when coupled with other site data, proper respect for ancestral remains, and the blessing of tribal descendants—have illuminated some of the ways that postcolonial approaches to cultural identity, practice, and agency have been successful in North American archaeology. Once attributed to the process of acculturation and assimilation, the changes documented in mortuary goods, burial orientation, grave shape, body treatment, and coffin use can reveal a more nuanced view of cultural hybridity and continuity. Paul Prince (2002) has shown that the Kimsquit, a Bella Coola nation on the Northwest Coast, began to adopt more "European" materials from the mid-19th to the early 20th century as a result of increased missionary and capitalist pressures beyond what they first experienced with British, Russian, and American traders in the preceding century. This adoption did not signal acculturation, but rather new avenues for emphasizing long-standing cultural "principles of rank, extended family, and group identity" in mortuary goods, memorials, and spatial configurations (Prince 2002: 53).

On the opposite side of the continent in southern New England, Patricia Rubertone (2001) approached a 17th-century Rhode Island Narragansett cemetery with a nuanced look at gender and age to tease apart the cultural practices surrounding lifestyle in an otherwise rapidly changing colonial world. She found that introduced and traditional materials were blended in such a way as to promote cultural continuity and community survival rather than to signal radical changes through new materials acquisition (see other discussions in Nassaney 1989, 2000; Rubertone 1989; Turnbaugh 1993). Nearby in southeastern Massachusetts, an 18th-century Christian Wampanoag cemetery in Dartmouth reveals another permutation of Native agency and cultural practice in colonial New England that comes from complicating the homogeneity of colonizer and colonized (Hodge 2005). With explicit postcolonial intent, Christina Hodge (2005) provides a counterpoint to those Native cemeteries in which grave goods are used to demarcate Native ceremonialism and culture from neighboring Anglo-Americans. In this case, this Wampanoag community cemetery had interments almost indistinguishable from neighboring Anglo, particularly Quaker, cemeteries: no mortuary goods, no clothing but use of shrouds and shroud pins, use of headstone and footstone markers, and highly variable grave shaft orientations. Hodge (2005) discusses how the cemetery reveals the ability of Native Americans to hybridize, mimic, appropriate, and lay ancestral claim to community in a subversion of colonialism's dominant narratives.

The case in 16th- and 17th-century Spanish "La Florida" in the southeastern United States offers another variation on the intersection of religious conversion, community life, and cultural continuity for Native Americans. Bonnie McEwan (2001) recently synthesized a wealth of cemetery data from Spanish missions across the modern states of Florida and Georgia and determined that the burials, in general, suggested strong connections between the deceased (or their buriers) and Catholic practices, even when mortuary goods were interred in the graves. She argues that Spanish Catholicism may have been more tolerated among local Native populations than such other colonial institutions as secular towns, military outposts, or labor requirements under *recomienda* and *repartimiento* (McEwan 2001). In part, this may reflect individual agency in Apalachee, Guale, and Timucua communities, but it may also be a feature encouraged by traditional Native leaders who used Spanish missions as a way to bolster their own power, even asking for friars to establish missions in their areas (e.g., McEwan 2001; Scarry and McEwan 1995). Either way, the power of this cultural syncretism is perhaps most visible in the Talimali Band of Apalachee Indians of today in Mobile, Alabama: practicing Catholics, they reside there as a result of the British expulsion of the Spanish from Florida in the early 1700s (McEwan 2001: 642).

Discussing cemeteries, particularly interments, leads to a focus on the body as a social and physical site where many of these negotiated practices and discourses take form. Diana Loren's (2000, 2001, 2003, 2008) work has captured the powerful interpretive potential of postcolonial perspectives when applied to archaeology, documentary evidence, and imagery dating to the early periods of Spanish and French colonization in the lower Mississippi River Valley. She describes the ways that Native American and French settlers, both as subjects of a colonial empire, used clothing not to mirror pre-established cultural identities, but to negotiate their positions through mixed dress and fashion—their "social skins"—in the contentious and equivocal process of "becoming colonial" (Loren 2001). Herein lay the potential for social agency, crossing boundaries, inconsistencies between colonial rule and colonial practice, contestations of the rigid colonial race/blood classifications, and engagements with ethnic, racial, sexual, and gender identities. This was particularly salient for "creoles" in the arena of household and bodily practices at the frontiers of Native American, French, and Spanish life in the region (Loren 2000); for Native Americans, "self-fashioning" in French dress to create new political identities in colonial Louisiana despite, or because of, colonial laws that attempted to regulate bodies and dress (Loren 2003); and for Native Americans and Spanish, negotiations of racialized *casta* categories of identity (Loren 2007).

Still other archaeological approaches to Native cultures and histories in colonial North America focus on the practices of households and gender. As Michael Nassaney (2004: 338) notes, understanding gender is important, but someone's experience of gender in colonial New England, or elsewhere, also varies as a function of age, status, and social group (see also Rothschild 2006). These social vectors, while not often considered through an explicitly postcolonial perspective, can be seen in the themes and interpretive schemes implicitly drawn from it or can contribute to it directly. At the 19th-century Russian colony of Ross on the northern California coast, Lightfoot and his colleagues (1998) have examined the ways that Native Alaskan men (who were brought on Russian merchant ships from Alaska) and California Indian women (who resided locally, near the settlement) negotiated the cultural and gender identities in village layout, food practices, and material culture of a multi-ethnic living area just outside the Russian stockade. While some practices indicate a reliance on material and spatial comforts for the diverse Indigenous social agents in contact at this mercantile outpost, others reveal the ways that households forged new or composite identities in this colonial milieu.

Farther north on the Oregon coast, in the decades following Russia's departure from California in the 1840s and well into the 20th century, Native women frequently developed inter-ethnic unions, but this time with white settlers (Tveskov 2007). However, the material, symbolic, and often subversively quiet ways of maintaining Native American heritage played out here as well. Although marrying white settlers, living in regular Euro-American homes, and attending Christian churches, these Indigenous mothers taught their children—through oral histories, ties to land, and the foods in their meals—that they were Indians (Tveskov 2007: 438). This accounts for how the 20th-century "revitalization" of certain groups, such as the Coos, Coquille, and Shasta, ties directly to elongated cultural strands across generations, through houses, and within communities.

Even farther north in Arctic Alaska, Lisa Frink (2005, 2006, 2007) has examined the ways that men and women confronted the Russian and successive American colonial fronts extending from the 18th to the 20th century. Her key point is that these men and women operated as "invested factions" (Frink 2006: 111) rather than as communities, a factor that led to divergent strategies when communities and individuals, women and men, young and old, confronted new economies or religious orders in an expanding colonial world in Alaska. She skillfully shows how Yup'ik Eskimo women lost access to one another as partners in learning, in social life, and in the economy, as well as to the mercantilist economy of the 19th century, when long-standing village tunnels were dismantled (Frink 2006). Frink (2007) also discusses the gendered impacts that occurred when storage was shifted from inside to outside the village house, thereby removing women from control over surplus subsistence products (furs, fish, and oil) and placing men in control over colonial market commodities in a patriarchal Anglo-American economic system. Frink's research is particularly relevant for this chapter, not only because it engages with postcolonial ideas about identity, gender, and agency for Native Alaskans, but also because her original, conventional excavation plan was reshaped into an array of spatial analyses, site surveys, oral histories, and ethnographic studies as a result of discussions with Yup'ik "hosts" who did not want extensive excavations conducted on their sites (Frink 2007: 367).

A focus on gendered social agents maneuvering in complex colonial worlds has salience in a diversity of studies that draw implicitly on postcolonial ideas. At the far northern reach of Spanish and Mexican-Californian settlements just north of San Francisco Bay, I found that Native men and women dealt differently with their laboring tasks on a 19th-century Mexican-Californian *rancho* (Silliman 2004a). Implements of women's labor appeared more frequently than those of men in residential debris, perhaps denoting different identity attachments to practices as a way to stake claims in the colonial labor regime. Individuals, perhaps men, also went to great lengths to procure and use obsidian as raw material for tool manufacture despite the availability of metal tools, a strategy that involves active choice among technological alternatives and likely statements about reformulated identities (Silliman 2001, 2003). As such, continuing to use lithic technology denoted change, rather than stasis or conservatism.

In 17th-century New England, Native women's negotiations of British and Dutch colonialism can be seen in material ways. Changes in pottery decoration to include certain rim decorations and greater numbers of effigy pestles seem to signal a symbolic investment in objects that not only represented but also facilitated women's production (Nassaney 2004; see also Nassaney and Volmar 2003). Tools for producing *wampum* (shell beads) and white ball clay pipes (for tobacco smoking) were found in several cemeteries, as well as in oral histories, indicating that women may have had access to both of these practices, something that pre-"contact" (that is, Late Woodland) women may not have had (Nassaney 2000, 2004). The incentive for smoking seems likely to have been a case of individuals, women or otherwise, seeking access to greater spiritual power as a challenge to male exclusivity, European infiltration, or both (Nassaney 2004, 2005). Nassaney notes that "they point to successful strategies of accommodation in a frequently hostile political environment that involved not merely the persistence of ancient practices and beliefs but active and creative responses that promoted social, biological, and cultural viability" (2004: 359). Herein, one may see both change and continuity in material practices that denote survivability of an Indigenous community. Using explicit postcolonial perspectives on materiality, practice, and social memory, my own research has recently developed similar insights for 18th- and 19th-century Native Americans in this same region who used market goods and "European" building practices to persist and to maintain community on a colonial Indian reservation (Silliman 2009b).

As illustrated in New England, the realm of cultural symbols, whether "artistic" or "religious," offers additional avenues for postcolonial visions of colonial-period Native histories. On the Pacific Northwest Coast, the Haida mediated their relationships with colonists through the production of particular kinds of imagery. Robert Paynter and Paul Mullins (2000) situate the production of Haida art in the negotiations among artists, consumers, and the larger colonial front. Depicting Europeans on Haida argillite objects in the first two-thirds of the 19th century and then dropping these representations later in the 19th century at a time when anthropologists and tourists alike sought "primitive art" reveals something other than a gauge of acculturation or aesthetic fads (see Brotherton 2000 for a discussion of Tlingit shamanic masks). As Paynter and Mullins point out, "for the Haida, trade goods likely were neither wholesale resistance nor covert cultural tradition; instead, they were a constant production whose stylistic shifts confronted, mediated, or evaded the material and social dynamism of colonization in the Queen Charlotte Islands" (2000: 81).

Interesting symbolic inversions and identity negotiations played out in the Pueblo Revolt period (1680–1692) in the American Southwest, a famous case of active resistance by the pueblo-dwelling agriculturalists of New Mexico who drove out the Spanish missionaries and other settlers for about 12 years (Preucel 2002). As Matthew Liebmann (2002) has argued, the Puebloans sought to remake themselves following the expulsion of the Spanish with nods both to pre-Spanish tradition and to colonial Catholic imagery. That is, they remade themselves just as they continued to be themselves, by incorporating some elements of Christian imagery. They did this not as an emblem of acculturative defeat, but as a declaration of how they might change to remain who they were in opposition to the Spanish. The same kind of process of remaking and resistance, albeit framed through slightly different material and social channels, could be seen with the Hopi after the destruction of the village of Awat'ovi in 1700 (Whiteley 2002). In both cases, what becomes visible is the nature of ethnicity and pan-Puebloism as a social process rather than a mapping of bounded colonial categories (Wilcox 2002: 174–176; 2009).

Conclusion

This chapter has provided a selective review of archaeology of the so-called contact, post-contact, colonial, and historic periods of North America with an eye toward highlighting the contributions of postcolonial theory. The full integration of postcolonial perspectives in the archaeological study of Indigenous people in North America has not been achieved, but the groundwork is in place to support those diverse theoretical structures. To end this chapter, I offer five points that not only capture the core issues brought to the fore in archaeological studies by postcolonial thinking, but that also can serve as guides for future interpretive refinement.

First, cultural practices and identities are *real* rather just a product of discourse, as some postmodern positions would imply. They are not "real" in the reified, bounded, and imposed ways that colonial categorization stipulates. Instead, they are real in the lived, negotiated, and material ways that social agents experience their existence as individuals, subgroups (or invested factions), and communities.

Second, we need to maintain (or return) our focus to colonialism as a complex, multiscalar, historical process operating throughout the last few centuries in Native North America, with poignant legacies today. At the same time, we must keep focusing on long-term Indigenous histories that set the stage for cultural action or that recognize Indigenous groups who maintained autonomy, economic viability, or political power—that is, were not colonized—for decades, even when colonial forces were on their doorstep.

Third, when used alone or simplistically, the labels of "colonizer" and "colonized" (or similarly broad terms such as "European" and "Native") do not capture social reality in colonial contexts with enough nuances. Even though colonialism was a powerful force orchestrated at times by very powerful colonizers, adhering to dichotomous thinking obscures the complex interdigitations of people themselves and the social vectors of gender, race, ethnicity, class, sexuality, and others that comprise them.

Fourth, sometimes people change to stay the same. The adoption of European material goods by Indigenous groups once meant acculturation to archaeologists (and other observers), but postcolonial ideas of mimicry and appropriation have revealed that these adoptions may well be strategies of holding together communities in the face of colonial pressures. This reminds us that our preferences for seeing material culture as an index of identity change may be more ambiguous than we have cared to admit.

Fifth, an assessment of changing or staying the same must take into account social agency and scale, since neither choice is possible without agency, and neither is identifiable without examining the rates and temporalities of social action as well as unintended consequences (Silliman 2009b). We must also ask who is assessing change or continuity and with what purpose, for this is a question of great political import.

Note

1. I do not include here a period termed "postcolonial" to refer to these centuries of Native American entanglements with European and Euro-American colonists and settlers (*contra* Stojanowski 2005). There was nothing "post" about the colonialism of these periods, whether in 17th-century Spanish Florida or in the late 19th century on the Great Plains. Instead, in the chapter I reserve this term to refer to particular political and theoretical frameworks.

References

Alexander, R. T. 1998. Afterward: Toward an archaeological theory of culture contact, in J. G. Cusick (ed.), *Studies in Culture Contact: Interaction, Culture Change, and Archaeology*, pp. 476–495. Occasional Papers, No. 25. Carbondale: Center for Archaeological Investigations, Southern Illinois University.

Atalay, S. 2006. Indigenous archaeology as decolonizing practice, in "Decolonizing—Efforts to Transform a Discipline," *The American Indian Quarterly* 30 (3–4): 280–310.

Blanton, D. B., and King, J. A. (eds.). 2004. *Indian and European Contact in Context: The Mid-Atlantic Region.* Gainesville: University Press of Florida.

Brotherton, B. 2000. Tlingit human masks as documents of culture, change and continuity, in M. S. Nassaney and E. S. Johnson (eds.), *Interpretations of Native North American Life: Material Contributions to Ethnohistory*, pp. 358–397. Gainesville: University Press of Florida.

Carlson, C. C. 2006. Indigenous historic archaeology of the 19th-century Secwepemc village at Thompson's River Post, Kamloops, British Columbia. *Canadian Journal of Archaeology* 30: 193–250.

Cobb, C. (ed.). 2003. *Stone Tool Technology in the Contact Era.* Tuscaloosa: University of Alabama Press.

Colwell-Chanthaphonh, C., and Ferguson, T. J. 2007. *Collaboration in Archaeological Practice: Engaging Descendant Communities.* Walnut Creek, CA: AltaMira Press.

Cusick, J. G. 1998. Historiography of acculturation: An evaluation of concepts and their application in archaeology, in J. G. Cusick (ed.), *Studies in Culture Contact: Interaction, Culture Change, and Archaeology*, pp. 126–145. Occasional Papers, No. 25. Carbondale: Center for Archaeological Investigations, Southern Illinois University.

Dartt-Newton, D., and Erlandson, J. M. 2006. Little choice for the Chumash:

Colonialism, cattle, and coercion in Mission Period California. *American Indian Quarterly* 30 (3/4): 416–430.

Deagan, K. 1983. *Spanish St. Augustine: The Archaeology of a Colonial Creole Community*. New York: Academic Press.

——. 1998. Transculturation and Spanish American ethnogenesis: The archaeological legacy of the quincentenary, in J. G. Cusick (ed.), *Studies in Culture Contact: Interaction, Culture Change, and Archaeology*, pp. 23–43. Occasional Papers, No. 25. Carbondale: Center for Archaeological Investigations, Southern Illinois University.

——. 2003. Colonial origins and colonial transformations in Spanish America. *Historical Archaeology* 37 (4): 3–13.

Deetz, J. F. 1963. Archaeological investigations at La Purísima Mission. *UCLA Archaeological Survey Annual Report* 5: 165–191.

Dongoske, K. E., Aldenderfer, M. S., and Doehner, K. (eds.). 2000. *Working Together: Native Americans and Archaeologists*. Washington, DC: Society for American Archaeology.

Ehrhardt, K. L. 2005. *European Metal in Native Hands: Rethinking Technological Change, 1640–1683*. Tuscaloosa: University of Alabama Press.

Ferguson, T. J. 1996. Native Americans and the practice of archaeology. *Annual Review of Anthropology* 25: 63–79.

Ferguson, T. J., and Colwell-Chanthaphonh, C. 2006. *History is in the Land: Multivocal Tribal Traditions in Arizona's San Pedro Valley*. Tucson: University of Arizona Press.

Ferris, N. 2003. Between colonial and indigenous archaeologies: Legal and extralegal ownership of the archaeological past in North America. *Canadian Journal of Archaeology* 27: 154–190.

Frink, L. 2005. Gender and the hide production process in colonial western Alaska, in L. Frink and K. Weedman (eds.), *Gender and Hide Production*, pp. 89–104. Walnut Creek, CA: AltaMira Press.

——. 2006. Social identity and the Yup'ik Eskimo village tunnel system in precolonial and colonial western Alaska, in W. Ashmore et al. (eds.), *Integrating the Diversity of 21st Century Anthropology: The Life and Intellectual Legacies of Susan Kent*, pp. 109–125. Archaeological Papers of the American Anthropological Association 16. Washington, DC: American Anthropological Association.

——. 2007. Storage and status in precolonial and colonial coastal western Alaska. *Current Anthropology* 48 (3): 349–374.

Gallivan, M. D. 2004. Reconnecting the contact period and late prehistory: Household and community dynamics in the James River Basin, in D. R. Blanton and J. A. King (eds.), *Indian and European Contact in Context: The Mid-Atlantic Region*, pp. 22–46. Gainesville: University Press of Florida.

——. 2007. Powhatan's Werowocomoco: Constructing place, polity, and personhood in the Chesapeake, C.E. 1200–C.E. 1609. *American Anthropologist* 109 (1): 85–100.

Gosden, C. 2004. *Archaeology and Colonialism: Cultural Contact from 5000 B.C. to the*

Present. Cambridge: Cambridge University Press.

Hall, M. 2000. *Archaeology and the Modern World: Colonial Transcripts in South Africa and the Chesapeake*. London: Routledge Press.

Handsman, R. G., and Lamb Richmond, T. 1995. Confronting colonialism: The Mahican and Scaghticoke peoples and us, in T. C. Patterson and P. Schmidt (eds.), *Making Alternative Histories: The Practice of Archaeology and History in Non-Western Settings*, pp. 87–117. School of American Research Advanced Seminar Series. Santa Fe: SAR Press.

Hantman, J. 1990. Between Powhatan and Quirank: Reconstructing Monacan culture and history in the context of Jamestown. *American Anthropologist* 92 (3): 676–690.

Hodge, C. J. 2005. Faith and practice at an early-eighteenth-century Wampanoag burial ground: The Waldo Farm site in Dartmouth, Massachusetts. *Historical Archaeology* 39 (4): 73–94.

Jordan, K. A. 2009. Colonies, colonialism, and cultural entanglement: The archaeology of post-Columbian intercultural relations, in T. Majewski and D. Gaimster (eds.), *International Handbook of Historical Archaeology*. New York: Springer.

Kelton, P. 2004. Avoiding the smallpox spirits: Colonial epidemics and southeastern Indian survival. *Ethnohistory* 51 (1): 45–71.

Liebmann, M. J. 2002. Signs of power and resistance: The (re)creation of Christian imagery and identities in the Pueblo Revolt era, in R. W. Preucel (ed.), *Archaeologies of the Pueblo Revolt: Identity, Meaning, and Renewal in the Pueblo World*, pp. 132–144. Albuquerque: University of New Mexico Press.

Lightfoot, K. G. 1995. Culture contact studies: Redefining the relationship between prehistoric and historical archaeology. *American Antiquity* 60 (2): 199–217.

——. 2003. Russian colonization: The implications of mercantile colonial practices in the North Pacific. *Historical Archaeology* 37 (4): 14–28.

——. 2004. *Indians, Missionaries, and Merchants: The Legacy of Colonialism on the California Frontiers*. Berkeley: University of California Press.

——. 2005. The archaeology of colonization: California in cross-cultural perspective, in G. J. Stein (ed.), *The Archaeology of Colonial Encounters*, pp. 207–235. Santa Fe: SAR Press.

——. 2006. Missions, gold, furs, and manifest destiny: Rethinking an archaeology of colonialism for western North America, in M. Hall and S. W. Silliman (eds.), *Historical Archaeology*, pp. 272–292. London: Blackwell Publishing.

Lightfoot, K. G., Martinez, A., and Schiff, A. M. 1998. Daily practice and material culture in pluralistic social settings: An archaeological study of culture change and persistence from Fort Ross, California. *American Antiquity* 63 (2): 199–222.

Loren, D. D. 2000. The intersections of colonial policy and colonial practice: Creolization on the 18th-century Louisiana/Texas frontier. *Historical Archaeology* 34 (3): 85–98.

——. 2001. Social skins: Orthodoxies and practices of dressing in the early colonial Lower Mississippi Valley. *Journal of Social Archaeology* 1 (2): 172–189.

——. 2003. Refashioning a body politic in colonial Louisiana. *Cambridge Archaeological Journal* 13 (2): 231–237.

——. 2004. Creolization in the French and Spanish colonies, in T. R. Pauketat and D. D. Loren (eds.), *North American Archaeology*, pp. 297–318. London: Blackwell Publishing.

——. 2007. Corporeal concerns: Eighteenth-century Casta paintings and colonial bodies in Spanish Texas. *Historical Archaeology* 41 (1): 23–36.

——. 2008. In Contact: *Bodies and Spaces in the Sixteenth- and Seventeenth-Century Eastern Woodlands*. Lanham, MD: AltaMira Press.

Mallios, S. 2006. *The Deadly Politics of Giving: Exchange and Violence at Ajacan, Roanoke, and Jamestown*. Tuscaloosa: University of Alabama Press.

McEwan, B. 2001. The spiritual conquest of La Florida. *American Anthropologist* 103 (3): 633–644.

Moussette, M. 2003. An encounter in the Baroque Age: French and Amerindians in North America. *Historical Archaeology* 37 (4): 29–39.

Mullins, P. R., and Paynter, R. 2000. Representing colonizers: An archaeology of creolization, ethnogenesis, and indigenous material culture among the Haida. *Historical Archaeology* 34 (3): 73–84.

Nassaney, M. S. 1989. An epistemological enquiry into some archaeological and historical interpretations of 17th century Native American-European relations, in S. J. Shennan (ed.), *Archaeological Approaches to Cultural Identity*, pp. 76–93. London: Unwin Hyman.

——. 2000. Archaeology and oral tradition in tandem: Interpreting Native American ritual, ideology, and gender relations in contact-period southeastern New England, in M. S. Nassaney and E. S. Johnson (eds.), *Interpretations of Native North American Life: Material Contributions to Ethnohistory*, pp. 412–431. Gainesville: University Press of Florida.

——. 2004. Native American gender politics and material culture in seventeenth-century southeastern New England. *Journal of Social Archaeology* 4 (3): 334–367.

——. 2005. Men and women, pipes and power in native New England, in S. M. Rafferty and R. Mann (eds.), *The Culture of Smoking: Recent Developments in the Archaeology of Smoking Pipes*, pp. 125–142. Knoxville: University of Tennessee Press.

Nassaney, M. S., and Volmar, M. 2003. Lithic artifacts in seventeenth-century native New England, in C. Cobb (ed.), *Stone Tool Traditions in the Contact Era*, pp. 78–93. Tuscaloosa: University of Alabama Press.

Nicholas, G. P. 1997. Education and empowerment: Archaeology with, for, and by the Shuswap Nation, British Columbia, in G. P. Nicholas and T. D. Andrews (eds.), *At a Crossroads: Archaeology and First Peoples in Canada*, pp. 85–104. Burnaby, B.C.: Archaeology Press.

Peck, T., Siegfried, E., and Oetelaar, G. A. (eds.). 2003. Indigenous people and archaeology: Honouring the past, discussing the present, building for the future. *Pro-*

ceedings of the 32nd Annual Chacmool Conference. Calgary: Archaeological Association of the University of Calgary.

Preucel, R. W. (ed.). 2002. *Archaeologies of the Pueblo Revolt: Identity, Meaning, and Renewal in the Pueblo World.* Albuquerque: University of New Mexico Press.

Prince, P. 2002. Cultural coherency and resistance in historic-period Northwest Coast mortuary practices at Kimsquit. *Historical Archaeology* 36 (4): 50–65.

Rothschild, N. A. 2003. *Colonial Encounters in a Native American Landscape: The Spanish and Dutch in North America.* Washington, DC: Smithsonian Institution Press.

——. 2006. Colonialism, material culture, and identity in the Rio Grande and Hudson River valleys. *International Journal of Historical Archaeology* 10 (1): 73–108.

Rubertone, P. 1989. Archaeology, colonialism, and 17th-century Native America: Towards an alternative interpretation, in R. Layton (ed.), *Conflict in the Archaeology of Living Traditions*, pp. 32–45. London: Unwin Hyman.

——. 2000. The historical archaeology of Native Americans. *Annual Review of Anthropology* 29: 425–446.

——. 2001. *Grave Undertakings: An Archaeology of Roger Williams and the Narragansett Indians.* Washington, DC: Smithsonian Institution Press.

Sahlins, M. 1981. Historical Metaphors and Mythical Realities: Structure in the Early History of the Sandwich Islands Kingdom. Ann Arbor: University of Michigan Press.

——. 1985. *Islands of History.* Chicago: University of Chicago Press.

Scarry, J. F., and McEwan, B. G. 1995. Domestic architecture in Apalachee Province: Apalachee and Spanish residential styles in the late prehistoric and early historic period Southeast. *American Antiquity* 60 (3): 482–495.

Scheiber, L. J., and Mitchell, M. (eds.) 2009. *Across a Great Divide: Continuity and Change in Native North American Societies, A.D. 1400–1900.* Amerind Studies in Archaeology 4. Tucson: University of Arizona Press.

Silliman, S. W. 2001. Agency, practical politics, and the archaeology of culture contact. *Journal of Social Archaeology* 1 (2): 184–204.

——. 2003. Using a rock in a hard place: Native American lithic practices in colonial California, in C. Cobb (ed.), *Stone Tool Technology in the Contact Era*, pp. 127–150. Tuscaloosa: University of Alabama Press.

——. 2004a. *Lost Laborers in Colonial California: Native Americans and the Archaeology of Rancho Petaluma.* Tucson: University of Arizona Press.

——. 2004b. Social and physical landscapes of contact, in T. R. Pauketat and D. D. Loren (eds.), *North American Archaeology*, pp. 273–296. London: Blackwell Publishing.

——. 2005. Culture contact or colonialism? Challenges in the archaeology of Native North America. *American Antiquity* 70 (1): 55–74.

——. 2009a. Blurring for clarity: Archaeology as hybrid practice. In P. Bikoulis, D. Lacroix, and M. Peuramaki-Brown (eds.), *Decolonizing Archaeology: Archaeology and the Post-colonial Critique.* Proceedings of the

39th Annual Chacmool Conference (2006), pp. 15–25. Calgary: Archaeological Association of the University of Calgary.

———. 2009b. Change and continuity, practice and memory: Native American persistence in colonial New England. *American Antiquity* 74 (2): 211–230.

Silliman, S. W. (ed.). 2008. *Collaborative Indigenous Archaeology at the Trowel's Edge: Exploring Methodology and Education in North American Archaeology*. Amerind Studies in Archaeology 2. Tucson: University of Arizona Press.

Stein, G. (ed.). 2005 *The Archaeology of Colonial Encounters*. Santa Fe, SAR Press.

Steward, J. 1942. The direct historical approach to archaeology. *American Antiquity* 7: 337–343.

Stojanowski, C. M. 2005. The bioarchaeology of identity in Spanish colonial Florida: Social and evolutionary transformation before, during, and after demographic collapse. *American Anthropologist* 107 (3): 417–431.

Stoler, A. L. 1989. Rethinking colonial categories: European communities and the boundaries of rule. *Comparative Studies in Society and History* 31 (3): 134–161.

Thomas, D. H. 2000. *Skull Wars: Kennewick Man, Archaeology, and the Battle for Native American Identity*. New York: Basic Books.

Thomas, D. H. (ed.). 1989. *Archaeological and Historical Perspectives on the Spanish Borderlands West*. Columbian Consequences, Vol. 1. Washington, DC: Smithsonian Institution Press.

———.1990. *Archaeological and Historical Perspectives on the Spanish Borderlands East*. Columbian Consequences, Vol. 2. Washington, DC: Smithsonian Institution Press.

———. 1991. *The Spanish Borderlands in Pan-American Perspective*. Columbian Consequences, Vol. 3. Washington, DC: Smithsonian Institution Press.

Thomas, N. 1994. *Colonialism's Culture: Anthropology, Travel, and Government*. Princeton: Princeton University Press.

Turnbaugh, W. A. 1993. Assessing the significance of European goods in seventeenth century Narragansett society, in J. D. Rogers and S. M. Wilson (eds.), *Ethnohistory and Archaeology: Approaches to Postcontact Change in the Americas*, pp. 133–160. New York: Plenum Press.

Tveskov, M. 2007. Social identity and culture change on the southern Northwest Coast. *American Anthropologist* 109 (3): 431–441.

Voss, B. L. 2005. From *Casta* to *Californio*: Social identity and the archaeology of culture contact. *American Anthropologist* 107 (3): 461–474.

———. 2008. *The Archaeology of Ethnogenesis: Race and Sexuality in Colonial San Francisco*. Berkeley: University of California Press.

Watkins, J. 2000. *Indigenous Archaeology: American Indian Values and Scientific Practice*. Walnut Creek, CA: AltaMira Press.

———. 2006. Communicating archaeology: Words to the wise. *Journal of Social Archaeology* 6 (1): 100–118.

Watkins, J., and Ferguson, T .J. 2005. Working with and working for Indigenous communities, in H. D. G. Maschner and C. Chippindale (eds.), *Handbook of Ar-*

chaeological Methods, Vol. 2, pp. 1372–1406. Walnut Creek, CA: AltaMira Press.

Wedel, W. R. 1938. The direct-historical approach in Pawnee archeology. *Smithsonian Miscellaneous Collections* 97 (7): 1–21.

Wesson, C. B. 2001. Creek and pre-Creek revisited, in T. R. Pauketat (ed.), *The Archaeology of Traditions: Agency and History Before and After Columbus*, pp. 94–106. Gainesville: University Press of Florida.

———. 2002. Prestige goods, symbolic capital, and social power in the protohistoric Southeast, in C. B. Wesson and M. A. Rees (eds.), *Between Contacts and Colonies: Archaeological Perspectives on the Protohistoric Southeast*, pp. 110–125. Tuscaloosa: University of Alabama Press

Wesson, C. B., and Rees, M. A. (eds.). 2002. *Between Contacts and Colonies: Archaeological Perspectives on the Protohistoric Southeast*. Tuscaloosa: University of Alabama Press.

Whiteley, P. J. 2002. Re-imagining Awat'ovi, in R. W. Preucel (ed.), *Archaeologies of the Pueblo Revolt: Identity, Meaning, and Renewal in the Pueblo World*, pp. 147–166. Albuquerque: University of New Mexico Press.

Wilcox, M. V. 2002. Social memory and the Pueblo Revolt: A postcolonial perspective, in R. W. Preucel (ed.), *Archaeologies of the Pueblo Revolt: Identity, Meaning, and Renewal in the Pueblo World*, pp. 167–179. Albuquerque: University of New Mexico Press.

———. 2009. *The Pueblo Revolt and the Mythology of Conquest: An Indigenous Archaeology of Contact*. Berkeley: University of California Press.

12

THE ARCHAEOLOGY OF HISTORICAL INDIGENOUS AUSTRALIA

Alistair Paterson

The roots of colonial Australia extend back into the 17th century, a past that continues to inspire debates across the nation's kitchens, universities, parliaments, and media. Matters of identity remain some of the most contested issues in the nation: in Australia the colonial past is important and will continue to be as long as we ask "how did we get here?" The contemporary importance of historical issues has been demonstrated in 2008 with an apology by the prime minister to Aboriginal Australians removed as children from their parents under official assimilation policies. The archaeology of the recent past, of the time since European and other settlers arrived, is important for providing a unique way of understanding the historical period and all its complexity. In this chapter, I aim to provide some historical depth to the archaeological study of Australian Indigenous people, as well as a focus on recent and particularly important archaeological work. This review is not comprehensive but illustrative, and more extensive studies are found elsewhere (for further overviews, see Harrison and Williamson 2002; Lilley 2000; Lydon and Ireland 2005; McGiven and Russell 2005; Murray 2004; Torrence and Clarke 2000; and Veth et al. 2008).

The Rise of Postcolonial Critique

Amateur archaeologists prior to the 1960s did little to critique the popular perception of Indigenous Australians as an unchanging isolated people (Murray and White 1981). With the advent of professionalism and the application of radiocarbon dating, archaeology revealed the great antiquity of human occupation and aspects of life on the Australian continent during the Pleistocene and

Holocene eras. While two early archaeological projects were concerned with historical sites related to Indigenous Australians (Allen 1969; Birmingham 1992), few others explicitly addressed this period of Indigenous life, although some evidence was recorded (e.g., Megaw 1968). The separation of archaeology into prehistoric and historical archaeology has complex causes (e.g., Colley and Bickford 1996), but in brief, prehistorians were concerned with the period prior to European arrival (except as a source for ethnographic analogy), and historical archaeologists remained largely concerned with non-Indigenous historical sites, with a major focus on European colonial activities and some attention to select ethnic groups (McGiven and Russell 2005; Paterson and Wilson 2000; Williamson and Harrison 2002: 2).

The last two decades have seen an increased body of work on historical contexts, in part fueled by (1) the demands of Indigenous people regarding heritage and archaeology (Langford 1983), which prompted the development of community archaeology and the participation of Indigenous Australians in archaeological research programs; (2) scholarly interest influenced by the work by Franz Fanon, Edward Said, and others in the results of colonialism and colonization taken up across a range of disciplines, including archaeology; and (3) interest elsewhere—particularly in North America and South America (Murray 2002: 214)—in cross-cultural encounters between Indigenous peoples and colonizing Europeans in the last half-millennium. The recent past is a period in which many Indigenous Australians have strong personal interest, for it may reveal information about immediate ancestors and Indigenous attachments to place. This is particularly significant for demonstration of Native Title, and for those attempting to understand the events of colonial and 20th-century Australia.

Across the continent, first encounters between Aboriginal people and outsiders took many forms, but were not limited to the interracial meetings between black and white people commonly described in the accounts of some explorers. Just as commonly, early encounters entailed coming across a flock of sheep being overlanded, seeing the smoke from a whaler's try-pot on the coast, finding trees blazed by explorers, viewing a rock engraving of a sailing ship, seeing the glint of an aircraft above the Western Desert, examining the flakes struck from glass bottles, or being stricken by a virus. Following these first encounters, Aboriginal people became enmeshed in the colonial world of settlers—although, it is important to point out, not necessarily in "history." Historical studies of colonial Australia, such as the work of Henry Reynolds (e.g., 1972, 1983, 1990) in reconstructing the Australian frontier and the nature and timing of cross-cultural interactions, have been particularly influential (and see Beckett 1958; Rowley 1970, 1971). Despite such research, many Aboriginal people and the actions that concerned them in "historical" Australia remained unreported, undescribed, and largely lost to us, unless accessed through people's memories or archaeological evidence. Archaeology's material- and place-based perspective is potentially critical to our understanding of Indigenous Australia, as a complement to Indigenous understandings and memories, as well as to historical analyses. Themes central to an understanding of the last few hundred years are amenable to archaeological research, such as European colonization, colonialism, cross-cultural encounters, and the continental-wide transformation of a nation of hunter-gatherers to a settler society replete with the social complexity inherent in such contexts.

The Archaeology of Culture Contact and Aboriginal History

Australia is a continental landmass of great environmental, cultural, and linguistic diversity. The pattern of Indigenous settlement and diversity results in part from the fact that rising sea levels at the end of the last Ice Age separated New Guinea, Tasmania, Kangaroo Island, Barrow Island, and many smaller islands around the Australian coastline (Figure 12.1) from the mainland.

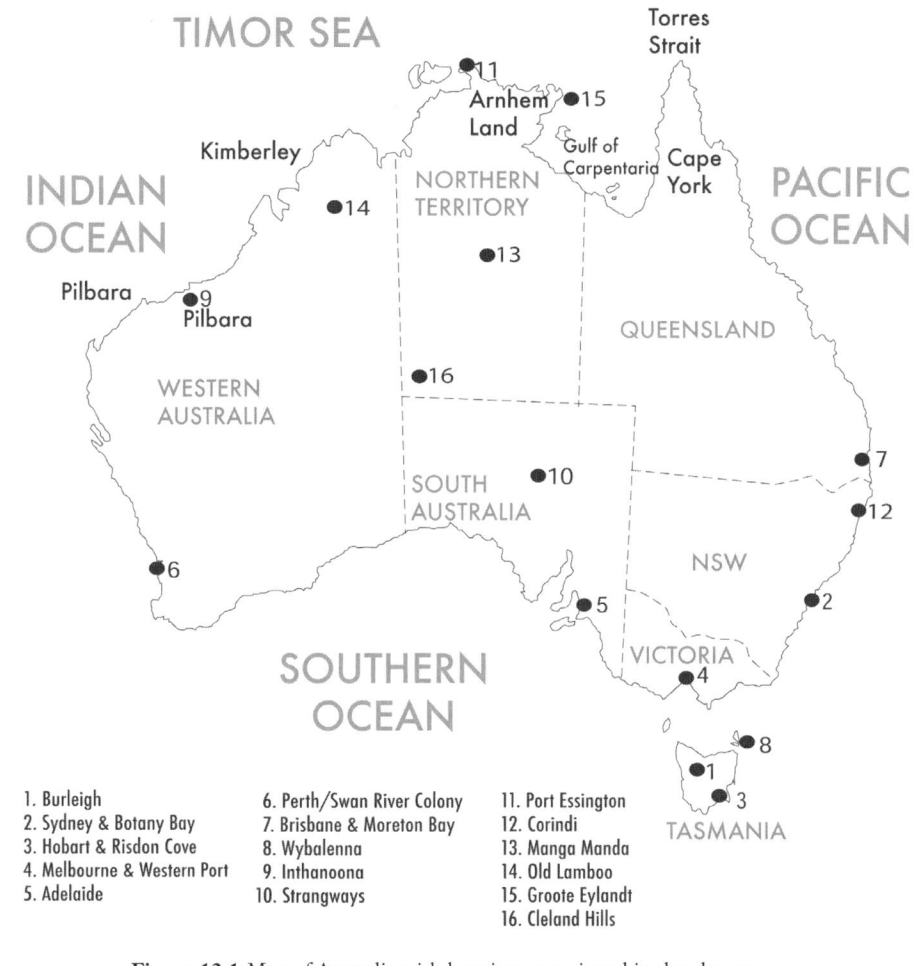

1. Burleigh
2. Sydney & Botany Bay
3. Hobart & Risdon Cove
4. Melbourne & Western Port
5. Adelaide
6. Perth/Swan River Colony
7. Brisbane & Moreton Bay
8. Wybalenna
9. Inthanoona
10. Strangways
11. Port Essington
12. Corindi
13. Manga Manda
14. Old Lamboo
15. Groote Eylandt
16. Cleland Hills

Figure 12.1 Map of Australia with locations mentioned in the chapter.

There is also environmental variation, from the temperate regions of southern Australia to the tropics of northern Australia, with areas of great aridity as seen in the range of deserts across the interior. At contact, Indigenous Australians were hunter-foragers, as well as environmental managers, as evidenced by practices like fire-stick farming and forms of intensive food collection.

The term "Aboriginal Australians" obscures the diversity of Indigenous Australians. Reference to regional groups—such as Torres Strait Islanders, Murri, Koori, Nyunger, Yolngu—and tribal groups allows for specific regional, linguistic, and cultural contexts to be made explicit (and see Arthur and Morphy 2005; Horton 1994).

Historical encounters between Indigenous Australians and outsiders preceded British colonization in 1788 (Mulvaney 1989). The best documented are of visiting Southeast Asian harvesters of *trepang* (also known as sea cucumber, or *bêche-de-mer*) which, when smoked and dried, were imported by China. The crews are commonly termed "Macassans" after the port of Macassar (Sulawesi), despite voyages originating from several islands (Madura, Flores, Timor, and Roti) with ethnically diverse crews. Archaeological remains of trepang-getting settlements on the coast and on offshore islands of northern Australia have been reported in the Gulf of Carpentaria, Arnhem Land (Baker 1984; Clarke 1994, 2000; Macknight 1976; Mitchell 1994), and the Kimberley (Crawford 1969; Morwood, and Hobbs 1997).[1]

This evidence reminds us that culture contact between Indigenous Australians and outsiders preceded European exploration and colonization. Indigenous people interacted with the Macassans, and the seafarers introduced new material culture, food, and ideas (possibly including the dugout canoe, as well as metal tools such as axes, cloth, fishhooks, pipes for tobacco, and beads). The archaeological record of cross-cultural interactions is reflected in rock art (Clarke and Frederick 2006), changes in settlement patterns and in intensity of site use to allow greater interaction with the Macassans during their seasonal visits (Clarke 2000; Mitchell 1994), the use of new material such as metal ax heads, and possible shifts in subsistence that accompanied new technology or patterns of settlement. In parts of northern Australia, these changes were accompanied by changes in symbolic systems and society, as well as in language. Trepang harvesting was only halted by the Australian government in the early 20th century.

The study of interactions between Indigenous Australians and outsiders has often been termed "contact archaeology," a term that has been critiqued for implying a focus on "first contact" rather than taking a longer perspective (Lightfoot 1995). However, in reality, most archaeologists using the term have set their frame wider, to take into account longer-term processes both preceding and following early interracial contacts. In this regard, Australians have developed approaches similar to those advocated in the Americas by Kent Lightfoot (1995) and Kathleen Deagan (1988), whose work recognizes the interpretive problems that arise from having disciplinary boundaries between prehistoric and historical archaeologies. As archaeologists move beyond models that draw a hard line at the point of cross-cultural contact, there may be no need for the term "contact." As an alternative, some argue that the term be subsumed into studies of colonialism (Gosden 2004; Silliman 2005; this volume, chapter 11). However, in the historical era in Australia, research centering on colonialism has tended to focus on the activities of Europeans and their descendants, rather than on external interactions.

From the 17th century onward, there were occasional contacts between European explorers and Indigenous people (Veth et al. 2008). Given the fleeting nature of exploration, few archaeological sites clearly reveal cross-cultural meetings between explorers and Aboriginal people; however, some rock art depicts these meetings (Bigourdan and McCarthy 2007; Silvester 1998). Some sites suggest early contact occurred prior to 1788; Dutch artifacts from the 1712 wreck of the Dutch East Indiaman *Zuytdorp* found in Aboriginal campsites on the cliffs of the nearby Western Australian coast (Morse 1988) may be evidence of Dutch survivors of the wreck, or Aboriginal salvage of material from the wreck.

European settlement in Australia was first initiated at Sydney Harbour in 1788 with the arrival of the First Fleet carrying convicts and their overseers. This and later settlements in coastal corners of the continent (such as Risdon Cove, Hobart, Moreton Bay, Norfolk Island, Albany, Port Essington, Western Port, and so on) established various communities of convicts and/or free settlers. While European explorers after 1600 were citizens of various European maritime powers, the permanent colonists after 1788 were largely British. However, during the 18th and 19th centuries, the colonies included people from the British dominions, including many unwilling participants, such as Irish revolutionaries. Many European colonists also arrived, including Germans, Moravians, Spanish religious groups, and Italian mine workers. Chinese migrants have also left their mark on Australian history; their importance in mining and urban contexts has led to extensive study by historical archaeologists. Another important Asian element was the arrival of cameleers who came during the 19th century from a range of South Asian locations and were often described collectively as "Afghan." Many Indigenous Australians are of mixed descent (Stevens 1989).

Other nations in Australian waters were represented by American, British, and French whalers and sealers. The early whaling and sealing settlements were significant places for cross-cultural encounters between white male sealers (located well beyond the reach of colonial administrations) and Aboriginal Australians in Tasmania (Lawrence 2007), Victoria, South Australia, New South Wales, and Western Australia (Kostoglou et al. 1991; Lawrence and Staniforth 1998). Some Tasmanian Aboriginals became involved in the New Zealand whaling industry (Prickett 1993). Aboriginal women were often present at sealing stations, some under duress, where they were companions and workers (Russell 2007). Some historical accounts reveal these to be places of violence as well as of survival.

Russell reviews the evidence from Kangaroo Island and argues that here (and elsewhere in southern Australia) these communities can potentially be viewed as creolized communities (Russell 2005).

There are numerous types of sites relevant to the archaeological study of Indigenous history and culture contact. In some instances, sites have been studied as isolated examples of culture contact, ranging from small huts on the European frontier (Murray 1993) to First Government House in Sydney (McBryde 1989a, 1989b; Proudfoot 1990). In their survey of historical Aboriginal sites in the Bowen Basin region, Queensland, Godwin and L'Oste-Brown (2002) identified numerous contact site types from oral, historical, and archaeological sources. These include sites of early interracial meetings, massacre sites, Native Mounted Police camps, cemeteries and burials, Indigenous campsites at the fringes of European towns and on pastoral sheep and cattle stations, drover's camps (these were campsites used when moving stock across the region), rock art sites, scarred trees, ceremonial and spiritual places, travel routes, missions, and reserves established by authorities.

One significant factor within Aboriginal history in some parts of Australia is the pastoral industry. Large tracts of the continent were taken up by sheep and cattle pastoralists, and the need for cheap labor was often supplied by Aboriginal people in whose traditional country the pastoralists arrived. Pastoral stations were settings for both resistance and accommodation in varying degrees. Studies of Aboriginal people and pastoralists have occurred across the nation, from the Kimberley (Harrison 2004b; Smith 2000), Northern Territory (Head and Fullagar 1997; Paterson et al. 2003), central Australia (Paterson 2005, 2008), Queensland (Godwin and L'Oste-Brown 2002), New South Wales (Harrison 2004a), Victoria (Wolski 2001; Wolski and Loy 1999), and Tasmania (Murray 1993; Williamson 2002). At Burleigh in northwestern Tasmania, where bitter conflict arose between Tasmanians and Europeans, archaeological research on a rare outstation reveals how a settler's hut was abandoned by the British and then reoccupied in the 1820s by surviving Indigenous Tasmanians, as demonstrated through two distinct phases of site use (Williamson 2002). Other sites elsewhere in Australia suggest contemporary uses by Aboriginal people and Europeans, such as a small shepherd's outstation on Strangways Springs Station in central Australia, where in the 1860s or 1870s, shepherds were based to protect a flock from dingoes in the desert. In and around their simple hut are the material remains of two systems of trade: a British system which brought clay pipes and whisky bottles (and other products) into remote Australian desert settlements, and local Indigenous trade networks which moved items like decorative ocher from distant mines via trading expeditions (Paterson 2008). The remains of ocher, pipes, bottles, clothes, and stone and glass tools in and around the hut reveal something of the overlapping use of this site, as do the station manager's letters, which indicate that Aboriginal people visited outstations and men and women worked as shepherds from a young age.

Some studies treat the pastoral domain as a holistic landscape, an approach that enfolds the head stations, Aboriginal camps, significant Indigenous sites, and resources into one interpretive frame (e.g., Harrison 2004a; Head and Fullagar 1997, 1999; Paterson 2008).

Another important area of research concerns Indigenous people and institutions, including missions, jails, depots, reserves, schools, homes, and hospitals. Some date from the earliest days of European colonization, such as the Blacktown Native Institution in colonial Sydney (Lydon 2005a), which played a seminal role in marking the beginnings of the removal of Aboriginal children by colonial authorities, and demonstrated the potential of the settlement's archaeological remains to reveal the experiences of pupils of the school and their Darug families camped nearby (Lydon 2005a: 213). Later in the 19th and 20th centuries, reserves were set aside for Aboriginal people, reflecting attempts to regulate their presence. Davison (1985) describes the remains of mud-brick structures at Manga-Manda settlement in the Northern Territory; detritus there reflects small camps around the settlement and the occasional homes of the many families living there for short and long periods, moving in and out of the world of officialdom. Their location reveals that tribal membership was a central organizing principle of the forced settlement of separate tribal groups. The counterpoint to these official settlements are the many more unofficial settlements that existed across Australia—the camps at the fringes of towns where Aboriginal people lived a life that moved parallel to, yet separate from, the rest of the nation. On the north coast of New South Wales, for example, archaeologists and Indigenous people have worked together to record the camps and huts at Corindi Beach, where during the 20th century the Gumbaingirr Aboriginal community lived in a "no-man's land" outside of town (Smith and Beck 2003).

Missions and farming villages established on Aboriginal reserves were a significant institutional setting for cross-cultural encounters, centering on the goal of conversion to Christianity. These have been studied in Tasmania (Birmingham 1992), central Australia (Birmingham 2000), Victoria (Lydon 2002; Rhodes and Stocks 1985), and Arnhem Land (Travers 1986). At Wybalenna ("Black Men's Houses"), Birmingham investigated one of the most significant institutions for Tasmanian Aboriginal people, which had been largely understood through the accounts of the government employee George Augustus Robinson. In the early 19th century, Robinson gathered surviving Indigenous Tasmanians, ravaged by years of resistance fighting, at a small settlement on Flinders Island. Wybalenna was eventually abandoned, but while it operated it aimed to convert the Tasmanians in a spiritual sense, as well as to enjoin them to adapt to more European modes of living. Birmingham's analysis tested the success of these intentions, revealing how certain households accommodated Europeans stipulations and sensibilities, while others clearly maintained traditional practices and rejected European values. The combination of archaeological and documentary data sets in studies such as these allows a more nuanced understanding of historical Aboriginal people whose lives were spent in times of great change.

Interpreting the Evidence

The archaeological study of Indigenous history encompasses the different techniques and research questions of "historical" and "prehistoric" archaeology and also illustrates the arbitrary construction of "prehistory" and "history" (McNiven and Russell 2005). The history we study as archaeologists is the story we tell about the past; and "history" is the name we give to the time we tell the story about. For most people, "history" is the product of writing, both because it is based on the study of written documents and because the story is written down. For these reasons, "history" generally refers to the past of literate peoples. But archaeological data can provide alternative evidence about the historical past, even where historical sources survive, particularly if these accounts neglect the people and contexts under scrutiny. Using documents to interpret "history" requires critical skills, for "most European writings in colonial contexts are not so much biased representations of history as culturally constructed texts that present eyewitness accounts from the vantage point of the elite, literate, Western males" (Lightfoot 2005: 16).

Another interpretive issue arises for archaeological material found in contact sites, because:

> Even today, Aboriginal people sometimes use "traditional" places (e.g. rock shelters, waterholes, campsites) without leaving any "European" materials behind. To label these Aboriginal sites as "prehistoric" because they contain no exotic materials is to render post-contact Aboriginal places, and the people who use them, invisible. (Colley and Bickford 1996: 8)

There is no easy solution to this problem. However, some work on historical Indigenous uses of material culture, the landscape, and artistic traditions attempts to better situate historical evidence in a long-term perspective that potentially allows for tracing changes and continuities in Aboriginal societies.

In what follows I review some of the main evidence used to interpret historical Indigenous archaeological material and sites in Australia. For archaeologists, the aim is to understand continuities in the use of materials and patterns of behavior, as well as to show how newly available material such as glass and ceramic fitted into daily life in a world with new demands and opportunities. The study of historical culture has been structured by studies of key materials such as glass and ceramic materials used for flaked tools (Figure 12.2). Glass tools have long been recognized as a marker of the historical presence of Aboriginal people in and around European settlements (Allen and Jones 1980), as well as reflecting Indigenous people's experiments with new materials like glass and ceramics (see, e.g., Balfour 1903; Wilson 2005). However, recent work has considered the technical and social aspects of glass artifacts. For example, in the Kimberley region around pastoral stations such as Old Lamboo (typi-

Figure 12.2 Nineteenth-century dark olive flaked glass bottle base, and conjoined base flakes, Strangways Springs contact site, central Australia. Photograph by the author.

cal of many other similar contexts around Australia), Aboriginal people used "new" materials such as metal artifacts in distinctively Indigenous ways (Harrison 2002b). The main value of this work is that the interpretation of these familiar materials in cross-cultural contexts requires considering potentially complex colonial relations (e.g., Harrison 2002a, 2006). While items such as modified glass artifacts were produced widely by Aboriginal people, Harrison's analysis also reveals the ways that Kimberley Points, a distinctive point formed by pressure-flaking the edges of glass and ceramic flakes, were highly desired by late 19th-century European collectors as well as archaeologists and entered into a cross-cultural process of colonial trade (Harrison 2006).

In fact, diverse types of exchange involving material culture were typical of colonial interactions from the earliest days of British settlement (McBryde 1989b). The theme of exchange is central to an understating of Aboriginal people's dealings with outsiders. The use of material culture in cross-cultural contexts is laden with cultural meanings, and as Nicholas Thomas (1991) points out, the exchange of objects, knowledge, gifts, or rations should not be understood as meaning the same thing to both sides. Historical objects became invested with new and different meanings by Indigenous people and were treated differently in Indigenous contexts. Phillip Jones has recently explored the many ways that objects reflect encounters on Australian frontiers, and how singular items reflect different historical contingencies (2007). Around the fledgling settlement of Sydney, objects moved among people, shifting meaning in the process: spear throwers, spears, fishing equipment, and shields were either traded for or pilfered by Europeans as curios, while, at the same time, other material was obtained by Aboriginal people, such as desirable metal objects (see also Taçon et al. 2003).

The barter of goods for work—commonly including such goods as flour, sugar, tea, tobacco, blankets, and clothing—was another form of exchange, as was the distribution of rations. The latter was a core type of transaction between employers and Indigenous Australians until the advocacy of wages for Aboriginal workers led to wage reform in the 1960s (Rowse 1998). Archaeological evidence reveals the extent of these practices, which varied for a range of reasons, such as distance from rationing, availability of work, the types of administration in place, and levels of cross-cultural

Figure 12.3 Aboriginal historical rock engravings, Inthanoona contact site, western Australia (Paterson 2004).

avoidance. Thus, the ways that objects were involved in processes of change and conservatism have become a focus for archaeological research (Harrison 2006; Torrence and Clarke 2000).

Decorated material culture holds a special fascination, given the increasing attention worldwide to Aboriginal art. In many places, rock art traditions extend into the historical period (Figure 12.3), such as in Sydney (McDonald 2008), central Australia (Frederick 1999), the Pilbara (Paterson 2008), and northern Australia (David and Wilson 2002). Rock art provides an Indigenous narrative of cross-cultural encounters and colonial contexts. This is particularly significant given the rarity of historical accounts by Aboriginal people in some regions. For instance, Annie Clarke and Ursula Frederick (2006) document how images of Macassan and later European ships are depicted in rock art on Groote Eylandt (eastern Arnhem Land) and how differences in their execution reflect different types of historically contingent cultural interaction. In another study of historical rock art, Paterson and Wilson (2009) consider how the rock engravings at 19th-century pastoral head stations reveal an Indigenous perspective on culture contact by expressing Ngaluma peoples' experience of work on pastoral stations (ranches). Rock art can also reflect Indigenous peoples' resistance to European colonization, as argued by David and Wilson (2002) for the Victoria River Downs. Europeans also depicted the colonial world and Indigenous people. For example, Jane Lydon (2002, 2005c) considered the ways that photography shows how people perceived and reproduced the colonial world of Victorian missions.

Like rock art, material culture provides evidence of the actions of historical individuals—that is, past Indigenous agency—as demonstrated in diverse archaeological contexts—for example, for pastoral workers in central Australia (Paterson 2008), Aboriginal men in the Kimberley (Harrison 2002a), Aboriginal women and European sealers (Russell 2005), and individuals in early colonial institutions (Lydon 2005b). An interest in past agency reflects the attempt by archaeologists to understand how people in the past reacted to colonial circumstances.

Aboriginal history is perhaps best understood by considering the social landscapes in which cross-cultural contacts occurred (e.g., Bender 1994; Gosden and Head 1994). Some studies have started to consider Aboriginal people's use of environments over the long term and into the historical era, such as Mike Smith's (2005) study of life in the Cleland Hills in central Australia. There are important physical parameters that are necessarily part of the picture at this level, such as the location of important resources, as described for a recent study of the cultural values that Gumbaingirr people ascribe to Corindi Beach, in New South Wales:

> The cultural values that Aboriginal people ascribe to the environment are many and complex. The active utilisation of wild foods and medicines is but one value, but it is linked to many aspects of contemporary culture and identity. Fishing, plant food collecting and hunting continue to play an important role in people's lives. Such activities may be viewed as embodying a continuation of cultural practice and as a primary means of passing on ecological knowledge, looking after and observing country, and maintaining links with valued places. (English 2002: ix)

Other ways of considering Indigenous historical landscape have focused on how they have been hidden (Rose 1991) by European narratives or the way that different narratives compete to be heard (Strang 1999). In recent years, the term "shared landscapes" has been advocated by Tim Murray (1996) and by Rodney Harrison, who states that this "is shared not in the sense in which it was homogenous, but through the mutual self-definitions of Aboriginal and non-Aboriginal people who lived and worked together (and were sometimes segregated from each other)" (Harrison 2004a: 219). The idea of separate and overlapping landscapes is a powerful way of changing prevailing ideas about the ways in which Australian landscapes and history are compartmentalized.

Conclusion

In conclusion, it is clear that the archaeological study of Aboriginal history in Australia has become increasingly significant and is closely aligned to the rise of collaborative research. This research has been driven by Indigenous concerns regarding their heritage, as well as by archaeologists' general interest in historical culture contact in Australia and elsewhere (although many Australian archaeologists working in the area of Aboriginal archaeology remain uninterested in developments in American historical archaeology).

Many countries have shown an interest in studies of culture contact and the historical archaeology of Indigenous peoples. These appear to have been very influential in some Australian quarters, particularly with the substantial work arising from the quincentennial of Columbus's voyages of discovery and colonization in the Americas, a body of work described by Tim Murray as "the great challenge thrown down to Australian archaeologists by their colleagues in North America and South Africa" (Murray 2002: 214). This work has included a substantial review of archaeological theory related to culture contact studies and the creation of a substantial body of research (see Silliman, this volume, chapter 11). Another arena influencing theoretical developments has been sustained interest in colonial Australia in a revisionist sense, inspired by a global consideration of colonialism and postcolonialism.

There are two hot topics in recent Australian historiography: frontier violence and land rights. It is worth briefly considering the recent and extensive debate in Australia about what happened to Aboriginal people in colonial contexts, most vividly the controversy about the numbers of Aboriginal casualties in frontier violence (Foster and Attwood 2003; Macintyre and Clark 2003; Manne 2003; Windschuttle 2003). These are localized debates driven by disagreements about the appropriate methodologies for historical research as well as broader ideological disagreements about the role of the past in the present. These studies are all explicitly concerned with frontier conflict, a debate that archaeologists have not been widely involved in. The legal basis for British appropriation of Aboriginal people's land has also been reviewed by the Australian legal system, culminating in the recognition of Aboriginal people's land rights (e.g., Lilley 2000). To date, archaeological evidence has been used within the Native Title process merely to demonstrate antiquity of practice rather than to explain the historical period, but potentially it may provide evidence for attachment to place, particularly where extensive disruption to Indigenous societies occurred (Harrison 2000; McDonald 2000). One future may see a better incorporation of Indigenous and non-Indigenous land uses, as demonstrated in part through archaeological evidence, into the management of cultural and natural heritage (see, e.g., Langton and David 2005).

Finally, recent research has developed new methods for recording Aboriginal historical sites. Some of this work has been driven by heritage agencies or by archaeologists working with Aboriginal groups, as well as by the growth of community archaeology approaches. The strongest driver has been Aboriginal concerns about their own heritage, a concern that has grown in recent decades and influenced archaeological practice: "This work reflects a sea-change in mainstream Australian attitudes towards the country's colonial past. . . . Since the 1960s, Aboriginal activism, coupled with an academic critique of colonialism, has revealed the tensions within the inclusive, pluralist model of nationhood" (Lydon 2006: 302). This work has fueled developments in methods of mapping heritage sites and linking oral histories (Beck and Somerville 2005) and historical evidence from documents and pictorial sources. Significant regional projects have been undertaken, particularly by heritage managers in New South Wales (Byrne and Nugent 2004; English 2002; Harrison 2004a). Collaborative heritage projects and community-driven research potentially improve relationships between Indigenous people and archaeologists (Davidson et al. 1995; Greer et al. 2002). This work requires rethinking analytical categories. For example, in their collaboration on the Waanyi Women's History Project, which aimed to find out from Waanyi women in far western Queensland what places they thought were significant, Smith, Morgan, and van der Meer (2003) argue that the definition of heritage by heritage experts excludes Indigenous understandings of significance, and that the community approaches should lead to a redefinition of cultural heritage management. In some instances, involvement with Indigenous stakeholders has changed the entire research process. In her study of Groote Eylandt, Anne Clarke initially expected to examine the prehistory of the island; however, her research process became transformed through working with the community, and she recast the research to encompass recent Macassan and European contexts as well as Indigenous understandings of time.

> [T]he development of a community approach to archaeology was integral to the transmutation of my research from a basic culture-historical project . . . to one concerned with . . . cross-cultural engagement. . . . The transformation of the . . . project occurred at two levels: first, through the interactions I had with Indigenous people as I negotiated the form of and content of my research and, second, as a result of the way in which my interests in old people's camping places were interpreted by people in terms of their Indigenous cultural and historical landscape. (Clarke 2002: 250)

As a result of these influences and events, the archaeological interpretation of Indigenous Australian people's history seems secure. The trends described here would suggest continued movement across the boundaries of "prehistory" and "history." The collaboration of Indigenous communities and archaeologists may help avoid the pitfalls of the past, although the question of who owns the right to discuss the past and the future of heritage remains unresolved.

Note

1. European accounts of trepang voyages and seasonal settlements, such as those of Matthew Flinders in 1801 (Flinders 1814), have led to researchers suggesting that these visits began around C.E. 1650 (Macknight, later revised to 1710; also C.E. 1660 in Crawford 1969). Dutch coins from the 18th and 19th centuries support these dates, while the interpretation of radiocarbon dates remains contested (Clarke 2000). The widely accepted dates for Macassan visits are ca. C.E. 1700 to 1900, although earlier visits would not be unlikely.

References

Allen, J. 1969. *Archaeology and the History of Port Essington*. Ph.D. thesis, Department of Prehistory, Australian National University, Canberra.

Allen, J., and Jones, R. 1980. Oyster Cove: Archaeological traces of the last Tasmanians and notes on the criteria for the authentication of flaked glass artefacts. *Papers and Proceedings of the Royal Society of Tasmania* 114: 225–233.

Arthur, B., and Morphy, F. (eds.). 2005. *Macquarie Atlas of Indigenous Australia: Culture and Society through Space and Time*. North Ryde: Macquarie Library.

Baker, R. 1984. *Macassan Site Survey and Bibliography*. Darwin: Report for Museums and Art Galleries of the Northern Territory.

Balfour, H. 1903. On the method employed by the natives of N. W. Australia in the manufacture of glass spear heads. *Man* 1903: 65.

Beck, W., and Somerville, M. 2005. Conversations between disciplines: Historical archaeology and oral history at Yarrawarra. *World Archaeology* 37: 468–483.

Beckett, J. 1958. A study of a mixed-blood Aboriginal minority in the pastoral west of New South Wales. M.A. thesis, University of Sydney.

Bender, B. (ed.). 1994. *Landscape: Politics and Perspectives*. Oxford: Berg.

Bigourdan, N., and McCarthy, M. 2007. Aboriginal watercraft depictions in Western Australia: on land, and underwater? *Bulletin of the Australasian Institute for Maritime Archaeology* 31: 1–10.

Birmingham, J. 1992. *Wybalenna: The Archaeology of Cultural Accommodation in Nineteenth Century Tasmania*. Sydney: Australian Society for Historical Archaeology.

———. 2000. Resistance, creolization or optimal foraging at Killalpaninna Mission, South Australia, in R. Torrence, and A. Clarke (eds.), *The Archaeology of Difference. Negotiating Cross-Cultural Engagements in Oceania*, pp. 360–405. London: Routledge.

Byrne, D., and Nugent, M. 2004. *Mapping Attachment: A Spatial Approach to Post-Contact Heritage*. Sydney: Department of Environment and Conservation.

Clarke, A. 1994. *Winds of Change: An Archaeology of Contact in the Groote Eylandt Archipelago, Northern Australia*. Ph.D. thesis, Australian National University, Canberra.

———. 2000. The "Moormans Trowsers": Macassan and Aboriginal interactions and the changing fabric of Indigenous social life. *Modern Quaternary Research in Southeast Asia* 16: 315–335.

———. 2002. The ideal and the real: Cultural and personal transformations of archaeological research on Groote Eylandt, Northern Australia. *World Archaeology* 34 (2): 249–264.

Clarke, A., and Frederick, U. 2006. Closing the distance: Interpreting cross-cultural engagements through Indigenous rock art, in I. Lilley (ed.), *The Archaeology of Oceania: Australia and the Pacific Islands*, pp. 116–133. Oxford: Blackwell.

Colley, S. M., and Bickford, A. 1996. "Real" Aborigines and "real" archaeology: Aboriginal places and Australian historical archaeology. *World Archaeological Bulletin* 7: 5–21.

Crawford, I. 1969. *Late Prehistoric Changes in Aboriginal Culture on Kimberley, Western Australia*. Ph.D. thesis, University of London.

David, B., and Wilson, M. 2002. Spaces of resistance: Graffiti and Indigenous place markings in the early European contact period of northern Australia, in B. David and M. Wilson, (eds.), *Inscribed Landscapes: Marking and Making Place*, pp. 42–60. Honolulu: University of Hawai'i Press.

Davidson, I., Lovell-Jones, C., and Bancroft, R. (eds.). 1995. *Archaeologists and Aborigines Working Together*. Armidale: University of New England Press.

Davison, P. 1985. *The Manga-Manda Settlement, Phillip Creek*. Townsville: James Cook University.

Deagan, K. A. 1988. Neither history nor prehistory: The questions that count in historical archaeology. *Historical Archaeology* 22 (1): 7–12.

English, A. 2002. *The Sea and the Rock Gives Us a Feed. Mapping and Managing Gumbaingirr Wild Resource Use Places*. Sydney: NSW National Parks and Wildlife Service.

Flinders, M. 1814. *A Voyage to Terra Australis*. London: G. W. Nicol.

Frederick, U. 1999. At the centre of it all: Constructing contact through rock art of Watarrka National Park, central Australia. *Archaeology in Oceania* 34: 132–144.

Foster, S. G., and Attwood, B. (eds.). 2003. *Frontier Conflict: The Australian Experience*. Canberra: National Museum of Australia.

Godwin, L., and L'Oste-Brown, L. 2002. A past remembered: Aboriginal "historic" places in central Queensland, in R. Harrison, and C. Williamson (eds.), *After Captain Cook: The Archaeology of the Recent Indigenous Past in Australia*, pp. 191–212. Sydney: Archaeological Computing Laboratory.

Gosden, C. 2004. Archaeology and Colonialism: Cultural Contact from 5000 B.C. to the Present. Cambridge: Cambridge University Press.

Gosden, C., and Head, L. 1994. Landscape—A usefully ambiguous concept. *Archaeology in Oceania* 29: 113–116.

Greer, S., Harrison, R., and McIntyre-Tamwoy, S. 2002. Community-based archaeology in Australia. *World Archaeology* 34 (2): 265–287.

Harrison, R. 2000. Challenging the "authenticity" of antiquity: Contact archaeology and Native Title in Australia, in I. Lilley (ed.), *Native Title and the Transformation of Archaeology in the Postcolonial World*, pp. 35–53. Sydney: Oceania Monographs.

———. 2002a. Archaeology and the colonial encounter: Kimberley spearpoints, cultural identity and masculinity in the north of Australia. *Journal of Social Archaeology* 2: 352–377.

———. 2002b. Australia's Iron Age: Aboriginal post-contact metal artefacts from Old Lamboo station, Southeast Kimberley, Western Australia. *Australasian Historical Archaeology* 20: 67–76.

———. 2004a. *Shared Landscapes: Archaeologies of Attachment and the Pastoral Industry in New South Wales*. Sydney: UNSW Press.

———. 2004b. Contact archaeology and the landscapes of pastoralism in the northwest of Australia, in T. Murray (ed.), *The Archaeology of Contact in Settler Societies*, pp. 109–143. Cambridge: Cambridge University Press.

———. 2006. An artefact of colonial desire? Kimberley Points and the technologies of enchantment. *Current Anthropology* 47: 63–88.

Harrison, R., and Williamson, C. 2002. *After Captain Cook: The Archaeology of the Recent Indigenous Past in Australia*. Sydney: University of Sydney.

Head, L., and Fullagar, R. 1997. Hunter-gatherer archaeology and pastoral contact: Perspectives from the Northwest Northern Territory, Australia. *World Archaeology* 28: 418–428.

———. 1999. Exploring the prehistory of hunter-gatherer attachments to place: An example from the Keep River area, Northern Territory, Australia, in P. Ucko and R. Layton (eds.), *The Archaeology and Anthropology of Landscape*, pp. 322–335. London: Routledge.

Horton, D. (ed). 1994. *The Encyclopaedia of Aboriginal Australia: Aboriginal and Torres Strait Islander History, Society and Culture*. Canberra: Aboriginal Studies Press.

Jones, P. 2007. *Ochre and Rust: Artefacts and Encounters on Australian Frontiers*. Adelaide: Australian History Wakefield Press.

Kostoglou, P., McCarthy, J., and Paay, J. 1991. *Whaling and Sealing Sites in South Australia*. Adelaide: Department of Environment and Planning.

Langford, R. 1983. Our Heritage—Your Playground. *Australian Archaeology* 16: 1–6.

Langton, M., and David, B. 2005. Nature and culture in a forest park: William Ricketts and his sanctuary, Victoria, in J. Lydon, and T. Ireland (eds.), *Object Lessons: Archaeology and Heritage in Australia*, pp. 71–88. Melbourne: Australian Scholarly Publishing.

Lawrence, S. 2007. *Whalers and Free Men: Life on Tasmania's Colonial Whaling Stations*. Melbourne: Australian Scholarly Publishing.

Lawrence, S., and Staniforth, M. (eds). 1998. *The Archaeology of Whaling in Southern Australia and New Zealand*. Australasian Society for Historical Archaeology and the Australian Institute of Maritime Archaeology Special Publication No. 10. Canberra: Brolga Press.

Lightfoot, K. G. 1995. Culture contact studies: Redefining the relationship between prehistoric and historical archaeology. *American Antiquity* 60: 199–217.

———. 2005. *Indians, Missionaries, and Merchants: The Legacy of Colonial Encounters on the Colonial Frontiers*. Berkeley: University of California Press.

Lilley, I. 2000. *Native Title and the Transformation of Archaeology in the Postcolonial World*. Oceania Monographs, No. 50. Sydney: University of Sydney.

Lydon, J. 2002. "This civilising experiment": Photography at Coranderrk Aboriginal station during the 1860s, in R. Harrison, and C. Williamson, (eds.), *After Captain Cook: The Archaeology of the Recent Indigenous Past in Australia*, pp. 59–74. Sydney: University of Sydney.

———. 2005a. "Men in black": The Blacktown Native Institution and the origins of the "Stolen Generation," in J. Lydon, and T. Ireland, (eds.). *Object Lessons: Archaeology and Heritage in Australia*, pp. 201–224. Melbourne: Australian Scholarly Publishing.

———. 2005b. "Our sense of beauty": Visuality, space and gender on Victoria's Aboriginal reserves, south-eastern Australia. *History and Anthropology* 16: 211–233.

———. 2005c. *Eye Contact: Photographing Indigenous Australians*. Durham, NC: Duke University Press.

———. 2006. Pacific encounters, or beyond the islands of history, in M. Hall and S. Silliman (eds.), *Historical Archaeology*, pp. 293–312. Malden, MA: Blackwell.

Lydon, J., and Ireland, T. 2005. *Object Lessons: Archaeology and Heritage in Australia*. Melbourne: Australian Scholarly Publishing.

Macintyre, S., and Clark, A. 2003. *The History Wars*. Melbourne: Melbourne University Press.

Macknight, C. 1976. *The Voyage to Marege*. Melbourne: Melbourne University Press.

Manne, R. 2003. *Whitewash: On Keith Windschuttle's Fabrication of Aboriginal History*. Melbourne: Black Inc.

McBryde, I. 1989a. *Guests of the Governor—Aboriginal Residents of the First Government House*. Sydney: The Friends of the First Government House Site.

———. 1989b. "… to establish a commerce of this sort": Cross cultural exchange at the Port Jackson settlement, in J. Hardy, and A. Frost, *Studies from Terra Australis to Australia*, pp. 169–182. Canberra: Australian Academy of the Humanities.

McDonald, J. 2000. Archaeology, rock art, ethnicity and Native Title, in I. Lilley, (ed.), *Native Title and the Transformation of Archaeology in the Postcolonial World*, pp. 54–64. Oceania Monographs, No. 50. Sydney: University of Sydney.

———. 2008. Rock art and cross-cultural interaction in Sydney: How did both sides perceive the other? in M. Neale, P. Sutton, and P. Veth (eds.), *Strangers on the Shore: Early Coastal Contact in Australia*, pp. 46–89. Canberra: National Museum of Australia Press.

McNiven, I., and Russell, L. 2005. *Appropriated Pasts: Indigenous Peoples and the Colonial Culture of Archaeology*. Walnut Creek, CA: AltaMira Press.

Megaw, V. 1968. Trial excavations in the Captain Cook Landing Place Reserve, Kurnell, N.S.W. Australian Institute of Aboriginal Studies: *Newsletter* 2: 9 (1968): 17–20.

Mitchell, S. 1994. *Culture Contact and Indigenous Economies on the Cobourg Peninsula, Northwest Arnhem Land*. Ph.D. thesis, Northern Territory University, Darwin.

Morse, K. 1988. An archaeological survey of midden sites near the *Zuytdorp* wreck, Western Australia. *Bulletin of the Australian Institute for Maritime Archaeology* 12 (1): 37–40.

Morwood, M. J., and Hobbs, D. R. 1997. The Asian connection: Preliminary report on Indonesian trepang sites on the Kimberley coast, N.W. Australia. *Archaeology in Oceania* 32: 197–206.

Mulvaney, J. 1989. *Encounters in Place: Outsiders and Aboriginal Australians, 1606–1985*. Brisbane: University of Queensland Press.

Murray, T. 1993. The childhood of William Lanne: Contact archaeology and aboriginality in Tasmania. *Antiquity* 67: 507–519.

——. 1996. Contact archaeology: Shared histories? Shared identities? in *Sites: Nailing the Debate: Archaeology and Interpretation in Museums*, pp. 200–213. Sydney: Historic Houses Trust of New South Wales.

——. 2002. Epilogue: An archaeology of Indigenous/ non-Indigenous Australia from 1788, in R. Harrison, and C. Williamson, *After Captain Cook: The Archaeology of the Recent Indigenous Past in Australia*, pp. 214–223. Sydney: Sydney University Press.

Murray, T. (ed.). 2004. *The Archaeology of Contact in Settler Societies*. Cambridge: Cambridge University Press.

Murray, T., and White, J. P. 1981. Cambridge in the bush? Archaeology in Australia and New Guinea. *World Archaeology* 13 (2): 255–263.

——. 2005. Early pastoral landscapes and culture contact in central Australia. *Historical Archaeology* 39: 28–48.

——. 2008. *The Lost Legions: Culture Contact in Colonial Australia*. Walnut Creek, CA: AltaMira Press.

Paterson, A. G., and Wilson, A. 2000. Australian historical archaeology: Retrospects and prospects. *Australian Archaeology* 50: 81–89.

——. 2009. Indigenous perceptions of contact at Inthanoona, Northwest, Western Australia. *Archaeology in Oceania* 44: 99–111.

Paterson, A. G., Gill, N., and Kennedy, M. 2003. An archaeology of historical reality? A case study of the recent past. *Australian Archaeology* 57: 82–89.

Prickett, N. 1993. The Tasmanian origins of New Zealand shore whaling. *Archaeology of New Zealand* 36 (4): 94–104.

Proudfoot, H. 1990. *Australia's First Government House*. Sydney: Allen & Unwin.

Reynolds, H. 1972. *Aborigines and Settlers*. North Melbourne: Cassell.

——. 1983. *The Other Side of the Frontier: Aboriginal Resistance to the European Invasion of Australia*. Ringwood: Penguin.

——. 1990. *With the White People*. Ringwood: Penguin.

Rhodes, D., and Stocks, R. 1985. Excavations at Lake Condah Mission 1984–1985. *Historic Environment* 4: 4.

Rose, D. B. 1991. *Hidden Histories: Black Stories from Victoria River Downs, Humbert River and Wave Hill Stations*. Camberra: Aboriginal Studies Press.

Rowley, C. D. 1970. *The Destruction of Aboriginal Society*. Canberra: Australian National University Press.

——. 1971. *Outcasts in White Australia: Aboriginal Policy and Practice*. Canberra: Australian National University Press.

Rowse, T. 1998. *White Flour, White Power: From Rations to Citizenship in Central Australia*. Melbourne: Cambridge University Press.

Russell, L. 2005. Kangaroo Island sealers and their descendants: Ethnic and gender ambiguities in the archaeology of a creolised community. *Australian Archaeology* 60: 1–5.

——. 2007. "Dirty domestics and worse cooks": Aboriginal women's agency and domestic frontiers, Southern Australia, 1800–1850. *Frontiers: A Journal of Women Studies* 28 (1–2): 18–46.

Sahlins, M. 1999. What is anthropological enlightenment? Some lessons of the twentieth century. *Annual Review of Anthropology* 28: 1–23.

Silliman, S. 2005. Culture contact or colonialism? Challenges in the archaeology of Native North America. *American Antiquity* 70: 55–74.

Silvester, L. 1998. *Strangers on the Shore. Shipwreck Survivors and Their Contact with Aboriginal Groups in Western Australia 1628– 1956*. Fremantle: Department of Maritime Archaeology, Western Australian Museum.

Smith, A., and Beck, W. 2003. The archaeology of no man's land: Indigenous camps at Corindi Beach, mid-north coast New South Wales. *Archaeology in Oceania* 38 (2): 66–77.

Smith, L., Morgan, A., and van der Meer, A. 2003. The Waanyi Women's History Project: A community partnership project, Queensland, Australia, in L. Derry and M. Malloy (eds.), *Archaeologists and Local Communities: Partners in Exploring the Past*, pp. 147–165 Washington DC: Society for American Archaeology.

Smith, M. 2005. *Peopling the Cleland Hills: Aboriginal History in Western Central Australia 1850–1980*. Canberra: Aboriginal History Inc.

Smith, P. A. 2000. Station camps: Legislation, labour relations and rations on pastoral leases in the Kimberley region, Western Australia. *Aboriginal History* 24: 75–97.

Stevens, C. 1989. *Tin Mosques & Ghantowns: A History of Afghan Cameldrivers in Australia*. Alice Springs: Paul Fitzsimmons.

Strang, V. 1999. Competing perceptions of landscape in Kowanyama, North Queensland, in P. J. Ucko and R. Layton (eds.), *The Archaeology and Anthropology of Landscape: Shaping Your Landscape*, pp. 206–218. London: Routledge.

Taçon, P. S. C., South, B., and Hooper, S. 2003. Depicting cross-cultural interaction: Figurative designs in wood, earth and stone from South-east Australia. *Archaeology in Oceania* 38: 89–100.

Thomas, N. 1991. *Entangled Objects: Exchange, Material Culture, and Colonialism in the Pacific*. Cambridge: Harvard University Press.

Travers, M. 1986. C. M. S. *Top End Missions (Emerald River, Angurugu, Umbakumba, Oenpelli)*. National Trust of Australia (NT).

Torrence, R., and Clarke, A. 2000. *The Archaeology of Difference: Negotiating Cross-Cultural Engagements in Oceania*. London: Routledge.

Veth, P., Sutton, P., and Neale, M. (eds.). 2008. *Strangers on the Shore: Early Coastal Contact in Australia*. Canberra: National Museum of Australia Press.

Williamson, C. 2002. Finding meaning in the patterns: The analysis of material culture from a contact site in Tasmania, in R. Harrison, and C. Williamson (eds.), *After Captain Cook: The Archaeology of the Recent Indigenous Past in Australia*, pp.76–101. Sydney University Archaeological Methods Series, No. 8. Sydney: Archaeological Computing Laboratory, University of Sydney.

Williamson, C., and Harrison, R. 2002. Introduction: "Too many Captain Cooks"? An archaeology of Aboriginal Australia after 1788, in R. Harrison, and C. Williamson (eds.), *After Captain Cook: The Archaeology of the Recent Indigenous Past in Australia*, pp. 1–13. Sydney University Archaeological Methods Series, No. 8. Sydney: Archaeological Computing Laboratory, University of Sydney.

Wilson, M. 2005. Variation amongst glass artefact assemblages at Cossack, Western Australia. M.A. thesis, School of Social and Cultural Studies, University of Western Australia, Perth.

Windschuttle, K. 2003. *The Fabrication of Aboriginal History*. Sydney: Macleay Press.

Wolski, N. 2001. All's not quiet on the western front—Rethinking resistance and frontiers in Aboriginal historiography, in L. Russell, (ed.), *Colonial Frontiers: Indigenous-European Encounters in Settler Societies*, pp. 216–236. Manchester: Manchester University Press.

Wolski, N., and Loy, T. 1999. On the invisibility of contact: Residue analyses on Aboriginal glass artefacts from western Victoria. *The Artefact* (Archaeological and Anthropological Society of Victoria) 22: 65–73.

13

SLAVERY, LIBERATION, AND EMANCIPATION: CONSTRUCTING A POSTCOLONIAL ARCHAEOLOGY OF THE AFRICAN DIASPORA

Theresa A. Singleton

The archaeological study of slavery and emancipation, and more generally of the African diaspora, can be considered a postcolonial area of study both chronologically and substantively. In chronological terms, it was initiated in the 1960s when most former colonies had become or were in the process of becoming independent. Substantively, it is a postcolonial pursuit because it was initiated in response to social movements of the 1960s and 1970s. Paramount among these was the Civil Rights movement in the United States, which influenced, and was influenced by, worldwide independence movements. The Civil Rights movement was a liberation movement that developed in response to legalized discriminatory practices against African Americans and other people of color, subordinating them to second-class citizenry. Legalized racism of the pre–Civil Rights Act era was very similar to colonial policies, such as apartheid in South Africa, which had been designed to maintain inequality between European colonizers and non-European colonized subjects. Given the temporal and sociopolitical context within which the archaeology of the African diaspora emerged, it is a postcolonial archaeology (although it has rarely been articulated as such) because it places the subaltern subject (the colonized, enslaved, and oppressed) front and center.

Now, over four decades later, despite the well-intentioned goals of archaeological studies of slavery and emancipation, we must ask ourselves: Has this work been true to the postcolonial analytic? That is, has this research successfully interpreted the perspectives of subaltern subjects, which was initially, and continues to be, a goal of this research? Or, has neocolonialism crept into archaeological interpretations of slavery and emancipation? How do we continue the work of decolonizing the archaeology of slavery and emancipation? These questions frame the following discussion of the archaeology of slavery and emancipation in the Atlantic world. Slavery was important in the conquest and colonization of other world areas as well—for example, the Indian Ocean—but archaeological research in this area is still in the early stages of development (Kusimba 2004; Walz and Brandt 2006).

In this essay, I begin by briefly summarizing the role slavery played in colonization and how archaeology has contributed to this understanding. Next, I look at the complex relationship between emancipation and independence in the Atlantic world to highlight the contradictions between independence struggles and slavery, and the failure of emancipation to deliver social equality for the descendants of enslaved people. Finally, I evaluate the influence of the postcolonial analytic within the archaeological study of slavery and emancipation by identifying areas of interpretation and practice that are in need of decolonization.

Archaeology, Civil Rights Movement, and Subaltern Subjects

Archaeologists attribute the rise of archaeology of the African diaspora in the United States to the Civil Rights movement of the 1960s, but they have not always appreciated or acknowledged the direct links between African-American activism and some of the early investigations at former African-American sites. While a few archaeologists initiated African-American projects on their own (e.g., Bullen and Bullen 1945), several studies—including investigations at Parting Ways (Deetz 1977), Project Weeksville in the Brooklyn neighborhood of Bedford-Stuyvesant (Bridges and Salwen 1980), and the African Meeting House (Bower and Rushing 1980), among others—were investigated at the prodding of African Americans. These black activists (rather than ivory-tower academicians) played a direct role in the emergence of this research interest. Black activists were not necessarily knowledgeable of the particulars of archaeology, but they understood how archaeological data could contribute to learning about the African-American past and to furthering grassroots preservation efforts of historic buildings, neighborhoods, and sites pertaining to African-American history and culture. Moreover, it was often through their political action that funds were made available for these initial investigations. This kind of black activism has also been seen in more recent archaeological projects, such as at Allensworth, California (Cox 2007: 3–4), the African Burial Ground Project in New York (LaRoche and Blakey 1997), and the Fort Mosé project in St. Augustine, Florida (Landers and Deagan 1999).

Archaeologists who directed pioneering archaeological investigations of African-American life during the Civil Rights Movement era did not make explicit connections between their political views and their archaeological interests, as archaeologists often do today; therefore, we can only speculate whether or not they saw such studies as contributing to the struggle for equal rights. Charles H. Fairbanks, whose initial testing at slave sites on the Georgia and Florida coasts in the late 1960s marked the beginning of the systematic study of slavery from archaeological resources, was an outspoken critic of racial segregation long before developing an archaeological interest in African-American life (Fairbanks and Smith 1958). Although his writings on the archaeology of slavery did not express his political sentiments, it is very likely Fairbanks saw a connection between the two. Fairbanks, along with other archaeologists of the Civil Rights Movement era, set in motion a shift away from the study of sites of "great white men" to the study of disenfranchised people such as African Americans and other ethnic minorities in historical archaeology. Their interest in oppressed communities may have been more influenced by intellectual trends developing from social movements of the 1960s such as the new social history or ethnic studies, rather than directly from civil rights or independence movements per se. Regardless of their political or intellectual persuasions, archaeologists of early studies in African diaspora archaeology paved the way for later archaeological studies of subaltern peoples.

Slavery and Colonialism

In the Americas, slavery was part and parcel of the colonization process from the very beginning. Africans and Afro-Spaniards accompanied Spanish explorers to the Caribbean, and their numbers greatly increased when the first sugar plantations were established on the island of Hispaniola in the 1510s and 1520s. As the Spaniards conquered areas in mainland America, they brought sugar and enslaved Africans with them (Andrews 2004: 13). Initially, enslaved Africans supplemented enslaved Native American labor in gold and silver mines and on plantations. Spanish, Portuguese, and later, English settlers utilized enslaved Native Americans to some degree. In most cases, Native American slavery was short lived, due in large part to declining Indigenous populations wrought by the introduction of Old World pathogens. After 1570, enslaved Africans became the preferred labor source for large-scale sugar production. Eventually, African slavery supplanted Native American slavery in the production of plantation staples. Sugar, more than any other export crop or extractive industry, set the stage for increased European imperialism in the Americas. By 1600, Brazil, a colony of Portugal, had become the world's leading producer of sugar. Later, in the 17th and 18th centuries, England, France, Holland, and Denmark established sugar operations in the Caribbean and intensified the importation of African laborers. The sugar revolution dictated the course of slavery in the Caribbean and tropical areas of mainland America well into the 19th century (Mintz 1985).

As the numbers of enslaved Africans imported to the Americas increased and slavery expanded to new geographic areas and economies, Africans played significant roles in the construction of colonial societies.

They provided labor, not only for the production of export crops and precious metals, but in diverse economic enterprises, including cattle-raising, factory work, maritime industries, ironworking, metalsmithing, transportation of goods, building and mechanical trades, and domestic service, among other occupations. Dependence on slave labor, however, varied from place to place and through time. Different crop or craft requirements, work routines, and organization of labor profoundly structured the lives of enslaved people and the character of the societies that were formed from their labor. Not all colonial economies with slave workers depended on slave labor, but those that did developed sizable black populations. In some cases, black communities constituted the numerical majority of the overall population within an area.

Wherever Africans and their descendants concentrated, they created discernible Afro-Atlantic cultures with certain beliefs, customs, practices, and behavioral patterns drawn from African, European, and Native American sources. Archaeologists use various terms to refer to the creative process by which these new cultures emerged, including "creolization" (Ferguson 1992), "hybridity" (Leone and Fry 1999), "transculturation" (Deagan 1998), and "ethnogenic bricolage" (Fennell 2007). All of these are in keeping with a core premise of postcolonial theory: that all participants in colonial cultures bring something of their own to the culture and have some power to shape their world, albeit nuanced and constrained in different ways (Gosden 2001: 242). Enslaved Africans and their descendants contributed to the creation of colonial cultures in ways that will never be fully comprehended because so much of their cultural knowledge was unrecorded. This is where archaeology offers the promise of unveiling little-known aspects of Afro-Atlantic cultures.

Archaeological investigations contribute to our understanding of slavery by providing material evidence of Afro-Atlantic cultures under different colonial regimes throughout the Americas. Although the vast majority of this research has been undertaken in the English-speaking world, studies have been conducted in the former Dutch (Haviser 2001), French (Gibson 2007; Kelly and Gibson 2005), Danish (Armstrong 2003), Spanish (Domínguez 1986; Singleton 2001, 2005), and Portuguese (Orser and Funari 2001) colonies. Analyses of archaeological materials recovered from the places enslaved Africans and their descendants lived, worked, sought refuge, or died provide information on their material world—housing, use of space, personal and household items, craft production, foodways—that can be used for making inferences about non-material aspects of slave lives, including their agency, group formations, survival strategies, religious beliefs, cultural practices, power struggles, and interactions with other peoples.

Slave resistance is an important theme of the archaeological study of slavery that is in keeping with postcolonial analyses of power. Resistance was manifested in various ways, from overt acts of running away and organized rebellions to more subtle acts of slowing down work by feigning illness or breaking and hiding tools. Slave runaways, referred to as "maroons" (derived from the Spanish word *cimarron*, meaning "wild"), formed their own communities, sometimes with Indigenous Americans, from the very beginning of colonization. Maroon settlements ranged from large, permanent settlements with hundreds of residents and complex forms of sociopolitical organization—for example, Palmares, a fugitive polity in Brazil (Orser and Funari 2001)—to small, temporary encampments in rock overhangs or some other secluded place. To elude capture and re-enslavement, slave runaways located their settlements in marginal environments—swamps, mountainous terrains, or dense tropical forests—that have proven difficult to rediscover for archaeological study. Despite this challenge, however, archaeologists have investigated slave runaway sites in Brazil (Orser and Funari 2001), Cuba, (La Rosa Corzo 2003, 2005), Dominican Republic (Arrom and García Arévalo 1986), Florida (Deagan and MacMahon 1995; Weik 2007), Jamaica (Agorsah 1993), and Suriname (Agorsah 2005, 2007). Archaeological findings from these sites provide insights into the survival strategies of maroon communities, such as their foraging activities, raiding of nearby plantations, and trading networks.

The subtleties of slave resistance on plantations are difficult to interpret from archaeological sources alone. But, when combined with written sources, the possibilities of interpreting everyday resistance are greatly enhanced. One of the most common examples of everyday slave resistance evident in the archaeological record is seen in modifications enslaved people made of their houses and yard areas. At different times and in different places, slaveholders imposed their ideals of cleanliness and orderliness upon the design and layout of slave quarters to promote their ideas of good hygiene as well as to increase their surveillance of slave activities within slave quarters (McKee 1992; Singleton 1988: 354–355; 2001). Enslaved people responded by modifying their living spaces in various ways: digging subfloor pits within the interior spaces of the houses (Samford 2007), enlarging or changing the orientation of house yards (Armstrong and Kelly 2000), or adding private entrances hidden from view of the slaveholders and overseers (Epperson 1990).

In addition to studies of resistance, archaeological findings have been important in analyzing slave agency, defined here as the capability of enslaved people to take some control of their situations on their own terms. Examples of slave agency inferred from archaeological findings are seen in efforts of enslaved people to shape their material lives beyond meager plantation rations provisioned to them, including such activities as hunting and fishing, recycling broken or discarded objects to make other kinds of tools and implements, crafting objects for sale or their own use, and bartering or purchasing household and personal objects. Studies of slave agency and slave resistance show that enslaved people were acting, thinking beings who sought to control their lives despite the overwhelming odds against them.

Independence and Emancipation

Independence and emancipation made for strange bedfellows throughout the Atlantic world. Independence from a colonial power did not necessarily result in the abolition of slavery, nor did abolition of slavery necessarily result in independence. When slaveholders supported independence, they often failed to acknowledge the contradiction between their desire for independence and their denial of freedom to the people they held in bondage. Enslaved people did not accept the contradiction between independence and slavery and used independence struggles to their advantage in the hope of obtaining their own freedom. The Haitian Revolution (1791–1804) was the preeminent example of this kind of slave action; it not only produced a new nation, but overturned slavery, implanted black and mulatto rule, and banished the white population from the new nation. Free segments of Saint-Domingue (Haiti)—the world's leading producer of sugar and coffee in the 18th century—began fighting among themselves in their efforts to gain greater autonomy from France during the French Revolution (1789–1799). These internal conflicts, in turn, created favorable conditions for a successful uprising of enslaved workers—90 percent of the population. Reactions to the Haitian Revolution varied throughout the Americas (see Geggus 2001 for specific examples). Haiti became the example of what could happen in colonial settings that were dependent on large numbers of coerced, non-white laborers, and this prospect may have deterred many colonial elites from seeking independence (Andrews 2004: 54). In some cases, it hastened the abolition of slavery and, in others, it delayed abolition. At the same time, it motivated the expansion of slavery among planters in Cuba, Brazil, Jamaica, and Trinidad eager to fill the void in sugar and coffee production left by the destruction of Saint-Domingue (Davis 2001: 5).

In North America, Thomas Jefferson—the most notable of the slaveholding architects of the American Revolution (1775–1783)—acknowledged the contradiction between independence and slavery, but he accepted slavery as a necessary evil until free labor could replace it. Despite the adoption of the Jeffersonian stance on slavery for the newly established United States, the American Revolutionary War—the first successful independence struggle in the Americas—aroused abolitionist sentiments. After the revolution, slavery was abolished in New England, where slave labor had been marginal, and, by 1830, in the remaining northeastern states (Pennsylvania, New York, and New Jersey) where slave labor often competed with free labor (Berlin 1998: 178–179). Even in the South, where slavery was firmly implanted, many slaveholders inspired by ideals of liberty granted manumissions to their enslaved laborers, usually through wills after the deaths of owners. The free black population in the southern United States tripled in size as a consequence of Revolutionary-era (1790–1810) manumissions (Johnson and Roark 1984: 33).

Other enslaved men and women, as well as some free blacks (perhaps uncertain of their fate among slaveholding patriots), sided with the British Army during the American Revolution. Known as "Black Loyalists," thousands of them were evacuated to Canada, England, and the British West Indies when the war ended and peace was declared. This secondary diaspora of African-descendant people was one of the largest in the Atlantic world (Pulis 2006: 194–195).

In many Spanish colonies, there was a close association between independence and abolition. Slave participation in the wars for independence not only provided opportunities for slave men to obtain freedom through military service, but also paved the way for the establishment of gradual emancipation programs. In colonies where the slave population was small and slavery was of minor economic importance (Chile, Mexico, Central America), emancipation came shortly after independence. Where slavery was economically important, emancipation was a long, slow process following independence. Because slaveholders were opposed to freeing enslaved people without getting compensated, emancipation sometimes involved civil wars, such those of Argentina, Columbia, Peru, Uruguay, and Venezuela (Andrews 2004: 65–67). Slave emancipation preceded independence in Cuba, the last Spanish colony to abolish slavery in 1886, but even there, the abolition of slavery came about after Cuba fought an unsuccessful 10-year war (1868–1878) with Spain for independence.

Slavery and independence were totally unrelated in many colonial situations. Brazil, the nation with the largest slave population, gained independence without warfare in 1822 but was the last nation in the Americas to abolish slavery, in 1889.

Great Britain, on the other hand, was among the first colonial powers to end slavery throughout its empire, in 1834–1838, but independence of the British West Indies did not come until 1962. Today, several Caribbean islands are still officially colonies or territories of industrialized countries, while neocolonialism has rendered many independent states dependent on wealthier nations. For many peoples of the Atlantic world, liberation from colonialism is not yet a reality.

Whether emancipation preceded, followed, or came about at the same time as independence, it simply put an end to slavery. It did not, however, alleviate racism, discrimination, and unequal social relations. People of African descent continue to be among the poorest and most undereducated social groups throughout of the Americas. Most of the archaeological research of post-emancipation has been undertaken in the United States, but some preliminary work has begun elsewhere (Armstrong 2003; Haviser 1999; Gibson 2007). Post-emancipation studies in the United States have shown how racial discrimination was manifested and how African-American communities responded to these conditions in both rural (Wilkie 2000) and urban settings (Mullins 1999). Growing both in number and in importance, archaeological studies of emancipation and post-emancipation are being undertaken at the sites of former black towns, post-emancipation plantations, and frontier settlements, among others. These investigations, unlike those associated with slavery, offer opportunities to work directly with descendant communities who often have firsthand knowledge of sites being studied. Archaeology of post-emancipation holds great promise for putting into perspective the aftermath of slavery and the historical struggles of people of African descent for equal rights.

Evaluating the Postcolonial Analytic in the Archaeology of Slavery and Emancipation

Archaeological study of slavery and emancipation contributes to postcolonial archaeology by yielding data from the application of postcolonial concepts and theories in the investigation of subaltern peoples. Because archaeological data provide direct evidence of lived experiences, it allows us to reevaluate colonialism and gain new insights into the lives of those who suffered from it. Despite potential contributions of archaeology to postcolonial analyses of slavery and emancipation, however, archaeologists seldom examine how archaeology's links with colonialism may have influenced how we interpret slavery and emancipation. Additionally, white privilege and middle-class values influence how archaeologists interpret their data and their perceptions of subaltern peoples. It may be easy to convince ourselves that because the archaeology of slavery and emancipation emerged from liberation movements of the 1960s and 1970s, it needs no decolonization.

Most discussions about the decolonization of the archaeology of the African diaspora have addressed issues concerning the audience or constituencies for this research (Farnsworth 1993; Leone et al. 1995; McKee 1994; Potter 1991), the roles of African-descendant communities within this research (Derry 2003; McDavid 2003; McDavid and Babson 1997; Singleton 1995; Singleton and Orser 2003; Wilkie and Bartoy 2000), or the small number of archaeologists of color engaged in this research and the profession of archaeology as a whole (Agbe-Davies 2002). All these important issues related to the practice of the archaeology of slavery and emancipation have had an impact on archaeological interpretations in recent years. Unfortunately, however, too much of the archaeological discussion of the African diaspora still remains unaffected by these changes; it is in this realm that research still needs to be decolonized.

In 1995, I suggested in a review essay on slavery in North America that archaeologists had created an archaeology of the Other by making racial minorities in the United States the focus of ethnicity studies (Singleton 1995: 121–122). This "Othering" was premised on the use of topdown approaches, or white middle-class perspectives, rather than sources derived from the people being studied or the abundant African-American scholarship on African-American life. Since that time, many practitioners of African diaspora archaeology utilize written, oral, or ethnographic sources generated from people of African descent to some extent.

Topdown interpretations of African diaspora archaeology, however, still persist in some areas—for example, in the study of slave consumption. In conference papers and other presentations, some archaeologists have characterized large quantities of objects or the acquisition and use of certain fashionable, expensive, or prestige items as "conspicuous consumption" on the part of enslaved people. Such statements not only reinforce the biased accounts written during the time of slavery by colonialists, but serve to demean subaltern subjects—the very people we are attempting to unveil from ethnocentric, colonialist narratives. Moreover, the use of the term "conspicuous consumption" in the context of slavery is particularly inappropriate and abuses the intended meaning of the term. Thorstein Veblen, Norwegian economist and sociologist, originally coined the term to refer to the lavish spending of a new upper class that emerged from industrial capitalism during the second half of the 19th century (1899). Later in the 20th century, the term was applied to middle-class individuals and households with expendable income who used their consumption as social masks to identify materially with the upper class while lacking the social position and power of the upper class (Wurst and McGuire 1999: 197). Neither should usage of "conspicuous consumption" be applied to slave laborers who were themselves human commodities. Archaeologists should seek alternative interpretations for the recovery of large quantities of objects or prestige items from slave contexts, and examine the social relations of slavery that might explain their presence. The issue that should concern archaeologists regarding consumption "is not what people buy, but the social relations that enable and constrain what they buy" (Wurst and McGuire 1999: 196). Furthermore, archaeologists' preoccupation with what enslaved people acquired or purchased misses the point regarding the significance of the informal economies in which enslaved people were engaged. That enslaved people were able to use slavery for their own ends provides insights into their agency. It is this kind of analysis that will further the development of a postcolonial archaeology of the African diaspora.

In the practice of African diaspora archaeology, archaeologists need to continue reevaluating how they see their role as specialists of the past. Despite two decades of discussion and debate concerning the ownership of the past, some archaeologists still project the attitude that they are the owners of the past, bringing aspects of a silenced or unrecorded history to oppressed communities, rather than perceiving their job as uncovering someone else's tradition and history (Singleton and Orser 2003: 150). Archaeologists should also be willing to admit they do not have all the answers and their research can best be described as "works in progress." The study of slavery and emancipation, in particular, requires archaeologists to confront, with sensitivity, a wide range of horrific and painful topics and to discuss these issues in ways that make them intellectually liberating.

Conclusion: Decolonizing Archaeologies of Slavery and Emancipation

How do we continue to decolonize the archaeology of slavery and emancipation? First, we must acknowledge that this research needs to be decolonized like any other area of archaeological study because of the ties archaeology has had with colonialism, and the tendency of archaeological practitioners to impose Western views on their data. We should not become complacent and assume that this research has been liberated because it developed in response to liberation movements of the 1960s and 1970s. Second, we must ask ourselves, What are the ultimate goals of postcolonial archaeology of the African diaspora? If decolonization means an archaeology based on non-Western precepts and assumptions, as has been proposed for anthropology as a whole (Harrison 1991: 7), then archaeology has a long way to go, and it is unlikely that such an archaeology will be realized in the near future. To realize such an archaeology requires us to rethink many concepts that we use and take for granted in our work or that we assume meant the same to the people we study as they do today (as in the previous discussion of consumption). On the other hand, if the goal is to apply core concepts of postcolonial theory to the archaeological study of slavery and emancipation, then this process has begun in earnest. We must not accept these concepts uncritically, however; instead, we should continue to critique our use of postcolonial theories and improve on them. Third, and finally, we must always be mindful of neocolonialist tendencies to revert back to older paradigms, models, or interpretations that impede rather than advance our understanding of subaltern people both in the past and in the present.

References

Agbe-Davies, A. S. 2002. Black scholars, Black pasts. *The SAA Archaeological Record* 4 (2): 24–28.

Agorsah, E. K. 1993. Archaeology and resistance history in the Caribbean. *African Archaeological Review* 11: 175–195.

———. 2005. Tracking down the maroons: Archaeogeography of marronage in the Caribbean, in C. Tavárez and M. A. García Arévalo (eds.), *Proceedings of the 20th International Congress for Caribbean Archaeology*, pp. 731–741. Santo Domingo, Dominican Republic: Museo del Hombre Dominican and Fundación García Arévalo.

———. 2007. New trends in maroon archaeology in Suriname: Transformation processes, in A. Curet, B. Reid, and H. P. Roget (eds.), *Proceedings of the 21st International Congress for Caribbean Archaeology*, pp. 555–563. St. Augustine, Trinidad & Tobago: School of Continuing Education, University of West Indies.

Andrews, G. R. 2004. *Afro-Latin America 1800– 2000*. New York: Oxford University Press.

Armstrong, D. V. 2003. *Creole Transformation from Slavery to Freedom: Historical Archaeology of the East End Community of St. John, Virgin Islands*. Gainesville: University Press of Florida.

Armstrong, D. V., and Kelly, K. G. 2000. Settlement patterns and the origins of African Jamaican society: Seville Plantation, St. Ann's Bay, Jamaica. *Ethnohistory* 47 (2): 369–397.

Arrom, J. J., and García Arévalo, M. A. 1986. *Cimarron*. Serie Monográfica No. 18, Fundación García-Arévalo, Santo Domingo, Dominican Republic.

Berlin, I. 1998. *Many Thousands Gone: The First Two Centuries of Slavery in North*

America. Cambridge: Harvard University Press.
Bower, B. A., and Rushing, B. 1980. The African Meeting House. The Center for the 19th-Century Afro-American community in Boston, in R. L. Schuyler (ed.), *Archaeological Perspectives on Ethnicity in America*, pp. 69–75. Farmingdale, NY: Baywood.
Bridges, S., and Salwen, B. 1980. Weeksville: The archaeology of a black urban community, in R. L. Schuyler (ed.), *Archaeological Perspectives on Ethnicity in America*, pp. 38–47. Farmingdale, NY: Baywood.
Bullen, A. K., and Bullen, R. P. 1945. Black Lucy's Garden. *Bulletin of the Massachusetts Archaeological Society* 6 (2): 17–28.
Davis, B. 2001. Impact of the French and Haitian revolutions, in D. Geggus (ed.), *The Impact of the Haitian Revolution in the Atlantic World*, pp. 1–14. Columbia: University of South Carolina Press.
Cox, B. R. 2007. The archaeology of the Allensworth Hotel: Negotiating the system in Jim Crow America. M.A. thesis, Cultural Management Resources Program, Sonoma State University.
Deagan, K. A. 1998. Transculturation and Spanish American ethnogenesis: The archaeological legacy of the Quincentenary, in J. Cusick (ed.), *Studies in Culture Contact Interaction, Culture, Change and Archaeology*, pp. 23–43. Carbondale: Center for Archaeological Investigations, Southern Illinois University.
Deagan, K. A., and MacMahon, D. 1995. *Fort Mose: Colonial America's Black Fortress of Freedom*. Gainesville: University Press of Florida.
Deetz, J. 1977. *In Small Things Forgotten: An Archaeology of Early American Life*. New York: Anchor Books.
Derry, L. 2003. Consequences of involving archaeology in contemporary community issues, in L. Derry and M. Malloy (eds.), *Archaeologists and Local Communities: Partners in Exploring the Past*, pp. 19–30. Washington, DC: Society for American Archaeology.
Domínguez González, L. 1986. Fuentes arqueológicas en le estudio de la esclavitud en Cuba, in *La esclavitud en Cuba*, pp. 267–269. Havana: Editora de la Academica de Ciencias de Cuba.
Epperson, T. W. 1990. Race and the disciplines of the plantation. *Historical Archaeology* 24 (4): 29–36.
Fairbanks, C. H., and Smith, H. 1958. Anthropology and the segregation problem. *Florida State University Studies* 28: 1–18.
Farnsworth, P. 1993. What is the use of plantation archaeology? No use at all, if no one else is listening! *History of Archaeology* 27 (1): 114–116.
Fennell, C. C. 2007. *Crossroad Cosmologies: Diasporas and Ethnogenesis in the New World*. Gainesville: University Press of Florida.
Ferguson, L. G. 1992. *Uncommon Ground: Archaeology and Colonial African America, 1650–1800*. Washington, DC: Smithsonian Institution Press.
Gibson, H. 2007. *Daily Practice and Domestic Economies in Guadeloupe: An Archaeological and Historical Study*. Ph.D. dissertation, Department of Anthropology, Syracuse University.

Geggus, D. P. 2001. *The Impact of the Haitian Revolution in the Atlantic World*. Columbia: University of South Carolina Press.

Gosden, C. 2001. Postcolonial archaeology: Issues of culture, identity, and knowledge, in I. Hodder (ed.), *Archaeological Theory Today*, pp. 241–261. New York: Polity Press.

Harrison, F. 1991. Anthropology as an agent of transformation: Introductory comments and queries, in F. V. Harrison (ed.), *Decolonizing Anthropology: Moving Further toward an Anthropology for Liberation*, pp. 1–14. Washington, DC: American Anthropological Association.

Haviser, J. B. 1999. Identifying a post-emancipation (1863–1940) African-Curaçaoan material culture assemblage, in J. B. Haviser (ed.), *African Sites: Archaeology in the Caribbean*, pp. 221–263. Princeton: Markus Wiener.

——. 2001. Historical archaeology in the Netherlands, Antilles and Aruba, in P. Farnsworth (ed.), *Island Lives: Historical Archaeologies of the Caribbean*, pp. 60–81. Tuscaloosa: University of Alabama Press.

Johnson, M., and Roark, J. L. 1984. *Black Masters: A Free Family of Color in the Old South*. New York: W. W. Norton.

Kelly, K., and Gibson, H. 2005. Plantation village archaeology in Guadeloupe, French West Indies, in C. Tavárez and M. A. García Arévalo (eds.), *Proceedings of the XX Congress for Caribbean Archaeology*, pp. 788–795. Dominican Republic.

Kusimba, C. M. 2004. Archaeology of slavery in East Africa. *African Archaeological Review* 21 (2): 59–88.

Landers, J., and Deagan, K. 1999. Fort Mosé: Earliest free African-American town in the United States, in T. Singleton (ed.), *I, Too, Am America: Archaeological Studies of African-American Life*, pp. 261–282. Charlottesville: University Press of Virginia.

LaRoche, C., and Blakey, M. 1997. Seizing intellectual power: The dialogue at the New York African Burial Ground. *Historical Archaeology* 31 (3): 84–106.

La Rosa Corzo, G. 2003. *Runaway Slave Settlements in Cuba: Resistance and Expression*. Translated by M. Todd. Chapel Hill: University Press of North Carolina.

——. 2005. Subsistence of *cimarrones*: An archaeological study, in L. A. Curet, S. L. Dawdy, and G. La Rosa Corzo (eds.), *Dialogues in Cuban Archaeology*, pp. 163–180. Tuscaloosa: University of Alabama Press.

Leone, M. P., and Fry, G.-M. 1999. Conjuring in the big house kitchen. *Journal of American Folklore* 112 (445): 372–403.

Leone, M., Mullins, P. R., Creveling, M., Hurst, L., Nash, B. J., Jones, L., Kaiser, H. J., Logan, G. C., and Warner M. S. 1995. Can an African American archaeology be an alternative voice? in I. Hodder, M. Shanks, A. Alexandri, V. Buchi, J. Carman, J. Last, and G. Lucas (eds.), *Interpretative Archaeologies*, pp. 110–124. London: Routledge.

McDavid, C. 2003. Collaboration, power, and the Internet: The public archaeology of the Levi Jordan Plantation, in L. Derry and M. Malloy (eds.), *Archaeologists and Local Communities: Partners in Exploring the Past*, pp. 45–66. Washington, DC: Society for American Archaeology.

McDavid, C., and Babson, D. (eds.). 1997. In the realm of politics: Prospects for public participation in African-American and plantation archaeology. *Historical Archaeology* 31 (3): 1–152.

McKee, L. 1992. The ideals and realities behind the design and use of 19th century Virginia slave cabins, in A. Yentsch and M. Beaudry (eds.), *The Art and Mystery of Historical Archaeology: Essays in Honor of Jim Deetz*, pp. 195–213. Boca Raton, FL: CRC Press.

———. 1994. Is it futile to try and be useful? Historical archaeology and the African-American experience. *Northeast Historical Archaeology* 23: 1–7.

Mintz, S. W. 1985. *Sweetness and Power: The Place of Sugar in Modern History*. New York: Viking.

Mullins, P. R. 1999. *Race and Affluence: An Archaeology of African America and Consumer Culture*. New York: Kluwer Academic/ Plenum Publishers.

Orser, C., Jr., and Funari, P. P. A. 2001. Archaeology of slave resistance and rebellion. *World Archaeology* 31 (1): 59–72.

Potter, P. 1991. What is the use of plantation archaeology? *Historical Archaeology* 25 (3): 94–107.

Pulis, J. 2006. "Important truths" and "pernicious follies": Texts, covenants, and the Anabaptist Church of Jamaica, in K. Yelvington (ed.), *Afro-Atlantic Dialogues: Anthropology in the Diaspora*, pp. 193–210. Santa Fe: SAR Press.

Samford, P. M. 2007. *Subfloor Pits and the Archaeology of Slavery in Colonial Virginia*. Tuscaloosa: University Press of Alabama.

Singleton, T. 1988. Archaeological framework for slavery and emancipation, 1740–1880, in M. Leone and P. Potter (eds.), *Recovery of Meaning: Historical Archaeology in the Eastern United States*, pp. 345–370. Washington, DC: Smithsonian Institution Press.

———. 1995. Archaeology of slavery in North America. *Annual Reviews in Anthropology* 24: 119–140.

———. 2001. Slavery and spatial dialectics on Cuban coffee plantations. *World Archaeology* 33 (1): 98–114.

———. 2005. An archaeological study of slavery on a Cuban coffee plantation, in G. La Rosa Corzo, A. Curet, and S. L. Dawdy (eds.), *Dialogues in Cuban Archaeology*, pp. 181–199. Tuscaloosa: University of Alabama Press.

Singleton, T., and Orser, Jr., C. E. 2003. Descendant communities: Linking people in the present with the past, in L. J. Zimmerman, K. D. Vitelli, and J. Hollowell-Zimmer (eds.), *Ethical Issues in Archaeology*, pp. 143–152. Walnut Creek, CA: AltaMira Press.

Veblen, T. 1899. *The Theory of the Leisure Class*. London: George Allen and Unwin.

Walz, J. R., and Brandt, S. A. 2006. Toward an archaeology of the other African diaspora: The slave trade and dispersed Africans in the western Indian Ocean, in J. B. Haviser and K. C. MacDonald (eds.), *African Re-genesis: Confronting Social Issues in the Diaspora*, pp. 246–268. New York: University College London Press.

Weik, T. 2007. Allies, adversaries, and kin in the African Seminole communities of Florida: Archaeology at Pilaklikaha, in A. Ogundiran and T. Falola (eds.), *Archaeology of Atlantic Africa and the African Diaspora*, pp. 311–331. Bloomington: Indiana University Press.

Wilkie, L. A. 2000. *Creating Freedom: Material Culture and African American Identity at Oakley Plantation, 1840–1950*. Baton Rouge: Louisiana State University Press.

Wilkie, L., and Bartoy, K. 2000. A critical archaeology revisited. *Current Anthropology* 41 (5): 747– 777.

Wurst, L. A., and McGuire, R. H. 1999. Immaculate consumption: A critique of the "shop till you drop" school of human behavior. *International Journal of Historical Archaeology* 3 (3): 191–199.

14

ENCOUNTERS WITH POSTCOLONIALISM IN IRISH ARCHAEOLOGY

Charles E. Orser, Jr.

The question of whether Ireland is non-colonial, colonial, or postcolonial is hotly contested, and archaeologists (like historians and other scholars) have yet to reach a consensus on an answer (Ruane 1992). One's view on the question of Irish postcolonialism, or even of a colonial past, is largely a reflection of one's political views. Though perhaps a gross oversimplification, those generally to the right of the political spectrum tend to downplay colonialism (and thus deny a postcolonial condition), while those to the left argue that Ireland was indeed colonial in the past and that it now exhibits many of the characteristics of a postcolonial society.

This brief essay cannot provide a definitive resolution to the question of Ireland's colonial past and postcolonial present, nor would it seek to do so even if final resolution were possible. Suffice it to say that the history of Ireland appears to encapsulate many of the elements identified by others as colonial and postcolonial experiences (see Childs and Williams 1997: 1–23). Perhaps the most enduring and visible aspect of Ireland's past is the division of the island into the Republic of Ireland, an independent nation, and Northern Ireland, part of the United Kingdom. That the creation of the republic is a 20th-century phenomenon should provide insight into the contested nature of Ireland's past, even for those with no knowledge of Irish history.

The history of Ireland is so complex and interwoven with European and Atlantic history that even scholars who acknowledge the island's colonial past disagree about the precise terminology to describe it. Some writers prefer the term "neocolonial" because it indicates that Ireland is irrevocably connected to the United Kingdom (even though the republic itself is independent), but others think "postcolonial" is more appropriate (Howe 2000: 146). Regardless, the last term usefully indicates that the island's character has been historically shaped by foreign rule and that the legacy of such rule continues to be felt by present-day inhabitants. The use of "colonial" and "postcolonial" neatly describes the initial development and much of the current character of contemporary Irish history and thus Irish archaeology, the subject of this essay. Given the contestation and the myriad interpretations of Irish history that are possible, the purpose of this chapter is to present a few examples to illustrate how Irish archaeology might be perceived as operating within a postcolonial framework. That the issue of colonialism in Ireland continues to be debated may be the best indicator that much exists here to be contemplated. The continuing contestation of Irish history, and particularly its many meanings in the contemporary world, indicates that this essay cannot be definitive.

Anyone the least bit cognizant of the history of the past four decades is aware of the tension that has been occasioned by the history of Ireland and the role of the British government on the island. Residents of Northern Ireland, and especially those living along the once disputed border (as well as in the larger cities of the republic), have experienced the conflict in personal, often devastating ways. The partition of Ireland in May 1921, which occasioned the establishment of the political entity called Northern Ireland, was a colonial act with far-reaching consequences (Adams 1994: 3). Conversely, the creation of the republic might be termed a postcolonial act because, though its earliest manifestations were centuries old, its most lasting rebellion occurred in 1916, just before the civil war that brought about partition (Boyce 1996: 170–175).

Irish politicians have appreciated the important role that the ancient history of the island has played in Irish culture, and they often entwine politics with famous archaeological sites. A well-known example is Daniel O'Connell's use of the Hill of Tara in the mid-19th century. O'Connell, the organizer of the Repeal movement (the goal of which was to create a quasi-independent Ireland), held one of his "monster meetings" at the ancient mound on August 15, 1843. This meeting at the renowned seat of the ancient Gaelic kings of Ireland was said to have attracted thousands of people (Mitchel 1868: 533–534). Governmental pressure forced O'Connell to temper his agitation, but his role as "The Liberator" has remained entrenched in Irish historical mythology (Uí Ógáin 1996). O'Connell was "no radical"; he was a landlord who respected private property (Metscher 2001: 59), and a radical interpretation has not judged him kindly (see Connolly 1983: 93–94). The fact that protesters are attempting, at the time of this writing, to change the route of the new M3 motorway to protect the Hill of Tara, now from its own government, demonstrates how the Irish archaeological landscape can be a focal point for mass political action. Similar protests within recent memory, such as those involving the Viking remains at Wood Quay (Heffernan 1988) and the medieval Carrickmines Castle (O'Keeffe 2005), demonstrate that archaeological sites have the ability to rally large numbers of non-archaeologists to fight for preservation and scientific analysis. That such sites have been eventually destroyed after varying amounts of archaeological research speaks more to the power of present-day capitalism (some would simply say "progress") than to the people's will to resist.

In addition to its political history, much of recent Irish cultural history is imbued with postcolonial meaning. Important contemporary writers have recounted the effects of colonialism and intervention in many literary styles. A poignant example is Brian Friel's (1981) *Translations*, in which he explores the impact the Royal Engineers had on a small Irish-speaking community in County Donegal in 1833 during the initial fieldwork for the Ordnance Survey. Friel tells the personal side of the colonial encounter in one tiny part of the Province of Ulster, but the essence of his tale was undoubtedly replayed wherever English surveyors established their camps and interacted with the local inhabitants (Doherty 2004; Ó Cadhla 2007).

Many contemporary social theorists easily associate present-day Ireland with postcolonialism. In fact, Edward Said (1993), a major architect of postcolonial theory, has given considerable thought to the history of Ireland in his major study of imperialism. Much of this research is based on literary sources, but other scholars have followed Said's lead, using both literary and historical analysis (e.g., Carroll and King 2003; Childs and Williams 1997: 66–73; Frame 1981; Gibbon 1975; Gibbons 1992; Graham 2001; Kiberd 1996; McDonough 2005; Ó Ceallaigh 1998; Smyth 2000).

The linkage between postcolonialism and Irish archaeology perhaps may be appreciated by examining two issues: the early history of Irish archaeology, and the way in which the archaeology of the plantation and post-plantation eras has allowed archaeologists working in Ireland to address issues of interest to postcolonial scholars. The plantation and post-plantation eras offer excellent avenues to investigate the colonial and postcolonial histories of Ireland using archaeological approaches and materials. Further research in these periods will help archaeologists to refine our perspectives on the relationships between the past and the present and the ways in which the two influence each other.

A Historical Perspective on Irish Archaeology

Archaeology in Ireland was founded as antiquarianism before the creation of the Irish Free State and Northern Ireland in 1921. The archaeology conducted during this period was overtly based on British methods and models and was usually conducted by members of the Anglo-Irish aristocracy. Archaeology by members of learned, elite families is not surprising, because these were individuals most likely to have the time and education to pursue such pastimes. When formally educated, such individuals typically received their training in elite institutions whose mandates generally involved the maintenance of the status quo.

These early archaeologists' interpretations tended to conform to their backgrounds and consequently often supported the desires, wishes, and goals of the ruling power. In keeping with this idea, Geoffrey Keating's early 17th-century analysis of the Hill of Tara has been interpreted as mirroring then-current aristocratic fears about parliamentary rule (Waddell 2005: 27–28).

The interpretations offered by the island's earliest antiquarians were often wrong and sometimes even far-fetched, with many prehistoric monuments being grossly misidentified. Given the long-term habitation of the island, it comes as no surprise that the earliest archaeology in Ireland was focused on sites that were ancient in date and readily visible on the landscape. Ireland has a rich store of world-class sites of great antiquity, so the earliest archaeologists' attention to these places is not unusual. But early in the history of Irish archaeology, two contemporary threads can be identified. One, academic and unimpassioned, represents the state of scientific archaeological practice. In this thread, pioneering archaeologists excavated sites to the best of their abilities and were largely content with merely describing what they had discovered. These kinds of "foundational histories" (Leone 2006: 139) presented the frequently dry, albeit vastly important, texts of archaeological primers. At the same time, however, a second thread was pursued as part of the Gaelic Revival movement of the late 19th century. This thread was overtly political in that it sought to make ancient archaeological sites part of the emerging nation's story.

The most important nationalist association was the Gaelic League, which promoted the idea that Ireland was a culturally definable nation (McCartney 1995: 297). The Gaelic Revival conflated politics and romanticism, a mix that is continued today by the mostly tourist-driven, mythical image of Ireland as the enchanted "Land of Saints and Scholars" (Brett 1996: 3). Douglas Hyde, Gaelic scholar and first president of the Republic of Ireland, wrote one of the most famous tracts of the revival, entitled "The Necessity for De-Anglicising Ireland." Speaking to the National Literary Society in 1892, Hyde argued that the Revival was not intended "as a protest against imitating what is *best* in the English people, for that would be absurd, but rather to show the folly of neglecting what is Irish, and hastening to adopt, pell-mell, and indiscriminately, everything that is English, simply because it 'is' English" (Hyde 1986: 153, emphasis in original). Significantly, Hyde opined that, even though "most Irishmen will naturally" view his position as one of nationalism, the idea of blending the Irish and the English really "ought also to claim the sympathies of every intelligent Unionist." Though the League attracted politically radical nationalists, Hyde is most accurately described as a cultural nationalist rather than a political nationalist (Crooke 2000: 25–26).

Until recently, archaeologists wrote texts that presented culture history devoid of social context (Ó Ríordáin 1964). Such authors tended to think pragmatically and atheoretically, seeking to eliminate (or at least to ignore) the political dimensions of archaeology (Cooney 1996; O'Keeffe 2006). Their texts provide abundant information about the various cultural expressions of Irish prehistory. Thus, they represent more foundational history but carefully avoid contextualizing the analyses in terms of contemporary society. Such careful dispassion is in clear evidence even though the authors, as citizens of the Republic of Ireland or Northern Ireland, could never entirely divorce themselves from the contemporary politics of their surroundings.

William F. Wakeman (1995: viii–ix), who in 1848 wrote the first book about Irish prehistory aimed at a popular audience (Waddell 2005: 138), argued that Irish tourists should learn to appreciate the ancient remains in their own country rather than travel to England and the Continent to see prehistoric ruins there. His position appears similar to Hyde's culturalist stance, but his typology for Irish archaeology is revealing because he divides the remains of Ireland's archaeological history into three temporal segments: pagan antiquities, early Christian antiquities, and Anglo-Irish remains. The first two categories provide insights into the general perception of Irish antiquities as uniquely tied to religion, but Wakeman's last category is perhaps most pertinent when thinking about the role of colonial thinking in early Irish archaeology. His use of "Anglo-Irish" is equally political and religious. It has a religious connotation because he includes ecclesiastical structures such as abbeys, cathedrals, and churches in this category. However, he broadens the term to include purely secular and administrative structures as well. Nonetheless, Wakeman is unclear here about how much British influence can be assigned to the design and construction of these structures, and so he appears uncertain how to characterize them. He identifies the mass settlement of the English in Ireland as "the Invasion," but adopts a gradualist view of cultural evolution over any sort of quick acceptance of foreign traits by Irish men and women (Wakeman 1995: 196–197).

Wakeman's use of religion as a typological key variable is open to interpretation. On one hand, his usage may simply represent a convention that he believed his readers would find understandable and meaningful. The official care of historic monuments in Ireland began in 1869 with the disestablishment of the Church of Ireland (see Milne 2003). Preservation-minded individuals realized at the time that important church buildings would be unprotected unless the state intervened to save them (Hamlin 1989: 171–172). Thus, Wakeman's use of religion as a variable would make contextual sense. It remains possible, however, that his usage may have been strictly personal or at least comfortable within his own way of thinking. A more contextualized interpretation might focus on the then-contemporary visibility of religious affiliation. His division of Christians and pagans might be understood as the historical version of the separation of Catholics and Protestants in mid-19th-century Ireland. It may be noteworthy that Wakeman's book appeared only nineteen years after Catholic Emancipation in Ireland (1829), and only two years before the creation of the Gaelic League. During this period of history, the term "Anglo-Irish" had particularly salient meanings to real men and women living in Ireland. Those outside that social category generally believed that the term denoted privilege, opportunity, and access to wealth and social advancement. The presence of the Anglo-Irish on the landscape was visible in great houses, well-manicured formal gardens, and huge demesnes.

Robert A. S. Macalister, who held the chair of archaeology at University College Dublin throughout the first half of the 20th century, was by all accounts a central figure in the development of scientifically oriented Irish archaeology (Waddell 2005: 192–197). He tackled the intricacies of sequencing Irish prehistory and used large-scale excavation methods. In a revealing moment of self-reflection that appears in the back of his *The Archaeology of Ireland*, first published in 1928 and revised in 1949, Macalister obliquely mentions the need to keep archaeology and Irish politics separate. Reacting against romanticizing Irish history by too strongly believing the truth of ancient tales (undoubtedly a reference to the use of archaeological themes by romantic writers, including those of the Gaelic League) Macalister (1996: 369) affirms that Irish archaeology must place unshakable reliance on "stern hard brutal facts" rather than sentiment. Specifically referring to the rejuvenation of the Irish language, a cause of many Irish nationalists and certainly of the Gaelic League, Macalister notes that the passing of the language was merely the result of normal cultural evolution; nothing sinister or overtly political was involved. Most Irish nationalists would strongly oppose this interpretation (e.g., Adams 1994: 122–123; Collins 1996:102).

In a guide to the collection of Irish antiquities housed in the National Museum of Ireland, Joseph Raftery, then Keeper of Irish Antiquities at the museum, presents a fairly standard chronology of Irish cultural materials. In a surprising passage, however, he presages a postcolonial critique by juxtaposing the poverty of the Irish countryside with the abundance often present in the towns of the Anglo-Irish. He characterizes 18th-century Ireland as a land of contrasts, where "poverty and misery [exist] on one side . . . great wealth and power on the other" (Raftery 1960: 96). Raftery (1976) was one of the few archaeologists in Ireland who would foresee and support the development of post-medieval archaeology (Orser 2006a: 12). His critique in a publication intended for visitors to the National Museum indicates that he believed that historic inequalities in wealth were worth considering and perhaps were well within the scope of archaeological research.

Archaeologists working in the Republic of Ireland generally avoided the archaeology of the Tudor plantation era, which began when the British decided to create "improved" settlements of immigrants in the 16th century. Such avoidance was generally not necessary in Northern Ireland, where the effects of colonization were always readily apparent. As cultural anthropologist William Kelleher (2003) has noted, many of the social spaces in Northern Ireland were designed as British and Protestant, unlike in the Republic, which was generally perceived as Irish and Catholic. The true social situation was much more complex, as Kelleher points out, but one implication of the easy acceptance of Britishness was that writers of guidebooks could include post-medieval remains as culturally significant archaeological sites. In fact, in the context of Northern Ireland, the presence of colonial outposts in guidebooks could be viewed as one way of promoting the Anglo-Irish ascendancy in Ireland and its relative "success" in Northern Ireland. The acceptance of plantation-era buildings as archaeological remains could be viewed as part of the state's ideological mandate. Authors of guidebooks could note, for example, that the castles of British planters in the north of Ireland required fortification because the Scottish and English settlers had been "[p]lanted among a more or less hostile population" (Jope 1952: 31), meaning the indigenous Gaelic Irish.

Some archaeologists have found it possible to ignore colonialism even at sites with clear associations to the historical process. A useful example derives from excavations at King John's Castle in Limerick (Sweetman 1980). This 13th-century fortification was designed using the mind-set of a conquering people. The Norman English originally built the castle on the River Shannon as a frontier stronghold demarcating the line between the Gaelic ("wild") west and the Norman ("civilized") east. In 1651, Cromwell's forces took the castle by force and maintained foreign control of the area. Sweetman's excavation uncovered abundant evidence of Cromwell's siege and the post-siege occupation, and he dutifully identifies and describes the material objects found during excavation. His research represents solid archaeological practice, and he provides a useful foundational history for the site. It may be unreasonable to expect a deeper analysis, given the nature of the discipline when he was conducting the study. Still, a more nuanced interpretation would have significantly improved our knowledge of the multicultural environment experienced in and around the castle.

Without question, Irish archaeology has generally suffered from an overreliance on what appears to be atheoretical description. But as noted above, the frequent mention of cultural evolution tends to refute that all past archaeological practitioners were truly atheoretical. Rather, it appears that many archaeologists, some of them quite prominent in the discipline, espoused a view that foregrounded the inevitability of gradual change. Viewed with a political lens, this gradualist perspective might be perceived as a safe way to practice scientific archaeology and yet stay above the political fray that has been apparent in Ireland for many years. The question, of course, is whether the position of true neutrality is ever really possible. Was the acceptance of gradual evolution acquiescence to British rule or a subtle clue about the belief that political change was sure to come?

Colonial and Postcolonial Archaeologies in Ireland

With noticeable exception, Irish archaeology has been almost totally focused on the era before the advent of writing, or before the Early Middle Ages. The beginnings of written history in Ireland extend to the 5th century C.E., but the archaeology of medieval history has been slower to develop in Ireland than in either Great Britain or the European continent. That the first academic chair in medieval archaeology was only appointed in the early 1970s and, in Northern Ireland, was "due in large measure to the history and politics of the island in the present century" (Barry 1987: 1). The ideologically forged connection between the new republic and the ancient Celtic past (overtly tangible by the stone circles, corbeled burial chambers, and massive earthworks on the pre-plantation landscape) made the archaeology of medieval Ireland, whose subject matter was the colonial past, seem less relevant and perhaps even dangerous. The archaeology of the medieval past raised the issue of how much Englishness should be tolerated in the Irish republic. In other words, was archaeology that began with the Middle Ages really the examination of Ireland's "true" past, or was medieval archaeology in Ireland merely the archaeology of foreigners? That the studied goal was to stay clear of the question (and the possible answer) is suggested by the fact that Ireland was unique in Europe for its scholarly neglect of castles until only recently (McNeill 1997: 1).

The unavoidable reality, however, is that the history of the Irish Middle Ages was readily accessible and difficult to ignore. Abundant physical remains, such as the tower houses of the landed gentry (including many Gaelic lords), were a constant presence and potent reminder (Leask 1951: 75–99). Given the nature of their data, medieval archaeologists generally have been less hesitant to consider the island's colonial past, even though a substantial body of literature in Irish medieval archaeology is devoid of any overt recognition of it. The word "colonial" has begun to appear in the literature of medieval Irish archaeology (e.g., O'Keeffe 2000: 12–14), but it remains true that archaeologists can present the Irish Middle Ages in a manner that is entirely consistent with the way in which textbooks of prehistory have been prepared, as solidly researched albeit carefully dispassionate overviews of housing types, artifact styles, and settlement patterns.

The archaeological investigation of the post-medieval era has generally developed in Ireland in much the same dispassionate manner as medieval archaeology (O'Keeffe 2006). The Society for Post-Medieval Archaeology publishes an annual list of excavations in Great Britain and Ireland for each preceding year. Surveys for the years 1990–1995 and 2000–2005 reveal that archaeologists have been extremely active in both the Republic of Ireland and Northern Ireland. Much of the research and publication, however, is descriptive in character. Perhaps the reliance on descriptive discourse is merely practical. After all, post-medieval archaeology is a fairly recent development in Ireland (Donnelly and Horning 2002), and first steps necessarily involve the identification and understanding of the relevant material culture. The path from description to interpretation has been the trajectory of historical archaeologies throughout the world. But since about 2004, the analyses of post-medieval archaeologists have grown increasingly visible (Horning et al. 2008).

Some of the sites archaeologists have investigated are especially ripe for postcolonial analysis. Post-medieval castles, fortified houses, and plantation landscapes provide prime arenas for postcolonial analysis. One example is Kilcolman Castle in County Cork. The castle and a huge, surrounding landscape were deeded to Edmund Spencer, English administrator and author of *The Faerie Queen*, who renovated the castle and lived there from 1588 to 1598. He and his family were forced to flee when forces involved in Tyrone's rebellion burned the castle and other seats of English power in the vicinity. Eric Klingelhöfer excavated at the castle site during the mid-1990s (Klingelhöfer 1999, 2005). His related research on the homes of English elites in Ireland (Klingelhöfer 2003) is especially important, because he seeks to unravel the distinctions between colonialism and imperialism. His research in this regard provides an example of comparative colonial archaeology, a line of inquiry that is just beginning to be explored in Ireland (Delle 1999b; Horning 2006a, 2006b).

Comparative colonial archaeology has a sporadic history in Ulster, where a few American archaeologists have shown interest (Blades 1986). This research began in the 1980s (Brannon 1999: 99), but it is likely that increasing numbers of archaeologists will take up this fruitful area of research in the immediate future (Mallory and McNeill 1991). A significant and highly contextualized examination in this vein is Colin Breen's (2005) study of the cultural landscape of southwestern County Cork. This study establishes a serious precedent for future research because his investigation tackles many of the issues, such as cultural change and identity formation, that have a prominent place in postcolonial studies.

In 2004, two issues of the *International Journal of Historical Archaeology* addressed the new directions some historical archaeologists were pursuing in Ireland. Most of the authors directly confronted issues of power and social control, prime areas of research in postcolonial archaeology. For example, James Boyle (2004) notes how archaeologists investigating early medieval Ireland have tended to overlook the poor. This propensity not to see the disadvantaged is consistent with an overly strong reliance on textual documentation, because the written evidence for the medieval period concentrates almost exclusively on the rights and responsibilities of the wealthy minority. Archaeology thus provides an important tool for investigating people erased from the dominant historical narrative. Alexandra Hartnett (2004) explores the illegal importation of tobacco in Galway City in the 17th century and investigates 19th-century smoking pipes that carried overt political statements, such as "Home Rule" and "Repeal" (Hull 2006: 52). Harnett's thinking about the "Politics of the Pipe" is especially important in helping archaeologists make the connection between specific artifacts and larger political issues. In addition, the presence of Irish-affiliated, politically charged smoking pipes in the United States and Canada (Brighton 2004;

Jelks 1973) indicates the transnational implications of some of the political movements that were important within the context of Ireland and Irish North America. Audrey Horning (2004) writes about cultural identity in the far north of the island. Her contention that the settlement at the Goodland site represents the remains of a 17th-century village of Highland Scots raises important issues about the nature of identity and cultural complexity in a social world that is often interpreted as consisting merely of a British-Irish duality.

In a particularly important article, Andrew Tierney (2004) directly confronts the connection between archaeology and the Gaelic Revival. He focuses on the way individuals in the 19th century variously perceived castles. For academics, castles were subjects of analysis and description, but for non-academic revivalists, castles functioned as romantic symbols of a great lost age. Using Leap Castle in County Offaly as an example, Tierney provides an insightful analysis that tacitly uses Henri Lefebvre's (1991: 38–39) three social spaces: "spatial practice," "representations of space," and "representational space." The Gaelic O'-Carroll clan built Leap Castle before 1514, but in the second half of the 17th century it fell to a family of British landed aristocracy. Tierney's analysis shows how the new owners confronted and wrestled with their identity in the politically charged atmosphere of late 19th-century Ireland.

Writing specifically about colonization, James Delle (1999a) has examined Irish tower houses and proposed that Gaelic designs incised into the stone on the top floor of one particular structure can be interpreted as a form of resistance to British colonizers of the plantation era. Colm Donnelly (2005) argues against Delle's interpretation, by noting that the presence of Gaelic designs may merely represent the early modern continuation of a medieval tradition to decorate secular homes with devotional iconography. Donnelly does not discount that signs of resistance may be found in Irish houses, but he proposes that the "I.H.S." (*Iesus Hominum Salvator* [Jesus, savior of mankind] or *In Hoc Salus* [In This (Cross) Salvation]) monogram may be a more evocative example of native Catholic resistance to English colonization and Protestantism. In either case, the idea that iconographic images can be used to identify elements of resistance against colonial authority situates this kind of Irish archaeology within a postcolonial perspective. Delle is concerned also with the way people can use space as a tool for both domination and resistance. Other historical archaeologists working in Ireland have also pursued this line of investigation. For example, Colin Breen (2006) has examined the spatial morphology and meaning of a utopian community established in County Clare in the 19th century, and I (Orser 2006b, 2007), using a late 17th-century L-shaped house in County Sligo as an example, have investigated the symbolic role that landscape can play in providing instruction about the nature of the social order. Wes Forsythe (2007) has pursued an important line of investigation by examining the role of land improvement on 18th- and 19th-century Rathlin Island. This research is important because it demonstrates the complex links between capitalism, landscape management, and indigenous peoples' responses to commercialization and the global marketplace. The study is also consistent with other research being conducted on the role of improvement in landscape modification in Ireland and Britain (Finch and Giles 2007; Tarlow 2007).

One particularly intriguing element of historical archaeology in Northern Ireland stems from the reality that a sizable amount of archaeological research has been conducted after terrorist bombings (Brannon 1999: 99; B. Lacey, pers. comm.). In the course of salvage efforts, archaeologists have amassed collections from Derry, Belfast, and other cities; and regardless of how one views the bombing campaigns, it might be reasonable to conclude that the Troubles in Ireland reflect a past that can be readily observed.

Other archaeologists working in Ireland will surely continue to explore elements of colonialism and its impacts in coming years. Research in medieval and post-medieval archaeology in particular appears best situated to make substantial contributions to knowledge useful for postcolonial interpretation. This short essay has sought only to introduce a few areas archaeologists are now exploring rather than to provide a complete inventory. A fuller analysis and engagement with postcolonial theory and action in Irish archaeology has yet to be written.

Conclusion

Irish archaeology represents an excellent arena in which to explore the application of postcolonial themes to the vagaries of archaeological practice. The idea that an archaeologist's interpretations might be affected by contemporary political realities appears as a given in today's archaeology. This conclusion raises important questions that many archaeologists have been confronting for the past two decades. When an archaeologist becomes cognizant of the pressing social issues of the present-day world, does he or she cease to be a dispassionate scientist? Should archaeologists even try to be dispassionate?

The role of politics in archaeology has never been easy to conceptualize. The writings of Irish archaeologists, from both the north and south, have indicated this reality in the past, and current-day writing continues to illustrate this point. Matthew Johnson (2003:29) has cogently observed that archaeologists "have all been very good at tracing the influence of politics on archaeology, but strikingly poor at making our archaeology address contemporary political debates." Sandra Scham, an archaeologist with excavation experience in the Middle East, agrees with Johnson that the study of conflict is both multidimensional and theoretical. She qualifies his assessment, however, with the comment that conflict is rooted in "real geography" and notes that "[s]ites and places are both the subjects and the scenes of conflict and because sites and places are what archaeological fieldwork is all about, archaeology in a conflict zone becomes a political statement in itself" (Scham 2006: 207). Scham's comment was elicited as part of a debate over the role of politics in Irish archaeology (Horning 2006a). This debate amply demonstrates the areas of very real contention in the archaeology of the two Irish polities that are still debatably colonial (and postcolonial). At a minimum, it seems obvious that the archaeology of Ireland has always been political, even if its political roots have been ignored, misidentified, or even denied. Attempts to remove politics in the early history of Irish archaeology merely masked historical and contemporary inequalities and removed archaeology from contemporary life. With today's calls for overtly accepting the role that archaeology plays in today's politics, broadly defined (McGuire 2008; Sabloff 2008; Saitta 2007), it appears that Irish archaeologists can play as large a role as they wish because they have much to say.

References

Adams, G. 1994. *Free Ireland: Towards a Lasting Peace*. Niwot: Roberts Rinehart.
Barry, T. B. 1987. *The Archaeology of Medieval Ireland*. London: Routledge.
Blades, B. S. 1986. English villages in the Londonderry Plantation. *Post-Medieval Archaeology* 20: 257–269.
Boyce, D. G. 1996 [1916]. Interpreting the rising, in D. G. Boyce and A. O'Day (eds.), *The Making of Modern Irish History: Revisionism and the Revisionist Controversy*, pp. 163–187. London: Routledge.
Boyle, J. W. 2004. Lest the lowliest be forgotten: Locating the impoverished in early Medieval Ireland. *International Journal of Historical Archaeology* 8: 85–99.
Brannon, N. 1999. Archives and archaeology: The Ulster Plantation in the landscape, in G. Egan and R. L. Michael (eds.), *Old and New Worlds*, pp. 97–105. Oxford: Oxbow.
Breen, C. 2005. *The Gaelic Lordship of the O'Sullivan Beare: A Landscape Cultural History*. Dublin: Four Courts Press.
——. 2006. Social archaeologies of "utopian" settlements in Ireland. *International Journal of Historical Archaeology* 10: 35–48.
Brett, D. 1996. *The Construction of Heritage*. Cork: Cork University Press.
Brighton, S. A. 2004. Symbols, myth-making, and identity: The red hand of Ulster in late 19th century Paterson, New Jersey. *International Journal of Historical Archaeology* 8: 149–164.
Carroll, C., and King, P. (eds.). 2003. *Ireland and Postcolonial Theory*. Notre Dame: University of Notre Dame Press.
Childs, P., and Williams, P. 1997. *An Introduction to Post-colonial Theory*. London: Prentice Hall.
Collins, M. 1996. *The Path to Freedom*. Boulder, CO: Roberts Rinehart.
Connolly, J. 1983. *Labour in Irish History*. Dublin: Dorset Press.
Cooney, G. 1996. Building the future on the past: Archaeology and the construction of national identity in Ireland, in M. Díaz-Andreu and T. Champion (eds.), *Nationalism and Archaeology in Europe*, pp. 146–163. London: University College London Press.
Crooke, E. 2000. *Politics, Archaeology, and the Creation of a National Museum in Ireland:*

An Expression of National Life. Dublin: Irish Academic Press.

Delle, J. A. 1999a. "A good and easy speculation": Spatial conflict, collusion, and resistance in late 16th-century Munster, Ireland. *International Journal of Historical Archaeology* 3: 11–35.

———. 1999b. Extending Europe's grasp: An archaeological comparison of colonial spatial processes in Ireland and Jamaica, in G. Egan and R. L. Michael (eds.), *Old and New Worlds*, pp. 106–116. Oxford: Oxbow.

Doherty, G. M. 2004. *The Irish Ordnance Survey: History, Culture, and Memory.* Dublin: Four Courts Press.

Donnelly, C. J. 2005. The I.H.S. monogram as a symbol of Catholic resistance in 17th-century Ireland. *International Journal of Historical Archaeology* 9: 37–42.

Donnelly, C. J., and Horning, A. 2002. Post-medieval and industrial archaeology in Ireland: An overview. *Antiquity* 76: 557–561.

Finch, J., and Giles, K. (eds.). 2007. *Design, Improvement, and Power in the Post-Medieval Landscape.* Woodbridge: Boydell and Brewer.

Forsythe, W. 2007. On the edge of improvement: Rathlin Island and the modern world. *International Journal of Historical Archaeology* 11: 221–240.

Frame, R. 1981. *Colonial Ireland, 1169–1369.* Dublin: Helicon.

Friel, B. 1981. *Translations.* London: Faber and Faber.

Gibbon, P. 1975. Colonialism and the great starvation in Ireland, 1845–9. *Race and Class* 17: 131–139.

Gibbons, L. 1992. Identity with a centre: Allegory, history, and Irish nationalism. *Cultural Studies* 6: 358–375.

Graham, C. 2001. *Deconstructing Ireland: Identity, Theory, Culture.* Edinburgh: Edinburgh University Press.

Hamlin, A. 1989. Government archaeology in Northern Ireland, in H. F. Cleere (ed.), *Archaeological Heritage Management in the Modern World*, pp. 171–181. London: Unwin Hyman.

Hartnett, A. 2004. The politics of the pipe: Clay pipes and tobacco consumption in Galway, Ireland. *International Journal of Historical Archaeology* 8: 133–147.

Heffernan, T. F. 1988. *Wood Quay: The Clash over Dublin's Viking Past.* Austin: University of Texas Press.

Horning, A. J. 2004. Archaeological explorations of cultural identity and rural economy in the north of Ireland: Goodland, County Antrim. *International Journal of Historical Archaeology* 8: 199–215.

———. 2006a. Archaeology, conflict and contemporary identity in the north of Ireland: Implications for theory and practice in comparative archaeologies of colonialism. *Archaeological Dialogues* 13: 183–219.

———. 2006b. English towns on the periphery: 17th-century town development in Ulster and the Chesapeake, in A. Green and R. Leech (eds.), *Cities in the World: Papers Given at the Conference of the Society for Post-Medieval Archaeology*, pp. 61–82. Leeds: Maney.

Horning, A., Ó Baoill, R., Donnelly, C., and Logue, P. (eds.). 2008. *The Post-Medieval*

Archaeology of Ireland, 1550–1850. Bray: Wordwell.

Howe, S. 2000. *Ireland and Empire: Colonial Legacies in Irish History and Culture*. Oxford: Oxford University Press.

Hull, K. L. 2006. History underground: Archaeological research history, methods and results, in C. Orser (ed.), *Unearthing Hidden Ireland: Historical Archaeology at Ballykilcline, County Roscommon*, pp. 37–71. Bray: Wordwell.

Hyde, D. 1986. *Language, Lore and Lyrics: Essays and Lectures*. Dublin: Irish Academic Press.

Jelks, E. B. 1973. *Archaeological Excavations at Signal Hill, Newfoundland, 1965–1966*. Canadian Historic Sites Occasional Papers in Archaeology and History 7. Ottawa: National Historic Sites Service.

Johnson, M. 2003. Muffling inclusiveness: Some notes towards an archaeology of the British, in S. Lawrence (ed.), *Archaeologies of the British: Explorations of Identity in Great Britain and Its Colonies, 1600–1945*, pp. 17–30. London: Routledge.

Jope, E. M. 1952. *Ancient Monuments in Northern Ireland not in State Charge*. Belfast: Her Majesty's Stationery Office.

Kelleher, W. F. 2003. *The Troubles in Ballybogoin: Memory and Identity in Northern Ireland*. Ann Arbor: University of Michigan Press.

Kiberd, D. 1996. *Inventing Ireland: The Literature of the Modern Nation*. London: Vintage.

Klingelhöfer, E. 1999. The castle of the *Faerie Queen*: Probing the ruins of Edmund Spencer's Irish home. *Archaeology* 52 (2): 48–52.

———. 2003. The architecture of empire: Elizabethan country houses in Ireland, in S. Lawrence (ed.), *Archaeologies of the British: Explorations of Identity in Great Britain and Its Colonies, 1600–1945*, pp. 102–115. London: Routledge.

———. 2005. Edmund Spencer at Kilcolman Castle: The archaeological evidence. *Post-Medieval Archaeology* 39: 133–154.

Leask, H. G. 1951. *Irish Castles and Castellated Houses*. Dundalk: Dundalgan Press.

Lefebvre, H. 1991. *The Production of Space*. Trans. D. Nicholson-Smith. Oxford: Blackwell.

Leone, M. P. 2006. Foundational histories. *Archaeological Dialogues* 13: 139–144.

Macalister, R. 1996 [1949]. *The Archaeology of Ireland*. London: Bracken.

Mallory, J. P., and McNeill, T. E. 1991. *The Archaeology of Ulster: From Colonization to Plantation*. Belfast: Institute of Irish Studies, Queens University of Belfast.

McCartney, D. 1995. From Parnell to Pearse, 1891–1921, in T. W. Moody and F. X. Martin (eds.), *The Course of Irish History*, pp. 294–312. Niwot: Roberts Rinehart.

McDonough, T., (ed.). 2005. *Was Ireland a Colony? Economics, Politics and Culture in 19th Century Ireland*. Dublin: Irish Academic Press.

McGuire, R. H. 2008. *Archaeology as Political Action*. Berkeley: University of California Press.

McNeill, T. 1997. *Castles in Ireland: Feudal Power in a Gaelic World*. London: Routledge.

Metscher, P. 2001. "Ireland her own": Radical movements in 19th-century Ireland. *The Republic* 2: 59–71.

Milne, K. 2003. Disestablishment, in B. Lalor (ed.), *The Encyclopedia of Ireland*, p. 301. New Haven: Yale University Press.

Mitchel, J. 1868. *The History of Ireland, from the Treaty of Limerick to the Present Time*. New York: D. and J. Sadlier.

Ó Cadhla, S. 2007. *Civilizing Ireland: Ordnance Survey, 1824–1842: Ethnography, Cartography, Translation*. Dublin: Irish Academic Press.

Ó Ceallaigh, D. (ed.). 1998. *New Perspectives on Ireland: Colonialism and Identity*. Dublin: Léirmheas.

O'Keeffe, T. 2000. *Medieval Ireland: An Archaeology*. Stroud: Tempus.

——. 2005. Heritage, rhetoric, identity: Critical reflections on the Carrickmines Castle controversy, in I. M. McCarthy (ed.), *Ireland's Heritage: Critical Perspectives on Memory and Identity*, pp. 139–151. Aldershot: Ashgate.

——. 2006. Starting as we mean to go on: Why we need a theoretically informed historical archaeology in Ireland. *Archaeological Dialogues* 13: 208–211.

Ó Ríordáin, S. P. 1964. *Antiquities of the Irish Countryside*. London: Methuen.

Orser, C. E., Jr.. 2006a. Discovering our recent pasts: Historical archaeology and early 19th-century rural Ireland, in C. E. Orser, Jr. (ed.), *Unearthing Hidden Ireland: Historical Archaeology at Ballykilcline, County Roscommon*, pp. 1–17. Bray: Wordwell.

——. 2006b. Symbolic violence and landscape pedagogy: An illustration from the Irish countryside. *Historical Archaeology* 40 (2): 28–44.

——. 2007. Estate landscapes and the cult of the ruin: A lesson of spatial transformation in rural Ireland, in J. Finch and K. Giles (eds.), *Estate Landscapes: Design, Improvement and Power in the Post-Medieval Landscape*, pp. 77–93. Suffolk, England: Boydell and Brewe.

Raftery, J. 1960. *A Brief Guide to the Collection of Irish Antiquities*. Dublin: The Stationery Office.

——. 1976. Things and people, in C. Ó Danachair (ed.), *Folk and Farm: Essays in Honour of A. T. Lucas*, pp. 235–238. Dublin: Royal Society of Antiquaries of Ireland.

Ruane, J. 1992 Colonialism and the interpretation of Irish historical development, in M. Silverman and P. H. Gulliver (eds.), *Approaching the Past: Historical Anthropology through Irish Case Studies*, pp. 293–323. New York: Columbia University Press.

Said, E. 1993. *Culture and Imperialism*. New York: Knopf.

Saitta, D. J. 2007. *The Archaeology of Collective Action*. Gainesville: University Press of Florida.

Sabloff, J. A. 2008. *Archaeology Matters: Action Archaeology in the Modern World*. Walnut Creek, CA: Left Coast Press.

Scham, S. 2006. Colony or conflict zone? *Archaeological Dialogues* 13: 205–207.

Smyth, W. J. 2000. Ireland a colony: Settlement implications of the revolution in military-administrative, urban, and ecclesiastic structure, c. 1550 to c. 1750, in T. Barry (ed.), *A History of Settlement in Ireland*, pp. 158–186. London: Routledge.

Sweetman, P. D. 1980. Archaeological excavations at King John's Castle, Limerick. *Proceedings of the Royal Irish Academy*, 80C: 207–229.

Tarlow, S. 2007. *The Archaeology of Improvement in Britain: 1750–1850*. Cambridge: Cambridge University Press.

Tierney, A. 2004. The Gothic and the Gaelic: Exploring the place of castles in Ireland's Celtic revival. *International Journal of Historical Archaeology* 8: 185–198.

Uí Ógáin, R. 1996. *Immortal Dan: Daniel O'Connell in Irish Folk Tradition*. Dublin: Geography Publications.

Waddell, J. 2005. *Foundation Myths: The Beginnings of Irish Archaeology*. Bray: Wordwell.

Wakeman, W. F. 1995. *Handbook of Irish Antiquities*. London: Bracken.

15

AN AFRICA-INFORMED VIEW OF POSTCOLONIAL ARCHAEOLOGIES

Peter R. Schmidt and Karega-Munene

The heterogeneity of the African colonial experience (e.g., Portuguese, Belgian, French, British, Italian, Spanish, Danish, Dutch, Omani, Ethiopian) defies easy generalization about the trajectories of postcolonial experiences and thought. One point of commonality that transcends postcolonial heterogeneity, however, is that African and Africanist archaeologists, unlike many postcolonial theorists, do not depend exclusively on written texts by colonial and postcolonial writers to assess how we might examine and understand colonial legacies that persist in past and contemporary historical representations.

Instead, there is a long-running tradition within the practice of African archaeology that draws extensively on oral testimonies—learning from and valorizing the representations of local historians. Archaeologists in other world areas often find that the materiality of archaeology provides the only alternative source, for example, to find and discuss subaltern lives, and they continually confront the conundrum of using a colonial library that privileges the colonizer, not the subaltern (Gullapalli 2008). Although Africanists constantly engage the colonial library, their distinctive methodology, especially the recovery and use of subaltern histories that challenge and help to deconstruct colonial narratives about the past, set them apart (e.g., Bugarin 2009; Meskell 2005; Reid and Segobye 1999; Schmidt 2006; Schmidt and Patterson 1995a, 1995b; Schmidt and Walz 2007; Van Schalkwyk and Smith 2004).

We focus here on how archaeologists are working to change their discipline in Africa and how their efforts have sometimes led to marginalization. Our assessment of practice also considers the power relationships that continue to limit opportunities and that constrain good scholarship through systems of patronage and corruption. A concentration on Africa also uncovers a number of themes and concerns that expand our understanding of postcolonial processes and trends, significantly enriching the insights gained from other world regions (Liebmann and Rizvi 2008). Among the shifts seen in the postcolonial archaeologies in Africa is the emergence of a discourse that uses auto-ethnography as well as autobiographical perspectives, both of which confer distinct advantages and points of leverage in decolonizing archaeology in Africa. These approaches more directly expose power relationships, hidden hierarchies, and how contributions outside of the canon are silenced. A necessary part of the decolonization process, they also invite misunderstandings, particularly by those who want critiques to fit within a normative framework of archaeological narrative. The escape from this conundrum, we believe, rests in the principle of transparency and open debate, not silence and fear of retribution.

Postcolonial studies reveal that political liberation has not ushered in a revolutionary disruption and overthrow of colonial ways of doing and thinking. Our consideration of postcolonial Africa is one that examines the continuing influences of colonial hegemonies, in this case those found within archaeology. Edward Said (1994: 323) observes that hegemony "is a system of pressures and constraints by which the whole cultural corpus retains its essentially imperial identity and its direction." This observation compels us to ask how to decolonize archaeology in Africa, a process much more subtle and elusive than the political decolonization of African nations. We turn now to several key themes that emerge from postcolonial archaeologies in Africa, with a special emphasis on how postcolonial archaeologies are silenced, how deep disenchantments dominate the daily lives of African peoples and the archaeologists who live and work among them, and how subaltern voices continue to be muted and erased through a rhetorical trope that falsely promises multivocality in archaeological inquiry.

Silencing Those Who Challenge Colonial Discourses

The silencing of African scholars who are not in the Western mainstream and who do not have access to recent literature because of poorly funded libraries in Africa (Schmidt and Patterson 1995a) is a condition that still persists during the postcolonial era. Silencing occurs when scholars proffer views outside the mainstream of Western scholarship and when peer review becomes a disguise to denigrate unorthodox viewpoints. Much more sinister are blatant attempts to silence those who challenge well-established paradigms that took root during the colonial era and have held sway since.

Beyond consigning work to the periphery by labeling it "controversial" or "inadequate," the most potent of the exclusionary dynamics is to ignore and to erase through silence. Joost Fontein's brilliant exegesis on this subject in his recent book

The Silence of Great Zimbabwe (2006) draws on Pierre Bourdieu's concept of symbolic violence, wherein professional status and objectivity are invoked to diminish and marginalize competing, alternative ways of seeing the past.

A poignant example is Felix Chami's (2006, 2009) experience with European responses to his research into the Neolithic along the East African littoral and offshore islands, research that contradicts the colonial and postcolonial taken-for-granted idea that human settlement along the East African littoral is linked to relatively recent in-migrations of other Africans as well as foreigners from the East. Attacks on his archaeological practice (his methods, not his broader theories about areas outside East Africa) take many forms. Rather than a full debate on the merits of the archaeological evidence, his antagonists cast doubts by affirming canonical texts and by representing his work as "inadequate" or technically sloppy. If Chami can be maneuvered to fill the role of the unreliable excavator or characterized pejoratively as an "unleashed nationalist"—through successive iterations—then his position becomes subaltern, with his voice muffled and eventually his research agenda appropriated by better-funded and more visible European expeditions.

Another domain of silencing is brought to light by Nkukuyakhe Ndlovu (2009), who unveils a dominant apartheid ideology that has yet to be purged from South African archaeology. Ndlovu describes the exclusive archaeology associations spread across South Africa, where an unspoken apartheid dampens black participation and inhibits interchange and entry into archaeological studies. Ndlovu's articulations of concern and disenchantment over the archaeological establishment in South Africa are met with skepticism and disdain by some who dismiss him as a malcontent.

Symbolic violence may also be recognized in Chaparukha Kusimba's (2009b) experiences when he recently challenged a sacrosanct paradigm in colonial interpretations of African technology (Kusimba 2001, 2009a) His important evidence that steel production on the Kenya coast entailed use of a crucible steel process for local production in the first and second millennia C.E. has been overshadowed by expert assertions that any crucible steel in sub-Saharan Africa must have been imported (e.g., Kusimba and Killick 2003; Kusimba et al. 1994),[1] relegating it to a mere footnote in African archaeology, another form of silencing (Killick 2001, 2009). Kusimba's interpretation that these materials represent local African technologists using technology from India is important on two counts: (1) that local craftsmen successfully used this technology; and (2) that the technology derived from India, suggesting a more complex interaction between the two continents at the time (Kusimba 2009a, 2009b). This interpretation, based on strong contextual evidence for local production, challenges ideas that privilege only trade, interpretive postures that place agency in the hands of outsiders and obscure the possibility of African ingenuity and agency.

Another species of silencing is seen in the experience of Simiyu Wandibba

(Karega-Munene, pers. comm.), whose petrological analysis of pottery samples from Manda on the Kenya coast was excluded from a monograph by a former and highly placed researcher in a European-funded and -controlled institute in Nairobi. The petrological evidence showed locally produced pottery, contradicting an entrenched colonialist position that Manda ceramics were imported. In both cases, Africans are thought of as passive bystanders, incapable of participating—a direct legacy of colonial thinking.

Silencing may take more clandestine and sinister expressions—all too reminiscent of colonial authoritarianism in Africa today. McIntosh (2009) discusses the "barons" who control much of the archaeological research in francophone Africa, including access to research funding, training, and publication. Their clients are *nos ancêtres*, contemporary African counterparts to colonial administrators, who block access to educational opportunities. They are gatekeepers who also control access to research, thus impinging on the well-being of nationals as well as foreign researchers.

The currents of silence run deep in the archaeology of Africa. The realization that an official can exact future payment in the form of an international trip or other payoffs in trade for research permission depends on the silence of all participants. Imperial prerogatives are at work when young African researchers are extorted, threatened with banishment or imprisonment (Schmidt 2009), or consigned to dark corners of museums and departments of antiquities without meaningful work (McIntosh 2009). The exercise of power in such circumstances creates pulsing silences.

Disenchantment and Ethical Practice

Disenchantment is a defining characteristic of the postcolonial era in Africa. Disenchantment with unrealized economic dreams and with political failures and collapse of civil society are ever present. Disenchantment with political leadership, corruption, autocratic states, human rights abuses—all of these inform the lives of Africans today, including African archaeologists as well as Africanists conducting archaeology in Africa. There are profound social and medical problems that deeply impact people as they conduct their daily lives, interpenetrating consciousness about the world in which archaeology is practiced.

It is our profound discomfort, our disenchantment about these vivid contrasts often involving the state and local peoples as well as what may be appropriate ethical practices in these circumstances, that drives us to confront and try to resolve some of the tensions and contradictions between archaeological practice and the welfare of people with whom we work and live. How is it possible to do archaeology in a community where people are dying every day from the HIV/AIDS epidemic? These profound contradictions, these disenchantments, have caused colleagues to engage in social activism as an integral part of their professional lives—for example, Alinah Segobye's (2006) employment with an HIV/AIDS intervention NGO in Botswana, Karega-Munene's (2004) involvement with human rights issues in Kenya, and Peter Schmidt's (1996) development of a Human Rights and Peace Institute in Uganda.

Walz (2009) draws some dramatic examples in which it is impossible *not* to engage the issues that are gripping a Tanzanian community. He and his team worked near an electoral polling station; the very act of archaeology—with its own contests and tensions in a community where strangers were viewed with deep suspicion and excavation team members were seen as government agents—created tensions that heightened when open, hostile political parades passed by the site. The tensions between the assigned political identities of the archaeologists and the political contests within the local community ask for a postcolonial archaeology that enters the lives of local people as a way to diminish alterity.

A study by Denbow, Mosothwne, and Ndobochani (2009) openly embraces disenchantment. Imagine their initial surprise when a religious assembly built structures on the Khubu la Dintša site in Botswana while they were conducting excavations nearby at the Botsutwe site. Avoiding a conventional archaeological response that sees such activities as violations of heritage laws, these archaeologists acknowledged the religious assembly as a legitimate presence, recognizing that the worshipers had needs pertaining to communication with the ancestors, a growing requirement and concern owing to high rates of HIV/AIDS in the region. Disenchantment with failures to overcome the current AIDS crisis has turned people of Christian sects back to the ancestors for solutions, a phenomenon that often incorporates ancient places where ancestors are readily engaged (see Robertshaw and Kamuhangire 1996 for a Uganda example).

Even more poignantly, local people accused the archaeological mission led by Denbow of causing deaths otherwise attributable to AIDS—a dramatic reminder that interactions between archaeologists and local peoples under stress may be used in unanticipated ways to challenge a mystifying archaeological enterprise as being dangerous. Such circumstances call for dialogue and engagement, not defensive postures and distancing, and such settings open the way to understanding long-term use of heritage sites—how heritage sites become places of refuge and longing under times of stress. A postcolonial archaeology embraces these encounters and goes beyond them to understand how disenchantment about the uncertainty of the present draws on the stability and continuity of ancestral places.

Karega-Munene argues (2009) that archaeologists today cannot ignore the call to address pressing local and national issues such as civil and political as well as economic, social, and cultural human rights as long as they are engaged with museums that are invested with public education. Seeing human rights issues as tightly linked to the study of the past, Karega-Munene believes that community museums have the capacity to draw on pertinent human rights lessons from the past, such as the brutal suppression of the Mau Mau, to provide understandings of conflicts over these rights today that parallel the oppression experienced during the colonial era. This is not a mission that state-supported schools or museums currently support or advocate.

The exercise of state power against the interests of local communities has a long legacy in Africa, starting with colonialism and sometimes increasing during the postcolonial period. As the newest state in Africa, Eritrea entered its post-liberation phase in 1991 with high hopes that local communities would experience self-rule implemented as part of the revolutionary reform process. Not long after independence, the Eritrean state erased local governance reforms. The disenchantment issuing from this experience is today palpable in Eritrea, creating extraordinary tensions for a postcolonial archaeology committed to collaboration with local communities. Multiple disenchantments unfold when (1) archaeologists are forced by the state and its agents not to interact with local communities; (2) archaeologists are alienated by such constraints and by censorship from colleagues who do not comprehend the power of state agents to manipulate archaeology; and (3) a state views archaeological engagement with local communities as disruptive, if not subversive, to its development agendas.

These layered disenchantments provide refractive insights into the role of the totalitarian state in Africa today. Walz (2009) illustrates a vivid case of local community disenchantment when state agencies failed to use their authority and power to stop the purposeful destruction of an important historic building in Pangani identified as a former slave depot. Local people, keenly aware of the building's important role as a symbol of oppression by Arab slavers—precursors to colonial oppression—expressed discontent over the state's refusal to mediate local tensions between descendants of former slaves and the Omani descendants of former slavers, who were eager to see the structure destroyed. Archaeologists in postcolonial Africa daily confront the failure of the state to intervene in issues of great importance for local identity.

Subaltern Voices: Ownership and Valorization

One of the most important schools of thought to arise in postcolonial studies is subaltern studies, in which the voices of the suppressed and marginalized are rediscovered, revitalized, and given free expression. But when subaltern voices are appropriated by archaeologists—for example, when local testimonies are represented with a generic, homogenized form—then the voice of each informant is silenced. For years this has been common practice: anonymity justified as protection of informant welfare, especially when sensitive or politically volatile subjects are discussed. Unfortunately, the broad application of such principles has done a great disservice to individuals and local groups who want to claim ownership of alternative histories. Oftentimes local historians want to be identified, no matter how volatile the subject.

Claiming ownership is central to the validation sought by the subaltern. Edward Said (1979: 293) observes, "It is always better to let them speak for themselves, to represent themselves (even though underlying this fiction stands Marx's phrase . . . for

Louis Napoleon: 'They cannot represent themselves; they must be represented')." Identifying self-representation as a fiction leads to the conundrum posed by Spivak (1988), who questions how elite academics can speak on behalf of the subaltern, while also recognizing that if we ignore subalterns, then we simply perpetuate the imperialist project of silencing (Liebmann 2008).

How may postcolonial archaeology provide an opportunity for subaltern voices—those who provide a dissonant way of seeing the past outside of the "official" histories—to be heard, other than writing "about" the subaltern (Hall 1999)? The best way is for members of communities to provide their own ways of seeing and representing their experiences and beliefs—in the form of texts that are not truncated, abbreviated, edited, or regurgitated by outside investigators.

One of the common tropes in archaeological discourse these days is the use of "multivocality." This trope has little relationship to the idea of multiple voices. Instead, it bundles together a host of different sources, such as the materiality of archaeology, evidence from ethnoarchaeology, and ecological evidence. The trope transforms these nonvocal and silent sources into multiple voices—all converging to provide a more powerful interpretive position. The metaphorical tension in this exercise arises from our awareness that these sources obviously cannot vocalize. They are dead, passive, and inarticulate. Rather, it is the archaeologist who speaks for each source of evidence, fashioning multiple voices. One of the issues that has steadily grown in postcolonial archaeology in Africa is the tension between this kind of rhetorical claim and the presence of multiple (sometimes hundreds) of local voices articulating histories that sometimes differ from those that dominate the meta-narratives of a region.

Archaeologists in Africa have a long record of deep engagement with local communities through studying and learning about their oral literature, their cosmologies, their technical knowledge systems—decades before "community engagement" became a catch-phrase of postcolonial archaeology. This perspective is depreciated, however, by continued failures to adequately record and represent alternative narratives, and to accept indigenous ownership of history—central concerns in postcolonial African archaeology.

Multivocality is also silenced when multiple testimonies—many with important differences—are summarized or when multiple oral traditions are reduced to the representation "oral traditions say . . . ," a process that filters out contradictions and contestations to arrive at comfortable syntheses. This excision of the critical variations of different historical testimonies leaves a skeletal narrative that erases dispute and the texture of history, creating a single narrative, bland and meaningless, a quintessentially colonial rejection of complicated disputes. A number of archaeologists draw on oral traditions in their study of local histories. What sets these discussions apart is their meticulous treatment of collaborators—careful attention to full documentation of texts, full recording of names of collaborating historians, and details on time and place—meeting the needs of recognized canons of historical documentation and diminishing the "othering" of African collaborators.

Kusimba's (2004, 2009b) research into the slave trade in eastern Kenya takes on much greater vividness because of his collaborators' stories about places of refuge and how people avoided detection during 19th-century slave raiding. As well, in a landscape represented in colonial literature as culturally barren and physically inhospitable (Schmidt and Walz 2007), the oral texts provided by various ethnic groups show how people cooperated in their use of the *nyika* (bush) landscape and then eventually abandoned it because of predatory slaving organized from the coast. This nuanced historical fabric of inter-ethnic cooperation contradicts and deconstructs colonial and immediate post-independence historical discourses that deny local identities with the *nyika*. These histories also fit closely with archaeological observations about the construction, use, and abandonment of dry-walled structures documented in remote rock shelters. These extant social memories capture profound bitterness about a 19th-century history that deeply informs ethnic relations in today's Kenya—an important intersection between postcolonial practice in the present and a revitalized past.

The themes of silencing, disenchantment, and multivocality by no means exhaust the range of issues confronting the practice of archaeology in postcolonial Africa today. Yet they help us to understand the problems faced in the struggle to decolonize archaeology, embrace issues of disenchantment, and practice an archaeology more consistent with the multiple voices, including those of subalterns, that have long been instrumental in constructing the history of the African continent.

Note

1. These publications powerfully illustrate the dilemma of a junior African scholar who initially demurs to the interpretations of a more senior expert until such time that the denial of archaeological context compels him to provide forthrightly evidence that favors local production.

References

Bugarin, F. T. 2009. Embracing many voices as keepers of the past, in P. R. Schmidt (ed.), *Postcolonial Archaeologies in Africa*, pp. 193–210. Santa Fe: SAR Press.

Chami, F. 2006. *The Unity of the African Ancient History*. Mauritius: E & D Publishers.

———. 2009. The atomic model view of society: Application in studies of the African past, in P. R. Schmidt (ed.), *Postcolonial Archaeologies in Africa*, pp. 39–56. Santa Fe: SAR Press.

Denbow, J., Mosothwne, M., and Ndobochani, N. M. 2009. "Everybody here is all mixed up": Postcolonial encounters with the past at Bosutwe, Botswana, in P. R. Schmidt (ed.), *Postcolonial Archaeologies in Africa*, pp. 211–230. Santa Fe: SAR Press.

Fontein, J. 2006. *The Silence of Great Zimbabwe: Contested Landscapes and the Power of Heritage*. New York: University College London Press.

Gullapalli, P. 2008. Heterogeneous encounters: Colonial histories and archaeological experiences, in M. Leibmann and U. Rizvi (eds.), *Archaeology and the Postcolonial Critique*, pp. 52–76. Lanham, MD: AltaMira Press.

Hall, M. 1999. Subaltern voices?: Finding the space between things and words, in P. Funari, M. Hall, and S. Jones (eds.), *Historical Archaeology: Back from the Edge*, pp. 193–203. London: Routledge.

Karega-Munene. 2004. Turning the chapter: The case for a national museum of shame as a deterrent to human rights abuse in Kenya. *The East African Journal of Human Rights and Democracy* 2 (1): 73–81.

———. 2009. Toward recognition of the right to a cultural past in the twenty-first century: An example from East Africa, in P. R. Schmidt (ed.). *Postcolonial Archaeologies in Africa*, pp. 77–94. Santa Fe: SAR Press.

Killick, D. J. 2001. Agency, dependency and long-distance trade: East Africa and the Islamic world, ca. 700–1500 C.E. Paper presented at Complex Society Group Fifth Biennial Meetings, October 31–November 2, 2001, in Tempe, Arizona.

———. 2009. Agency, dependency and long-distance trade: East Africa and the Islamic world, ca. 700–1500 C.E., in S. Falconer and C. Redman (eds.), *Polities and Power: Archaeological Perspectives on the Landscapes of Early States*, pp. 179–207. Tucson: University of Arizona Press.

Kusimba, C. M. 2001. Landscape, economy, and trade in the Afrasian littoral: Archaeological evidence from eastern Africa. Paper presented at Complex Society Group Fifth Biennial Meetings, October 31–November 2, 2001 in Tempe, Arizona.

———. 2004. Archaeology of slavery in East Africa. *African Archaeological Review* 21 (2): 59–88.

———. 2009a. Landscape, economy, and trade in the Afrasian littoral: Archaeological evidence from eastern Africa, in S. Falconer and C. Redman (eds.), *Polities and Power: Archaeological Perspectives on the Landscapes of Early States*, pp. 163–178. Tucson: University of Arizona Press.

———. 2009b. Practicing postcolonial archaeology in Africa from the United States, in P. R. Schmidt (ed.), *Postcolonial Archaeologies in Africa*, pp. 57–76. Santa Fe: SAR Press.

Kusimba, C. M., and Killick, D. 2003. Iron Age ironworking on the Swahili coast of Kenya, in C. M. Kusimba and S. B. Kusimba (eds.), *East African Archaeology: Foragers, Potters, Smiths, and Traders*, pp. 99–116. Philadelphia: MASCA, The University Museum of Pennsylvania.

Kusimba, C. M., Killick, D. J., and Cresswell, R. G. 1994. Indigenous and imported metals at Swahili sites on the coast of Kenya, in S. T. Childs (ed.), *Society, Culture and Technology in Africa*. Philadelphia: MASCA, University of Pennsylvania Museum of Archaeology and Anthropology.

Liebmann, M. 2008. Introduction: The intersections of archaeology and postcolonial studies, in M. Liebmann and U. Rizvi (eds.), *Archaeology and the Postcolonial Critique*, pp. 7–32. Lanham, MD: AltaMira Press.

Liebmann, M., and Rizvi, U. (eds.). 2008. *Archaeology and the Postcolonial Critique*. Lanham, MD: AltaMira Press.

Meskell, L. 2005. Archaeological ethnography: Conversations around Kruger National Park. *Archaeologies* 1 (1): 81–100.

McIntosh, R. J. 2009. Barons, Anglo-Saxons, and *nos ancêtres*: Or, eating the young in francophone West Africa, in P. R. Schmidt (ed.), pp. 115–128. *Postcolonial Archaeologies in Africa*. Santa Fe: SAR Press.

Ndlovu, N. 2009. Decolonizing the mindset: South African archaeology in a postcolonial, post-apartheid era, in P. R. Schmidt (ed.), *Postcolonial Archaeologies in Africa*. Santa Fe: SAR Press.

Reid, A., and Segobye, A. 1999. The archaeology of the Makgadikgadi Pans, Botswana. Paper presented at the Fourth World Archaeological Congress, January 10–14 in Cape Town, South Africa.

Robertshaw, P., and Kamuhangire, E. 1996. The present in the past: Archaeological sites, oral traditions, shrines and politics in Uganda, in G. Pwiti and R. Soper (eds.), *Aspects of African Archaeology: Papers from the 10th Congress from the Pan-African Association for Prehistory and Related Studies*, pp. 739–743. Harare: University of Zimbabwe Publications.

Said, E. 1979. *Orientalism*. New York: Vintage Books.

———. 1994. *Culture and Imperialism*. New York: Vintage Books.

Schmidt, P. R. 1996. The human right to a cultural heritage: African applications, in P. R. Schmidt and R. J. McIntosh (eds.), *Plundering Africa's Past*, pp. 18–28. Bloomington: Indiana University Press.

———. 2006. *Historical Archaeology in Africa: Representation, Social Memory, and Oral Traditions*. Lanham, MD: AltaMira Press.

———. 2009. Postcolonial silencing and the state: Perspectives from Eritrea, in P. R. Schmidt (ed.), *Postcolonial Archaeologies in Africa*, pp. 95–114. Santa Fe: SAR Press.

Schmidt, P. R., and Patterson, T. C. (eds.). 1995a. Introduction: From constructing to making alternative histories, in P. R. Schmidt and T. C. Patterson (eds.), *Making Alternative Histories: The Practice of Archaeology and History in Non-Western Settings*, pp. 1–24. School of American Research Advanced Seminar Series. Santa Fe: SAR Press.

———. 1995b. *Making Alternative Histories: The Practice of Archaeology and History in Non-Western Settings*. School of American Research Advanced Seminar Series. Santa Fe: SAR Press.

Schmidt, P. R., and Walz, J. R. 2007. Re-representing African pasts through historical archaeology. *American Antiquity* 72 (1): 53–70.

Segobye A. 2006. Historias estratificadas e identidades en el desarrollo de la arqueología pública en el sur de Africa. *Arqueología Suramericana* 2 (1): 93–118.

Spivak, G. 1988. Can the subaltern speak?, in C. Nelson and L. Grossberg (eds.), *Marxism and the Interpretation of Culture*, pp. 217–313. Urbana: University of Illinois Press.

Van Schalkwyk, J. A., and Smith, B. W. 2004. Insiders and outsiders: Sources for reinterpreting a historical event, in A. M. Reid and P. J. Lane (eds.), *African Historical Archaeologies*, pp. 325–346. New York: Kluwer Academic/Plenum Publishers.

Walz, J. R. 2009. Archaeologies of disenchantment, in P. R. Schmidt (ed.), *Postcolonial Archaeologies in Africa*, pp. 21–38. Santa Fe: SAR Press.

16

COMMENTARY:
ARCHAEOLOGICAL SURVEY OF INDIA AND THE SCIENCE OF POSTCOLONIAL ARCHAEOLOGY

Ashish Chadha

The Archaeological Survey of India (ASI) is grounded in a colonial epistemology that can be characterized as somewhere between what Bernard Cohn calls the "historical modality" and the "survey modality" (Cohn 1996: 5). Cohn defines these categories as the "investigative modalities" of knowledge production mechanisms invented by imperial ideology, subsequently perfected in colonies to produce "facts" that could be classified to govern their subjects. For Cohn, the historical modality is a means of knowledge production instrumental in "the ideological construction of Indian civilizations," whereas the survey modality is involved in "mapping and bounding to describe and classify the territory's zoology, geology, botany, ethnography, economic products, history, and sociology" (Cohn 1996: 7). On the one hand, ASI (established in 1861) was an instrument of survey that scientifically discovered, excavated, and classified India's past, and, on the other, it was an agency that provided empirical evidence for the construction of an ideological history of India's past through the analysis of architectural remains, epigraphical inscriptions, and archaeological excavations. In its postcolonial incarnation, ASI continues to embody this colonial, ideological, and epistemological framework in the scientific-bureaucratic construction of Indian civilization.

Postcolonial Evolution of ASI

The partition of South Asia in 1947 forced ASI to reevaluate the archaeological heritage that came under its purview. By 1948, ASI had relinquished jurisdiction of a substantial portion of the Old Frontier Circle, covering the entire region of erstwhile West Pakistan and parts of its Eastern Circle, comprising areas in East Pakistan. This necessitated the reconfiguration of the boundaries and personnel and the creation of new areas of operations. As a result of this reconfiguration, the number of circles went from seven to nine (Thakran 2000: 45). Some of the most prominent Buddhist archaeological sites, such as Taxila and the northwestern Buddhist Gandhara complex, had gone to Pakistan. Furthermore, the loss of jurisdiction over Harappa and Mohenjodaro represented the biggest blow to the organizational subjectivity of postcolonial ASI, since these sites had constituted the professional essence of ASI in the last decades of its colonial legacy. However, soon after partition, by the early 1950s, ASI began a systematic exploration of the western states of independent India (Ghosh 1952, 1956, 1959; Thakran 2000: 48). Eventually, these explorations led to the large-scale excavation of the Harappan sites of Lothal (1955–1963), Rangpur (1953–1956), Kalibangan (1960–1969), and Surkotada (1971–1972).

With the Constitution of India coming into effect in 1950, archaeology was made a concurrent subject under the Seventh Schedule of the Indian Constitution. ASI was now the central authority involved in all aspects of archaeological exploration and excavation: maintenance, conservation, and preservation of archaeological sites; chemical preservation of monuments and antiquarian remains; architectural survey of monuments; epigraphical and numismatic studies; setting up and running site museums; training students in archaeology; bringing out archaeological publications; archaeological expeditions outside India; running horticultural operations in and around ancient monuments and sites; and implementation and regulation of the Ancient Monuments and Archaeological Sites and Remains Act (1958) and the Antiquities and Art Treasures Act (1972). It had the legal jurisdiction to provide licenses and permission for any archaeological exploration and excavation throughout the country. This jurisdiction gave ASI not only power over the vast archaeological heritage of the subcontinent, but also hegemonic control over the nature of archaeological knowledge produced in the country. No individual or institution could undertake any form of archaeological work without a legal license issued by the ASI.

Today, ASI is an organization attached to the Department of Culture, Ministry of Tourism and Culture, with its headquarters in New Delhi. ASI has its own head, designated as the director general, who is assisted by an additional director general, a joint director general, and a group of other directors. Administratively, the country is divided into 24 circles, each headed by a superintending archaeologist responsible for the upkeep of the protected monuments in its jurisdiction. Alongside, there are six excavation branches, one prehistory branch, one building survey project, two temple survey projects, two epigraphy branches, and one science branch functioning in the ASI. ASI employs several thousand workers throughout the country, is responsible for the protection of 3,663 monuments, and has excavated close to 292 sites since independence. Its annual budget in 2005–2006 was Rs. 251 crores ($56,114,000), which was almost 30 percent of the total budget of the Ministry of Culture.

ASI and Its Scientific Aspirations

The postcolonial (post-partition) evolution of ASI has been shaped by a series of review committees set up by the government to assess its departments every two decades. This evaluative convention originated with the Leonard Woolley Report of 1939. Until 2001, there were three similar high-profile reviews of postcolonial ASI. The first of these reports was the Wheeler Review Committee Report of 1965 (Ministry of Education 1965), followed by the Mirdha Review Committee Report of 1984, and the B. B. Lal Review Committee Report of 2001. These review reports have had an important role in the career of ASI as a postcolonial statist institution and represent both its apathy to transformation and its lack of agency—arising from the maze of systemic entanglements of postcolonial bureaucracy. The quasi-legal status of these review committee reports was responsible for bringing about major bureaucratic changes, causing a significant organizational transformation of the ASI. The recommendations of these review reports were taken seriously by the bureaucratic system, although implementation was more often than not delayed by years, if not decades.

Of the several recommendations that gathered dust in the files of the postcolonial bureaucratic system, one of them had the potential of transforming the professional essence of ASI. In 1984, the Mirdha Committee Report announced that, based on the context and content of the work that the ASI conducts, the organization should be declared a scientific institution (Basu 2005: 8). This mandate was the outcome of decades of aspiration on the part of ASI bureaucrat-archaeologists to be considered scientists. The ASI considered itself scientific on the basis of its disciplinary intervention with regard to protecting the heritage of ancient India and, more importantly, its knowledge production capabilities. All the other major survey organizations came under the purview of the Department of Science and Technology, and there was a simmering professional discontent that ASI was still attached to the Ministry of Culture. However, the concern also had professional ramifications, the most prominent among them the possibility of acquiring a higher pay scale. In 1989, a group set up by the Department of Science and Technology further recommended that ASI be declared a scientific and technological department; however, the shift has not occurred to date. The Ninety-First Report of the Department-related Parliamentary Standing Committee of Transport, Tourism, and Culture was devoted to the functioning of ASI. Headed by Nilotpal Basu, a senior member of the Parliament, the report severely pronounced:

> No concrete action was taken by Ministry of Culture and Archaeological Survey of India for developing Archaeological Survey of India as a Scientific and Technical Department, which amply indicates the administrative apathy towards the whole issue. . . . The Committee is of the view that the Archaeological Survey of India needs to reinvent itself, not merely as an administrative wing of the government, but as an agency for protecting and safeguarding our national heritage, which involves a lot of scientific and technical work. Unless the Archaeological Survey

of India converts itself fully into a scientific and technical organization, the basic role and function of the organization will be defeated. (Basu 2005: 10)

The links between science, state, and bureaucracy within archaeology are best illustrated by the existing struggle between the Ministry of Culture, which does not want to transfer the ASI, the most financially prized organization under its ministry, and the Department of Science and Technology, which, although administratively willing to admit the ASI under its wing, is still disciplinarily reluctant (Basu 2005: 9–10). The tension was between ASI's bureaucratic character as a large heritage management and conservation organization and its aspiration as a scientific organization. This tension—between governmentality and science, bureaucracy and archaeology—which is at the center of ASI's postcolonial archaeology, has had a powerful impact in the way it produces knowledge, such as in the context of the Ayodhya Babri Mosque controversy.

ASI and Ayodhya Archaeology

The political blending of science, history, nationalism, and mythic past was an intrinsic historical process through which archaeology evolved in postcolonial India, culminating in the demolition of the Babri Masjid in 1992 (Bernbeck and Pollock 1996; Shaw 2000). For all those who were involved in the archaeological and historical knowledge production of the Indian past, this ultra-nationalist disciplinary collusion was apparent (Engineer 1992); however, it came to the attention of the international archaeological community in a disturbing way during the 1994 meetings of the World Archaeological Congress in New Delhi (Colley 1995; Golson 1995; Hassan 1995; Muralidharan 1994; Rao 1994, 1999). The destruction of the 16th-century Babri Masjid in Ayodhya by Hindu fundamentalists brought into sharp focus the politics of ethics (Vitelli 1996), the science of archaeology, and nationalism, not just in India but also in the world of archaeology at large.

ASI was central to this controversy.[1] First, it was the excavation in Ayodhya, conducted as part of the Archaeology of the Ramayana project (1970–1985) by B. B. Lal, that provided the scientific rationale for the destruction of the Babri Masjid by the Hindu fundamentalist forces (see Archaeological Survey of India 1977). ASI was ordered by the Lucknow bench of the Allahabad high court to conduct scientific excavation of Ayodhya once again, to ascertain if there was indeed a temple under the mosque. In 2003, ASI conducted the most high-profile postcolonial archaeological excavation in India. The four-month-long excavation was conducted under the daily surveillance and sharp public scrutiny of the national media and the judiciary. An excavation report was tabled in the court in less than two months—the fastest archaeological report ever written by the ASI. This was a miraculous feat, considering that out of 292 excavations conducted by the ASI between 1950 and 2002, only 45 had seen detailed publication. The most recent archaeological report of the Kalibangan excavation was published more than 30 years after the completion of the excavations (Lal et al. 2003). Dilip Chakrabarti, in an op-ed written in the *Hindustan Times*, entitled "It's the Archaeology, Stupid!" (2003b), notes with mock jubilation and a shade of cynicism the completion of the Ayodha report in two months: "Considering that only 15 percent of all the archaeological excavations undertaken in India since Independence are properly published, the submission of a full report on any excavated site in the country should be a matter of great rejoicing among archaeologists" (see also Chakrabarti 2003a).

If ASI intended to fashion the Ayodhya report under the jurisdiction of the court as evidence of scientific archaeology, then its legitimacy was seriously challenged. Stringent criticism was leveled against the conclusion the ASI came to: that a temple did exist under the Babri Mosque. Methodological discrepancies were noted by critics who challenged the general premise of the archaeological excavation as conducted by the ASI. Most critics argued that by conducting a methodologically flawed excavation, the ASI came to a preconceived conclusion—which had the political sanction of the Hindu nationalist government in power. They argued that by employing archaeo-juridical evidence, the ASI justified the destruction of the Babri Masjid by Hindu fundamentalist forces (Bhan 2004; Mandal 2004a, 2004b; Roy 2004). This report, although tabled in the court in 2003, has yet to be published, further jeopardizing the scientific credibility of ASI. More recently, the role of ASI came under sharp public scrutiny in the controversial Sethu Samudran project. Its expertise was seriously undermined by the present Congress regime, which withdrew the affidavit filed by the ASI in the Supreme Court questioning the historical existence of the Hindu god Ram. Thus the postcolonial subjectivity of the ASI as a knowledge production organization has been fraught with the tension between its role as a postcolonial statist organization and a scientific institution.

Conclusion

Contemporary ASI archaeology is driven more by the thrust of postcolonial bureaucracy than by the desire to produce knowledge—although the eminence of knowledge has been employed to increase its authority about the Indian past. Science and its rhetoric play a central role in emphasizing the influence of ASI. The scientific practice of archaeology is subverted and exploited by the governmentality of ASI to essentialize its objective authority over the Indian past. Although science in ASI archaeology is craft, it has a powerful objective valence. This craft is viewed as the most efficient and ideologically objective practice in the production of knowledge (Shanks and McGuire 1996). ASI is simultaneously both a postcolonial bureaucratic institution and an organization that produces archaeological knowledge. There is a disjunctural tension between these two professional practices, embodied in a single institutional organization, which affects the way knowledge is produced at an archaeological site. ASI is at once a symbol of the postcolonial state and practitioner of a marginal science struggling to produce objective knowledge about the past. It is the dual character of this institution that makes it distinctive from an organization that solely produces knowledge, because ASI is significantly also an instrument of postcolonial governmentality.

Note

1. See Ratnagar 2004; Abraham 2005; Mandal 2003; 2004a, 2004b; Roy 2004; Chakrabarti 2003a; Johnson-Roehr 2008.

References

Abraham, J. 2005. Archaeology and politics: A case study of the Ayodhya issue. *Material Religion* 1 (2): 253–260.

Archaeological Survey of India. 1977. *Indian Archaeology Review 1976–77*. New Delhi: ASI.

Basu, N. 2005. *Ninety-first Report on the Functioning of the Archaeological Survey of India*. New Delhi: Rajya Sabha Secretariat.

Bernbeck, R., and Pollock, S. 1996. Ayodhya, archaeology, and identity. Special issue, *Current Anthropology: Anthropology in Public* 37 (S1): S138–S142.

Bhan, S. 2004. Ayodhya Report (2002–03): Mockery of Indian Archaeology. *Social Science Probing* 16 (1): 75–84.

Chakrabarti, D. 2003a. Archaeology under the judiciary: Ayodhya 2003. *Antiquity* 77 (297): 579–80.

———. 2003b. It's the Archaeology, Stupid! *Hindustan Times*, August 29.

Cohn, B. 1996. *Colonialism and Its Form of Knowledge: The British in India*. Princeton: Princeton University Press.

Colley, S. 1995 What happened at WAC-3? *Antiquity* 69 (1): 16–18.

Engineer, Asghar A. (ed.). 1992. *The Babri-Masjid Ramjanmabhoomi Controversy Runs Riot*. Delhi: Ajanta Publications.

Ghosh, A. 1952. The Rajputana Desert: Its archaeological aspect. *Bulletin of the National Institute of Sciences of India* 1: 37–42.

———. 1956. Exploration in Bikanir, India. *Miscellanea Asiatica Occidentalis* 18: 102–115.

———. 1959. Explorations in Bikanir, in H. Field (ed.), *An Anthropological Reconnaissance in West Pakistan, 1955*. Papers of the Peabody Museum of Archaeology and Ethnology. Cambridge, MA: Harvard University.

Golson, J. 1995. What went wrong with WAC 3 and an attempt to understand why. *Australian Archaeology* 41: 48–54.

Hassan, F. A. 1995. The World Archaeological Congress in India: Politicizing the past. *Antiquity* 69 (266): 874–877.

Johnson-Roehr, S. 2008. The Archaeological Survey of India and communal violence in post-independence India. *International Journal of Heritage Studies* 14 (6): 506–523.

Lal, B. B. 2001. Report of the Review Committee on the Functioning of Archaeological Survey of India. New Delhi: Archaeological Survey of India.

Lal, B. B., Joshi, J. P., Thapar, B. K., and Bala, M. 2003. *Excavations at Kalibangan: The Early Harappans (1961–69)*. New Delhi: Archaeological Survey of India.

Mandal, D. 2003. *Ayodhya: Archaeology after Demolition*. New Delhi: Orient Longman.

——. 2004a. Report of the Ayodhya Excavation (2002–03): A document of unscientific archaeology. *Social Science Probing* 16 (1): 37–65.

——. 2004b. Ayodhya Excavation Report 2002–03: Some observations on the main question. *JISHA* 1 (1): 151–155.

Ministry of Education, Archaeological Review Committee, Chaired by Sir Mortimer Wheeler, 1965. Republished report in *Committees and Commissions in India 1964–65*, Vol. 6, edited by V. Kumar. New Delhi: Concept Publishing Company.

Muralidharan, S. 1994. Questions of ethics: World Archaeological Congress, Delhi. *Frontline*, November 19: 99–101.

Rao, N. 1994. Interpreting silences: Symbol and history in the case of Ram Janmabhoomi/Babri Masjid, in G. C. Bond and A. Gilliam (eds.), *Social Construction of the Past: Representation as Power*. London: Routledge.

——. 1999. Ayodhya and the ethics of archaeology, in T. Insoll (ed.), *Case Studies in Archaeology and World Religions*. Oxford: Archaeopress.

Ratnagar, S. 2004. Archaeology at the heart of a political confrontation: Case of Ayodhya. *Current Anthropology* 34 (1): 429–449.

Roy, S. R. 2004. Communal content in Ayodhya Excavation Report 2002–03. *Social Science Probing* 16 (1): 67–74.

Shanks, M., and McGuire, R. H. 1996. The craft of archaeology. *American Antiquity* 61 (1): 75–88.

Shaw J. 2000. Ayodhya's sacred landscape: Ritual memory, politics and archaeological "fact." *Antiquity* 74: 693–700.

Thakran, R. C. 2000. Implications of partition on protohistoric investigations in the Ghaggar-Ganga Basins. *Social Scientist* 1/2 (Jan.–Feb.): 42–67.

Vitelli, K. D. 1996. *Archaeological Ethics*. Walnut Creek, CA: AltaMira Press.

17

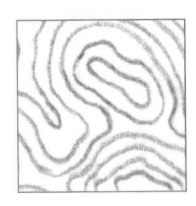

***COMMENTARY:
SHADES OF THE COLONIAL***

O. Hugo Benavides

> My name is Karim Amir, and I am an Englishman born and bred, almost. I am often considered to be a funny kind of Englishman, a new breed as it were, having emerged from two old histories. But I don't care—Englishman I am (though not proud of it), from the South London suburbs and going somewhere. Perhaps it is the odd mixture of continents and blood, of here and there, of belonging and not, that makes me restless and easily bored.
>
> Hanif Kureishi, *The Buddha of Suburbia*

Anthropology started as, and continues to be, a colonial discipline. In various respects, anthropology and archaeology are essentially invested in reproducing global knowledge in ways that structure us and others and that, in the process, reconstitute the West in unconscious forms of constant reidentification. As such, the anthropological enterprise is at best, in the words of Mexico's poet laureate, Octavio Paz, "the conscience of the West"; and at its worst, it is the rearticulation of old new (Hall 1987) ways of political and cultural domination.

Since the 1960s there has been a growing concern with the politics of domination in the West's liberal project of academic and intellectual production. Specifically in anthropology, this was marked by the presence of (so-called) Natives in the subjective production of the discipline, who until then had been completely excluded from this noble enterprise, other than as objects (and not subjects) of knowledge. In hindsight, this Native categorization is interesting in its own right since, as Jamaica Kincaid (1997) elaborates, everybody is a Native of somewhere, except that in the development period of late capitalism, clearly some of us are more Native than others, and as she adds, there is a whole world in that.

In archaeology, this Native conundrum featured a significant paradigmatic shift, away from the (now) traditional postulates of the New Archaeology and toward a more relative understanding of the study of the past marked by a postprocessual archaeology. As a postmodern enterprise, "postprocessual archaeology" is an umbrella term that signifies a host of interests, endeavors, and claims that differ significantly but still vehemently share a more complex understanding of the past than its positivistic ancestors. In this manner, Western academia, including archaeology, had made way for numerous groups of Third World scholars that no longer could be kept to the margins of intellectual production and many times set the pace of new Western fields of knowledge (e.g., Spivak 1999; Said 1989).

To some degree, the reductionist dichotomy of peoples' identities as Western *and* other (as highlighted by Kureishi above) was severely overlooked. This allowed many to declare the postcolonial project as a simplistic inclusion of "Native" scholars to the Western enterprise of archaeological research. Although more inclusive than its previous Western embodiments, this project of inclusion fails in quite an essential manner.

This cultural undertaking ignored the greater paradigmatic implication that it was less about opening spaces to Native scholars, inasmuch as many of these (supposedly) non-Western scholars had already erupted onto the scene in a central manner. Perhaps more importantly, it further overlooked the fact that Natives had always played a fundamental role in the production of the world's past. Not only did Natives make up most of the crews that excavated any site outside of the United States and Europe, but also, even in these reified Western territories, the past had always been *about* Natives; elusive Natives, then, were being erased from the intellectual landscape as fast as they were hailed at conferences, international exhibitions and museums.

The postcolonial enterprise was less about marking the inclusion of Natives than it was about recognizing the central role that these marginalized groups (and identifications) had already played in the excavation (both literally and intellectually) of the past. For many of us in Latin America, this meant the powerful commitment to an explicit political identification with our role as archaeologists: researching the past was no longer contained within an academic heading, but rather directly connected us to the Indian and colonial legacy of our continental history. Excavating the Latin American (in my case, the Ecuadorian) past was directly linked to the trying neocolonial conditions of the present, and in that sense what we were excavating was our own past, a past that had been dutifully denied and repressed by the Western-inspired national governments and the "objective" national histories of each of our countries (see Lumbreras 1981; Vargas 1990).

This particular postcolonial endeavor would be revisited several decades later when members of the Confederation of Indian Nationalities of Ecuador (CONAIE) would state that their history, an Indian history, had never been written, because until then anything written was the white/mestizo's version of the past (see CONAIE 1989, 1997, 1998). The alternative histories put forward by the Indian movement in Ecuador and other similar groups around the world represented yet another way to question the traditional archaeological enterprise of the West, highlighting the political implications of researching the past and the frequently obsolete manner in which this knowledge had been produced and articulated both in the ancestral and larger national communities.

Both the political commitment of Latin American (and other so-called Third World) archaeologists and the uprising of Indian (Native) communities all over the world reflected two very different postcolonial ways of connecting to the past, while highlighting archaeology's essential political enterprise. These approaches also provided an opening to reidentify the archaeological landscape in the continent with markers of gender (Silverblatt 1987), sexuality (Trexler 1995), race (de la Cadena 2005), and class (Bate 1977, 1978) in ways that had not been possible before. This also manifested a renewed interest in colonial archaeology—again, not just for the reproduction of a European other, but rather as a detailed study of the hybrid consolidation of the different American (continentally speaking) nation-states.

This development of historical archaeology highlighted another area of postcolonial focus: the indivisible fusion of Natives with Europeans, Arabs, and Africans (among many other groups) in the reproduction of new American populations. This particular approach is one—perhaps even the most—interesting area of contemporary research, one of ideological discursive practice. To this degree, it is no longer about merely including Natives in the research enterprise, recognizing the political commitment of archaeological discourse, or even the political emancipation of historically oppressed racialized groups. Rather, it is about the recognition of how all of these elements are caught within the web of our own historical production; that is to say, we are all historical subjects in the making, fed by continuous discursive practices about the past that can never fully escape our ideological repositioning. On the contrary, these positionings themselves, as well as our moments of transgression and agency, are central maneuvers in the politics of the past (see Baldwin 1984, 1990; Foucault 1980), which define what we want to see and when and how we are able to see it.

In the archaeological landscape, this is reflected in new journals and publications that look to reconfigure the manner of reproducing archaeological knowledge, moving from a nostalgic look toward the north to a view comprising complete agency from the south. This same ideal is behind cultural projects at many archaeological sites that are interested in furthering interdisciplinary research by incorporating the Native other (Silberman 1997). And yet, these cultural projects must be quite necessarily aware that even these new postcolonial conundrums cannot fully escape the historical conditions of our times —a history not of our making, but ours nonetheless. Moreover, they must take into account that these new re-foundational shifts about the other are necessarily responding to a global market that looks to reify difference as the essential cultural commodity of the 21st century.

Unlike previous schemes of global domination, today's power moves are less about eradicating difference (at least not in explicitly genocidal terms) than they are about transnational capital essentializing cultural difference as a mechanism of maintaining similar forms of racial differentiation and hierarchies. In the archaeological landscape, this development imperative (to support and fund Natives throughout the world) has quite complicated configurations. In this regard, postcolonial archaeologists have to seriously contend not only with transnational forces that weigh in upon their understanding of the past, but also quite uniquely with seeing themselves as the personal embodiment of these greater global forces at work.

The contemporary setting highlights processes where interest groups such as oil companies decimate contemporary Indian communities while simultaneously being forced to invest in recovering Native ancestral pasts. Quite similarly, we now witness imperatives to support environmental or other NGOs that coincidentally continue to uphold racial hierarchies that can no longer be deemed innocent or well intentioned. One of the crucial contributions of a postcolonial enterprise is to consciously avoid images of well-intentioned Natives or Native-saving agents and rather more mindfully recognize the rocky boat (or ship of fools) that we are all equally sailing in. That is why new approaches to the past, such as that of the Taller Etnohistórico Andino in Bolivia or the CONAIE's lack of concern with direct ancestral claims to archaeological sites, are both equally valid means of recognizing and affirming the complex manner in which we are one and the other, Western and not, at the same time.

In the same vein, it is this necessity to recognize that any refusal to accept our complicity in this pervasive Western discourse of differentiation could only continue the geno- and ethnocidal path that has brought us to reflect at this place (Malkki 1995). Perhaps it is the recognition that we are one and the same, from an "odd mixture of continents and blood, of here and there, of belonging and not" that may provide the most singular forms of transient agency (Kureishi 1990: 3). As James Baldwin (1990: 481) states:

> Our history is each other. That is our only guide. One thing is absolutely certain: one can repudiate, or despise, no one's history without repudiating or despising one's own.

And in the postcolonial project, that means recognizing that the colonizer's past is always one's own.

References

Baldwin, J. 1984. *Notes of a Native Son.* Boston: Beacon Press.
——. 1990. *Just Above My Head.* New York City: Laurel Press.
Bate, L. F. 1977. *Arqueología y materialismo histórico.* Mexico: Editorial Nueva Imágen.

CONAIE (Confederación de Nacionalidades Indígenas del Ecuador). 1989. *Las nacionalidades indígenas en el Ecuador: Nuestro proceso organizativo.* Quito: Ed. TINCUI-CONAIE and Abya-Yala.

———. 1997. *Proyecto Político de la CONAIE.* Quito: CONAIE.

———. 1998. *Las nacionalidades indígenas y el estado plurinacional.* Quito: CONAIE.

de la Cadena, M. 2005. *Indigenous Mestizos: The Politics of Race and Culture in Cuzco, Peru, 1919–1991.* Durham, NC: Duke University Press.

Foucault, M. 1980. *Power and Knowledge: Selected Interviews and Other Writings 1972–1977.* New York: Pantheon Books.

Hall, S. 1987. The local and the global: Globalization and ethnicity, in A. King (ed.), *Culture, Globalization and the World-System: Contemporary Conditions for the Representation of Identity.* Minneapolis: University of Minnesota Press.

Kincaid, J. 1997. *My Brother.* New York: Farrar, Straus and Giroux.

Kureishi, H. 1990. *The Buddha of Suburbia.* Kent: Faber and Faber.

Lumbreras, L. 1981. *La arqueología como ciencia social.* Lima: Ediciones Histar.

Malkki, L. 1995. *Purity and Exile: Violence, Memory, and National Cosmology among Hutu Refugees in Tanzania.* Chicago: University of Chicago Press.

Silberman, N. A. 1997. Structuring the past: Israelis, Palestinians, and the symbolic authority of archaeological monuments, in N. Silberman and D. Small (eds.), *The Archaeology of Israel: Constructing the Past, Interpreting the Present.* Sheffield: Sheffield Academic Press.

Silverblatt, I. 1987. *Moon, Sun, and Witches: Gender Ideologies and Class in Inca and Colonial Peru.* Princeton: Princeton University Press.

Said, E. 1989. Representing the colonized: Anthropology's interlocutors. *Critical Inquiry* 15: 205–225.

Spivak, G. 1999. *A Critique of Postcolonial Reason: Toward a History of the Vanishing Present.* Cambridge, MA: Harvard University Press.

Trexler, R. 1995. *Sex and Conquest: Gendered Violence, Political Order, and the European Conquest of the Americas.* Ithaca: Cornell University Press.

Vargas, I. 1990. *Arqueología, ciencia, y sociedad.* Caracas: Editorial Abre Brecha.

PART III
ADDRESSING/REDRESSING THE PAST: RESTITUTION, REPATRIATION, AND ETHICS

This section presents concrete strategies that aim to redress injustice in the present. As a result of intellectual critique as well as Indigenous and minority demands for control over land and cultural heritage, important changes have taken place at the intersection between academic knowledge and public practice—for example, in current developments in Indigenous intellectual property and archaeology (e.g., Nicholas and Bannister 2004, 2009). Among the most prominent of these processes is repatriation, or the return of human remains and sacred objects to their source communities, a process that perhaps most clearly crystallizes many of the problems and incommensurabilities posed by attempts to redress the inequities of colonialism. In the United States, analysis has centered on the Native American Graves Protection and Repatriation Act (NAGPRA), the central means of repatriation employed since 1990.

What many would see as NAGPRA's shortcomings are exemplified by the 15-year struggle over the discovery, analysis and repatriation of the "Ancient One" or "Kennewick Man." This landmark case began in 1996 when a skull and other bones were found eroding from the bank of the Columbia River, near Kennewick, Washington. Immediately, conflict flared between Native Americans demanding reburial, and archaeologists who wished to analyze the 9,000-year-old (or older) remains (e.g., Burke et al. 2008; Watkins 2004). While some scientists argue that they have a "responsibility to the people they study" who might otherwise remain without a history (Meighan 2006: 168), for Indigenous and minority peoples, such a position threatens their right *"not to be a scientist"* (Marks 2005: 40, original emphasis) and their distinct world view, in which the importance of the return of such significant cultural patrimonies, entailing respectful burial of the dead, may transcend all other potential values. By equating Indigenous and scientific views as equal and commensurable, in a universalizing "stakeholder model" of interest (and see, e.g., Brady and Crouch's [chapter 32] and Nakata and David's [chapter 33] contributions to this volume), relativist instruments such as NAGPRA may serve to deny the distinct cultural perspectives and moral claims of Indigenous descendants.

Jon Daehnke and Amy Lonetree (this volume, chapter 18) evaluate NAGPRA's benefits and shortcomings, in recapitulating the history of collecting Native American bodies and artifacts and the continuing struggle over "culturally unidentifiable human remains," which they suggest indicates the current limits of decolonization. The process of repatriation raises issues of identity and difference, as well as those involving making amends for wrongs done, as Michael Green and Phil Gordon point out in their chapter (chapter 19). The repatriation movement was impelled by Indigenous activism during the 1970s around the world. As colonial institutions, museums were targeted, prompting new policies and practices that encourage community access and employment of Indigenous people and respond to Indigenous concerns to restore the human identity of the remains of their ancestors, initially defined as "specimens." Many institutions around the globe are now responding to claims for the return of cultural patrimony: the return of Sarah Baartman, "the Hottentot Venus" from France, for example, represented a triumph for the "new" South Africa in 2002 (Tobias 2002).

In their review of Australian developments, Michael Green and Phil Gordon trace the ways that repatriation has responded to specific claims of significance made by certain Aboriginal traditional owners or descent groups. Unlike the uniform federal legislation passed in the United States, case-by-case negotiation, rather than law, is needed for successful repatriation in Australia, although the policy of all major museums now requires collaboration with appropriate Indigenous groups. The authors foreshadow growing demands for the return of "all" Indigenous cultural property and suggest that this might properly take place on the basis of legitimate Indigenous ownership rather than illegitimate collection in the first place.

Peter Veth (chapter 20) reviews the role of archaeological research within processes of Native Title, focusing on Australia. He traces the disjunction between Indigenous "lore" and Western law, demonstrating the artificial constraints imposed on Indigenous claims by legal frameworks, and he argues for the role of archaeology in providing more satisfactory accounts of cross-cultural exchange within colonialism.

Alexander Bauer (chapter 21) reviews international cultural property disputes provoked by Indigenous demands for reparation, providing an account of the main ways that international law and policy regulate cultural property. Colonial inequalities are being challenged by a growing trend toward acknowledgement of national or cultural rights to retain control of cultural—and intellectual—property, but this same trend also poses difficult questions about the eventual consequences of linking material heritage to cultural identity in ways that promote narrow and limiting conceptions of ownership and meaning.

The colonial history of such conceptions is discussed by Lina Tahan (chapter 22), who explores how French colonialism continues to affect the display of collections in archaeological museums in Lebanon, as well as within the Louvre Museum in France. French archaeologists drew upon Lebanese prehistory in constructing a genealogy for Lebanon that originated in the ancient Near East but saw modern descendants as degenerate. Through the representation of archaeological research in museums, the French expressed this relationship of power and defined a national identity.

The two commentaries in this section provide a critical lens for analyzing the discourse of "universal" in relation to heritage. Magnus Fiskesjö (chapter 23) focuses our attention on the larger structures of inequity and on pathways toward change within archaeology and museum policy. He reflects on the 2002 "Declaration on the Importance and Value of Universal Museums" issued by a coalition of Western museums, which opposes repatriating cultural material to their countries of origin. By dissociating artifacts from their past on the basis that modern nation-states did not exist at the time of their creation and acquisition, this manifesto expands the argument that modern Indigenous identities or groups are spurious inventions with no real connection to the past. As he shows, the modern universal museum purports to present antiquities in a new context as art that is universally accessible and meaningful—masking their culturally and temporally explicit meanings as foundation-stones for a triumphant enlightened West.

In a more specific study from Great Zimbabwe, Joost Fontein (chapter 24) discusses cases in which local pasts were silenced, and the creation of a heritage center angered the spirits associated with the site, "silencing the *Voice* that once spoke there." Fontein posits that Indigenous archaeological reinterpretations are no longer only about competing representations of the past, but also concern the ways in which "authority to represent the past is established and contested," an important issue that challenges the emic/etic distinctions of traditional anthropology.

References

Burke, H., Smith, C., Lippert, D., Watkins, J., and Zimmerman, L. (eds.). 2008. *Kennewick Man: Perspectives on the Ancient One.* Walnut Creek, CA: Left Coast Press.

Marks, J. 2005. Your body, my property: The problem of colonial genetics in a postcolonial world. In L. Meskell and P. Pels (eds.), *Embedding Ethics*, pp. 29–45. Oxford: Berg.

Meighan C. W. 2006. Burying American archaeology, in K. D. Vitelli and C. Colwell-Chanthaponh (eds.), *Archaeological Ethics*, pp. 167–169. Lanham, MD: Altamira Press.

Nicholas, G., and Bannister, K. 2004. Copyrighting the past? Emerging intellectual property rights in archaelogy. *Current Anthropology* 45 (3): 327–350.

——. 2009. Intellectual property issues in cultural heritage, http://www.sfu.ca/ipinch (accessed 23 December 2009).

Tobias, P. V. 2002. Saartje Baartman: Her life, her remains, and the negotiation for their repatriation from France to South Africa. *South African Journal of Science* 98: 107–110.

Watkins, J. 2004. Becoming American or becoming Indian? *Journal of Social Archaeology* 4 (1): 60–80.

18

REPATRIATION IN THE UNITED STATES: THE CURRENT STATE OF NAGPRA

Jon Daehnke and Amy Lonetree

Repatriation in the United States today is synonymous with the passage of the Native American Graves Protection and Repatriation Act (NAGPRA). While repatriations of Native American ancestral remains and cultural objects certainly occurred—and continue to occur—outside of the purview of NAGPRA, this law remains the centerpiece of repatriation activities in the United States. NAGPRA is important human rights legislation, designed first and foremost to address the historical inequities created by a legacy of past collecting practices, the continual disregard for Native religious beliefs and burial practices, and a clear contradiction between how the graves of white Americans and graves of Native Americans have been treated. NAGPRA attempts to address these inequities by giving Native American communities greater control over the remains of their ancestors and cultural objects, and the law has provided some measure of success in this regard. But in the nearly 20 years since its passage, significant shortcomings of NAGPRA have become readily apparent.

Therefore, part of the purpose of this chapter is to look at some of these shortcomings in NAGPRA—specifically, the problems associated with the large numbers of "culturally unidentifiable human remains" that remain in museums and federal agencies throughout the United States. Ultimately, our goal is to question whether NAGPRA actually represents a moment of decolonization in practice or, rather, a modified continuation of the status quo. Before reaching that point, however, we provide a brief history of past collecting practices that moved Native American objects and human remains into museums, universities, and federal agencies in the first place and necessitated the passage of a law like NAGPRA. While this story certainly has been told elsewhere, we argue that it is a story that needs to be told and retold, and that this troubling history is far from a closed chapter. We then provide a background to the history of the development of NAGPRA legislation in the United States, as well as a brief discussion on the requirements of the law. This chapter is not designed to discuss either repatriation as a philosophical construct or the comparative repercussions that repatriations have had on Native American and scientific communities (see Burke et al. 2008; Gabriel and Dahl 2008; Killion 2008; Mihesuah 2000), but rather to look specifically at the development of NAGPRA and the lingering problems associated with its implementation in the United States.

Background: History of Collection

Fascination with Native American material culture and the violation of Native American graves occurred almost immediately after European settlement of North America. In 1620, Pilgrims uncovered the remains of a small Native American child while searching for caches of corn to rob. They eventually reinterred the corpse, but not before removing and taking the beaded necklaces and bracelets that had been buried with the child (Thornton 1998: 387–388). Violation of Native American graves continued into the 18th century, and perhaps the most famous incident during this time period involved Thomas Jefferson. Before becoming the third president of the United States, Jefferson excavated a Native American burial mound located near his estate. The excavation was undertaken in order to answer one of Jefferson's questions about Native American burial practices. Although he knew that living Native Americans occasionally visited the mound, he did not ask for permission to excavate, nor did he consider simply asking these groups about their burial practices (Riding In 2002: 296).

The collecting of Native American objects, specifically human skeletal remains, dramatically increased in the early 19th century, as scholars utilized human remains to explain physical and cultural differences between peoples. Scholars such as Samuel G. Morton—often recognized as the father of physical anthropology—actively collected human remains for their studies. The collection of crania, especially, became more widespread as "scholars attempted to relate intelligence, personality, and character to skull and brain size" (Thornton 1998: 388). Morton believed that a person's intelligence directly correlated to the size of their brain, and he and others conducted "experiments" measuring several hundred skulls belonging to members of different races. The measurements of cranial capacity and skull shape were really a way to racialize ethnic groups and "to validate theories of white supremacy" (Riding In 2002: 298). Morton quickly discovered that there were few skulls available for study. He therefore provided economic incentives to soldiers, settlers, and government agents to enter Native American graves and collect the remains. The task of these collectors was facilitated by the high incidence of Native American deaths due to disease and other forces of colonization (Riding In 2002: 298).

The desire for Native American skulls and bodies for scientific research continued throughout the 19th century. In 1867, George A. Otis, the curator of the Army Medical Museum (AMM), urged field doctors to send Native American human remains to the AMM. Otis later entered into an agreement with the Smithsonian in which the AMM would receive osteological remains and send the burial and cultural items associated with the remains to the Smithsonian. In 1868, U.S. Army Surgeon General Joseph Barnes also issued a request to medical officers and field surgeons to collect human remains for scientific research. As a result of these orders, roughly 4,500 Native American crania ended up in the collections of the AMM, many of which were transferred to the Smithsonian Institution in the 1890s (Harjo 1996: 3–4; see also Riding In 1992). Numerous other sets of Native American remains ended up in European collections as well.

Anthropologists certainly played a role in the early collecting of Native American human remains. Franz Boas, who in part made his reputation by gathering the oral traditions of the Native American cultures of the Northwest Coast, also collected their physical bodies. While conducting ethnographic work with the Kwakwaka'wakw, Boas robbed graves at night, noting that "it is most unpleasant work to steal bones from a grave, but what is the use, someone has to do it" (cited in Riding In 2002: 306). During his early research on the Northwest Coast, Boas collected roughly 100 complete skeletons and 200 skulls belonging to Kwakwaka'wakw and Coast Salish populations. Boas sold most of these human remains to the Field Museum in Chicago, but also later sold some sets of remains to parties in Berlin, Germany (Riding In 2002: 306). Numerous other celebrated figures of anthropology, such as Aleš Hrdlička and George Dorsey, were also voraciously collecting Native American human remains during this time.

The passage of the Antiquities Act of 1906 also had ramifications for the relationship between anthropology and Native Americans, both living and dead. The Antiquities Act, which was intended to protect the cultural resources of the United States by creating a permitting process for archaeological excavation and establishing punishments for looting, in effect further sustained the authority that anthropologists held over Native American material culture, including human remains. The act failed to directly consider the interests that Native Americans might have in their own material culture, and it legislated the appropriation of that culture by anthropologists. In effect, it turned Native American human remains into archaeological resources and the property of the federal government (Watkins 2006: 192–193). As Clayton Dumont notes, "the legislation made no distinction between graves that were thousands of years old and the internment of one's mother at a tribal cemetery a week or even day prior" (Dumont 2003: 117).

It is important to note the broader social and demographic context of collecting human remains and other cultural objects in North America. The time period during which many important museum collections in the United States were formed and collecting flourished is viewed as the nadir of

Native American existence. Tribal nations across the Western Hemisphere experienced great population declines as a result of European colonization of the Americas. By the turn of the 20th century, it is estimated that only 250,000 Indians were alive in the United States, a drop from what may have been a pre-contact population of 15 million. Scholars have called this dramatic demographic decline, resulting from the combination of disease and genocidal governmental polices, the "American Indian Holocaust" (Thornton 1987). Owing to their demographic collapse, Native people were believed to be a "vanishing race," and at the turn of the 20th century, anthropologists saw themselves in a race against time and engaged in "salvage anthropology" to collect the remnants of what they viewed as a dying people.

Surviving Native American communities were at the same time experiencing extreme pressures to assimilate. The U.S. government enacted a series of assimilation policies, and government-funded boarding schools subjected American Indian children to an educational program aimed at destroying traditional cultures. During this period of assimilation, collectors aggressively searched for the "most authentic" artifacts for their collections. It was during this time of enormous upheaval and suffering that most of the collecting took place. Native American people were told there was no place for them as tribal people, yet the material culture that identified their tribal uniqueness—as well as their physical bodies—were highly valued. The scale of the transfer of material culture from Native Americans to anthropologists and collectors was truly staggering (see Cole 1985). By the time NAGPRA passed in 1990, it was estimated that museums, federal agencies, and private collectors held anywhere between 300,000 to 2.5 million Native American bodies and millions of cultural objects (Echo-Hawk and Echo-Hawk 2002: 180).

Legal Framework: A Brief History of NAGPRA Legislation

The vast number of Native American objects and ancestral bodies held in museums and federal agencies led to vocal Native American activism beginning in the 1960s. This activism eventually led to the passage of repatriation and burial laws in the United States at both the state and federal levels (Riding In 2005, 2008). The United States was the first nation to pass comprehensive repatriation legislation at the federal level, including the National Museum of the American Indian Act (NMAIA) and NAGPRA (McKeown 2008: 134). The NMAIA applies exclusively to the collections of the Smithsonian Institution and grew out of the 1986 discovery by Cheyenne religious leader William Tallbull that the Smithsonian's National Museum of Natural History held the remains of roughly 18,500 Native Americans (McKeown 2008: 134). Provisions for the repatriation of these human remains (as well as Native American human remains held by other Smithsonian Museums) were included in legislation that established the National Museum of the American Indian. This legislation required the Secretary of the

Smithsonian Institution "to inventory and identify the origin of human remains and associated funerary objects in the Smithsonian's possession or control and expeditiously return them upon the request of lineal descendants or culturally affiliated Indian tribes and Native Hawaiian organizations" (McKeown 2008: 136). The NMAIA became law in November 1989.

The following year, the U.S. Congress passed legislation that applied similar repatriation procedures to *all* federal agencies and any institutions that receive federal funding (most notably museums). NAGPRA was passed in 1990 and signed into law by President George H. W. Bush. NAGPRA is designed to provide "various repatriation, ownership and control rights to Native American individuals and families who are the lineal descendants of a deceased Native individual and to Indian tribes and Native Hawaiian organizations" (Trope 1996: 8). It is principally human rights legislation crafted in response to the disparate treatment of Native American graves in comparison to non-Native American graves. It is also, however, American Indian law, property law, and administrative law (see McKeown and Hutt 2003; Trope and Echo-Hawk 1992). NAGPRA does not apply to private individuals or institutions that do not receive federal funds.

Like the NMAIA, NAGPRA requires affected institutions to produce both general summaries and specific inventories of cultural objects that are subject to NAGPRA. The four principal types of cultural objects subject to NAGPRA are human remains, funerary objects (associated and unassociated), sacred objects, and items of cultural patrimony. Summaries are designed to provide information about collections of unassociated funerary objects, sacred objects, and objects of cultural patrimony to Native American tribes and Native Hawaiian organizations that might be interested in requesting repatriation of these objects. Summaries are not object-by-object inventories of collections, but rather estimates of the number of objects in collections, description of the kinds of objects, and reference to the methods, dates, and locations from which the collections were acquired. Inventories are an item-by-item list of human remains and associated funerary objects and are designed to facilitate the repatriation of these objects to Native American tribes and Native Hawaiian organizations. Inventories are supposed to provide a clear description of these cultural objects and are intended to help establish the "cultural affiliation" between these objects and present-day organizations. Importantly, inventories and the resulting determinations of cultural affiliation "must" be completed in consultation with potentially affected Native American tribes and Native Hawaiian organizations. Some tribal voices, however, have questioned how extensive these consultations have been in practice.

NAGPRA requires that human remains and associated funerary objects must be repatriated to direct descendants or culturally affiliated Native American tribes or Native Hawaiian organizations. Cultural affiliation requires a reasonable connection between the present-day organization making the repatriation request and the earlier tribe or group from which the cultural objects come. Geographical, kinship, biological, archaeological, linguistic, and folkloric information, together with oral tradition, historical evidence, expert opinion, and other relevant data can be used to establish cultural affiliation (Trope 1996: 11). Cultural affiliation is determined by a "preponderance" of the evidence and does *not* need to be demonstrated with scientific certainty. Additionally, no single line of evidence is supposed to be given more weight than any other. This aspect of NAGPRA is very important to tribal communities, as it is one means by which the law attempts to overcome some of the strong bias previously shown in favor of "scientific" evidence. For the first time, legislation codified the equality of Indigenous evidence, such as oral histories, alongside the "scientific" evidence of archaeologists and physical anthropologists.

We should note that repatriations of cultural objects and ancestral remains have occurred outside of and prior to the passage of the NMAIA and NAGPRA. For instance, in 1989 the Nebraska state legislature passed an unmarked burial law which forced the Nebraska State Historical Society to repatriate the remains of over 400 Pawnee (Riding In 2002: 316), and numerous other states have passed similar unmarked burial laws. A few institutions, like Stanford University, repatriated human remains to tribal communities prior to the passage of NAGPRA. Still, the primary mechanism for repatriation in the United States is NAGPRA, and any understanding of the repatriation landscape in this country must place this law at the center.

"Unfinished Business": Culturally Unidentifiable Human Remains

The central contentious issue concerning NAGPRA implementation in the United States is the treatment and disposition of "culturally unidentifiable human remains" (CUHRs). CUHRs are human remains for which no cultural affiliation with a present-day Native American tribe or Native Hawaiian organization can be sufficiently determined. There are three primary reasons that human remains are designated as CUHRs: (1) insufficient evidence or provenience to identify the affiliation of remains, (2) identification of remains to an earlier group for which there is no present-day tribal organization, and (3) affiliation of human remains to a modern-day tribal organization that is *not* federally recognized as an Indian tribe. Due to the contentiousness of this issue, regulations for the appropriate disposition of CUHRs were not issued when NAGPRA regulations were initially promulgated. Instead, a section of the regulations was reserved for future use, leaving this very central aspect of repatriation as "unfinished business." In October 2007, the U.S. Department of the Interior finally proposed regulations for the disposition of CUHRs and opened the proposal to public comment. Responses to the proposed regulations, however, demonstrate that they remain highly contentious (see Marek-Martinez 2008 for an overview), and currently the time and form of their final adoption is uncertain.[1] While there are certainly a variety of nuanced views on the issue of CUHRs, in general the differences in viewpoint reflect whether one interprets NAGPRA principally as a repatriation law for the return of human remains to tribal organizations, or rather as legislation reflecting a compromise between Native American interests and those of the scientific community (Riding In 2008: 39).

The issue of CUHRs is so central, in part because of the magnitude of the numbers of human remains designated as "culturally unidentifiable." Riding In (2008: 39; see also Kline 2007) notes that institutions having NAGPRA responsibilities reported holding at least 150,887 Native American human remains. Of this number, however, only slightly more than 32,000 have been culturally affiliated, leaving nearly 119,000 sets of human remains as "culturally unidentifiable." This means that roughly 80 percent of the human remains currently in the collections of museums and federal agencies have been determined to be "culturally unidentifiable," and therefore the status of their disposition is in question. Additionally, Kline (2007: 9) notes that the majority of CUHRs came into institutional collections via scientific excavations, and therefore theoretically their designation as unaffiliated cannot be due to lack of adequate provenience.

This data has led some to view the disproportionately high number of CUHR designations as a reflection of continued colonialism and racism in the repatriation process. For instance, Riding In (2008; see also Riding In 2005) argues that the high number of CUHR designations is indicative of institutional barriers established to reinforce archaeologists' control over archaeological collections and a way to circumvent repatriations. This includes the possibility that museums and federal agencies, especially those that view NAGPRA as anti-science legislation, often use a standard for affiliation that exceeds the "preponderance of the evidence" standard that NAGPRA requires. Furthermore, as Riding In (2008: 39) notes, NAGPRA is fatally flawed by the fact that federal agencies and museums—rather than tribal organizations—are ultimately the ones empowered to make the final decisions about affiliation, and their determinations are principally based on "scientific" rather than tribal views. And while designations of affiliation are expected to be made in full consultation with Native American tribes, in practice consultation is too often cursory at best and at times entirely nonexistent.

An additional issue surrounding CUHRs centers on the status of non-recognized tribes. Indian nations that are not federally recognized have no direct standing to make NAGPRA claims. Therefore, human remains ancestral to such tribes are automatically considered "culturally unidentifiable." Although there is nothing in NAGPRA to preclude the transfer of human remains to non-recognized tribes, these transfers must be approved by the national NAGPRA Review Committee. Furthermore, transfers to non-recognized Indian nations are purely voluntary and solely at the discretion of the federal agency or museum that holds the collections. In response to this weakness in NAGPRA, some groups have made NAGPRA claims as coalitions consisting of both recognized and non-recognized Indian nations. But despite the approval of such coalitions by the national NAGPRA Review Committee, the formation of tribal coalitions has been opposed by the Society for American Archaeology (SAA).

There is also concern among tribal communities that remains designated as CUHRs will forever be considered as such, predicating a permanent status that signifies de facto ownership by the archaeological and museum community. These human remains would always be available for research and use as teaching collections. As many tribal communities note, however, guidance for NAGPRA clearly states that "culturally unidentifiable" status is not a fixed category and can change as a result of either the introduction of new information or a change in recognized status. These communities note that the goal of NAGPRA is repatriation of *all* human remains, not the determination of which human remains are to be left behind for analysis.

Conclusion: NAGPRA as Decolonization?

There is no underestimating the importance of NAGPRA as an act that extends to Indigenous people the same burial rights and protections over their dead as afforded all U.S. citizens. Additionally, NAGPRA forces the anthropological and museum communities to at least acknowledge the hard truths of the history of past collecting practices and to do what is morally and legally right in the present by repatriating human remains and cultural objects in museums and federal agencies affiliated with contemporary Indigenous people. Since its passage in 1990, a number of successful repatriations have taken place that brought great healing and comfort to Native people and also helped the scientific community to begin taking the necessary steps to put things right. However, while we recognize these positive collaborations and repatriations, we caution against subscribing to a narrative of progress when assessing the current situation of NAGPRA compliance in the United States, or equating NAGPRA with decolonization. This same caution is also noted by Clayton Dumont, who in a review of *Opening Archaeology* (Killion 2008) has stated the following:

> I worry that the text [*Opening Archaeology*] is part of a larger effort to minimize the ugly, racist history of archaeology and physical anthropology so that scientists can avoid taking responsibility for examining how their research-driven agendas are complicit in the legacy of atrocities committed by their anthropological predecessors. And all of this, I fear, is a strategy for maintaining the upper hand in the emerging fight for the nearly 120,000 ancestors and millions of stolen objects that they have declared "culturally unidentifiable." I am concerned that stories full of flowery relationships between the tribes and scientists are political cover for a legally mandated consultation process that has been minimized, trivialized, obfuscated, and in too many instances not happened at all. (Dumont 2009: 118)

As suggested by Dumont, the current struggle over the status of CUHRs illustrates that NAGPRA implementation as it stands today does not represent an act of decolonization. Regardless of whether the status of these ancestral remains as "culturally unidentifiable" is due primarily to poor record-keeping, attempts by museums and agencies to keep these remains from being repatriated, or the historical ambiguities of federal recognition and non-recognition, the result is the same: under NAGPRA, the vast majority of Native American human remains are not presently being repatriated. Furthermore, many members of the anthropological community have remained steadfast in their opposition to the repatriation of CUHRs. A truly decolonized view of repatriation would start from the position that "all" Native American human remains—including CUHRs—be under the control of tribal communities, that repatriation of CUHRs, if desired by tribes, be completed in accordance with protocols established by Native American groups, and that all scientific study and use of CUHRs stop immediately (see Riding In 2005: 64–65). While collaborations between anthropologists and Native Americans have grown in recent years, the current state of NAGPRA compliance illuminates that there is still unfinished business. Repatriation, we argue, is the most important aspect of collaboration, and if archaeologists cannot collaborate with tribes by standing up for tribal primacy in determining what happens to all Native American human remains, then other forms of collaboration become much less relevant. There remains, therefore, a great deal of work to do before we can assert that NAGPRA is an act of decolonization in a postcolonial world.

Note

1. The regulations for the disposition of CUHRs were published on March 15, 2010, and went into effect on May 14, 2010. The regulations are controversial, to the point that some scientific organizations and museums have threatened lawsuits. Exactly how the regulations will play out in practice remains to be seen.

References

Burke, H., Smith, C., Lippert, D., Watkins, J. and Zimmerman, L. (eds.) 2008. *Kennewick Man: Perspectives on the Ancient One*. Walnut Creek, CA: Left Coast Press.

Cole, D. 1985. *Captured Heritage: The Scramble for Northwest Coast Artifacts*. Seattle: University of Washington Press.

Dumont, Jr., C. W. 2003. The politics of scientific objections to repatriation. *Wicazo Sa Review* 18: 109–128.

——. 2009. Review essay: Opening archaeology: Repatriation's impact on contemporary research and practice. *Wicazo Sa Review* 24: 113–118.

Echo-Hawk, W. R., and Echo-Hawk, R. C. 2002. Repatriation, reburial and religious rights, in S. Evans (ed.), *American Indians in American History, 1870–2001: A Companion Reader*, pp. 177–193. Westport, CT: Greenwood Publishing Group.

Gabriel, M., and Dahl, J. (eds.). 2008. *Utimut: Past Heritage—Future Partnerships*. Copenhagen: IWGIA.

Harjo, S. S. 1996. Introduction, in B. Mesiter (ed.), *Mending the Circle: A*

Native American Repatriation Guide, pp. 3–7. New York: American Indian Ritual Object Repatriation Foundation.

Killion, T. W. (ed.). 2008. *Opening Archaeology: Repatriation's Impact on Contemporary Research and Practice*. Santa Fe: SAR Press.

Kline, A. 2007. Who are the culturally unidentifiable? National NAGPRA Report, www.nps.gov/history/nagpra/review/Who%20are%20the%20Culturally%20Unidentifiable.pdf.

Marek-Martinez, O. V. 2008. NAGPRA's Achilles heel: The disposition of culturally unidentifiable human remains. *Heritage Management* 1 (2): 243–260.

McKeown, C. T. 2008. Considering repatriation legislation as an option: The National Museum of the American Indian Act (NMAIA) & The Native American Graves Protection & Repatriation Act (NAGPRA), in M. Gabriel and J. Dahl (eds.), *Utimut: Past Heritage—Future Partnerships*, pp. 134–147. Copenhagen: IWGIA.

McKeown, C. T., and Hutt, S. 2003. In the smaller scope of conscience: The Native American Graves Protection & Repatriation Act twelve years after. *UCLA Journal of Environmental Law and Policy* 21 (2): 153–212.

Mihesuah, D. A. (ed.). 2000. *Repatriation Reader: Who Owns American Indian Remains?* Lincoln: University of Nebraska Press.

Riding In, J. 1992. Six Pawnee crania: The historical and contemporary significance of the massacre and decapitation of Pawnee Indians in 1869. *American Indian Culture and Research Journal* 16 (2): 101–117.

———. 2002. Our dead are never forgotten: American Indian struggles for burial rights and protections, in P. Weeks (ed.), *"They Made Us Many Promises": The American Indian Experience, 1524 to the Present*, pp. 291–323. Wheeling, IL: Harlan Davidson, Inc.

———. 2005. Decolonizing NAGPRA, in W. A. Wilson and M. Yellow Bird (eds.), *For Indigenous Eyes Only: A Decolonization Handbook*, pp. 53–66. Santa Fe: SAR Press.

———. 2008. Graves protection and repatriation: An unresolved universal human rights problem affected by institutional racism, in *Human Rights in Global Light: Selected Papers, Poems, and Prayers, SFSU Annual Human Rights Summits, 2004–2007. Treganza Museum Anthropology Papers*, 24–25 (2007–2008): 37–42.

Thornton, R. 1987. *American Indian Holocaust and Survival: A Population History since 1942*. Norman: University of Oklahoma Press.

———. 1998. Who owns our past?: The repatriation of Native American human remains and cultural objects, in R. Thornton (ed.), *Studying Native America: Problems and Prospects*, pp. 385–415. Madison: University of Wisconsin Press.

Trope, J. F. 1996. The Native American Graves Protection and Repatriation Act, in B. Mesiter (ed.), *Mending the Circle: A Native American Repatriation Guide*, pp. 8–18. New York: American Indian Ritual Object Repatriation Foundation.

Trope, J. F., and Echo-Hawk, W. R. 1992. The Native American Graves Protection and Repatriation Act: Background and legislative history. *Arizona State Law Journal* 24: 35–77.

Watkins, J. E. 2006. The Antiquities Act at one hundred years: A Native American perspective, in D. Harmon, F. P. McManamon, and D. T. Pitcaithley (eds.), *The Antiquities Act: A Century of American Archaeology, Historic Preservation, and Nature Conservation*, pp. 187–198. Tuccon: The University of Arizona Press.

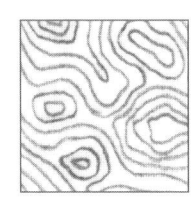

19

REPATRIATION: AUSTRALIAN PERSPECTIVES

Michael Green and Phil Gordon

In its broadest sense, "repatriation" is the act of returning or restoring something, usually a person, to the country of origin. It is an action that occurs worldwide, probably on a daily basis, as the bodies of recently deceased tourists, soldiers on overseas tours of duty, and traveling businessmen and women (among others) are recovered by local authorities and returned to their homelands, to waiting families and friends. From a cultural heritage perspective, however, the word has recently been imbued with a more specific meaning—namely, the return, back to their communities of origin, of Indigenous cultural patrimony (ancestral property) whose historical removal was facilitated by a colonial regime. An inference often attached to such acts of repatriation is that the initial removal was undertaken in a way that would not be sanctioned by today's ethical or legal standards (this is not to say that these same actions were condoned at the time). The act of repatriation then becomes an act of reparation (Skrydstrup 2005), an action of making amends for a wrong done. At this point, all sorts of values can be, and often are, applied to the act itself and should be supported, indeed endorsed, by us all.

This chapter provides an Australian perspective on issues relating to the repatriation of Indigenous cultural property and human remains. We present a brief historical commentary on how relevant collections came to be created and how Indigenous Australian communities reacted to them. This is followed with a discussion of the contemporary legal, policy, and political repatriation landscape in Australia. The chapter concludes with some personal observations on the future of repatriation in Australia, and touches on the issues that we believe are mostly likely to occupy Australians over the next decade.

Historical Overview

Australia is one of the places in the world where European colonists encountered hunter-gatherers (Pardoe 2004). Knowledge of Australian Aboriginal society became vital to 18th- and 19th-century European thinkers who were pondering the place of the human in nature. While some romantically viewed Aboriginal peoples as being the closest to a pure state of nature, others saw them as occupying the bottom of various biological and cultural evolutionary trees.

Consequently, there was a great demand for Australian Aboriginal and other Indigenous cultural material and biological specimens (e.g., bodies, skulls) to be made available to the scholars of the day, most of whom directed their intellectual campaigns remotely from the armchairs of Europe. Large amounts of ethnographic material culture and Indigenous skeletal remains (hereafter referred to as ancestral remains) were shipped to Europe and used to inform the further development of these varied and often contradictory ideas (MacDonald 2005: 96–135; Turnbull 1999, 2001, 2007). The newly acquired materials required storage with easy accessibility, and in a short time they found their way into recently created museums of natural history and ethnography. Hundreds of Aboriginal and Torres Strait Islander crania and other skeletal elements were sent to museums and universities across Europe, and a few made their way to North America. Many more were collected and held in newly established Australian museums in Sydney, Hobart, Melbourne, and Adelaide. These activities commenced very shortly after the establishment of the first European settlement at Botany Bay in 1788, and, at least in Victoria, continued well into 1950s (Sunderland and Ray 1959). The collections of ancestral remains held in Australia, Europe, and North America have been used to investigate general theories of human evolution and the origins of anatomically modern humans; human variation and such evolutionary mechanisms as selection, migration, and drift; palaeopathology; and osteometric and nonmetric anatomical variation (see Donlon 1994; Pardoe 1991, 2004).

The systematic repatriation of Australian Aboriginal and Torres Strait Islander artifacts and ancestral remains to their Indigenous communities of origin is a relatively recent phenomenon. In New South Wales, the Australian Museum Trust has been actively implementing a policy of sympathetic consideration of repatriation requests since 1974. Their first formal repatriation was of an artifact to the Solomon Islands National Museum and Cultural Centre, in honor of that county's impending independence; and their first repatriation of ancestral remains occurred in 1980 to a south coast New South Wales Aboriginal community. In each case, the repatriations occurred in response to specific claims of cultural and spiritual significance made by the respective traditional Indigenous owners. In the case of Victoria's state museum (Museum Victoria), the first formal record of repatriated ancestral remains relates to the public reburial in 1985 of the remains of eight Aboriginal people in the

King's Domain, adjacent to Melbourne's Royal Botanic Gardens, during a memorial ceremony conducted by Aboriginal communities from across Victoria.

Repatriation is now vigorously and routinely pursued by Australian territory, state, and federal governments and cultural institutions as a matter of public policy. It did not always receive such a high level of support, however, and many in the museum profession and related disciplines of anthropology and archaeology considered the disposal of material culture and ancestral remains in this way as something akin to scientific or intellectual vandalism (Mulvaney 1989, 1991).

Although Indigenous concerns about holding ancestral remains in museum collections goes back many years, the genesis of the repatriation movement in Australia lies in the worldwide Indigenous political activism of the 1970s. The political and cultural environment at that time was quite foreign to many Australian museums. During this period, the quest for independence by many colonized nations reached its zenith across the globe. This growing independence movement and associated political world view manifested itself in many ways that affected a host of cultural institutions, including museums. The very existence of some museums, especially those holding extensive ethnographic collections, was viewed by many as an explicitly tangible expression of colonial power. It is no surprise that museums became targets for the many frustrations felt by Indigenous people worldwide, and these led to demands for the return of cultural patrimony, especially that held outside of their home countries (for other examples, see chapters 14, 24, and 25, this volume).

The Pacific region was not isolated from these worldwide trends. In fact, Australia was, and still is, viewed by many Aboriginal and Torres Strait Islanders as a colonial power, and many of the demands being made of European cultural institutions at that time were also being made of Australian museums, which soon became the target of vocal protests regarding the treatment of Indigenous cultural property. Many Aboriginal people began to lobby for a say in the management and display of ethnographic collections. Such calls become increasingly prevalent as Australia moved from a conservative to a more liberal federal government approach to Indigenous land rights and the development of a legitimate Aboriginal political voice.

The late 1970s also saw a generational change in museum employment at all levels, from directors through to curators and collection managers. Many of the people employed at this time came from outside the "classic" museum environment, which had previously encouraged promotion from within. They came from universities and Indigenous communities and brought with them few preconceptions about how collections could or should be accessed or used. New intellectual frameworks were applied to the development of museum policy. This, in turn, facilitated great change in the ways that museums and Indigenous communities communicated with each other and how they each perceived the other's point of view with regard to the significant issues confronting them. In the

1980s and 1990s, these changes translated into new institutional policies relating to a whole range of cultural issues that Indigenous people saw as critically important, such as community access to collections, the appropriate display of cultural objects, and training and employment within the museum sector.

From a historical perspective, a number of events in the early to mid 1980s crystallized issues surrounding increasing calls for the repatriation of Indigenous cultural patrimony in Australia. Two in particular had a major influence on the Australian repatriation scene. The first was the delivery of a paper by Ros Langford of the Tasmanian Aboriginal Centre to the annual conference of the Australian Archaeological Association in 1982 (Langford 1983), titled "Our heritage—your playground," in which she argued that archaeologists had appropriated Aboriginal cultural heritage under a colonial paradigm for personal, professional, and intellectual gain. Langford demanded that full control of that culture should be in the hands of Aboriginal people, saying "it is our past, our culture and our heritage, and forms part of our present life. As such it is ours to control and it is ours to share on our terms" (1983: 2). Much of Langford's argument challenges concepts of ownership and control, issues central to the rationales underpinning repatriation today.

The second event was the 1984 action brought against the University of Melbourne by the Victorian Aboriginal Legal Service for holding a collection of Aboriginal skeletal remains without a permit, contrary to the provisions of the Archaeological and Aboriginal Relics Preservation Act 1972 (Victoria). The Legal Service managed to obtain an injunction against the university, and the remains in question (the Murray Black Collection, named after the Victorian collector who assembled it during the 1940s and 1950s) were temporarily transferred to the National Museum of Victoria (now Museum Victoria) for safekeeping while the Victorian state government determined how it should act with respect to demands by Aboriginal communities for the return of the remains for reburial. The state government passed legislative amendments that, although not requiring the repatriation of ancestral remains, did allow it to return these and other ancestral remains held in the National Museum of Victoria's collections to Indigenous communities across Australia. This was the first repatriation of an entire Australian collection of ancestral remains, representing over 800 individuals. This policy position was again invoked in 1990 when the Victorian state government responded positively to requests from the Yorta Yorta Aboriginal community for the repatriation and reburial of 9,000- to 14,500-year-old ancestral remains from Kow Swamp in central Victoria.

Contemporary Repatriation Landscape in Australia

There is no nationally uniform federal or state legislation in Australia that compels museums to repatriate cultural patrimony to Indigenous communities, unlike in the United States where the Native American

Graves Protection and Repatriation Act (1990) requires that all federal agencies and museums and all state and private museums in receipt of federal funding make holdings of Native American ancestral remains and other significant cultural patrimony available for repatriation. The most relevant Australian Commonwealth legislation is the Aboriginal and Torres Strait Islander Heritage Protection Act of 1984 (Commonwealth), which contains provisions for issuing protective declarations over significant Aboriginal cultural property that is under threat of injury or desecration (Section 12), and directs the relevant minister to consult with Aboriginal communities regarding the possible repatriation of remains that are delivered to the minister (Section 21).

Each Australian state and territory has passed legislation that protects Aboriginal cultural heritage, and in some instances these contain specific repatriation provisions. The most comprehensive and specifically relevant piece of legislation to date is probably Victoria's Aboriginal Heritage Act of 2006 (Victoria), which recognizes Aboriginal people with a traditional or familial link to Aboriginal ancestral remains as the owners of those remains (Section 13). The act further identifies Museum Victoria as the official repository for ancestral remains in the care of the State (Section 14); requires the museum to repatriate ancestral remains to identified Aboriginal owners on request (Section 15); and requires that all other Aboriginal ancestral remains found in Victoria be passed to the custody of the relevant departmental secretary for repatriation to identified Aboriginal owners (Sections 19–20). The same provisions effectively apply to Aboriginal secret-sacred objects found in Victoria, although non-state holders of secret-sacred objects are not compelled to surrender them to the state.

Generally speaking, the successful repatriation outcomes achieved by Australian state and territory governments are the result of negotiated policy rather than legislatively imposed obligation. The level of consultation with Aboriginal communities on these polices has varied from state to state, but as a rule there has been significant Indigenous involvement in the drafting of these documents. All major Australian national, state, and territory museums now have policies that require them to negotiate with relevant Indigenous interests regarding the management and display of Aboriginal cultural heritage. Many of these institutions also maintain Aboriginal cultural heritage advisory committees, which actively engage in the development of relevant policy and also provide day-to-day advice on its operational implementation. These policies generally require that significant Aboriginal cultural patrimony, especially ancestral remains and secret-sacred objects, be made available to relevant Indigenous interests for repatriation. Australia's national museums association, Museums Australia, also maintains a policy titled *Continuous Cultures, Ongoing Responsibilities*, which requires collaborative relationships between museums and Indigenous Australian communities and the repatriation of ancestral remains and secret-sacred objects on request (Museums Australia Inc. 2005).

Currently, there is a national Australian scheme, the Return of Indigenous Cultural Property (RICP) Program, that deals specifically with the repatriation of human remains and secret-sacred objects in Australia. The program is an initiative of the Cultural Ministers Council, which is comprised of Australian state and territory ministers, in association with ministers from New Zealand who generally oversee the arts. The RICP Program represents a collaborative effort between the Australian and state/territory governments and the museum sector to resolve issues surrounding collections of ancestral remains and sacred objects. The major aim is the return of cultural material and/or the implementation of negotiations with appropriate Indigenous people about objects and remains held by the main state and territory museums across Australia. Since 2000, over $7.7 million has been provided by the Cultural Minister's Council for the RICP Program. This includes a recent Australian government grant of $4.7 million to be spent over the next four years (2008– 2012). The aim of the RICP Program is to repatriate all ancestral remains and secret-sacred objects from eligible participating museums to their communities of origin. The four specific objectives of the program are to:

1. identify (where possible) the origins of all ancestral remains and secret-sacred objects held in participating museums;
2. notify all communities who have ancestral remains and secret-sacred objects held in these museums;
3. appropriately store ancestral remains and secret-sacred objects held in these museums at the request of the relevant community; and
4. arrange for repatriation where and when it is requested.

The RICP Program has two major funding categories: the Museum Support Program provides funds for museums to prepare collections for return to Indigenous communities, while the Community Support Program funds Indigenous communities' participation in the repatriation process.

Present and Future Issues in Australian Repatriation

According to unpublished statistics compiled by the Australian Department of Communications, Information Technology and the Arts, the government department that administers the RICP Program, over 1,200 lots of ancestral remains and 380 secret-sacred objects were returned to Indigenous communities across Australia during the last six years. Ownership of a further 340 lots of ancestral remains and 230 secret-sacred objects was transferred during that time from museums to Indigenous communities. However, conservative estimates put the number of lots of ancestral remains and secret-sacred objects still remaining in Australian museums at 8,200 and 11,200, respectively. The job has only just begun, and it is clear that repatriation will continue to be a focus of museum and Indigenous community activities for many years to come.

Here we identify eight issues that we believe must be dealt with if Australia is going to be able to claim a satisfactory result in its repatriation engagement with its Indigenous communities:

1. Indigenous communities require assistance and resources to establish and maintain infrastructure, such as for the upkeep of organizations that support repatriation outcomes. These are critical to the appropriate management of cultural heritage material such as secret-sacred objects, which require ongoing curation within the community.

2. A very large proportion of the ancestral remains still held in Australian museums are effectively unprovenanced. A real challenge for Australia's Indigenous communities will be to develop a sustainable and effective solution to this issue, with support from all levels of government.

3. Australia's Indigenous communities are engaged in an ongoing struggle to have ancestral remains returned from overseas institutions. Advocacy by the Australian government has been crucial in advancing this issue in the United Kingdom over the last few years, and more recently in France, Germany, and the United States, on a government-to-government basis. A downside to this, however, is that Indigenous communities, and sometimes the overseas collecting institutions themselves, feel sidelined and sometimes excluded from the process. A secondary aspect to this is the strong likelihood that Australian Indigenous communities will demand the repatriation of secret-sacred objects. These, as well as ancestral remains, are automatically available for repatriation from Australian museums under the RICP Program, and it is likely that Indigenous communities will demand that both classes of cultural patrimony should also be repatriated from overseas.

4. There is currently a confusing array of state, territory and federal bureaucratic structures that all have a stake in repatriation. Sometimes they get in one another's way in the effective delivery of successful repatriation outcomes. The challenge for governments and the museum sector is to collaborate in the development of effective whole-of-government processes that minimize unnecessary impacts on Indigenous communities.

5. Australian museums hold Indigenous ancestral remains derived from other countries, a legacy of the historical body trade. The Australian government has indicated that in the next round of the RICP Program, commencing in 2008, it will develop a repatriation policy in relation to these remains.

6. There is an urgent need for biological anthropologists to reopen a dialogue with Australian Indigenous communities regarding the potential for access to biological data that may be recorded from ancestral remains prior to their reburial. Over the last 20 years, there has been almost no research conducted into prehistoric Australian Indigenous skeletal biology. As Pardoe points out, the complete repatriation of all Australian human remains without the chance to record useful, meaningful biological data would be a great loss to science and to the representation of Indigenous Australians in the story of human evolution (2004: 144).

7. The RICP Program has made many Indigenous communities aware of their rights under various existing museum policies. Many of these policies make reference not only to ancestral remains and secret-sacred objects, but to all Indigenous cultural property. Museums are already grappling with requests for the repatriation of "open" or non-restricted cultural material, and the likelihood is that such requests will only increase in number.
8. We need to refine and clarify the language of repatriation. For many Australians, "repatriation" has come to mean the return of something to its place of origin in an effort to right a perceived or acknowledged wrong, and museums and governments are happy to oblige, given their policy positions and reactions to the often unsavory historical circumstances under which many ancestral remains and secret-sacred objects were collected. Should this perspective extend to all traditional Indigenous material culture? Although open material may be requested for return, should the rationale for the request be differently couched? Rather than phrasing the action in terms of righting a wrong (i.e., questioning the legitimacy of the collecting action), should it not be considered in terms of acknowledging a legitimate and legal ownership of the material in the first place as a basic right of Indigenous peoples?

Conclusion

Repatriation, along with other activities that Australian museums are pursuing to support Indigenous cultural objectives, is a positive response to reconciliation, even if not always voluntary. Museums have reacted to Indigenous political and cultural concerns in a variety of supportive ways, and in conjunction with flexible and supportive management structures, they will continue to build on the foundational relationships established over the last 25 years. In having to deal with such a highly emotional subject as repatriation, these relationships have been tested and strengthened over time. We hope that they will deliver opportunities such as the use of new and emergent digital technologies to facilitate the repatriation of material to communities. Repatriation has led to increasing collaboration with Australia's Indigenous communities in the development, management, and public understanding of Australia's rich Indigenous history.

References

Donlon, D. 1994. Aboriginal skeletal collections and research in physical anthropology: An historical perspective. *Australian Archaeology* 39: 73–82.

Langford, R. 1983. Our heritage—your playground. *Australian Archaeology* 16: 1–6.

MacDonald, H. 2005. *Human Remains: Episodes in Human Dissection*. Carlton: Melbourne University Press.

Mulvaney, D. J. 1989. Reflections on the Murray Black Collection. *Australian Natural History* 23: 66–72.

———. 1991. Past regained, future lost: The Kow Swamp Pleistocene burials. *Antiquity* 15: 100–102.

Museums Australia Inc. 2005. *Continuous Cultures, Ongoing Responsibilities: Principles and Guidelines for Australian Museums Working with Aboriginal and Torres Strait Islander Cultural Heritage*. Canberra: Museums Australia Inc.

Pardoe, C. 1991. Competing paradigms and ancient human remains: The state of the discipline. *Archaeology in Oceania* 26: 79–85.

——. 2004. Australian biological anthropology for archaeologists, in T. Murray (ed.), *Archaeology from Australia*, pp. 131–150. Melbourne: Australian Scholarly Publishing.

Skrydstrup, M. 2005. Claiming cultural property across international borders. Paper presented at the conference, The Meanings and Values of Repatriation: A Multidisciplinary Conference, The Australian National University, Canberra, Australia, 8–10 July 2005.

Sunderland, S., and Ray, L. J. 1959. A note on the Murray Black Collection of Australian Aboriginal skeletons. *Royal Society of Victoria Proceedings* 71: 45–48.

Turnbull, P. 1999. Enlightenment anthropology and the bodily remains of Indigenous Australian peoples, in A. Calder, J. Lamb, and B. Orr (eds.), *Voyages and Beaches: Pacific Encounters, 1769–1840*, pp. 202–225. Honolulu: University of Hawai'i Press.

——. 2001. "Rare work amongst the professors": The capture of indigenous skulls within phrenological knowledge in early colonial Australia, in B. Creed and J. Hoorn (eds.), *Body Trade: Captivity, Cannibalism and Colonialism in the Pacific*, pp. 3–23. New York: Routledge.

——. 2007. British anatomists, phrenologists and the construction of the Aboriginal race, *c.* 1790–1830. *History Compass* 5: 26–50.

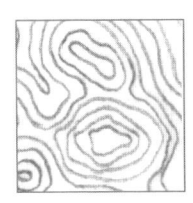

20

AUSTRALIAN AND INTERNATIONAL PERSPECTIVES ON NATIVE TITLE, ARCHAEOLOGY, AND THE LAW

Peter Veth

Native Title is Australia's acknowledgment that some Indigenous peoples have a continued beneficial legal interest in and rights to land that survived acquisition of title by the Crown when Empress Queen Victoria gained sovereignty of Australia in 1901. The concept embraces two distinct systems of law—traditional Indigenous law and the English-derived law—operating within the same geographic, national, and jurisdictional space. Following the *Mabo* decision of 1992, which overturned the legal fiction of *terra nullius* (that the land was "unoccupied" by people), and then with the passage of the Native Title Act (1993), a juggernaut of cases asserting Native Title rights has been mobilized. While many Aboriginal groups have avoided full litigation and received a consent determination[1] (after meeting certain conditions), others have been involved in extremely protracted and costly (both monetarily and culturally) court cases running to the tens of millions of dollars. There is currently a backlog of over 600 Native Title cases in the federal courts of Australia.

Under the Evidence Act,[2] litigants must deal with such issues as who has standing to make claims, what kinds of evidence are admissible, and whose opinions are reliable. Claimants' oral testimonies come in for particular scrutiny—but they are acknowledged to constitute a direct form of proof. Expert witnesses from such disciplines as archaeology, under the Evidence Act, must navigate pathways through the often opaque boundaries of expert opinion and hearsay evidence.

In this paper, I begin by exploring these issues generally and examine three high-profile Australian cases in some detail in order to argue that the integrity of Aboriginal cultural heritage (both tangible and intangible) is impaired by the artificial imposition of the rules of evidence and Western disciplinary hegemonies. I then argue that archaeology and allied disciplines dealing with the "time of contact" between First Australians and settlers can provide more satisfactory narratives that stitch together the realities of cross-cultural exchange—incorporating histories of resilience, resistance, and power asymmetry—that ultimately transcend legal historiography and the manacle of precedent. Finally, I profile the governances of some other countries and explain why professional archaeology–Indigenous Native Title and land tenure dialogues have common elements around the globe, yet also differ on account of their different forms of Indigenous representation and state relations.

Foundational Issues and History: The Use of Archaeology in Native Title

Archaeological data, together with claimant connections to sites with such evidence, have historically been seen as integral to land determinations in settler societies, such as in New Zealand, Canada, and the United States (cf. Bartlett 1993; Lilley 2000). I have long argued (Veth 2000) that archaeology is relevant to Native Title because it can provide independent evidence for continuing and referable occupation, use, and exploitation of lands before, during, and after colonization that is consistent with the laws and customs of the original inhabitants. Archaeology also highlights transitions that groups may have experienced through enforced changes to social organization, economy, and technology, such as the imposition of pastoral regimes.

An examination of some major cases in Australia where archaeology has been deployed successfully, such as *Martu* (Federal Court of Australia 2002), *Birriliburu; Ngarluma-Yindjibarndi* (Federal Court of Australia 2005), De Rose Hill (Federal Court of Australia 2003), and *Miriuwung-Gajerrong* (Federal Court of Australia 1998), suggests that the kinds of evidence that may be addressed in Native Title include Aboriginal presence on the land demonstrated through transformed European materials (e.g., glass, metal, and ceramics, often on pre-contact sites); the depiction of European cross-cultural objects (e.g., boats, horses and guns), especially in painted rock art; hunting and gathering patterns in the form of food-processing sites; dietary suites showing use and enjoyment of the resources of the land; shelters/caves with modified European materials, showing evidence for ongoing occupation; ceremonial activity, such as engravings and ongoing regeneration ceremonies at sites with known time depth such as *thalu* (sacred) sites in the Pilbara region of northwestern Australia; quarrying of stone and ocher (and glass) still in contemporary circulation; ongoing distribution of prized commodities, such as pearl shell and ochers; structured and repeated occupation of sites on groups' homelands; the establishment and maintenance of totemic estates as seen in the production and repainting of art, such as the *Wandjina* paintings of the Kimberley region (see O'Connor et al. 2008); and specifically the mass reproduction of glass artifacts at contact sites, often in the same technological forms as their precursors, which is seen as some kind of identifying behavior in the changed social circumstances of contact.

Main Issues and Concerns in Relation to the Use of Archaeology and History in Native Title

My focus here is on the unnatural impositions made by Native Title law on archaeological and claimant narratives about sites and places, particularly the separation of the tangible and intangible aspects of cultural heritage. It is an assumption of archaeology expert witness reports (Harrison et al. 2005; Veth 2000; Veth and O'Connor 2005) that archaeological investigations are intermeshed as much as possible with sites that are foreknown to claimants, especially if claimants have connections of a historic, ethnographic, ceremonial, or ritual nature. Such convergences, and the social context within which cultural heritage is reproduced in the recent past, can provide powerful bodies of proof where required by the adversarial legal system.

As expert witnesses, historians face many of the same problems as archaeologists, and some of these have been analyzed recently in a volume addressing history, law, and Indigenous peoples (Curthoys et al. 2008), and specifically issues surrounding Native Title, proof and historical evidence, and judicial historiography. Here I focus primarily on Australian examples—specifically, the long-running De Rose Hill, Daniels (*Ngarluma-Yindjibarndi*), and *Martu* (including the more recent *Birriliburu* consent determination) cases (Figure 20.1)—and I provide some comparative data from other settler societies and the Philippines. These large claims have taken up to 10 years to run their course; one case involved tracts of land covering 140,000 square kilometers (*Martu*); another comprised the mineral-rich province of the Pilbara. In the case of De Rose Hill, it was a question as to whether pastoral leases (non-Indigenous property rights granted by the Australian government for agricultural use) and Native Title could coexist on the same piece of land. The unique circumstances of each case, then, dictated they would not be straightforward; however, the court requirements meant that highly charged "test cases" became, as noted before, processes of attrition of funding and human resources, with far too little attention, in my opinion, to the heritage content of the cases themselves.

There are four main concerns for both archaeologists and historians (cf. Curthoys et al. 2008). First is the use of courtroom techniques for denying past phenomena such as genocide and for establishing "abandonment" of country and essentialist notions of "tradition" (*sensu* Yorta Yorta)—so critical to the concept of ongoing connection to country as a tenet of proving Native Title. Second are the inconsistent rules for defining hearsay, opinion, and oral testimony. Sites with archaeological evidence for occupation and use may also have claimant connections, may have been visited historically, and/or may be of ongoing ceremonial use. The parallel narratives from claimants working with expert witnesses on both tangible and intangible heritage sources (including historic textual ones) can actually

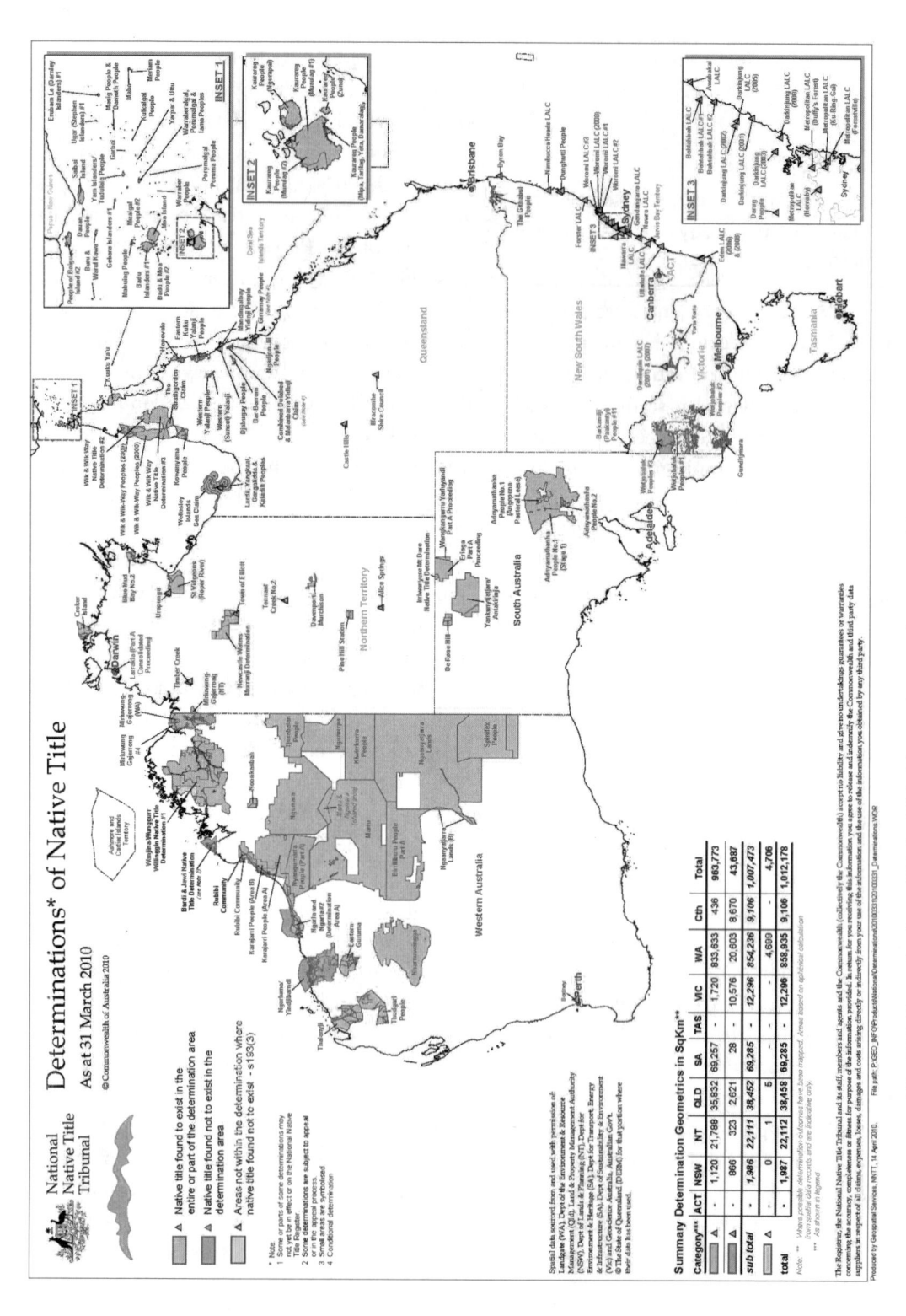

Fig. 20.1 Determinations of Native Title. To see a larger scale version of this map, go to www.nntt.gov.au

represent the heritage *values*, but the rules of evidence make for a highly complex legal brew that dissects those narratives in a way that both weakens the case and is contrary to Aboriginal law and lore. Why should oral accounts and physical evidence (about the same sites) be treated as incompatible? The Evidence Act can treat tangible and intangible strains in these cases as having different probative weight, yet the holistic nature of these sites is very well documented. Third, the standard of evidence required for the proof of Native Title has become unnaturally high. The burden should be a "reasonable one," meaning that all admissible evidence (e.g., oral testimonies from claimants, and anthropological, linguistic, and archaeological evidence) is taken into account and a decision made on the balance of the facts. Instead, the logic of falsification appears to be operating (sometimes termed the "forensic tack"), and this approach may be taken by counsel with up to seven cognate expert disciplines in parallel, each drawn upon to falsify the claims of others. If that weren't difficult enough, efforts are made to cross-corroborate. This is in addition to the cross-corroboration of claimant testimony with each specific discipline's reports, despite profound difficulties of equating diverse epistemological and disciplinary protocols. And finally, fourth, the Federal Court trials and preparation of connection reports (where there has been no litigation) have generated volumes of high-quality material on Aboriginal–settler relations that generally have not been mobilized or repatriated to communities after being released from legal privilege. Some of this cutting-edge research (and critique) has costs many millions of dollars to produce and is unquestionably of interest to the claimant groups and the wider community. Yet surprisingly, much of it remains inaccessible.

Key issues from the Daniels (*Ngarluma-Yindjibarndi*) Case

One of the key ceremonial places of extreme importance in the non-restricted category is the *thalu* site of the Pilbara, in northwestern Australia. *Thalus* are essentially places where Indigenous people, through the observance and maintenance of a range of actions and invocations, help ensure the perpetuation of key economic species (e.g., fish and kangaroo) and the reliable onset of rainfall (including the more malevolent forces such as flooding and even an increase in sand flies). Often these sites are represented by man-made structures, such as circular stone arrangements and standing stones; however, they can also comprise natural features such as rock formations and water holes (cf. Daniel and Reynolds 1990). Therefore, the *thalu* site has both a tangible cultural heritage component (usually a structure or feature that can be assessed archaeologically and sometimes dated) and intangible elements, such as the actions and songs that occur in a particular sequence and which have been recorded since the beginning of the last century (cf. Withnell 1901). Unquestionably, they provide firm evidence (where they are still part of the social repertoire) for ongoing practices and traditions from the pre- to post-contact era. This was certainly found to be the case by the trial judge, but the strands required to prove this were far from interwoven.

For example, in this case (*Daniel v State of Western Australia* [2005] FCA 536), key claimants, including David Daniel, provided direct oral testimony at these sites as to how they were "looked after" and how they fitted into *Ngarluma* cosmology. His coauthored bilingual booklet (Daniel and Reynolds 1990), published before *Mabo*, had photos and drawings of these *thalu* sites, with detailed descriptions of how they should be sung to and what practices should be carried out there. A mosaic of such sites was known to him and his kinsmen through the west Pilbara, and some of these were already registered sites with the West Australian Department of Indigenous Affairs. This was treated as a single and separate line of evidence during the trial—even though the curators (see below) of these sites gave direct oral evidence.

The archaeology expert witness report, while noting the traditional owner connections, additionally attested to the human construction of many of the features, indicated that some of them likely dated to before contact and sovereignty for Western Australia (1829), and showed that they were part of larger Aboriginal cultural landscapes. Importantly, the superimposition of more modern acrylic paints on older paints, and then before that on ocher, demonstrated diachronic and repeated curation of these sites. The bases of these stone structures can also be dated using techniques such as optically stimulated luminescence (OSL) (as recently used for large stone arrangements in the Pilbara uplands) and could then have demonstrated that their original construction occurred in the order of several thousand years ago. Again, the archaeology was used as a separate line of evidence, with little cross-discovery between expert reports allowed or encouraged before trial.

Ethnohistoric accounts, especially from the western Pilbara area, show that pastoralists, early magistrates, and ethnologists had recorded the specific regenerative powers of these sites for well over 100 years and that this practice appears to have continued despite the disruptive imposition of pastoral and pearling industries. The locations and names of the sites and even some of the traditional owners are cited in these records. During trial, the court was taken to these very same sites. This again constituted a separate line of evidence (history) and had to pass its own thresholds of probity.

Anthropological research included detailed genealogies that identified the nature of the families and groups who resided in and maintained these sites post-contact; it also included details of the ceremonies performed by *Ngarluma* today at these sites and the likely continuities through, and transformations brought about by, the start of the pastoral, pearling, and mining industries. Specifically, the research showed that despite major massacres that occurred on what was once known as Dampier Island (now Burrup Peninsula) and elsewhere (cf. Veth et al. 1993), the groups still perpetuated their traditional practices, demonstrating remarkable resilience and connection to the land. Indeed, the early entrepreneur and parliamentarian Charles Broadhurst began a diving venture for pearl shell in the Dampier Archipelago only three years after the "Flying Foam Massacre" of 1868 in which many local people were killed. He apparently used inmates from Fremantle Prison, some of whom it appears may have been brought back to the very place where their kinsmen were gunned down on the mudflats only three years earlier (Sutton and Veth 2008). Once again, anthropological data was artificially quarantined or confined to its "silo"; thus the historical context of *Ngarluma* (*Yabuarra* and others) being killed or forcibly removed from what is now called Burrup Peninsula was nearly silenced in the court proceedings—despite detailed anthropological and ethnohistorical data.

Finally, *thalu* sites are found within the boundaries of what is seen to be *Ngarluma*, *Yindjibarndi*, *Mardudunnerah*, *Yabuarra*, *Kariera*, and other adjacent language groups of the west Pilbara. Both the physical manifestation of these sites and the associated mythology do vary by language group (see transcripts in Federal Court of Australia 1998) and were relevant to a consideration of the shared *and* different cultural values of *Ngarluma-Yindjibarndi*, as compared with other coastal Pilbara groups (the exclusive possession principle). These intersections again were heard as separate evidence and tested and cross-examined as if the other body of supporting data were near silent.

In summary, the claimant testimony and expert witness reports from the different disciplines were stored away, allowing very little opportunity to integrate the narratives in their historic context (to explain, for example, that connections for the Burrup [*Murajuga*] were fewer because of their history of massacre and indentured labor). Because of this phenomenon of "parallel evidence thresholds," it is fair to conclude that the burden on such a Native Title case might be characterized as unnatural. The tangible and intangible elements of sites were artificially dissected, kept separate, and subject to exceptionally vigorous cross-examination during trial.

Key Issues from the *Martu* Native Title (and adjacent *Birriliburu*) Determinations

The final consent determination for the *Martu* Native Title claim, located in the western third of the Western Desert, took 10 years from the original lodgment of the claim for their country in 1992. It must be stressed that these were some of the last forager-hunters on earth to come into contact with settlers, some as late as 1963 to 1976 (Tonkinson 1991; Veth 1993). In addition to numerous claimants still being alive who had met their first European only one generation back (such as Yuwali, coauthor of the book *Cleared Out* [Davenport et al. 2005]), their knowledge of totemic, domestic, ritual, ceremonial, and historic sites was second to none.

Despite this, the numerous occupation sites and vast painted and engraved bodies of art located within *Martu* over the last 20 years had to be placed within a chronological framework covering the period before sovereignty and after contact. Indeed, the final expert witness report documented sites of extreme mythological significance (like *Katjarra*) with 25,000 years of occupation evidence (O'Connor et al. 1998). This locale displayed multiple painting episodes (the most recent of which date to sometime within the last millennium up until around the 1960s) and contained evidence of thousands of grindstones used mainly by women to process seeds via wet milling, presumably to support very large aggregations of people during large regional meetings.

Once again, the evidence that the claimants were required to produce had a burden of proof that seemed more appropriate to a criminal trial than the demonstration of the existence of Native Title with the last "nomads" on the planet. It is worth noting that the only communities extant within the claim are Aboriginal; that the only industries (bar a few mines and exploration camps) are Indigenous harvesting initiatives; and that the main non-Indigenous users comprise some 1,500 "intrepid" four-wheel-drive enthusiasts who make the three-week trek along the 1,800-kilometer-long Canning Stock Route, which passes through the middle of the *Martu* and *Buirriliburu* determined area.

Despite the clear unity of the physical fabric of the art of the *Martu* and *Birriliburu* and its human and Dreaming origins and connections, Native Title law required proof of the age of the art, whether it was consistent with Western Desert traditions and customs, the "ethnicity" of the producers (through time), and claimant knowledge and connection to the art.

Key Issues Arising from the De Rose Hill Case

De Rose Hill Station has hosted many Aboriginal stockmen and women who were either born on these *Anangu* lands of the Central and Western Australian Desert or worked this station, some from as early as the 1920s (see Figure 20.1). The station lies adjacent to the Central lands, and was granted land rights during the 1970s, in a highly charged test case that aimed to establish whether Native Title rights could coexist on a pastoral lease—a precedent of more than passing interest to regional lessees and the Pastoralist and Grazier's Board. The case by the claimants revolved around issues of access and use of traditional resources on the land, not diminution of existing improvements or the viability of the cattle concern itself.

Both of the key expert archaeology witnesses—for the claimants, Peter Veth from the Aboriginal Legal Rights Movement; and for the main respondent, Jo McDonald from the Solicitor General's Office of South Australia—concluded that there was an overwhelming case for the claim of Native Title. Paintings of stockmen on horses adjacent to *Anangu* pigment art attested to ongoing occupation on the claim area.

Over 1,000 objections were lodged by another respondent, including a request for the name of the person carrying out particular ritual activities at a recorded site in 1837 (when sovereignty was established). Many of these objections were rejected by the trial judge as lacking sufficient relevance to the case. As in *Martu*, many examples of overwhelming connection to the land, requiring forensic levels of proof, also occurred with the De Rose Hill case.

Indigenous Governance and the International Context

This section presents, first, a comparison of Canadian and Australian Native Title law, followed by a review of National Indigenous Representative Bodies. Studies in the international context (e.g., Danlag Tribal Council 1996; Harrington 2004; Klimko and Wright 2000; Lilley 2000; McCarron-Benson 2004; Riches 2002; Williamson and Harrison 2002; Veth 2003; Veth et al. 2008; Wood 2007) raise a number of issues similar to those outlined above for both settler societies and such former colonies as the Philippines and Thailand. These relate to (1) the difficulty of establishing "connection" and "authenticity" in the most populous urban areas where most Indigenous people actually reside for historical reasons (e.g., the *Yorta Yorta* case in Victoria); (2) shifts in the way archaeology is practiced, given that the politics surrounding ownership of tangible and intangible cultural heritage is moving toward a greater focus on narratives of contact, cross-cultural exchange, and resilience in the face of European settlement; and (3) the need for a revised methodology relevant to requirements of Native Title and land tenure that does not abort the tenets of good archaeological practice (cf. Lilley 2000: 3).

Canadian and Australian Native Title Law

Much of what now follows draws on a recent study of Canadian and Australian Native Title law and the role and practice of archaeology (Wood 2007). Specifically, Wood looks at the treatment of Aboriginal oral history in the original Canadian trial of *Delgamuukw*[3] (1991) and how, on appeal, two evidence streams (archaeology and oral history) were given the opportunity to advance a joint story. The Canadian approach is founded on dual sources of title (i.e., proof of occupation *and* Aboriginal customs and laws), which diverges from the Australian foundation of entitlement in Aboriginal laws and customs, where the "Aboriginal systems of law existing at the time of sovereignty . . . show title" (Yurkowski 2000: 479). Indigenous title countries—namely, Canada, the United States, and New Zealand— have tended to use historic occupation as a criterion for title while also extending varying degrees of consideration to the transformations caused by white settlement.

As Wood (2007: 6) notes of the *Delgamuukw* decision in Canada, "[t]he rights of Aboriginal People in Canada [were] greatly expanded" (Rush 2000: 171), and "the legal environment. . . changed overnight" (Nicholas 2000: 134). This case was responsible for stipulating that archaeological evidence could be used as a requirement for proof of occupancy. Archaeology has the ability to represent "both material culture and [Indigenous] intellectual property" (Nicholas 2005: 97) . . . and to reflect "past Indigenous knowledge systems . . . symbols of cultural identity and worldview" (Nicholas 2005: 97). The global impact of this and related Canadian decisions cannot be underestimated: there are over 100 references to the Canadian authorities in *Mabo* (Bartlett 1999: 94). It has been said that the Canadian Supreme Court has been more progressive overall than the Australian Federal and High Courts following the *Delgamuukw* decision (Bartlett 1999; Yurkowski 2000) regarding, for example, issues of continuity and determining where the onus of proof lies. In Australia, the onus is on the plaintiffs to prove a traditional connection to the land and that Native Title has not been extinguished, whereas in Canada the onus is on the Crown to prove abandonment and extinguishment (Bartlett 1999: 96).

The Canadian Supreme Court in *Delgamuukw* rejected the notions of title as "merely a bundle of Aboriginal rights," or simply a property right (Strelein and Muir 2000: xii). Title was defined in this decision as "an interest in the land itself" and implied "management of land and resources and of self-government and jurisdiction" (Strelein and Muir 2000: xii). Despite the requirements of the Court to give "due deference" to Indigenous evidence in either Canada or Australia, ingrained bias against what in court effectively amounts to hearsay (oral histories) or opinion (relaying cultural information) has continued in Native Title determinations.

While believing the claimants to be truthful, Chief Justice McEachern in *Delgamuukw* 1991 was unmoved by the reliability of such evidence and accorded their *adaawk* and *kungax*[4] little weight despite having no concerns with their admissibility (Yurkowski 2000, cited in Wood 2007: 21). He found that there was a "romantic view of history," which therefore could not be "literally true." This unfortunate attitude also played out in *Yorta Yorta* in Australia, reflecting the "common law exception to the hearsay rule" (Ketley and Ozich 2003: 85), the "ghost of hearsay" and the "preference of the written over the spoken word." Pro-archaeology First Nations people believe archaeology can be used to "illuminate past cultural diversity; to correct false images of the past; to address issues relating to land claims; to restore, supplement or extend oral histories and traditions; and to assist in the process of cultural revival and political unification" (Nicholas 2005:96). Yet some First Nations are more cautious, fearful that archaeology is a threat to aspects of their culture "because it ultimately seeks to replace their view of the past with one that is explicitly 'scientific'" (Nicholas 2005: 96). This plurality of views is also mirrored in the Australian context.

The 1997 appeal to the Supreme Court in *Delgamuukw* was perhaps most significant in that it allowed recognition of Indigenous knowledge structures. The dual sources of title formalized the inclusion of archaeological evidence "as one means to demonstrate the pre-existence of aboriginal societies and their entitlement to land" (Klimko and Wright 2000: 89). The proof of occupation requirement allows for the proof of physical presence, which is defined by proof of (historical and contemporary) construction of dwellings, cultivation, and so on, and thus the gateway for archaeology (Roberts 2001: 41). The Supreme Court of Canada essentially enshrined the principles and innovative strategies of Neil Sterrit and the *Gitxsan* and *Wet'suwet'en* groups through the dual source (and therefore dual proof) system by setting out the blueprint for collaborative research and corroborated evidence.

Wood (2007: 48) notes that both Hanks (1997: 187–88) and Harris (1997: 194) concur that oral histories and archaeology fill the gaps in the other's stories. They agree that data from archaeology are commonly used to addresses technological and stylistic change in material culture, frequently absent in Indigenous accounts, whereas oral histories canvass broader pictures of momentous events. Likewise, Nicholas (1997: 93) refers to "verification" or "legitimization" of oral histories through archaeology, in the service of "translat[ing] Native culture into a form that can be understood and appreciated more readily by our society". Nicholas argues that through education and empowerment—particularly with reference to archaeological fieldwork and control over non-Indigenous activities and access—archaeology allows First Nations to "articulate their position more clearly" to the public, through utilizing the more common language of tangible evidence combined with testimony. Wood (2007: 49) concludes that the *sui generis* nature of Native Title has resulted in a change in the admissibility of certain forms of evidence. Hearsay and opinion rules have been "pushed" in consideration of oral histories and Indigenous testimony on cultural information (cf. Riches 2002). The dual "source of title" model from Canada recognizes that European settlement was culturally and physically disruptive and so allows choice in proving title.

Different National Indigenous Representative Organizations

Most of the following comments regarding the United States, Canada, Sami, and Maori derive from a recent Options Paper prepared for the (re)establishment of a new Indigenous representative organization in Australia (HREOC 2008). Currently, Australia has *no* national Indigenous representative *body* of Indigenous representation similar to those that have been established internationally, such as the National Congress of the American Indian (NCAI) in the United States, the Assembly of First Nations (AFN) in Canada, the Sami Parliament of Sweden, and *Te Puni Kōkiri* (TPK) of New Zealand.

The critical difference between the models is whether self-governance is aspired to and what "purchase" or persuasiveness they have with government. Here I give a précis of each to profile why professional–Indigenous relations might vary even when experiences of archaeologists might be similar. To ignore such basic differences in governances and control of heritage between countries is to gloss over the contexts of how and why particular disciplinary issues and tensions have arisen.

The National Congress of American Indians—United States

The National Congress of American Indians (NCAI) is currently addressing a range of issues, including service programs for Indian families; promotion and support of Indian education; enhancement of health care; support of environmental protection and natural resources management; protection of Indian cultural resources and religious freedom rights; promotion of the rights of Indians to economic opportunity; and protection of the rights of Indian people to housing. The supreme powers of the Congress reside with the members of the general assembly. The general assembly meeting of members may delegate its powers to the executive and officers of the NCAI, which has 250 member tribes and thousands of individual members from throughout the United States, where there are over 550 recognized tribes.

The NCAI has developed a policy statement that provides direction on tribal sovereignty, treaty rights, federal trust responsibilities, health, housing, education, environmental quality, and physical, spiritual, traditional, and cultural customs and practices. When Indian lands were ceded to the United States, the government's ensuing legal commitment was codified in treaties, federal law, executive orders, judicial opinions, and international doctrine that created three general obligations: (1) the protection of Indian trust lands; (2) the protection of tribal self-governance; and (3) the provision of basic social, medical, and educational services for tribal members.

The United States and Indian tribes have a broad range of common interests and shared responsibilities to use available public resources effectively. A central aim is to coordinate and realize the objectives of 50 state governments and 550 tribal governments with respect to education, health, economic development, law enforcement, and cultural and environmental maintenance.

The Assembly of First Nations—Canada
The Assembly of First Nations (AFN) is a national Aboriginal advocacy organization representing First Nations citizens in Canada, regardless of age, gender, or place of residence. There are over 630 First Nations communities in Canada. The AFN presents the views of various First Nations through their leaders in areas such as Aboriginal and treaty rights, economic development, education, languages and literacy, health, housing, social development, justice, taxation, land claims, environment, and a whole array of issues that are of common concern to Aboriginal Canadians and can arise at any given time.

Chiefs meet between the annual assemblies every three to four months in a forum called the Confederacy of Nations. The membership of the confederacy consists of chiefs and other regional leaders chosen according to a formula based on the population of each region. First Nations chiefs in Canada are elected in accordance with federal Indian Act regulations or by traditional governance practices of the country's First Nations. The AFN mandate is primarily to lobby government on behalf of First Nations in Canada, and to use political and moral persuasion to influence government.

One of the biggest challenges faced by the AFN at the moment is in representing all of its members. In the past, the AFN has focused more on "on-reserve" status members. However, at least 50 percent of all status Indians now reside in urban centers, especially in some of Canada's larger cities. In response, the Congress of Aboriginal Peoples (CAP) was established to represent so-called non-status Indians in Canada (that is, Aboriginal people who lack "status" under the Indian Act). By default, they represent Indians in urban Canada in meetings with the federal government.

The Sami Parliament—Sweden
Sami comprise about 70,000 people spread across portions of Russia, Sweden, Norway,

and Finland. Around 20,000 Sami live in Sweden. The Sami are renowned for their pastoralist reindeer herding and have a long history of organizing themselves into polities. The Sami parliament in Sweden is a publicly elected body established in 1993, and is regarded as a state authority with the overall objective of achieving a living Sami culture. Its form is tightly controlled by the Sami Assembly Act, being both a publicly elected body and an authority that is controlled by the Swedish government. The Sami still have no political representation in the Swedish parliament. Sweden was required to agree to a Sami Protocol as part of its conditions of membership to the European Union and to recognize the domestic and international legal obligations and responsibilities Sweden has to Sami people in their country. The protocol states that Sweden is committed to preserving and developing the Sami people's living conditions, language, culture, and way of life.

Maori Representation—New Zealand

Maori, the Indigenous people of New Zealand, today number about 632,900 (14 percent of the total population) spread across the nation's North and South Islands. There are numerous ways in which Maori interests are represented across the political system. Distinct from the Australian, Canadian, and Swedish situation, the New Zealand scheme primarily revolves around the provision of guaranteed Maori seats in the legislative system, as opposed to a separate national Indigenous representative body or Indigenous parliament.

The interests of New Zealand's Indigenous people are embodied in the Ministry of Maori Development, *Te Puni Kōkiri* (TPK), which is a governmental advisory body that links the Crown with the Maori population. A branch of this body, the Maori Trusts Office, exists to support Maori land and asset management. Importantly, however, recent consultations by the New Zealand government with Maori groups have proposed that the Trust become independent of the TPK and be required to report on an annual basis to Parliament. *Te Puni Kōkiri* is the principal government body that advises on policy and legislation regarding Maori well-being. It currently has no service delivery role but acts as an intermediary between government agencies and other external organizations to ensure that "Maori succeed as Maori" and that their concerns are reflected in policy development. It is responsible for providing independent policy advice to, and coordinating the legislative obligations of, the Minister of Maori Affairs. A policy framework was developed by the TPK that informs and coordinates the Maori Affairs portfolio and the development and implementation of Maori public policy. The focus of their Maori Potential framework is on building knowledge and skills (*mātauranga*); on strengthening Maori culture, leadership, and decision-making (*whakamana*); and on managing, developing, and using natural, financial, and physical resources (*rawa*).

An additional point worth noting is that TPK is charged with the responsibility of facilitating Treaty of Waitangi settlements.

The Treaty of Waitangi is a founding document in New Zealand history that affirms the status of Maori as its Indigenous inhabitants, including the rights of Indigenous peoples to the land and natural resources.

It should be clear from this brief tour of Indigenous governances and Indigenous–state relations that differences in how title is addressed by archaeology and Indigenous people will necessarily vary even if United Nations covenants on the rights of Indigenous people and cultural heritage are finally taken up by the settler countries. In the same vein, Lilley (2000: 99–120) has undertaken a comparison of professional responses to Native Title in the settler countries (Australia, Canada, New Zealand, the United States, and South Africa; also see Prins 2000). Lilley concludes that because the first three are still technically colonies of the British Crown (a situation hopefully soon to be remedied in Australia), unlike the United States and South Africa, the dynamics among archaeologists, Aboriginal peoples, and the nation-state differ—as necessarily does the legislation. For example, potentially strong federal heritage legislation applies on private land in Australia but not in the United States. Large reserves and treaties exist in the United States and Canada, while freehold Aboriginal land in Australia (as opposed to that held in Native Title) is proportionally very small.

Lessons Learned and Future Developments for Archaeology and Native Title

These case studies clearly illustrate that major reforms are needed in how Native Title is adjudicated in Australia following the common law elements of the original *Mabo* decision and, specifically, in how archaeology is deployed as an "expert" body of evidence in both trials and connection reports. In addition to the obvious limitations and disciplinary imposts of the Evidence Act, there are considerations of diverging origin narratives where claimant testimonials and archaeology may not be in congruence. While they often are, the instances of divergence serve to illustrate that contact-period archaeology and the archaeology of the recent past must engage with Indigenous knowledge systems even if the explanatory pathways are not the same. Here I have discussed high-profile cases where Indigenous narratives of ongoing site use were well supported by independent lines of archaeological evidence—which, it must be said, were well received by the trial and appellant judges, being perceived to be somewhat akin to the positivist robustness of medical forensic evidence—even if the inferential bases in fact differ.

There is a clear need to marry the archaeology of the recent past with Indigenous knowledge systems and to maintain the integrity of the tangible and intangible cultural heritage of both sites and places—whether it is a regeneration site or something as large as a seascape off the Arnhem Land coast of northern Australia. To dissect these sites and places because of the disciplinary boundaries of the Evidence Act or the gray boundaries between expert and opinion evidence is akin to mocking the Aboriginal lore from which these narratives ultimately derive.

Disciplinary experts must work in unison and with knowledgeable traditional owners to give value to sites and places that have names, mythology, human-made forms, and certain laws and customs associated with them. To deconstruct these elements through a process of isolating relevant bodies of evidence from one another is to discourage integration and produce potentially flawed case law. The Federal Court must create new opportunities for hearing tangible and intangible values as unified bodies of evidence.

Notes

1. Section 87 of the Native Title Act empowers the Federal Court to make a consent determination where agreement about a claim is reached between the parties. Section 94A requires all determinations of Native Title, including consent determinations, to set out details of the matters mentioned in Section 225 (which defines "determination of native title").
2. The Evidence Act sets out federal rules of evidence. For the entire act, see *http://www.comlaw.gov.au/ComLaw/Legislation/ActCompilation1.nsf/0/5D76721765AF47F5CA25760400065606/$file/EvidenceAct1995_WD02.pdf* (last accessed 11/11/ 2009).
3. *Delgamuukw v. British Columbia* [1997] 3 S.C.R. 1010 is a decision of the Supreme Court of Canada, in which the Court made its most definitive statement on the nature of Aboriginal title in Canada. The proceedings, initiated in 1984 by the Gitxsan Nation and the Wet'suwet'en Nation, bypassed the Federal Land Claims process due to a non-participating British Columbia Provincial Government. The nations claimed ownership and legal jurisdiction over 133 individual hereditary territories, using oral histories as principal evidence in the case.
4. *Adaawk* and *kungax* are oral histories of a special kind.

References

Bartlett, R. H. 1993. *The Mabo Decision*. Butterworths: Sydney.

———. 1999. Australia's museum mentality, in R. H. Bartlett, and J. Milroy (eds), *Native Title Claims in Canada and Australia: Delgamuukw and Miriuwung Gajerrong*, pp. 94–97. Perth: Centre for Aboriginal Programmes and Centre for Commercial and Resources Law, University of Western Australia.

Curthoys, A., Genovese, A., and Riley, A. 2008. *Rights and Redemption: History, Law and Indigenous People*. Sydney: UNSW Press.

Daniel, D., and Reynolds, R. 1990. *Thalu Sites of West Pilbara*. Perth: Unpublished Booklet, DAA.

Danlag Tribal Council. 1996. The Danlag Bla-an Ancestral Domain Claim/Tampakan, South Cotabato, Mindanao, Philippines. Fremantle: Unpublished Report for WMC held by Archeo-Aus.

Davenport, S., Johnson, P., and Yuwali. 2005. *Cleared Out: First Contact in the Western Desert*. Canberra: Aboriginal Studies Press.

Federal Court of Australia. 1998. *Ben Ward and Ors v State of Western Australia and*

Ors [1998] 1478 FCA (24 November 1998).
———. 2002. *James on Behalf of the Martu People v State of Western Australia* [2002] FCA 1208 (27 September 2002).
———. 2003. *De Rose v State of South Australia* [2003] FCAFC 286 (December 2003).
———. 2005. *Daniel v State of Western Australia* [2003] FCA 666 (3 July 2003).
Hanks, C. 1997. Ancient knowledge of ancient sites: Tracing Dene identity from the late Pleistocene and Holocene, in G. Nicholas and T. Andrews (eds.), *At a Crossroads: Archaeology and First Peoples in Canada*, pp. 178–189. Burnaby: Archaeology Press, Department of Archaeology, Simon Fraser University.
Harrington, J. 2004. *Being Here: Heritage, Belonging and Place Making. A Study of Community and Identity Formation at Avebury (England), Magnetic Island (Australia) and Ayutthaya (Thailand)*. Ph.D. thesis, James Cook University, Townsville.
Harris, H. 1997. Remembering 10,000 years of history: The origins and migrations of the Gitksan, in G. Nicholas and T. Andrews (eds.), *At a Crossroads: Archaeology and First Peoples in Canada*, pp. 190–251. Burnaby: Archaeology Press, Department of Archaeology, Simon Fraser University.
Harrison, R., McDonald, J., and Veth, P. 2005. *Native Title and Archaeology. Australian Aboriginal Studies*. Canberra: Australian Aboriginal Studies Press.
HREOC. 2008. Building a sustainable National Indigenous representative body—Issues for consideration. An issues paper prepared by the Aboriginal and Torres Strait Islander Social Justice Commissioner, in accordance with section 46C(1)(b) of the *Human Rights and Equal Opportunity Commission Act 1986* (Cth). Prepared by the National Centre for Indigenous Studies, The Australian National University, Canberra.
Ketley, H., and Ozich, C. 2003. Snapshots of adventitious content: The assessment of oral and historical evidence in Native Title claims. *Studies in Western Australian History* 23: 83–94.
Klimko, O., and Wright, M. 2000. Old rocks and hard places: Archaeology and land claims/treaty in British Columbia, Canada, in I. Lilley (ed.) *Native Title and the Transformation of Archaeology in the Postcolonial World*, pp. 88–98. Oceania Monograph 50. Sydney: University of Sydney.
Lilley, I. (ed.). 2000. Native Title and the transformation of archaeology in the postcolonial world, in I. Lilley (ed.), *Native Title and the Transformation of Archaeology in the Postcolonial World*, pp. 1–9. Oceania Monograph 50. Sydney: University of Sydney.
McCarron-Benson, A. A. 2004. Native Title archaeology. Honours Thesis. School of Archaeology and Anthropology and Archaeology, The Australian National University, Canberra.
Nicholas, G. P. 1997. Education and empowerment: Archaeology with, for, and by the Shuswap people, in G. Nicholas and T. Andrews (eds.), *At a Crossroads: Archaeology and First Peoples in Canada*, pp. 85–104. Burnaby: Archaeology Press, Department of Archaeology, Simon Fraser University.

———. 2000. Indigenous land rights, education, and archaeology in Canada: postmodern/ postcolonial perspectives by a non-Canadian white guy, in I. Lilley (ed.), *Native Title and the Transformation of Archaeology in the Postcolonial World*, pp. 121–137. Oceania Monographs 50. Sydney: University of Sydney.

———. 2005. The persistence of memory; the politics of desire: Archaeological impacts on Aboriginal peoples and their response, in C. Smith and H. M. Wobst (eds.), *Indigenous Archaeologies: Decolonizing Theory and Practice*, pp. 81–103. London and New York: Routledge.

O'Connor, S., Barham, A., and Woolagoodja, D. 2008. Painting and repainting in the West Kimberley, in L. Taylor and P. Veth (eds.), *Aboriginal Art and Identity*. Australian Aboriginal Studies 2008 (1). Canberra: Australian Aboriginal Studies Press.

O'Connor, S., Veth, P., and Campbell, C. 1998. Serpent's Glen: A Pleistocene archaeological sequence from the Western Desert. *Australian Archaeology* 46: 12–22.

Prins, F. 2000. Forgotten heirs: The archaeological colonization of the Southern San, in I. Lilley (ed.), *Native Title and the Transformation of Archaeology in the Postcolonial World*. Sydney: Oceania Publications.

Riches, L. 2002. Legislating the past: Native Title and the history of Aboriginal Australia, in C. Williamson and and R. Harrison (eds.), *After Captain Cook: The Archaeology of the Indigenous Recent Past in Australia*, pp. 75–101. Sydney University Archaeological Methods Series 8. Sydney: Archaeological Computing Laboratory, University of Sydney.

Roberts, A. 2001. Using archaeology as evidence. *Alternative Law Journal* 26 (1): 41, 52.

Rush, S. 2000. *Native Title in Perspective: Selected Papers from the Native Title Research Unit 1998–2000*. Canberra: Aboriginal Studies Press, Native Title Research Unit, Australian Institute of Aboriginal and Torres Strait Islander Studies.

Strelein, L., and Muir, K. (eds.). 2000. *Native Title in Perspective: Selected Papers from the Native Title Research Unit 1998–2000*. Canberra: Aboriginal Studies Press, Native Title Research Unit, Australian Institute of Aboriginal and Torres Strait Islander Studies.

Sutton, P., and Veth, P. 2008. Introduction and themes, in P. Veth, P. Sutton, and M. Neale (eds.), *Strangers on the Shore: Early Coastal Contacts in Australia*, pp. 1–5. Canberra: National Museum of Australia.

Tonkinson, R. 1991. *The Mardu Aborigines: Living the Dream in Australia's Desert*. New York: Holt, Rinehart and Winston.

Veth, P. M. 1993. *Islands in the Interior: The Dynamics of Prehistoric Adaptations within the Arid Zone of Australia*. International Monographs in Prehistory. Archaeological Series 3. Ann Arbor: University of Michigan.

———. 2000. Origins of the Western Desert language: Convergence in linguistic and archaeological space and time models. *Archaeology in Oceania* 35 (1): 11–19.

———. 2003. "Abandonment" or maintenance of country? A critical examination of mobility patterns and implications for Native Title, in *Land, Rights, Laws: Issues of Native Title*, Vol. 2. Issues Paper No. 2. Canberra: Native Title Research Unit,

Australian Institute of Aboriginal and Torres Strait Islander Studies.

Veth, P., Bradshaw, E., Gara, T., Hall, N., Haydock, P., and Kendrick, P. 1993. Burrup Peninsula Aboriginal Heritage Project. Perth: Unpublished report to the Department of Conservation and Land Management.

Veth, P., and O'Connor, S. 2005. Archaeology, claimant connection to sites, and Native Title: Employment of successful categories of data with specific comments on glass artefacts, in R. Harrison, J. McDonald, and P. Veth (eds.), *Native Title and Archaeology. Australian Aboriginal Studies* 2005 (1): 2–15. Canberra: AIATSIS.

Veth, P., Sutton, P., and Neale, M. 2008. *Strangers on the Shore: Early Coastal Contacts in Australia*. Canberra: National Museum of Australia.

Williamson, C., and Harrison, R. (eds.). 2002. *After Captain Cook: The Archaeology of the Indigenous Recent Past in Australia*, pp. 75–101. Sydney University Archaeological Methods Series 8. Sydney: Archaeological Computing Laboratory, University of Sydney.

Wood, A. 2007. The role of archaeological evidence in Native Title determinations: An international perspective. Honours thesis, University of Queensland, St. Lucia.

Withnell, J. 1901. The *Customs and Traditions of the Aboriginal Natives of Western Australia*. Roebourne: Private Printing.

Yurkowski, R. 2000. "We are all here to stay": Addressing Aboriginal Title Claims after Delgamuukw v British Columbia. *Victoria University of Wellington Law Review* 31: 471–496.

21

CULTURAL PROPERTY: INTERNATIONALISM, ETHICS, AND LAW

Alexander A. Bauer

In December 2002, under increasing pressure to disavow antiquities collecting and return some of the objects they had in their collections, the directors of 19 of the world's most prestigious art and archaeology museums issued the Declaration on the Importance and Value of Universal Museums. They noted in no uncertain terms that:

> The international museum community shares the conviction that illegal traffic in archaeological, artistic, and ethnic objects must be firmly discouraged. We should, however, recognize that objects acquired in earlier times must be viewed in the light of different sensitivities and values, reflective of that earlier era. The objects and monumental works that were installed decades and even centuries ago in museums throughout Europe and America were acquired under conditions that are not comparable with current ones.[1]

Given these different values, they argued that museums should not be obligated to return objects that were acquired according to the law and morality of the time. And in any case, such "universal museums" (i.e., those that contain and display an encyclopedic range of cultural materials for an international audience) should be recognized for their value to society and not be dismantled or made to "narrow [their] focus."

In spite of the spirited defense of collecting practices put forward by this Declaration, there is plenty in it that fails to withstand the scrutiny of the more ethically engaged archaeological and museological practices developing today. The collections of many Western museums were developed during a time of colonial expansion and subjugation (both physically and conceptually) of "others" and were built to reinforce Enlightenment-based notions of progress and national identity among Western powers.[2]

Maintaining these collections, even as historically contingent "relics," let alone continuing to expand them as suggested in the Declaration, may be seen as continuing to sanction the symbolic violence of the collecting practices and the mind set they represent (see Barkan 2002). Citing the "sensitivities and values" of the time (which rationalized the taking of objects as well as the people themselves because they were considered less than human) may be a convenient way to maintain the status quo; however, it assumes that these values are tolerated today and that the values of the collecting nation are the only ones that matter.

As Daniel Shapiro (1998) has pointed out, it is the recognition and respect of people today and their claims that count and are the underlying issue in most cultural property claims. Taking as an example the ongoing debate over the "Elgin" Parthenon marbles (classical Greek sculptures taken from the Parthenon in Athens beginning in 1801, on display in the British Museum since 1816, and the subject of dispute from the beginning), Shapiro argues that the marbles' importance to modern Greek identity is what must be recognized. Their continued possession by the British Museum (and the related claim that it can take better care of them than the Greeks can) implies that the modern Greeks are not the proper stewards and inheritors of past Greek achievements, relegating them to an "inferior" status as a people. The fact that many art museums (and several of those which signed the Declaration) have now made it a blanket policy, as a moral imperative, to return art and objects looted by the Nazis from Jewish families during World War II (AAMD n.d.) indicates that even they acknowledge that keeping objects taken from those regarded at one point as inferior is not acceptable, even if they are not willing to apply the principle more generally.

It is clear, then, that collecting antiquities and the institutions and policies built around such acquisition over the past 200 years deserve, and in fact are undergoing, increased scrutiny and reevaluation in the 21st century. Nations continue to adopt stricter antiquities laws in an effort to stem the looting of archaeological sites and the export of cultural objects. Moreover, a push to repossess objects obtained under dubious circumstances by collectors and museums over the past generation has resulted in a flurry of high-profile repatriations, new agreements, and even criminal proceedings against those involved in the antiquities trade. At the same time, while the holdings and scope of such museums as the British Museum in London, the Louvre in Paris, or the Metropolitan Museum of Art in New York are undeniably impressive, the fact that so-called universal museums seem to exist only in North America and Europe (the Global North) has not been lost on critics, who have raised legitimate questions about how universal they really are. Specifically, how well do they serve the interests of and provide access to a global public, given the prohibitive costs of international travel for a great majority of the world's population? (Prott 2005: 231; Urice 2004: 150).

The aim of this chapter is to review the ways in which current international cultural property disputes have developed and continue to develop in both the regulatory (legal) and ethical spheres. Moreover, this chapter assesses the extent to which these developments address postcolonial concerns regarding reparation for past injustices and respect for the rights of present-day groups to control their culture and to dictate the terms under which it is shared (or not) with the rest of the world. A brief review of the main ways in which cultural property is regulated in international law and policy is initially presented, followed by a discussion of important recent developments that have challenged international collecting practices developed over the past century. The chapter concludes with some brief thoughts on prospects for the future.

Regulating the International Trade in Cultural Property

Regulating the international movement of cultural property involves international treaties, international and local customary law, national laws, and codes of practice.[3] It is a subject that has provoked a wide range of policy perspectives (for recent statements from opposing positions, see Merryman 2005; Prott 2005). The most important multilateral treaty in this area is the 1970 UNESCO Convention on the Means of Prohibiting and Preventing the Illicit Import, Export and Transfer of Ownership of Cultural Property (UNESCO 1970), which is aimed at protecting cultural property by limiting the movement of works that have been illegally exported or stolen.[4] A generation after its implementation, the Convention has arguably had a greater moral than legal impact, but its ratification and implementation by more than 100 nations during this period—including, recently, an increasing number of so-called market nations such as Switzerland and the United Kingdom—marks a major shift in international attitudes toward the movement of stolen and illegally exported cultural property.

Although nations rarely discourage the importation of cultural property, most have laws that carefully regulate their export. These export regulations may be characterized as one of three basic types: (1) strict regulations that effectively embargo all export; (2) schemes that permit some trade through either licensing or, conversely, the embargo of only specific works of national significance; and (3) a laissez-faire approach that effectively allows movement without restriction.

The United States, for example, has a policy that is quite liberal in both directions. Import is generally allowed without restriction (except in cases where there are treaties with specific other nations in place). If a work of cultural property is properly declared on its entry into the United States, it may be brought into the country legally and without customs duties. Export regulation is similar; only a small number of objects, primarily Native American materials found on federal or public lands, are subject to export restrictions. In the United States, whether an object is on its way into or out of the country, federal law is violated only if the work is not properly declared to U.S. Customs officials or if an object is known to have been stolen and moves across state or federal borders.

Many countries, however, have much more comprehensive antiquities laws, which stipulate that any cultural object over a certain age, as well as any yet to be discovered archaeologically, is the property of the state and cannot be exported without express permission, which is rarely granted, unless for scientific analysis of unexceptional objects (Prott and O'Keefe 1988). The application of these "vesting statutes" (so called because they vest ownership in the state) has been a subject of much debate. Specifically, it is debated whether illegal export (i.e., without a permit) from a nation with a vesting law in place could itself constitute theft in terms of international law. The reason for this distinction is important, because while many nations will not enforce another nation's export laws, violations of property law tend to be enforced across borders. In addition, in those (mostly Anglophone) nations with common-law systems, a stolen object can never be transferred legally to a new owner, even if that purchaser was innocent, had done due diligence, and purchased it at a fair market price; those latter requirements will merely absolve a purchaser from criminal liability, but will not allow him or her to have gained good title to the object.[5]

Market nations like the United States and the United Kingdom resist interpreting the export of antiquities without a permit as "theft" in part because doing so would mean recognizing the rights of nations to nationalize their heritage and to effectively call the shots in controlling the trade in those antiquities. The idea that some groups should have the right to dictate the terms of cultural sharing and use is directly at odds with the notion of a "universal" heritage advanced by the Universal Museums, which declares that all peoples have a shared stake in the preservation and enjoyment of all the world's heritage and that objects should be distributed widely to ensure those goals (Appiah 2006a: 115–135; 2006b; Merryman 2005). The "universal" nature of this view, however, like that of the Universal Museums themselves, is in reality more often used by advocates of the antiquities trade to rationalize the rights of the individual to collect and own those parts of it they wish, and as Prott (2005: 228) points out, this "looks far more like cultural imperialism, based as it seems to be on the activities of those from trading between wealthy countries with each other and between wealthy countries and with poorer states whose cultural resources are flowing in one direction, without an equal exchange.[6]

The practice of collecting from the art market is not given up so easily, although it is clear that the assertion and recognition of national and local rights in the postcolonial era is demanding a reconfiguring of legal and disciplinary structures and practices, in both intranational and international contexts (Prott 2005; Watkins 2005). Domestic cultural property and repatriation laws, such as the Native American Graves Protection and Repatriation Act (NAGPRA) in the United States and the Protected Objects Act in New Zealand, are forcing museums and archaeologists to relinquish their monopoly on controlling heritage and to begin a dialogue with descendent communities (see this volume, Armstrong-Fumero and Hoil Gutierrez [chapter 31]; Brady and Crouch [chapter 32]; Daehnke and Lonetree [chapter 18]; Green and Gordon [chapter 19] ; and Silliman [chapter 11]). Similarly, it is due to both changing laws and the increasing success of efforts to prosecute the global trade of antiquities that museums that collect such materials are turning to develop similar kinds of relationships internationally.

Recent Developments

A series of legal and policy developments over the past few years have considerably changed how cultural property claims are considered. In spite of the plea of the Universal Museums, the general trend has been to move away from a largely unfettered market in antiquities in favor of the rights of individual nations to dictate the terms under which objects are exchanged. In 2003, a key criminal ruling in the United States against antiquities dealer Frederick Schultz (and the prior conviction in the United Kingdom of his conspirator, Jonathan Tokeley-Parry) definitively settled the debate about whether illegal export alone would be treated as theft in U.S. law, as his illegal smuggling of antiquities out of Egypt was prosecuted as a theft (Gerstenblith 2006; Yasaitis 2005). At the same time, so-called source nations are also increasing their prosecution of antiquities traffickers at home and abroad, with the recent trials in Italy of the well-known art dealer Robert Hecht, and (now ex) curator at the Getty Museum, Marion True, serving as the most high-profile examples (Watson and Todeschini 2006). Together, these cases have effectively expanded the remedies available for recovering cultural property internationally, and have already had a significant impact on the international trade in antiquities.

A second development has been the somewhat unexpected ratification of the 1970 UNESCO Convention and the passage of new cultural property laws by some important market countries. One of the long-standing weaknesses of the UNESCO Convention was that some of the most prominent market nations were not signatories (the United States was a significant exception, having become a signatory in 1972 and then implementing the Convention in United States law in 1983). Without the participation of these countries, the Convention's effect on antiquities trafficking remained more moral than legal. However, this situation changed when the United Kingdom and Japan signed in 2002, followed by Switzerland in 2004. This was a significant development given that Switzerland, with its civil law structure and its independence from the European Union and other international frameworks, long played a primary role in the smuggling and "laundering" of antiquities (Weber 2006).[7]

Against this backdrop of increasing acceptance on the part of market nations to join international efforts against antiquities trafficking and the increasingly successful prosecutions of smugglers, it may come as little surprise that some major (even "universal") museums are rethinking their collections policies and entering into agreements with nations making repatriation claims. Most significantly, in February 2006, the Metropolitan Museum of Art agreed to return a host of important works, the legality of whose purchase had long been questioned, including the famed "Euphronios Krater," as well as the cache of Hellenistic silver vessels believed to have been looted from Morgantina in Sicily. Since then, similar agreements have been made or attempted with a host of other museums, including the Museum of Fine Arts, Boston, the Princeton University Art Museum, and the Getty Museum in Malibu, California (Gill and Chippendale 2006, 2007). Interestingly, and perhaps most positively, these agreements are not simply concessions on the part of the museums, but include provisions for the reciprocal sharing of cultural materials and the development of new cooperative endeavors between Italy and the museums. These developments suggest positive steps toward cultural sharing along the lines that the Universal Museums seem to support. Ironically, these may never have come about without the more aggressive prosecutions of antiquities smugglers.

Future Prospects

While increasing adoption and enforcement of cultural property laws and agreements such as those between the Metropolitan Museum and Italy do limit the possibilities for a continuing antiquities trade, they may not signal the end of archaeological museums. Rather, they signal the end of these museums as we have known them, that is, as products of an Enlightenment-based and colonialism-facilitated era of acquisition. In these postcolonial times, exchanges of objects will likely continue, but will depend more on international and intercultural relationships and good will. Fears about the "emptying of the world's museums" are overstated and very much parallel similar fears voiced by museums of Native American history and archaeology at the time NAGPRA was passed in 1990 (Meighan 1992). Yet, almost two decades later, not only have those fears proven to be largely unfounded, but NAGPRA itself is now widely seen as having opened up important new avenues for cooperation and sharing between museums and the communities whose objects they curate (Nafziger and Dobkins 1999; Preucel et al. 2003). It is likely that the cooperative agreements born from international repatriation disputes will promote similar structures that will allow archaeology museums to operate in new and important ways.

Another example of the development of a new, cooperative middle-ground satisfying the concerns of both the "universalists" and specific national or descent groups is the Afghan Museum-in-Exile initiative, which was maintained until recently in the town of Bubendorf, Switzerland, with the support of UNESCO and other groups in the archaeological and museum communities. That museum acted as a repository for materials thought to have been looted from Afghanistan's sites and museums and donated to them by individuals, institutions, and governments with the aim of eventually returning them to Afghanistan when the region became sufficiently stable (Bucherer-Dietschi 2002). While many statements about the ability of Western countries to take better care of another's objects are paternalistic and often inaccurate (and to some, beside the point), there are clearly cases where international intervention to safeguard a culture's heritage is necessary and a moral imperative (the looting of Iraq's museum and sites since the U.S. invasion of that country is another example). However, rather than serve as an excuse to claim indefinite ownership of those materials in the name of a universal heritage, these circumstances might provide additional opportunities for intercultural cooperation and understanding in line with the growing trend of postcolonialism in international law and policy (Orford 2007; Pahuja 2005). Certainly, recognition of the sovereignty of cultures and nations to call the shots when it comes to their heritage requires a critical rethinking of those universalist claims that have underpinned the international trade in and ownership of antiquities since at least the 19th century.

Yet, there are also ambivalences here that deserve to be raised, even if their answers are not easy or straightforward. While the developing trend of local and national assertion of control over archaeological materials and practice is important for challenging colonialist, Western narratives that have long dominated the archaeology of many regions, it is equally important to identify and understand their unanticipated and perhaps less beneficial ramifications, such as the promotion of narrow nationalist perspectives and the suppression of alternative discourses about the objects. As McIntosh et al. write, this would be simply to replace "one set of limiting conditions with another" (1996: 189). At the same time, the fact that archaeologists' scrutiny and critique of power and politics in archaeological practice comes just as that power is being asserted by previously disenfranchised groups is an irony not lost on many local and Indigenous activists, who see a "strategic essentialism" vital to their successful assertion of control over their culture and past (Robbins and Stamatopoulou 2004). Being mindful of these tensions is important as the field continues to confront issues of control over cultural heritage.

Notes

1. Though the British Museum was not initially one of the declaration's signatories, it has since become its most vocal proponent. For the full text of the declaration, see *ICOM News* 2004/1, p. 1, available online at *http://icom.museum/pdf/E_news2004/p4_2004-1.pdf* (last accessed 19 March 2008). The British Museum is listed as a signatory there.
2. For more on these issues, see Ana Filipa Vrdoljak's (2006) masterful analysis of the growth of museum collections and their relationship to nationalism and the colonial endeavor, as well as their contribution to shaping international law and policies regarding cultural property.
3. For more in-depth, if in some cases outdated, treatments of this subject, see

Bator 1982; Gerstenblith 2004; Merryman et al. 2007; and Prott and O'Keefe 1984, 1990.
4. The treaty is not self-executing: it requires the adoption of legislation in each state party to give effect to its provisions. For example, although the United States ratified the treaty in 1972, Congress could not reach a compromise on enabling legislation until 1983, when it adopted the Convention on Cultural Property Implementation Act, or CCPIA (19 U.S.C. 2601 et seq. [1983]). Under the CCPIA, foreign nations petition the U.S. to place import restrictions on certain classes of cultural items that are under threat in part because of their trade. The United States currently has bilateral agreements with 11 nations (see "Chart of Emergency Actions & Bilateral Agreements" at *http://exchanges.state.gov/culprop/chart.html* [last accessed 19 March 2008]).
5. This is distinct from nations with civil law systems, where satisfying those requirements (i.e., being a "bona fide purchaser for value") will allow that purchaser to acquire good title to the object, even if it had originally been stolen. This is one of the principal reasons many antiquities have been trafficked through Switzerland, where, combined with privacy protections there, the civil law system allowed buyers to gain good title to objects that the sellers may not have had to give (though the fact that purchasers knew to go to Switzerland for this very reason casts doubt on whether purchasers were acting in good faith). For example, in the classic case of *Autocephalous Greek-Orthodox Church of Cyprus* v. *Goldberg and Feldman Fine Arts. Inc.*, 917 F.2d 278 (7th Cir. 1990), the court's analysis of Swiss law found that art dealer Peg Goldberg's lack of suspicion about the transaction's circumstances indicated that she did not act in good faith about it, and thus could not have acquired good title even under that nation's law.
6. While Appiah's "cosmopolitan" view recasts the free-market perspective in more contemporary terms, he has remarked that ideally objects should circulate both ways, even if perhaps not the best objects should go to poor or unstable countries. In the symposium "Who Owns Art" held at the New School in New York City on March 6, 2006, Appiah remarked, "[O]ne thing that Mali is not short of is Malian art. If you want to, if you care about the aesthetic experience of Malians, you'll be more concerned to see how to get the second-rate Impressionists in." A complete transcript of the symposium is available online at *http://www.nytimes.com/packages/pdf/arts/29panel.pdf* (last accessed 16 April 2008).
7. For the implementing legislation in the United Kingdom, Dealing in Cultural Objects (Offences) Act 2003, see *http://www.opsi.gov.uk/acts/acts2003/ukpga_20030027_en_1* (last accessed 6 April 2008); for the implementing legislation in Switzerland, Swiss Federal Act on the International Transfer of Cultural Property, see *http://www.nb. admin.ch/ bak/themen/kulturguetertransfer/index.html?lang=en* (last accessed 6 April 2008).

References

Association of Art Museum Directors (AAMD). n.d. *Art Museums and the Identification and Restitution of Works Stolen by the Nazis*. New York: Association of Art Museum Directors. www.aamd.org/pdfs/Nazi%20Looted%20Art.pdf.

Appiah, K. A. 2006a. *Cosmopolitanism: Ethics in a World of Strangers*. New York: W. W. Norton.

———. 2006b. Whose culture is it? *The New York Review of Books* 2: 53.

Barkan, E. 2002. Amending historical injustices: The restitution of cultural property—an overview, in E. Barkan and R. Bush (eds.), *Claiming the Stones/Naming the Bones: Cultural Property and the Negotiation of National and Ethnic Identity*, pp. 16–46. Los Angeles: Getty Research Institute.

Bator, P. M. 1982. *The International Trade in Art*. Chicago: University of Chicago Press.

Bucherer-Dietschi, P. 2002. Protection and restitution of Afghan cultural heritage in the framework of the Afghanistan-Museum in Exile, in K. Warikoo (ed.), *Bamiyan: Challenge to World Heritage*, pp. 164–183. New Delhi: Bhavana Books and Prints.

Gerstenblith, P. 2004. *Art, Cultural Heritage, and the Law*. Durham, NC: Carolina Academic Press.

———. 2006. Recent developments in the legal protection of cultural heritage, in N. Brodie, M. M. Kersel, C. Luke, and K. W. Tubb (eds.), *Archaeology, Cultural Heritage, and the Antiquities Trade*, pp. 68–92. Gainesville: University Press of Florida.

Gill, D. W. J., and Chippendale, C. 2006. From Boston to Rome: Reflections on returning antiquities. *International Journal of Cultural Property* 13: 311–331.

———. 2007. From Malibu to Rome: Further developments on the return of antiquities. *International Journal of Cultural Property* 14: 205–240.

McIntosh, R. J., McIntosh, S. K., and Togola, T. 1996. People without history, in K. D. Vitelli (ed.), *Archaeological Ethics*, pp. 185–197. Walnut Creek, CA: AltaMira.

Meighan, C. W. 1992. Some scholars' views on reburial. *American Antiquity* 57: 704–710.

Merryman, J. H. 2005. Cultural property internationalism. *International Journal of Cultural Property* 12 (1): 1–29.

Merryman, J., Elsen, A. E., and Urice, S. K. 2007. *Law, Ethics, and the Visual Arts*. Alphen aan den Rijn: Kluwer Law International.

Nafziger, J. A. R., and Dobkins, R. J. 1999. The Native American Graves Protection and Repatriation Act in its first decade. *International Journal of Cultural Property* 8: 77–107.

Orford, A. (ed.). 2007. *International Law and Its Others*. New York: Cambridge University Press.

Pahuja, S. 2005. The postcoloniality of international law. *Harvard International Law Journal* 46: 459–469.

Preucel, R. W., Williams, L., Espenlaub, S. O., and Monge, J. 2003. Out of heaviness, enlightenment. *Expedition* 45 (3): 21–27.

Prott, L. V. 2005. The international movement of cultural objects. *International Journal of Cultural Property* 12: 225–248.

Prott, L. V. and O'Keefe, P. J. 1984. *Law and the Cultural Heritage*, Vol. I: *Discovery and Excavation*. Abingdon: Professional Books Ltd.

———. 1988. *Handbook of National Regulations Concerning the Export of Cultural Property*. Paris: UNESCO.

———. 1990. *Law and the Cultural Heritage*, Vol. III: *Movement*. London: Butterworths.

Robbins, B., and Stamatopoulou, E. 2004. Reflections on culture and cultural rights. *South Atlantic Quarterly* 103: 419–434.

Shapiro, D. 1998. Repatriation: A modest proposal. *NYU Journal of International Law and Politics* 31: 95–108.

UNESCO. 1970. *Convention on the Means of Prohibiting and Preventing the Illicit Import, Export and Transfer of Ownership of Cultural Property*. Paris: UNESCO.

Urice, S. K. 2004. The beautiful one has come—to stay, in J. H. Merryman (ed.), *Imperialism, Art, and Restitution*, pp. 135–165. New York: Cambridge University Press.

Vrodoljak, A. F. 2006. *International Law, Museums, and the Return of Cultural Objects*. Cambridge: Cambridge University Press.

Watkins, J. 2005. Cultural nationalists, internationalists, and "intra-nationalists": Who's right and whose right? *International Journal of Cultural Property* 12: 78–94.

Watson, P., and Todeschini, C. 2006. *The Medici Conspiracy: The Illicit Journey of Looted Antiquities from Italy's Tomb Raiders to the World's Greatest Museums*. New York: Public Affairs.

Weber, M. 2006. New Swiss law on cultural property. *International Journal of Cultural Property* 13: 99–113.

Yasaitis, K. E. 2005. National ownership laws as cultural property protection policy: The emerging trend in *United States v. Schultz*. *International Journal of Cultural Property* 12: 95–113.

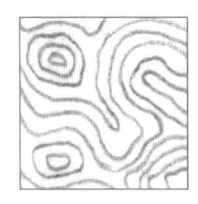

22

NEW MUSEOLOGICAL WAYS OF SEEING THE WORLD: DECOLONIZING ARCHAEOLOGY IN LEBANESE MUSEUMS

Lina G. Tahan

> Larger imperial and colonial projects had influenced each country's museums, but such projects varied in their respective philosophical underpinnings, time frames, geography, and outcomes.
>
> *Kreps 2003: xii*

The objective of this chapter is to present a model for studying the history of Lebanese archaeological museums. This chapter sets the background for an investigation of how Lebanese museums are still influenced by colonial ideas in terms of the display of artifacts. First, Edward Said's (1978, 1993) philosophy of the history of the "Orient" is evaluated in order to answer a broader critical question: Is museum history missing an account of the history of the "Orient" and is there such a thing as an "archaeological Orient"? Through the discussion of Said's works, the meaning of an "archaeological Orient" is analyzed. Second, the concept of museums and the postcolonial critique are examined with regard to the shaping of museums in the postcolonial period. Finally, models are presented and applied in my assessment of the role of museums within the context of colonialism and postcolonialism.

The Creation of an Archaeological Orient and the Birth of the Museum in Lebanon

The discussion of the archaeology of the postcolonial period can be introduced from the point of accepting the basic distinction between the "East" and the "West." This distinction is shown through the various means employed by the West in its domination of the East—culturally, politically, economically, socially (Said 1978: 2–3), and, I argue, even archaeologically.

Researching colonialism and archaeology has become a timely issue in today's world. The connection among colonialism, museums, and archaeological artifacts is very interesting, as it brings together four major disciplinary areas: colonial and postcolonial theories, archaeology, museum studies, and material culture. Reevaluating the political and theoretical connotations of this postcolonial world has affected our perception of museums as institutions (Barringer and Flynn 1998: 2), and many studies have been devoted to elucidating this colonial representation. Among the most influential contributions is Edward Said's *Culture and Imperialism*. Said's aim is "to connect these different realms [culture and imperialism] to show the involvements of culture with expanding empires, to make observations about art that preserve its unique endowments and at the same time map its affiliations" (1993: 5). This chapter is intended as a contribution to such a project by looking at Lebanese archaeological museums and at Lebanon's heritage as displayed in the Louvre Museum. From *Orientalism* (1978) and *Culture and Imperialism* (1993) onward, Said's critiques laid the foundations of my project for an inquiry into colonial material culture which has wide reverberations across humanity.

The "Orient," a European invention, has been perceived since antiquity as "a place of romance, exotic beings, haunting memories, landscapes and remarkable experiences" (Said 1978: 1). The scholar, the scientist, the missionary, the soldier, or the trader was in the "Orient," or thought about the "Orient," because he could be there, or could think about it with very little resistance on the "Orient's" part. "Under the general heading of knowledge of the Orient, and within the umbrella of Western hegemony over the Orient during the period from the end of eighteenth century, there emerged a complete Orient suitable for study in the academy, for display in the museum, for reconstruction in the colonial office, for theoretical illustration in anthropological, biological, linguistic, racial and historical theses about mankind and the universe" (Said 1978: 7). To this list should be added an "archaeological Orient."

Colonialism, with its ideologies and power relations, influences the ways in which archaeological artifacts are understood (Barringer and Flynn 1998: 1). We can see this by looking at the changing narratives of archaeological artifacts and how they are displayed in museum exhibits. An artifact removed from a colonial periphery to an imperial center radically alters our understanding of that object. Therefore, one cannot address a museum's collections in isolation, and one needs to know the historical circumstances of how each object ended up in that particular museum collection. Hence, a museum can be seen as a "cultural formation" (Barringer 1998: 12) and as consisting of artifacts arranged into a specific classification system and interpreted accordingly by the use of display panels, labels, guidebooks, and catalogs (Barringer 1998: 12). Moreover, it is evident that if a museum chooses to focus on colonialism, that intellectual framework can elicit a range of historical, archaeological, as well as interpretive issues essential to museum professionals and their publics in the postcolonial era. And by raising the issue of who and what are being represented in a museum, we pose important questions not only about how the ideologies and doctrines of colonialism impact the interpretation and definition of archaeology in museums, but also how these same ideas affect the ways that appropriated objects are displayed.

During the colonial period, vast quantities of cultural material were collected in Lebanon and placed in museums in France. In many instances, particularly in the early years of collecting, the items collected were very poorly documented. Indeed, the the details of acquisition and ownership of cultural artifacts are rarely analyzed in French museum exhibitions, despite the fact that the behavior of French colonialists and the detrimental effects of expansionist policies are part of the biography of a museum's archaeological objects as well as part of the history of both colonizer and colonized (Simpson 1996: 25).

Museums have long served as repositories of a diverse heritage. Often beginning with the private collections of elites obtained through conquest and exploitation, museums also came to conserve their own national and cultural heritage, along with the heritage of the "other," and to educate the public about these topics (Kaplan 1994: 9). It is the nature of these collections, and the way they are used to illuminate and interpret the past, that is of interest to us. In the West, museum professionals seem to be discovering the impact of colonialism in their respective museums (Kaplan 1994: 9); while, in the developing world, museum professionals seem unconcerned with the influence of the colonial legacy in their own museums as they make new choices that move toward a postcolonial future.

Lebanon resembles any other developing country in assigning national roles to its museums. The objective is to present the past and create a coherent picture of Lebanon's heritage—a national identity, if you will. The Lebanese past has particular qualities, encompassing as it does the colonial experience, which is often viewed negatively. As Lowenthal (1976: 89) has observed, countries freeing themselves from colonial rule may seek to erase the colonial experience and try to find an autonomous national identity in the precolonial past.

The interest in archaeological museums is fairly recent, and in some parts of the world, such as Lebanon, archaeological museums have been affected by recent "Western" intellectual developments. "The national and racial discourses of the nineteenth century established a self-evident and 'natural' tie among identity, history and territory" (Olsen 2001: 50). In this light, the museum becomes a fixed cultural space where the present frameworks of identities are shaped. Our challenge lies in reconsidering the idea of colonial legacy and its impact on Lebanese archaeological museums. This involves questioning the meaning and social values of the past and readdressing and reassessing these within the context of modern society.

Under this model, the museum becomes a space where the demand for reevaluation is constantly needed (Bennett 1995: 90).

However, the discourse of reform that initiated these demands has remained relatively static in Lebanon over the last century, due to the political constituencies that operate within the museum space. In my view, reform should be characterized by two principles: (1) museums should be accessible and equally open to all members of the public, and (2) they should represent adequately the cultures and values of different sections of the public. Unfortunately, this is not happening in Lebanon: adequacy in representation is not practiced and not all archaeological periods are given equal weight. Indeed, there are no comprehensive narratives present in the Lebanese museum space, and the contents of the displays remain traditional in that they carry an embedded view of how the past was perceived by the French. This does not apply to the technical methods of display, which are very modern.

The relationship between colonizer and colonized in the museum space is extremely relevant to the Lebanese case, in that artifacts can be seen as "active agents" in tracing the history of colonialism. In particular, I argue that the French archaeologists were influenced by political and research agendas when interpreting "ancient Phoenicia" in the Beirut museum (more on this below), and this affected the way the Christian Lebanese used the "Phoenician" histories within their own rhetoric. This representation within the museum helped to shape attitudes about the past, as some periods were made invisible and some groups saw their sense of identity downgraded. While the French controlled the archaeology of Lebanon (for almost a century), local voices were silenced. Even in the 19th and early 20th centuries, when locals were involved in digging sites or shipping their artifacts to the Louvre Museum in Paris, the French used them as a tool to advance their own interests. For their part, locals were mainly concerned with pleasing the French with archaeological objects, rather than engaging themselves with their own past. Now, the Lebanese museums have a role to fulfill in the new millennium: to represent the past adequately and attract more local visitors, who deserve to become active agents and to have a say in the reconstruction and representation of their past.

It is relevant here to briefly express how France's *mission civilisatrice* was wielded as a weapon of French imperialism and came to shape Lebanese archaeology. As is typical in a "civilizing mission," the French purposefully employed the best qualities of their civilization to woo the locals in order to more easily impose their foreign policy in North Africa and the Levant before World War I:

> Cultural imperialism in the form of the diffusion of a national culture is immeasurably less mechanical and disciplinary, but not necessarily less effective, than the totalitarian kind. While the latter makes use primarily of the affinities of political ideology, the former impresses the intellectually influential groups of a foreign country with its attractive qualities of civilisation until these groups tend to find the political objectives and methods of that civilisation equally attractive.
> (Morgenthau 1960: 62–63)

Seen in this light, cultural imperialism is the most subtle and triumphant of imperialistic policies. Its purposes are not only the invasion of territories and/or the control of the economy and resources, but also the exercise of authority over the minds of men and women, as a tool for altering the power relations between two nations (Morgenthau 1960: 60–61).

Cultural imperialism is still alive and well in the recently founded museums of Lebanon. The historical links between Lebanon's archaeological museums and colonialism show why this is so. The first museums were initiated by the French and by American missionaries. Within the French mandate, Lebanon was largely a Christian (Maronite) enclave; Muslims were in the minority. Christian Lebanese considered France a "Mother Nation" or *Puissance Protectrice*, whereas the Muslims associated themselves with the other Arab nations, whom they saw as "protectors." It was the French who initiated research in "Phoenician archaeology"—ideas that appealed to the Maronite Christian intellectual elites and were reused in order to claim that they were of "Phoenician" descent. This discourse, as we have seen, was perpetuated later by many other Christian Lebanese to suit their own ideological needs and fragment the Lebanese society; it became a colonial residue and is still present among Lebanese museum narratives. The responsibility of the curators in museums today needs to be urgently reviewed, and the voices of what was the Muslim minority (prior to the Lebanese Civil War) but became a Muslim majority (in contemporary Lebanese post–Civil War society) need to be heard. Their past needs to be given more weight within the museum exhibits.

While conducting a visitors' survey at the National Museum of Beirut (NMB), visitors were asked whether they thought that the Islamic period was satisfactorily represented in their national museum; 72 percent of the 79 Lebanese visitors responded "no" (NMB visitors' survey, 2002, Q12).[1] Most of those Lebanese visitors were pupils or university students in attendance with their teachers and professors. One can infer from these statistics that perhaps the majority of the Lebanese public do not visit museums. Perhaps the local Lebanese communities are not as interested in their past as are the Lebanese elites, for whom it is prestigious and a symbol of political power and control over a national heritage that should belong to all Lebanese regardless of religious sect or social background.

Colonialism/Postcolonialism in Lebanon

Colonialism can be defined as the capture and seizure of other people's land and goods (Loomba 1998: 2). Archaeology became part of these goods because the past was appropriated by the colonizers and used for various political purposes. Of course, colonialism takes different forms in different parts of the world. Lebanon was part of the Ottoman Empire until the latter's defeat in World War I, after which it was ruled by France as a mandated territory from 1918 until 1943 (in 1918, it was part of the French

Mandate of Greater Syria; in 1920 France formed the State of Greater Lebanon as an enclave of Syria). During this time, Lebanon's boundaries were redefined. It is in this period that archaeological heritage was also redefined; a National Museum in Beirut was constructed in 1930, and an Antiquities Law was put into action in 1933.

In 1921, soon after the French took over Lebanon as a mandate, Claude Prost, the official representative of the Antiquities Service in Syria and Lebanon, questioned why it was necessary for Syria to have three museums (in Beirut, Damascus, and Aleppo). It was decided at that time to give each museum a unique focus: the Beirut museum would be entirely devoted to "Phoenician" antiquities; the Damascus museum to the Arabic and Islamic periods; and the Aleppo museum to the Christian and Byzantine periods. Greek and Roman periods would be distributed across the three museums depending on the objects' provenance.[2] The National Museum of Beirut opened its doors to the public in 1937. It was the chief repository of archaeological material excavated in the country (Chéhab 1937).

One can say that the history of archaeology in Lebanon can be attributed to France. In short, it was initiated by Western travelers, those commercial and diplomatic agents who had an interest in archaeological digs and artifacts as well as in maintaining a political and diplomatic career through their consulates. It is thus argued that colonialism first began with the arrival in 1855 of the travelers and agents who started exploring Lebanon and taking archaeological artifacts to ship back to their respective countries. All these practices contributed to the history of the colonized country and the colonizing power.

Because of Lebanon's rich heritage, archaeology has played a significant role in the creation of the Lebanese state. In Lebanon's colonial context, its archaeological heritage was appropriated by France with Ernest Renan's expedition, *Mission de Phénicie*, in 1860. French archaeologists began their archaeological investigations in the 19th century. Their research focused on the historical influence that Lebanon (and other countries) had on France. Such a connection is quite interesting, as those links between colonizer and colonized contributed to the image of superiority of the conquerors as "true heirs" of the historical rulers, in contrast to the degenerated local populations who were to be patronized (cf. Trigger 1984).

I should like to end this chapter by reflecting on the complexities of the present postcolonial world. Gosden (1999: 203) has argued that archaeology and anthropology were both products of colonialism in their origins and early years, but what we, as archaeologists and museologists, are predisposed to forget is that these colonial influences are still with us. Their residues are certainly still extant in the Lebanese archaeological museums. Undeniably, we have all been created as colonial subjects (Gosden 1999: 203). The independence of Lebanon as a republic did not make us—the Lebanese people—truly postcolonial in thought and instinct. It is in this sense that archaeological museums should be engaged in teaching us two sets of tasks: "One is to learn about the state of the modern world and its antecedents; the second is to unlearn the habits of thought which we bring to bear on the world through a thorough examination of their histories and antecedents. This process of unlearning will be helped by the realisation that the set of unequal relations which compose the modern world is just the latest in a series of global relations, historical and prehistorical" (Gosden 1999: 203).

Postcolonial studies are now generally accepted as a field of interdisciplinary studies that encompasses a wide variety of types of analysis. What links these forms of analysis is a concern with the imperial past, with the different varieties of colonialism within the imperial framework, and with the links between the imperial past and the postcolonial present. It is these links concerning museums in Lebanon that interest us, although such ideas have not infiltrated Lebanon yet. It is true that Lebanese museums are temporally in a postcolonial era, but colonialism as a narrative is still present within museum displays.

It is important to think of postcolonialism as not just literally coming after colonialism and implying its end, but rather as contesting colonial domination and the legacies of colonialism (Loomba 1998: 12). Such a position allows us to think of archaeological material culture displaced by colonialism as having a colonial narrative as well—for example, objects such as the sarcophagus of Eshmounazar II or the Yehawmilk stele displayed in the Louvre Museum. A country such as Lebanon may be regarded as postcolonial in that it achieved its independence from France in 1943, but it is still colonial in the sense that it has remained culturally dependent on France and other Western countries. This is reflected in the museums of archaeology. Lebanon is still dependent on foreign expertise to create museums, and there is a foreign influence in particular kinds of displays and even in the decision to retain the same museological content while revamping only its appearance, as is the case at the National Museum of Beirut.

Conclusions: Toward a Bright Future for a Postcolonial Archaeology

This chapter has presented possible solutions to the problem of colonial/postcolonial interactions within the museum space. Moreover, an examination of the history of this interaction—one that reveals power and knowledge—provides a starting point for the formulation of further solutions for future directions of Lebanese museology and museography. In viewing the relationship of colonizer versus colonized as a complex one, the power that museums hold in Lebanese and French society becomes apparent. This perspective aids in the formulation of answers to the following enquiry: Why are Lebanese and French museums still elitist in nature, and why is the focus only on the aesthetic nature of the artifacts rather than on their historical and archaeological contextual value?

Finally, the interaction of colonizers and colonized has remained largely ignored in museum exhibitions in France and Lebanon. Archaeological displays have tended to focus on the material culture of Lebanon, but have failed to explore the behaviors and approaches of the colonialist period. Hence, this "cultural colonialism" continues to control the representations of Lebanese archaeology and culture.

Notes

1. A visitors' survey was conducted in 2002 at the National Museum of Beirut and the American University of Beirut Archaeological Museum. It showed that very few Lebanese visit their museums. The only Lebanese visitors are students and their teachers.
2. Annual Report No. 527 from C. Prost to the High Commissioner of the French Republic in Syria and Lebanon, dated Beirut, 11 August 1921. Archives of the Institut Français du Proche-Orient (IFAPO)-Service des Antiquités du Haut-Commissariat (SAHC).

References

Barringer, T. 1998. The South Kensington Museum and the Colonial Project, in T. Barringer and T. Flynn (eds.), *Colonialism and the Object: Empire, Material Culture and the Museum*, pp. 11–27. London: Routledge.

Barringer, T., and Flynn T. 1998. Introduction, in T. Barringer and T. Flynn (eds.), *Colonialism and the Object: Empire, Material Culture and the Museum*, pp. 1–8. London: Routledge.

Bennett, T. 1995. *The Birth of the Museum*. London: Routledge.

Chéhab, M. 1937. *Le Musée National*. Beirut: Imprimerie Catholique.

Gosden C. 1999. *Anthropology and Archaeology: A Changing Relationship*. London: Routledge.

Kaplan, F. S. 1994. *Museums and the Making of Ourselves*. London: Leicester University Press.

Kreps, C. F. 2003. *Liberating Culture: Cross-Cultural Perspectives on Museums, Curation, and Heritage Preservation*. London: Routledge.

Loomba A. 1998. *Colonialism/Postcolonialism*. London: Routledge.

Lowenthal, D. 1976. The place of the past in the American landscape, in D. Lowenthal and M. J. Bowden, (eds.), *Geographies of the Mind: Essays in Historical Geography in Honour of John Kirtland Wright*, pp. 89–117. New York: Oxford University Press.

Morgenthau, H. 1960. *Politics among Nations: The Struggle for Power and Peace*. New York: Knopf.

Olsen, B. J. 2001. The end of history? Archaeology and the politics of identity in a globalised world, in R. Layton, P. G. Stone, and J. Thomas, (eds.), *Destruction and Conservation of Cultural Property*, pp. 42–54. One World Archaeology 41. London and New York: Routledge.

Said, E. W. 1978. *Orientalism*. London: Penguin Books.

——. 1993. *Culture and Imperialism*. London: Vintage Books.

Simpson, M. G. 1996. *Making Representations: Museums in the Post-Colonial Era*. London: Routledge.

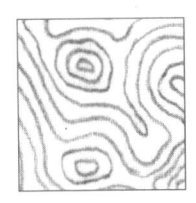

23

COMMENTARY:
THE GLOBAL REPATRIATION DEBATE AND THE NEW "UNIVERSAL MUSEUMS"

Magnus Fiskesjö

The Declaration on the Importance and Value of Universal Museums was issued unilaterally in 2002 by 19 of the richest and most prominent museums of the world.[1] To date, it is the most forceful general counterattack on rising repatriation demands. It is part of a new, powerful counter-trend to not just defend existing collections, but also to favor the continued collecting of looted antiquities, in the name of "art" for a global audience.

Archaeologists should take note: Arguments against looting and in favor of repatriations are not necessarily winning this momentous new battle. In what follows, I take the Declaration as a starting point for addressing some of the major issues of museums and repatriation in the world today—including the enduring force of the values of Western modernity that sustain the top museums, often with the tacit acceptance of archaeologists.

Only European and American museums were found in the Declaration's exclusive line-up, from the Art Institute of Chicago and New York's Metropolitan Museum of Art, to the Louvre and the Hermitage. Not one great museum from "the rest" of the world was asked to join, to legitimate the Declaration's "universal" claims—not Cairo or Calcutta, Istanbul or Shanghai, Japan or Mexico. There are two possible explanations for this glaring omission (discussed almost solely by Africans [e.g., Abungu 2004] and others historically at the receiving end of Western colonialism).[2] Perhaps the signatories simply were not thinking,[3] as they launched a 21st-century Westerners-only rich-club defense of holding onto objects amassed on the principle that colonial and imperial might is right. More plausibly, in the light of that history, they simply assumed that contemporary non-Western colleagues would not sign. Their line in the sand even crossed the code of ethics of the International Council of Museums for museums, which demands open-minded engagement with every repatriation demand[4] —probably the bare minimum expected by any non-Westerner (even as most are actually not demanding the wholesale return of old collections).

As ethnographic material (which is how we should approach it), the Declaration is fascinating. It begins with a gesture toward the growing global opinion against the ongoing illicit trade in culturally meaningful objects, stating that the signatories share the "conviction that illegal traffic in archaeological, artistic, and ethnic objects must be firmly discouraged." It then lays out two main arguments to justify holding onto existing collections:

1. "Objects acquired in earlier times must be viewed in the light of different sensitivities and values, reflective of that earlier era" (a reference to the once self-evident right of Westerners to dismantle the monuments of others, for redisplay at home); and

2. the "objects so acquired ... have become part of the museums that have cared for them, and by extension part of the heritage of the nations which house them" (ICOM 2004: 4).

These arguments are clearly also to justify the principles underpinning the acquisition of more such objects. These museums, as argued in the text of the Declaration, "provide a valid and valuable context for objects that were long ago displaced from their original source. The universal admiration for ancient civilizations would not be so deeply established today were it not for the influence exercised by the artifacts of these cultures, widely available to an international public in major museums..."; and "We should acknowledge that museums serve not just the citizens of one nation but the people of every nation.... To narrow the focus of museums whose collections are diverse and multifaceted would therefore be a disservice to all visitors" (ICOM 2004: 4).

The point about serving the tourists of the world provided a convenient first target for critics. For example, Ethiopia's Association for the Return of Ethiopia's Maqdala Treasures (AFROMET)[5] retorted: "Few of Ethiopia's sixty or so million inhabitants are in a position to visit the great museums of Europe or America to inspect their heritage; ... it is unseemly of the museum directors to expect those robbed of their rightful inheritance to have always to grovel for it" (AFROMET 2002). Indeed, the directors' formulation of the Declaration assumes that the world is flat, void of inequalities, so that every farmer from Bihar or Bahía might as well be flying into JFK or Heathrow airport for weekend museum-going, and never have a care regarding the history of these collections' "multifaceted diversity." The result is that, regardless of any benign intentions among the signatories, the Declaration is seen around the world as yet another confirmation of Western intent to hold onto unfair privilege.

AFROMET stressed that "the principle of restitution of cultural artifacts to their country of origin is now increasingly accepted," as demonstrated when Italy, in 2005, did return to Ethiopia the enormous Aksum obelisk that had been stolen by Mussolini, one of the most spectacular of postcolonial repatriations to date (but poorly reported in Western media). Still, I think AFROMET's optimism is premature. Yes, Bruno Latour (1993) famously theorized that we really "have never been modern," but the formidable power of the modern imaginary is far from exhausted. We need only look at these museums—massively wealthy institutions lodged in imposing, city-center edifices—to notice that the Western modern framework of value formation remains in full force. The Metropolitan in New York, for instance, a major cathedral for the mass worship of "art," orchestrates these rites in the terms of Fine Arts and the like, as if these notions had never been questioned. And most visitors, anyway, have never heard of such doubts. Instead, drawn by the fame of the treasures, they unthinkingly accept their designation as "art" (which, of course, isn't a given, but a "learned disposition," as Pierre Bourdieu [1984] noted). These top-tier museums were never primarily about *explaining*; they offer a powerful spectacle that awes the visitors, inculcating them with the tenets that these museums simultaneously embody and preach.

In this grand process of mystification, visitors are encouraged to consider the antiquities on display, now considered "art," as ends in themselves, as *the real source* of such enduring values—as in the Declaration's formulation (in a fit of classic fetishism!) of how, supposedly, the ancient artifacts *themselves* have "exercised their influence" on us, transmitting the essence of "civilization" and its privileges. Their suggestion itself forms a beautiful illustration of how "art" is created as the reified vanguard of "the West" and as a social value believed to sustain the civilized. This was key to Western self-identity already in the heyday of nation-states, and this is still why non-Western collections typically are organized to suggest the *pastness* of others, in contrast with the *forward* West (or, we might now say, "North"),[6] a master narrative in which archaeologists are cast mainly in secondary roles, as suppliers and authenticators of supporting evidence.

Riding post–Cold War waves of globalization, the new defenders of the old "universal" museums are aiming for a new high ground, portraying themselves as above what they call old-style nation-state ethno-"retentionism," which those archaeologists who do speak up against looting can then be accused of caving in to—never mind that the same museums have long relied on nation-state property laws to defend their ownership of contested objects! Drawing on the key theorists of a global free trade in cultural heritage (such as John Henry Merryman, the "internationalist" legal scholar [e.g., 2000, 2006] and Kwame Anthony Appiah, the "cosmopolitan" philosopher [2006]), the argument is made that contemporary and postcolonial nation-states are simply latter-day modern political constructs, and people there can have no special claim to a heritage created by "their" ancestors.[7] For example, the modern Italian state was established in 1861, and it is thus only about as old as the Metropolitan Museum of Art, which, founded in 1870, holds many items from civilizations once thriving on Italy's territory but on which it would have no claim.[8] The same argument is made for modern Ethiopia (where Aksum once flourished), Cambodia, Greece, and so on. The idea is that, despite the international legal and property system based on the nation-state framework introduced and enforced by Western powers, we are now *not* supposed to support the efforts of custodian "source" states like Cambodia to curb the looting rampage that supplies a global buyers' market, but instead *applaud* the trade in such objects, "freed" from ancient sites in those nations! What we are seeing is an attempt of an increasingly "globalized" elite (Fiskesjö 2007; Friedman 2001) justifying the hoarding of a fresh supplies of antiquities. The argument should be recognized as a variant of the notion that "Indigenous peoples" are but recent constructs with spurious connections to the past: the intention is to obscure the underlying issues of inequality and power, and the Declaration attempts the same—on a planetary scale.

If we understand the Declaration's purported universalism in this way,[9] we see that it actually has a point when it indignantly emphasizes (against the archaeologists who decry the orphaned looted antiquities on display) that these museums *do* provide a "valid and valuable" (new) context for objects removed from their original sociocultural anchoring. Not universal, of course, but very much historically and culturally specific: the assumption that the West is the gold standard can be seen as one component of a strategy of *encompassment*, in the technical sense suggested by Baumann and Gingrich (2004): The "other," while crucial to one's identity, is cast as an inferior *version* of the self. Since such otherings and ritualized belonging are mutually constitutive, the true meaning of the Declaration's seemingly innocuous aside about how long-held museum collections (from Parthenon marbles to Maqdala treasures) have become "part of the heritage of the nations that house them" is, then, that these tokens of the other cannot be relinquished because they are a key foundation of the particular identity of a civilizing, triumphant West.[10]

This is why the mighty museums are scrambling for viable new justifications for their perpetuation as dominant, prestigious social institutions, complete with the system of donations and acquisitions that is vital to their sustenance. All this is threatened when, as recently happened repeatedly, formerly clandestine supporting networks of looters and smugglers are exposed or even prosecuted, and when global public opinion begins to shift as a result. It is not simply the survival of the antiquities traffic (and associated profits) that is at stake, but the ideological basis of Western identity. This is why influential museums have long refused to stop acquisitioning fresh loot, even though no real threat to the existing collections (or even to the continuing traffic in loot) has emerged through the international conventions or other recent constraints listed by Neil Brodie and Colin Renfrew (2005), who were left baffled by their reluctance.

Brodie and Renfrew were right that the current pillaging is the more urgent, and that the Declaration's defense of old collections does deflect attention from the new "age of piracy" that we seem to be entering. But they were wrong to conclude that this reduces "what might otherwise have been coherent arguments in [the] Declaration to little more than pretentious sophistry" (Brodie and Renfrew 2005: 355). It does not, since there is really nothing baffling about these museums, especially the American ones, trying to continue their basic *modus operandi* of accepting prestige-building donations and purchases from dubious dealers still busy unloading smuggled goods from the global conveyor belts of trafficking in art, antiquities, and heritage items from the impoverished (and therefore often mostly defenseless) sections of the global South—or to now scramble for new arguments.

Against this background, the new guidelines agreed upon in 2008 by both the American Association of Museums and the Association of Art Museum Directors (AAMD) must be noted. Member museums now are advised to try to ensure that new acquisitions have not been illegally exported from their countries of origin, and also to trace documentation for such objects to at least 1970. Will this actually mean that leading art museums like the Metropolitan Museum of Art will discontinue acquiring and displaying fresh loot, or will they use the caveats from the AAMD and devise new practices like the "ten-year rule" of the recent past (i.e., a waiting period, effectively a "looters' charter" [Brodie and Renfrew 2005: 353]), or even build on the intellectual coherence of the Declaration for openly justifying such acquisitions, explicitly linking this with the defense of the existing collections? This remains to be seen.

Note too that there is little mention in the Declaration or other similar pronouncements of even the *possibility* of sharing or borrowing from contemporary nation-states such as Honduras, Libya, or others, whose citizens and governments are the *de facto* present-day custodians of world cultural heritage. The obsession with "acquisition" indulged in every new and current catalog is another indication of just how "modern" these powerful model museums still are. This may make such novel borrowing more difficult (the British Museum, the missing link of the Declaration, is trying). But it is not just that they could never make do with copies or reproductions, insisting on the aura of the original in this era of mass reproduction.[11] The default obsession with ownership of collected objects and *property* as the only meaningful relation to heritage (Carman 2005) is reflective of an anxiety in the face of the loss of mastery, which is really identical with that felt in regard to the loss of the power to define history in the terms of the former colonial and imperial masters.

The battle is on.

Notes

1. For the Declaration text, see the special issue of *ICOM News*, 57.1 (2004), p. 4; also the commentaries included, as well as Curtis 2006, Mathur 2005, Muthoni Thang'wa 2007, and O'Neill 2004.

2. See, e.g., Abungu 2004 on why the National Museums of Kenya was not called.
3. In 2003, I asked a leading representative of a German signatory museum why there were only Western nations involved. At first, he drew a blank and then offered that during the drafting this had not been considered at all.
4. The International Council of Museums, taken by surprise, cited this duty in its surly commentary (2002) on this self-appointed declaration on behalf of "the international museum community."
5. AFROMET—The Association for the Return of The Maqdala (or Magdala) Ethiopian Treasures—is an international organization dedicated to retrieving priceless treasures. For more information, see *www. afromet.org* (last accessed 11/10/2009).
6. In China and other contending centers of world capitalism, the original Western model is duplicated as Chinese museums and collectors embrace and reformulate Western values, while their country joins the global North (see Fiskesjö 2005, 2006, 2010).
7. See, for example, Atwood 2008; Cuno 2008a, 2008b; Kimmelman 2006.
8. There are no publications regarding the official position of the Opificio delle Pietre Dure (the Italian Ministry for Cultural Heritage) in Florence, as a signatory, regarding this both simplistic and radical theory.
9. Here, I am drawing on recent advances in the theory of value, notably by David Graeber (2001).
10. It is not just because they've become part of "national heritage" that the Parthenon marbles in the British Museum are retained, but also because they sustain British self-identification as a torchbearer of ancient civilization. The fight over them arises because both Greek and British identity formation builds on that past (Friedman 1992); their symbolic value can be gleaned from the absence of the museum among the original signatories. The Declaration was initiated in support of the British Museum against internecine Greek demands (O'Neill 2004).
11. See Sherman's excellent discussion (1994).

References

Abungu, G. 2004. The Declaration: A contested issue. *ICOM News* 57 (1): 5.

AFROMET. 2002. AFROMET replies to European, American museum directors. *Addis Tribune* (Addis Ababa), December 13, 2002. http://allafrica.com/stories/200212130027.html (last accessed 11/10/2009).

Appiah, K. A. 2006. *Cosmopolitanism: Ethics in a World of Strangers*. New York: W.W. Norton.

Atwood, R. 2008. Guardians of antiquity? *Archaeology* 18: 66–70.

Baumann, G., and Gingrich, A. (eds.) 2004. *Grammars of Identity/Alterity: A Structural Approach*. New York: Berghahn Books.

Bourdieu, P. 1984. *Distinction: A Social Critique of the Judgment of Taste*. Cambridge, MA: Harvard University Press.

Brodie, N., and Renfrew, C. 2005. Looting and the world's archaeological heritage: The inadequate response. *Annual Review of Anthropology* 34: 343–61.

Carman, J. 2005. *Against Cultural Property: Archaeology, Heritage and Ownership*. London: Duckworth.

Cuno, J. 2008a. Who owns the past? *Yale Global*. http://yaleglobal.yale.edu/display.article?id=10678 (last accessed 11/10/2009).

———. 2008b. *Who Owns Antiquity? Museums and the Battle over Our Ancient Heritage*. Princeton: Princeton University Press.

Curtis, N. G. W. 2006. Universal museums, museum objects and repatriation: The tangled stories of things. *Museum Management and Curatorship* 11 (1): 79–82.

Declaration on the Importance and Value of Universal Museums. (2004). [Signed by the directors of The Art Institute of Chicago and 17 other museum directors, December 11, 2002]. *ICOM News* 57 (1): 4, http://icom.museum/universal.html (last accessed on 11/10/2009).

Fiskesjö, M. 2005. En främmande fågel i en förgylld bur: Reflektioner kring svenska Asiensamlingar [A foreign bird in a gilded cage: Reflections on Sweden's Asia collections]. *Res Publica* (Stehag, Sweden) 65: 68–80. [In Swedish].

———. 2006. Chinese collections outside China: Problems and hopes. *Public Archaeology* 5 (2): 111–126.

———. 2007. The trouble with world culture: Recent museum developments in Sweden. *Anthropology Today* 23 (5): 6–11.

———. 2010. Politics of cultural heritage, in C. K. Lee and You-tien Hsing (eds.), *Reclaiming Chinese Society*, pp. 225–245. London: Routledge.

Friedman, J. 1992. Past in the future: History and the politics of identity. *American Anthropologist* 94 (4): 837–859.

———. 2001. Museums, the state and global transformation: From Temple of the Muses to Temple of Amusements. *Folk* (Copenhagen) 43: 251–267.

Graeber, D. 2001. *Toward an Anthropological Theory of Value: The False Coin of Our Own Dreams*. New York: Palgrave.

International Council of Museums (ICOM). 2002. Repatriation of cultural property. Press release, 13 December 2002. http://icom.museum (last accessed 11/10/2009).

———. 2004. *ICOM News* 57 (1): 4.

Kimmelman, M. 2006. Is it all loot? Tackling the antiquities problem. *New York Times*, March 29, 2006.

Latour, B. 1993. *We Have Never Been Modern*. Cambridge, MA: Harvard University Press.

Mathur, S. 2005. Museums and globalization. *Anthropological Quarterly* 78.3: 697–708.

Merryman, J. H. 2000. *Thinking about the Elgin Marbles: Critical Essays on Cultural Property, Art and Law*. The Hague and Boston: Kluwer Law International.

Merryman, J. H. (ed.). 2006. *Imperialism, Art and Restitution*. Cambridge: Cambridge University Press.

Muthoni T. 2007. Africa: It's time to return what was stolen. *East African Standard* (Nairobi), 27 June 2007. www.elginism.com/20070627/774/ (last accessed 11/10/2009).

O'Neill, M. 2004. Enlightenment museums: Universal or merely global? *Museum and Society* 2.3: 190–202.

Sherman, D. J. 1994. Quatrèmere/Benjamin/ Marx: Art museums, aura, and commodity fetishism, in D. J. Sherman and I. Rogoff (eds.), *Museum Culture: Histories, Discourses, Spectacles*, pp. 123–143. Minneapolis: University of Minnesota Press.

24

COMMENTARY:
THE EFFICACY OF "EMIC" AND "ETIC" IN ARCHAEOLOGY AND HERITAGE

Joost Fontein

If the poststructuralist turn began in the late 1970s with a profound questioning of the status of anthropological, historical, and archaeological knowledge and representations about the past (or indeed any representations at all), then the birth of postcolonial studies that accompanied it provoked particularly acute insights into the intense political implications of the colonial legacies of these disciplines (Asad 1973; Said 1978). Everywhere representations of the past, place, and "the Other" were shown to be imbricated with the imprint of the politics and power of the context of their production and indeed consumption. While the birth of anthropology was recognized as having been inevitably enabled by the European imperial project (Asad 1973; Fabian 1983), archaeology's emergence as a discipline was suffused in the 19th-century project of imagining the world as divided into discrete "nations" (Díaz-Andreu 1995; Kohl and Fawcett 1995). And like anthropology, archaeology and its representations too were "offshoots of the colonial enterprise" (Holl 1995: 185; Trigger 1984). When the outing of these disciplines' colonial legacies prompted some scholars to take up the baton of anti-colonial nationalisms, and when these efforts too came under scrutiny in a broader search for alternative or subaltern histories to fill the multiple silences of marginalized or denigrated pasts, then examinations (Ortner 1995) of these efforts have in turn reinforced the perspective that any kind of representation of the past is inevitably political. The politics of the past is omnipresent, and the past is everywhere a "scarce resource" (Appadurai 1980), and a "battleground of rival attachments" (Lowenthal 1990: 302).

In African archaeology, the complexity of the discipline's political imbrications—as a colonial science and for the purposes of administering settler states, under apartheid, as well as in resistances to colonialism and for the purposes of anti-colonial nationalisms—has come under increasing scrutiny (Robertshaw 1990; Schmidt 2006; Shepherd 2002). Debates have become more sophisticated in their critiques of archaeology's Eurocentric legacies, recognizing, for example, that "efforts to counter negative images of Africa through the production of new histories questioned the *details* of the narrative but 'not its underlying presumptions'" (Stahl 2005: 11). Archaeologists seeking to demonstrate "that Africa's past was continuous with the standard of world prehistory" often failed to recognize that "the unquestioned standard that continues to lurk behind the distinctive qualities of Africa's past are the supposedly 'universal' qualities of Europe's past" (Stahl 2005: 12). Hence, there continue to be calls for African archaeology to become "Indigenized" and to respond to both "local" pasts, and to "local" interpretations of those pasts (Andah 1995; Schmidt 1995, 2006; Shepherd 2003). If archaeology's initial, and often problematic, flirtations with cognitive archaeology and ethnoarchaeology derived from its central problem (Beach et al. 1997; Beach et al. 1998; Huffman 1996)—namely, that things of the past do not themselves easily reveal past meanings and values (Ndoro 1996: 774)—then recent reformulations of ethnoarchaeology "as the study of non-western, Indigenous archaeological practices" (Lane 1996: 731; 2006) demonstrate a growing recognition that the postcolonial challenge for archaeology in Africa is not only to provide alternative histories to fill the silences and upturn the biases of denigrated colonial-era pasts, but also to explore alternative ways of seeing and understanding the past itself (Andah 1995; Schmidt 1995, 2006; see also Benavides, this volume, chapter 17).[1]

Such calls for the emergence of new kinds of "Indigenous archaeology" are centered on an implicit, if not explicit, challenge to the emic-etic[2] distinction that Bassey Andah has described as "the cornerstone of scientific anthropology, including archaeology" (Andah 1995: 166). If postmodern deconstructions of claims to "objectivity" in the production of archaeological knowledge mirrored critiques of the distinction between history and memory in other disciplines (Klein 2000; McGregor 2005; Nora 1989), then it has also been recognized that the politics of the past does not simply revolve around competing representations of it, but also concerns the ways in which authority to represent the past is established and contested. In the example that I am most familiar with, the intensely politicized controversy over origins that dominated debates about Great Zimbabwe for much of 20th century (Garlake 1983; Kuklick 1991), archaeology's claims to a professional, objective, or "etic" perspective were used to debase not only the absurd fantasies of colonial antiquarians (e.g., Bent 1896; Hall 1905), but also the deeply felt "history-scapes" of local clans which were silenced and ignored (Fontein 2006: 3–17). Another result of this "disembedding" (Giddens 1990; Walsh 1992) and distancing effect of the professionalization of archaeological discourses was that the determined effort to depoliticize Great Zimbabwe's past also threatened to make archaeology irrelevant for most of society (Fontein 2006: 202; Garlake 1983: 4; Ucko 1994: 274–275). Calls for "Indigenous archaeologies" are therefore responses both to theoretical challenges to archaeology's ontological, "etic" authority, as well as a growing recognition of the "violence" perpetrated by archaeology's claims to it.[3]

However, the politics of the past is not simply about competing representations of, or contested authority over, the past; it is also finely intertwined with practices having to do with the materiality of the past. Although postcolonial studies have been dominated by literary studies (van Dommelen 2006: 108, 110), there has been a great deal of literature on museums, heritage, and landscape that focuses on the idea that the politics of the past is also about material culture in its widest terms (Bender 1993, 1998; Layton and Ucko 1999; Rowlands and de Jong 2008). This literature has clearly revealed that what practices of archaeology and its "entwined" (Ucko 1994: 271), if sometimes estranged (Lowenthal 1990), sibling, heritage, do with objects, monuments, and landscapes (not to mention bodies) can often be deeply problematic. Demands for the repatriation of ancestral objects and bodies that have been looted or "scientifically" collected from Indigenous peoples in North America, Australia, and elsewhere are perhaps the noisiest examples (e.g., Fforde et al. 2002; Curtis 2003) of this, but there are plenty of others (e.g., Chalcraft 2005; Pwiti and Mvenge 1996; Ranger 1999). At Great Zimbabwe, the silencing of local pasts was not the only troublesome feature of archaeological engagement within the site; also problematic were the excavations, the removal and museumification of objects, and the ways in which the site was turned into national and international heritage, which for locals desecrated the site and angered the spirits associated with it, silencing the *Voice* that once spoke there (Fontein 2006: 87–116). If such examples illustrate the postcolonial nature of the politics of archaeological and heritage practices, then Barbara Bender's work on Stonehenge (1998) reminds us that everywhere such practices can be subject to contestation and dispute (see also Herzfeld 1991). As she notes, everywhere "the contemporary obsession with preserving and commodifying the past 'freezes' the landscape as a palimpsest of past activity ... [allowing] the landscape or monuments in it to be packaged, presented and turned into museum exhibits" (Bender 1998: 26).

These distancing (and sometimes commodifying) effects of both archaeology and heritage practices have been well recognized, and efforts to acknowledge other ways of dealing with the materiality of the past have begun to emerge, in much the same way as calls have proliferated for alternative histories and archaeologies (Lane 1996, 2005, 2006). More often than not the two coincide, reflecting how archaeology and heritage practices are in no way unique in the materiality of their engagement with the past, even if other forms of such engagement may involve destructive, iconoclastic practices (Brown 1980; Küchler 1987; Rowlands 1993) as often as they do the preservation of objects (Lane 2005: 28). If in archaeology the "trend ... has been to encourage acknowledgement of such differing interpretations and to accord respect for local narratives" (Lane 2005: 29),[4] then heritage discourses, particularly at the international level of UNESCO's world heritage "system," have focused increasing attention on both widening definitions of "heritage" to encompass "other pasts" and "other" practices and materialities of it, particularly with innovative notions of living, spiritual, and intangible heritage, and by making "local participation" an essential component of heritage management.

However, notwithstanding the fact that such emphases on local participation are often more real in rhetoric than in practice (Pwiti 2004), and that concerns continue about "the extent to which UNESCO's conservation programme still reflects a Eurocentric heritage conception" (Rowlands and de Jong 2008: 11), questions also remain about the extent to which such efforts to acknowledge "other pasts" and "other ways" of engaging with the materiality of the past actually undermine the implied emic/etic distinction in either archaeology or heritage discourses (Schmidt 2006). UNESCO's inevitable insistence on the *universal* value of whatever is designated "world heritage" is perhaps the most audacious illustration of how such efforts to acknowledge "alternative pasts" can fail to collapse the emic/etic distinction; one is still inevitably subsumed under the other (Fontein 2006: 185–194). In archaeology, as Paul Lane has noted, "although well intentioned, such strategies have nevertheless encouraged an implicit evaluation of the different accounts whereby the 'local' is contrasted unfavourably with the 'universal' as being more partial and selective, even though there is widespread recognition that 'scientific' archaeology is far from being objective and free from interpretative bias" (Lane 2005: 30).

Lane, like others (Fontein 2006: 19–45; McGregor 2005), points to the urgency of recognizing that within "other pasts" there also exist inherent silences and contests over authority to represent the past. McGregor argues that the continued saliency of Nora's romantic distinction between premodern "memory" and modern "history" (Nora 1989) de-historicizes and depoliticizes "traditional" connections with the past (McGregor 2005). Similarly, in terms of heritage management, there has been increasing recognition that the notion of "local community" is not quite as wholesome or straightforward as heritage policy planners might have imagined.[5] Ironically, however, critiques that stress the need to historicize what has too often been enveloped conveniently as "local pasts" and "local heritage values" risk contributing to the very problem they aim to address: reification of archaeological and heritage professionals' common self-ascription as overseers or intermediaries in complex webs of conflicting perspectives and practices of heritage (e.g., Fontein 2006: 194–199). The danger posed by archaeologists and heritage managers, who prefer to see themselves as the "etic" interpreter standing outside of troublesome but necessarily complex emic perspectives, is that this prevents them from exploring the situatedness of their own positions. At Great Zimbabwe, the continued "veto" by the National Museums and Monument over the conduct of ancestral ceremonies at the site is a good illustration of this effect (Fontein 2006: 224).

More than just nuancing and historicizing other "emic" practices and materialities of the past, the challenge that remains is historicizing and contextualizing the so-called etic side of the equation: the practices of archaeology and heritage management themselves. This requires more than simply tracing the roots of these practices to the European Enlightenment, the emergence of "modernity," or the rise of nationalism. Such approaches all too easily posit a rupture between radically opposed representations, practices, and materialities of the past, whether "premodern" and "modern," or "Western" and "Other." Rather, what is required is careful empirical study into the specific, situated contexts within which encounters between so-called alternative pasts and heritage and archaeological practices actually take place. Just as Florence Bernault argues that "a premise of historical proximity," rather than one of "working misunderstandings," better explains the "refetishizing" and "resacralization of bodies as political resources" by both Europeans and Africans during the colonial encounter in Equatorial Africa, so postcolonial "heritage encounters" need, perhaps, to be understood less in terms of epistemic boundaries between "Western and African imaginaries" and practices of the past, and more in terms of the situated proximity of archaeologists, heritage managers, and many "others" "within" the complex webs of interests that are emergent in specific historical and political contexts. In this way, the politics of the past that surrounds archaeological and heritage practices might be revealed as having, to quote Bernault, "crystallized less from existing symbolic or material discrepancies than from conscious or unconscious strategies of organising ... difference" (Bernault 2006: 238). Perhaps the continuing efficacy (however latent or implied) of the emic/etic distinction in archaeology and heritage practices lies, then, in the ways it creates distance where it doesn't actually exist.

The comparison with Bernault's enlightening work on the "refetishization" of bodies by both Europeans and Africans during the colonial encounter in Equatorial Africa is not entirely fortuitous here. It may be that what archaeological and heritage practices do with bodies and human remains offers the clearest glimpse into the "emic situatedness" that lies behind the continuing "etic" veneer of "distanced" professionalism and "universalism" lurking as latent claims in their own discourses. For example, Williams's work on medieval mortuary practices points to a deep historical continuity in archaeology's engagement with the materiality of the dead that defies common accounts of the discipline's "modern" roots (Williams and Williams 2007: 47; Williams 2006, 2008). Similarly, studies of archaeologists' involvement in excavations of war remains, whether in World War I battlefields (Filippucci forthcoming) or among the mass graves of Zimbabwe's liberation struggle, illustrate that, in practice, archaeological excavations are not necessarily cold "distancing" techniques, but can become emotive engagements—indeed, much "like a funeral," as one archaeologist involved in the Southern African Development Community's (SADC) Liberation heritage project described (Fontein 2009). At the same time, the sensitivity about the status of human remains in British museum collections clearly situates museum practices of reburial and return in the political and historical context of the present (Jenkins 2008; Swain 2002), even as the arguments of those virulently opposed to reburial—"that the practice not only infringes academic freedom and prohibits future research through the application of new techniques, but also curtails understandings of universal aspects of human behaviour, genetic heritage and physiology in favour of local partisan interests" (Lane 2005: 30)—illustrate exactly the continuing efficacy of the emic/etic distinction that I have been trying to describe.

Conclusion

In postcolonial studies, a lot of excitement and interest has been provoked by the ambiguous processes of mimicry that Homi Bhabha (1994) and others (Taussig 1993) have identified in the cultural politics of colonialism. The notion of the "slippage" of the mimic, in particular, allowed scholars to identify spaces of genuine subalternity, resistance, and "authenticity" in what otherwise appeared as uncomfortably "derivative" discourses and practices of the subaltern. We can apply a similar logic to archaeology and the heritage practices that have been my focus here. Thus, if it is "undeniable that, as a consequence of colonialism and the impact of European derived models of nationalism, the state in Africa has a tendency to monumentalise itself," then exploring "what kind of memorialising tactics and strategies attach themselves to technologies of memory, such as heritage sites, museums, rituals, performances and projects" offers a useful way to bridge the persistent but problematic gulf between "local" "alternative memory" practices and the "globalising and/or state building acts" of heritage and commemoration (Rowlands and de Jong 2008: 1).

Yet as Ferguson has warned, studies of mimicry too easily become a means by which "anthropological otherness is salvaged" (2002: 554) and premises of cultural distance and heterogeneity restored. This is similar to how, as I have suggested, the search for and accommodation of "Indigenous pasts" in archaeological and heritage discourses risk recreating an "emic" "Other." Ferguson's well-judged critique can serve as an important reminder that heritage projects in postcolonial Africa are as much about continuing claims to "full membership rights in world society" as they are about appropriating Western discourses of heritage "within the terms of an 'Indigenous' logic" (Ferguson 2002: 554, 559). Hence, it is no surprise that even in the context of the renewed anti-colonialist vigor of Zimbabwe's recent "patriotic history" (Ranger 2004) the aims of UNESCO and ICOMOS can be "synonymous with Zimbabwe's philosophy," committed as it is to "preserving its heritage . . . through the agrarian reform programme" (Ranger 2004: 228). Nor should we be surprised that Rangi people around Mungumi wa Kolo in

Tanzania are not necessarily adverse to that site's nomination to the World Heritage list, even if it will undoubtedly "necessitate a reorientation of the 'loci' of cultural reproduction, as a landscape of different values and practices reframes the history that locals at present negotiate for themselves" (Chalcraft 2005: 48–50). Similarly, at Great Zimbabwe, the country's independence in 1980, its adoption of the name "Zimbabwe," and that site's elevation to World Heritage status in 1986, clearly rekindled or reanimated existing local contests over the site (Fontein 2006: 22, 213).

The best illustration is provided by Michael Rowlands's discussion of Fon palace museums in the Cameroon Grasslands (2007) as examples of how differing temporalities and "processes of cultural transmission" coexist and are "cross cut by the heritage/memory distinction," as both heritage as technology and "memory evoked . . . as ancestral time . . . may enter the experiences of the past of the same person or group" (Rowlands 2007: 1–2). He concludes that there is no contradiction in the often cited multiple roles of Fons as "ritual leaders," politicians, businessmen, and modernizers, even if it may appear so from the outside (Rowlands 2007: 19). This conclusion echoes the broader challenge that Rowlands and de Jong's edited collection throws down to analyses that posit a distinction between "memory" and "heritage" in terms of "personal and collective acts defined in resistance to the public sphere" (2008: 2). They conclude that "material monuments and intangible heritage do trigger memory-work and do not thereby offer to bear the burden of memory, but open up spaces for reflexive engagements" (2008: 13–14). "In that respect," they suggest, "heritage and monuments in Africa can be as productive as they are in Europe" (Rowlands and de Jong 2008: 14).

Notes

1. There is also a growing body of literature that explores how alternative ways of remembering and relating to the past can take the form of oral history and embodied performances (see, e.g., Barber 1991; Connerton 1989; Lambek 2002; Shaw 2002; Stoller 1995; Tonkin 1992).

2. The emic/etic distinction has a particular history in anthropology. It derived from distinctions between phonetic and phonemic levels of analysis in linguistic anthropology and was first put to use in Pike's work (1967), which was later seen as a founding text for the emergence of cognitive anthropology in the 1960s (cf. Tyler 1969). Here I am using these terms in the looser sense that they are most commonly employed today, which posit the "etic" as reflecting a "universal model" and the "emic" as culture-specific. For more on "emic" and "etic," see Barnard's useful discussion (1996).

3. As Layton and Ucko (1999: 5) have put it, quoting Derrida: "[T]he violence of anthropology occurs at 'the moment when the [cultural] space is shaped and re-orientated by the gaze of the foreigner' (Derrida 1976: 113). The colonial act of 'discovering' and renaming places is an example of such oppression. So too

is the rereading as wild or barren a landscape that, to its Indigenous inhabitants, is filled with tradition."
4. There is also a growing body of anthropological literature that has explored the possibilities of a "vision of reciprocity in academic research" (Clifford 2004: 21) offered by co-curated or collaborative heritage projects. For good examples relating to Alaska, see Clifford (2004) and Fienup-Riordan (1996, 2000).
5. See Sinamai (2003: 3). Also, Pikirayi (see Fontein 2006: 224 fn. 16) made comments to this effect in the final plenary session of an international conference entitled "Heritage in Southern & Eastern Africa: Imagining and Marketing Public Culture and History" held in Livingston, Zambia, in July 2004.

References

Andah, B. W. 1995. Studying African societies in cultural context, in P. R. Schmidt and T. C. Patterson (eds.), *Making Alternative Histories: The Practice of Archaeology and History in Non-Western Settings*, pp. 149– 181. Santa Fe: SAR Press.

Appadurai, A. 1980. The past is a scarce resource. *Man* 16 (2): 201–219.

Asad, T. 1973. *Anthropology and the Colonial Encounter*. London: Ithaca Press.

Barber, K. 1991. *I Could Speak until Tomorrow: Oriki, Women and the Past in a Yoruba Town*. Edinburgh: Edinburgh University Press.

Barnard, A. 1996. Emic and etic, in A. Barnard and J. Spencer (eds.), *Encyclopedia of Social and Cultural Anthropology*, pp. 180– 183, London: Routledge.

Beach, D., Bourdillon, M., Denbow, J., Hall, M., Pikirayi, I., Pwiti, G., and Huffman, T. 1997. Review feature. *South African Archaeological Bulletin* 52: 125–143.

Beach, D., Bourdillon, M., Denbow, J., Liegang, G., Joubser, J., Pikirayi, I., Schoenbrun, D., Soper, R., and Stahl, A. 1998. Cognitive archaeology and imaginary history at Great Zimbabwe. *Current Anthropology*, 39 (1): 47–72.

Bender, B. 1993. *Landscape, Politics and Perspectives*. Oxford: Berg

——. 1998. *Stonehenge: Making Space*. Oxford: Berg.

Bent, T. J. 1896 [1893]. *The Ruined Cities of Mashonaland*. 2nd ed. London: Longman's Green.

Bernault, F. 2006. Body, power and sacrifice in equatorial Africa. *Journal of African History* 47: 207–239.

Bhabha, H. K. 1994. Of mimicry and man: The ambivalence of colonial discourse, in H. K. Bhabha, *The Location of Culture*, pp. 85–92. New York: Routledge.

Brown, J. L. 1980. Miji-Kenda grave and memorial sculptures. *African Arts* 13 (4): 36–39, 88.

Chalcraft, J. 2005. "Varimu Valale": Rock art as world heritage in a ritual landscape of central Tanzania, in W. James and D. Mills (eds.), *The Qualities of Time, Anthropological Approaches*, pp. 35–53. Oxford; Berg.

Clifford, J. 2004. Looking several ways. Anthropology and Native heritage in Alaska. *Current Anthropology* 45 (1): 5–30.

Connerton, P. 1989. *How Societies Remember.* Cambridge: Cambridge University Press.

Curtis, N. G. W. 2003. Human remains: The sacred, museums and archaeology. *Public Archaeology* 3: 21–32.

Derrida, J. 1976. *Of Grammatology.* Baltimore: Johns Hopkins University Press.

Díaz-Andreu, A. 1995. Archaeology and nationalism in Spain, in P. L. Kohl and C. Fawcett (eds.), *Nationalism, Politics and the Practice of Archaeology,* pp. 39–56. Cambridge: Cambridge University Press.

Ferguson, J. 2002. Of mimicry and membership: Africans and the "new world society." *Cultural Anthropology* 17 (4): 551–569.

Fforde, C., Hubert, J., and Turnbull, P. 2002. *The Dead and Their Possessions: Repatriation in Principle, Policy and Practice.* London: Routledge.

Fontein, J. 2006. *The Silence of Great Zimbabwe: Contested Landscapes and the Power of Heritage.* London and Harare: UCL Press and Weaver Press.

———. 2009. The politics of the dead: Living heritage, bones and commemoration in Zimbabwe. *ASAOnline* 1/2: 1–2.

Fienup-Riordan, A. 1996. *The Living Tradition of Yup'ik Masks: Agayuliyaraput (Our Way of Making Prayer).* Seattle: University of Washington Press.

———. 2000. *Hunting Tradition in a Changing World: Yup'ik Lives in Alaska Today.* New Brunswick: Rutgers University Press.

Filippucci, P. Forthcoming. Archaeology and memory on the western front, in D. Boric (ed.), *Archaeology and Memory.* Oxford: Oxbow Books.

Garlake, P. 1983. Prehistory and ideology in Zimbabwe, in J. D. Y. Peel and T. Ranger (eds.), *Past and Present in Zimbabwe,* pp. 1–19. Manchester: Manchester University Press.

Giddens, A. 1990. *The Consequences of Modernity.* Cambridge: Polity.

Hall, R. N. 1905. *Great Zimbabwe, Mashonaland, Rhodesia. An Account of Two Years Examination Work 1902–4 on Behalf of the Government of Rhodesia.* London: Methuen.

Herzfeld, M. 1991. *A Place in History: Social and Monumental Time in a Cretan Town.* Princeton: Princeton University Press.

Holl, A. F. C. 1995. African history: Past, present, future. The unending quest for alternatives, in P. R. Schmidt and T. C. Patterson (eds.), *Making Alternative Histories: The Practice of Archaeology and History in Non-Western Settings,* pp. 183–211. Santa Fe: SAR Press.

Huffman, T. N. 1996. *Snakes and Crocodiles: Power and Symbolism in Ancient Zimbabwe.* Johannesburg: Wits University Press.

Jenkins, T. 2008. How museum professionals relate to human remains. Paper delivered at Social Anthropology Departmental Seminar, University of Edinburgh, January 25, 2008.

Kohl, P. L., and Fawcett, C. 1995. Archaeology in the service of the state, in P. L. Kohl and C. Fawcett (eds.), *Nationalism, Politics and the Practise of Archaeology,* pp. 3–18. Cambridge: Cambridge University Press.

Klein, K. L. 2000. On the emergence of memory in historical discourse. *Representations* 69: 127–150.

Kuklick, H. 1991. Contested monuments, in G. W. Stocker (ed.), *Colonial Situations,* pp. 135–169. London and Madison: University of Wisconsin Press.

Küchler, S. 1987. Malangan: Art and memory in a Melanesian society. *Man* 22: 238–255.

Lambek, M. 2002. *The Weight of the Past*. New York: Palgrave Macmillan.

Lane, P. J. 1996. Rethinking ethnoarchaeology, in G. Pwiti and R. Soper (eds), *Aspects of African Archaeology: Papers from the 10th Congress of the Pan African Association for Prehistory and Related Studies*, pp. 727–732. Harare: University of Zimbabwe Publications.

———. 2005. The material culture of memory, in W. James and D. Mills (eds.), *The Qualities of Time, Anthropological Approaches*, pp. 19–34. Oxford: Berg.

———. 2006. Household assemblages, lifecycles and the remembrance of things past among the Dogon of Mali. *South African Archaeological Bulletin* 61: 40–56.

Layton, R., and Ucko, P. 1999. Introduction: Gazing upon landscape and encountering the environment, in R. Layton and P. Ucko (eds.), *The Archaeology and Anthropology of Landscape*, pp. 1–20. London: Routledge.

Lowenthal, D. 1990. Conclusion: Archaeologists and others, in P. Gathercole and D. Lowenthal (eds.), *The Politics of the Past*, pp. 302–314. London: Unwin Hyman.

McGregor, J. 2005. The social life of ruins: Sites of memory and the politics of a Zimbabwean periphery. *Journal of Historical Geography* 31: 316–337.

Ndoro, W. 1996. Towards the meaning and symbolism of archaeological pottery assemblages, in G. Pwiti and R. Soper (eds), *Aspects of African Archaeology: Papers from the 10th Congress of the Pan African Association For Prehistory and Related Studies*, pp. 773–780. Harare: University of Zimbabwe Publications.

Nora, P. 1989. Between memory and history: Les lieux de mémoire. *Representations* 26: 7–24.

Ortner, S. 1995. Resistance and the problem of ethnographic refusal. *Comparative Studies in Society and History* 37 (1): 173–193.

Pike, K. L. 1967 [1954]. *Language in Relation to a Unified Theory of the Structure of Human Behaviour*. 2nd ed. Hague and Paris: Mouton.

Pwiti, G. 2004. The management of the cultural heritage of the people, by the people, for the people: How close have we come? Paper presented at Heritage in Southern & Eastern Africa: Imagining and Marketing Public Culture and History Conference, Livingston, Zambia, July 2004.

Pwiti, G., and Mvenge, G. 1996. Archaeologists, tourists and rainmakers: Problems in the management of rock art sites in Zimbabwe, a case study of Domboshava National Monument, in G. Pwiti and R. Soper (eds.), *Aspects of African Archaeology: Papers from the 10th Congress of the Pan African Association for Prehistory and Related Studies*, pp. 815–823. Harare: University of Zimbabwe Publications.

Ranger, T. 1999. *Voices from the Rocks; Nature, Culture and History in the Matopos Hills of Zimbabwe*. Oxford: James Currey.

———. 2004. Nationalist historiography, patriotic history and the history of the nation: The struggle over the past in Zimbabwe. *Journal of Southern African Studies* 30 (2): 215–234.

Robertshaw, P. 1990. *A History of African Archaeology*. Oxford: James Currey.

Rowlands, M. 1993. The role of memory in the transmission of culture. *World Archaeology* 25: 141–151.

———. 2007. Africa on display: Curating postcolonial pasts in the Cameroon Grassfields. Paper presented at Image as Embodiment Symposium, SRU Norwich University, November 2007.

Rowlands, M., and de Jong, F. 2008. Reconsidering heritage and memory in Africa, in M. Rowlands and F. de Jong (eds.), *Reclaiming Heritage, Alternative Imaginaries of Memory in West Africa*, pp. 1–19. Walnut Creek, CA: Left Coast Press.

Said, E. W. 1978. *Orientalism*. London: Routledge and Kegan Paul.

Schmidt, P. R. 1995. Using archaeology to remake history in Africa, in P. R. Schmidt and T. C. Patterson (eds.), *Making Alternative Histories: The Practice of Archaeology and History in Non-Western Settings*, pp. 119–147. Santa Fe: SAR Press.

———. 2006. *Historical Archaeology in Africa: Representation, Social Memory, and Oral Traditions*. Lanham, MD: AltaMira Press.

Shaw, R. 2002. *Memories of the Slave Trade: Ritual and Historical Imagination in Sierra Leone*. Chicago: University of Chicago Press.

Shepherd, N. 2002. The politics of archaeology in Africa. *Annual Review of Anthropology* 31: 189–209.

———. 2003. State of the discipline: Science, culture and identity in South African archaeology, 1870–2003. *Journal of Southern African Studies* 29 (4): 823–844.

Sinamai, I. 2003. Cultural shifting-sands: Changing meanings of Zimbabwean sites in Zimbabwe, South Africa and Botswana. Paper presented to ICOMOS Conference, Victoria Falls, available at *http://www.international.icomos.org/ victoriafalls2003/papers/c3-7%20%-%7sinamaipdf*.

Stahl, A. B. (ed.) 2005. *African Archaeology: A Critical Introduction*. Blackwell Studies in Global Archaeology Series. Oxford: Blackwell.

Stoller, P. 1995. *Embodying Colonial Memories: Spirit Posession, Power and the Hauka in West Africa*. London: Routledge.

Swain, H. 2002. The ethics of displaying human remains from British archaeological sites. *Public Archaeology* 2: 95–100.

Taussig, M. 1993. *Mimesis and Alterity: A Particular History of the Senses*. New York: Routledge.

Tonkin, E. 1992. *Narrating Our Pasts: The Social Construction of Oral History*. Cambridge: Cambridge University Press.

Trigger, B. 1984. Alternative archaeologies: Nationalist, colonialist, imperialist. *Man* 19: 335–370.

Tyler, S. A. (ed.) 1969. *Cognitive Anthropology*. New York: Holt, Rinehart and Winston.

Ucko, P. 1994. Museums and sites: Cultures of the past within education—Zimbabwe, some ten years on, in P. G. Stone and B. L. Molyneaux (eds.), *The Presented Past*, pp. 237–282. London: Routledge.

Van Dommelen, P. 2006. Colonial matters: Material culture and postcolonial theory in colonial situations, in C. Tilley, W.

Keane, S. Kuchler, M. Rowlands, and P. Spyer (eds.), *Handbook of Material Culture*, pp. 104–124. London: Sage.

Walsh, K. 1992. *The Representation of the Past: Museums and Heritage in the Post-Modern World.* London: Routledge.

Williams, H. 2006. *Death and Memory in Early Medieval Britain.* Cambridge: Cambridge University Press.

——. 2008. Anglo-Saxonism and Victorian archaeology: William Wylie's *Fairford Graves. Early Medieval Europe* 16 (1): 49–88.

Williams, H., and Williams, E. J. L. 2007. Digging for the dead: Archaeological practice as mortuary commemoration. *Public Archaeology* 6 (1): 47–63.

PART IV
COLONIAL AND POSTCOLONIAL IDENTITIES

The articulation of identities emerges as one of the central issues advanced by new forms of collaboration and interpretation and is key to postcolonial scholarship and cultural politics more generally within contemporary societies. Identity politics are dialogical, intersecting in complex ways with diverse postcolonial locales, as this fourth section of the volume explores.

Discourses of gender, race, and class have been central to analyses of colonialism and are touched on in many of the preceding chapters, but here they are the focus of analysis. As Meskell's chapter (chapter 34) emphasizes, researchers must grapple with the ongoing question of how identities grounded in material goods and practices are reified. In South Africa, for example, the political effects of this process, in producing static constructions of ethnicity and culture promoted by government-sponsored tourism and heritage programs, risk reanimating the essentialist and oppressive racist categories of apartheid.

Yet elsewhere, Indigenous peoples assert such identities as a means of righting colonial wrongs and gaining access to resources and heritage. Intellectual trends that emphasize the mutability and contingency of identity have been perceived as undermining Indigenous claims. Within settler societies such as Canada, Australia, New Zealand, and the United States, Indigenous peoples are often required to demonstrate the continuity of their connections to place and culture—for example, under Native Title legislation—and any transformation of practice or view is often interpreted as inauthentic. Many have noted that Gayatri Spivak's notion of "strategic essentialism"—that is, choosing what is useful in essentialist discourse and then finding its limits in practice—has proved empowering to Indigenous peoples, especially at a collective level (e.g., Spivak 1999: 10–12; for an archaeological example, see Liebmann 2008). Academic concerns about this disjunction tend to oppose these conceptions of identity in an absolute sense, but several critics have pointed out that the meaning and effects of particular representations of identity depend on their immediate sociopolitical context and should be assessed accordingly.

In her contribution, Louise Ströbeck (chapter 25) considers feminist interventions, providing a global framework and a postprocessual, multivocal approach to explore practical applications in fieldwork, geopolitical mapping of research sites, formation of theory and theorists, and the process of making plausible and convincing interpretations from data to visualize and narrate the past.

Sarah Croucher (chapter 26) provides a lucid review of the fundamental role played by notions of cultural identity within the discipline of archaeology. The culture-historical paradigm, linked to a conception of cultural exchange as acculturation, was implicated in colonialism in various locales around the globe, until it began to be subjected to postprocessual critique from the 1980s onward. More recent ideas of cultural exchange entailed by colonial contact have included creolization, an emphasis on power relations (including domination and resistance), and an interest in practice theory (Bourdieu 1977) and the role of material culture in signifying shared identity.

Gavin Lucas (chapter 27) explores the applicability of class as an analytic category in the study of colonialism. Through a range of historical archaeological studies, he explores the intersection between class and other social categories such as race, and the ways that inequality within one sphere (such as slavery) masked inequality within another (such as class). Consumption choices allowed racially subordinate peoples to assert equality and respectability, while exposing the contradictions within colonial ideology. Despite the centrality of class to Marxism, which provided postcolonial scholars with a range of theoretical tools, recent work has shifted from considering capitalism as a mode of production, and class identity as ideology, to a broader focus on the mutually constitutive role of social categories such as class, race, and gender.

Building on this type of analysis, Paul Mullins (chapter 28) explicitly considers the relationship between race and class, understood as social constructions, as interacting systems of inequality. Race is closely linked to class as a material basis for the mode of exploitation that enables capitalism, as "reinforcing systems of oppression," yet race has been a neglected framework in archaeological research, despite its integral role within modernity and expression through material consumption and the ways it structures everyday life (e.g., Epperson 2004). Mullins reviews projects that have begun to trace the role of power inequalities structured by race and class and have effects in the present.

Finally, in the commentaries for this section, Whitney Battle-Baptiste (chapter 29) and John Norder (chapter 30) provide stirring accounts of the crucial role that identity plays in understanding the past. Battle-Baptiste gives us a personal view into ways that race and gender intersect with archaeology. From the perspective of an African-American woman, she is able to contextualize just how different a conversation might be when archaeologists (and others) recognize the voice that racialized minorities speak with. That form of recognition has significant ramifications for archaeological practice as a whole, and for any movement toward social justice and social change.

John Norder's commentary moves from the soul to the body. In an interesting shift within identity studies, Norder indexes the body, not only as a scientific object of study, but as a move to preserve the "self" in opposition to the colonial "other." By introducing the idea of the "body ancient," Norder creates an implicit link between contemporary understandings of the sensual body and the ancient body, with significant ramifications for the consideration of the body as scientific object, as it reinvigorates "bones" into "identity." Norder argues that DNA research creates a form of scientifically defined identity that paradoxically violates its own sanctity and iconic status for Native groups, which might then erase identity altogether.

References

Bourdieu, P. 1977. *Outline of a Theory of Practice*. Cambridge: Cambridge University Press.

Epperson, T. 2004 Critical race theory and the archaeology of the African diaspora. *Historical Archaeology* 38: 101–08.

Liebmann, M. 2008. Postcolonial cultural affiliation: Essentialism, hybridity, and NAGPRA, in M. Liebmann and U. Z. Rizvi (eds.), *Archaeology and the Postcolonial Critique*, pp. 73–90. Lanham, MD: AltaMira Press.

Spivak, G. C. 1999. *A Critique of Postcolonial Reason: Toward A History of the Vanishing Present*. Cambridge, MA: Harvard University Press.

25

GENDER AND SEXUALITY

Louise Ströbeck

The relationship between Indigenous peoples and European and Euro-American feminists—and later feminist and gender archaeological research—has a history of its own during the colonial era and the period of postcolonial critique and reconsideration. This chapter elicits how Indigenous gender systems have been used to expand and elaborate feminist theory since the mid-19th century. Indigenous cultures and their social organizations were adopted as models by advocates of the early and the modern movements for women's rights, and in research throughout feminist and gender archaeological scholarship. These initiatives shed light on various specific aspects of gender and sexuality in Indigenous societies, in order to generate knowledge about alternatives to Western patriarchy and the male/female dichotomy therein.

Despite early interest in the dissimilarities between the social organizations of Indigenous and Euro-American societies, and despite the suffragists' and later the scholars' contact with Indigenous cultures, the feminist and gender archaeological interpretations of Indigenous peoples' gender and sexuality formations have undergone continuous critical scrutiny for biases of sex, gender, and sexuality. After critique, revisions and elaborations of feminist and gender perspectives have followed, demonstrating that feminist and gender archaeological perspectives are informed by changes in the formation and representations of sex, gender, and sexuality in societies from the 19th to the 21st centuries. Moreover, this indicates the changing images that European and Euro-American feminist and gender interpreters, as well as Indigenous peoples, have had of themselves and others, and of their relationships, during the colonial era and the period of postcolonial critique and reconsideration.

The chapter is structured as a history of feminist and gender perspectives in archaeology. It distinguishes the theoretical breakthroughs and much of the landmark writing on specific topics in the history of feminist and gender archaeological research, and it specifically considers the role that Indigenous peoples, and additionally anthropological case studies of non-Western peoples, have played in Western feminist initiatives and interpretations. The outline takes as its point of departure the establishment and argumentation of the suffrage movement among Euro-American middle-class women, and it ends with scholars' recent comments about the issues they would like to see raised and elaborated in future feminist and gender archaeological research. Additionally, the chapter focuses on references in English, most often studies that are performed and published in the United States and to some extent in Canada and northwestern Europe. Additional information on feminist and gender archaeological research in other countries and different languages can be found in databases on the Internet.[1]

On Waves, Interpretations, and Identities

There have been recurrent encounters, in person and in writings and readings, between feminists and Indigenous peoples in North America. Here the relationship between them is illustrated through three waves of feminism. The feminist influences in the society at large and in academia are commonly categorized, by archaeologists and other scholars, according to a chronology of waves of feminism, although the idea of three consecutive waves has its limits. There is, for example, disagreement with the perception of the women's suffrage movement as feminism (Meskell 1999: 54; cf. Ströbeck forthcoming). Moreover, the perception of feminist and gender perspectives as constituting a linear development of theory through three gradually advancing stages is problematic, as there is much branching and much dissimilarity within the stages and because waves of feminist theory coexist.

The women's suffrage movement of the 19th and early 20th centuries was formed in a context of European colonialism and patriarchy. The Euro-American women who founded the movement for women's rights in the United States had contact with Indigenous North American peoples, and they were influenced by the extensive rights of women in the cultures of the Iroquois, or Haudenosaunee, and the Huron (Allen 1988; Landsman 1992: 259; Roesch Wagner 2001). In the suffragists' initial celebration of the Iroquois, they pictured matriarchy as natural and original, and an alternative to their own society's male dominance (Landsman 1992: 259, 261, 263). Later, the suffragists transformed their strategy for attaining the right to vote, and concurrently switched focus in their reference to Indigenous North American societies. When facing the changing conditions in the industrialized and urbanizing Euro-American society, as well as in the Indigenous societies under Western influence, the suffragists emphasized women's special caring and nurturing skills and moral superiority as qualities that the entire Euro-American society could benefit from (Landsman 1992: 252–255; Spencer-Wood 1991a: 238–239). The perception of the community as a household for women to engage in and reform has been archaeologically researched, by analyzing how women's reform institutions transformed culture in the United States (Spencer-Wood 1991b). In arguing for their cause, the suffragists then brought forward individual Indigenous women, whom the suffragists praised for the key role that these women had played in the expansion of Euro-American society and for the domestic skills associated with women (Landsman 1992: 269, 271, 273).

The patriarchal Euro-American society of the time made women's contributions invisible in the study of the past. However, women were carrying out archaeological excavations and analyses even though they did not have a formal academic education, and continued to do so once granted the right to university degrees, thus officially turning their work into fieldwork. It was during the 1990s that these women's work began to be officially recognized, primarily in Australia, Europe, and the United States (Claassen 1994; Díaz-Andreu and Sørensen 1998; du Cros and Smith 1993; Irwin-Williams 1990; Reyman 1992; White et al. 1999).

Moreover, a postcolonial feminist analysis of women from the United Kingdom, South Africa, and the United States who were Africanist archaeologists between the 1860s and the 1960s has revealed that African archaeology has excluded the contributions of female archaeologists to this field. Originating in a gendered colonial context, and thereafter continuously formed under Western domination, African archaeology has a history in which the accomplishments of female archaeologists were occasionally appropriated by male archaeologists or neglected altogether. This practice of exclusion meant that many studies of early goddess worship, Indigenous origins of "native civilizations" (Weedman 2001: 12, 18), discovery of early hominid finds, interest in the relationship between the early hominids and prehistoric landscapes, and complementary ethnographical studies, whether concerning Indigenous Egypt, Zimbabwe, East Africa, or southern Africa, were forgotten for a long time. More generally, to operate with a specific African—instead of a European—archaeological terminology, and to have Africans studying the remains of African prehistory and history were yet other initiatives by women that the contemporary male archaeologists hardly acknowledged (Weedman 2001: 3–29).

The modern—or second-wave—feminist movement asserted the legacy of the women's suffrage movement in the United States and updated its interest in gender relations among Indigenous peoples. This was illustrated, for example, by the predominantly Euro-American "Women's Encampment for a Future of Peace and Justice" of 1983. It drew on the history of women's action and its preoccupation with Indigenous, as well as historically enslaved, peoples when setting up the camp in Seneca County, in the northeastern United States.

The heritage of the modern feminist movement includes the First Women's Rights Convention held at Seneca Falls in 1848, the prohibition of women delegates speaking at the 1840 international abolitionist conference (which instigated the Seneca Falls meeting), and early knowledge of Iroquois women's greater powers and rights compared with Euro-American married women (Landsman 1992: 249–252, 259). The establishment of a feminist anthropology followed the establishment of the modern feminist movement in the United States, and in conjunction with this came the introduction of feminist perspectives in archaeology. Feminist primatologists, physical anthropologists, and cultural anthropologists stimulated the formulation of questions about gender in the past, as they discussed the origins and historical changes of gender (cf. Linton 1971; Rosaldo and Lamphere 1974: 3–7). The archaeologists adopted the anthropologists' questions, and addressed new ones as well, in discussions about archaeological material (cf. Conkey and Spector 1984; Wylie 1991: 48).

In the mid 1970s, cultural anthropologists established a critique of the assumption that gender roles were biologically determined. The concept of a sex/gender system was formulated, which served to highlight "the set of arrangements by which a society transforms biological sexuality into products of human activity," and by which "a female becomes an oppressed woman" (Rubin 1975: 159). Here, sex and gender were differentiated, and while sex was perceived to be based on biology, gender was argued to be a cultural formation. Although male domination and female subordination were recorded as a general structure of human societies, the asymmetry between male and female was believed to be socially and culturally organized and therefore possible to change in contemporary society (Ortner 1974: 71, 73, 87; Rosaldo 1974: 22–23, 42).

In her article, "Is Female to Male as Nature is to Culture?," Sherry Ortner (1974), focused on the association between woman and nature, and between man and culture, in theorizing about women's supposedly universal secondary status. A structural model was concurrently published that related aspects of psychology and cultural and social organization to a supposedly universal opposition between women's subordinate domestic sphere and men's dominant public sphere. It was intended to help categorize the general characteristics of male and female roles in human societies (Rosaldo 1974: 22–35), and it was later elaborated by ascribing to men public influence, prestige, forging of relationships, determining of enmities, and use of force, while ascribing to women the daily maintenance of children, spouse, and kin (Rosaldo 1980: 394). A review of cultural expressions of universal sexual asymmetry drew on studies published between the 1930s and the 1970s of the Iroquois in the United States, the New Guinea Arapesh and Tchambuli, the African Yoruba, the Merina in Madagascar, Australian "[A]boriginal groups" (Rosaldo 1974: 19), as well as Jewish communities in eastern Europe (Rosaldo 1974: 19–23). The influential feminist anthropological texts by Ortner (1974) and Rosaldo (1974) did not elaborate on the authors' selection of case studies in modeling universal sexual asymmetry. However, the issue of an inherent male-centered perspective in much ethnographic research began to be debated in feminist anthropological research in the early 1970s (Ardener 1972; Reiter 1975: 12–17; Rohrlich-Leavitt et al. 1975), and thereafter also continuously by archaeologists who used ethnographic data in modern feminist as well as in postmodern feminist archaeological studies (Conkey and Spector 1984: 3–13; Spector 1983: 80, 94; Hollimon 1997).

Feminist and gender archaeological research has thereafter successively revealed biases inherent in mainstream archaeology. At the inception of feminist critical analysis, traditional archaeological writing was shown to be androcentric, or male biased. The critique of the often unreflective male-centered perspective in archaeology was frequently presented together with new case studies, which made women in the past visible and active (Arnold et al. 1988; Balme and Beck 1995; Bertelsen et al. 1987; Claassen 1992a; Conkey and Spector 1984; du Cros and Smith 1993; Ehrenberg 1989; Gero and Conkey 1991; Gero et al. 1983; Miller 1988; Olsen Bruhns and Stothert 1999; Seifert 1991a; Walde and Willows 1991). Attention was additionally drawn to the ways in which androcentric theories and practices marginalized proposed feminist perspectives in archaeology (Engelstad 1991; Gero et al. 1983; Spencer-Wood 1992; Wylie 1991).

The first published archaeological approach to conceptualize and analyze gender in the past came from the United States. The roots of gender archaeology in the United States, in feminist anthropological works from the 1970s and in the modern feminist movement, are recognizable in research interests in sexual division of labor, universality in gender roles, and the relationship between reproduction and gender roles (Gilchrist 1999: 6). In 1971, the theory of Woman the Gatherer was initiated, in a critique of the previous Man the Hunter model. It was based on studies of primate behavior and was supported by ethnographic research among foraging societies (Gilchrist 1999: 20–21; Linton 1971). In 1983, a task differentiation framework for analyzing who did what among men and women in the past was constructed in archaeological research on the 19th-century Hidatsa on the Great Plains in the United States (Spector 1983). This framework implied gender power dynamics that were not theorized in archaeology until later (Sweely 1999). A seminal article that critically theorized aspects of gender in the past was published in 1984 (Conkey and Spector 1984). The article presented an analytical perspective with dimensions—social, temporal, spatial, and material—on male and female activity patterns within a culture. Also, it embraced the possibility for cross-cultural study of variability in male and female gendered task-differentiation (Conkey and Spector 1984: 24–27).

The first significant feminist revision of scholarly interpretation in archaeology came out of modern feminism, or second-wave feminism. Early academic research by women had interpreted exclusively women, domestic artifacts, and activities within the conventional gender roles of wife and mother, as women knew them from their own contemporary society and traditional research (Díaz-Andreu and Sørensen 1998: 6–7, 9–10). There was a shift from this early research of female gender roles to modern feminist research that challenged traditional androcentric constructions of the past. Research influenced by modern feminism elucidated the male-centered perspective in the foundations of archaeological knowledge, with such formulations as "Were they all men?" (Bertelsen et al. 1987), "Those of little note" (Scott 1994), "What this awl means" (Spector 1991), and "Challenging the Three-Age system" (i.e., the Stone Age, the Bronze Age, and the Iron Age) (paper abstract by Ströbeck 1998, 1999). Issues were raised concerning knowledge production within the prevailing frameworks that once had been drawn up for studies of past societies. Analyses of representations in source materials, and in typology and chronology in archaeological research, revealed that these frameworks for interpreting roles, relationships, and identities of peoples in the past were male biased and Eurocentric.

"What this awl means" was a critical analysis of the established typology of awls from Indigenous cultures in the United States, which had been derived from the study of the iron tips on awls. The tip, being a European item of exchange and trade, was mediating the story about European colonists' appearance and their contact with Indigenous peoples of North America. This is a male-associated history that was researched at the expense of the work and accomplishments of Indigenous women who used awls—for example, among the Wahpeton of the Dakota culture in Minnesota. The feminist analysis found that the Indigenous context for differentiating among types was located in women's repeated engravings of antler or bone awl handles (Spector 1991; 1993: 30–39). Concurrent research on African archaeology concluded that the archaeological chronology systems for Africa, which had been established during colonization, obviously favored European prehistory as a point of departure and reference (Robertshaw 1990; Trigger 1990: 313; Weedman 2001: 4–5, 28). Interestingly, in another critique, the system for sorting prehistory in northern Europe into three periods was challenged for being androcentric. The Three-Age system for Scandinavia, which was published in 1836, was found to favor male-associated artifacts and activities in its characteristics of the different time periods and in its designation of the periods (Ströbeck 1999).

Throughout the 1990s, new ethnographic and archaeological studies revised the former models of domestic or private and public spheres, which at that point were perceived as more or less essentialist in the distinction of roles of women and men (Claassen 1997: 85; Meskell 1999: 85). Research among, for example, the Efe in Zaire, the Iñupiat in Alaska, and the Chipewyan and Cree in Canada now showed that overlap, integration, and flexibility exist in the formation of male and female activities in these cultures, and also that there can be a non-gendered differentiation between public and private spheres (Boderhorn 1993; Brumbach and Jarvenpa 1997; Peacock 1991). The earlier interpretation of power and prestige as universal male characteristics was also questioned and reconceptualized for ancient and historic societies. Case studies of, for example, the Maya in Mesoamerica, the Moche in Peru, the Aztec in Mexico, the societies of the Mississippian period in the southeastern United States, and societies in the Bronze and Iron Ages and the Viking Age in Scandinavia all analyzed power in relation to gender and distinguished power in terms of dynamic relations, as a continuum, circumstantial, negotiated, and as small-scale individual action.

These studies highlighted the constructions of leadership, as well as heterarchically organized societies that combined relationships of dominance and subordination with complex lateral social relationships, and women in public positions such as leaders, traders, healers, innovators, and producers. Also, cases were found of powerful historic men whose dress was not ostentatious, and of men in ancient times who showed ostentatious display because they were powerless— not powerful, as is usually assumed (Alcalde 2004; Gräslund 2001; Nelson 2004 [1997]: 131–149; Spencer-Wood 1991b, 1994; Stalsberg 1991; Sweely 1999; Wright 1991). The prevailing typology of gender systems, which generally consisted of mutually exclusive systems of either gender hierarchy or gender complementarity, was critically reviewed. It was rejected as being too general to accommodate variations of gender systems and nuances within the systems. In addition, it was criticized for favoring a replacement of gender complementarity with gender hierarchy (Gero and Scattolin 2002: 155–158). The typology of gender systems was revised to include variations and coexistence of the two gender modes with reference to, among others, analyses of settlement remains dated to 200 B.C.–A.D. 500 in northwest Argentina and of human images of production and reproduction in pre-Hispanic southern Central America (Gero and Scattolin 2002:155–158; Joyce 1993).

Postmodern—or third-wave—feminism took shape in the 1980s as women of color, lesbian feminists, queer theorists, and postcolonial feminists reacted against the prevailing feminist apprehension of women as a homogeneous category of people all sharing white middle-class women's experiences (Gilchrist 1999: 3, 8; Meskell 1999: 55). The interest in experiential difference was redirected from differentiation between the sexes in matters of equality, toward differences within the group of women and within the group of men (Lesick 1997; Meskell 1999: 86–87). This new perspective was theoretically supported by poststructuralism and postcolonialism.

Earlier research on ancient and historic societies was thereafter viewed as being age-skewed, due to the absence of children. Since then, the young peoples in the past have been dealt with in archaeological studies of Scandinavia (Lillehammer 1989; Welinder 1998), in European and ancient Egyptian contexts (Sofaer Derevenski 1994; Moore and Scott 1997), in ancient Mesoamerica and the prehistoric Puebloan Southwest (Ardren and Hutson 2006; Kamp

2002), in historical contexts (Spencer-Wood 1991b: 265–269; 2003: 35– 50), as well as more generally (Baxter 2005; Kamp 2001; Sofaer Derevenski 2000). Some have also researched the previously overlooked activities of childbirth and mothering in ancient and historical societies (Beausang 2000, 2005; Bonfante 1997; Wilkie 2003). The elderly make up another omitted category of people, which later caught the interest of gender archaeology (Hollimon 2000: 182–183, 185; Toivari-Viitala 2001: 204–213; Welinder 2001). Also, the monolithic and normative masculinity in previous studies of the past was rejected in some gender analyses of the constructedness, complexity, and plurality of masculinities in ancient, medieval, and later historical societies (Hadley and Moore 1998; Harrison 2002; Treherne 1995). Once these biases were uncovered and "remedial" research—a term used by Alison Wylie (1991: 31)—and sex and gender integrative theorization had been initiated, archaeological analysis could become more inclusive, as more people—of female and male gender and of various ages—were studied. This research also led to an approach that elucidated the human life cycle and socialization into cultural norms and society in the past (Gilchrist 2000; Joyce 2000a; Sofaer Derevenski 1997). Moreover, feminist and gender archaeological analyses contributed to laying bare the ethnocentric bias and its gender implications in mainstream research, most often in terms of Western-oriented and Eurocentric interpretations of ancient or historic societies and non-Western Indigenous cultures (Spector 1991, 1993). Western bias was apparent in the distinction of exclusively binary male/female gender identities and in perceptions of ancient and historic sexualities. Archaeologists have for a long time thought about, or made assumptions about, sexuality in accordance with a heterosexual matrix. This was excluding same-sex sexuality in the past as well as all non-reproductive sexual practices, and sexuality was perceived as being static throughout (pre-) history.

The traditional interpretation of the encounter between colonists and Indigenous peoples perceived the parties in this cultural contact as two groups only, and it centered on binary and hierarchical relations between the two. The traditional image can be analyzed from a gender perspective, which adds yet another dimension to the aspects of dichotomy and hierarchy revealed, researched, and revised in colonial and postcolonial perspectives. Former narratives about cultural contacts in the colonial era have now been modeled to see continents, as well as colonists and Indigenous peoples, through the lenses of gender and sexuality. The colonized land is often now perceived as female, passive, and subordinate, while the colonizing Europe is characterized as male, active—as in conquest—and superior (Scully 2005). The gendering of cultural contact has been personalized as well, through stories about three Indigenous women: Malintzin in Mexico, Pocahontas in Virginia, United States, and Krotoa in the Cape of South Africa. Common characteristics assigned to these women are that they were helpful young women of a relatively noble status, who married European men, had children with them, and died at a young age. The children later integrated into European society, either in Europe or in the colonized areas (Scully 2005). As has been emphasized in archaeology in the United States since the 1980s and the early 1990s, the imperative male/female gendered relation between the categories of colonist and colonized conceals the existence of multiple gendered relationships between colonists and Indigenous peoples living in the colonies. The former imperative also downplayed the complexity of gender constructions and gender relations among colonists, and among Indigenous peoples who lived in colonized areas (Clements 2004; Voss 2005, 2008). Also, we can now examine the specific gendered conditions of Indigenous peoples in the colonial era who were removed from various areas—for example, from different places on the African continent—and then placed in North America or elsewhere (Samford 2004; Voss 2005: 461–462). Narratives about Indigenous female elites and their heterosexual, and procreative, relationships with colonizing men remain to be altered (McCafferty 2009; Perdue 1997; Scully 2005; Voss 2008).

The establishment of the field of sexology in the late 1800s provided a subject field as well as analytical categories for research about sexuality and sexual identities (Voss 2004: 56). Early sexuality research in archaeology was, however, stimulated and structured primarily by the book *Sexual Meanings: The Cultural Constuction of Gender and Sexuality* (Ortner and Whitehead 1981) and its ethnographic case studies of Indigenous North American peoples, the Bimin-Kuskusmin and Mount Hageners of New Guinea, Samoans, the Mundurucú in South America, and the African Maasai (Ortner and Whitehead 1981; cf. Voss 2000: 186). The prominent use of the sex/gender system in this publication impeded for some time the analysis of multiple and changing sexual behaviors and identities in archaeological feminist research (Voss 2000: 186). Moreover, such scholarship has documented sexual relationships and marriages between European colonists and the Indigenous peoples living in or being relocated to North America, which include events of sexual violence, premarital sexual relations and pregnancy, divorce due to adultery, and more. Historians also note that sexual standards changed over time in colonial society (Castañeda 1993; D'Emilio and Freedman 1988: 22–30; Perdue 1997; Spear 1999).

Initial studies of sexuality in archaeology, in the early 1990s, followed excavations of brothels from the Victorian period in urban settings (Seifert 1991b; 1994). Archaeological study of gendered contact—including sexual liaisons—between Indigenous North American peoples and Europeans appeared later on. For example, material remains of short-term as well as long-term sexual relations, some of which resulted in offspring, between Inuit women and whalers were elucidated at Inuit sites from the 16th, 19th, and 20th centuries on Baffin Island, Canada (Gullason 1999).

Studies of sexuality in archaeology also grew out of postmodern case studies of two-spirit, or third-gender, people in Indigenous North American cultures. The

Chumash, Hidatsa, and Eastern Dakota were some of the cultures studied (Hollimon 1991; 1997; Whelan 1991; Prine 2000). The existence of two-spirit individuals was taken as evidence of multiple genders in social organization, which was in contrast to the binary constructions in the previously distinguished gender system (Claassen 1992b:3; Duke 1991). Influential writing on queer theory later was put into service for deconstructing the formerly identified sexual categories or constructions. The previously established stereotype of woman, and the former distinction between the categories of biological sex and cultural gender, were destabilized through deconstruction, discourse theory, and the idea of "the performative" (Conkey and Gero 1997: 420–421; Gilchrist 1999: 3, 8). Archaeological analyses applied the concept of performance to material remains from the past, arguing for the general significance of material culture in the repetitive acts that constitute gender performance. These analyses also revealed time depth in the cultural formation of sexual identities that have changed throughout the past in accordance with various societies' norms (Perry and Joyce 2001). Ancient pictorial and textual discourse among the Maya and in ancient Egypt were prominent research areas for this approach (Joyce 2000b; Meskell 2000).

Postmodern research on third, and occasionally fourth, genders and historically and culturally specific sexual practices shed light on their existence in the past, overturning previously set ideas of connections between male and female genders and particular sexual practices (Dowson 2000; Gero 2004; Hollimon 2006; Schmidt and Voss 2000). Third-wave feminist research even deconstructed the notion of genders being first and foremost interconnected with sexuality, after studies distinguished occupational and spiritual characteristics as significant of a third gender (Hollimon 1997, 2000).

Genders that fall outside the binary categories of male and female had already been recognized in anthropological research on culturally and historically gender-variant behavior in many parts of the world (cf. Nanda 1990, 2000). New studies, as well as reinterpretation of early analyses of two-spirits, followed during the 1990s. Early research had focused on aspects of sexuality (particularly homosexuality) in the formation of the third gender. Later, the politicizing of Western ideas of homosexuality in interpretations of the Indigenous two-spirits was highlighted and criticized. This critical approach took shape in writings by both Indigenous North Americans and anthropologists of non-Indigenous origin and identity (Epple 1998; Goulet 1996; Jacobs et al. 1997a). The term "berdache," which had sexually derogatory meanings in its colonial context (Fulton and Anderson 1992: 603–604), was rejected at the Third Native American/First Nations Gay and Lesbian Conference in 1990, in favor of the "two-spirit" concept (Jacobs et al. 1997b: 2).

Archaeological studies of two-spirits in the Indigenous societies of the Chumash, Yokuts, Mono, and Tubatulabal in California revealed that the tasks performed by two-spirits were of a ritual and transcendent character, often associated with supernatural power. Two-spirits have often been specialists responsible for handling the deceased and conducting mourning rituals (Hollimon 1997). Critical analysis also pointed out that it may well be due to informants' and ethnographers' perceptions of these figures as men with female characteristics that made this type of two-spirit dominant in research. The possibility of temporary gender modification during the performance of the gender-transcendent activity was highlighted in analysis as well (Hollimon 1997: 182–183). Critiques of Western societies' romanticizing of the Indigenous third gender thereafter began to appear in forums for Western gay and lesbian scholarship as well (Towle and Morgan 2002).

A comparison between feminist and gender research in the United States and the United Kingdom shows differences, but these should not be overemphasized because the diversity in gender archaeology has increased within both countries throughout the 1990s and into the 21st century. The division into two major research traditions, as characterized by these two countries, is sometimes supplemented by the early tradition of feminist archaeology that emerged in Norway in the 1980s. This was similar to the dominant woman-centered perspective in the United States (Engelstad 2007: 217; Gilchrist 1999: 7).

Gender archaeology in the United Kingdom emerged simultaneously with the breakthrough of postprocessual archaeology. In the United States, gender research came in response to the early feminist perspective, with its preference for binary structure. It is therefore considered indicative that in research on later medieval monasteries and castles in the United Kingdom, the archaeological analyses of the layout of the built space elucidated the intersection of male and female genders with economic conditions and social status (Gilchrist 1994; 1999). The subject of gendered norms for usage of space at settlements was later implemented in archaeological analyses of some 19th-century plantations in the United States, Jamaica, and the east African island of Zanzibar. There it could also be shown how class and race ideologies have intersected with, and affected, gendered norms for access to and use of dwellings. This approach also drew attention to the particular sexual relationships that have taken form on plantations as a result of the many intersecting ideologies represented at this type of historical site (Croucher 2007; Delle 2000).

From History and Now Onward

Beginning in the 1990s, there have been recurring initiatives in the United States to research gender in archaeology. Continuing interest was stimulated by a conference series on the theme of gender, held every second year.[2] Furthermore, two book series have been established that encourage research and publishing on gender and archaeology: Regendering the Past, begun in 1994, and Gender and Archaeology, in 2001. Some books in these series have centered entirely on women's lives and female gender roles in past societies around the world, and to some extent in archaeology. Others have additionally included approaches for analyzing children, life cycles, men, masculinity, non-binary genders, and sexuality (Ardren 2002; Arnold and Wicker 2001; Baxter 2005; Bolger 2003, 2008; Claassen 1994; Claassen and Joyce 1997; Frink and Weedman 2005; Hays-Gilpin 2003; Linduff and Rubinson 2008; Linduff and Sun 2004; Nelson 2001, 2003, 2004 [1997], 2006, 2007a, 2007b, 2007c; Peterson 2002; Rautman 2000).

Volumes are continuously being published in the Gender and Archaeology series. Recent works include a reference book on gender and archaeology (Nelson 2006), which also was published as a subseries in 2007 (Nelson 2007a, 2007b, 2007c). In 2007, a theme issue of the *Journal of Archaeological Method and Theory* focused on feminist methods and practices. The theme developed from concern with gender archaeology's dissociation from feminist scholarship and feminist activism. Most of the articles in the issue originated from a research seminar in the United States nine years earlier, although with updated references. The lack of a feminist dimension in gender archaeology was considered a current matter. Altogether these initiatives show that what is generally considered the focus of second-wave—or modern—feminism is currently used in archaeological research, along with the third-wave—or postmodern—feminist perspective. This is also true for Europe (cf. Hamilton et al. 2007). From this, one can assume that both modern feminist and postmodern feminist perspectives will continue to be recognized and used in the near future, by scholars as well as students learning and performing gender analysis in archaeology.

The feminist critical perspective continues to draw attention to biased frameworks in both older traditional and recent archaeological knowledge production (e.g., *Journal of Archaeological Method and Theory* 14 (3); Nelson 2003, 2004 [1997]). Male bias—for example, the favoring of male-associated colonist activity—was identified and critiqued in an earlier analysis (Spector 1993). By applying a feminist critical perspective in various research contexts, and with methods not used before, new and additional dimensions of biases have been elucidated. In Peru, the Killka project, running in the 1990s and early 21st century, embraced an analysis of cultural continuity from pre-contact times to the present through the study of two multi-gendered figures. In this study, it was concluded that the term "millennium" as it relates to Christianity should be replaced, in the area under study, with a concept of continuity based on non-binary genders of the Andean calender (Lizárraga 2000: 7). Since the questioning of traditional chronologies, typologies, analogies, and cultural identities in archaeological research can be followed up with revised and altered frameworks only after years of thorough deconstruction and ground-breaking case studies, we can expect further studies on the subject of gendered archaeological basics in the future as well.

Moreover, the feminist archaeological perspective responds to the call for decolonization and empowerment of Indigenous peoples, in society as well as in archaeological scholarship. Meg Conkey (2005) published a comparative analysis of the shared issues of feminist and Indigenous archaeologies, and its conclusions were reviewed. The proposed intersection of feminist and Indigenous archaeologies has raised concerns about linking two marginalized perspectives, and whether their very foundations and power relationships actually are the same (Lippert 2005: 64; Million 2005: 69). Moreover, as was pointed out in a review, both feminist and Indigenous archaeologies aim for impact and intersection, but primarily with mainstream archaeology (Million 2005: 69). Future publications will show if interest is strong enough for these two perspectives to operate together in the struggle for turning feminist and Indigenous issues into mainstream matters. Recently, the feminist Indigenous perspective has drawn attention to ways in which the lingering norms of Euro-American colonialism, patriarchy, and Christian ideology have structured the lives of Indigenous women in North America, in the historic past as well as in the present (Clements 2004; Mihesuah 2003). And a few archaeologists have researched how Indigenous women ideologically and materially resisted Englishmen's attempts to impose Christian patriarchy on matrilineal societies in southern New England during the 17th century (Clements 2004; Nassaney 2004). Today Indigenous women have to consider both their interest in decolonization and empowerment of Indigenous society, as well as their situation as women within an Indigenous society, when they consider a joint project with feminist archaeology.

Multivocality was an issue introduced in the early 1990s, and it continues to be elaborated (Beaudry 1991: 165, 179; Spencer-Wood 1991a: 239). The theoretical and methodological orientations in feminist archaeology in the late 1990s and the early 21st century have led to new realms of studying inequalities and of instituting multivocality within archaeological practices such as fieldwork (Moser 2007), geopolitical mapping of research sites (Tomášková 2007), formation of theory and theorists (Conkey 2007), the process of making plausible and convincing interpretations from data (Gero 2007), and visualizing and narrating the past (Joyce and Tringham 2007). We wait for discussions and proposals on these matters to be applied more widely in archaeological practice, in order to further reflect on their respective formation and outcome.

In recent reviews of gender analyses in historical archaeology and in archaeology of the pre-Hispanic Americas, scholars call for further elaboration and implementation of a gender perspective that embraces multiple femininities and masculinities. It is argued in these reviews, as elsewhere since the introduction of the postmodern feminist perspective in the 1990s, that social identity preferably be studied as a concept constituted through various intersections, such as race, class, and gender (Ardren 2008: 18; Spencer-Wood 2006: 77; Wilkie and Howlett Hayes 2006: 253–254). Recent work by Barbara Voss (2008) looks at Spanish colonization of the Americas and argues for the importance of deconstructing the male/female binary, as well as of contesting the prevailing perception of female as being relegated to the domestic (or private) and Indigenous spheres, and the male to the public and colonial—each of these on multiple scales from the macro to the micro of social relations, including gender (Voss 2008). Furthermore, reviewers of archaeological gender analyses currently draw special attention to the rich opportunities for studies of gendered landscapes in the ancient Americas, and the generally multifaceted source material from cultures of the New World. There is a wish to establish a closer dialogue and exchange of ideas and experiences between archaeologists who analyze extant source material from the ancient and historic Americas and those who use elaborate theoretical approaches to the study of gender (Ardren 2008: 18–19). As has been revealed in this chapter, this endeavor offers opportunities. It also means constant critical scrutiny of sex, gender, and sexuality biases, followed up by revision and elaboration of feminist and gender interpretations, with regard to changes in the formation of sex, gender, and sexuality in contemporary society and in relation to changing images of the self.

Notes

1. For example, to find out more about studies in the Nordic countries—in English and the Nordic languages—search the "Nordic Archaeological Abstracts' (*www.naa.dk*). In Germany, scholars who are interested in and who perform feminist and gender archaeological research have established a network on the Internet—the "FemArc—Netzwerk archäologisch arbeitender Frauen"—with book publications primarily in German (*www.femarc.de*). For further information about archaeological research on gender in Mesoamerica (in both English and Spanish), search the "Bibliografía Mesoamericana" (*www.famsi.org/research/bibliography.htm*) at the website of the Foundation for the Advancement of Mesoamerican Studies, Inc. Also, the *Handbook of Gender in Archaeology* (Nelson 2006) contains essays that summarize the feminist and gender archaeological research performed in different world regions (Nelson 2006: 595–874).

2. Information about the three conferences may be accessed at *www.uwm.edu/~barnold/gender.html; www2.nau.edu/~gender-p; www.geocities.com/gender_conference/home.html* (last accessed 11/10/ 2009).

References

Alcalde, C. 2004. Leaders, healers, laborers, and lovers. Reinterpreting women's roles in Moche society, in K. A. Pyburn (ed.), *Ungendering Civilization*, pp. 136–155. New York: Routledge.

Allen, P. G. 1988. Who is your mother? Red roots of white feminism, in R. Simonson and S. Walker (eds.), *The Graywolf Annual Five: Multicultural Literacy*, pp. 13–27. St. Paul: Graywolf Press.

Ardener, E. 1972. Belief and the problem of women, in J. S. La Fontaine (ed.), *The Interpretation of Ritual: Essays in Honour of A. I. Richards*, pp. 135–158. London: Tavistock Publications.

Ardren, T. 2008. Studies of gender in the preHispanic Americas. *Journal of Archaeological Research* 16 (1): 1–35.

Ardren, T. (ed.). 2002. *Ancient Maya Women*. Gender and Archaeology Series. Walnut Creek, CA: AltaMira Press.

Ardren, T., and Hutson, S. R. (eds.). 2006. *The Social Experience of Childhood in Ancient Mesoamerica*. Boulder: University Press of Colorado.

Arnold, B., and Wicker, N. L. (eds.). 2001. *Gender and the Archaeology of Death*. Gender and Archaeology Series. Walnut Creek, CA: AltaMira Press.

Arnold, K., Graves, P., Gilchrist, R., and Taylor, S. (eds.).1988. Women in archaeology. *Archaeological Review from Cambridge* 7 (1): 2–8.

Balme, J., and Beck, W. (eds.). 1995. *Gendered Archaeology: Proceedings of the Second Australian Women in Archaeology Conference*. Research Papers in Archaeology and Natural History 26. Canberra: Australian National University.

Baxter, J. E. 2005. *The Archaeology of Childhood. Children, Gender, and Material Culture*. Gender and Archaeology Series. Walnut Creek, CA: AltaMira Press.

Beaudry, M. C., Cook, L. J., and Mrozowski, S. A. 1991. Artifacts and active voices: Material culture as social discourse, in R. Paynter and R. H. McGuire (eds.), *The Archaeology of Inequality*, pp. 150–191. Oxford: Basil Blackwell.

Beausang, E. 2000. Childbirth in prehistory: An introduction. *European Journal of Archaeology* 3 (1): 69–87.

——. 2005. *Childbirth and Mothering in Archaeology*. Department of Archaeology, University of Gothenburg. GOTARC Series B, Gothenburg Archaeological Theses 37.

Bertelsen, R., Lillehammer, A., and Næss, J. (eds.). 1987. *Were They All Men? An Examination of Sex Roles in Prehistoric Society. Acts from a Workshop Held at Utstein Kloster, Rogaland 2–4. November 1979* (NAM-Forskningsseminar nr. 1). AmsVaria 17. Stavanger, Norway: Arkeologisk Museum i Stavanger.

Bibliografía Mesoamericana. http://www.famsi.org/research/bibliography.htm (accessed June 13, 2008).

Boderhorn, B. 1993. Gendered spaces, public places: Public and private revisited on the North Slope of Alaska, in B. Bender (ed.), *Landscape: Politics and Perspectives*, pp. 169–203. London: Berg.

Bolger, D. 2003. *Gender in Ancient Cyprus: Narratives of Social Change on a Mediterranean Island*. Gender and Archaeology Series. Walnut Creek, CA: AltaMira Press.

Bolger, D. (ed.). 2008. *Gender through Time in the Ancient Near East*. Gender and Archaeology Series. Lanham, MD: AltaMira Press.

Bonfante, L. 1997. Nursing mothers in Classical art, in A. O. Koloski-Ostrow and C. L. Lyons (eds.), *Naked Truths. Women, Sexuality, and Gender in Classical Art and Archaeology*, pp. 174–196. London and New York: Routledge.

Brumbach, H., and Jarvenpa, R. 1997. Woman the Hunter: Ethnoarchaeological lessons from Chipewyan life-cycle dynamics, in C. Claassen and R. Joyce (eds.), *Women in Prehistory*, pp. 17–32. Philadelphia: University of Pennsylvania Press.

Castañeda, A. I. 1993. Sexual violence in the politics and policies of conquest: Amerindian women and the Spanish conquest of Alta California, in A. de la Torre and B. M. Pesquera (eds.), *Building with Our Hands: New Directions in Chicana Studies*, pp. 15–33. Berkeley: University of California Press.

Claassen, C. 1997. Changing venue: Women's lives in prehistoric North America, in C. Claassen and R. A. Joyce (eds.), *Women in Prehistory: North America and Mesoamerica*, pp. 65–87. Philadelphia: University of Pennsylvania Press.

Claassen, C. (ed.). 1992a. *Exploring Gender through Archaeology*. Madison, WI: Prehistory Press.

———. 1992b. Questioning gender: An introduction, in C. Claassen (ed.), *Exploring Gender through Archaeology*, pp. 1–9. Madison, WI: Prehistory Press.

———. 1994. *Women in Archaeology*. Regendering the Past Series. Philadelphia: University of Pennsylvania Press.

Claassen, C., and R. A. Joyce (eds.). 1997. *Women in Prehistory: North America and Mesoamerica*. Regendering the Past Series. Philadelphia: University of Pennsylvania Press.

Clements, J. M. 2004. "… *A winding sheet for Deborah George* …": *Searching for the women of Ponkapoag*. Doctoral thesis, Women's Studies, York University, York, Ontario.

Conkey, M. W. 2005. Dwelling at the margins, action at the intersection? Feminist and Indigenous archaeologies. *Archaeologies* 1 (1): 9–59.

———. 2007. Questioning theory: Is there a gender of theory in archaeology? *Journal of Archaeological Method and Theory* 14 (3): 285–310.

Conkey, M. W., and Gero, J. M. 1997. Programme to practice: Gender and feminism in archaeology. *Annual Reviews Anthropology* 26: 411–437.

Conkey, M. W., and Spector, J. D. 1984. Archaeology and the study of gender. *Advances in Archaeological Method and Theory* 7: 1–38.

Croucher, S. 2007. Clove plantations on nineteenth-century Zanzibar. Possibilities for gender archaeology in Africa. *Journal of Social Archaeology* 7 (3): 302–324.

Delle, J. A. 2000. Gender, power, and space: Negotiating social relations under slavery on coffee plantations in Jamaica, 1790–1834, in J. A. Delle, S. A. Mrozowski, and R. Paynter (eds.), *Lines that Divide: Historical Archaeologies of Race, Class, and Gender*, pp. 168–204. Knoxville: University of Tennessee Press.

D'Emilio, J., and Freedman, E. B. 1988. *Intimate Matters. A History of Sexuality in America*. New York: Harper & Row.

Díaz-Andreu, M., and Sørensen, M. L. S. (eds.). 1998. *Excavating Women: A History of Women in European Archaeology*. London and New York: Routledge.

Dowson, T. A. (ed.). 2000. *World Archaeology* 32 (2), Queer Archaeologies.

Duke, P. 1991. Recognizing gender in Plains hunting groups: Is it possible or even necessary?, in D. Walde and N. D. Willows (eds.), *The Archaeology of Gender: Proceedings of the 22nd Annual Chacmool Conference*, pp. 280–283. Calgary: Archaeological Association of the University of Calgary.

du Cros, H., and Smith, L. (eds.). 1993. *Women in Archaeology. A Feminist Critique*. Canberra: Australian National University.

Ehrenberg, M. 1989. *Women in Prehistory*. Norman: University of Oklahoma Press.

Engelstad, E. 1991. Images of power and contradiction: Feminist theory and post-processual archaeology. *Antiquity* 65: 502–514.

——. 2007. Much more than gender. *Journal of Archaeological Method and Theory* 14 (3): 217–234.

Epple, C. 1998. Coming to terms with Navajo "nádleehí": A critique of "Berdache," "gay," "alternate gender," and "two-spirit." *American Ethnologist* 25 (2): 267–290.

FemArc—Netzwerk Archäologisch Arbeitender Frauen. *http://www.femarc.de* (accessed June 13, 2008).

Frink, L., and Weedman, K. (eds.). 2005. *Gender and Hide Production*. Gender and Archaeology Series. Walnut Creek, CA: AltaMira Press.

Fulton, R. and Anderson, S. W. (eds.). 1992. The Amerindian "man-woman": Gender, liminality, and cultural continuity. *Current Anthropology* 33 (5): 603–610.

Gero, J. M. 2004. Sex pots of ancient Peru: Post-gender reflections, in T. Oestigaard, N. Anfinset, and T. Saetersdal (eds.), *Combining the Past and the Present. Archaeological Perspectives on Society*, pp. 3–22. BAR International Series 1210. Oxford: Archaeopress.

——. 2007. Honoring ambiguity/problematizing certitude. *Journal of Archaeological Method and Theory* 14 (3): 311–327.

Gero, J., M., and Conkey, M. W. 1991. *Engendering Archaeology. Women and Prehistory*. Oxford and Cambridge: Blackwell.

Gero, J. M., Lacey, D. M., and Blakely, M. L. (eds.). 1983. *The Socio-Politics of Archaeology*. Research Reports No. 23. Amherst: University of Massachusetts.

Gero, J., and Scattolin, C. 2002. Beyond complementarity and hierarchy: New definitions for archaeological gender relations, in S. M. Nelson and M. Rosen-Ayalon (eds.), *In Pursuit of Gender: Worldwide Archaeological Perspectives*, pp. 155–171. Walnut Creek, CA: AltaMira Press.

Gilchrist, R. 1994. *Gender and Material Culture. The Archaeology of Religious Women*. London and New York: Routledge.

——. 1999. *Gender and Archaeology. Contesting the Past*. London and New York: Routledge.

Gilchrist, R. (ed.). 2000. *World Archaeology* 31 (3), Human Lifecycles.

Goulet, J. A. 1996. The "Berdache"/"two-spirit": A comparison of anthropological and Native constructions of gendered identities among the northern Athapaskans. *The Journal of the Royal Anthropological Institute* 2 (4): 683–701.

Gräslund, A. 2001. The position of Iron Age Scandinavian women: Evidence from graves and rune stones, in B. Arnold and N. Wicker (eds.), *Gender and the Archaeology of Death*, pp. 81–102. Walnut Creek, CA: AltaMira Press.

Gullason, L. 1999. *Engendering Interaction: Inuit-European Contact in Frobisher Bay, Baffin Island*. Doctoral thesis, Department of Anthropology, McGill University, Montreal.

Hadley, D. M., and Moore, J. 1998. "Death makes the man": Burial rite and the construction of masculinities in the early Middle Ages, in D. M. Hadley (ed.), *Masculinity in Medieval Europe*, pp. 21–38. London: Longman.

Hamilton, S., Whitehouse, R. D., and Wright, K. I. (eds.). 2007. *Archaeology and Women. Ancient and Modern Issues*. Walnut Creek, CA: Left Coast Press.

Harrison, R. 2002. Archaeology and the colonial encounter: Kimberley spearpoints, cultural identity and masculinity in the north of Australia. *Journal of Social Archaeology* 2 (3): 352–377.

Hays-Gilpin, K. 2003. *Ambiguous Images: Gender and Rock Art*. Gender and Archaeology series. Walnut Creek, CA: AltaMira Press.

Hollimon, S. 1991. Health consequences of the division of labor among the Chumash Indians of southern California, in D. Walde and N. D. Willows (eds.), *The Archaeology of Gender: Proceedings of the 22nd Annual Chacmool Conference*, pp. 462–469. Calgary: Archaeological Association of the University of Calgary.

——. 1997. The third gender in Native California: Two-spirit undertakers among the Chumash and their neighbors, in C. Claassen and R. A. Joyce (eds.), *Women in Prehistory: North America and Mesoamerica*, pp. 173–188. Philadelphia: University of Pennsylvania Press.

——. 2000. Archaeology of the *'Aqi*: Gender and sexuality in prehistoric Chumash society, in R. A. Schmidt and B. L. Voss (eds.), *Archaeologies of Sexuality*, pp. 179–196. London and New York: Routledge.

——. 2006. The archaeology of non-binary genders in Native North American societies, in S. M. Nelson (ed.), *Handbook of Gender in Archaeology*, pp. 435–450. Lanham, MD: AltaMira Press.

Irwin-Williams, C. 1990. Women in the field. The role of women in archaeology before 1960, in G. Kass-Simon and P. Farnes (eds.), *Women of Science. Righting the Record*, pp. 1–41. Bloomington and Indianapolis: Indiana University Press.

Jacobs, S.-E., Thomas, W., and Lang, S. (eds.). 1997a. *Two-Spirit People: Native American Gender Identity, Sexuality, and Spirituality*. Urbana: University of Illinois Press.

——. 1997b. Introduction, in S.-E. Jacobs, W. Thomas, and S. Lang (eds.), *Two-Spirit People: Native American Gender Identity, Sexuality, and Spirituality*, pp. 1–18. Urbana: University of Illinois Press.

Joyce, R. A. 1993. Women's work. Images of production and reproduction in pre-Hispanic southern Central America. *Current Anthropology* 34 (3): 255–274.

——. 2000a. *Gender and Power in Prehispanic Mesoamerica*. Austin: University of Texas Press.

——. 2000b. *A Precolumbian Gaze: Male Sexuality among the Ancient Maya*, in R. A. Schmidt and B. L. Voss (eds.), *Archaeologies of Sexuality*, pp. 263–283. London and New York: Routledge.

Joyce, R. A., and Tringham, R. E. 2007. Feminist adventures in hypertext. *Journal of Archaeological Method and Theory* 14 (3): 328–358.

Kamp, K. 2001. Where have all the children gone? The archaeology of childhood.

Journal of Archaeological Method and Theory 8 (1): 1–29.

Kamp, K. (ed.). 2002. *Children in the Prehistoric Puebloan Southwest*. Salt Lake City: University of Utah Press.

Landsman, G. H. 1992. The "other" as political symbol: Images of Indians in the woman suffrage movement. *Ethnohistory* 39 (3): 247–284.

Lesick, K. S. 1997. Re-engendering gender: Some theoretical and methodological concerns on a burgeoning archaeological pursuit, in J. Moore and E. Scott (eds.), *Invisible People and Processes: Writing Gender and Childhood into European Archaeology*, pp. 31–41. New York: Leicester University Press.

Lillehammer, G. 1989. A child is born: The child's world in an archaeological perspective. *Norwegian Archaeological Review* 22 (2): 89–105.

Linduff, K. M., and Rubinson, K. S. 2008. *Are All Warriors Male? Gender Roles on the Ancient Eurasian Steppe*. Gender and Archaeology series. Lanham, MD: AltaMira Press.

Linduff, K. M., and Sun, Y. (eds.). 2004. *Gender and Chinese Archaeology*. Gender and Archaeology series. Walnut Creek, CA: AltaMira Press.

Linton, S. 1971. Woman the Gatherer: Male bias in anthropology, in S.-E. Jacobs (ed.), *Women in Perspective: A Guide for Cross-Cultural Studies*, pp. 9–21. Urbana: University of Illinois Press.

Lippert, D. 2005. Comment on "Dwellings at the Margins, Action at the Intersection? Feminist and Indigenous Archaeologies," *Archaeologies* 1 (1): 63–66.

Lizárraga, K. 2000. Unkunakuchkan and Waylis: An archaeolinguistic study of two Andean radicals. Paper presented at the Sixth Gender and Archaeology Conference, October 6–7, 2000, Flagstaff, AZ. http://www2.nau.edu/~gender-p/Papers/Lizzarrga2.pdf. (accessed June 13, 2008).

McCafferty, G. 2009. De-colón-izing Malintzin: Feminism to the rescue!, in P. Bikoulis, D. LaCroix, and M. Peuramaki-Brown (eds.), *Postcolonial Perspectives in Archaeology: Proceedings from the 39th Annual Chacmool Conference*, pp. 183–192. Calgary: University of Calgary Press.

Meskell, L. 1999. *Archaeologies of Social Life. Age, Sex, Class et cetera in Ancient Egypt*. Oxford: Blackwell.

——. 2000. Re-em(bed)ding sex: Domesticity, sexuality, and ritual in New Kingdom Egypt, in R. A. Schmidt and B. L. Voss (eds.), *Archaeologies of Sexuality*, pp. 253–262. London and New York: Routledge.

Mihesuah, D. A. 2003. *Indigenous American Women: Decolonization, Empowerment, Activism*. Lincoln: University of Nebraska Press.

Miller, V. E. (ed.). 1988. *The Role of Gender in Precolumbian Art and Architecture*. Lanham, MD: University Press of America.

Million, T. 2005. Comment on "Dwellings at the Margins, Action at the Intersection? Feminist and Indigenous Archaeologies, 2005." *Archaeologies* 1(1): 67–70.

Moore, J., and Scott, E. (eds.). 1997. *Invisible People and Processes: Writing Gender and Childhood into European Archaeology*. New York: Leicester University Press.

Moser, S. 2007. On disciplinary culture: Archaeology as fieldwork and its gendered associations. *Journal of Archaeological Method and Theory* 14 (3): 235–263.

Nanda, S. 1990. *Neither Man nor Woman: The Hijras of India*. Belmont, CA: Wadsworth Publishing.

———. 2000. *Gender Diversity: Crosscultural Variations*. Illinois: Waveland Press Inc.

Nassaney, M. S. 2004. Native American gender politics and material culture in seventeenth-century southeastern New England. *Journal of Social Archaeology* 4 (3): 334–367.

Nelson, S. M. (ed.). 2001. *In Pursuit of Gender: Worldwide Archaeological Approaches*. Gender and Archaeology series. Walnut Creek, CA: AltaMira Press.

———. 2003. *Ancient Queens: Archaeological Explorations*. Gender and Archaeology series. Wanut Creek, CA: AltaMira Press.

———. 2004 [1997]. *Gender in Archaeology. Analyzing Power and Prestige*. Gender and Archaeology series. Walnut Creek, CA: AltaMira Press.

———. 2006. *Handbook of Gender in Archaeology*. Gender and Archaeology series. Lanham, MD: AltaMira Press.

———. 2007a. *Women in Antiquity: Theoretical Approaches to Gender and Archaeology*. Gender and Archaeology series. Lanham: AltaMira Press.

———. 2007b. *Identity and Subsistence: Gender Strategies for Archaeology*. Gender and Archaeology series. Lanham, MD: Rowman & Littlefield Publishers.

———. 2007c. *Worlds of Gender: The Archaeology of Women's Lives around the Globe*. Gender and Archaeology series. Lanham, MD: AltaMira Press.

Nordic Archaeological Abstracts. 2008. http://www.naa.dk (accessed June 13, 2008).

Olsen Bruhns, K., and Stothert, K. E. 1999. *Women in Ancient America*. Norman: University of Oklahoma Press.

Ortner, S. B. 1974. Is female to male as nature is to culture?, in M. Rosaldo and L. Lamphere (eds.), *Woman, Culture and Society*, pp. 67–88. Stanford, CA: Stanford University Press.

Ortner, S. B., and Whitehead, H. (eds.). 1981. *Sexual Meanings: The Cultural Constuction of Gender and Sexuality*. Cambridge: Cambridge University Press.

Peacock, N. R. 1991. Rethinking the sexual division of labour: Reproduction and women's work among the Efe, in M. di Leonardo (ed.), *Gender at the Crossroads of Knowledge: Feminist Anthropology in the Post-Modern Era*, pp. 339–360. Berkeley: University of California Press.

Perdue, T. 1997. Columbus meets Pocahontas in the American South. *Southern Cultures* 3 (1): 4–21.

Perry, E. M., and Joyce, R. 2001. Providing a past for "Bodies That Matter": Judith Butler's impact on the archaeology of gender. *International Journal of Sexuality and Gender Studies* 6 (1/2): 63–76.

Peterson, J. 2002. *Sexual Revolutions: Gender and Labor at the Dawn of Agriculture*. Gender and Archaeology series. Walnut Creek, CA: AltaMira Press.

Prine, E. 2000. Searching for third genders: Towards a prehistory of domestic space in middle Missouri villages, in R. A. Schmidt and B. L. Voss (eds.), *Archaeologies of Sexuality*, pp. 197–219. London and New York: Routledge.

Rautman, A. E. (ed.). 2000. *Reading the Body: Representations and Remains in the Archae-

ological Record. Regendering the Past series. Philadelphia: University of Pennsylvania Press.

Reiter, R. R. 1975. Introduction, in R. R. Reiter (ed.), *Toward an Anthropology of Women*, pp. 11–19. New York: Monthly Review Press.

Reyman, J. E. 1992. Part 2, in J. E. Reyman (ed.), *Rediscovering Our Past: Essays on the History of American Archaeology*, pp. 69–136. Avebury and Brookfield: Ashgate Publishing Company.

Robertshaw, P. 1990. A history of African archaeology: An introduction, in P. Robertshaw (ed.), *A History of African Archaeology*, pp. 3–12. London: James Curry Publishers.

Roesch Wagner, S. 2001. *Sisters in Spirit: Haudenosaunee (Iroquois) Influence on Early American Feminists*. Summertown, TN: Native Voices.

Rohrlich-Leavitt, R., Sykes, B., and Weatherford, E. 1975. Aboriginal woman: Male and female anthropological perspectives, in R. R. Reiter (ed.), *Toward an Anthropology of Women*, pp. 110–126. New York: Monthly Review Press.

Rosaldo, M. 1974. Woman, culture and society: A theoretical overview, in M. Rosaldo and L. Lamphere (eds.), *Woman, Culture and Society*. pp. 14–42, 321–324. Stanford, CA: Stanford University Press.

——. 1980. The use and abuse of anthropology: Reflections on feminism and cross-cultural understanding. *Signs: Journal of Women in Culture and Society* 5 (3): 389–417.

Rosaldo, M. and Lamphere, L. 1974. Introduction, in M. Rosaldo and L. Lamphere (eds.), *Woman, Culture and Society*, pp. 1–16. Stanford, CA: Stanford University Press.

Rubin, G. 1975. The traffic in women: Notes on the "Political Economy" of sex, in R. R. Reiter (ed.), *Toward an Anthropology of Women*, pp. 157–210. New York: Monthly Review Press.

Samford, P. 2004. Engendering enslaved communities on Virginia's and North Carolina's eighteenth- and nineteenth-century plantations, in J. E. Galle and A. L. Young (eds.), *Engendering African American Archaeology: A Southern Perspective*, pp. 151–177. Knoxville: University of Tennessee.

Schmidt, R. A., and Voss, B. L. (eds.). 2000. *Archaeologies of Sexuality*. London and New York: Routledge.

Scott, E. M. 1994. *Those of Little Note. Gender, Race, and Class in Historical Archaeology*. Tucson: University of Arizona Press.

Scully, P. 2005. Malintzin, Pocahontas, and Krotoa: Indigenous women and myth models of the Atlantic world. *Journal of Colonialism and Colonial History* 6 (3).

Seifert, D. J. (ed.). 1991a. *Gender in Historical Archaeology* 25 (4): 1–155.

Seifert, D. J. 1991b. Within sight of the White House: The archaeology of working women. *Gender in Historical Archaeology* 25 (4): 82–108.

——. 1994. Mrs. Starr's profession, in E. M. Scott (ed.), *Those of Little Note: Gender, Race, and Class in Historical Archaeology*, pp. 149–174. Tuscon: University of Arizona Press.

Sofaer Derevenski, J. (ed.). 1994. *Archaeological Review from Cambridge* 13 (2).

———. 1997. Age and gender at the site of Tiszapolgár-Basatanya, Hungary. *Antiquity* 71: 875–889.

———. 2000. *Children and Material Culture*. New York: Routledge.

Spear, J. M. 1999. "They Need Wives": Métissage and the regulation of sexuality in French Louisiana, 1699–1730, in M. Hodes (ed.), *Sex, Love, Race: Crossing Boundaries in North American History*, pp. 35–59. New York: New York University Press.

Spector, J. D. 1983. Male/female task differentiation among the Hidatsa: Toward the development of an archeological approach to the study of gender, in P. Albers and B. Medicine (eds.), *The Hidden Half: Studies of Plains Indian Women*, pp. 77–99. Lanham, New York, and London: University Press of America.

———. 1991. What this awl means: Toward a feminist archaeology, in J. M. Gero and M. W. Conkey (eds.), *Engendering Archaeology. Women and Prehistory*, pp. 388–406. Oxford and Cambridge: Blackwell.

———. 1993. *What This Awl Means: Feminist Archaeology at a Wahpeton Dakota Village*. St. Paul: Minnesota Historical Society Press.

Spencer-Wood, S. M. 1991a. Toward a feminist historical archaeology of the construction of gender, in D. Walde and N. Willows (eds.), *The Archaeology of Gender: Proceedings of the 22nd (1989) Chacmool Conference*, pp. 234–244. Calgary: University of Calgary Archaeological Association.

———. 1991b. Toward an historical archaeology of materialistic domestic reform, in R. H. McGuire and R. Paynter (eds.), *The Archaeology of Inequality*, pp. 231–286. Oxford and Cambridge: Blackwell.

———. 1992. A feminist program for nonsexist archaeology, in L. Wandsnider (ed.), *Quandaries and Quests: Visions of Archaeology's Future*, pp. 98–114. Carbondale, IL: Center for Archaeological Investigations Occasional Paper No. 20.

———. 1994. Diversity and nineteenth-century domestic reform. Relationships among classes and ethnic groups, in E. M. Scott (ed.), *Those of Little Note: Gender, Race and Class in Historical Archaeology*, pp. 175–208. Tucson: University of Arizona Press.

———. 2003. Gendering the creation of green urban landscapes in America at the turn of the century, in D. L. Rotman and E.-R. Savulis (eds.), *Shared Spaces and Divided Places: Material Dimensions of Gender Relations and the American Historical Landscape*, pp. 24–61. Knoxville: University of Tennessee Press.

———. 2006. Feminist theory and gender research in historical archaeology, in S. Milledge Nelson (ed.), *Handbook of Gender in Archaeology*, pp. 59–104. Lanham, MD: AltaMira Press.

Stalsberg, A. 1991. Women as actors in North European Viking Age trade, in R. Samson (ed.), *Social Approaches to Viking Studies*, pp. 75–83. Glasgow: Cruithne Press.

Ströbeck, L. 1998. Challenging the three-age system in Scandinavian prehistory. Paper abstract for the Fifth Gender and Archaeology Conference, October 9–10, Milwaukee. *http://www.uwm.edu/~barnold/*

abstracts.html#talk33 (accessed June 13, 2008).

———. 1999. Möjligheter, begränsningar och utmaningar inom genusarkeologi-några reflektioner, in C. Caesar, I. Gustin, E. Iregren, B. Petersson, E. Rudebeck, E. Räf, and L. Ströbeck (eds.), *Han, Hon, Den, Det. Att integrera genus och kön i arkeologi*, pp. 17–25. Report Series No. 65. Lund: Institute of Archaeology, Lund University.

———. Forthcoming. *Engendering the Roman Iron Age and Society in Southeast Scandinavia 0–AD 400*. Ph.D. dissertation, Lund University.

Sweely, T. L. 1999. *Manifesting Power. Gender and the Interpretation of Power in Archaeology*. London and New York: Routledge.

Toivari-Viitala, J. 2001. *Women at Deir el-Medina. A Study of the Status and Roles of the Female Inhabitants in the Workmen's Community during the Ramesside Period*. Egyptologische Uitgaven 15. Leiden: Netherlands Institute for the Near East (NINO).

Tomášková, S. 2007. Mapping a future: Archaeology, feminism, and scientific practice. *Journal of Archaeological Method and Theory* 14: 264–284.

Towle, E. B., and Morgan, L. M. 2002. Romancing the transgender Native. Rethinking the use of the "third gender" concept. *GLQ: A Journal of Lesbian and Gay Studies* 8(4): 469–497.

Treherne, P. 1995. The Warrior's beauty: The masculine body and self-identity in Bronze-Age Europe. *Journal of European Archaeology* 3 (1): 105–144.

Trigger, B. 1990. The history of African archaeology in world perspective, in P. Robertshaw (ed.), *A History of African Archaeology*, pp. 309–319. London: James Curry Publishers.

Voss, B. 2000. Feminisms, queer theories, and the archaeological study of past sexualities. *World Archaeology* 32 (2): 180–192.

———. 2004. Sexual subjects. Identity and taxonomy in archaeological research, in E. C. Casella and C. Fowler (eds.), *The Archaeology of Plural and Changing Identities. Beyond Identification*, pp. 55–77. New York: Springer.

———. 2005. From *Casta* to *Californio*: Social identity and the archaeology of culture contact. *American Anthropologist* 107 (3): 461–474.

———. 2008. Gender, race, and labor in the archaeology of the Spanish Colonial Americas. *Current Anthropology* 49 (5): 861–893.

Walde, D., and Willows, N. D. (eds.). 1991. *The Archaeology of Gender: Proceedings of the 22nd Annual Chacmool Conference*. Calgary: Archaeological Association of the University of Calgary.

Weedman, K. 2001. Who's "That Girl": British, South African, and American women as Africanist archaeologists in colonial Africa (1860s–1960s). *African Archaeological Review* 18 (1): 1–47.

Welinder, S. 1998. The cultural construction of childhood in Scandinavia, 3500 BC– 1350 AD. *Current Swedish Archaeology* 6: 185–205.

———. 2001. The archaeology of old age. *Current Swedish Archaeology* 9: 163–178.

Whelan, M. K. 1991. Gender and historical archaeology: Eastern Dakota patterns in the 19th century. *Historical Archaeology* 25 (4): 17–32.

White, N. M., Sullivan, L. P., and Marrinan, R. A. (eds.). 1999. *Grit-Tempered: Early Women Archaeologists in the Southeastern United States*. Gainesville: University Press of Florida.

Wilkie, L. A. 2003. *The Archaeology of Mothering: An African-American Midwife's Tale*. New York: Routledge.

Wilkie, L., and Hayes, K. H. 2006. Engendered and feminist archaeologies of the recent and documented pasts. *Journal of Archaeological Research* 14 (3): 243–264.

Wright, R. P. 1991. Women's labor and pottery production in prehistory, in J. M. Gero and M. W. Conkey (eds.), *Engendering Archaeology*, pp. 194–223. Oxford: Blackwell.

Wylie, A. 1991. Gender theories and the archaeological record: Why is there no archaeology of gender?, in J. M. Gero and M. W. Conkey (eds.), *Engendering Archaeology. Women and Prehistory*, pp. 31–54. Oxford and Cambridge: Blackwell.

26

CULTURAL IDENTITY AND COLONIAL AND POSTCOLONIAL ARCHAEOLOGIES

Sarah K. Croucher

Cultural identities draw together multiple people within a notion of shared cultural practice and a shared sense of "sameness." Conceiving of identities at this scale has been foundational to the way in which archaeology has conceptualized past societies and related these to identities within the present. These concepts were created within a framework of colonial politics, but the ideas formulated decades ago continue to be pervasive in dividing particular groups from their cultural heritage today. Moving forward, postcolonial theory is providing a framework with which to critique past conceptions of cultural identity, as well as to highlight the importance of archaeological formations of cultural identities to contemporary postcolonial identities. These critiques are vital, given the central importance of cultural identities to our classification of archaeological remains.

Colonial history and postcolonial theory impact the realm of cultural identity at a number of levels, explored throughout this chapter. The notion of "archaeological cultures" as clearly identifiable groups relating to past peoples was first articulated in the late 19th and early 20th centuries. The creation of archaeological cultures during this period was closely related to the colonial politics of the wider sociopolitical context in which archaeologists were working, including the intertwining of racial and cultural identities. This chapter begins by demonstrating how firmly conceptions of culture are embedded within these particular strands of colonial history and discourse. After first introducing the general theme, I explore two divergent strands: postcolonial critiques of constructions of cultures and their place in past colonial systems, and the importance of cultural identities in contemporary archaeological politics. These two areas are linked through recent theoretical debates over archaeological interpretations of cultural identities. In these arguments, fluidity and complexity within and among cultures are emphasized, which helps to demonstrate that the relationships among material symbols, cultural practices, and cultural identities are not fixed. If these critiques are to be utilized in practice, then we must reexamine both archaeology's endeavor to track cultures through time by following material culture patterning, and the reliance on this by governments who require clear demonstrations of "cultural continuity" by Indigenous groups who wish to take charge of their own archaeology. Directions for future practice, discussed at the end of this chapter, focus on how this might be achieved.

Cultural Identities in Archaeology

The idea of cultural identity has two sometimes conflicting uses within archaeology. The first refers to the manner in which people recognize themselves as belonging to some kind of corporate group, sharing values and practices with others within their culture. Attempting to interpret cultural identities in this manner represents an emic perspective. The second way of approaching past cultural identities is through the construct of *archaeological cultures*, founded in the culture-historical theoretical phase of the discipline. For the most part, this approach equates patterning in material remains with bounded groups of homogeneous people. This takes an etic perspective

to such identities, interpreting them through the visible traces of past action instead of seeking to understand the way in which those materials were bound up in practice with past cultural identities. This production of clearly discernible groups is highly problematic, but is nevertheless a pervasive approach within archaeology today (Jones 1997; Shennan 1989).

The conception of archaeological cultures lies embedded within the colonial regimes and classificatory schemes of modernity. Archaeologists drew the idea of cultural identity from the theories of late 19th-century anthropologists. Definitions of "culture" as referring to knowledge, beliefs, and materials such as art were espoused by English ethnologist Edward Tylor in his 1871 work *Primitive Culture* (Trigger 2006: 233). At that time, archaeologists had yet to speak of past cultures, although they had already recognized patterning in past material cultures, which Europeans had carefully ordered chronologically into ages (Lucas 2001: 28–29; Trigger 2006: 233). The German archaeologist Gustaf Kossina, working in the early 20th century, sought to trace an Aryan past through the archaeology of Germany and Eastern Europe and was a key figure in equating archaeological typologies with conceptions of clearly bounded and named ethnic groups—the root of conceptions of archaeological cultures (Shennan 1989: 8; Veit 1989). In his clear aims of using archaeology to serve the political goals of German nationalism and the ideologies of the Nazi party, it is easy to see the way in which sociopolitical contexts and the development of ideas of culture within archaeology are inseparable (Arnold and Hassmann 1995; Veit 1989). Kossina's underlying concept argued cogently for the equation of groupings of material culture with past peoples, assumed to have a clear shared identity. As Kossina traced back cultural sequences through time, rather than seeing these as cultural groupings alone, he instead equated them squarely with racial identities, particularly the "Aryans" (Barkan 1992: 55; Jones 1997: 47; Stepan 1982: 98). While Kossina's racial basis of culture was particularly appalling owing to the fact that it later became a part of the justification for the Jewish Holocaust, he was not alone in equating the idea of bounded identities and race (Jones 1997: 41–43). Many of those working on archaeological remains, particularly burials, during the 19th and early 20th centuries viewed racial and cultural identities as closely related, usually in tandem with deeply prejudiced views with regard to the superiority of particular racial groups (e.g., Hawkes 1942; Putman 1875; Wilson 1865). For these archaeologists, tracing past identities was as much about biological racial identities as it was about cultural materials.

Following World War II, most of the archaeologists who had been influenced by Kossina tried to distance themselves from his political stance and terminology. Such a distancing also resonated with wider debates within the field of anthropology about the relationship between biological race and culture, particularly through the work of the American anthropologist Franz Boas (e.g. 1887; 1912). By the 1920s, the concept of archaeological cultures, owing much to Kossina's work and yet expunged of blatant racial linkage, was fairly widespread in broader archaeological literature (Jones 1997: 16).

Genealogically, we can trace the formative ideas of Kossina into a wider international archaeological discourse through the work of Vere Gordon Childe (1892–1957). The early work of Childe in the 1920s "has come to be regarded as the defining moment in the establishment of the culture historical archaeology in Britain, and the development of the culture concept in the sense of the distinctive ways of life of discrete groups of people" (Jones 1997: 16). As Childe was tied into the colonial experience from his birth as part of a white Australian family (Mulvaney 1994: 56), it is easy to see the projection of British colonial ideas into interpretations of archaeological cultures. Childe argued that past cultural identities, defined through archaeological cultures as "certain types of remains—pots, implements, ornaments, burial rites, house forms —constantly recurring together" were among the most traceable elements of past societies (Childe 1929: v–vi; Jones 1997: 17; Shennan 1989: 5). The culture-historical approach advocated by Childe had its roots in the wider modernist discipline of archaeology as it was then being developed (Thomas 2004: 66), a central component of which was the colonial political matrix.

V. Gordon Childe's scholarship clearly marks the beginning of the culture-historical phase of archaeological research, in which identifying past cultural groupings and their movements through time and space became *the* goal of much archaeological research. This work was, however, dependent on the colonial politics of certain regions. Most European archaeologists focused their efforts first on the European continent, then in an area extending from the Mediterranean to North Africa, and then in an easterly direction through Southeast Asia to India. These were the areas seen as foundational for understanding the past (through patterns of migrating cultures and the diffusion of cultural norms) of their own contemporary European states (Trigger 2006: 256). The demonstration of cultural sequences through this geo-temporal space supported modern European states as being the true heirs to the Mediterranean and to southwestern Asia, providing a historical underpinning to justify colonial interventions in these regions (Trigger 1984: 365). This was also a part of the process of developing colonial frameworks of knowledge about the history of colonized subjects, a fundamental part of the power and control of colonial rule (Asad 1973; Said 1978; Wright 1998: 8). Archaeologists working to establish past cultural identities were therefore a fundamental part of the colonial process of creating Otherness (Gosden 2004: 162). Even within Britain itself, the colonial political matrix influenced how British cultural sequences were interpreted. For example, the supposed acculturation of Iron Age British subjects to Roman cultural norms was seen to be analogous to the proper process of acculturation for Indian subjects under British imperial rule (Jones 1997: 33).

Within the United States, archaeological recognition of past bounded cultural traditions occurred from the late 1920s onward, at a similar point in time to the growth of culture-historical archaeology in Europe (Fowler 2005: 22; Willey and Sabloff 1993: 121). The quite different approach to past cultures taken by American archaeologists, compared with their European counterparts (Trigger 1984: 361), has been attributed to the particular colonial politics of the United States in the early 20th century with regard to Native Americans. Instead of tracing direct cultural continuity through time, the cultural units sought by U.S. archaeologists were geographic taxonomic units rather than historically known ethnic groups (Fowler and Cordell 2005: 8). The term "tradition" often became shorthand for the groupings perceived to be carrying some kind of cultural identity in the North American past, although ideas of past tribes, bound into groups by clear cultural identities, were implicitly behind this terminology (Jones 1997: 21; Lightfoot 2001: 239).

Moving outside of Europe and North America to sub-Saharan African archaeology, it is clear that the interpretation of past cultural identities was similarly entwined within the milieu of European colonial rule and with early struggles for African independence. The large stone-built settlement of Great Zimbabwe provides perhaps the best-known example of this. White settler ideology was confirmed by the first interpretations of the site, attaching the material remains to external cultural influence (Hall 1990: 61). Throughout the first half of the 20th century, debates continued over the cultural origins of the site. While these offered various interpretations, colonial archaeologists were almost all united on the lack of cultural continuity between Great Zimbabwe and contemporary local African communities. This lack of continuity has been argued to have been an implicit aim of the earliest practitioners of African archaeology, largely drawn from the ranks of European colonial settlers and administrators, as they insidiously attempted to "deny their conquered subjects a past" (Robertshaw 1990: 4).

The pattern of attempting to demonstrate a clear cultural discontinuity with the past as a way of divorcing contemporary African populations from their past was also carried out on the East African coast. Here, Islamic stone town sites were argued by archaeologists to be the product of Arab colonizers (LaViolette and Fleisher 2005: 339). As politics changed in the region, however, a backlash against this emerged in the search for clear Indigenous cultural continuity through apparent developmental sequences of architecture and ceramics from the 8th century to the present (e.g., Chami 1998; Chami and Msemwa 1997; Horton 1996). Despite this shift in political positions, culture-historical assumptions that material culture patterning represented the past cultural identities of East African coastal residents remained at the heart of later postcolonial interpretations of the development of East African urbanism.

From the 1960s onward, as postcolonial nations sought to redefine links with their cultural heritage, processual theory began to influence archaeological interpretations.

Within this framework, rather than being equated with cultural differences alone, patterning in material culture could be derived from functional differences within a single group (Jones 1997: 107). Still, the essential characterization of cultural identities remained the same. Even as archaeologists rejected culture classifications as the sole goal of archaeological practice, they continued to attempt to order the "untidiness" of archaeological remains into past bounded groups (Shennan 1989: 11). This has meant that despite processual critiques of culture-historical approaches, until recently the specter of a bounded, monolithic "cultural *cum* ethnic unit" has continued to underlie almost all archaeological interpretations (Jones 1997: 104) and often continues to do so today.

Redefining Cultural Identities: Postcolonial Critiques

Following the questioning of "common sense" interpretations of past cultures by postprocessual critiques beginning in the 1980s, many archaeologists have come to recognize that the cultural identities created by archaeologists are themselves a historical construction (Hill 1998: 162; Shanks and Tilley 1987: 29). Under the influence of works such as Frederick Barth's (1969) *Ethnic Groups and Boundaries*, archaeologists began to place a clear theoretical emphasis on the subjective aspects of group identity (Jones 1997: 60). Included within this general move was the incorporation of new ethnoarchaeological studies which clearly demonstrated that stylistic elements of material-culture patterning do not dovetail in a straightforward one-to-one correlation with cultural identities. Ian Hodder's (1982) *Symbols in Action* was a key study in examining this relationship, although many authors have engaged in sustained debates as to the precise relationship between the style of material culture and identity (e.g. Sackett 1985; Weissner 1985).

In such research, archaeologies of colonial periods have been at the forefront of critiquing the way in which material culture is often directly correlated to conceptions of static cultural identities. Research into past colonial periods formerly also relied on such ideas, through the theory of "acculturation." This had its roots in the colonialism and anti-immigrant fervor of early 20th-century America, where Anglo-American culture was assumed to be dominant to any other cultural form (Cusick 1998: 127). Acculturation models argued that in colonial situations, distinct bounded "donor"' cultures forced their material ideas onto a "recipient" culture (Silliman 2005: 65). Within such a model, the new material culture is accepted by the recipient culture, and through this process the recipient culture becomes increasingly like the donor culture (Cusick 1998: 128). As with the culture-historical approach outlined above, no steps were taken toward actually interpreting the way in which material culture was itself meaningful as a marker of identity for those who used it (Loren 2005: 312; Stahl 2002).

Critiques of this model have drawn on several historical theoretical models. One of these is the theory of creolization. This has its roots in linguistics and proposes that as new artifacts available in colonial regimes are adopted by colonized cultures, they are incorporated into underlying cultural grammars. While new forms of material culture may be adopted, behind this material veneer the original cultural identity of colonized groups can remain the same (Ferguson 1992). This approach has been widely used, particularly to examine the archaeology of plantation sites and enslaved Africans (e.g., Ferguson 1992; Wilkie 2000), as well as other North American colonial situations (e.g., Ewen 2000; Groover 2000), and it has even been applied to changing patterns of material culture within the Roman Empire (e.g., Webster 2001). Creolization is one way of accounting for the fact that within colonial situations, adopting new forms of material culture did not necessarily equate to a change in cultural identity. Such an approach has, however, also been critiqued as shorthand for acculturation models (Cusick 1998: 47), since the idea of cultural identity as a static entity often remains unchallenged within a creolization model.

A further direction in understanding the ways in which past cultural identities were created in colonial contexts has come from highlighting the power relations that structured cultural change in these situations. In many colonial situations, different groups of people with distinct cultural identities who came into contact with one another had their engagements structured by violent and unequal power relations. Archaeologists must therefore examine the ways in which these complex relationships intersected with changes in material-culture use and, in turn, how this related to changing cultural identities (Silliman 2005: 63). The formation of new African-American cultural identities within enslaved communities has been one key area in which archaeologists have successfully examined the importance of power, domination, and resistance to cultural identity (e.g., Epperson 2001; Howson 1990; Singleton 1995: 130).

Despite a growing understanding of the relationships between material culture and identity, the problem remains that etic historical categorizations of cultural identity still lie behind the majority of interpretations. These may be quite different from how the groups in question interpret their lived experience (Deagan 1997: 7). This problem plagues most attempts to understand archaeological cultures, since categorizing material culture in relation to past identities usually results in merely reducing it to a simple sign within an archaeological classificatory system (Thomas 2004: 23). One way archaeologists have attempted to move beyond this problem is through the utilization of Pierre Bourdieu's (1977) theory of practice. The creation of meaningful identities in reality is tied to specific historical conditions. Communities conceptualize identities through a process of objectifying cultural practices in the recognition and signification of difference between one group and another (Jones 1997, 1999; see also contributions to Barth 1969). In doing so, they draw upon preexisting social knowledge but only as it intersects with the historical conditions of the given moment in which a conception of a clear shared group identity exists. In any practice of cultural identification, then, the cultural realities drawn upon are thus "highly variable and contingent upon the cultural transformations engendered by the nature of identification and power relations between groups of people" (Jones 1997: 128).

Within such a theoretical framework of reference, it has become possible to interpret the relationships between material culture and cultural identities in new and exciting ways. Archaeological studies of colonial periods are at the forefront of this. For example, in a study of Native American artifacts from Rancho Petaluma, California, under a period of Spanish colonial rule, interpretations of either acculturation or traditionalism were seen to be "insufficient for handling the complex engagements of indigenous people with colonialism" (Silliman 2004: 152). Instead, Silliman (2004: 152) places emphasis on how material culture in both "traditional" and "introduced" forms was a product of active choices of Native Americans at the Rancho, situated as they were within a complex colonial scene. Use of newly introduced forms of material culture did not necessarily equate to a loss of Native American cultural identity. But the continued use of traditional lithic artifacts within this new colonial situation would have had new signification in relation to cultural identity, as it would indicate an active choice rather than an unquestioned daily practice (Silliman 2001).

As practice theory becomes further embedded within interpretations of cultural change in colonial periods (alongside the inclusion of the differential power relations among the cultural groups in question), new directions for interpreting past identities become increasingly open. Other examples that place material culture in an active role in the practice of producing past cultural identities include work on Mexicano America (Clark 2005), East Africa (Croucher and Wynne-Jones 2006), and Australia (Harrison 2002; 2003). Such theoretical applications require a careful contextual analysis of the archaeological materials in question, taking on a diachronic perspective which in turn accommodates the subtleties and importance of any continuities or changes in material-culture patterns and use as related to past cultural identities (Jones 1997: 132).

Relating Past Cultural Identities to the Present

The interpretation of cultural identities by archaeologists is a key area of praxis within postcolonial archaeologies. In many areas of the world, archaeological cultures have come to stand in for ethnic identities. Through this process, archaeological cultures have come to have a political role as "legitimators of the claims of modern groups to territory and influence" (Shennan 1989: 6). Archaeological constructions of past cultures are therefore very important for potentially legitimizing or disproving claims of the continuity of cultural identities (Jones 1997: 10; Ucko 1989). In the contemporary world, archaeology has a key role to play in negotiating for the recognition of particular cultural identities, since a sense of historicity is generally required for any claim to "authentic" cultural heritage and identity (Sahlins 1998: 401). This recognition is not just a part of academic discourse but is crucial to the way in which Indigenous groups gain power in heritage debates today. Demonstrations of cultural "continuity" through archaeology have been particularly important to the successful repatriation of human and/or cultural remains (T. J. Ferguson 1996; Watkins 2003) and for land claims cases, especially where Indigenous groups are no longer currently living on important cultural landscapes (Weiner 1999).

This highlights the fact that tracing cultural identities in the past involves far more than neutral scientific investigation, for even naming cultures and providing a terminology with which to describe them goes beyond simple semantics (Silliman 2005: 57). Within postcolonial frameworks, Indigenous groups are attempting to redefine power relationships, as in the debates over the nomenclature of the Ancient Pueblo/Anasazi archaeological culture in the American Southwest. The roots of the naming of this culture lie in the so-called Pecos classification, developed by non-Indigenous North American archaeologists in the 1920s, which became fixed terminology by the 1940s (Preucel 2005: 178; Willey and Sabloff 1993: 122). This classification is still in use today in regard to architecture and pottery, and it remains a useful and convenient device with which to organize archaeological data, despite the fact that it stands divorced from the realities of past social units (Cordell 1997: 23).

In recent years, Indigenous groups in the southwestern United States have called for a change in terminology, arguing for renaming the "Anasazi" cultural group as "Ancestral Pueblo" in order to reconnect past and present for contemporary Hopi and Pueblo groups in New Mexico. Sites representing part of the cultural knowledge of these groups' past migrations are archaeologically known as "Anasazi," including Chaco Canyon and Mesa Verde. Renaming the cultural association of these sites to "Ancestral Pueblo" strengthens the argument that the cultures related to these sites have not died, disappeared, or vanished (Bolstetter 2007; Weixelman 2004). The word "Anasazi" in Navajo means "ancient enemy," thereby denoting hostility between Navajo and the Ancestral Pueblo. As some Navajo clans trace their ancestry back to so-called Anasazi communities (such as Chaco Canyon), archaeology and ethnohistory suggest a close relationship, rather than hostility, between the two. Past hostility is no longer presumed when "Ancestral Pueblo" is the cultural label adopted for these sites (Bolstetter 2007). Contemporary Native Americans also point to the disjuncture between their own ideas about the cultural identities of their ancestors and archaeological conceptions of Anasazi identity. Modern groups are adamant, for instance, in pointing out that their ancestors did not speak "Anasazi" as a language, further distancing the use of this word from any past social reality (Fowler and Cordell 2005: 8).

Yet this remains a matter of dispute within archaeological spheres. One recent book, entitled *Anasazi America* (Stuart 2000), begins with a statement of why the term "Anasazi" was chosen rather than "Ancestral Pueblo." While the author acknowledges there are political dimensions to this nomenclature that relate to the identity politics of the present, he argues that his choice was motivated by the fact that library catalogs and Internet databases all over the world continue to use the word "Anasazi" (Stuart 2000: 9). The names of cultural units play a powerful pedagogical role, as they are taught to students and to the public as pre-established facts resulting from archaeological interpretations. It seems worrisome, therefore, that the discipline as a whole might argue that the existing taxonomies of identity are fixed forever, due to their presence within catalogs and indexes. While this example of nomenclature is a powerful one, there are other ways in which archaeology acts to divorce past cultural identities from identities claimed by oppressed Indigenous groups in the present. Examples of archaeology's role in this process abound, including incidents in Chile (Jofré 2007) and Guatemala (Frühsorge 2007; Pyburn 2006; Ren 2006), along with numerous instances on the African continent (Andah 1995; Holl 1995; Reid 2005). These examples show the ongoing pervasiveness of separating named past cultural groups from local Indigenous groups in the present, and the effect this has in disempowering them from important historical aspects of their own cultural identity.

Future Directions

Archaeologists working to interpret the complexities of cultural identities during colonial periods seem set to remain at center stage in deepening our theoretical understandings of the relationship between material culture and identities. However, despite the strength of these critiques at present, the older definitions of culture, outlined in the first section of this chapter, have moved into public and popular discourse (Wright 1998: 8). In this realm, the mere categorization of archaeological remains is seen to confirm past "authentic" cultures. The examples cited above show the importance of taking a more critical approach to understanding past cultural identities and interpreting these along lines that consider the power of archaeological narratives in the present. We are faced with a challenge in this sphere: how to transmit complex ideas out of our discipline, and how to move away from academic practice that justifies the taxonomy of library catalogs, past reports, and museum interpretations over the wishes of contemporary Indigenous groups.

If archaeology is to recognize its ethical commitments in the present, including the way in which these participate in the formation of contemporary identities (Thomas 2004: 238), then this is a challenge that must be met. I am optimistic that the next 10 years will see a move away from conceptions of cultural identities in the past that rest upon the colonial theoretical foundations of early 20th-century culture history. As this takes place, I hope that it may also be possible to rapidly communicate changing perspectives on archaeological cultures beyond the archaeological community, allowing for engagements between past and present cultures that rely on more than just a trail of what seems to be unchanging material culture.

Acknowledgments

My thanks to Brianne Bolstetter, Joe Watkins, Kehaulani Kauanui, and Doug Charles, who all provided me with ideas and information with regard to the Anasazi/Ancestral Pueblo case study. Emma Poulter kindly read and provided comments on an earlier draft of this paper. Many thanks also to the editors for inviting me to write this piece.

References

Andah, B. W. 1995. Studying African societies in cultural context, in P. R. Schmidt and T. C. Patterson (eds.), *Making Alternative Histories: The Practice of Archaeology in Non-Western Settings*, pp. 149–182. Santa Fe: SAR Press.

Arnold, B., and Hassmann, H. 1995. Archaeology in Nazi Germany: The legacy of the Faustian bargain, in P. L. Kohl and C. Fawcett, *Nationalism, Politics, and the Practice of Archaeology*, pp. 70–81. Cambridge: Cambridge University Press.

Asad, T. (ed.). 1973. *Anthropology and the Colonial Encounter*. New York: Humanities Press.

Barkan, E. 1992. *The Retreat of Scientific Racism: Changing Concepts of Race in Britain and the United States between the World Wars*. Cambridge: Cambridge University Press.

Barth, F. (ed.). 1969. *Ethnic Groups and Boundaries: The Social Organization of Culture Difference*. Boston: Little, Brown.

Boas, F. 1887. Museums of ethnography and their classification. *Science* (9) 228: 587–589.

——. 1912. Changes in the bodily form of descendants of immigrants. *American Anthropologist* 14 (3): 530–562.

Bolstetter, B. 2007. Personal communication via email, 29 August 2007.

Bourdieu, P. 1977. *Outline of a Theory of Practice*. Cambridge Studies in Social and Cultural Anthropology. Cambridge: Cambridge University Press.

Chami, F. 1998. A review of Swahili archaeology. *African Archaeological Review* 15 (3): 199–218.

Chami, F., and Msemwa, P. 1997. A new look at culture and trade on the Azania coast. *Current Anthropology* 38 (4): 637–677.

Childe, V. G. 1929. *The Danube in Prehistory*. Oxford: Clarendon.

Clark, B. J. 2005. Lived ethnicity: Archaeology and identity in *Mexicano* America. *World Archaeology* 37 (3): 440–52.

Cordell, L. S. 1997. *Archaeology of the Southwest*. 2nd ed. San Diego: Academic Press.

Croucher, S. K., and Wynne-Jones, S. 2006. People, not pots: Locally produced ceramics and identity on the 19th century East African coast. *International Journal of African Historical Studies* 39 (1): 107–124.

Cusick, J. G. 1998. Historiography of acculturation: An evaluation of concepts and their application in archaeology, in J. G. Cusick (ed.), *Studies in Culture Contact: Interaction, Culture Change, and Archaeology*, pp. 126–145. Occasional Paper No. 25. Carbondale: Southern Illinois University, Center for Archaeological Investigations.

Deagan, K. 1997. Cross-disciplinary themes in the recovery of the Colonial Middle Period. *Historical Archaeology* 31 (1): 4–8.

Epperson, T. W. 2001. Constructing difference: The social and spatial order of the Chesapeake Plantation, in T. A. Singleton (ed.), *"I, Too, Am America": Archaeological Studies of African-American Life*, pp. 159–173. Charlottesville: University Press of Virginia.

Ferguson, L. G. 1992. *Uncommon Ground: Archaeology and Early African America*. Washington, DC: Smithsonian Institution Press.

Ferguson, T. J. 1996. Native Americans and the practice of archaeology. *Annual Review of Anthropology* 25: 63–79.

Fowler, D. D. 2005. The formative years: Southwest archaeology, 1890–1910, in L. S. Cordell and D. D. Fowler (eds.), *Southwest Archaeology in the Twentieth Century*, pp. 16–26. Salt Lake City: University of Utah Press.

Fowler, D. D., and Cordell, L. S. 2005. Introduction, in L. S. Cordell and D. D. Fowler (eds.), *Southwest Archaeology in the Twentieth Century*, pp. 1–15. Salt Lake City: University of Utah Press.

Frühsorge, L. 2007. Archaeological heritage in Guatemala: Indigenous perspectives on the ruins of Iximché. *Archaeologies* 3 (1): 39–58.

Gosden, C. 2004. *Archaeology and Colonialism: Cultural Contact from 5000 BC to the Present*. Cambridge: Cambridge University Press.

Groover, M. D. 2000. Creolization and the archaeology of multiethnic households in the American South. *Historical Archaeology* 34 (3): 99–106.

Hall, M. 1990. "Hidden history": Iron Age archaeology in southern Africa, in P. Robertshaw (ed.), *A History of African Archaeology*, pp. 59–77. London and Portsmouth (NH): James Currey and Heinemann.

Harrison, R. 2002. Archaeology and the Colonial encounter: Kimberley spear points, cultural identity and masculinity in the north of Australia. *Journal of Social Archaeology* 2 (3): 352–377.

——. 2003. "The magical virtue of these sharp things": Colonialism, mimesis and knapped bottle glass artefacts in Australia. *Journal of Material Culture* 8 (3): 311–336.

Hawkes, C. F. C. 1942. Race, prehistory, and European civilization. *Man* 42: 125–130.

Hill, J. D. 1998. Violent encounters: Ethnogenesis and ethnocide in long-term contact situations, in J. G. Cusick (ed.), *Studies in Culture Contact: Interaction, Culture Change, and Archaeology*, pp. 146–171. Occasional Paper No. 25. Carbondale: Southern Illinois University, Center for Archaeological Investigations.

Hodder, I. 1982. *Symbols in Action: Ethnoarchaeological Studies of Material Culture*. Cambridge: Cambridge University Press.

Holl, A. F. 1995. African history: Past, present, and future: The unending quest for alternatives, in P. R. Schmidt and T. C. Patterson (eds.), *Making Alternative Histories: The Practice of Archaeology in Non-Western Settings*, pp. 183–212. Santa Fe: SAR Press.

Horton, M. 1996. *Shanga: The Archaeology of a Muslim Trading Community on the Coast of East Africa*. London: British Institute in Eastern Africa.

Howson, J. E. 1990. Social relations and material culture: A critique of the archaeology of plantation slavery. *Historical Archaeology* 24 (4): 78–91.

Jofré, D. 2007. Reconstructing the politics of Indigenous identity in Chile. *Archaeologies* 3 (1): 16–38.

Jones, S. 1997. *The Archaeology of Ethnicity: Constructing Identities in the Past and Present*. London: Routledge.

——. 1999. Historical categories and the praxis of identity: The interpretation of ethnicity in historical archaeology, in P. P. Funari, M. Hall, and S. Jones (eds.), *Historical Archaeology: Back from the Edge*, pp. 219–32. London: Routledge.

LaViolette, A., and Fleisher, J. 2005. The archaeology of sub-Saharan urbanism: Cities and their countrysides, in A. Bower Stahl (ed.), *African Archaeology*, pp. 327–352. Malden, MA: Blackwell.

Lightfoot, K. G. 2001. Traditions as cultural production: Implications for contemporary archaeological research, in T. R. Pauketat (ed.), *The Archaeology of Traditions: Agency and History before and after Columbus*, pp. 237–252. Gainesville: University Press of Florida.

Loren, D. D. 2005. Creolization in the French and Spanish colonies, in T. R. Pauketat and D. D. Loren (eds.), *North American Archaeology*, pp. 297–318. Oxford and Malden, MA: Blackwell.

Lucas, G. 2001. *Critical Approaches to Fieldwork: Contemporary and Historical Archaeological Practice*. New York: Routledge.

Mulvaney, D. J. 1994. "Another university man gone wrong": V. Gordon Childe 1892–1922, in D. R. Harris (ed.), *The Archaeology of V. Gordon Childe*, pp. 55–74. Chicago: University of Chicago Press.

Preucel, R. W. 2005. Ethnicity and southwestern archaeology, in L. S. Cordell and D. D. Fowler (eds.), *Southwest Archaeology in the Twentieth Century*, pp. 174–193. Salt Lake City: University of Utah Press.

Putman, F. W. 1875. Archaeological explorations in Indiana and Kentucky. *The American Naturalist* 9 (7): 410–415.

Pyburn, K. A. 2006. The politics of collapse. *Archaeologies* 2 (1): 3–7.

Reid, A. 2005. Interaction, marginalization, and the archaeology of the Kalahari, in A. Bower Stahl (ed.), *African Archaeology*, pp. 353–377. Malden, MA: Blackwell.

Ren, A. C. 2006. Maya archaeology and the political and cultural identity of contemporary Maya in Guatemala. *Archaeologies* 2 (1): 8–19.

Robertshaw, P. 1990. The development of archaeology in East Africa, in P. Robertshaw (ed.), *A History of African Archaeology*, pp. 78–94. London and Portsmouth (NH): James Currey and Heinemann.

Sackett, J. R. 1985. Style and ethnicity in the Kalahari: A reply to Weissner. *American Antiquity* 50 (1): 154–159.

Sahlins, M. 1999. Two or three things that I know about culture. *Journal of the Royal Anthropological Institute* (New Series) 5 (3): 399–421.

Said, E. W. 1978. *Orientalism: Western Conceptions of the Orient*. London: Penguin.

Shanks, M., and Tilley, C. 1987. *Social Theory and Archaeology*. Albuquerque: University of New Mexico Press.

Shennan, S. J. 1989. Introduction: Archaeological approaches to cultural identity, in S. J. Shennan (ed.), *Archaeological Approaches to Cultural Identity*, pp. 1–32. London: Unwin Hyman.

Silliman, S. W. 2001. Agency, practical politics and the archaeology of culture contact. *Journal of Social Archaeology* 1 (2): 190–209.

——. 2004. *Lost Laborers in Colonial California: Native Americans and the Archaeology of Rancho Petaluma*. Tucson: University of Arizona Press.

——. 2005. Culture contact or colonialism? Challenges in the archaeology of Native North America. *American Antiquity* 70 (1): 55–74.

Singleton, T. A. 1995. The archaeology of slavery in North America. *Annual Review of Anthropology* 24: 119–140.

Stahl, A. Bower 2002. Colonial entanglements and the practices of taste: An alternative to logocentric approaches. *American Anthropologist* 104 (3): 827–845.

Stepan, N. 1982. *The Idea of Race in Science: Great Britain 1800–1960*. Hamden, CT: Archon Books.

Stuart, D. E. 2000. *Anasazi America*. Albuquerque: University of New Mexico Press.

Thomas, J. 2004. *Archaeology and Modernity*. London and New York: Routledge.

Trigger, B. G. 1984. Alternative archaeologies: Nationalist, colonialist, imperialist. *Man* (New Series) 19 (3): 355–370.

———. 2006. *A History of Archaeological Thought*. 2nd ed. Cambridge: Cambridge University Press.

Ucko, R. 1989. Foreword, in S. Sherman (ed), *Archaeological Approaches to Cultural Identity*, pp. ix–xx. London: Unwin Hyman.

Veit, U. 1989. Ethnic concepts in German prehistory: A case study on the relationship between cultural identity and archaeological objectivity, in S. J. Shennan (ed.), *Archaeological Approaches to Cultural Identity*, pp. 33–56. London: Unwin Hyman.

Watkins, J. E. 2003. Beyond the margin: American Indians, First Nations and archaeology in North America. *American Antiquity* 68 (2): 273–285.

Webster, J. 2001. Creolizing the Roman provinces. *American Journal of Archaeology* 105 (2): 209–225.

Weiner, J. F. 1999. Culture in a sealed envelope: The concealment of Aboriginal heritage and tradition in the Hindmarsh Island Bridge affair. *The Journal of the Royal Anthropological Institute* 5 (2): 193–210.

Weissner, P. 1985. Style or isochrestic variation? A reply to Sackett. *American Antiquity* 50 (1): 160–166.

Weixelman, J. O. 2004. *Hidden Heritage: Pueblo Indians, National Parks, and the Myth of the "Vanishing Anasazi."* Ph.D. dissertation, University of New Mexico.

Wilkie, L. A. 2000. Culture bought: Evidence of creolization in the consumer goods of an enslaved Bahamian family. *Historical Archaeology* 34 (4): 10–26.

Willey, G. R., and Sabloff, J. A. 1993. *A History of American Archaeology*. 3rd ed. New York: W. H. Freeman and Company.

Wilson, D. 1865. Inquiry into the physical characteristics of the ancient and modern Celt of Gaul and Britain. *Anthropological Review* 3 (8): 52–84.

Wright, S. 1998. The politicization of "culture." *Anthropology Today* 14 (1): 7–15.

27

CLASS IDENTITY AND POSTCOLONIALISM

Gavin Lucas

The concept of class is a highly complex and contested notion used in various ways by different authors (e.g., Wright 2004; Wurst and Fitts 1999). However, there are perhaps two critical dimensions to consider. The first is the distinction between class as a question of ideology (i.e., class consciousness) and class as an economic division within society (i.e., inequalities in material standards of living). The second is the distinction between a gradational characterization of class versus a relational one—that is, between class as an empirical, economic division based on a simple hierarchy or ranking (usually after income), on the one hand, and as a relational term between a person or group and the social organization of material resources, on the other (Wright 2004). Of the latter, the two most influential and important approaches are those of Weber and Marx. For Weber, this relationship is defined in terms of the opportunities (or life chances) that inherited resources give to a person or group. It is very much a relational concept of class focused on consumption. For Marx, class identity is based primarily on the relationship to the means of production. The latter essentially divides classes into two antagonistic types: those who own the means of production (bourgeoisie/capitalists) and those who do not (labor/proletariat).

One of the more particular points regarding class in the context of archaeology is whether it is applicable to non-capitalist societies—an issue of some relevance in discussions of postcolonialism, as we shall see below. This question has largely been discussed from the Marxist perspective and, for many, is a basic given insofar as class is defined in a general way to denote groups with contradictory interests forged through a particular mode of production. Engels, in his classic *The Origin of the Family, Private*

Property and the State (1954 [1891]), argued that the concept of class can be applied to feudalism and slavery, and indeed can even be extended to the distinction of the sexes. In recent times, French Marxist anthropologists have been the most vocal in exploring this theme, especially P. P. Rey, who affirmed the applicability of the class concept to all societies and argued that history was fundamentally a history of class struggle (Rey 1975; 1977; also see Terray 1975). In general, the idea of class analysis, even if the term "class" is not always used, has been taken up by many Marxist anthropologists (e.g., Wolf 1987) and archaeologists (Gilman 1984; Saitta 1988). Others, however, prefer to confine the concept of class to capitalist or at least stratified or state societies and, even though inequality and conflicting interests can be identified in nonstratified societies, argue that "class" is not the appropriate term to define such interest groups (e.g., Godelier 1986; McGuire 2002: 180–187). Similar arguments occur when we examine the concept of class in relation to postcolonialism.

Marxist Foundations:
Class, Colonialism, and Imperialism

The Weberian and Marxist concepts of class were both articulated in the context of European capitalist societies, but how does one envisage class in relation to postcolonialism? To answer this question, it is important to review the key concepts and ideas that link capitalism to colonialism, an endeavor that has, for the main, been conducted within Marxist circles. European colonialism, like capitalism, is generally perceived to have its origins in the 16th century as a movement toward expanding trade and increasing wealth. Colonies were primarily about extending, consolidating, or protecting the trade networks of European nation-states and not necessarily about political expansion. This only happened under the rise of imperialism in the later 19th century, which was an explicit attempt to extend the boundaries of the nation-state. Thus, Lenin regarded imperialism as the inevitable next step after the establishment of industrial capitalism within the nation-state in the late 18th and early 19th centuries; in order to continue its inexorable expansion and accumulation, capital had to become global (Lenin 1987; Luxembourg 2003). By incorporating older colonies or annexing new ones more directly into the capitalist system, capitalist forms of social and economic organization were also exported globally: class (in the capitalist sense) became a global rather than a European phenomenon.

This is not to say that capitalism did not have a global aspect prior to late 19th-century imperialism. As argued by dependency theorists such as Andre Gunder Frank or, more famously, world systems theorists such as Immanuel Wallerstein, European mercantile expansion since the 16th century led to a world system divided into core and periphery countries marked by unequal exchange and unequal control of resources and wealth (Wallerstein 2004). However, even though the emergence of a world system and colonialism may have been linked to capitalism, this was primarily mercantile rather than industrial (or, as some would maintain, "true" capitalism). Only with the emergence of industrial capitalism in Britain and then continental Europe in the late 18th and early 19th centuries did new social classes emerge based on new sets of relations to the means of production: the bourgeoisie who owned the means of production or capital, and the proletariat who sold their labor to the capitalists. Under late 19th-century imperialism, these new relations were transported to the colonies, replacing existing forms of relations, particularly slavery. The Leninist theory of Imperialism has recently been developed by Italian Marxist Antonio Negri, who, with Michael Hardt, has argued for a third stage after Imperialism, called Empire. Empire represents the limits of Imperialism, where capitalism has expanded to its fullest and can expand no more. Characteristic of Empire is the dispersed and decentered location of capital (allied to no particular place or nation-state) and a concomitant and equally dispersed or decentered model for resistance, which they call the Multitude (Hardt and Negri 2000).

Class Identity and Slavery in Historical Archaeology

Archaeologies of capitalism vary in their approaches, although most appear to share the longer-term view of capitalism as emerging around the 16th century in Europe (e.g., Johnson 1996; Leone and Potter 1999). However, positions vary on whether the concept of class can be extended outside the more conventional realm of capital and wage labor. For example, James Delle's study of early 19th-century coffee plantations in Jamaica is quite clear in applying the terminology of class to slavery, distinguishing between a planter class and an enslaved class (Delle 1999). A more constrained approach is taken by Christopher Matthews in his analysis of class formation in the Chesapeake (Matthews 2001). He appears to confine the concept of class to the free white population and argues that slavery, and especially the ideology of slavery, was used to mask class inequalities among the white population by making the issue of freedom the only relevant one (Matthews 2001: 75–76).

This question of slavery/freedom, however, was importantly overlain by an ideology of race, which was materialized through the color of one's skin. On the surface, therefore, it appears as if race and freedom were the principal dimensions of identity, yet in fact they also acted to mask class inequalities among the white/free population. However, Matthews is not necessarily asserting that class is therefore deeper and more primary than race, only that inequality in one sphere was used to conceal inequality in another. A final example is Paul Shackel and David Larsen's study of the position of African Americans within the newly emerging industrial wage labor nexus in Harpers Ferry (Shackel and Larsen 2000). This study resonates with Matthews's in exposing the significance attached to an ideology of freedom and equality among whites; in pre-emancipation times, enslaved African Americans were employed alongside free white laborers, even sharing housing. Upon emancipation, however, African Americans were excluded and marginalized from the wage labor system because of their prior identification as slaves —wage labor had to be seen as the free man's choice.

What seems to tie all these approaches together is an emphasis on the economic realities of exploitation, usually with ideology serving to mask this exploitation. Sometimes this exploitation is explicitly articulated in terms of class identity, but just as often it is not; indeed terms such as "elites" serve to cover the ambiguity of the application of the class concept. Class therefore remains a somewhat under-theorized term within those archaeologies of capitalism that focus on the pre-industrial/pre-wage labor system in colonial or postcolonial contexts. Unwittingly, this actually decenters class from a study of capitalism and is perhaps an inevitable consequence of taking a longer-term perspective on capitalism.

Decentering Class: Post-Marxism and Postcolonialism

Postcolonialism represents something of a quandary for the Marxist concept of class (or indeed Marxism as a whole). This is because it questions the primacy of class as the key concept in articulating social relationships. The situation is by no means straightforward, however. While many black activists challenged the race-blindness of Marxist class theory, some of the early postcolonial writers had close links to Marxism. The Trinidadian scholars C. L. R. James and Eric Williams both wrote about slavery largely from the perspective of capitalism, subsuming issues of race and racism under those of class and economic exploitation (e.g., Williams 1944). More ambiguously, Franz Fanon, perhaps one of the key figures in the early phases of postcolonialism and influenced by the Negritude Movement, nonetheless partly linked colonial consciousness to social and economic oppression rather than race (Fanon 1967). Many Marxist scholars continue to argue for class as the privileged term to explain racial ideologies and conflict (Balibar and Wallerstein 1991; Callinicos 1993; Cox 1972; Geshwender and Levine 1994; Wolf 1982; also see Mullins, this volume, chapter 28); within postcolonialist discourse, Aijaz Ahmad has been a vociferous proponent of this view (Ahmad 1992).

However, the more popular and widely accepted position within academic circles today is to accept that class is just one subject position among many—particularly gender and race. Ironically, it was the work of a leading Marxist theorist, Antonio Gramsci, and in particular two of his critical concepts—the subaltern and hegemony —that inspired much of the literature used to decenter class. "Subaltern" is used in postcolonial theory to refer to any marginalized group, specifically one with diminished or constrained agency in certain spheres. Unlike the concept of working class or proletariat, it focuses on issues of political and ideological power, rather than economic relations. It came to prominence through the Subaltern Studies Group, a collection of South Asian scholars whose most famous exponent is undoubtedly Gayatri Spivak (e.g., see Spivak 1999). "Hegemony" is another Gramscian concept, which refers to the dominance of one social group over another, specifically through ideology rather than brute force. It was taken up by post-Marxist scholars Chantal Mouffe and Ernesto Laclau in their highly influential book *Hegemony and Socialist Strategy*, in which they replace a class-based notion of struggle with the concept of social antagonism or agonistic pluralism, arguing that political struggles cannot be privileged to one site (e.g., class) but rather are dispersed according to different subject positions (Laclau and Mouffe 1985). For many scholars today, it is the intersection of these different subject positions—especially race, class, and gender—which constitute the most interesting issues, not a singular focus on one.

The Intersection of Class and Race in Historical Archaeology

In 2000, Laurie Wilkie and Kevin Bartoy launched a broadside at archaeologies of capitalism, particularly the Critical Archaeology of Mark Leone and the "Annapolis School" (Wilkie and Bartoy 2000). Their criticism was largely focused on what they perceived to be a lack of concern with the individual and agency in such studies of capitalism; but in the process, they raised two important issues relevant to this chapter. The first was whether capitalism could really be extended to cover forms of exploitation outside of the normal wage labor situation, singling out for criticism Delle's extension of capitalism as a mode of production to slavery. The second was to question the primacy of class as a dimension of social identity within capitalism, arguing that other exploitative relations are equally significant, such as gender, sexuality, or race (Wilkie and Bartoy 2000: 754). These criticisms, and others raised in their paper, may have been partially misrepresentative, as the responses that followed the paper testify. Nonetheless, in pointing out the heterogeneous nature of capitalism (especially if taking the long-term approach), they also, perhaps unintentionally, destabilized it. Wilkie and Bartoy emphasized class identity in an ideological sense—that is, as something constructed by people and something of which people are conscious. This does not mean it has no economic reality (e.g., in terms of wealth difference), but rather that, because it is something actively constructed, it allows more complex intersections of identity to be examined, such as race and class, without having to privilege one over the other.

Paul Mullins, in a study of African Americans in 19th-century Annapolis, explicitly makes consumption the focus for exploring the construction of class identity (Mullins 1999a, 1999b; also this volume, chapter 28). Although he is still aware of the important role of production, Mullins argues that class identity, as articulated through consumption, was largely structured by race. Mirroring the arguments by Matthews and Shackel, Mullins suggests that equality and classlessness were ideologies promoted within the spheres of consumption and the labor market. Mass marketing that targeted white or European sectors of the population drew explicitly on racial difference as a way of promoting the idea of a material consumption accessible to all (whites). Yet emancipated African Americans subverted this marketing by participating in the new consumer culture through, for example, favoring the purchase of national brand goods over local products. In doing so, they also asserted their equality and destabilized the ideological basis of a classless consumer society.

Lucas presents a similar example in his study of an ex-slave mission community in South Africa (Lucas 2004). He argued that in the transition from slave labor to wage labor, working conditions and relations barely changed after emancipation, with former slaves generally working on the same farms and for the same masters as before, often with little change in working conditions and rights. Despite this continuity, many ex-slaves sought to articulate their freedom as wage laborers in the sphere of consumption, through their new lives on the mission station. While the directors of the mission station sought to maintain a distinction through a racial ideology of subtle segregation about who lived where on the station, governmental policy explicitly adopted a race-based classification to divide the population, often seen as the precursor to the apartheid system. In reaction, the community sought to define themselves in terms of class, specifically through notions of respectability and economic status expressed in the homes they built and the goods they acquired. Their aspiration was to achieve political autonomy and enfranchisement, which was defined in economic terms of property value.

In many ways, their actions exposed the ambiguity of the colonial system, which used and conflated racial and class divisions to separate the population. This very ambiguity, however, ultimately operated in the favor of those in power insofar as it helped to disperse the possibility of any combined resistance, even while it multiplied the sites of inequality. Within South African historical archaeology, for example, Martin Hall has pioneered postcolonial theory, especially through his adoption of the concept of the subaltern, which he uses to great effect in unraveling the contradictions between documentary and archaeological sources to explore marginalized groups (Hall 1999, 2000).

Class Identity: Foundation of Inequality?

The decentering of class can be seen as part of the larger influence of postmodernism on social theory and its concern to deconstruct any fixed or privileged claims to authority. More specifically, the whole Marxist program has been severely criticized through the lens of postcolonialism by Robert Young, whose book *White Mythologies* challenges the Marxist version of history as Eurocentric (Young 1990). Nonetheless, the problem faced in postcolonial discourse (and indeed within postmodernism in general) is that without a master narrative or privileged point from which to claim authority, resistance to dominant ideologies becomes almost impossible. Indeed, a dominant ideology may thrive on the very fragmentation and disunity of such counter discourses, which cannot assemble a coherent opposition. One strategy is to argue for a "logic of equivalence" between the counter discourses in the manner of Laclau and Mouffe; another is to posit a strategic essentialism à la Spivak, where a privileged point is adopted but recognized as a pragmatic move rather than an absolute position (Moore-Gilbert 1997: 198–199). What distinguishes these approaches from mainstream Marxism, therefore, is that social conflict or inequality is primarily perceived as a dispersed phenomenon as opposed to being anchored in a set of fundamental economic relations expressed through class. None of this is to deny the economic dimension to inequality, only to remove its foundational status.

There is no doubt that the postcolonial critique that decenters class holds a strong position; however, class identity seen in Marxist terms occupies a somewhat different status and carries with it the burden of an explanatory role for a broad range of other inequalities that might be manifested through racial, ethnic, and national divisions. The difference is not simply about an opposition between ideology and economy, but rather the privileging of one term over the other. Mainstream Marxists well recognize the important role of ideology, while many postcolonial critics no doubt appreciate the significance of economic context. However, when it comes to defining class identity, there seems little doubt that scholars tend to defer to one of these terms as the primary one. Perhaps in many ways, this is simply a symptom of a much older and deeper philosophical antinomy between idealism and materialism. Scholars such as Wright may argue that the Marxist concept of class is sturdy enough to incorporate both ideological and economic elements in all their variants (Wright 2004), but it is equally arguable that the stress imposed on a concept covering so much ground weakens its plausibility. Whether this signals the end of class as a useful concept is another matter.

References

Ahmad, A. 1992. *In Theory. Classes, Nations, Literatures*. London: Verso.

Balibar, E., and Wallerstein, I. 1991. *Race, Nation, Class: Ambiguous Identities*. London and New York: Verso.

Callinicos, A. 1993. *Race and Class*. London: Bookmarks.

Cox, O. C. 1972. Race and exploitation: A Marxist view, in P. Baxter and B. Sansom (eds.), *Race and Social Difference*. Baltimore: Penguin Books.

Delle, J. 1999. The landscapes of class negotiation on coffee plantations in the Blue Mountains of Jamaica: 1790–1850. *Historical Archaeology* 33 (1): 136–158.

Engels, F. 1954 [1891]. *The Origin of the Family, Private Property and the State*. Moscow: Foreign Languages Publishing House.

Fanon, F. 1967. *The Wretched of the Earth*. London: Penguin.

Geshwender, J., and Levine, R. 1994. Classical and recent theoretical developments in the Marxist analysis of race and ethnicity, in P. McGuire and D. McQuarie (eds.), *From the Left Bank to the Mainstream*. New York: General Hall Publishing.

Gilman, A. 1984. Explaining the Upper Palaeolithic revolution, in M. Spriggs (ed.), *Marxist Perspectives in Archaeology*, pp. 115–126. Cambridge: Cambridge University Press.

Godelier, M. 1986. *The Mental and the Material*. London: Verso.

Hall, M. 1999. Subaltern voices? Finding the spaces between things and words, in P. A. Funari, M. Hall, and S. Jones (eds.), *Historical Archaeology. Back from the Edge*, pp. 193–203. London: Routledge.

——. 2000. *Archaeology and the Modern World*. London: Routledge.

Hardt, M., and Negri, A. 2000. *Empire*. Cambridge, MA: Harvard University Press.

Johnson, M. 1996. *An Archaeology of Capitalism*. Oxford: Blackwell.

Laclau, E., and Mouffe, C. 1985. *Hegemony and Socialist Strategy. Towards a Radical Democratic Politics*. London: Verso.

Lenin, V. I. 1987 [1917]. *Imperialism. The Highest Stage of Capitalism*, in H. Christman (ed.), *The Essential Works of Lenin*, pp. 179–270. New York: Dover.

Leone, M., and Potter, P. B. (eds.). 1999. *Historical Archaeologies of Capitalism*. New York: Kluwer.

Lucas, G. 2004. *An Archaeology of Colonial Identity. Power and Material Culture in the Dwars Valley, South Africa*. New York: Kluwer.

Luxembourg, R. 2003 [1913]. *The Accumulation of Capital*. London: Routledge.

Matthews, C. 2001. Political economy and race: Comparative archaeologies of Annapolis and New Orleans in the eighteenth century, in C. Orser (ed.), *Race and the Archaeology of Identity*, pp. 71–87. Salt Lake City: University of Utah Press.

McGuire, R. 2002. *A Marxist Archaeology*. New York: Percheron Press.

Moore-Gilbert, B. 1997. *Postcolonial Theory. Contexts, Practices, Politics*. London: Verso.

Mullins, P. 1999a. Race and the genteel consumer: Class and African-American consumption, 1850–1930. *Historical Archaeology* 33 (1): 22–38.

——. 1999b. *Race and Affluence. An Archaeology of African America and Consumer Culture*. New York: Kluwer.

Rey, P. P. 1975. The lineage mode of production. *Critique of Anthropology* 1.

——. 1977. Contradiction de classe dans les Sociétiés Lignagères. *Dialectique* 21.

Saitta, D. 1988. Marxism, prehistory and primitive communism. *Rethinking Marxism* 1 (4): 146–168.

Shackel, P., and Larsen, D. 2000. Labor, racism, and the built environment in early industrial Harpers Ferry, in J. Delle, S. Mrozowski, and R. Paynter (eds.), *Lines That Divide. Historical Archaeologies of Race, Class and Gender*, pp. 22–39. Knoxville: University of Tennessee Press.

Spivak, G. 1999. *A Critique of Postcolonial Reason*. Cambridge, MA: Harvard University Press.

Terray, E. 1975. Class and class consciousness in an Abron Kingdom of Gyaman, in M. Bloch, (ed.), *Marxist Analysis and Social Anthropology*. London: Malaby Press.

Wallerstein, I. 2004. *World Systems Analysis. An Introduction*. Durham, NC: Duke University Press.

Wilkie, L., and Bartoy, K. 2000. A critical archaeology revisited. *Current Anthropology* 41 (5): 747–777.

Williams, E. 1944. *Capitalism and Slavery*. Chapel Hill: University of North Carolina Press.

Wolf, E. 1982. *Europe and the People without History*. Berkeley: University of California Press.

——. 1987. An interview with Eric Wolf. *Current Anthropology* 28 (1): 107–117.

Wright, E. O. 2004. Social class, in G. Rizter (ed.), *Encyclopedia of Social Theory*. London: Sage.

Wurst, L., and Fitts, R. (eds.). 1999. Confronting class. *Historical Archaeology* 33 (1).

Young, R. 1990. *White Mythologies. Writing History and the West*. London: Routledge.

28

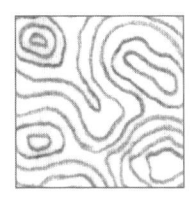

RACE AND CLASS

Paul R. Mullins

Racial ideology and class inequality have profoundly shaped the last half millennium, but archaeologists have been oddly reticent about the material impression of the color line and its entanglement with class structure. An archaeology that examines race across time and space can underscore the complexity of the color line and illuminate the genesis of contemporary privileges. Politically, though, some archaeologists have been hesitant to wrestle with race and racism or to link color and class inequalities to contemporary systems of privilege. Instead, they have considered race as a social construction without critically examining the concrete realities of racial identities, the distinctive epistemic privileges of differing positions along the color line, and the ways in which an archaeology of race is compelled to scrutinize the impression of class on race. Archaeology risks ignoring perhaps the most fundamental structural features of the colonial and postcolonial world if it evades questions about race and racism, casts class in reductionist terms disconnected from race, or poses these considerations as somehow methodologically or politically outside the appropriate sphere of archaeological scholarship. This paper focuses on how a broad range of archaeologists might profit from examining how American historical archaeologists have linked race and class in some forms but disregarded them in other ways that tend to squander many of the most interesting implications of an archaeology of race and class.

Linking Race and Class

Race has long been long approached by archaeologists as a social construction whose power is either largely rhetorical or so complexly interwoven with other dimensions of identity that it cannot be evoked in material analysis. Virtually all archaeologists appear to have accepted that racism is a social process that has some generalized material dimensions, and race and racism clearly have had a profound impact on archaeological research since the late 19th century, but actual archaeological interpretations that explicitly use race as a framing mechanism are not especially common. Class shares a comparable prominence in its central role in shaping archaeological practice over the last century, and fundamental structural relations of inequality are a feature of every complex society. Class has been defined in myriad ways, and yet it has rarely been linked to race as a paired system of inequality in the post-Columbian world. Most scholars examining the last half millennium recognize that race privileged some agents over others, and few could dispute that material inequalities were routinely paired with various forms of racial inequality. When archaeologists minimize the interdependence of race and class, the discipline risks evading their status as fundamental constitutive features of modernity that are constantly reproduced in the intimate material details of life that archaeology so powerfully illuminates.

In 1945, Oliver Cox (1945) argued that racism was inextricably wound into class relations, suggesting that racism was a form of class exploitation that lay at the heart of capitalism and did not exist before 1492 (Hier 2001: 75). Cox portrayed capitalism as a patchwork of mutually reinforcing systems of oppression (cf. Brewer et al. 2002). Rather than paint racism as simply another form of timeless ethnocentrism, Cox criticized scholars who defined "race prejudice as essentially a belief," indicating that such a position "gives almost no attention to the materialistic source of the rationalization" (Reed 2001). Cox's broader analysis of capitalism and the colonial world eventually formed the basis of world systems theory, but his effort to focus on related systems of racism and class inequality has generally been ignored. W. E. B. Du Bois (1933: 104) saw the 20th-century world in similar terms, as shaped by class and racial exploitation, arguing that "the extension [sic] of the world market by imperial expanding industry has established a world-wide new proletariat of colored workers, toiling under the worst conditions of 19th-century capitalism, herded as slaves and serfs and furnishing by the lowest paid wage in modern history a mass of raw material for industry." Du Bois (1933: 118) soberly acknowledged the power of racial privilege, even in the face of a depression "that levels all in mighty catastrophe." Du Bois believed that while the "fantastic industrial structure of America is threatened with ruin . . . white labor is too frightened at Negro competition to attempt united action" (1933: 118).

Such challenges to acknowledge racism and class inequality as reinforcing systems of oppression remain largely unanswered in archaeology (exceptions include Babson 1990; Delle et al. 2000; Franklin 1997; McDavid 2004; Mullins 1999; Orser 1998; Perry and Paynter 1999; Schrire 1995; Scott 1994; see also McDavid and McGhee, this volume, chapter 37). Anthropologists have scrutinized race and racism in their research and activism for well over a century, and few contemporary anthropological topics have a richer scholarly lineage (Baker and Patterson 1994). Archaeology has played an especially powerful role in both perpetuating and confronting racialized inequalities in scholarship on Indigenous peoples since the late 19th century, and race could be argued to be one of the central factors driving the development of comparative archaeologies since the 19th century.

Nevertheless, for many scholars, race's status as a social construction appears to render it an inappropriate analytic category. Archaeologists occasionally invoke race as one of many dimensions of a generalized identity, but such analyses rarely probe how racial subjectivity was fashioned in material consumption or how systemic racializing processes impacted even the most prosaic everyday details of material life (Epperson 2004: 101–102). Class was long disconnected from race and routinely expunged from prehistoric archaeologies, which once took kinship as the central organizing principle in prehistory and placed class on the historic side of the divide (McGuire 1992: 182). Randall McGuire (1992: 182) argues that until the 1980s, most prehistorians who employed the term "class" used it to refer to craft specialization or a functional division of labor. LouAnn Wurst and Robert Fitts (1999: 1) argue that historical archaeologists have rarely defined class in terms of exploitative social relations and instead favor a notion of a gradational class ladder based on income, occupation, and status distinctions. While class has an exceptionally rich scholarly pedigree distinct from that of racial inquiries, this chapter focuses on how race and class might be most productively coupled in archaeologies that examine the development of capitalism over the last half millennium. Questions of race and class are pertinent to any critical assessment of archaeology's history and practice, and scholarship linking race and class could be foregrounded in virtually any archaeological inquiry (e.g., see González-Ruibal [chapter 2], Atalay [chapter 4], and Orser [chapter 14], this volume).

Dismantling Race

Scholars in many disciplines have productively de-essentialized race since the 1960s, but this has often been accompanied by the sentiment that such dispassionate deconstruction will inevitably dispel unfounded prejudices (cf. Olson 2001). In archaeology, the effort to push "beyond" race and racism has deemphasized structural determinism and shifted the analytical focus to individuals, small social collectives, and hyperfragmented identities. This has certainly complicated archaeological identity, but efforts to dismiss race as an organizing principle for social life and deny its existence in "color blind" analysis hazards becoming its own racist discourse (Harrison 1998: 610). Terrence Epperson (2004) acknowledges that race is indeed a social construction without any claim to biological reality, but he argues that archaeological efforts to anti-essentialize race must still recognize it as a lived reality with concrete material consequences that archaeologists are well situated to interpret.

Racism is a material process that positions social subjects based primarily on physical variation and a now-transparent ideological appeal to biology as a mechanism of distinguishing social collectives. Much of what is accepted as the salient evidence of race is body ideologies and color hierarchies that were most clearly defined in the post-Columbian world. It is not unreasonable, of course, to suggest that physical variations were used to distinguish between social collectives much earlier (Gosden 2006). Yet body distinction in itself means nothing unless those characteristics are situated within a defining framework, and that framework has been quite distinctive in the last half millennium. Colonialism rooted such distinctions in a geographical place, as with the connection between Blackness and Africa, situating race in spaces that were being contested by European states. Biology also was invoked, providing a scientifically verifiable interpretation for apprehensible reality. Perhaps more importantly, in the colonial world race has been a basis for legitimizing power inequalities.

In the 1970s, historical archaeologists began to extend the discipline's reach throughout the world and confront the power tensions between European colonizers and Indigenous peoples, a move that lay a foundation to examine broadly shared systems of race and class inequalities. One of the first statements championing worldwide archaeologies came from Robert Schuyler (1970: 84), when he advocated for a historical archaeology that examined the "expansion of European culture into the non-European world." Schuyler (1970: 87) envisioned in European colonization an "overpowering and global presence" in which colonizers negotiated "indigenous cultures ranging from the band level to civilization." Such positions championed a global historical archaeology that recognized broad colonial inequalities and the migrations and dispersals that capitalism fostered, all essential to an archaeology of either race or class. For instance, an archaeology of plantations emerged that initially simply documented captives' presence, then stressed their African cultural continuities, and gradually expanded its scope to transatlantic power relationships. Nevertheless, little of the work following Schuyler's ambitious challenge explicitly considered race and the color line, and considerations of class were restricted to reductive notions of status hierarchies (e.g., Otto 1977). This is especially true of the many ethnic archaeologies that surfaced during those years; these produced rich archaeological evidence from a wide range of ethnic collectives, but rarely linked racism and inequality to concrete material patterns. Race and racism, in particular, tended to be subsumed within and conflated with ethnic subjectivities, naturalizing categories like Irish American and overseas Chinese, and inelegantly sidestepping how those categories were themselves born from racist inequalities.

Race brings with it sticky philosophical and political issues that reach deeply into the ways in which contemporary archaeologists define identity in a global context characterized by dislocation, migration, and inequalities. To some extent, archaeology's apparently delayed attention to race and racism reflects that colonial archaeologies found their first substantial foothold in the 1960s. The archaeology of the colonial world was initially the province of archaeologists in the eastern United States whose research focused on famous figures, old sites, and conventional historical questions that steered clear of issues of inequality. A few of the earliest historical archaeologists, though, envisioned a discipline that would weave counter-narratives or at least relate tales of everyday life that featured marginalized peoples otherwise ignored in dominant narratives. In 1971, for instance, Robert Ascher and Charles H. Fairbanks examined a 19th-century Georgia slave cabin, arguing that conventional histories and first-person narratives had largely distorted or ignored African-American captives' experiences. They creatively incorporated what they called a "soundtrack," a series of African-American textual voices ranging from Frederick Douglass's autobiography (1845) to Solomon Northrup's 1855 study, *Twelve Years a Slave*. Ascher and Fairbanks aimed to complicate plantation histories with a rich picture of captives' everyday lives, an effort that remains a commonplace ambition of archaeologists who aspire to give "voice" to historically ignored peoples. Their modest inclusion of African-American voices countering dominant narratives resisted painting life along the color line in monolithic and implicitly White terms.

The equation of certain goods with a particular collective ethnic identity is similar to archaeologies of class that revolve around analyses of material value, assuming that expensive goods and assemblages reflect affluence within an economic continuum. This departs from Marxian usage focused on consciousness and the ways in which marginalized peoples experience and articulate shared oppression, and it does not acknowledge race and class as mutually constitutive systems of inequality. Class has often been reduced simply to relative poverty, failing to contemplate the racist symbolism routinely linked with impoverishment and ignoring the multivalent meanings of otherwise commonplace things. Scholarship on agency has complicated reductive notions of class as a monolithic social ladder by focusing on consumption as the product of individual decision-making, but such scholarship often has evaded broader structural constraints and ideologies that lurk within consumption's perceived self-empowerment (Mrozowski 2006; Wurst and McGuire 1999). Charles Orser (2004: 170) argues that the archaeological fixation on the household unit has also moved attention away from race and class, fabricating the household as a locus for consumer decision-making ambiguously linked to either structural influences or consumer agency.

Conventional archaeological definitions of ethnicity and class have been gradually destabilized and complicated, and this has had a paradoxical effect. On the one hand, it has illuminated dynamism and contextual power relations, but, on the other hand, it has also produced some reluctance to embrace any concrete subjectivity, which has yielded especially fluid definitions of identity (McGuire and Wurst 2002). Lynn Meskell (2001: 200) has championed an archaeological focus on "vectors of difference" that de-essentialize identities while situating them within structural inequalities. Archaeological attention to marginalized social groups, though, has increasingly revolved around somewhat ambiguous notions of "identity" that do not systematically assess power and inequality that are routinely invested in class and racial structures. The destabilization of ethnicity in particular and identity in general has encouraged a hyper-contextualized scholarship that revolves around the specificities of a given place, time, and consumer that tends to distance social agents from dominant determining mechanisms. This apparent scholarly wariness of structural determinism and the movement toward an archaeology of specific contexts and individuality has often taken aim on race and class, suggesting that such categories focus on structural determinism and misrepresent individual agency.

Race and Class in Ethnic Archaeologies

Overseas Chinese archaeologies reveal many of the persistent shortcomings of ethnic identity archaeologies and suggest how an archaeological analysis of race might profoundly shape at least one corner of archaeological thought. Overseas Chinese archaeological research began to be conducted in scattered reaches of the American West, Australia, and New Zealand in the 1970s. Much of this scholarship was framed in terms of acculturation, aspiring to assess the degree to which overseas Chinese embraced dominant Western material practices and culture. Acculturation has a rich anthropological lineage, with John Wesley Powell (1883: 206) defining it in 1883 as "subjective adjustment of the lower to the higher" and Franz Boas (1896: 11) arguing that acculturation embodies "the mutual transformation of the old culture and the newly acquired material." The transparent melting-pot dimensions of acculturation models declined significantly in the 1960s in favor of perspectives that stressed cultural boundary maintenance. Archaeologists contributed by examining a host of ethnic collectives, but these studies championed clear and unique ethnic material patterns that distinguished individual collectives. Internal variation in such categories was largely evaded, and virtually no attention was devoted to exactly what defined the backdrop against which difference was being defined and evaluated.

The archaeological scholarship on the overseas Chinese was especially rigid. Archaeologies of overseas Chinese painted a picture of Chinese immigrants as overwhelmingly insular communities removed from the otherwise dynamic social landscapes around them (Voss 2005: 426). To some extent, this notion of segregated Chinese enclaves reflects the scholarly belief that Chinese immigrants rejected dominant practices because they were "sojourners" who migrated simply to accumulate resources for their return to China. The stereotype of utter insularity and cultural resistance among Chinese immigrants is remarkably similar to that wielded by 19th-century racists who peripheralized the Chinese by criticizing their apparent material and social distinctions. Contemporary archaeologists risk reproducing such stereotypes by recurrently painting the Chinese as protecting cultural traditions, resisting assimilation, and otherwise fortifying ethnic difference (Voss 2005: 427–428). It is unlikely that many archaeologists examining acculturation among overseas Chinese communities embrace its potential racist implications, but acculturation remains a powerful theme in overseas Chinese archaeologies long after its demise in most other corners of the discipline.

The gravitation toward unique patterns considered to be ethnic boundary mechanisms is commonplace throughout historical archaeology. African-American archaeology has long focused on goods associated with African cultural practice, what are commonly referred to as "Africanisms," despite the overwhelming predominance of mass-produced European goods within most African-American contexts (cf. Ferguson 1992). Yet those material patterns that seem to distinguish collectives may simply reflect ideological assumptions scholars make about specific groups; that is, the "recognition" of a specific identity is conditioned by disciplinary frameworks that encourage archaeologists to search out particular goods, ignore conflicting or anomalous evidence, and reinforce contemporary assumptions about specific collectives.

The argument has often been made that overseas Chinese assemblages exhibit significant material distinctions from mainstream patterns (cf. Voss 2005). This reflects that archaeological assemblages from overseas Chinese sites included Asian goods that were rarely, if ever, found in other assemblages. Many archaeologists interpreted this as evidence for cultural self-segregation that generations of previous scholars had attributed to overseas Chinese. This maneuver opposes the sway of Chinese tradition to Western modernity and fortifies a commonplace Oriental/Occidental polarization, but it conveniently ignores whether such ethnic isolation is truly reflected in material culture. Barbara Voss (2005: 428) suggests that significant portions of Chinese material assemblages are composed of standard mass-produced goods that upset the picture of conscious self-exclusion from dominant practices. Yet archaeologists' attention to overseas Chinese material culture has revolved around distinctive goods, including opium bowls, coins, and gaming pieces, while mass-produced goods pass without equally thorough analysis.

Very little archaeology has looked closely at class as an expression of consumers' consciousness of racial subjectivity by examining the material tactics that consumers use to negotiate interdependent class and racial inequalities. The most significant exception is Orser's (2004, 2007) work on racialization which examines overseas Chinese, 19th-century Ireland, and African America. Orser's (2004) analysis of Irish consumers argues for dual racial and class consumption strategies among 19th-century residents of Ballykilcline who resisted definition as a lowly racial group through material consumption and grassroots activism. Orser argues that the Irish cultivated what Du Bois called "double consciousness," with the Ballykilcline residents conscious of their conflicting identities as British citizens and Irish subjects. He suggests that printed ceramic patterns with idyllic pastoral scenes were one of the material forms that provided a symbolic means to distance community consumers from racist and class caricatures of Irish rural life.

Race and Class in Contemporary Historical Archaeology

Many archaeologists with interests in race and class inequalities have assertively focused on how such historical inequalities reach into the contemporary world. Mark Leone, Parker Potter, and Paul Shackel's (1987) formulation of critical theory argues for a self-reflective archaeology that concentrates on capitalist inequalities and embeds the scholarly discussion of them in public interpretation programs. Their case study in Annapolis, Maryland, contends with the ideological separations made in mainstream Annapolis histories, in which the division between Black and White was especially prominent. They argue that the presentation of Black and White history as separate phenomena evades contemporary racial tensions, so they instead advocate an archaeology that probes how race was constructed and reproduced in everyday material culture. Elaine-Maryse Solari's (2001) study of urban renewal in Oakland, California, links the landscape of Oakland to contemporary inequalities, examining the relationships between racism and landscape transformation and arguing that resistance to renewal projects fostered community politicization among African-American targets. Solari positions Oakland's historic landscape in relation to recent urban renewal projects that rationalized themselves by seeing Oakland as a slum landscape peopled by poor African Americans and European descendants (cf. Mayne and Murray 2001).

Increasingly, more archaeologists have begun to wrestle with the power inequalities between scholars and descendant communities, and these discourses along class and color lines are particularly contested (cf. Franklin 1997; McDavid 2004; Singleton 1997). Ultimately, relationships along and across the color line seem infeasible without acknowledging color and class privilege (Singleton and Orser 2003). Terrence Epperson (2004) argues that archaeologists' willingness to ignore race, suggesting that it is simply a social construction or yet another dimension of identity, is itself an effect of White racial privilege by scholars who either cannot recognize, or hope to evade, their own racial privileges. A central challenge likely will be to move beyond simply dismantling racist and class caricatures. For instance, Lu Ann De Cunzo (1998: 43) reaches the surprising conclusion that racism's "influences and injustices have received heightened attention in archaeologists' stories about African Americans in recent years," so she advocates an archaeology that produces less "inaccurate images" shaped by racist stereotypes. This sentiment aspires to paint African-American life in some form that is not determined by racism, but it risks artificially isolating African America from the social and structural influences of race. Illuminating White privilege in the past, situating it at the heart of colonial and postcolonial life, and connecting it to contemporary inequality carries much more transformative potential.

Michael Blakey (1997) argues that archaeologies of the color line are inevitably discourses about contemporary life, and the most productive archaeological discourses must acknowledge the continuity of racism and confront its relationship with class inequalities. In 1933, W. E. B. Du Bois maintained that scholars and activists must acknowledge the connections between racism and class inequality, but it "is no sufficient answer to say that capital encourages this oppression and uses it for its own ends. This may have excused . . . some of the poor whites of the South today. But the bulk of American white labor is neither ignorant nor fanatical. It knows exactly what it is doing and it means to do it." For Du Bois, racism was indeed a social construction, but it was also one that privileged people willingly accepted (cf. Roediger 1991). The archaeological challenge may be to confront this conscious 500-year acceptance of racism and examine how concrete material consumption patterns reproduced racial inequality while other consumers used the same goods hoping to defuse racism. Stressing the mutually dependent structural frameworks of race and class will not inevitably rob consumers of agency, but it will productively complicate agency and privilege. Ultimately, this will paint a half millennium in which a vast range of consumers negotiated color and class lines in distinctive ways that were creative and thoughtful, but this scholarship also will underscore the remarkable persistence of class and color privileges shaping everyday life. Archaeologists are especially well positioned to illuminate the most intimate material details of everyday life and examine how apparently commonplace consumption resisted, embraced, and complexly negotiated class and color lines.

References

Ascher, R., and Fairbanks, C. H. 1971. Excavation of a slave cabin: Georgia, U.S.A. *Historical Archaeology* 5: 3–17.

Babson, D. W. 1990. The archaeology of racism and ethnicity on southern plantations. *Historical Archaeology* 24 (4): 20–28.

Baker, L. D., and Patterson, T. C. 1994. Race, racism, and the history of U.S. anthropology. *Transforming Anthropology* 5 (1–2): 1–7.

Blakey, M. L. 1997. Past is present: Comments on "In the realm of politics: Prospects for public participation in African-American plantation archaeology." *Historical Archaeology* 31 (3): 140–145.

Boas, F. 1896. The growth of Indian mythologies. A study based upon the growth of the mythologies of the North Pacific coast. *The Journal of American Folklore* 9 (32): 1–11.

Brewer, R. M., Conrad, C. A., and King, M. C. 2002. The complexities and potential of theorizing gender, caste, race, and class. *Feminist Economics* 8 (2): 3–18.

Cox, O. C. 1945. Race and caste: A distinction. *The American Journal of Sociology* 50 (5): 360–368.

De Cunzo, L. 1998. A future after freedom. *Historical Archaeology* 32 (1): 42–54.

Delle, J. A., Mrozowski, S. A., and Paynter, R. (eds.). 2000 *Lines That Divide: Historical Archaeologies of Race, Class, and Gender.* Knoxville: University of Tennessee Press.

Douglass, F. 1845. *Narrative of the Life of Frederick Douglass, an American Slave.* Boston: The Anti-Slavery Office.

Du Bois, W. E. B. 1933. Marxism and the Negro problem. *Crisis* 40 (5): 103–104, 118.

Epperson, T. W. 2004. Critical race theory and the archaeology of the African diaspora. *Historical Archaeology* 38 (1): 101–108.

Ferguson, L. 1992. *Uncommon Ground: Archaeology and Early African America, 1650–1800.* Washington, DC: Smithsonian Institution Press,

Franklin, M. 1997. "Power to the People": Sociopolitics and the archaeology of Black Americans. *Historical Archaeology* 31 (3): 36–50.

Gosden, C. 2006. Race and racism in archaeology: Introduction. *World Archaeology* 38 (1): 1–7.

Harrison, F. V. 1998. Introduction: Expanding the discourse on "Race." *American Anthropologist* 100 (3): 609–631.

Hier, S. P. 2001. The forgotten architect: Cox, Wallerstein and World-System Theory. *Race & Class* 42 (3): 69–86.

Leone, M. P., Potter, Jr., P. B., and Shackel, P. A. 1987. Towards a critical archaeology. *Current Anthropology* 28 (3): 283–302.

Mayne, A., and Murray, T. (eds.). 2001. *The Archaeology of Urban Landscapes: Explorations in Slumland.* Cambridge: Cambridge University Press.

McDavid, C. 2004. From "traditional" archaeology to public archaeology to community action, in P. A. Shackel and E. J. Chambers (eds.), *Places in Mind: Public Archaeology as Applied Anthropology*, pp. 35–56. New York: Routledge,.

McGuire, R. H. 1992. *A Marxist Archaeology.* San Diego: Academic Press.

McGuire, R. H., and Wurst, L. 2002. Struggling with the past. *International Journal of Historical Archaeology* 6 (2): 85–94.

Meskell, L. 2001. Archaeologies of identity, in I. Hodder (ed.), *Archaeological Theory Today*, pp. 187–213. Malden, MA: Polity Press.

Mrozowski, S. A. 2006. *The Archaeology of Class in Urban America.* Cambridge: Cambridge University Press.

Mullins, P. R. 1999. *Race and Affluence: An Archaeology of African America and Consumer Culture.* New York: Kluwer/Plenum.

Northup, S. 1855. *Twelve Years a Slave: Narrative of Solomon Northup, A Citizen of New-York, Kidnapped in Washington City in 1841, and Rescued in 1853, from a Cotton Plantation near the Red River in Louisiana.* Miller, Orton.

Olson, S. 2001. The genetic archaeology of race. *The Atlantic Monthly* (April): 69–80.

Orser, C. E., Jr. 1998. The challenge of race to American historical archaeology. *American Anthropologist* 100 (3): 661–668.

——. 2004. *Race and Practice in Archaeological Interpretation.* Philadelphia: University of Pennsylvania Press.

——. 2007. *The Archaeology of Race and Racialization in Historic America.* Gainesville: University Press of Florida.

Otto, J. S. 1977. Artifacts and status differences: A comparison of ceramics from planter, overseer, and slave sites on an antebellum plantation, in S. South (ed.), *Research Strategies in Historical Archaeology*, pp. 91–118. New York: Academic Press.

Perry, W., and Paynter, R. 1999. Artifacts, ethnicity, and the archaeology of African Americans, in T. A. Singleton (ed.), *"I, Too, am America": Archaeological Studies of African-American Life*, pp. 299–310. Charlottesville: University Press of Virginia.

Powell, J. W. 1883. Human evolution. Annual address of the president, J. W. Powell, delivered November 6, 1883. *Transactions of the Anthropological Society of Washington.* 2: 176–208.

Reed, A. 2001. Race and class in the work of Oliver Cromwell Cox. *Monthly Review* 52 (9). http://www.monthlyreview.org/201reed.htm (last accessed 08/1/07).

Roediger, D. R. 1991. *The Wages of Whiteness: Race and the Making of the American Working Class.* New York: Verso.

Schrire, C. 1995. *Digging through Darkness: Chronicles of an Archaeologist*. Charlottesville: University Press of Virginia.

Schuyler, R. L. 1970. Historical and historic sites / archaeology as anthropology: Basic definitions and relationships. *Historical Archaeology* 4 (1): 83–89.

Scott, E. M. (ed.). 1994. *Those of Little Note: Gender, Race, and Class in Historical Archaeology*. Tucson: University of Arizona Press.

Singleton, T. A. 1997. Facing the challenges of a public African-American archaeology. *Historical Archaeology* 31 (3): 146–152.

Singleton, T. A., and Orser, Jr., C. E., 2003. Descendant communities: Linking people in the present to the past, in L. J. Zimmerman, K. D. Vitelli, and J. Hollowell-Zimmer (eds.), *Ethical Issues in Archaeology*, pp. 143–152. Walnut Creek, CA: AltaMira Press.

Solari, E. 2001. The making of an archaeological site and the unmaking of a community in West Oakland, California, in A. Mayne and T. Murray (eds.), *The Archaeology of Urban Landscapes: Explorations in Slumland*, pp. 22–38. Cambridge: Cambridge University Press.

Voss, B. L. 2005. The archaeology of overseas Chinese communities. *World Archaeology* 37 (3): 424–439.

Wurst, L., and Fitts, R. K. 1999. Introduction: Why confront class? *Historical Archaeology* 33 (1): 1–6.

Wurst, L., and McGuire, R. H. 1999. Immaculate consumption: A critique of the "Shop Till You Drop" school of human behavior. *International Journal of Historical Archaeology* 3 (3): 191–199.

29

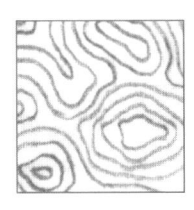

COMMENTARY:
AN ARCHAEOLOGIST FINDS HER VOICE: A COMMENTARY ON COLONIAL AND POSTCOLONIAL IDENTITIES

Whitney Battle-Baptiste

"My foremost priority is taking care of myself and keeping my soul intact...."

Wallace 2004: 15

Each morning before I leave my house, I stop by a small altar that stands just at the edge of my kitchen. I say a few words of thanks—for the new day, the positive things in my life, and the ability to maintain an open relationship with my ancestors. On this altar are pictures of family members who have passed away, glasses of water (symbolizing the medium that separates the world of the living from the world of the dead), flowers, a portion of food my family has eaten for breakfast, a cup of coffee sweet with sugar, unprocessed cotton (the sugar, coffee, and cotton are representative of those crops cultivated by my enslaved ancestors), several small bottles of liquor, and a source of light. This altar is for my *Egun*, which in the Yoruba language means "bones." These bones are the bones of my ancestors, not in the physical sense, but in the spiritual sense, a way to acknowledge the connection between the living and the dead. Let me explain further. I was raised in a religious community of Orişa traditionalists based in New York City. Followers of Orişa (pronounced "orisha") are part of an ancient spiritual tradition indigenous to contemporary Nigeria and Benin. Throughout the African diaspora it is called by different names: Santería, Shango, Lucumí, Candomblé, or Ifá. I was raised in this tradition among a very active and vibrant Orişa community in New York City.

When I was younger, I often kept my faith as a private matter. As an adult, I have generally kept my faith a part of my non-public self. As an anthropologist, I am learning that my subject position enhances, rather than inhibits, the work I do; therefore I wanted to begin this commentary with this bit of information about myself to perhaps give some insight into why I think the future of historical archaeology will be about connections, genealogies, honest dialogues, and *Egun*. The connection to the past can mean learning and understanding the very rich and lengthy black intellectual traditions of Vindicationist, Critical Race, Black feminist, African Diaspora, and Afrocentric/Africana theories; the genealogies are about those scholars and African-American anthropologists who have maintained a marginalized position in the anthropological canon; the honest dialogues begin with being able to convey to descendant communities that we are versed in the African and African-American past; and *Egun* is about continuing a dialogue with our Africanist brothers and sisters also engaged in the struggle of interpreting the African past.

What does postcolonialism have to do with a historical archaeology based in *Egun*? Well, I did some soul searching to understand what a postcolonial archaeology might be. I began to try to understand what postcolonialism sets out to accomplish as it is related to the issues so central to African diaspora archaeology. Postcolonialism, as a theory, is still marginal to many of us doing archaeology in the United States. Or so I thought. Although I had never perceived myself as directly fighting colonialism, I did relate to using archaeological interpretation to confront and critique this fluid thing we call colonialism. For me, postcolonialism had always been about the search for redefining one's identity, writing against imperialist notions of truth, and finding ways to create viable critiques of the colonial past and centering the cultural and political needs of the Indigenous somewhere else. I have read a lot of material on the subject to figure out how to handle my research and the challenges of interpreting life under slavery. Yet, I still had not connected what I had read with the types of struggles I was engaged in here in the United States. However, is the United States of America not a former colonial site? I am not only the product of a long colonial moment, but also a child of the so-called inner city, the concrete jungle, the playground of the urban social scientist, who in many ways plays a part in maintaining a form of imperialist (read "culture of poverty" here) discourse. This is about connections.

I believe that at times, as archaeologists are coming to grips with the needs of various publics and shifting their focus to descendant communities, we often believe we are coming from a place of knowing. We are fully aware of what descendant communities need, what they are looking for—before they even understand what it is that we do. However, we rarely engage in these critical conversations with a sense of who they are and what they already know. I will give an example from my own life experience. My arrival at the Hermitage plantation, where I would do my dissertation research, was a reality check about what historical archaeologists did. I immediately recognized that my training (although in history) was not only different, but was opposed to that of many of the archaeologists I would meet in those first few years in the field. My connection to an African world view, a solid foundation in contemporary African history and African-American culture, felt misplaced. It gave me a variety of factors that marked my difference: my faith, race, gender, class, and knowledge base.

To some extent, I began to do my own ethnography of African-American archaeology. I had long conversations about how those around me were trained. I asked questions about their background in African history, African-American history and culture, African-American anthropology, Caribbean literature, and black women's fiction. To my dismay, many of those I talked to had bits and pieces of these elements, but never enough to hold a lengthy conversation about an intellectual tradition that continues to be relegated to African-American/African studies departments. This was real for me, and it has taken me almost 10 years to come to grips with this reality and be able to write about it. This is about genealogies.

A topic that figures prominently in this literature and in popular culture is the historical position of Africa, and the ongoing relations we have with African governments, institutes, and specific individuals. In other words, what are our relations with our colleagues on the African continent? They can tell us about the African past; we can tell them about the implications of that past. In this conversation, we can all better understand that the transatlantic trade in African captives adversely affected both the African continent and the New World. Without these conversations, we have no connection and are without a genealogy, without an ancestral line, without *Egun*.

Recently I was asked by a colleague, whom I respect, about ways to enrich her understanding of the intersection of race and gender in her work. Based on this conversation, I realized that I could use my commentary in this book as a means to push archaeologists to think about scholarship that is overlooked in anthropology and to consider other works that are outside the discipline. I feel that passing along even a preliminary sketch of the genealogical literature that African-American archaeologists should be familiar with is the first step to shifting the focus from "margin to center" (hooks 2000). Please understand that this is not all there is out there, and there are many scholars I have omitted. In many ways, I need my colleagues to understand that for me to be a conscious member of African America, it is vital to understand the connection that race and racism have on the perspectives of African diasporic peoples, so I have to be able to turn around or look up and find the book or the article that may have something I can use or that at times can be the source of inspiration when I am writing or preparing to teach a class. This is another part of my personal practice or routine. It enters into all aspects of my work—in my office, when I write, and when I am in the field. I am familiar with this literature and these experiences, which is to say I have a grasp of the genealogies.

Here is a brief list of some of my mainstays (also included in the references, below); Aimé Césairé, Edward Said, Frantz Fanon, Angela Davis, bell hooks, Leith Mullings, Michele Wallace, Audre Lorde,

Toni Morrison, Robert Farris Thompson, Chandra Mohanti, Chinua Achebe, Paul Gilroy, Walter Rodney, Ron Eyerman, Derrick Bell, Kimberlé Crenshaw, Lee Baker, St. Claire Drake, W. E. B. Du Bois, John Gwaltney, and Theresa Singleton. Another reason I have listed these authors is because they have become my guides to understanding the impact of race and racism on people of African descent. What would an archaeological interpretation look like with some of these works woven into them? How would an anthropology program benefit from including some of this scholarship in graduate seminars? Imagine coming to a site or a conversation with a descendant community with questions informed by a world that reflects the everyday issues and critiques of American society that are important to many marginalized groups of people. Imagine a world where we can have conversations that are not just about making up for lost time and misunderstandings, but realizing the role of oppression and white supremacy before the community outreach programs are constructed. There should be a moment when archaeologists are no longer concerned about struggles of power and control of archaeological knowledge, because once we as archaeologists recognize that there is a different voice from which racialized minorities and other oppressed communities speak, the dialogue, in my opinion, becomes a different conversation. This could be an honest dialogue.

So with this commentary, I hope to put some ideas out there that have been on my mind for some years. It is also a moment to reflect and give thanks to all of those *Egun* scholars who have gone before me and helped me to understand that this work can be difficult, but at the center of it all is the ability to keep your soul intact.

Peace & light.

References

Achebe, C. 1994. *Things Fall Apart*. New York: Anchor Books.

Baker, L. 1998. *From Savage to Negro: Anthropology and the Construction of Race, 1896–1954*, Berkeley: University of California Press.

Battle-Baptiste, W. 2007. The other from within: A commentary, in J. Jameson, Jr. and S. Baugher (eds.), *Past Meets Present: Archaeologists Partnering with Museum Curators, Teachers, and Community Groups*. New York: Springer.

Bell, D. A. 2000. *Race, Racism and Amerian Law*. Maryland: Aspen Law & Business.

Césairé, A. 2000. *Discourse on Colonialism*. New York: Monthly Review Press.

Crenshaw, K., Gotanda, N., Peller, G., and Thomas, K. 1995. *Critical Race Theory: The Key Writings That Formed the Movement*. New York: New Press and W. W. Norton & Company.

Davis, A. 1983. *Women, Race and Class*. New York: Vintage Books.

Drake, St. Clare 1987. *Black Folk Here and There: An Essay in History and Anthropology*. Los Angeles: University of California Press.

Du Bois, W. E. B. 1997. *The Souls of Black Folk*. Boston: Bedford Books.

Eyerman, R. 2001. *Cultural Trauma: Slavery and the Formation of African American*

Identity. Cambridge: Cambridge University Press.

Fanon, F. 1991. *Black Skin, White Masks*. New York: Grove Weidenfield.

Farris Thompson, R. 1984. *Flash of the Spirit: African & Afro-American Art and Philosophy*. New York: Vintage Press.

Franklin, M. 2001. A Black feminist-inspired archaeology? *Journal of Social Archaeology* 1 (1): 108–125.

Gilroy, P. 1993. *The Black Atlantic: Modernity and Double Consciousness*. Cambridge, MA: Harvard University Press.

Gomez, M. 1998. *Exchanging Our Country's Marks*. Durham: University of North Carolina Press.

Gwaltney, J. 1993. *Drylongso: A Self Portrait of Black America*. New York: W. W. Norton.

hooks, b. 1990. *Yearning: Race, Gender and Cultural Politics. Feminist Theory: From Margin to CenterCenter*. Cambridge, MA: South End Press.

Lorde, A. 1984. *Sister Outsider: Essays and Speeches*. Trumansburg: Crossing Press.

Mohanti, C. T. 2003. *Feminism without Borders: Decolonizing Theory, Practicing Solidarity*. Durham, NC: Duke University Press.

Morrison, T. 1992. *Playing in the Dark: Whiteness and the Literary Imagination*. New York: Vintage Books.

Mullings, L. 1997. *On Our Own Terms: Race, Class, and Gender in the Lives of African American Women*. New York: Routledge.

Rodney, W. 1981. *How Europe Underdeveloped Africa*. Washington, DC: Howard University Press.

Said, E. 1994. *Orientalism*. New York: Vintage Books.

Wallace, M. 2004. *Dark Designs and Visual Culture*. Durham, NC: Duke University Press.

30

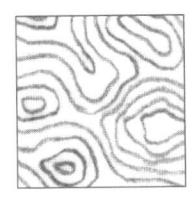

COMMENTARY:
ARCHAEOLOGY, ANCESTRAL BODIES, AND NATIVE AMERICAN IDENTITY IN THE NEW MILLENNIUM: COMMENTARY ON COLONIAL AND POSTCOLONIAL IDENTITIES

John Norder

In graduate school, a friend of mine was studying variation in tooth morphology of Native American populations from a series of archaeological sites. She had developed a coding system for the curvature of shovel-shaped incisors, and one afternoon while we were in the osteology lab, she asked if I would do an impression for her. I agreed, and she produced a piece of molding clay that I pressed over my upper front teeth. Giving the impression back to her, she pulled out her coding chart and a caliper and proceeded to measure and compare. I knew that my incisors were shovel-shaped, and being Native American, I was confident in the outcome. However, after a minute or so, she informed me that I was only a "two," which fell within the range that included Europeans and several other world populations. If I had been a "five," she said, there would have been no question that I was Native American. We were both disappointed by the results, and at the time, I also felt compromised in some way by them.

Walking away from this experience and reflecting on it years later, what I had taken to be a simple act of indulging intellectual curiosity had encapsulated the essentialized relationship archaeologists and physical anthropologists have with the human body. In this relationship, the body is viewed as an object rather than as a person. As such, it is something to be measured, codified, and solved. In the context discussed here, it is also an object of colonization. In North America, ancestral remains of Native Americans have been studied for centuries, and, throughout it all, the history of aboriginal

America has been appropriated and written through the lens of Western empirical discourse. As a result, the body, as reflected by my own naive participation in my friend's study, has been used as a tool to empower the master narrative of anthropology in defining the past, and identity, of Native Americans.

In contrast, many Native Americans view the human body as the "ancestral body," a focus of communal identity and linkage to the world before European contact. In extremity, it is the pristine and prime self around which identity is formed. As such, it is sacrosanct and therefore inviolable in its meaning to Native American communities. It is, simply, "ancestor," and as an objectification of the core self, it can be argued that it is what defines North American Indigenous peoples as "Indians," separate both culturally and biologically from the European colonizers with whom they have been interacting for the past 500 years. As such, the body is an object that is to be spoken for, as by its very presence it must be defended in order to preserve the contemporary self through emerging postcolonial discourses.

At the present time, these colonial and postcolonial discourses have become increasingly intertwined in the post-NAGPRA (Native American Graves Protection and Repatriation Act) era and with emerging developments in the use of DNA analysis on ancient human remains. NAGPRA, ostensibly, was meant to address the historic legacy of the unwanted removal and study of ancestral Native American remains from burial sites across the United States. For Native Americans, this issue was one of the rallying points of the American Indian Civil Rights movements of the 1970s, which did not see fruition until 20 years later with passage of the legislation. Unfortunately, the legislation proved problematic with the absence of critical language on certain sets of human remains left undefined and, subsequently, contested in terms of their ownership under the law. This has changed with the addition of this language, but challenges remain. DNA analysis, on the other hand, has opened an entirely new chapter in the biocolonial exploitation of ancestral remains. Promoted by endeavors such as the Human Genome Diversity Project (Crigger 1995; Gillis 1994; Lewin 1993; Roberts 1993; Ross 1993), National Geographic Society's Genographic Project (Harry and Kanehe 2006; Tallbear 2007; Wells 2006), and numerous corporate ventures for DNA collection,[1] it has insinuated itself into the relationship between Native Americans and the ancestral body, capitalizing on shifting identity politics and political economy within Native American communities with sometimes disastrous results.

Subjugating Identity of the Ancestral Body

The controversy over the appropriation of Native American ancestral remains by archaeologists and physical anthropologists in North America is one that can be framed by notions of intimacy. There are few things more intimate to us than the body itself, either as an object of study or as one of identity. From an individual perspective, we frequently study ourselves and others in order to learn more about who we are in the contexts in which we engage on a daily basis, and we do this most effectively through intimate acts. We see, hear, smell, touch, and feel others around us; in an ideal world, this is a consensual process. With those who die, the process is obviously different, but consent remains an implied component. It is expected that the body will be handled and cared for in a respectful way by those remaining, which again is an act of intimacy. Within Western society, a person's last wishes, which typically include how their remains are to be treated, are considered almost a sacred obligation, and it is rare for those wishes to be ignored.

Archaeology exists as an anomaly that inherently violates this process. As a Western science, it defines itself outside of this framework. With objectivism as a central principle, the discipline appropriates human remains as a source of data used to understand past human behaviors. The interpretive process, with its hybrid of scientific and inferential approaches, creates identity that is imposed on the past in ways that both recognize and ignore social and cultural diversity and continuity. The discipline has recognized the artificiality of this process and has problematized the issue for the past few decades in both critical studies (Harke and Wolfram 1992; Hodder 1991; Johnson and Olsen 1992; Meskell 2002) and applied research (Díaz-Andreu et al. 2005; Jones 1997). However, despite successes in examining the colonial structure of archaeological practice (McNiven and Russell 2005; Nicholas 2006), the cultural relativism of the discipline remains a significant challenge. Ian Hodder, for example, cautions that "it would be wrong to assume that there is some continuous connection between past and present ... [or that] local communities are an 'other' that is somehow closer to prehistory than [archaeologists] are" (Hodder 2002: 177).

To use a well-known case study that highlights this tension, we can briefly examine Kennewick Man, an individual whose remains were recovered in Washington State in 1996 and have been dated to be as old as 8,000–8,500 years B.P. (Taylor et al. 1998). The controversy over Kennewick Man arose from the scientific study of the cranium, which, based on extensive research, did not share features with any of the known contemporary Indigenous populations in North America (Chatters 2000). However, these results were irrelevant to several Native American tribes, who sought to claim the individual who came to be known as the "Ancient One,"[2] using the process outlined in the Native American Graves Protection Repatriation Act. This claim was based on their oral history and historically documented presence in the region.[3] This claim was subsequently denied through a series of court battles initiated by eight archaeologists and physical anthropologists who argued that, based on the cranium, the remains were not Native American and therefore not subject to legally required repatriation (Bruning 2006). As a result, Kennewick Man became one of the more significant precedents used to deny repatriation due to a lack of cultural affiliation.

While there are more complicating elements of this case study, such as the controversy over concepts of cultural affiliation and identity, the essential nature of the argument is clear. For Native Americans, Kennewick Man represents a source of core identity, and that identity was denied not only by the academics who brought suit, but by the court decision as well. This action sought to break the continuity of self between the past and the present of the tribes who claimed the Ancient One as one of their own. The implications of this outcome challenged the relationship of Native Americans to the ancestral body that was theirs by right of history and place; and as subsequent headlines asked the question, "Who were the first Americans?" it also altered the ability to self-define in terms of both individual and corporate identity.

Native American Identity Politics in the Age of DNA

DNA was brought into the Kennewick case as an ostensibly objective tool that would be used as an additional line of evidence. The analysis itself did not generate results, but it set the stage, along with the earlier Human Genome Diversity Project, for a proliferation of studies on ancient human remains in archaeological research. In this case, ancient DNA has become an alternative to answering questions that were traditionally approached through material-culture remains. Where once identity and culture were defined through material similarities in lithic and ceramic assemblages, DNA has been used as a means to both challenge and support these inferences (Bolnick and Smith 2003, 2007; Kaestle and Horsburgh 2002).

At the same time, DNA has taken on a political dimension among Native American tribes, who have engaged with archaeologists and physical anthropologists in using this type of analysis to answer questions regarding ancestry.

As an example, while serving on the National Congress of American Indians Repatriation and Burial Sites Protection Commission, I chaired a meeting where a tribal member brought forth the issue of "outsiders" participating in DNA research that was looking to find a link between individuals from a 1,000-year-old Native American cemetery and contemporary populations. The concern of the tribal member was that these outsiders would use a positive test to somehow force the tribe to allow them to enroll. In another example discussed by Kimberly Tallbear (2003), the state of Vermont introduced legislation that would allow for DNA testing as a means to prove that an individual was of Native American descent. The purpose was to provide support for a tribal federal recognition case for a group that had failed using other available avenues. The implications of both of these examples is the assertion that the biological "truth" of the ancestral body, its DNA, could be used as a means to override or support the contested "belief" of the ancestral body as a source of both individual and sovereign identity.

For Native American communities, this assertion of "truth" has become yet another form of biocolonialism,[4] which has inserted itself into an already complicated realm of identity politics. The concepts of "mixed bloods" and "blood quantum" have been political tools of the postcolonial era that have factionalized tribal communities for over a century. Assertions of who is or is not a "real" Native American, or even what percentage or fraction of Native American an individual is, have consistently served to inflame community tensions and undermine unifying attempts toward a greater sovereignty. Into this, DNA has become the new tool being dangled like a carrot that, as some have advertised, can answer all questions and end all debate. Once again, it is a "truth" that can define the self in a manner that the vagaries and inconsistencies of genealogies sometimes can, or will, not.

Conclusion

The use of human remains to subvert and create identity by archaeologists and physical anthropologists remains a continuing challenge that bridges the colonial enterprise of these disciplines with the postcolonial politics of Native American communities. While NAGPRA seemed to provide a tool to help empower tribes in the United States to repatriate ancestral remains, the very notion of ancestral identity has become caught up within the evolving biocolonial practices of these sciences, whether it is studies of tooth morphology, cranial features, or DNA. DNA can be a tool with utility to those who have been or could be disenfranchised from Native American tribal communities. In conjunction with the interests of archaeologists, it also has the potential to support claims of ancestry of a people at a particular place and time, which has become critical in the political economic discourse of land claims and federal recognition. Yet at what cost does this pursuit come? Prior to the use of DNA, the ancestral body served as an unquestioned, iconic identity for tribes and a rallying point for assertions of sovereignty. However, to support the ancestral body's use as a scientifically defined support of identity is paradoxically to violate its sanctity and iconic status, which could be used, as some have argued (Tallbear 2007), to erase identity altogether. For Native Americans and Indigenous peoples worldwide, the intimacy of the ancestral body to the modern self is being redefined yet again, with the ultimate question of control over this process remaining elusive, a problem that still remains to be suitably addressed.

Notes

1. See *Frequently Asked Questions about DNA Tribes® Genetic Ancestry Analysis*, revised April 29, 2010. DNA Tribes, 25 July 2008, *http://www.dnatribes.com/faq.html*; Ancestry ByDNA FAQs: *http://www.ancestrybydna.com* (accessed June 23, 2010.
2. Confederated Tribes of the Umatilla Indian Reservation statement on the Ancient One/Kennewick Man, 19 July 2004; Confederated Tribes of the Umatilla, 27 July 2008. *http://www.umatilla.nsn.us/ancient.html*.
3. U.S. Department of the Interior/National Park Service Kennewick Man Scientific Investigations. May 2004; U.S. Department of the Interior/National Park Service Archaeology Division, 27 July 2008. *http://www.nps.gov/archeology/kennewick/*.

4. Indigenous People's Council on Biocolonialism, Our Mission. 25 July 2008 (revision date unknown). http://www.ipcb.org.

References

Bolnick, D. A., and Smith, D. G. 2003. Unexpected patterns of mitochondrial DNA variation among Native Americans from the southeastern United States. *American Journal of Physical Anthropology* 122: 336–354.

———. 2007. Migration and social structure among the Hopewell: Evidence from ancient DNA. *American Antiquity* 72 (4): 627–644.

Bruning, S. B. 2006. Complex legal legacies: The Native American Repatriation Act, scientific study, and Kennewick Man. *American Antiquity* 71 (3): 501–521.

Chatters, J. C. 2000. The recovery and first analysis of an early Holocene human skeleton from Kennewick, Washington. *American Antiquity* 65 (2): 291–316.

Crigger, B. J. 1995. The Vampire Project (Human Genome Diversity Project). *The Hastings Center Report* 25 (1): 2.

Díaz-Andreu, M., Lucy, S., Babic, S., and Edwards, D. 2005. *The Archaeology of Identity: Approaches to Gender, Age, Ethnicity, Status and Religion.* New York: Routledge.

Gillis, A. M. 1994. Getting a picture of human diversity. *Bioscience* 44 (1): 8–11.

Harke, H., and Wolfram, S. 1992. The power of the past. *Current Anthropology* 34 (2): 182–184.

Harry, D., and Kanehe, L. M. 2006. Collecting blood to preserve culture? *Cultural Survival Quarterly* 29 (4): 34.

Hodder, I. 1991. Interpretive archaeology and its role. *American Antiquity* 56 (1): 7–18.

———. 2002. Ethics and archaeology: The attempt at Çatalhöyük. *Near Eastern Archaeology* 65 (3): 174–181.

Johnson, H., and Olsen, B. 1992. Hermeneutics and archaeology: On the philosophy of contextual archaeology. *American Antiquity* 57 (3): 419–436.

Jones, S. 1997. *The Archaeology of Ethnicity: Constructing Identities in the Past and Present.* New York: Routledge.

Kaestle, F., and Horsburgh, K. A. 2002. Ancient DNA in anthropology: Methods, applications, and ethics. *Yearbook of Physical Anthropology* 45: 92–130.

Lewin, R. 1993. Genes from a disappearing world. *New Scientist* 138 (1875): 25–29.

McNiven, I. J., and Russell, L. 2005. *Appropriated Pasts: Indigenous People and the Colonial Culture of Archaeology.* Lanham, MD: AltaMira.

Meskell, L. 2002. The intersections of identity and politics in archaeology. *Annual Review of Anthropology* 31: 279–301.

Nicholas, G. 2006. Decolonizing the archaeological landscape: The practice and politics of archaeology in British Columbia. *American Indian Quarterly* 30 (3–4): 350–380.

Roberts, J. 1993. Global project underway to sample human diversity. *Nature* 361 (6414): 675.

Ross, P. E. 1993. Endangered genes: Human genome diversity project to catalog endangered genes. *Scientific American* 268 (1): 17.

Tallbear, K. 2003. DNA, blood, and racializing the tribe. *Wicazo Sa Review* 18 (1): 81–107.

———. 2007. Narratives of race and indigeneity in the Genographic Project. *Journal of Law, Medicine, and Ethics* 35 (3): 412–424.

Taylor, R. E., Kimer, D. L., Southon, J. R., and Chatters, J. C. 1998. Radiocarbon dates of Kennewick man. *Science* 280 (5366): 1171–1172

Wells, S. 2006. *Deep Ancestry: Inside the Genographic Project*. Washington, DC: National Geographic.

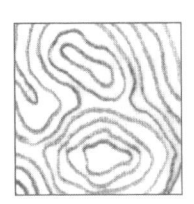

PART V
STRATEGIES OF PRACTICE:
IMPLEMENTING THE POSTCOLONIAL CRITIQUE

This final section canvasses new approaches toward decolonizing the discipline of archaeology. Criticized for its lack of engagement with on-the-ground political struggle, the discipline of archaeology has imagined itself as dealing in the past, not in the present, focusing on objects rather than people. In response to such criticisms, new archaeological practices provide important contributions to the postcolonial project (e.g., Liebmann and Rizvi 2008; Schmidt 2009; Smith and Wobst 2005). Postcolonial theory and archaeology have inspired new forms of practice that have become platforms for critical interventions with communities and publics (e.g., Green et al. 2003; McDavid 2004; Moser et al. 2002; Rizvi 2006). These innovative forms of collaborative practice acknowledge the ethical necessity to engage with descendant communities—that is, with "the groups that link themselves intensely to archaeological heritages because of their cultural, social, and historical affinities" (Colwell-Chanthaphonh and Ferguson 2008: 8).

Collaboration itself has come under scrutiny, in sociopolitical, discursive, and practical contexts, as new relationships are deliberately forged. Indigenous community involvement is growing through formal training and education programs, but also by theorizing collaboratively and creating new means of working together, in the field and afterward. These new strategies of practice show that archaeologists have moved beyond simply acknowledging Indigenous perspectives and adding them to the mix of interpretive strands (Colwell-Chanthaphonh and Ferguson 2008). Such shifts point toward alternative or postcolonial ways of writing archaeology (e.g., Conkey 2005) and have very clear antecedents in recent archaeological theory. The establishment of the feminist critique in archaeology (Gero and Conkey 1991) and the poststructuralist emphasis on multivocality (Preucel and Hodder 1996) fundamentally destabilized the discipline by both questioning the single authoritarian male voice and allowing for a dialogue to emerge between local communities and the archaeologist (e.g., Atalay 2006; Smith and Wobst 2005)

This new strain of community-oriented anthropology has integrated its approaches with archaeological methodologies as an activist response to the need for decolonization, combining public advocacy and public interest anthropology with applied archaeology (Rizvi 2006). This includes new ways to incorporate classic ethnographies within archaeological discourses, thereby dissolving intradisciplinary boundaries within anthropology (e.g., Edgeworth 2006; Castañeda and Matthews 2008; Hamilakis and Anagnostopoulos 2009; Mortensen and Hollowell 2009). These practitioners are critically engaging with the diversities and power inequalities within "publics" and "communities," indicating a promising future for the discipline.

Fernando Armstrong-Fumero and Julio Hoil Gutierrez (chapter 31) explore new forms of collaborative research among state institutions, anthropologists, and local Yucatec Maya–speaking communities in Mexico. Using an inclusive and community-based notion of cultural heritage, they investigate overlapping local perceptions of landscape, memory, and institutional heritage practice to produce a new model of partnership and knowledge repatriation.

Liam Brady and Joe Crouch (chapter 32) focus on issues raised by archaeological collaboration with Indigenous peoples, tracing the emergence of "community archaeology" during the early 1990s and more recent developments in partnership approaches, using the example of research with Torres Strait Islander communities. For Brady and Crouch, it is not enough to relinquish (some) control and "allow" Indigenous peoples to participate in archaeological research: acknowledging the power inequalities that continue to structure Australian society compels a more radical reconceptualization of collaborative practice. Instead, they explore how living peoples' relationships with ancestral spirits have shaped their research agenda, producing a powerful narrative that combines oral tradition and archaeological evidence to link generations.

Martin Nakata and Bruno David (chapter 33) also take tensions that emerge within collaborative practice as the basis for a more extended consideration of Indigenous interpretive frameworks—what Nakata has termed the "cultural interface." They propose an "Indigenous standpoint theory" which provides a means of understanding Indigenous "perspectives" and positions Indigenous people as more active participants in a self-reflexive practice grounded in acknowledgment of the colonial past and its legacies.

Similarly, Lynn Meskell's archaeological ethnography (chapter 34) provides a methodology that involves living and working among modern communities in a process of long-term immersion. Meskell strongly emphasizes the contemporary dimensions of this approach, necessarily concerned with cosmopolitan transnational alliances and their imbrications with the local in new modes of political community that transcend simple dichotomies of scale.

Sandra Scham (chapter 35) is also critical of remedial, consensual approaches that squander archaeology's radical potential to illuminate marginal experience by recapitulating orthodox histories—for example, that African Americans "did everything that other Americans did and simply were not given credit for it." While Scham suggests that inclusion as reparation is a peculiarly American response, we can also see this process at work across many societies, in a conception of the past as shared and consensual, its meaning universally accessible.

The last two chapter-commentaries in this section deal most directly with the issues of an applied anthropology and archaeological practice. Peggy Reeves Sanday (chapter 36) focuses on epistemological and philosophical issues within developing public-interest theory, and Carol McDavid and Fred McGhee (chapter 37) discuss cultural resource management (CRM), public archaeology, and the role of advocacy in archaeology. Providing a broader anthropological perspective, Sanday illustrates the modes of practice through which there are ethical engagements in critical social issues, and shows how the practice of anthropology is a viable form of social change. McDavid and McGhee's commentary furthers that possibility, strategizing "creative, moral and practical ways" by which the intersections between archaeology and the requirements of descendant groups can be better understood and met. They are particular in contextualizing their work as practitioners in both the CRM and public archaeology spheres—both of which are also further understood through their respective standpoints as a Euro-American and an African American working in the United States.

References

Atalay, S. 2006. Decolonizing archaeology. Special Issue. *American Indian Quarterly* 30 (3).

Castañeda, Q., and Matthews, C. 2008. *Ethnographic Archaeologies: Reflections on Stakeholders and Archaeological Practices.* Rowman and Littlefield.

Colwell-Chanthaphonh, C., and Ferguson, T. J. 2008. Introduction: The collaborative continuum, in C. Colwell-Chanthaphonh and T. J. Ferguson (eds.), *Collaboration in Archaeological Practice: Engaging Descendant Communities*, pp. 1–32. New York: AltaMira Press.

Conkey, M. W. 2005. Dwelling at the margins, action at the intersection? Feminist and indigenous archaeologies. *Archaeologies* 1 (1): 9–59.

Edgeworth, M. (ed.). 2006. *Ethnographies of Archaeological Practice: Cultural Encounters, Material Transformations.* Oxford: AltaMira Press.

Gero, J. M., and Conkey, M. 1991. *Engendering Archaeology: Women and Prehistory* Oxford: Blackwell.

Green, L. Fordred, Green, D. R., and Góes Neves, E. 2003. Indigenous knowledge and archaeological science: The challenges of public archaeology in the reserva Uaça. *Journal of Social Archaeology* 3 (3): 366–398.

Hamilakis, Y., and Anagnostopoulos, A. (eds.). 2009. Archaeological ethnographies. *Public Archaeology* 8 (2–3).

Liebmann, M., and Rizvi, U. Z. (eds.). 2008. *Archaeology and the Postcolonial Critique*. Lanham, MD: AltaMira Press.

McDavid, C. 2004. From "traditional" archaeology to public archaeology to community action, in P. A. Shackel and E. J. Chambers (eds.), *Places in Mind: Public Archaeology as Applied Anthropology*. New York: Routledge.

Mortensen, L., and Hollowell, J. (eds.). 2009. *Ethnographies and Archaeologies: Iterations of the Past*. Florida: University Press of Florida.

Moser, S., Glazier, D., Phillips, J. E., N. el Nemr, L., Saleh Mousa, M., Nasr Aiesh, R., Richardson, S., Conner, A., and Seymour, M. 2002. Transforming archaeology through practice: Strategies for collaborative archaeology and the community archaeology project at Quseir, Egypt. *World Archaeology* 34 (2): 220–248.

Preucel, R. W., and Hodder, I. 1996. *Contemporary Archaeology in Theory*. Oxford: Blackwell Publishers.

Rizvi, U. Z. 2006. Accounting for multiple desires: Decolonizing methodologies, archaeology, and the public interest. *India Review* 4 (3–4): 394–416.

Schmidt, P. R. 2009. *Postcolonial Archaeologies in Africa*. Santa Fe: SAR Press.

Smith, C., and Wobst, H. M. 2005. *Indigenous Archaeologies: Decolonizing Theory and Practice*. London: Routledge.

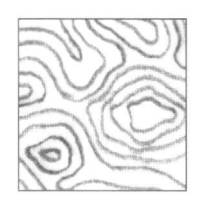

31

COMMUNITY HERITAGE AND PARTNERSHIP IN XCALAKDZONOT, YUCATÁN

*Fernando Armstrong-Fumero and
Julio Hoil Gutierrez*

For the past several years, we have worked together on ethnographic and oral history research in a series of Yucatec Maya–speaking communities in the eastern part of the Mexican state of Yucatán. Our respective backgrounds, as an anthropologist based in the United States (Armstrong-Fumero) and an archaeologist based in Mexico (Hoil Gutierrez, born and raised in the same communities where he conducts research), have brought together the methods and experiences of two national traditions of social science, as well as the distinct personal perspectives of each. Currently, we are conducting preliminary research on a project that explores new forms of partnership among state institutions, anthropologists, and local communities in preserving tangible and intangible forms of cultural heritage. The first phase of this project will be the creation of an ethnographic map of Xcalakdzonot, a community of close to a thousand people in the municipality of Chan Kom, just a 30-minute drive from the world-famous archaeological site of Chichén Itzá.

In this chapter, we discuss how the inclusive and community-based definitions of cultural heritage that inform this project can provide a more general model for exploring points of overlap and collaboration between local forms of landscape perception and historical memory and the heritage practices of official institutions.

Historical Background

For generations, the relationship between Maya-speaking communities and heritage professionals in this part of Yucatán has tended to be marked by hierarchical labor relations, informal collaborations, and occasional tensions. People in the communities where we conduct research have inherited a tradition of intense interactions with archaeology that span back at least to the 1920s, when excavations at Chichén Itzá sponsored by the Carnegie Institute of Washington and the Mexican government drew upon the labor of the residents of Pisté, Xcalakoop, Kaua, and other communities near the archaeological site (Brunhouse 1973; Castañeda 1996). Through the ethnographic studies of Robert Redfield and Alfonso Villa Rojas (1934), this same micro-region also became the *topos* for some of the canonical ethnographic studies of Yucatec Maya people. In the decades since, local people have worked as laborers in the excavation projects conducted by foreign and Mexican archaeologists; have seen a range of legal and institutional changes brought on through the consolidation of national heritage institutions in Mexico (Bernal 1980; Breglia 2006; Vásquez León 2003); and have experienced sweeping economic changes after the emergence of tourism as a major economic resource in the 1970s (Castañeda 1996).

Given the emphasis on cultural continuity that has been at the heart of Mayanist archaeology and anthropology, the relationship between the communities that provided labor for excavation projects and the original builders of pre-Hispanic ruins has been a recurring theme in scholarly writing on the region. As the first generation of professional archaeologists and ethnohistorians noted, many of the towns on the periphery of the archaeological zones had been populated by descendants of the builders of the pre-Hispanic ruins throughout the colonial and modern periods (Coe 1992; Roys 1941). Having an intimate knowledge of a landscape in which they planted their crops, hunted, and extracted forest products, these descendant communities were familiar with the archaeological remains that could be found inside of their own towns, villages, and collectively held agricultural lands. However, as the Carnegie-era researchers also noted, contemporary Maya speakers often interpreted these remains through oral narratives and cosmological principles that were very distinct from the cultural lens of Western anthropology (Redfield 1932). More than half a century later, the great-grandchildren of those who worked in the Carnegie project or who were interviewed by Robert Redfield have been much more influenced by a discourse on the ancient past and cultural patrimony that is promoted by government institutions. Nevertheless, local engagements with contemporary and historical landscapes continue to reflect culturally distinct forms of resource use and historical consciousness (Hanks 1990; Quintal et al. 2003).

Unfortunately, bilateral dialogue between local knowledge of the landscapes that ensconce archaeological remains and the expert knowledges that have greater currency within official heritage institutions has been relatively sparse in this particular micro-region of Yucatán. Today, the only sanctioned interactions between members of rural communities and objects that are designated as cultural patrimony take place through archaeological projects that are initiated and ultimately controlled by foreign researchers or official institutions. Outside of this, the most direct engagement that residents in rural communities have with heritage resources is when they seek to earn a living as wage laborers or as self-employed vendors in the tourist industry, spaces from which their claims on the interpretation or management of the past are given little formal legitimacy. In the worst cases, contentions regarding access to tourist sites have created moments of real tension between heritage workers and local communities. Over the decades, this lack of mutual understanding has tended to impede the repatriation of anthropological knowledge to Maya-speaking descendant communities, and limited other forms of community-based research.

Nowhere are the limits of existing interactions between local communities and archaeological projects more evident than in the relationship between heritage workers and the Maya-speaking laborers who work as groundskeepers, excavators, and masons in research and restorations projects. Through these projects, local people with no previous experience in archaeological work are trained in the basic principles of excavation and restoration. But in most cases, formal communication between archaeologists or workers does not extend beyond what is necessary to create a viable workforce and to provide basic local monitoring of sites during the off-seasons. At the close of a project, the archaeologists will have provided the workers with basic technical training, but only a limited knowledge of the ultimate goals of archaeological research and the protection of heritage.

Although this kind of relationship between heritage workers and community members is less than ideal, the potential for more significant forms of partnership and collaboration can sometimes emerge, albeit informally. After participating in one or more projects, the laborers' experience and knowledge of archaeology can become quite substantial, and some begin to ascribe more importance to archaeological remains and to other sites that could be classified as heritage resources. In many cases, former excavation workers lead local efforts to prevent members of nearby communities or foreign parties from conducting unauthorized excavations, and report such activities to the relevant authorities.

Unfortunately, there are few official mechanisms through which the local knowledge and archaeological training that are combined in the experience of excavation workers from rural communities is used to bridge institutional and Indigenous forms of managing the lived landscape and cultural heritage. In most cases, the representatives of official heritage institutions are required to speak to project workers and other residents of local communities about the need to preserve specific objects of archaeological heritage, even if they might lack the necessary knowledge to reconcile these institutional notions of the past with local forms of human–landscape interactions and historical consciousness. Thus, many members of local communities are left with the impression that they are excluded from a process of defining and managing heritage resources, even when these are found within the traditional territory of their towns and villages.

A good example of the tension between institutional and local experiences of cultural heritage is the number of cases in which government heritage institutions have banned the practice of lighting candles in some colonial churches in order to prevent staining of painted surfaces. Although these measures will certainly help to preserve colonial remains, this protection comes at the expense of a traditional religious practice. Without open communication regarding the potential smoke damage suffered by heritage resources, or serious debate weighing the value of these material resources against that of the traditional religious practices associated with candle lighting, this ban was seen by many as an infringement of local rights to a particular form of religious expression. Similar issues have emerged regarding the right to enjoy tourist incomes generated by archaeological remains that are situated in or adjacent to agricultural lands that are titled to local communities.

The Xcalakdzonot Project

One goal of our exploration of notions of landscape and community patrimony in the town of Xcalakdzonot is to establish a series of useful points of reference for future dialogues between perspectives on the landscape and the past derived from anthropological research and institutional heritage work and the emic perspective of members of Maya communities. In contrast to notions of "national" and "global" heritage, which tend to regard state institutions and expert knowledges as the ultimate arbiters of the value of the past, our approach to community patrimony will highlight productive points of overlap and collaboration between these two distinct cultural perspectives. This implies more than a simple recognition that different discourses on the past and landscape exist; it also includes the members of the host community as partners in defining a research agenda and as custodians of the data that they themselves have produced.

One of the key elements of the dialogue that we hope to develop through this project is an expansion of the kinds of places that can be treated as heritage resources. Our map of the community of Xcalakdzonot will include the remains of some pre-Hispanic monuments that are protected within the juridical and conceptual frameworks that guide formal heritage work in Mexico. But greater emphasis will be placed on aspects of the landscape that have accrued cosmological and thus practical importance within the historical experience of the populations that currently occupy these territories, even if these fall outside of more traditional notions of "national" heritage. Although the role of landscapes in constituting collective memories and identities has received ample discussion in archaeological (Ashmore and Knapp 1999; Dunning et al. 1999; Tilley 1994), ethnographic (Basso 1996; Rosaldo 1980; Slyomovics 1985), and other theoretical literatures (e.g., de Certeau 1984; Norá 1996), it has played a much less significant role in the actual practice of heritage management in this part of Mexico.

Places that will take a prominent place in this extended definition of heritage include caves, sinkholes (*k'oop* or *rejollada*), *cenotes*, and other elements of the natural landscape, as well as material traces of more recent human activity that often fall by the wayside of heritage practices that focus almost exclusively on the pre-Hispanic and colonial periods. We will, for example, locate the foundations of peripheral settlements and house sites that were settled and abandoned over the course of the 20th century and that figured in a series of conflicts that emerged during the first decades of the agrarian reform instituted after the Mexican Revolution of 1910 (see Armstrong-Fumero 2007). These events proved pivotal in defining the contemporary social and political makeup of Xcalakdzonot and occupy a central role in the collective memory of the community. But just as emic forms of landscape perception rarely figure in institutional heritage discourse in Mexico, these local instantiations of processes that helped to consolidate the modern Mexican state are generally excluded from the official narratives that schoolchildren in Xcalakdzonot encounter in their textbooks (see Benjamin 2000).

The ideas of community patrimony and partnership that are at the center of this project address a number of current debates regarding the inclusion and involvement of descendant communities in the process of archaeological research (Ardren 2002; Colwell-Chanthaphonh and Ferguson 2008; González-Ruibal 2003; Marshall 2002; Watkins 2000). Our first extended season of fieldwork begins with a number of open meetings with the local agrarian committee and members of the community at large, through which we will finalize the list of sites that the members of the community consider the most significant for preserving the history and traditional knowledge of the town. The research team will then visit these sites along with collaborators from Xcalakdzonot, to record their exact location with GPS equipment, document the sites photographically, and conduct preliminary interviews with our local guides regarding the uses of the sites or events that previously occurred there. Afterward, these photos and preliminary interview data will be used to conduct semistructured interviews with members of the community, which will generate a record of oral narrative regarding these sites.

The final product of this research will be an interactive map that will permit the user to locate different sites that have been documented by the researchers and to access narratives in which members of the community relate different events that have occurred at these sites, the uses for which they have served the community, and the different cosmological or social values they have accrued over time. The researchers will also train members of the community in the use of the relevant software so that they can revise and expand the map. Copies of all the materials generated by this study—images, paper and electronic copies of maps and interviews, audio recordings, and a computer containing the necessary mapping software —will be kept in the local primary school.

Ultimately, we hope that this map will serve a fourfold purpose for the community, region, and heritage workers in general. First, it will preserve a record of the location and local significance of a series of cultural resources—whether these are archaeological remains that are protected under existing heritage laws or sites that play a more specific emic role within community patrimony—in the hands of the people of Xcalakdzonot. Second, in collaboration with local municipal authorities and the directors of the local school, the data generated by this study can be used to supplement existing school curricula and make knowledge of certain forms of community patrimony more accessible to younger generations who have less direct experience in traditional forms of interacting with the local landscape. Third, this same record of a local history of interactions with the landscape can also educate publics outside of the community about a valuable and endangered form of intangible heritage that documents part of the diversity of human interactions with the environment. Finally, the model of partnership and the repatriation of anthropological knowledge that is operationalized through this project can generate important insights for the development of more inclusive, postcolonial, and critically multicultural heritage practices.

References

Ardren, T. 2002. Conversations about the production of archaeological knowledge and community museums at Chunchucmil and Kochol, Yucatan, Mexico. *World Archaeology* 34 (2): 379–400.

Armstrong-Fumero, F. 2007. *Before There Was Culture Here: The Making and Unmaking of Revolutionary Modernity in Yucatán, Mexico*. Ph.D. dissertation. Department of Cultural and Social Anthropology, Stanford University.

Ashmore, W., and Knapp, A. B. (eds.). 1999 *Archaeology of Landscape: Contemporary Perspectives*. New York: Blackwell.

Basso, K. 1996. *Wisdom Sits in Places: Landscape and Language among the Western Apache*. Albuquerque: University of New Mexico Press.

Benjamin, T. 2000. *La Revolución: Mexico's Great Revolution as Memory, Myth and History*. Austin: University of Texas Press.

Bernal, I. 1980. *A History of Mexican Anthropology*. New York: Thames and Hudson.

Breglia, L. 2006. *Monumental Ambivalence: The Politics of Heritage*. Austin: University of Texas Press.

Brunhouse, R. L. 1973. *In Search of the Maya: The First Archaeologists*. Albuquerque: University of New Mexico Press.

Castañeda, Q. E. 1996. *In the Museum of Maya Culture: Touring Chichén Itzá*. Minneapolis: University of Minnesota Press.

Certeau, M. de 1984. *The Practice of Everyday Life*. Minneapolis: University of Minnesota Press.

Coe, M. 1992. *Breaking the Maya Code*. New York: Thames and Hudson.

Colwell-Chanthaphonh, C. and Ferguson, T. J. (eds.). 2008. *Collaboration in Archaeological Practice: Engaging Descendant Communities*. Lanham, MD: AltaMira Press.

Dunning, N., Scarborough, V., Valdez, Jr., F., Luzzadder-Beach, S., Beach, T., and Jones, J. G. 1999. Temple mountains, sacred lakes, and fertile fields: Ancient Maya landscapes in northwestern Belize. *Antiquity* 73 (281): 650–660.

González Ruibal, A. 2003. *La experiencia del Otro: Una introducción a la etnoarqueología*. Madrid: Ediciones Akal.

Hanks, W. 1990. *Referential Practice: Language and Lived Space among the Maya*. Chicago: University of Chicago Press.

Marshall, Y. (2002). What is community archaeology? *World Archaeology* 34 (2): 211–219.

Norá, P. 1996. *Realms of Memory: Rethinking the French Past*. New York: Columbia University Press.

Quintal, E. F., Bastarrachea, J. R., Briceño, F., Medina, M., Repetto, B., Rejón, L., and Rosales, M. 2003. *U Lu'umil Maaya Wíiniko'ob: La Tierra de los Mayas*. In Alicia Barabas (ed.), *Diálogos con el territorio: Simbolizaciones sobre el espacio en las culturas indígenas de México*, pp. 275–360. México: INAH.

Redfield, R. 1932. Maya archaeology as the Mayas see it. *Sociologus; Zeitschrift fur Volker-psychologie und Soziologie* 8: 299–309.

Redfield, R., and Villa Rojas, A. 1934. *Chan Kom: A Maya Village*. Washington, DC: Carnegie Institution of Washington.

Rosaldo, R. 1980. *Ilongot Headhunting, 1883–1974: A Study in Society and History*. Stanford, CA: Stanford University Press.

Roys, R. 1941. *The Indian Background of Colonial Yucatán*. Washington DC: Carnegie Institute.

Slyomovics, S. 1985. *The Object of Memory: Arab and Jew Narrate the Palestinian Village*. Philadelphia: University of Pennsylvania Press.

Tilley, C. 1994. *A Phenomenology of Landscape: Places, Paths and Monuments*. Oxford: Berg.

Vásquez León, L. 2003. *El Leviatán arqueológico. Antropología de una tradición científica en México*. México: CIESAS.

Watkins, J. 2000. *Indigenous Archaeology: American Indian Values and Scientific Practice*. Walnut Creek, CA: AltaMira Press.

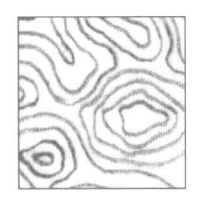

32

PARTNERSHIP ARCHAEOLOGY AND INDIGENOUS ANCESTRAL ENGAGEMENT IN TORRES STRAIT, NORTHEASTERN AUSTRALIA

Liam M. Brady and Joe Crouch

Archaeologists who engage in research with Indigenous communities are inherently confronted with a complex intersection between Western-oriented archaeological agendas and powerfully tangible aspects of Indigenous cultural heritage (e.g., ancestral remains). Over the last three decades, Indigenous communities have increasingly, and rightly, demanded control over research agendas intimately connected to *their* heritage. Consequently, the relationship between archaeologists and Indigenous communities has undergone a major episode of restructuring, with the challenge to create an ethically, politically, and socially acceptable working environment.

We begin this chapter with a review that traces the historical trajectory of this relationship to the notion and emergence of "community archaeology." Next we explore the scale and scope of the Indigenous "community" in conjunction with the recent development of "partnership approaches" exemplified and articulated in terms of McNiven and Russell's (2005) host–guest model. Lastly, we provide some reflexive case studies linked to our research experiences as archaeologists and guests of Indigenous Torres Strait Islander communities to illustrate how partnership archaeology can provide greater insight and clarity into (1) the notion of ancestors as active and equal partners in the research process, and (2) the privileges, responsibilities, and protocols we face today when practicing archaeology in a postcolonial world.

Tensions and Ethics

Instances of disagreement and tension between archaeologists and Indigenous communities regarding issues such as control of material culture, repatriation, reburial, and ethical conduct by archaeologists have attracted considerable attention worldwide. High-profile examples include the battle between Native American groups and anthropologists for control of "Kennewick Man" (e.g., Holden 2004; Watkins 2000, 2004), and the forced repatriation of excavated material culture in Tasmania (e.g., Murray and Allen 1995; Tasmanian Aboriginal Land Corporation 1996).

In an Australian context, the early 1980s was a pivotal phase in the archaeologist–Indigenous community relationship; archaeologists were confronted with Indigenous demands for greater control, power, and recognition in research involving Indigenous communities. Papers presented at national conferences by Ros Langford (1983), presenting on behalf of the Tasmanian Aboriginal Community, and later Henrietta Fourmile (1989) publicly criticized the way archaeologists worked with Indigenous communities and their cultural heritage. These influential papers introduced Aboriginal perspectives on archaeological research in Australia to archaeologists and played a crucial role in the development of specific ethical codes of conduct for archaeologists working with Aboriginal communities (e.g., Davidson 1991; Lewis and Bird Rose 1985; Veth 1991). While ethical orientations in archaeology have changed over time (see Tarlow 2006: 200), the 1980s saw ethical codes of conduct being created by professional archaeology organizations for their members (e.g., Australian Archaeological Association, World Archaeological Congress), and discussion continues today on issues regarding the ethical practice of archaeology with Indigenous communities (see, e.g., Hanna 2003; Lynott and Wylie 2000; Scarre and Scarre 2006; Zimmerman et al. 2003, among others). Alternatively, Indigenous elders and organizations have also created guidelines and ethical protocols for archaeologists to follow if they wish to engage in research involving their cultural heritage (e.g., Central Land Council 2003; Pikwàkanagàn Council 2004; Wiynjorroc et al. 2005). Although recognition of the inalienable rights of Indigenous communities with regard to their cultural heritage has been slow, the proliferation of projects and initiatives aimed at "working together" is indicative of an important change in the Indigenous community–archaeologist relationship.

"Community Archaeology" in a Global Context

The concept of "community archaeology" developed in the early 1990s and has meant different things to different people. Community archaeology refers broadly to archaeologists and Indigenous communities working together, although it has also been used as an approach to moderate tensions between Indigenous communities and archaeologists, promote collaboration between the two groups on issues related to Indigenous heritage, and recognize Indigenous rights to their cultural places and histories. This development was in stark contrast to early archaeological endeavors involving Indigenous heritage which saw archaeology carried out largely without any Indigenous participation, consultation, or communication of results. The notion of community archaeology is probably most associated today with a *World Archaeology* volume (Marshall 2002) containing a range of examples and discussions regarding the practice and concept of community archaeology. Taking this collection as a starting point, we go further to consider some of the difficult issues it raises.

A review of Indigenous community-based archaeological initiatives from around the globe reveals that there is no single formula or methodology for practicing collaborative research—each project is unique and contextual. However, some key features can be identified that archaeologists and Indigenous communities alike consider crucial to a successful collaboration: cooperative attitude, trust, return of information, plain English reports, community participation, obtaining permission to conduct research, identification of benefits to the community, and Indigenous review of published material (e.g., Jackson and Smith 2005; Watkins and Ferguson 2005).

From a geographical perspective, the community-based paradigm is most visible in archaeological research projects throughout Australasia and North America. As George Nicholas (2001: 38) notes, much of the 1990s was devoted to the "working together" theme, where archaeologists and Indigenous communities sought ways to collaborate and develop "greater awareness and sensitivity on the part of archaeologists, and a more complete understanding of what archaeology can offer to indigenous people." While an in-depth, cross-cultural examination of different collaborative research arrangements is beyond our scope here, some of the approaches used in community-based research include research by invitation, research by inquiry, and research by consultancy (Brady 2005). Key themes identified through these various research approaches focus on (but are certainly not limited to) the role of archaeology in cultural education, training, and conservation (e.g., Brady et al. 2003; Krall 2003; Mills 2000; Nicholas 1997, 2001), ecotourism (e.g., Beck et al. 2005; Colwell-Chanthaphonh 2003), and cultural site documentation, protection, and management (e.g., Allen et al. 2002; Anyon and Ferguson 1995; Friesen 2002; Ross and Coghill 2000). Many of the issues associated with the practice and results of research projects involving archaeologists and Indigenous communities have been the focus of international forums and edited volumes, and also formed a section of the Society for American Archaeology's *Archaeological Record* entitled "Working Together" (e.g., Davidson et al. 1995; Derry and Malloy 2003; Dongoske et al. 2000; Nicholas and Andrews 1997; Swidler et al. 1997). However, in spite of the development of collaborative ventures between archaeologists and Indigenous communities, critical evaluation of this relationship and an understanding of the complexity associated with a community remain ongoing challenges.

Scale and Scope of "Community"

While "community" can be defined as anything one chooses to group together (e.g., a body of individuals [see Anderson 1983]), Indigenous communities are dynamic and cannot be considered as static or finite entities. In the context of defining and understanding the composition of an Indigenous community, we need to consider a community's scale (e.g., individuals linked by name, clan, totem, or language affiliations) and scope (e.g., ancestors and objects as other potential actors). And although "community" implies some degree of homogeneity in terms of group affiliations, there is also an innate heterogeneity. In an Australian colonial context, Attwood (1989) links the European imposition of a homogenizing (and disempowering) Aboriginal identity with the creation (and empowerment) of European "Australians."

The ambiguous nature of collective identities is also critically significant at the scale of community-based projects. In the United States, for example, Larry Zimmerman (2005: 301–304) recently recounted the difficulties and politics related to the identification of communities associated with the Crow Creek Massacre Project in South Dakota. During community meetings, several groups and subgroups emerged, each claiming a relationship to the site and each with different opinions and perceptions of the work. Zimmerman's research highlights the complexities involved with identifying living communities who might have an interest in an archaeological project involving Indigenous cultural heritage. Similarly, Yannis Hamilakis (2007: 35) has recently advocated combining the ethical and political arenas in community archaeology (a political-ethical approach) to engage with the broader sociopolitics of the past. In particular, he noted that the politics of community archaeology should also be considered at both micro- (e.g., micro-politics of a community) and macro-scales (e.g., colonialism, nationalism).

The historical imposition of collective identities and the dynamic nature of Indigenous communities can also create considerable difficulty in ascertaining *which* communities to deal with. In Torres Strait, for example, prior to European contact, identity tended to focus inward—primarily on the family, clan, and home island levels (Shnukal 2004: 113), but today Islanders identify at a range of social scales: families, totems, islands, island groups, the Torres Strait region, and Australia as a whole. Martin Nakata (2003: 133) has also drawn attention to the colonial imposition of a collective "Torres Strait Islander" identity resulting in an "umbrella Islander community," one that sometimes blurs the distinction between local and regional identities. Yet this collective identity was used strategically by Islanders in the 1930s as a source of empowerment in their struggle for increased political power as a regional organization involved in the 1936 Maritime Strike and the development of an inter-island council (Sharp 1993: 210).

The composition of Indigenous communities is also constantly changing. Deaths of community elders, promotion of younger community members to positions of power, and changes in committee members are examples of community dynamism. As a consequence, research agendas need to be constructed with built-in flexibility capable of shifting with changing circumstances. Furthermore, as we discuss below, understanding the nature of a "community" is not limited to the living—the role and inclusion of ancestors in the research process is proving to be an important consideration when working in a collaborative context.

The Struggle for Power and Control: Toward Partnership Archaeology

In the 2002 *World Archaeology* volume dedicated to "Community Archaeology," the introductory essay by guest editor Yvonne Marshall (2002: 211) began with a key statement describing community archaeology: "Its most important distinguishing characteristic is the relinquishing of at least partial control of a project to the local community." Furthermore, "[r]elinquishing the right to total control over an archaeological project and allowing local communities to make critical decisions on research directions, questions and priorities may at first seem like a loss" (Marshall 2002: 218).

By "allowing" Indigenous communities to take part in a project involving *their* heritage and *relinquishing* control to the local community, there remains an overt non-Indigenous sense of control, power, and Western hegemony over the "collaborative" project involving Indigenous heritage. Indeed, as Ian McNiven and Lynette Russell (2005: 234) have remarked in their analysis and critique of the community archaeology literature, "a trend is emerging where archaeologists are positioning themselves as the agents of change and as the source of Indigenous empowerment.... [S]uch a position denies the agency and political activism of Indigenous people." Indigenous agency is likewise diluted through the stakeholder model—where Indigenous communities, archaeologists, developers, and curators are identified as having an equal controlling interest in Indigenous heritage. And while it is beyond our scope here to provide a detailed critique of the stakeholder model (but see McNiven and Russell 2005; Nicholas 2001), its inadequacy as an approach is exemplified by its inability to cope with Indigenous ancestral agency and dead "stakeholders."

This dissatisfaction with the continuing Western hegemony in the Indigenous community–archaeologist relationship has led to McNiven and Russell's (2005: 235–242) proposition of a further development of the discipline: an ethically acceptable host–guest paradigm which sees archaeologists as *guests* of Indigenous communities, and who have obtained community consent to undertake research on Indigenous cultural heritage. In this sense, Indigenous communities are not just stakeholders in archaeological research; they retain full power and control of the project. This paradigm is viewed as a fundamental step to redressing the problem of empowerment when dealing with Indigenous heritage and property. Furthermore, as a research *partnership*, the agenda, process, interpretation of data, and presentation of results must be negotiated together and reflect both Indigenous and scientific perspectives. This process enables both parties to work together to minimize the risk of alienating either group. As archaeologists working in partnership with Indigenous communities, we have certain responsibilities including (but not limited to) clarifying limitations and error margins involved with a particular method (e.g., surveys, radiocarbon dating), establishing a regular process of community feedback in a user-friendly format for the community, educating community members interested in archaeology, and educating ourselves with community protocols and traditional knowledge, and retaining a degree of research flexibility, where the agenda can be adjusted and refined as appropriate.

As we discuss in the next section, the partnership approach also leads to a more complex understanding of how the research process works. Our experience as doctoral researchers working in partnership with local Torres Strait Islander communities has furthered our awareness of methods for engaging in a research dialogue that includes active ancestral engagement. In addition, this experience represents our first major foray into practicing archaeology with Indigenous communities. As such, our positions as early career researchers has resulted in the partnership process being the *only* way we have known how to practice archaeology with Indigenous communities.

Meeting the Ancestors in an Islander Spiritscape

As invited members of the Western Torres Strait Culture History Project (WTSCHP) —a project co-directed by Ian McNiven, Bruno David, various local community organizations (e.g., Native Title bodies, community councils), and community elders from across Western Torres Strait, we were fortunate enough to participate in a range of archaeological projects focused on Indigenous and scientific agendas. As such, our examples involve shared experiences and interpretations as part of the research team.

Islander ancestral engagement has been documented in many forms. McNiven (2003: 333) notes that "Saltwater People," such as Torres Strait Islanders, "believe they share the world with spirits of the dead (the 'old people')." In Torres Strait, "death dances" were held to help ensure the ghost of the deceased individual was conveyed safely to *Kibu*, the "land of the dead" where they became a *markai*, or "spirit of the dead" (Haddon 1904: 355–356) (Figure 32.1). Evidence of *markai* was commonly observed by Islanders. Waterspouts were considered a means for *markai* to harpoon turtle and dugong, while canoe rock-paintings were said to represent the canoes' *markai* used to paddle on calm nights (Haddon 1904: 358). Skulls of relatives were used to ask questions concerning outcomes of events or causes of an individual's death (Haddon 1904: 358). Additionally, many of the physical features of the landscape and seascape were also created by ancestors, and actions by ancestors are enshrined in oral traditions still regularly told today.

Hunters have also engaged with ancestors by visiting a "graveyard to ask ancestors for good luck" (Nietschmann and Nietschmann 1981: 61; see also McNiven and Feldman 2003: 180), while McNiven and Feldman (2003: 180) also note an association between dugong hunting and ancestral powers via oral tradition. These examples reveal that engagement with the ancestors

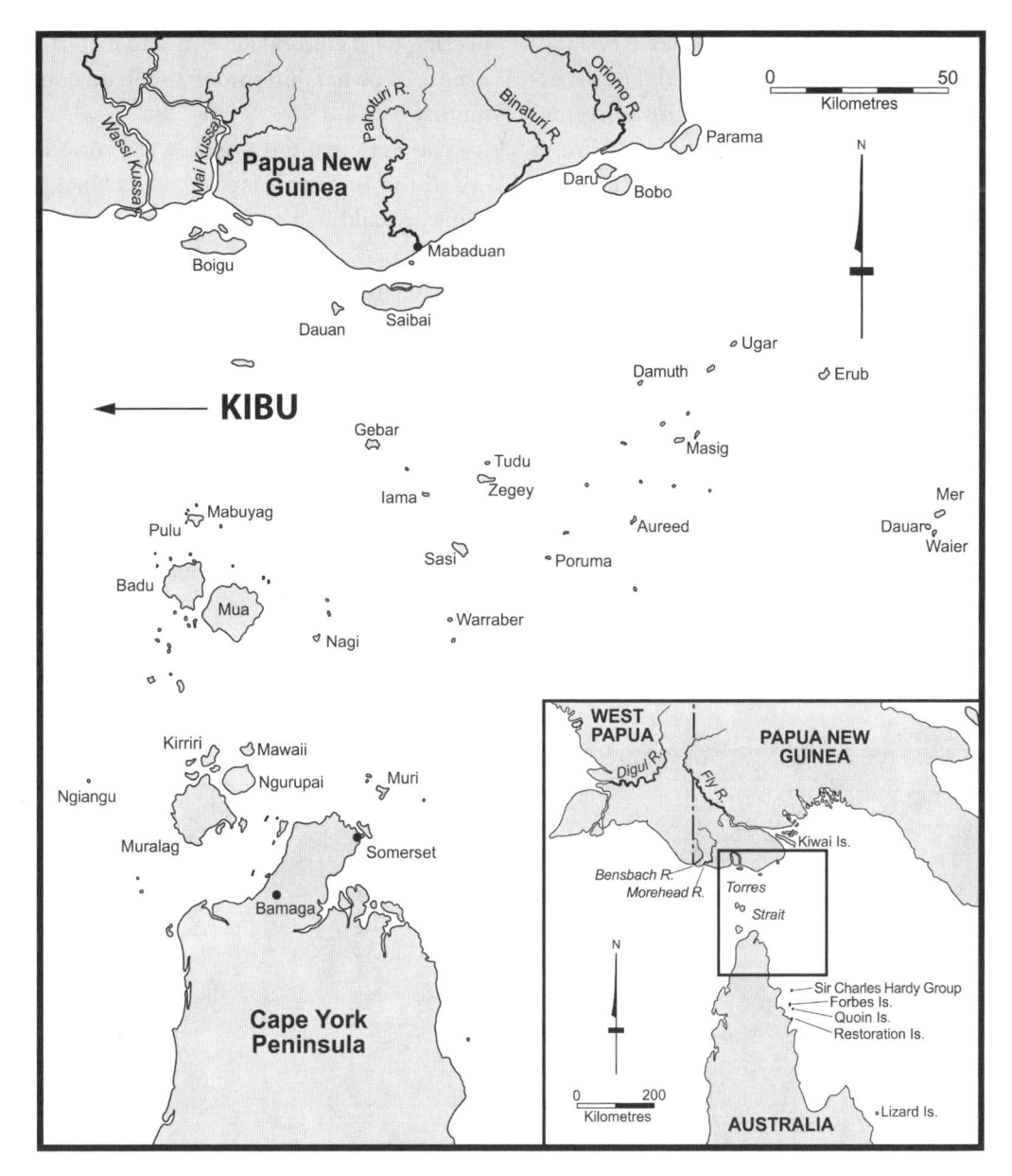

Figure 32.1 Map of Torres Strait showing location of Kibu.

and the spirit world was not—and is not—uncommon. As we discuss below, this practice also helps direct and shape archaeological research.

The Ikis Turtleshell Mask

During the early contact period, turtleshell masks were a common element in Islander ceremonial and ritual activities (see Haddon 1912). Yet until recently, all known examples were part of museum collections scattered around the world (e.g., Fraser 1978). In 2001, joint surveys on the island of Badu targeted Ikis, a place of special significance, at the request of Badu elders. At Ikis we documented the first turtleshell mask to be recovered in an archaeological context in Torres Strait (see David et al. 2004) (Figure 32.2). The local pride within the community in recovering such a significant cultural heritage object was obvious; the community decided to remove the mask and store it in a safe place until a cultural center was operational on the island. The mask is today considered symbolic of past cultural practice on Badulgal [Badu Islander] traditional lands and is viewed as reflecting local cultural identity and fostering a sense of ownership among the Badu community.

The Badulgal did not view the discovery of the Ikis turtleshell mask as "lucky." We were told by the Badulgal community that the mask was *meant* to be found; when we made important discoveries (such as the Ikis turtleshell mask), it was because the ancestors had guided us; the ancestors wanted these items to be found and to be recorded by and for the community. Badulgal also explained that the spirits must have approved of the collaborative research, and the discovery of the Ikis turtleshell mask was testament to their approval. In this sense, active ancestral engagement is a Badulgal explanation for the discovery of material culture, and for shaping local archae-

Figure 32.2 *(Left):* Discovery of the Ikis turtleshell mask on Badu in 2001. *(Upper right):* Ikis turtleshell mask. *(Lower right):* Piece of decorated turtleshell (probably from a headdress) collected from an unknown location in Torres Strait (courtesy of the Pitt-Rivers Museum; PRM 1906.20.50).

ology projects. However, it is important to note that this dynamic also operates the other way: if a survey proves fruitless, or a problem is encountered (e.g., someone becomes sick), this can lead to a consideration of whether proper protocols have been followed.

Celebrating an Oral Tradition

A cultural celebration on the island of Mua in 2002 also reveals how archaeologists and Islanders—and their ancestors—worked together in a project aimed at promoting cultural education and awareness of cultural history. The impetus for this project came from respected elders Wees Nawia and his son Morris who, in the 1960s, told the Mualgal community they wanted to commemorate the Mualgal oral tradition of Goba of Mua (see Brady et al. 2003; David et al. 2004). The story tells of a fishing expedition where Goba's father was killed by Badu headhunters while Goba escaped by climbing and hiding in a tree (see Lawrie 1970: 45–46 for details). Both Wees and Morris hoped to construct a memorial at Goba's father's grave at Uma, so younger generations would remember the Goba story and the Goba landscape. Unfortunately, both men passed away before this desire could be realized.

In 2001, as part of a cultural heritage project, elders invited archaeologists to visit a rock-shelter called Turao Kula (near Uma). Computer enhancement of rock paintings revealed a human figure—identified by elders as Goba—climbing a palm tree. An excavation directly below the panel of paintings uncovered a piece of red ochre in the stratified cultural deposit, which was subsequently dated to between C.E. 1750 and 1850 (see David et al. 2004 for further details).

The cultural celebration that followed these archaeological discoveries commemorated the wishes of Wees and Morris Nawia, and the Goba story and landscape. At the celebration, a plaque featuring the computer-enhanced rock paintings and the Goba narrative was placed at Goba's father's grave (Figure 32.3). Goba's direct descendants were also present, and lengthy genealogies related to Goba were read aloud. As Brady et al. (2003: 46) note, the results of the project were instrumental in "linking the present generations to the history of the island via the ancestors." By linking archaeology with an oral tradition involving their ancestors, the Mualgal community was revealing a research agenda that was guided by deceased members of their community and focused on events directly involving both ancestors and descendants.

While the significance of ancestors in Indigenous archaeology has been noted in recent years (e.g., Syms 1997; Webb 1995), our research partnership with Torres Strait Islander communities has reinforced the notion that partnership archaeology goes beyond the realm of the living. Whereas James Whitley (2002: 119) has recently argued that there are "too many ancestors" in archaeological interpretations, especially in relation to British prehistory, this is certainly not the case in Indigenous archaeology.[1] The case studies described in this

Figure 32.3 *(Left):* Celebration at Goba's father's grave on Mua in 2002. *(Upper right):* Black and white computer tracing of the rock-art panel depicting Goba climbing between two palm trees. *(Lower right):* Traditional dancing at the Goba celebration.

chapter resonate with Tim Ingold's (2000: 140–151) relational (versus genealogical) model of ancestry, whereby the ancestors have a role in actively guiding and "nurturing" current generations as opposed to only being connected through lines of descent. Our experiences have revealed that the partnership we are involved in is effectively made up of three parties: living Islanders, dead Islanders, and archaeologists. Moreover, this partnership is mediated by powerful items of local material culture, which link living and dead traditional custodians with the partnership research agenda.

Conclusion

A fundamental aspect of archaeology with Indigenous communities is dealing with an ancestral past in the present. Through the partnership research process, our hosts have introduced us to their ancestors and affirmed their role as active and equal participants in the community: we consider this partnership both a great privilege and responsibility. Ultimately, long-term commitment to partnership research can lead to friendships and attachments that begin to blur the host–guest distinction. Furthermore, long-term partnerships help build trust and respect and create a momentum that promotes pan-generational relevance in the research process.

The way we have come to meet the ancestors has involved "mediating objects" (Dant 1999) imbued with local cultural significance that connect living and dead custodians. Such mediating objects are potentially another class of unseen agency in the research process that needs to be acknowledged and explored further in the future. The intimate interrelationship that we have documented between archaeological sites, contemporary Torres Strait Islanders, and their ancestors is complex and often a highly personal affair. Further understanding of this interrelationship will require an interdisciplinary approach that includes the combined skills of local elders, anthropologists, and cultural theorists. Not only is this next level of understanding beyond the scope of this chapter, but Torres Strait Islander elders, both living and dead, may decide that it remains beyond the gaze of outsiders.

Acknowledgments

We thank Ian McNiven for many insightful discussions that inspired ideas in this chapter and for providing valuable comments on an earlier draft, and also Bruno David and two anonymous referees for helpful comments on an earlier draft. *Kaima esso* to our Islander hosts, in particular the Badulgal and Mualgal, for their hospitality, generosity, and for introducing us to their ancestral landscape and seascape.

Note

1. While Mike Pitts (2003) and James Whitley (2002, 2003) engage in a semantic debate regarding whether "people who came before us" is an appropriate definition of "ancestors" in terms of the British Neolithic, it is worth considering that for the Yanyuwa people of the Gulf of Carpentaria (northeastern Australia) "ancestors" literally translates as "those who stand in front of us" (John Bradley, pers. comm., 2007).

References

Allen, H., Johns, D., Phillips, C., Day, K., O'Brien, T., and Mutunga, N. 2002. *Wahi ngaro* (the lost portion): Strengthening relationships between people and wetlands in North Taranaki, New Zealand. *World Archaeology* 34 (2): 315–329.

Anderson, B. 1983. *Imagined Communities: Reflections on the Origin and Spread of Nationalism*. London: Verso.

Anyon, R., and Ferguson, T. J. 1995. Cultural resources management at the Pueblo of Zuni, New Mexico, USA. *Antiquity* 69: 913–930.

Attwood, B. 1989. *The Making of the Aborigines*. Sydney: Allen and Unwin.

Beck, W., Murphy, D., Perkins, C., Perkins, T., Smith, A., and Somerville, M. 2005. Aboriginal ecotourism and archaeology in coastal NSW, Australia: Yarrawarra Place Stories Project, in C. Smith and H. M. Wobst (eds.), *Indigenous Archaeologies: Decolonising Theory and Practice*, pp. 226–241. London: Routledge.

Brady, L. 2005. *Painting Patterns: Torres Strait Region Rock-Art, NE Australia*. Ph.D. dissertation, Monash University, Australia.

Brady, L., David, B., Manas, L., and the Mualgal Torres Strait Islanders Corporation. 2003. Community archaeology and oral tradition: Commemorating and teaching cultural awareness on Mua Island, Torres Strait. *Australian Journal of Indigenous Education* 31: 41–49.

Central Land Council 2003. Protocol for the Conduct of Archaeological Work. http://www.clc.org.au/media/publications/protocols/Protocol%20for%20archaeological%20work.pdf (accessed November, 2004).

Colwell-Chanthaphonh, C. 2003. A new future for the past: Ecotourism, indigenous peoples, and archaeologists in Belize, in T. Peck, E. Siegried, and G. A Oetelaar (eds.), *Indigenous People and Archaeology: Honouring the Past, Discussing the Present, Building for the Future*, pp. 191–197. Calgary: Archaeological Association of the University of Calgary.

Dant, T. 1999. *Material Culture in the Social World: Values, Activities, Lifestyles*. Buckingham: Open University Press.

David, B., McNiven, I. J., Manas, L., Manas, J., Savage, S., Crouch, J., Neliman, G., and Brady, L. 2004. Goba of Mua: Archaeology working with oral tradition. *Antiquity* 78 (299): 158–172.

David, B., McNiven, I., Bowie, W., Nomoa, M., Ahmat, P., Crouch, J., Brady, L., Quinnell, M., Herle, M., and Herle, A. 2004. Archaeology of Torres Strait turtle-shell masks: The Badu Island cache. *Australian Aboriginal Studies* 1: 18–25.

Davidson, I. 1991. Archaeologists and aborigines. *The Australian Journal of Anthropology* 2 (2): 247–258.

Davidson, I., Lovell-Jones, C., and Bancroft, R. (eds.). 1995. *Archaeologists and Aborigines Working Together*. Armidale: University of New England Press.

Derry, L., and Malloy, M., (eds.). 2003. *Archaeologists and Local Communities: Partners in Exploring the Past*. Washington, DC: Society for American Archaeology.

Dongoske, K. E., Aldenderfer, M., and Doehner, K. (eds.). 2000. *Working Together: Native Americans and Archaeologists*. Washington, DC: Society for American Archaeology.

Fourmile, H. 1989. Who owns the past?—Aborigines as captives of the archives. *Aboriginal History* 13 (1): 1–8.

Fraser, D. F. 1978. *Torres Strait Sculpture: A Study in Oceanic Primitive Art*. London: Garland Publishing.

Friesen, T. M. 2002. Analogues at Iqaluktuuq: The social context of archaeological inference in Nunavut, Arctic Canada. *World Archaeology* 34 (2): 330–345.

Haddon, A. C. 1912. *Reports of the Cambridge Anthropological Expedition to Torres Straits*, Vol. 4: *Arts and Crafts*. Cambridge: Cambridge University Press.

Haddon, A. C. (ed.). 1904. *Reports of the Cambridge Anthropological Expedition to Torres Straits*, Vol. 5: *Sociology, Magic and Religion of the Western Islanders*. Cambridge: Cambridge University Press.

Hanna, M. G. 2003. Old bones, new reality: A review of issues and guidelines pertaining to repatriation. *Canadian Journal of Archaeology* 27 (2): 234–257.

Hamilakis, Y. 2007. From ethics to politics, in Y. Hamilakis and P. Duke (eds.), *Archaeology and Capitalism: From Ethics to Politics*, pp. 15–40. Walnut Creek, CA: Left Coast Press.

Holden, C. 2004. Court battle ends, bones still off-limits. *Science* 305: 591.

Ingold, T. 2000. *The Perception of the Environment: Essays in Livelihood, Dwelling and Skill*. London: Routledge.

Jackson, G., and Smith, C. 2005. Living and learning on Aboriginal lands: Decolonizing archaeology in practice, in C. Smith and H. M Wobst (eds.), *Indigenous Archaeologies: Decolonizing Theory and Practice*, pp. 328–351. London: Routledge.

Krall, A. 2003. The Ute Conservation Corps: Archaeology and ancestral landscape, in T. Peck, E. Siegried, and G. A. Oetelaar (eds.), *Indigenous People and Archaeology: Honouring the Past, Discussing the Present, Building for the Future*, pp. 185–190. Calgary: Archaeological Association of the University of Calgary.

Langford, R. F., [for the Tasmanian Aboriginal Community]. 1983. Our heritage, your playground. *Australian Archaeology* 16: 1–6.

Lawrie, M. 1970. *Myths and Legends of Torres Strait*. St. Lucia: University of Queensland Press.

Lewis, D., and Bird Rose, D. 1985. Some ethical issues in archaeology: A methodology of consultation in northern Australia. *Australian Aboriginal Studies* 1: 37–44.

Lynott, M., and Wylie, A. (eds.). 2000. *Ethics in American Archaeology*. 2nd edition. Washington, DC: Society for American Archaeology.

McNiven, I. J. 2003. Saltwater People: Spiritscapes, maritime rituals and the archaeology of Australian indigenous seascapes. *World Archaeology* 35 (3): 329–349.

McNiven, I. J., and Feldman, R. 2003. Ritual orchestration of seascapes: Hunting magic and dugong bone mounds in Torres Strait, NE Australia. *Cambridge Archaeological Journal* 13 (2): 169–194.

McNiven, I. J., and Russell, L. 2005. *Appropriated Pasts: Indigenous Peoples and the Colonial Culture of Archaeology*. Walnut Creek, CA: AltaMira Press.

Marshall, Y. 2002. What is community archaeology? *World Archaeology* 34: 211–219.

Mills, B. J. 2000. The archaeological field school in the 1990s: Collaboration in research and Training, in K. E. Dongoske, M. Aldenderfer, and K. Doehner (eds.), *Working Together: Native Americans and Archaeologists*, pp. 121–128. Washington, DC: Society for American Archaeology.

Murray, T., and Allen, J. 1995. The forced repatriation of cultural properties to Tasmania. *Antiquity* 69: 871–874.

Nakata, M. 2003. Better, in M. Grossman (ed.), *Contemporary Critical Writing by Indigenous Australians*, pp. 132–144. Carlton: Melbourne University Press.

Nicholas, G. P. 1997. Education and empowerment: Archaeology with, for, and by the Shuswap Nation, British Columbia, in G. P. Nicholas and T. D. Andrews (eds.), *At a Crossroads: Archaeology and First Peoples in Canada*, pp. 85–104. British Columbia: Archaeology Press.

——. 2001. The past and future of Indigenous archaeology: Global challenges, North American perspectives, Australian prospects. *Australian Archaeology* 52: 29–40.

Nicholas, G. P., and Andrews, T. D. (eds.). 1997. *At a Crossroads: Archaeology and First Peoples in Canada*. British Columbia: Archaeology Press.

Nietschmann, B., and Nietschmann, J. 1981. Good dugong, bad dugong: Bad turtle, good turtle. *Natural History* 90 (5): 54–63.

Pikwàkanagàn Council 2004. Umbrella Protocol of the Algonquins of Pikwàkanagàn for the Management of Archaeological Resources in Unceded Algonquin Territory. http://www.algonquinsofpikwakanagan.com/Umbrella%20Protocol%20for%20Archaeology.mht (accessed 8August, 2007).

Pitts, M. 2003. Don't knock the ancestors. *Antiquity* 77 (295): 172–178.

Ross, A., and Coghill, S. 2000. Conducting a community-based archaeological project: An archaeologist's and a Koenpul man's perspective. *Australian Aboriginal Studies* 1–2: 76–83.

Scarre, C., and G. Scarre. (eds.). 2006. *The Ethics of Archaeology: Philosophical Perspectives on Archaeological Practice*. Cambridge: Cambridge University Press.

Sharp, N. 1993. *Stars of Tagai: The Torres Strait Islanders*. Canberra: Aboriginal Studies Press.

Shnukal, A. 2004. Language diversity, pan-Islander identity and "national" identity in Torres Strait, in R. Davis (ed.), *Woven Histories, Dancing Lives: Torres Strait Islander Identity, Culture and History*, pp. 107–123. Canberra: Aboriginal Studies Press.

Swidler, N., Dongoske, K. E., Anyon, R., and Downer, A. S. (eds.). 1997. *Native Americans and Archaeologists: Stepping Stones to Common Ground*. Walnut Creek, CA: AltaMira Press.

Syms, E. L. 1997. Archaeological native internships at the Manitoba Museum of Man and Nature, in G. P. Nicholas, and T. D Andrews (eds.), *At a Crossroads: Archaeology and First Peoples in Canada*, pp. 224–234. British Columbia: Archaeology Press.

Tarlow, S. 2006. Archaeological ethics and the people of the past, in C. Scarre and G. Scarre (eds.), *The Ethics of Archaeology: Philosophical Perspectives on Archaeological Practice*, pp. 199–218. Cambridge: Cambridge University Press.

Tasmanian Aboriginal Land Corporation 1996. Will you take the next step?, in S. Ulm, I. Lilley and A. Ross (eds.), *Australian Archaeology '95: Proceedings of the 1995 Australian Archaeological Association Annual Conference*, pp. 293–299. St. Lucia: Anthropology Museum, University of Queensland.

Veth, P. 1991. Archaeological ethics in WA: The formalisation of Aboriginal consultation. *Australian Aboriginal Studies* 1: 63–65.

Watkins, J. 2000. *Indigenous Archaeology: American Indian Values and Scientific Practice*. Walnut Creek, CA: AltaMira Press.

——. 2004. Becoming American or becoming Indian: NAGPRA, Kennewick and cultural affiliation. *Journal of Social Archaeology* 4 (1): 60–80.

Watkins, J., and Ferguson, T. J. 2005. Working with and working for Indigenous communities, in H. D. G. Maschner and C. Chippindale (eds.), *Handbook of Archaeological Methods*, pp. 1372–1406. Walnut Creek, CA: AltaMira Press.

Webb, S. 1995. *Palaeopathology of Aboriginal Australians: Health and Disease across a Hunter-Gatherer Landscape*. Cambridge: Cambridge University Press.

Whitley, J. 2002. Too many ancestors. *Antiquity* 76 (291): 119–126.

——. 2003. Response to Mike Pitt's "Don't Knock the Ancestors." *Antiquity* 77 (296): 401.

Wiynjorroc, P., Manabaru, P., Brown, N., and Warner, A. 2005. We just have to show you: Research ethics *blekbalawei*, in C. Smith and H. M. Wobst (eds.), *Indigenous Archaeologies: Decolonizing Theory and Practice*, pp. 316–27. London: Routledge.

Zimmerman, L. 2005. First, be humble: Working with Indigenous peoples and other descendant communities, in C. Smith and H. M. Wobst (eds.), *Indigenous Archaeologies: Decolonizing Theory and Practice*, pp. 301–314. London: Routledge.

Zimmerman, L. J., Vitelli, K. D., and Hollowell-Zimmer, J. (eds.). 2003. *Ethical Issues in Archaeology*. Walnut Creek, CA: AltaMira Press.

33

ARCHAEOLOGICAL PRACTICE AT THE CULTURAL INTERFACE

Martin Nakata and Bruno David

Archaeological practice conventionally aims to employ scientific methodologies to investigate the pasts of (usually) other people.[1] Many Indigenous communities have enthusiastically yet apprehensively embraced such attempts to characterize and understand their own pasts through professional archaeological research. This guarded Indigenous interest in archaeological historicism reflects tensions between, on the one hand, community desires for one's own history to be investigated, told locally and/or in the broader world and, on the other hand, Indigenous historical experience of intruders' practices in producing knowledge about them.

This chapter reflects on the emergence of community archaeology to address these tensions by examining the issues at the level of knowledge production and Indigenous historical experience as they emerge in community archaeology. We suggest that attention needs to shift from internal disciplinary concerns to include a better understanding of the contemporary Indigenous interpretive frameworks employed in collaborative spaces of knowledge production. We propose that theorizing Indigenous standpoints at the cultural interface (Nakata 2007) opens up possibilities for more robust and critical engagement on the part of both Indigenous peoples (whose history is being investigated) and non-Indigenous researchers in the tensions between Indigenous and archaeological accounts of the past.

From the onset, we position ourselves in the view that communities whose history is being studied, and/or on whose ancestral lands archaeological research is being undertaken, and non-Indigenous interested parties (e.g., archaeologists, developers, government cultural heritage authorities) are not simply "stakeholders," for this term presumes a degree of equality in rights of access, history, research, and reporting. Rather, as Ian McNiven and Lynette Russell (2005: 235–237) suggest, Indigenous peoples whose ancestry or lands are being researched should be considered as *hosts*, while outsiders are *guests* to the research process. A decolonized research partnership can thus be more appropriately approached as a collaboration between hosts and guests, with all the appropriate protocols that such a partnership entails (see McNiven and Russell 2005 for details on a host–guest approach to archaeological research; also Brady and Crouch, this volume, chapter 32). Needless to say, archaeological research that does not meet such standards of approach into other people's lives and homelands are unacceptably intrusive and problematic.

Contested Knowledge Spaces and Tensions within Community Archaeology

The underlying assumptions of colonial knowledge production about Indigenous peoples have been well critiqued across a number of disciplines (e.g., Atalay 2006; David et al. 2002; McNiven and Russell 2005; Nakata 1998; Linda T. Smith 1999). Such critiques follow broader structuralist, poststructuralist, feminist, and postcolonial commentaries (e.g., Fanon 1986; Freire 1972; Foucault 1972; Weedon 1987; Said 1995). The contestation by the formerly colonized, subordinated, and "othered" subjects of an assumed scientifically objective, apolitical, and "universal" knowledge of human history has produced a deeper and more complicated struggle over meaning and legitimacy at various sites of contemporary knowledge production (Nakata 2007).

To Maori scholar Linda Tuhiwai Smith, the "collective memory of imperialism" and its ongoing offshoots have ensured that much present-day research constitutes "a significant site of struggle between the interests and ways of knowing of the West and the interests and ways of resisting of the Other" (1999: 1–2). And in constructing notions of Indigenous pasts, outside researchers are in receipt of privileged information. They may interpret it within an overt theoretical framework, but also in terms of a covert ideological framework. They have the power to distort, to make invisible, to overlook, to exaggerate, and to draw conclusions, based not on factual data, but on assumptions, hidden value judgments, and often downright misunderstandings. They have the potential to extend knowledge or to perpetuate ignorance (Linda T. Smith 1999: 176).

Following this strand of analysis, constructing other peoples' pasts through archaeological practice is seen to perpetuate processes of "cultural' colonization" as the archaeologist's cultural assumptions and historicist logic are then implicitly grafted onto community histories, irrespective of any explicit intention of the archaeologist to do otherwise. Furthermore, in interactions between outside specialists and those whose history is being investigated, the latter, whose existence is being historicized, are positioned somewhere between their own being and the historicizer's cultural location. This posits Indigenous subjects in terms of Homi Bhabha's (1994) notion of the "third space," between being and representation. This is a space where social identity appears and where a person neither *is* nor *is not* quite the person *re*presented by others—a hyperreality, as Eco (1986) described it.

On the other hand, it can also be asserted that those "others," when involved in self-representation, historicize standpoints in ways that are also limited by their own particular knowledge assumptions and logic. And so, as elsewhere in the social sciences, in the Indigenous–archaeology intersection we end up in the bind of epistemic relativism—that is, where claims to truth over the meaning and significance of material evidence are contingent on particular epistemic frameworks, those finely grooved systems of thought that shape how we make sense of our observations and experience of the social and material world. The collaborative space in which archaeologists and Indigenous people work together to construct accounts of the past becomes a contested knowledge space of relative but competing "truth" claims where, as Joan Gero (1999) asserts, "it must be generally conceded that there are many pasts and they will be known differently from many views."

A subfield of the profession has embraced this "multivocality" (Hodder 2003) as an opportunity to build much richer archaeological accounts and more "textured" narratives of the past in collaboration with descendant communities "at the peripheries" (e.g., Clarke 2002; Gero 1999; Greer et al. 2002; Moser et al. 2002). Community archaeology (used here broadly to encompass a range of community-inclusive practices; see Brady and Crouch, this volume, chapter 32, for a discussion of this term) is therefore an important disciplinary shift that recognizes archaeological research as a sociopolitical endeavor (Clarke 2002) which promotes reflexive practices by valuing different positions or standpoints and encourages examination of taken-for-granted assumptions that researchers bring to their inquiry (Hodder 2003).

Community-based archaeology also stresses the interactive processes of a practice whose prerequisite "is the definition of elements of contemporary community identity that underpin the development of research interests and which inform issues of methodology and practice" (Greer et al. 2002: 268). In this interactive and collaborative space, crossovers between archaeology and other disciplines, subdisciplines, and discourses that investigate Indigenous peoples become evident: examples include ethnographical practice (Clarke 2002), oral history (Greer et al. 2002; Whitely 2002), Indigenous archaeology (Atalay 2006), historic archaeology (Beck and Somerville 2005; Rubertone 2000), cultural heritage management (Smith 2000), Indigenous political discourse (Fourmile 1989; Langford 1983), and oral tradition (Hodder 2003), to name several.

Since the 1970s, in particular, and despite long-held cross-disciplinary collaborations, epistemic relativism and new forms of cross-disciplinary influences in the humanities and social sciences, together with a greater awareness of the significance of non-academic voices (such as community views) to academic practice, have meant an unsettling of disciplinary conventions both in terms of determining and legitimating avenues of inquiry and in ways of "doing" archaeology. For example, some collaborative practices have raised questions about non-Indigenous assumptions when determining sites of archaeological interest as Indigenous or non-Indigenous (e.g., Greer et al. 2002).

In some cases, Indigenous communities are demonstrating that "historic" or "settler" archaeology is valued as a shared space of historical experience—as much about Indigenous histories as about settler histories (e.g., see papers in Russell 2001). As Greer, R. Harrison, and S. McIntyre-Tamwoy note, this disturbs the accepted and arguably persistent divisions between prehistory and historic archaeology in the study of the "deep" past of Aboriginal communities and the study of the "recent" past of settler communities, respectively (2002: 266; see also David and Denham 2006 for discussion of the problematic term "prehistory"). Furthermore, the meanings associated with *place*, rather than time, have emerged as a central focus for inquiry where living, continuing, contemporary communities have opportunities to historicize the past in terms of their own present.

It is relatively easy to demonstrate that collaborative practice produces additional layerings of Indigenous meanings that draw from epistemic continuities from "traditional" pasts, through the era of colonial intrusion, to give expression to a reconstructed contemporary community standpoint embedded in contemporary cultural landscapes. Collaborative practice both contextualizes and brings an Indigenous perspective to bear on the meaning of colonial intrusion and also helps communities to reestablish continuities with past Indigenous relationships attached to a particular place or activity. It does indeed go some way to provide the conditions for Indigenous people to historicize their own past and in the process extends community constructions of their own contemporary identities on their own terms (e.g., Wilson et al. 2000). It should also be noted that changes to the "doing" of archaeology have occurred in the broader context of Indigenous political activity and agendas of self-determination (Fourmile 1989; Kelly 1975; Langford 1983).

It is more difficult, however, to articulate the tensions that occur in this collaborative space and their implications for the theory-practice nexus at the heart of disciplinary knowledge production. Differences in the concepts of *origin, time, history,* and *place,* as well as in what counts as *evidence* and *validity in argument,* are rooted in the deeper foundational conditions of knowledge systems (see also Barker 2006). These deeper differences emerge in practice as the taken-for-granted and less-reflected-on aspects of knowledge production (Barthes 1973). When the knowledge that archaeologists and Indigenous participants draw on is operationalized at the level of collaborative practice, it is not so clear what informs and is being brought through to the dialogue. When the meanings of material or intangible evidence are negotiated, it is not so clear what ontological and epistemological anchors are attached below the surface of collaborators' statements. For example, where do the boundaries between different knowledge systems and cultural location begin and end? What is the epistemological basis of particular strands of thinking, reasoning, and logic? Whose knowledge or experience counts? Is Indigenous experience or "narrative" to be understood as knowledge? Who makes those judgments? What assumptions are reflected on and which remain uncontested? Whose knowledge can be validated and by whose standards is it to be tested? How is Indigenous-generated "data" to be seen in this? And what is the accepted nature of *archaeological* knowledge in general?

Nor is it so clear how Indigenous "interests" in archaeology are constituted in this space in relation to other "stakeholder" interests. Apart from disciplinary interests, governments in Australia still have a large stake in controlling and managing Indigenous interests and to a large extent frame Indigenous political and cultural discourse as an ongoing (often oppositional or resistant) response to government agendas. Contemporary Indigenous perspectives are constructed within these complex relations, and archaeology is complicit in one or more of these epistemic agendas and their attitudinal, structuring, and practical outcomes.

Creating this complex web of social and knowledge relations is an array of historical and contemporary objectified discourses about Indigenous peoples, intersecting with regulatory and bureaucratic mechanisms. These sets of relations have shaped the everyday experiences of what it means to be an Indigenous person in Australia. Also produced within this web of discursive relations are those inter-subjective relations constructed and codified within Indigenous discourse and experience and not easily accessible to outsider analysis. Anne Clarke may appeal that community archaeology "is an explicit restructuring of power relations and a political recognition of the rights of communities to have a role in directing how research about their lives (past or present) is conducted" (2002: 252). But in these complex and fluid interactions on the ground, who is to adjudicate the lines of control and authority?

At its best, the purposes and intentions of collaborative practice are rooted in the quest for deeper and fuller understanding of a human social past. At its worst, collaborative practice is tokenistic and patronizing to the descendant communities whose ancient connections to the land are the object of archaeological interest. But whether "people's" history is at the heart of collaborative projects or not, collaborative practice is also rooted in the politics of Indigenous and non-Indigenous relations, and these relations have a long, unhappy history and are in a constant state of tension. As Laurajane Smith (1999) points out, the privileged position of archaeology as an "objective" and "scientific" authority legitimates contemporary governments' cultural heritage management practice which, in turn, reinforces archaeological authority over Indigenous cultural heritage (see also Barker 2006).

Indigenous peoples clearly have agency but are usually constrained in this particular collaborative space. They make the most of a political and moral position to exploit opportunities to assert their interests. But they continuously enter the discourse of archaeology as the less knowledgeable, the less skilled, and put forward their understanding to be "tested" by those "authorized" to validate Indigenous "interpretation." To satisfy disciplinary knowledge standards, community archaeologists are required at the very least to cross-reference Indigenous-generated data with other related accounts. But from where are these to be drawn? From oral tradition via other Indigenous people who may contradict, or may be unable to confirm, a particular piece of information? Or from oral tradition as recorded in the Western corpus or historical accounts of non-Indigenous people, or from Western understanding? Under these conditions, Indigenous collaborators may unsettle the practices of archaeology but cannot become the authors of their own pasts, much less be recognized as legitimate authorities on their own pasts, at least not in the intersections with the relevant disciplines. However, the Indigenous side of the account is held up on political, moral, or relativist grounds—Indigenous efforts to forge "collaborative archaeological" accounts require that Indigenous meanings have some coherence with what is already known and understood of Indigenous peoples and histories in order to establish a field of mutual intelligibility and some sort of conclusion.

The production of negotiated accounts demonstrates disciplinary interest in Indigenous theorizing of the past and historicizing of the present; nevertheless, the grounds of negotiation are not devoid of the politics and power relations that have always subjugated Indigenous meanings in the processes of knowledge construction.

Rather than thinking of one party as authoritative and the other as "partner," perhaps it is rather incumbent on us all to remember that all parties in a collaboration are trying to make sense of history through their own frames of meaning, using the various tools and sets of knowledge at their disposal, with each party coming from a particular cultural perspective and for which no party has all the answers.

Collaborative practice, then, as a site of contemporary knowledge production concerned with Indigenous pasts, can be theorized as a site of struggle for and over meaning (Nakata 1998, 2007). To reach consensus over meanings and to construct coherent accounts that satisfy both Indigenous and professional communities requires a complex negotiation (e.g., Biolsi and Zimmerman 1997; Echo-Hawk 2000; Nicholas and Andrews 1997). The complexity of these negotiations can be described in terms of what it means *for archaeology*—that is, for how the discipline can serve the interests of contemporary Indigenous communities. But we would argue that these professional accounts are not so adept at bringing to light the complexities of the *Indigenous experience* of participating in contemporary knowledge production at the site of such knowledge entanglements.

We also argue that Indigenous theorizing of knowledge practice tends to embed its critical analysis within resistant or oppositional standpoints, as the earlier statement from Linda T. Smith (1999) noted earlier in this article. We do not dispute the grounds for this; the evidence of subjugation, dismissal, exclusion, and omission in representations of Indigenous knowledge and experience is overwhelming and well documented. Indeed, this reality provides the motivation for Indigenous people to engage the Western academy in the first place, and it provides the motivation for both separate and collaborative knowledge production.

However, we propose that there is space for Indigenous people, particularly theorists and those engaged in knowledge construction, to begin to problematize their own standpoints as well, especially with regard to the way these are brought to bear in critical engagements with the assumptions of Western knowledges. Unless theorizing moves deeper into the muddied entanglements in the intersections between Indigenous and Western ways of "knowing," the focus will remain on teasing knowledge strands apart and arguing their truth claims on political, moral, relativist, or essentialist grounds. It is in the entanglements of knowledge and discourse that Indigenous peoples struggle to reconstruct contemporary identities in the broader world and to articulate the meanings of their experience. We suggest that the entanglement itself is an entry point for inquiry and can inform a method for analysis that gives representation to Indigenous positions. As with all attempts to represent who and what people were or are, this approach cannot get to the truth of Indigenous positions, but it can, we argue, produce more critically engaged Indigenous narratives in contemporary discourses where different grounds of knowledge interact and inform the way we interpret the world. Indeed, the epistemological turn must be about what can be assembled from both sides to achieve the most comprehensive interpretation of the evidence at archaeological sites.

Theorizing Collaborative Practice: The Cultural Interface and Indigenous Standpoints

In relation to practice in Indigenous contexts, the contestation about knowledge production that historicizes the present through examination of Indigenous pasts is a deep one that produces a dialogue played out in the space between systems of knowledge with different cosmological, ontological, and epistemological foundations. Also layered into this space are the effects of colonial intervention into Indigenous worlds. However, discussions about theory have so far tended to remain internal to the discipline (e.g., Murray 1995) and so involve interpretation and translation of Indigenous interests across the terrains of Indigenous political discourse, research ethics for Indigenous contexts (itself an outcome of the political discourse), knowledge built through relationships with Indigenous people in practice, other disciplinary knowledge about Indigenous people (e.g., history, anthropology), and broader social theory development in the human sciences. And yet at the heart of theory are the conceptual parameters and the interpretive frameworks through which a range of decisions are rationalized: the research hypothesis, the contextual knowledge that helps determine sites and entry points to inquiry, the methods used, the analysis of "data," and the conclusions reached.

In collaborative practice with Indigenous people, not only are different conceptual grounds and interpretive frames at work in Indigenous "voices" or "stories," but both Indigenous and disciplinary frames are conditioned within a broader field of politics. It is one thing to develop practice that can "include" Indigenous interpretations, but quite another to develop theory that can encompass the presence of two interpretive frameworks that reach back into different cosmologies.

To attempt to get beyond the dilemma of relativism would seem to risk that neither scientific nor Indigenous conditions of knowledge can be satisfied. However, whether the inclusion of Indigenous interpretation is seen to undermine the "scientific" practice of archaeology, or whether the scientific interpretations of archaeology subordinate or "colonize" Indigenous knowledge practice and ways of historicizing the present, is perhaps a futile argument. What is arguably much more productive is to consider more deeply the interpretive framework that Indigenous participants bring to the collaborative space. If interpretive frameworks are embedded in deeper cognitive schemas for understanding and interpreting the world, then what can be understood of contemporary Indigenous interpretive frameworks that are at work in collaborative practice to produce accounts of the past?

Shelley Greer, Rodney Harrison, and Susan McIntyre-Tamwoy have described the Indigenous–archaeology intersection as a space "where community perspectives [become] entangled with archaeological practices and interpretations" (Greer et al. 2002: 272). Although that does describe what happens in collaborative practice, we argue that Indigenous people come to archaeological sites already entangled and enmeshed in historical experience of the intersection between Indigenous and Western ways of knowing the world. In considering contemporary Indigenous interpretive frameworks, it is useful to consider how Indigenous or community "perspectives" come to be constituted.

Indigenous entanglement is not the result of a simple intersection between Western and Indigenous knowledge systems or cultures or perspectives or interpretations in any single instance. The contemporary Indigenous position is born out of colonial experience and of living in the world and is enmeshed in the historical effects of colonial knowledge production and regulatory practices. This space has been conceptualized elsewhere as a *cultural interface* (Nakata 2007: 199) and is a deep, complex, and both horizontally (inter-textually) and vertically (historically) layered discursive and lived space. In the Australia-Pacific region generally, Indigenous life worlds are, and have been for over 100 (and in some places 200) years, circumscribed by the knowledge and discourses of Western thought. Part of Indigenous experience is to have been enacted upon through the Western corpus that has constructed knowledge "about" Indigenous people and has also defined the parameters of what constitutes Indigenous knowledge, culture, experience, communities, and identities today.

Indigenous peoples have considerable experience of working between different systems of meaning over time. But they do not work neatly between these systems of meaning. To the contrary, making sense in this space involves making sense of contradictory and ambiguous meanings as they emerge in everyday life. From Indigenous standpoints, the frames of reference for Indigenous meaning-making are constituted within a complex matrix of discourses and discursive practices. Here, traditional and Western discourses circulate and shape meaning. But it is also the case that living in this complex and, at times, confusing space—the articulation of discourses at the intersection of meaning systems—shapes Indigenous dispositions to make meaning in particular but fluid ways.

Implicit in much of the negotiation process in contemporary knowledge production is the representation of Indigenous analysis as "voice," "story", "narrative," and "perspective." This is not problematic in itself, and we would agree that this expresses an Indigenous analysis in relation to the possible meanings attached to any particular site or evidence. But we would also argue that this characterization, however well intentioned and "reasonably" accurate from the profession's perspective, strips the negotiated, collaborative process of opportunities to position Indigenous collaborators as more than "informants."

To "shake out" and "reweave" the complex knowledge relations at the cultural interface, we suggest an *Indigenous standpoint theory* (Nakata 2007) that prioritizes three constituting elements that shape Indigenous and non-Indigenous interpretation in collaborative spaces. These are the *locale*, *agency*, and *tensions* that sit in this cultural interface. In proposing a consideration of Indigenous standpoint theory to straddle the epistemic divide in community archaeology, we make use of feminist standpoint theorizing, which contends that "the social position of the knower is epistemically significant; where the knower is socially positioned will both make possible and delimit knowledge ... more objective knowledge is not a product of mere observation or a disinterested perspective on the world, but is achieved by struggling to understand one's experience through a critical stance on the social order within which knowledge is produced" (Polhaus 2002: 285).

The notion of *locale*, then, refers to the "situatedness" of the Indigenous and non-Indigenous position within complex sets of social relations constituted within knowledge-power relations (Foucault 1972). *Locale* signifies not just a physical, but rather a hermeneutic space *as a hegemonic space*. For example, *locale* signifies that even on local, scientific, or traditional grounds, Indigenous and non-Indigenous contributions will be framed within the broader sociopolitical relations at play in any interaction. Generally unrecognized, the *locale* naturalizes the epistemic position as neutral (which it is not). Mobilizing this sense of *locale*, the collaborative space can then be seen as a single moment in a complex environment, where the effects of historical experience and discursive positioning converge, entangle, and generate points of coherence for a perspective to be imparted. Importantly, perspectives taken in this space will contain evidence of the presence of a priori elements that condition the possibilities for what can be said or not said in the collaboration. Thus, the complexity at any particular site should not be viewed as a fixed point from which an Indigenous "truth" is generated, or an archaeological "truth" is confirmed, or an Indigenous–archaeological "dilemma" is resolved. Rather, consideration of the *locale* leads us to view the complexity that emerges in a particular collaboration as a shifting one, conditioned in different moments by such things as what is being asked, who is doing the asking, where it is asked, who it is asked of, and so forth. Explicating the elements that condition the possibilities for contributions from both sides in the collaboration will inevitably shed light on the limits or constraints of those possibilities; and thus begins the process of investigating the points of coherence that can be assembled to interpret evidence at a particular archaeological site. When all "the cards are on the table," pathways will open up for resolving a more comprehensive and mutually satisfying interpretation of evidence at an archaeological site.

In this collaborative space, then, the role of Indigenous participants requires further consideration. In the collaborative space (and we illustrate this here in relation to Indigenous positions), Indigenous participants have *agency* in the mix of things as described above and can manifest representations from their own vantage points to contribute or not. It is not an already resolved position that one simply asserts, as structuralists would contend. Indigenous agency can be seen as enabled rather than constrained, as it has been in the past. However, to produce an account that represents an Indigenous perspective, knowledge production processes work at fixing a particular knowledge position or "claim to know" by finding coherence with broader knowledge positions. In the collaborative space, these accounts are forged in dialogue and conversation with archaeologists.

Indigenous participants, experienced in the positioning that occurs at the *cultural interface*, "fix" their positions according to the elements they assume an account needs in order to cohere in that moment. That is, we assert that Indigenous participants at an archaeological site (and in other research sites) are already disposed to "read" not just the "traditional" or "local" or "material" evidence, but are disposed to "read" this within the moment of cross-cultural interaction, as gauged through their particular historical experience of reading their position in the non-Indigenous world.

In other terms, the knowledge and social relations that have orchestrated Indigenous experience in the historical sense are also read into the moment of interpretation. This is like an Indigenous lens that filters "what will I say, what will I withhold, with whom can I share, will they understand it or should I twist it to make sense to them?" and so on. This is the subtext often at work in cross-cultural interactions—cross-cultural interactions that non-Indigenous people often take at face value unless they have long experience of Indigenous contexts. In this context, at different times, different elements emerge to produce different positions, and this both illustrates changing perspectives and explains inconsistencies, ambiguities, and con-traditions that emerge in and between Indigenous accounts and also between Indigenous and non-Indigenous knowledge claims. This is constitutive of an agency, we suggest, with continual opportunities and risks as Indigenous and non-Indigenous collaborators attempt to resolve what Marcia Langton and Lisa Palmer (2002) describe as a "co-incidence of interest."

Reconsidering Indigenous locale and agency in this way highlights the *tensions* at work at the cultural interface where Indigenous people engage daily to manage the meanings associated with the trajectories of different histories, cultures, and identities. These tensions emerge in a myriad of intersections in the everyday context where Indigenous people must manage their daily engagements entangled and enmeshed in the web of complex discursive and social relations. Unlike structuralist positions of power that configure those with authority as determining outcomes, tensions help configure discursive elements as a constellation of a priori conditions that allow us to see relations between them as primary referents for the perspectives taken on things. These tensions are not insignificant when trying to understand Indigenous contributions in collaborations. Out of generations of experience with these tensions, the conditional nature of Indigenous perspectives can be understood. But the conditional nature of Indigenous perspectives is no more than for other knowledge perspectives; it is merely anchored in a different trajectory, now projected on a different course from former times. These anchors are attached to the deeper foundations of systems of thought, which are always in the process of transformation, always being tested, contested, and retested under the changing conditions produced by, and which produce the conditions for, both innovative and conventional thinking. Nor are these tensions insignificant in the way Indigenous participants interpret or add to archaeological evidence. Indigenous participants work to make sense from their own standpoints and to cohere or reject, or at least correspond with, knowledge put forth by archaeologists.

Theorizing practice to incorporate or synthesize Indigenous and archaeological knowledge to produce a fuller account of the past, rather than merely straddling the epistemic divide and producing an alternative reading, may seem daunting or fraught from the discipline's perspective and risky from Indigenous perspectives. But some community archaeologists are producing much more fine-grained accounts that are reaching toward this end (see McNiven and Russell 2005: 232–260), and some Indigenous participants are interested in using and shaping the tools of Western knowledge to investigate their own world, to continue Indigenous knowledge trajectories from their own vantage point (e.g., Mualgal [Torres Strait Islanders] Corporation and David 2006). Further work in this area can only but bring new content, dimensions, and meta-narratives that will inform archaeological practice at the disciplinary level.

Understanding the complexity and diversity of Indigenous standpoints at the cultural interface and the discursive and knowledge space in which Indigenous people must make sense of the world provides an entry point that can inform the types of discussion and dialogue between Indigenous participants and archaeologists. And while some archaeologists and Indigenous communities have already entered into new and inspiring forms of partnership, in general much richer and more complicated dialogue is now required to produce negotiated accounts that are more than an inclusion of Indigenous "stories" or "perspectives."

Conclusion

Our intent in this paper has been to further enable collaborative practice in community archaeology rather than focus on its limits and risks for Indigenous people. However, issues of control and authority (cf. McNiven 1998) are serious ones at the heart of all research in Indigenous contexts. We suggest more consideration of notions of the *cultural interface* and *Indigenous standpoints* to overcome the dilemmas that emerge when questions of control and authority become the central issue that conditions the sorts of research investigations that can occur, who can own them, and who can control the processes involved in knowledge and representation. Issues of control and authority contextualize the political grounds of practice, but we argue that these are also contained within Indigenous standpoints as an element of conditions in the collaborative process. Issues of control and authority emerge as critical tensions within any knowledge contestation or in any negotiation process where Indigenous people attempt to reconstruct and project themselves as peoples with distinct histories, cultures, and experiences, which are significant to the way they make analytical judgments of their position.

Professionals who understand archaeology as a sociopolitical practice and who are alert to what conditions interpretive frameworks from Indigenous standpoints have opportunities to write these elements into their accounts in ways that also reveal the often fragile and culturally embedded grounds of their own interpretations. Indigenous participants also have opportunities to explicate the murky grounds of knowledge entanglement, rather than be cast to the peripheries once again to assert from there the reified, idealized, or romantic notions of past Indigenous traditions that have their moorings in the imagination of those who have written Indigenous people into the corpus from their own epistemic vantage points.

Over time, as collaborative practice of this nature proceeds, a corpus of accounts may emerge to provide substantial examples of knowledge construction that give better representations of Indigenous life and historicism (a corpus that has already begun to develop). Archaeology as a method of investigating the past is not in itself antithetical to Indigenous life and historicism. The struggle in this space is not just to focus on bias and omission in archaeological representations of Indigenous peoples, or to raise the problematics of Indigenous memory or oral accounts rooted in Indigenous knowledge traditions. Nor is it productive to collapse into an intellectual malaise of epistemic indifference. The difficult task is to draw both sides of the debate into the unfamiliar, decolonized but "curiously" shared ground at sites of collaborative practice to make opportunities out of different knowledge practices.

The challenge is to generate fuller accounts of history that might serve us all in the way we come to understand one another. The test is to write people, in all their diversity and complexity, into an intelligible space, and to embrace the very complicated, but often speculative, stories of human history that we have all inherited. Whether Indigenous peoples do it on their own or not, the grounds, terms, and conditions of knowledge construction are now extremely complex and entangled. Archaeologists cannot credibly write about sites or places once (or still) occupied by Indigenous peoples as accounts of human history if they dismiss and exclude how Indigenous people make meaning of their continuing presence. Indigenous theorists and practitioners, on the other hand, could also be a little less dismissive of the usefulness of science as a method of investigation and more attentive to their own theorizing of contemporary Indigenous standpoints.

Note

1. In this paper, we address only processes of historicism involving outside archaeologists working on Indigenous pasts. We fully recognize that there are also many Indigenous archaeologists around the world who research their own community histories, but some of the issues discussed here do not apply to the archaeology of one's own history.

References

Atalay, S. 2006. Indigenous archaeology as decolonizing practice. *American Indian Quarterly* 30 (3–4): 280–310.

Barker, B. 2006. Hierarchies of knowledge and the tyranny of text: Archaeology, ethnohistory and oral traditions in Australian archaeological interpretation, in B. David, B. Barker, and I. J. McNiven (eds.), *The Social Archaeology of Australian Indigenous Societies*, pp. 72–84. Canberra: Australian Institute of Aboriginal and Torres Strait Islander Studies.

Barthes, R. 1973. *Mythologies*. London: Paladin.

Beck, W., and Somerville, M. 2005. Conversations between disciplines: Historical archaeology and oral history at Yarrawarra. *World Archaeology* 37 (3): 468–483.

Bhabha, H. 1994. *The Location of Culture*. London: Routledge.

Biolsi, T., and Zimmerman, L. J. (eds.). 1997. *Indians and Anthropologists: Vine Deloria Jr. and the Critique of Anthropology*. Tucson: University of Arizona Press.

Clarke, A. 2002. The ideal and the real: Cultural and personal transformations of archaeological research on Groote Eylandt, Northern Australia. *World Archaeology* 34 (2): 249–264.

David, B., and Denham, T. 2006. Unpacking Australian prehistory, in B. David, B. Barker, and I. J. McNiven (eds.), *The Social Archaeology of Australian Indigenous Societies*, pp. 52–71. Canberra: Australian

Institute of Aboriginal and Torres Strait Islander Studies.

David, B., Langton, M., and McNiven, I. J. 2002. Re-inventing the wheel: Indigenous peoples and the master race in Philip Ruddock's wheel comments. *Philosophy, Activism, Nature* 2: 31–45.

Echo-Hawk, R. C. 2000. Ancient history in the New World: Integrating oral traditions and the archaeological record in deep time. *American Antiquity* 65 (2): 267–290.

Eco, U. 1986. *Travels in Hyperreality: Essays*. San Diego: Harcourt Brace Jovanovich.

Fanon, F. 1986. *Black Skin, White Masks*. New York: Pluto Press.

Foucault, M. 1972. *The Archaeology of Knowledge*. London: Routledge.

Fourmile, H. 1989. Who owns the past? Aborigines as captives of the archives. *Aboriginal History* 13 (1): 1–8.

Freire, P. 1972. *Pedagogy of the Oppressed*. Middlesex: Penguin.

Gero, J. 1999. The History of the World Archaeology Congress. http://www.worldarchaeologicalcongress.org/site/about_hist.php.

Greer, S., Harrison, R., and McIntyre-Tamwoy, S. 2002. Community-based archaeology in Australia. *World Archaeology* 34 (2): 265–287.

Hodder, I. 2003. Archaeological reflexivity and the "local" voice. *Anthropological Quarterly* 76 (1): 55–68.

Langford, R. 1983. Our heritage—your playground. *Australian Archaeology* 16: 1–6.

Langton, M., and Palmer, L. 2002. Treaties and agreements as instruments of order in and between civil societies: A rational choice approach. Paper presented to the National Treaty Conference, Canberra, 27–29 August 2002.

McNiven, I. J. 1998. Shipwreck saga as archaeological text: Reconstructing Fraser Island's Aboriginal past, in I. J. McNiven, L. Russell, and K. Schaffer (eds.), *Constructions of Colonialism: Perspectives on Eliza Fraser's Shipwreck*, pp. 37–50. London: Leicester University Press.

McNiven, I. J., and Russell, L. 2005. *Appropriated Pasts: Indigenous Peoples and the Colonial Culture of Archaeology*. Lanham, MD: AltaMira Press.

Moser, S., Glazier, D., Phillips, J. E., el Nemr, L. N., Mousa, M. S., Aiesh, R. N., Richardson, S., Connor, A., and Seymour, M. 2002. Transforming archaeology through practice: Strategies for collaborative archaeology and the community archaeology project at Quseir, Egypt. *World Archaeology* 34 (2): 220–248.

Mualgal Torres Strait Islanders Corporation, and David, B. 2002. *Keeping Culture Strong: Archaeology and Oral Traditions Working Together*. DVD. Kubin: Mualgal Corporation.

Murray, T. 1995. On Klejn's agenda for theoretical archaeology. *Current Anthropology* 36 (2): 290–292.

Nakata, M. 1998. Anthropological texts and Indigenous standpoints. *Journal of Aboriginal Studies* 2: 3–15.

———. 2007. *Disciplining the Savages: Savaging the Disciplines*. Canberra: Aboriginal Studies Press.

Nicholas, G. P., and Andrews, T. D. (eds.). 1997. *At the Crossroads: Archaeology and*

First Peoples in Canada. Publication 24. Burnaby: Archaeology Press.

Pohlhaus, G. 2002. Knowing communities: An investigation of Harding's standpoint epistemology. *Social Epistemology* 16 (3): 283–293.

Rubertone, P. E. 2000. The historical archaeology of Native Americans. *Annual Review of Anthropology* 29: 425–446.

Russell, L. (ed.). 2001. *Colonial Frontiers: Indigenous–European Encounters in Settler Societies*. Manchester: Manchester University Press.

Said, E. 1995. *Orientalism*. London: Penguin.

Smith, Laurajane. 1999. The last archaeologist? Material culture and contested identities. *Australian Aboriginal Studies* 1999 (2): 25–34.

——. 2000. "Doing archaeology": Cultural heritage management and its role in identifying the link between archaeological practice and theory. *International Journal of Heritage Studies* 6 (4): 309–6.

Smith, Linda T. 1999. *Decolonizing Methodologies: Research and Indigenous Peoples*. London: Zed Books.

Weedon, C. 1987. *Feminist Practice and Poststructuralist Theory*. Oxford: Basil Blackwell.

Whitely, P. 2002. Archaeology and oral tradition: The scientific importance of dialogue. *American Antiquity* 67 (3): 405–415.

Wilson, M., Sanhambath, J., Senembe, P. D., David, B., Hall, N., and Abong, M. 2000. "*Tufala kev blong* devil": People and spirits in north west Malakula, Vanuatu: Implications for management. *Conservation and Management of Archaeological Sites* 4: 151–166.

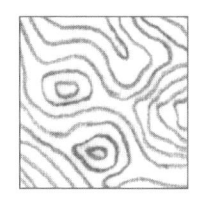

34

ETHNOGRAPHIC INTERVENTIONS

Lynn Meskell

This paper presents new work that bridges archaeological and ethnographic practice and describes the possibilities for fieldwork and, more importantly, for crafting a more engaged and ethical archaeology. In recent years, there has been a growing number of ethnographers analyzing archaeological practices, sites, and landscapes from various national, disciplinary, and political perspectives. This trend has been followed by hybrid methodological research in archaeology itself.

Using case studies from my own archaeological ethnography in South Africa, which was designed to track the progress of archaeology after 10 years of democracy, I advocate a larger framing for heritage that encompasses global conservation movements, the role of culture in development and empowerment strategies, and the differential impacts of state, private, and nongovernmental interventions. The specters of colonialism, paternalism, and even tacit racism sometimes surface through the well-meaning efforts of aid, education, development, conservation, and uplift. These are just some of the reasons why an "archaeology of archaeology" alone does not suffice: researchers are increasingly impelled to enter new fields and disciplines, address global concerns and movements, and promote issues of social justice, often before their own scholarly interests.

Archaeological Ethnography

Throughout the 1980s and 1990s, many archaeologists deepened their awareness and application of social theory, while the 1990s and 2000s were marked by the recognition of archaeology's sociopolitical embedding. In recent years, practitioners have become increasingly concerned with the ethical implications of their research and, more importantly, the politics of fieldwork and collaborations with local people, descendants, Indigenous groups, and other communities of connection (e.g., Hall 2005; Hodder 1998; Joyce 2005; Lilley and Williams 2005; Meskell 2005a, 2005b; Smith 2004; Watkins 2004; Zimmerman et al. 2003). Ethics itself has become the subject of numerous volumes (e.g., Lynott and Wylie 2000; Meskell and Pels 2005; Messenger 1999; Vitelli and Colwell-Chanthaphonh 2006), as had politics and nationalism before that, and these were not simply Euro-American trends but were more often driven by archaeologists from Latin America, Australasia, Africa, and the Middle East (see Abdi 2001; Funari 2004; Ndoro 2001; Politis 2001; Scham and Yahya 2003; Shepherd 2002).

Indigenous issues and potential collaborations have slowly become mainstream in archaeological discussions, and while there is much that needs redressing, the concerns of restitution, repatriation, and reconciliation have gradually gained ground. Today, such organizations as the World Archaeology Congress acknowledge the discipline's colonial history and present, and have a public mandate of social justice that seeks not only to instantiate a model of best practice, but to go beyond in terms of reparations and enhanced livelihoods to make a positively felt impact for the communities within which archaeologists work. The time when archaeologists considered their subjects dead and buried has long passed (Meskell 2005c). These are all vital disciplinary developments that have irrevocably changed how we undertake our research. Yet it is not simply our situated contexts that have been exposed and challenged: our methodologies have also recently been expanded and reimagined. As a result, the discipline has recently witnessed emergent hybrid methodologies, such as archaeological ethnography (Meskell 2007a).

Archaeological ethnography is a holistic anthropology that is improvisational and context dependent. It can encompass a mosaic of traditional forms, including archaeological practice, museum, or representational analysis, as well as long-term involvement, participant observation, interviewing, and archival work. Good examples are Denis Byrne's research in Southeast Asia on the theme of Indigenous heritage conservation and spiritual materiality (Byrne 2007); Alfredo González-Ruibal's unpacking of modernity and its destructions in Ethiopia and its material aftermath (González-Ruibal 2006), and the long-term work of T. J. Ferguson and Chip Colwell-Chanthaphonh in the American Southwest working collaboratively with Native American communities (Colwell-Chanthaphonh and Ferguson 2004; Ferguson et al. 2004; Ferguson and Colwell-Chanthaphonh 2006).

In Denis Byrne's writing, we clearly see the benefits of a long-term immersion in the field: living and working with and among people not simply as a means of extracting specific information about the archaeological past, but as a way of uncovering what matters most about the past in people's lives today. In his work across Southeast Asia, Byrne is interested not simply in the material remains of the past, but in understanding people's contemporary practices, histories, and discussions about the afterlives of landscapes, monuments, and objects. His writing presents a personal account of those interactions and bears a strong resemblance to travel writing, which he sees as having great connection with archaeological narratives.

My own archaeological ethnography has been ongoing since 2004. In one facet of the project, I spent many months on an annual basis living and working in Kruger National Park, side by side with my non-archaeological colleagues, accompanying them on their daily duties, attending meetings, and visiting sites. Like traditional sociocultural field projects, archaeological ethnography entails "deep hanging out," as Geertz famously described it, but may also involve different periodicities, such as returning to the field over successive years, as archaeologists do traditionally. Taking the classic notion of "participant observation" and examining its semantics, I have previously suggested (2005a) that the experience of "participation" is formative, an immersion in a cultural setting over an extended period of time and taking part in the richness and diversity of everyday practice. This experience is a "culture-from-within" approach. "Observation," the second component, involves witnessing or critically viewing the values, dynamics, internal relationships, structures, and conflicts as they play out in communities. Personal observation often counters the normative statements given in interviews, and the two can operate successfully in a dialogic relationship. While archaeological fieldwork must be similarly ethically guided, ethnographic projects must specifically follow human subject protocols and be passed by institutional review boards (IRBs) at the researcher's university, and often within the host institutions.

Archaeological ethnography is very different from the existing tradition of ethnoarchaeological work (David and Kramer 2001; Hodder 1982; Moore 1982, 1987; Parker Pearson 1982). In archaeology, the term "archaeological ethnography" has been variously used to describe ethnoarchaeological work in Iran (Watson 1979), social archaeology in a Neolithic Syrian settlement (Verhoeven 1999), and archaeological place making (Robin and Rothschild 2002), among other things. My understanding of archaeological ethnography entails a reorientation, albeit with many of the same techniques; it has not evolved *sui generis*. From my perspective, the term "the past" is not always a privileged locale, nor are the core concerns necessarily ancient technology, roles of material culture, subsistence, or symbolic systems, which are all valid research interests and could be included.

Archaeological ethnography entails a serious ethnographic engagement, one that is significantly different from the more casual encounters many archaeologists experience in the field when simply talking to various stakeholders or seeking information to aid their research. The latter occurs frequently, and I take this form of conversation to task for a number of reasons. The notion of "local" or "locals" is a trope that has become an easy catchall for the complex and ethically necessary encounters we have with various constituencies in and around archaeological locales. But "locals" and "local communities" are not passive constituencies there for our intellectual mining; nor are they there awaiting our theoretical insights into their situations or histories. They are directly enmeshed in their own critical reformulations, political negotiations, and constitutions of theory and interpretation.

Obviously, archaeologists have a certain requisite insider expertise to conduct various forms of archaeological ethnography, and we benefit from our knowledge of the craft and its results, so that one initial stage of our training has already been achieved. Such reflexive research can similarly be positioned as the "ethnography of us," of what we do as practitioners, thus lessening the exotic patina and keeping our work closely aligned to what was once described as an "anthropology at home" (Marcus and Fischer 1986: 112). We have a knowledge of the field, a deep experiential understanding, yet that too is challenged by engaging with other stakeholders and the modalities through which we come to take their accounts seriously—namely, through encounters and interviews. The seemingly discrete positions of *insider* and *outsider* become more permeable, and that porosity undoubtedly operates as an ethical check on our interpretations and our politics more broadly (see chapters in Meskell and Pels 2005).

Given the current climate of research briefly outlined here and the types of transnational ethical and political work undertaken, it is not surprising that a younger generation of archaeologists is actively pursuing a broader suite of attendant techniques and multi-sited field methods. Blurring the conventional disciplinary divides, archaeologists have increasingly conducted ethnographic work around the construction of archaeological heritage, excavated the archives, investigated media-based productions of knowledge, and worked creatively in conjunction with living communities. Sometimes this work is focused on the materiality of the past. For instance, Susan Kus (1987, 1997, 2000, 2005) has conducted collaborative research that traverses archaeological and ethnographic boundaries, following questions relating to complexity, state formation, and monumentality by sharing insights gleaned from historic and contemporary society. This could be described as one form of archaeological ethnography. More frequently, however, archaeological ethnography maintains a strong contemporary emphasis and is concerned with unpacking the micro-politics of archaeological practice, the impacts of heritage on an international scale, and the entwined global networks of tourism, development, and heritage agencies, nongovernmental organizations, and so on. Additionally, there is a burgeoning literature by anthropologists on archaeological and heritage projects (Abu el-Haj 2001; Benavides 2005; Breglia 2006; Castañeda 1996; Wynn 2007). Archaeological ethnography thus brings a new set of connections and conversations to the fore (see chapters in Meskell 2009). Yet where this work diverges from mainstream ethnography is with the foregrounding of materiality, specifically those traces of the past that have residual afterlives in living communities, which are often considered spiritually significant and that invite a kind of governmental monitoring and control that many Indigenous communities and archaeologists increasingly find problematic. Moreover, archaeological ethnography often entails collaborating with, rather than studying, the people with whom we work in the heritage sphere.

Many archaeologists increasingly want to examine the ways in which our discipline comes to work in the world. What kinds and intensities of connection exist? How is archaeology potentially transformative in the fashioning of possible futures? Addressing these questions necessarily foregrounds ethnographic method as practiced by sociocultural anthropologists, a stronger commitment to contemporary situations centering on archaeology and its primary stakeholders, the role of the state and new forms of governmentality, and a recognition of archaeology's political embeddedness and of the expanded possibilities for ethical participation, advocacy, and outreach. The latter entails ethical responsibility for one's participation, as does all archaeological and ethnographic praxis (see Herzfeld 2003). After all, we each chose the particular research topics we engage with.

I would argue that the subject of our research, the archaeological past and present, is situated firmly within a suite of cosmopolitan dispositions and practices: extensive mobility and travel; consuming places and environments; curiosity about people, places, and cultures; experiencing risks in encountering others; mapping various cultures and societies; semiotic skills in interpreting others; and openness to different languages and cultures (Szerszynski and Urry 2006: 114–115). Archaeologists now recognize that particular "locals," "communities," and "national" bodies have complex interactions with various international sponsors and universities, conservation agencies, development organizations, and NGOs, thus challenging simplistic notions of globalization or homogenization (see chapters in Meskell 2009). The shorthand of "local versus global," caricatured by imputed cultural designations of traditional versus capitalist, falls short of the current complexities we all necessarily face on the ground. Nor can we conversely consider the local, situated contexts in which we work as archaeologists or ethnographers as isolated, traditional, disengaged, or disconnected from larger processes, institutions, organizations, consumer networks, and knowledges.

Making Heritage Pay

My own ethnographic work in South Africa makes clear that it is not possible to parse out heritage from other issues of ancestral land, forced dislocation, landscape, power, oppression, and recent histories, among other matters. Rather than diluting archaeology, the methodological hybridity of archaeological ethnography enriches it significantly and recenters our discipline in contemporary cosmopolitan societies (Hall 2005; Hall and Bombardella 2005). The heritage sector is booming in South Africa; there are new heritage agencies, NGOs, and UNESCO-proclaimed sites, reflecting the fact that heritage is vitally connected to various government ministries and parastatals (quasi-governmental organizations, corporations, businesses, or agencies). However, the growth of the heritage sector is a decidedly post-1994, post-apartheid enterprise, and it reflects the specific neoliberal strategies of entrepreneurship and private-public partnerships. The state is contributing less in the way of infrastructure and expecting private enterprise—national and international—to fill in the voids. Many of these new national initiatives are expected to be self-sustaining through private partnerships with business, all based on the tender system, and end up largely being promoted as centers for weddings, receptions, corporate events, and the *indabas* (i.e., workshops) South Africans are so fond of.

Quite recently, the tourist figures for South Africa's first UNESCO cultural heritage site, Mapungubwe, boasted impressive numbers of black visitors, pushing the total average of black visitation in parks from 4% to 19.7% nationally. In 2007, it was discovered that the Mapungubwe figure of 62.2% black visitors (South African National Parks 2006) resulted from conferences and workshops rather than site visitations. This trend is also reflected in such magazines as *Explore!*, which showcases archaeological imagery such as San rock art, but employs the past purely as a marketing device rather than to promote archaeological significance. The magazine's July 2007 issue was devoted to heritage sites as new destinations for holidays, conferences, and weddings, all of which were touted economically and without historic or political specificity—a clear example of the nation's new heritage consumption. Another is the production of cultural villages with their attendant replication of apartheid racial categories. These are deeply problematic commercial ventures that are growing rapidly in the new South Africa (Rassool 2000; Rassool and Witz 1996; Witz et al. 2001).

As JoAnn McGregor and Lyn Schumaker note (2006: 658), tourism has encouraged the proliferation of "traditional villages" and commodified reinventions of authentic local life, working through particular configurations of local and national interests. They suggest, however, that many local civic initiatives are motivated by a desire for recognition or acknowledgment rather than for financial reward. One need only think of local museums in poor urban communities such as Kliptown that lack an obvious tourist market but want to commemorate their role in the struggle, specifically (in this case) as the place where the Freedom Charter was signed (Meskell and Scheermeyer 2008). As one of the organizers explained during our interview, "what drove our people to do this is the pride of heritage obviously. Because what happens tomorrow when we are all not here, two or three years down the line? Our children won't know anything. They won't know about Kliptown. They won't know about history. It's for us to write history, and not for history to be forgotten. And that is very important."

The possibility that local heritage projects may attract both financial benefits and recognition has undoubtedly stimulated local demand for the creation of ever-new heritage sites (e.g., Apartheid Museum, Hector Pietersen Museum, Constitution Hill) and tours (WEKAT Trauma Tours)

(Meskell 2007b). However, as James Clifford (2004: 8) asserts, "heritage is not a substitute for land claims, struggles over subsistence rights, development, educational, and health projects, defense of sacred sites, and repatriation of human remains or stolen artifacts, but it is closely connected with all these struggles." Since heritage can play a recuperative role in allowing otherwise marginalized histories to be brought to the fore, communities invest their aspirations and needs into such heritage prospects.

On the more extreme front, there now exists quite a spectrum of cultural villages. These range from those of single ethnic groups, such as the San (Meskell and Weiss 2006; Robins 2001) or the Shangaans on the edge of Kruger National Park, or Shakaland in KwaZulu Natal (which pays homage to the TV series *Shaka Zulu* rather than to a proud history [see Hamilton 1998]), to such multi-ethnic enclaves as Lesedi Cultural Village outside of Johannesburg. While cultural villages or ethnic villages enjoy widespread popularity with tourists, they retain a number of troubling aspects—namely, their cultural fixity, the performance of primitivism, and the reinforcement of ethnic stereotypes and cultural hierarchies, not to mention the repetitive futility of labor for those employed in such enterprises. Previously I have written about Egypt's famed Pharaonic Village in Cairo and the replication of the roles of colonized and colonizer enunciated through tourist practices (Meskell 2005c). These problematics are similarly present in the South African examples, yet the specter of apartheid's ethnic categorizations and segregations, as well as the notorious Bantustans (apartheid's construction of ethnic homelands), looms rather too closely.

In 2005, I spent time at Lesedi Cultural Village, outside of Johannesburg, with a group of students and scholars from the Rock Art Research Institute at the University of the Witwatersrand. Each of us was researching various aspects of heritage, and the students were from South Africa and other African countries. The village was very busy, and some several hundred visitors were there at one time, being funneled through their own segregated villages: Xhosa, Sotho, Zulu, and Pedi. Ironically, I was told that there was so much intermarriage between the cultural performers that the ideal of keeping spatially and socially discrete cultural groups was becoming difficult to manage, even at the level of artifice. In fact, there was a tacit materialist focus on educating tourists about cultural types: Khosa people smoke these type of pipes; Zulu wear these type of skins; Sotho make these types of mats; and so on. Not surprisingly, these depictions were trapped in time: there were no modern Zulus or Pedi; they each were portrayed very much as a product of colonial times and points of contact.

Cultural villages are all about people crafting significant objects of ethnic specificity, thus allowing visitors to be privy to cultural secrets: in fact, the entire performance of object making is key. In Lesedi Cultural Village, for example, visitors view the art of weaving or house decoration, and in Shakaland the forging of a metal spear, the processes of which are formulaically explained by a tour guide. Modern material culture is strictly taboo, as we discovered when plastic bags littered the enclosure where certain "ancient arts" were being performed. Our guide chastised the performer in Zulu for allowing such intrusions. Of course, visitors can catch glimpses of people in their jeans and Nikes before they have had a chance to change into their impala-skin costumes for the various performances.

It is materiality—particularly the fiction of a specific ethnically bounded materiality—that sediments identity in a pre-modern era, that stands as an unchanging hallmark of "black" and "colored" peoples, situated within the very tribal constituencies that the apartheid government sought to maintain for much of the 20th century. These contemporary "primitivisms" reflect the earlier, and much critiqued, reifications and fetishizations of a notionally simple way of life. More seriously, their distinctive character derives from the politics of identity in the present (Douglas 1997: 63) and serves to reinforce the tribalisms of the colonial and later apartheid eras. As archaeologists, we might ask, Why are particular communities deemed to be trapped in the past, shot through with their particular materialities? Indeed, why fossilize culture in such ways? As many interviewees have asked me directly, Why is it that Afrikaner culture is not historicized in this way? And why is it not the subject of theme parks and craft stalls? White Afrikaners too claim to be African, of course; some even desire to be considered "indigenous" (see Kuper 2003: 389). Perhaps this inequity resides in the judgment that "Boer" culture is not deemed exotic, much less aesthetically appealing, and lacks the necessary historical substrate of real tradition.

As both an archaeologist and ethnographer, I keep returning to the question, What does it imply to know a people by their things? As the 19th-century social evolutionist Edward Tylor famously argued, a rough scale of civilization could be instigated on the basis of industrial arts, metalworking, manufacture of vessels and implements, scientific knowledge, social and political organization and so on, leading to a definite basis of compared facts (Tylor 1977: 27). He specifically pointed to South Africa as one context in which colonial forces have brought previously primitive people in line with European civilization (1977: 53). In fact, he went as far as to impute that the role of the ethnographer was to expose "crude old cultures . . . and to mark these out for destruction," which was "urgently needful for the good of humanity" (see Tambiah 1999: 44). Tylor had his own hierarchy of substances, where certain practices and techniques were directly correlated to a primitive age—indeed, Stone, Bronze, and Iron are still the pertinent taxonomies. The technologies of contemporary peoples were also hierarchically ordered along the same schema, and correlated back into prehistoric time. This is worrisome because these ideas continue to hold sway in the modern mind, implying that technology equals progress and that material sophistication is an index of social complexity and, ultimately, worth. Impoverished material culture equals impoverished culture in general. A paucity of goods is a material shortfall, another index of the evolution of culture and society: we are fixated by material lack—especially in such "underdeveloped" contexts as the African continent. Discourses of development also fasten firmly onto this view of material impoverishment and technical backwardness, in a self-fulfilling and destructive cycle where anthropologists, governments, and international organizations affix social and cultural value to modern technologies, whereas other traditional industries are "deprivileged" (Escobar 1995; Ferguson 1994, 1996; Hobart 1993). It would be a national shame for a post-apartheid society to encourage the same rigid constructions of ethnicity and culture enforced by their now vilified predecessors.

What I find troubling in conducting this particular form of archaeological ethnography is the degree to which options are limited and people are trapped by the very heritage for which they were so recently persecuted. Not enough has changed in the new South Africa, and ethnic identities are often seemingly enforced and publicly reified rather than embraced. Such identity politics are "constituted as much by our response to others and to the context we find ourselves in, as they are the product of processes of self-identification and determination" (Ivison 2002: 10). Put simply, what concerns me here are matters of agency: Indigenous peoples, whether the San, Venda, Zulu, or other groups, require clear social and economic choices in their crafting and performing of identity and should not be impelled to perform de facto as unchanging minorities, especially in the new South Africa where black empowerment and mobility are high on the agenda. The material expression of those solidarities and the creative new directions being forged should be of great interest to archaeologists and anthropologists alike and have the potential for great import in the lives of many. One way around this thorny issue—with black empowerment and benefits firmly in mind—is to develop local tourism that presents contemporary black culture in all its complexity. Such moves are now happening around world-class conservation areas such as Kruger and Hluhluwe Umfolozi National Parks. For some years, I have worked at such lodges as Bongani and Phinda, run by Conservation Corporation Africa, which actively contribute to community development and profit sharing. By taking tourists out into adjacent communities, at the request of tribal leaders, visitors have been educated into the ways of life and basic socioeconomic needs of rural South Africans, and those same communities are reaping the benefits through the building of schools and clinics and the creation of jobs and futures (Buckley 2002; Carlisle 2003).

Conclusions

Archaeological ethnography might have heritage and the archaeological past as an organizing principle, as the above examples demonstrate, yet it can also embrace much broader research and ethical concerns, whether local livelihoods, conservation and management, social justice, or Indigenous rights. The suite of methodologies applied might involve ethnography, archival analysis, oral histories, excavation and survey, site recording, or museum and collections study, and any of these may entail long-term immersion in the field. Its blend of archaeological and anthropological techniques bridges past and contemporary cultures, yet we acknowledge that these are not always neatly overlapping groups or concerns. Archaeological ethnography does not always privilege the past, nor does it see living communities as resources to be mined in an attempt to interpret archaeological materials or landscapes. As research around heritage ethics expands and new forms of collaborative fieldwork become instantiated, archaeological ethnographies will become increasingly valuable contributions to our ever-expanding disciplinary program.

References

Abdi, K. 2001. Nationalism, politics, and the development of archaeology in Iran. *American Journal of Archaeology* 105: 51–76.

Abu el-Haj, N. 2001. *Facts on the Ground: Archaeological Practice and Territorial Self-Fashioning in Israeli Society*. Chicago: University of Chicago Press.

Benavides, O. H. 2005. *Making Ecuadorian Histories*. Austin: University of Texas Press.

Breglia, L. C. 2006. *Monumental Ambivalence*. Austin: University of Texas Press.

Buckley, R. 2002. Public and private partnerships between tourism and protected areas: The Australian situation. *The Journal of Tourism Studies* 13: 26–28.

Byrne, D. 2007. *Surface Collection: Archaeological Travels in Southeast Asia*. Walnut Creek, CA: AltaMira Press.

Carlisle, L. 2003. Private reserves: The Conservation Corporation African model, in R. Buckley, C. Pickering, and D. B. Weaver (eds.), in *Nature-based Tourism, Environment and Land Management*, pp. 17–23. Wallingford: CABI Publishing.

Castañeda, Q. 1996. *In the Museum of Maya Culture: Touring Chichén Itzá*. Minneapolis: University of Minnesota Press.

Clifford, J. 2004. Looking several ways: Anthropology and Native heritage in Alaska. *Current Anthropology* 45: 5–30.

Colwell-Chanthaphonh, C., and Ferguson, T. J. 2004. Virtue ethics and the practice of history: Native Americans and archaeologists along the San Pedro Valley of Arizona. *Journal of Social Archaeology* 4: 5–27.

David, N., and Kramer, C. 2001. *Ethnoarchaeology in Action*. Cambridge: Cambridge University Press.

Douglas, S. 1997. Reflections on state intervention and the Schmidtsdrift Bushmen. *Journal of Contemporary African Studies* 15: 45–66.

Escobar, A. 1995. *Encountering Development: The Making and Unmaking of the Third World*. Princeton: Princeton University Press.

Ferguson, J. 1994. *The Anti-Politics Machine: "Development," Depoliticization, and Bureaucratic Power in Lesotho*. Minneapolis: University of Minnesota Press.

——. 1996. Development, in A. Barnard and J. Spence (eds.), *Encyclopedia of Social and*

Cultural Anthropology, pp. 154–160. London: Routledge.

Ferguson, T. J., and Colwell-Chanthaphonh, C. 2006. *History is in the Land: Multivocal Tribal Traditions in Arizona's San Pedro Valley*. Tucson: University of Arizona Press.

Ferguson, T. J., Colwell-Chanthaphonh, C., and Anyon, R. 2004. One valley, many histories: Tohono O'odham, Hopi, Zuni, and Western Apache history in the San Pedro Valley. *Archaeology Southwest* 18: 1–16.

Funari, P. P. A. 2004. The archaeological study of the African diaspora in Brazil, in T. Falola and A. Ogundiran (eds.), *The Archaeology of Atlantic Africa and the African Diaspora*. Studies in African History and the Diaspora series. Rochester: University of Rochester Press.

González-Ruibal, A. 2006. The dream of reason: An archaeology of the failures of modernity in Ethiopia. *Journal of Social Archaeology* 6.

Hall, M. 2005. Situational ethics and engaged practice: The case of archaeology in Africa, in L. M. Meskell and P. Pels (eds.), *Embedding Ethics: Shifting the Boundaries of the Anthropological Profession*, pp. 169–194. Oxford: Berg.

Hall, M., and Bombardella, P. 2005. Las Vegas in Africa. *Journal of Social Archaeology* 5: 5–24.

Hamilton, C. 1998. *Terrific Majesty: The Powers of Shaka Zulu and the Limits of Historical Invention*. Cambridge: Harvard University Press.

Herzfeld, M. 2003. Pom Mahakan: Humanity and order in the historic center of Bangkok. *Thailand Journal of Human Rights* 1: 101–119.

Hobart, M. (ed.). 1993. *An Anthropological Critique of Development: The Growth of Ignorance*. London: Blackwell.

Hodder, I. 1982. *Symbols in Action*. Cambridge: Cambridge University Press.

——. 1998. The past and passion and play: Çatalhöyük as a site of conflict in the construction of multiple pasts, in L. M. Meskell (ed.), *Archaeology under Fire: Nationalism, Politics and Heritage in the Eastern Mediterranean and Middle East*, pp. 124–139. London: Routledge.

Ivison, D. 2002. *Postcolonial Liberalism*. Cambridge: Cambridge University Press.

Joyce, R. A. 2005. Solid histories for fragile nations: Archaeology as cultural patrimony, in L. M. Meskell and P. Pels (eds.), *Embedding Ethics*, pp. 253–273. Oxford: Berg.

Kuper, A. 2003. The return of the Native. *Current Anthropology* 4: 389-395.

Kus, S. 1987. Notes on and for friends and enemies, in R. Auger, M. F. Glass, S. MacEachern, and P. H. McCartney (eds.), *Ethnicity and Culture*, pp. 77–80. Calgary: Archaeological Association at the University of Calgary.

——. 1997. Archaeologist as anthropologist: Much ado about something after all? *Journal of Archaeological Method and Theory* 4: 199–213.

——. 2000. Ideas are like burgeoning grains on a young rice stalk: Some ideas on theory in anthropological archaeology, in M. B. Schiffer (ed.), *Social Theory in Archaeology*, pp. 156–172. Salt Lake City: University of Utah Press.

——. 2005. Materials and metaphors of sovereignty in central Madagascar, in C.

Renfrew, C. Gosden, and L. DeMarrais (eds.), *Rethinking Materiality*. Cambridge: McDonald Institute for Archaeology.

Lilley, I., and Williams, M. 2005. Archaeological and Indigenous significance: A view from Australia, in C. Mathers, T. Darvill, and B. Little (eds.), *Heritage of Value, Archaeology of Renown: Reshaping Archaeological Assessment and Significance*, pp. 227–247. Gainesville: University of Florida Press.

Lynott, M. J., and Wylie, A. (eds.). 2000. *Ethics in American Archaeology*. Washington, DC: Society for American Archaeology.

Marcus, G., and Fischer, M. J. 1986. *Anthropology as Cultural Critique: An Experimental Moment in the Human Sciences*. Chicago: University of Chicago Press.

McGregor, J., and Schumaker, L. 2006. Heritage in Southern Africa: Imagining and marketing public culture and history. *Journal of Southern African Studies* 32: 649–665.

Meskell, L. M. 2005a. Archaeological ethnography: Conversations around Kruger National Park. *Archaeologies: Journal of the World Archaeology Congress* 1: 83–102.

——. 2005b. Recognition, restitution and the potentials of postcolonial liberalism for South African Heritage. *South African Archaeological Bulletin* 60: 72–78.

——. 2005c. Sites of violence: Terrorism, tourism and heritage in the archaeological present, in L. M. Meskell and P. Pels (eds.), *Embedding Ethics*. Oxford: Berg.

——. 2007a. Falling walls and mending fences: Archaeological ethnography in the Limpopo. *Journal of Southern African Studies* 33: 383–400.

——. 2007b. Living in the past: Historic futures in double time, in N. Murray, M. Hall, and N. Shepherd (eds.), *Desire Lines: Space Memory and Identity in the Postapartheid City*. London: Routledge.

Meskell, L. M. (ed). 2009. *Cosmopolitan Archaeologies*. Durham, NC: Duke University Press.

Meskell, L. M., and Pels, P. (eds.). 2005. *Embedding Ethics*. Oxford: Berg.

Meskell, L. M., and Scheermeyer, C. 2008. Heritage as therapy: Set pieces from the New South Africa. *Journal of Material Culture* 13 (2): 153–173.

Meskell, L. M., and Weiss, L. W. 2006. Coetzee on South Africa's past: Remembering in the time of forgetting. *American Anthropologist* 108: 88–99.

Messenger, P. M. (ed.). 1999. *The Ethics of Collecting Cultural Property*. Albuquerque: University of New Mexico Press.

Moore, H. L. 1982. The interpretation of spatial patterning in settlement residues, in I. Hodder (ed.), *Symbolic and Structural Archaeology, New Directions in Archaeology*, pp. 74–79. Cambridge: Cambridge University Press.

——. 1987. Problems in the analysis of change: An example from the Marakwet, in I. Hodder (ed.), *Archaeology as Long Term History, New Directions in Archaeology*, pp. 88–104. Cambridge: Cambridge University Press.

Ndoro, W. 2001. *Your Monument, Our Shrine: The Preservation of Great Zimbabwe*. Studies in African Archaeology 19. Uppsala: Uppsala University.

Parker Pearson, M. 1982. Mortuary practices, society and ideology: An ethnoarchaeological study, in I. Hodder (ed.), *Symbolic and Structural Archaeology*, pp. 99–114. Cambridge: Cambridge University Press.

Politis, G. 2001. On archaeological praxis, gender bias and Indigenous peoples in South America. *Journal of Social Archaeology* 1: 90–107.

Rassool, C. 2000. The rise of heritage and the reconstitution of history in South Africa. *Kronos: Journal of Cape History* 26: 1–21.

Rassool, C., and Witz, L. 1996. South Africa: A world in one country; moments in international tourist encounters with wildlife, the primitive and the modern. *Cahiers d'etudes africaines* 143: 335–371.

Robins, S. 2001. NGOs, "Bushmen" and double vision: The Khomani San land claim and the cultural politics of "community" and "development" in the Kalahari. *Journal of South African Studies* 27: 833–853.

Robin, C., and Rothschild, N. A. 2002. Archaeological ethnographies: Social dynamics of outdoor space. *Journal of Social Archaeology* 2: 159–173.

Scham, S., and Yahya, A. 2003. Heritage and reconciliation. *Journal of Social Archaeology* 3: 399–416.

Shepherd, N. 2002. The politics of archaeology in Africa. *Annual Review of Anthropology* 31: 189–209.

Smith, C. 2004. *Country, Kin and Culture: Survival of an Australian Aboriginal Community*. Adelaide: Wakefield Press.

South African National Parks. 2006. *Go Wild* (staff newsletter), April. Pretoria: SANP.

Szerszynski, B., and Urry, J. 2006. Visuality, mobility and the cosmopolitan: Inhabiting the world from afar. *The British Journal of Sociology* 57: 113–131.

Tambiah, S. J. 1999. *Magic, Science, Religion and the Scope of Rationality*. Cambridge: Cambridge University Press.

Tylor, E. B. 1977. *Primitive Culture: Researches into the Development of Mythology, Philosophy, Religion, Language, Art and Custom*, Vol. 1. New York: Gordon Press.

Verhoeven, M. 1999. *An Archaeological Ethnography of a Neolithic Community: Space, Place and Social Relations in the Burnt Village of Tell Sabi Abyad, Syria*. Leiden: Nederlands Historisch-Archaeologisch Instituut te Istanbul.

Vitelli, K. D., and Colwell-Chanthaphonh, C. (eds.). 2006. *Archaeological Ethics*. Walnut Creek, CA: AltaMira Press.

Watkins, J. 2004. Becoming American or becoming Indian? NAGPRA, Kennewick, and cultural affiliation. *Journal of Social Archaeology* 4: 60–80.

Watson, P.-J. 1979. *Archaeological Ethnography in Western Iran*. Tucson: University of Arizona Press.

Witz, L., Rassool, C., and Minkley, G. 2001. Repackaging the past or South African tourism. *Daedalus* 130.

Wynn, L. L. 2007. *Pyramids and Nightclubs: A Travel Ethnography of Arab and Western Imaginations of Egypt, from King Tut and a Colony of Atlantis to Rumors of Sex Orgies, Urban Legends about a Marauding Prince, and Blonde Belly Dancers*. Austin: University of Texas Press.

Zimmerman, L. J., Vitelli, K. D., Hollowell-Zimmer, J., and Maurer. R. D. (eds.). 2003. *Ethical Issues in Archaeology*. Walnut Creek, CA: AltaMira Press.

35

COLONIALISM, CONFLICT, AND CONNECTIVITY: PUBLIC ARCHAEOLOGY'S MESSAGE IN THE BOTTLE

Sandra Scham

> Whereas earlier globalization produced nationalism, colonialism and epistemological universalism, globalization presently is postcolonial, challenges the nation-state, and is marked by a break-down of universalism.
>
> *Dirlik 2003: 13*

Historian Arif Dirlik, unlike many of his colleagues in the social sciences, sees the benignities of our brave new world. Selling globalization as the antidote to our fractious world disorder has, in fact, become a ubiquitous theme in our popular and political culture. While many scholars and social activists remain decidedly skeptical about it, the ranks of those who believe that the new economic "comity of nations" will bring benevolent social and cultural advances are increasing. In contrast, many of us believe that the philosophy that has developed as a counterweight to colonialism can bear no possible correlation to a system of values whose major manifestations are the pursuit of cheap labor, international banking, and the easing of trade restrictions. In fact, few social scientists are certain that globalization is anything less than wholly insidious.

Among them is Manuel Castells, who, at the end of a particularly harrowing discussion on the abuse of children in the global political economy, concludes, "[g]lobalization proceeds selectively, including and excluding segments of economies and societies" (Castells 2000: 165). Furthermore, he states that it results in "a hardened form of capitalism" that relies on production and competition "to generate wealth, and to appropriate it selectively" (2000: 369). What Dirlik sees as a valid and beneficial historical paradigm, Castells views as a pernicious blight on the establishment of international human and economic rights. For archaeologists, the globalization controversy has necessarily taken on a different form. Ian Hodder has suggested that "the fragmentation within and across globalisation processes needs to be reflexively engaged with" (Hodder 1998: 139). Does this mean, however, that we must admit to providing the fodder for what Castells views as an insidious preserver of inequality (Castells 2000: 167)? Does an encouragement to local, national, and global communities to connect to archaeological sites represent simply a new form of invented and commodified culture?

The answer to the first of these questions seems evident. Archaeologists have bought into our very own version of globalization with a vengeance (Appadurai 2002), directing a great deal of attention to sites on the UNESCO endangered list while disregarding the fact that the ways in which these sites are selected are blatantly opportunistic (Joyce 2005). Removing heritage issues from their own backyards to the global arena has provided nations with a means to dilute their contentious pasts. Additionally, some UNESCO participants, by giving the occasional nod to the existence of less threatening heterogeneous groups within their borders, have used the global heritage movement to deflect sectarian tensions (Meskell 2002). Jordan, for example, a country where the tiny Christian minority is rapidly disappearing as a result of a growing discomfort with the Muslim majority, has nominated Um er-Rasas, a site with 7th-century (post-Islamic) Christian remains. Similarly, Turkey, with its wealth of archaeological sites, nominated several places with Christian associations—but, interestingly, not a single Hellenic site (see *http://whc.unesco.org*).

As world heritage becomes increasingly defined in accordance with a nation-state-serving mosaic model, even the most repressive of governments can feel comfortable with this kind of controlled sharing of the past. The second question posed above, which presupposes more of a confrontation with the past, is the more complex of the two. The question of what kind of connections, if any, between present groups and past sites are to be promoted and built upon by archaeologists has consumed practitioners of public archaeology in many debates over the past decade—not the least of which is the debate over what public archaeology is, what it should be, and why it has been such a disappointment.

Homing in on our own field, we find more of a willingness to address this development as morally ambiguous, albeit with different degrees of concern. More negatively, we have Ruth Tringham's critique that "globalization can lead to an essentializing of the past and a quashing of the diversity of voices and alternative interpretations" (Tringham 2003). Adding to this is Michael Shanks's warning that "a key tension or contradiction in globalisation involves the fluid free market between nations.... Here, the nation, nation state and nationalism remain potent" (Pearson and Shanks 2001: 291). Obviously, these are not the only archaeologists willing to address the issue (see, e.g., Kane 2003; Kohl 2004; Kristiansen and Rowlands 1998; Rowan and Baram 2004), but no one has really clarified what our role in all of this should be. We have accustomed ourselves, inadvertently, to providing the symbolic ammunition for contentious nationalisms.

The Advent of Heritage Studies and the Yawn of Public Archaeology

We archaeologists know that our work is interesting to the public. At urban gatherings, whenever the inevitable question emerges—"What do you do?"—others in our humble economic category might be dismissed if they reveal that they do not have the requisite license to practice something or other. We are not. People like archaeology and, by extension, they like to talk to archaeologists. They want to know about our work and we want to tell them. Out of this most serendipitous of circumstances, we might be expected to have developed a host of fascinating approaches for involving the public in archaeology. Nevertheless, at least in the minds of many archaeological practitioners (McDavid 1999), this promise has never come to fruition. Indeed, if some of us are honest with ourselves, we must acknowledge that we envision public archaeology projects as falling into mutually exclusive types. The first are those that have a high level of community involvement and a low level of academic rigor, and the second are those that have a high level of academic rigor and are, consequently, of no interest to the community (Green et al. 2003). There is no third type.

The amount of busy backpedaling in the archaeological community relating to public archaeology is, consequently, becoming increasingly apparent. Some scholars, for understandable reasons, want to differentiate the term from "community" and "public interest" archaeology (Morris 1998; Rizvi 2006). Others remain adamant that public archaeology as a concept can be salvaged. Paul Shackel, in his edited volume, takes the position that it is still compatible with notions of "community-based archaeology" (2004: 2), though it is difficult to countenance this in the face of a realization that today's primary promoters of public archaeology have become those very institutions that were once the objects of its incisive critique. Hence, we now have the National Park Service defining for us what public archaeology is—according to them, a practice dedicated to "increasing public awareness and education about archaeology" and promoting "legislative attempts to provide funding and protection for archaeological sites" (*http://www.nps.gov/history/seac/terms.html*). In other words, it is a means whereby experts (archaeologists) can program whole segments of the population into mobilizing against looting and destruction.

Surely this is not what practitioners like Shackel, Mark Leone, Carol McDavid, and countless others had in mind when they began this enterprise. In this regard, it should be a matter of particular concern to those same practitioners that the Daughters of the American Revolution (see, e.g., *www1.umn.edu/marp/dig/site1.html*) and the Daughters of the Confederacy (Gallaher and Aycock 2001), groups that were once famous for discriminating in their memberships on the basis of race, are now quite enamored of public archaeology. Once the transition was accomplished from grass roots to appropriation as an adjunct to historical preservation—a cause dear to the hearts of the "blue-blooded blue-hairs" (in the unkind words of one frustrated archaeologist), this was inevitable. This is not to say that archaeological concepts of either heritage or the public must exclude elite individuals, but it is undoubtedly a fear on the part of every archaeologist that the interested public will, in time, degenerate into a dedicated and privileged corps of moneyed volunteers (Rizvi 2006: 413; Morris 1998). Thus, public archaeology, once the experimental enclave of a few zealous and radical practitioners, has in many places devolved into a preoccupation with colonial houses, commemorations and "twee museums."[1]

How did this misalliance come to pass? An initial observation is that the diffuse goals and fuzzy methodology of public archaeology lent themselves to it. The attempt of many would-be public archaeologists to enshrine marginalized voices in an ordered narrative that merely echoes the narrative that originally excluded them couldn't have helped either. For example, for want of a truly alternative perspective on the past of African Americans, such as that being painstakingly developed by Jeppson (1997) and La Roche and Blakey (1997), we are told at federal, state, local, and private heritage factories that African Americans did everything that other Americans did and simply were not given credit for it. This convenient gloss over hundreds of years of slavery, violence, and discrimination gives us an idea of how public archaeology came to be synonymous with heritage and historical preservation. It also reflects a peculiarly American approach to reparation and contrition—namely "inclusion" as the remedy for past wrongs.

Which leads me to a second observation: to the extent that public archaeology has fulfilled its original mandate to truly involve living communities in archaeological sites, it has done so outside of the United States where it is much more likely to be labeled "public interest archaeology" or "community archaeology" (Green et al. 2003; Greer et al. 2002; Rizvi 2006). Public interest archaeology is not necessarily the same as community archaeology (Marshall 2002), but I would suggest that their goals are similar and they both deserve being considered as distinct from public archaeology and its discontents as practiced in the United States. Laying aside for the moment the issue of when and how much power over archaeological sites can be shared with the public, both of these archaeologies are concerned with the public as archaeology's primary beneficiary. Site preservation is secondary to site relevance. These archaeologies make the issues of parochial identity that every site represents significant for a greater public and have been far more cautious in embracing associations with heritage and historical preservation.

There is yet hope, both in this country and abroad, for making public archaeology closer to the ideal envisioned by Shackel (2004). In spite of its failures, like the castaway of numerous Victorian novels, public archaeology has encapsulated its story in a hopeful message. The tale, from promising embarkation to shipwreck in a sea of misunderstanding, is one of having *not* overcome colonialism or succeeding in adequately addressing conflict. In our culture of "real virtuality" (Castells 2000: 403), however, the means of rescue is more dependent on Google Earth than on chance ship sightings. Connectivity, in both its online and psychosocial implications, may yet make possible the synthesis of global and local identities that public archaeology was intended to achieve.

A Play in Hypertext

Archaeology that matters to the public is not represented by overblown world heritage claims but rather by telling the stories of both us and them with some degree of panache. One of the best venues for telling archaeological stories has, quite naturally, been the Internet (Hodder 2003; Keene 2004). This kind of connectivity, in order to become a valid means for exploring identities in the past and present, provides the best medium for multiple interpretations (Merriman 2004)—namely, hypertext. Hypertext does not only apply to website material, however. As Rosemary Joyce explains, hypertext is any communication that maintains "the immediacy of different points of view" (Joyce 2002: 60). An archaeological story in hypertext, she suggests, like any narrative, has a plot and dialogue.

Hypertext literature can take many forms, but it is specifically the play, to borrow Hodder's simile (1998), that I believe best suits archaeology. Therefore, as a performance genre, effective archaeological communication involves more than plot and dialogue, both of which we have managed to incorporate into our projects with little difficulty. It also includes subtext (realized through action), drama (emotional effect), and theater (conscious staging). What follows is a discussion of how these elements have been used in archaeological settings and what the strengths and weaknesses have been in applied contexts.

Plot has been the element that has received the most attention from public archaeology practitioners. Successful archaeological plots provide a definable beginning, middle, and end (White 1987: 2)—but not in the kind of "march of time" order familiar in traditional archaeology and history. Hypertextual plots branch or perform in accordance with the needs and requests of the users. The multimedia investigations of Maria Franklin (1998) and Carol McDavid (1999, 2002) at the Levi Jordan Plantation (Brazoria, Texas) are an excellent example. As an ongoing and interactive exploration of power, class, and race relations in a society of slaves, tenant farmers, and wealthy landowners, this project can be seen as something of a continuation of Leone's original work in Annapolis that began as a study of the fragmented ways in which Annapolis was presented to the public (Leone et al. 1987). The degree to which archaeologists using Internet technology can and will guide the interactions of users has been a matter of some concern (McDavid 2004) that has not been effectively resolved.

Dialogue is another area in which hypertextual archaeological projects have done well. Interactivity with the past may have begun with the devices used by public and private museums to draw in visitors, but it has now become a mainstay for archaeological sites, both physical and virtual (Keene 2005). Archaeological projects all over the world are presenting findings on the Web, and there are numerous online forums permitting "visitors" to express their views.[2] Additionally, physical sites are incorporating interactive technology, although the resources necessary in order to do this can be substantial. The best examples are the well-organized explorations of Ian Hodder at Çatalhöyük (Hodder 2000) and Lynn Meskell at Kruger National Park (Meskell 2005).

Nevertheless, true dialogue between the public and archaeologists is not a matter of increased resources and technology so much as increasing an awareness of voices "unheard" and "unseen," to use Joyce's terminology (2002: 39). Julia Costello (1998) and Jeanie Lopiparo (2002) have experimented with ways to accomplish this, in the first case by placing the archaeologist as an actor within the reported narratives, and in the second by creating the opportunity to connect to figures from polychrome vessels through vocal animation. Both are interesting approaches that, if further developed, might accomplish something.

Archaeologists have long been familiar with *subtext* in our work, but planned subtext is another thing entirely. In a typical play, plot is expressed through specifically controlled dialogue, but subtext can only be realized through performance. Thus, there is an aspect of the uncontrolled in subtext even while the actors are exhorted to adhere as closely as possible to the author's intentions. Claire Smith was among the first archaeologists to attempt to control subtext in her community-based project. Her discussion with the Barunga about establishing rules for outsiders to visit their sacred sites (Smith and Wobst 2005) actually combines a couple of subtexts. The first is that of the archaeological and historical meaning of the site, which is the one likely to draw visitors. The second is the right of the Aboriginal communities to control access to their land and culture.

Australia, in general, seems to be a particularly rich place for exploring subtext. Postcolonial methodology apparently can thrive in a climate of subaltern histories (Derry and Malloy 2003; Field et al. 2000; Gosden 2001; Marshall 2002; Porter and Salazar 2005). Casella (2004) recently posited that it is confinement and incarceration, dominant themes in the colonialist peopling of Australia, that have encouraged Anglo-Australians to both differentiate themselves from Europeans and seek to discover a pre-colonialist, unconfined past among the Indigenous inhabitants of the continent.

Many people would argue that there is enough drama in the past without scholars attempting to create more of it, but we, as archaeologists, have a rather established habit of generating or supporting dull solutions to interesting problems. Archaeologists disregard the sensitivities of Native

Americans toward their ancestors' remains and sacred objects? Provide a complex bureaucratic structure to address the issue. America's superhighway mania is running roughshod over sites? Cultural Resource Management to the rescue. Similarly, our answer to making the public more interested in the past has often been to couch information in the form of persistently neutral narratives, designed to neither engage nor offend. There are, of course, some bold scholars willing to confront history that "hurts" (Jameson 1981). Of particular interest in recent years has been the so-called African Renaissance projects (Manyanga 2003; Malegapuru 1999; Muringaniza 1999), in which heritage has become a focus for local communities to confront the deprivation of their rights by reviving traditions relating to archaeological sites. Elsewhere, histories of subjugation and slavery are now being told with emotion by scholars. Some of these projects have resulted in a détente of sorts between archaeologists and communities (Derry and Malloy 2003; Dowdall and Parrish 2002; Fagerstrom 1998; Pyburn 2003), but others maintain the controversy as an honest exploration of how past injustices fragment modern communities (Ardren 2002; La Roche and Blakey 1997).

Theater, which requires a separation between actors and spectators at the same time as it ostensibly brings them together to engage in common emotions, is something few of us have been comfortable in creating at our sites. Good theater also entails a respect for the audience that seems to be, sadly, lacking among historians and archaeologists. The kind of production that one finds at Williamsburg, St. Mary's City, Deerfield, and elsewhere on the "colonial" circuit are cases in point (Hodder 1999: 163). The stimulus for truly good archaeological theater should be strongest in developing a site for visitors. Here, the distribution of power—Who represents "the community"? Who is the decision-maker? Who will benefit from the site? (Green et al. 2003; Marshall 2002: 215)—become central questions that have to be resolved within the production itself. This aspect of archaeology as theater may be particularly unappealing to scholars who are known for spinning out their resolutions for many years. Further, many would scorn the theatrical as popularizing the site. Ultimately, unless we as archaeologists become more involved in the staging of a site for the public, someone else will, as likely as not, turn it into a theme park.

Conclusion

Public archaeology has been largely appropriated by heritage, which, in turn, has itself been appropriated by global informational capitalism (Castells 2000). The local manifestations of this development can be seen in the ever-expanding, and elitist, historical preservation movement. Consequently, it is no surprise that today the practice is largely understood as an approach to preserving cultural property. In contrast, public interest and community archaeology, which developed from the original (and still largely unrealized) goals of public archaeology, have become more concerned with the preservation, and presentation, of cultural identities. At its best, public interest and community archaeology are undertaken with a conscious effort to engage, inform, and be informed in return. They impose roles upon scholars that we cannot easily adapt to, as we can neither commodify nor trivialize the identities we explore.

Seeing the past as public education, entertainment, identity support, and sustainable development is relatively new for archaeologists, yet it is important to remember that these have always been the primary ways in which communities have connected with sites (e.g., Rowan and Baram 2004). Some projects can effectively balance the interests of scholars and the public, but, all too often, archaeologists are stymied by the problem of making sites both profitable and purposeful for researchers and the public alike (Howell 1996; McEwan et al. 1993). Here, drama, honest dialogue, and audience participation may operate on a collision course, particularly where economics are involved. However, if the balancing act is successful, it will result in an experience that, like the best of theatrical productions, is both inspiring and memorable.

Notes

1. "Twee" means overly quaint. Twee museums are those little places that preserve the flotsam and jetsam of small town gentry.
2. Many of these are listed at *http://www.archaeology.org/wwwarky/index.html*.

References

Appadurai, A. 2002. The globalization of archaeology and heritage. *Journal of Social Archaeology* 1: 35–49.

Ardren, T. 2002. Conversations about the production of archaeological knowledge and community museums at Chunchucmil and Kochol, Yucatan, Mexico. *World Archaeology* 34 (2): 379–400.

Casella, E. 2004. Legacy of the "Fatal Shore": The heritage and archaeology of confinement in post-colonial Australia. *Journal of Social Archaeology* 4 (1): 99–125.

Castells, M. 2000. *The Information Age: Economy, Society and Culture*, Vol. 1: *The Rise of the Network Society*. Oxford: Blackwell.

Costello, J. 1998. Bread fresh from the oven: Memories of Italian breadmaking in the California mother-lode. *Historical Archaeology* 32: 66–73

Derry, L., and Malloy, M. (eds) 2003. *Archaeologists and Local Communities: Partners in Exploring the Past*. Washington, DC: Society for American Archaeology.

Dirlik, A. 2003. Globalization as the end and the beginning of history: The contradictory implications of a new paradigm. Working Paper Series, Institute on Globalization and the Human Condition, McMaster University.

Dowdall, K., and Parrish, O. 2002 A meaningful disturbance of the earth. *Journal of Social Archaeology* 3(1): 99–13.

Fagerstrom, J. 1998. Golovin Field School. Paper presented at Beringian Days Conference, Anchorage Alaska, October 11–12, 1998.

Field, J., Barker, J., Barker, R., Coffey, E., Coffey, L., Crawford, E., Darcy, L., Fields, T., Lord, G., Steadman, B., and Colley, S. 2000. "Coming back": Aborigines and archaeologists at Cuddie Springs. *Public Archaeology* 1: 21–33.

Franklin, M. 1998. Comments on "Perspectives on the evolution of African American culture: The historical archaeology of the tenant community at the Levi Jordan Plantation," Society for Historical Archaeology Conference, Atlanta, GA. *www.webarchaeology.com/html/maria.htm*.

Gallaher, T., and Aycock, G. 2001. Opportunities analysis for AHC properties; Analysis of programs in other states. Report prepared for the Alabama Historical Commission. Birmingham, AL: Economics Research Associates.

Gosden, C. 2001. Postcolonial archaeology: Issues of culture, identity, and knowledge, in I. Hodder (ed.), *Archaeological Theory Today*. Cambridge: Polity Press.

Green, L. F., Green, D. R., and Neves, E. G. 2003. Indigenous knowledge and archaeological science: The challenges of public archaeology in the Reserva Uaça. *Journal of Social Archaeology* 3 (3): 366–398.

Greer, S., Harrison, R., and McIntyre-Tamwoy, S. 2002. Community based archaeology in Australia. *World Archaeology* 34 (2): 265–287.

Hodder, I. 1998. The past as passion and play: Çatalhöyük as a site of conflict in the construction of multiple pasts, in L. Meskell (ed.), *Archaeology under Fire: Nationalism, Politics and Heritage in the Eastern Mediterranean and Middle East*, pp. 124–139. London: Routledge.

———. 1999. *The Archaeological Process: An Introduction*. Oxford, UK, and Malden, MA: Blackwell Publishers.

———. 2003. *Archaeology beyond Dialogue*. Salt Lake City: University of Utah Press.

Hodder, I. (ed.). 2000. *Towards Reflexive Method in Archaeology: The Example at Çatalhöyük*. BIAA Monograph No. 28. Cambridge: McDonald Institute for Archaeological Research.

Howell, C. 1996. Daring to deal with huaqueros, in K. D. Vitelli (ed.), *Archaeological Ethics*. Walnut Creek, CA: AltaMira.

Jameson, F. 1981. *The Political Unconscious: Narrative as a Socially Symbolic Act*. Ithaca: Cornell University Press.

Jeppson, P. 1997. Leveling the playing field in the contested territory of the South African past: A "public" versus a "people's" form of historical archaeology outreach, in Historical Archaeology Symposia Issue on "In the Realm of Politics: Prospects for Public Participation in African-American and Plantation Archaeology, *Society for Historical Archaeology* 31 (3): 65–83.

Joyce, R. 2002. *The Languages of Archaeology: Dialogue, Narrative, and Writing*. Oxford: Blackwell.

———. 2005. Solid histories for fragile nations: Archaeology as cultural patrimony, in L. Meskell and P. Pels (eds.), *Embedding Ethics*. New York: Berg.

Kane, S. (ed.). 2003. *The Politics of Archaeology and Identity in a Global Context*. Boston: Archaeological Institute of America.

Keene, S. 2004. The future of the museum in the digital age. *ICOM News* 57 (3): 4.

———. 2005. *Fragments of the World: Uses of Museum Collections*. Oxford: Elsevier.

Kohl, P. 2004. Making the past profitable in an age of globalization and national ownership: Contradictions and considerations, in Y. Rowan and U. Baram (eds.), *Marketing Heritage: Archaeology and the Consumption of the Past*. Walnut Creek, CA: AltaMira Press.

Kristiansen, K., and Rowlands, M. (eds.). 1998. *Social Transformations in Archaeology: Global and Local Perspectives*. New York: Routledge.

La Roche, C., and Blakey, M. 1997. Seizing intellectual power: The dialogue at the New York African Burial Ground. *Historical Archaeology* 31 (3): 84–106.

Leone, M. P., Potter, P. B. Jr., and Shackel, P. A. 1987. Toward a critical archaeology. *Current Anthropology* 28 (3): 283–302.

Lopiparo, J. 2002. A second voice: Crafting cosmos, in R. Joyce (ed.), *The Languages of Archaeology: Dialogue, Narrative, and Writing*, pp. 68–99. Oxford: Blackwell.

Malegapuru, W. M. (ed.). 1999. *African Renaissance: The New Struggle*. Sandton: Mafube Publishing.

Manyanga, M. 2003. Intangible cultural heritage and the empowerment of local communities. Paper presented at ICOMOS Conference, 14th General Assembly and Scientific Symposiums, Victoria Falls, Zimbabwe.

Marshall, Y. 2002. What is community archaeology? *World Archaeology* 34 (2): 211–219.

McDavid, C. 1999. From "traditional" archaeology to public archaeology to community action, in P. Shackel and E. Chambers, (eds.), *Places in Mind: Public Archaeology as Applied Anthropology*, pp. 35–56. Oxford: Blackwell.

———. 2002. Archaeologies that hurt; descendants that matter: A pragmatic approach to collaboration in the public interpretation of African-American archaeology. *World Archaeology* 34 (2): 303–314.

———. 2004. Towards a more democratic archaeology? The Internet and public archaeological practice, in N. Merriman (ed.), *Public Archaeology*, pp. 159–187. London: Routledge.

McEwan, C., Hudson, C., and Silva, M.-I. 1994. Archaeology and community: A village cultural center and museum in Ecuador. *Practicing Anthropology* 16 (1): 3–7.

Merriman, N. (ed.). 2004. *Public Archaeology*. London: Routledge.

Meskell, L. 2002. Negative heritage and past mastering in archaeology. *Anthropological Quarterly* 75 (3): 557–574.

———. 2005 Archaeological ethnography: Conversations around Kruger National Park. *Journal of the World Archaeology Congress* (Archaeologies) 1: 83–102.

Morris, R. 1998. *Collapse of Public Interest Archaeology*. British Archaeology No. 31. York: Council for British Archaeology.

Muringaniza, J. S. 1999. Heritage that hurts: The case of the grave of Cecil Rhodes in the Matopos National Park of Zimbabwe. Paper presented at the World Archaeological Congress 4, Cape Town, 10–16 January 1999.

Pearson, M., and Shanks, M. 2001. *Theatre/Archaeology*. London: Routledge.

Porter, B., and Salazar, N. 2005. Heritage tourism, conflict, and the public interest:

An introduction. *International Journal of Heritage Studies* 11 (5): 361–370.

Pyburn, A. 2003. Archaeology for a new millennium: The rules of engagement, in L. Derry and M. Malloy (eds.), *Archaeologists and Local Communities: Partners in Exploring the Past*. Washington, DC: Society for American Archaeology.

Rizvi, U. Z. 2006. Accounting for multiple desires: Decolonizing methodologies, archaeology, and the public interest. *India Review* 5 (3–4): 394–416.

Rowan, Y., and Baram, U. (eds.) 2004. *Marketing Heritage: Archaeology and the Consumption of the Past*. Walnut Creek, CA: AltaMira Press.

Shackel, S. 2004. Introduction: Working with communities: Heritage development and applied archaeology, in P. Shackel and E. J. Chambers, (eds.), *Places in Mind: Public Archaeology as Applied Anthropology*, pp. 1–18. New York and London: Routledge.

Smith, C., and Wobst, H. M. 2005. *Indigenous Archaeologies: Decolonizing Theory and Practice*. London: Routledge.

Tringham, R. 2003. Interview with the Society for California Archaeology. http://www.scahome.org/educational_resources/2003_Tringham.html.

White, H. 1987. *The Content of the Form: Narrative Discourse and Historical Representation*. Baltimore: Johns Hopkins University.

36

PUBLIC INTEREST ANTHROPOLOGY: A MODEL FOR ENGAGED RESEARCH TIED TO ACTION

Peggy Reeves Sanday

Public interest anthropology (PIA) was named as such at a 1996 faculty seminar at the Department of Anthropology, University of Pennsylvania. The goal of this seminar was to find ways to join research and action, to cut across the subfields of anthropology, and to bridge teaching and community action in service learning programs.[1] Among many other subjects, we discussed the possibilities for anthropologizing public interests, which we labeled "public interest anthropology," building on the title of my 1976 edited book, *Anthropology and the Public Interest*. We agreed that, regardless of the subdiscipline, anthropologists who address public issues must deal not just with specific publics motivated by certain interests or characterized by definable needs, but with contested interests as well.

This commentary focuses on the broad epistemological and philosophical issues that I see as crucial in developing public interest–related culture theory, and which frame this section. Given PIA's focus on diverse *publics* and *interests*, the primary focus orienting cultural analysis is on the description and mapping of ethnographic *particulars* so that the immediacies of human thought, behavior, action, and production are in the forefront. The emphasis on diversity and engagement means that rather than fitting the particulars into existing theory (the "bifocal" approach), theory evolves with PIA's engagement with the many different levels described below, requiring a multifocal approach to analysis.

Bifocality refers to the practice of tacking between the "the experience-near"—that is, the particulars of ethnography—and what Geertz calls "the experience-distant" (Geertz 1983: 55–72). By this meaning, bifocality involves assessing local facts in terms of wider theoretical models drawn from a number of sources. Multifocality addresses the local and the global, the theoretical and the political, the moral order and the social imaginary, along with strategies for action. The analysis phase may also address macro-social guarantees, meta-cultural discourse, and the future in terms of generalizable human interests such as social justice and human rights. Another consideration might be the historical and social trajectories of public(s) and interest(s) in relations of power. Observing the patterning of such trajectories provides the baseline for building theoretical models of and for the social life of specific interests.

In its emphasis on action and change, PIA has its roots in the foundational Boasian anthropological paradigm that evolved during the 20th century through the work of a legion of engaged anthropologists. It is also inspired by the work of critical theorists, Karl Marx's "Thesis on Feuerbach," which represents the classic foundation for a public interest social science,[2] and by Pierre Bourdieu's "reflexive sociology."

The conceptual framework recognizes the power of human social agency to affect the future through reflection, social engagement, negotiation, consensus building, and political action. The theoretical issues evolve from the assumption that if humans constitute their world, they then have the capacity to change it, even though it is lodged in the *habitus* of the cultural worlds they have constructed. Today, engaged anthropologists who tie theory to research, explication, and action in addressing public audiences play a central role in the reconstitution of these worlds. While the approach may be seen as fitting under the rubric of Public Anthropology (the book series announced in 1998 by Robert Borofsky), PIA is more specifically focused on public interests.

The core conceptual framework for PIA is shaped by the *concept of culture* and an appreciation for the meaning and implications of *cultural diversity*. Diversity refers to the myriad ways human groups have found to solve the problems that face them, along with the imaginaries that guide or develop solutions passed down through the generations. Taking Clifford Geertz's (1973: 5) concept of culture as "webs of significance" in which humans are "suspended" but which they also spin, a dialectical relationship between *order* and *freedom* grounds PIA's approach to observation and analysis; *freedom* refers to the spinning and *order* refers to the being suspended. Both are tied to the structure of the web formed by social fields that are upheld and legitimated by historical cultural meanings justifying values and norms. Human social creativity is part of the freedom/order dialectic as groups (publics) form to promote, reflect on, and act with respect to certain interests. Public interest anthropology identifies the moments of choice, the resolution of conflict, and the construction of solidarity, which yield new webs of meaning supporting social bonding.

Critical theory's emphasis on human agency, along with its goal of bridging action and theory so that the two are mutually constitutive, is key. "Critical theory," Craig Calhoun (1995: 13) explains, "was the name chosen by the founders of the Frankfurt School in the period between two world wars to symbolize their attempt to achieve a unity of theory and practice, including a unity of theory with empirical research and both with an historically grounded awareness of the social, political, and cultural problems of the age." According to Max Horkheimer, one of the founders, critical theory conceptualizes humans as "producers of their own historical way." A major goal is to emancipate humans "from the relationships that enslave [them]" (Horkheimer, quoted by Benhabib 1986: 3). Emancipation used in this sense is defined not just in terms of finding the means to free people from oppressive social forces, but also to free them from a world view that narrows the realm of the possible (see discussion in Calhoun 1995: 14).

Critical theory illuminates the social and historical grounds for an oppressed consciousness by "defetishizing critique" (Benhabib 1986: 9). Calhoun (l995: 20) compares this aspect of critical theory with "positivist social science" to demonstrate that while the former uses science for change, the latter accepts the world as it exists and precludes recognition of the possibilities for change. Critical theory is unique among the social sciences in privileging human freedom in its research practice.

The use of anthropology to free human thought is reminiscent of Franz Boas's (1969: 1–2) goal of using science to "engender the habit of clear thinking" so that people will be weaned "from a complacent yielding to prejudice," the "tyranny of custom," and "the love of traditional lore" (Benedict 1943). This goal can be compared with the "reflexive sociology" of Pierre Bourdieu.

In the last decade of his life, Pierre Bourdieu was outspoken in his engagement with "the public" and "the public interest." In writing and talking about "the public interest," he freely uses concepts like the "public good," the "collective interest," "collective responsibility," and "civic virtue" (Bourdieu 1998: 4–7). He is blistering in his attack on intellectuals and politicians who "are terribly short of ideals that can mobilize people" (p. 5). Like Boas, Bourdieu sees humans as both imprisoned yet capable of freedom. In place of Boas's "tyranny of custom," he speaks of "social fields" which "necessitate the world" (Bourdieu and Wacquant 1992: 19–20). Like Boas, Bourdieu believes that social science can be an avenue to freedom. What he calls "reflexive sociology" opens "the possibility of identifying true sites of freedom, and thus of building small-scale, modest, practical morals in keeping with the scope of human freedom," however narrow it may be.

PIA begins with the assumption that human beings and groups are in a constant state of change and flux—contesting, adopting, abandoning, and reflecting on past, present, and future norms when developing new positions and adaptations. Interests are tied to norms and values, to hopes and dreams for the future, and to relations of production and systems of domination. The major question is not how populations are oppressed, but how (and whether) people join together to find common ground to resolve tensions and quality-of-life concerns. Another major question revolves around the cultural manifestation of ideas about shared substance, the common good, and well-being in the face of social, cultural, and institutional diversity.

In cultural anthropology, the vantage point from which I write, data collection and analysis are grounded in ethnography, the study of discourse, cultural critique, and the use of reflection. Cultural critique and reflection work at several levels. First, there is the critical reflection of citizens thinking about, and acting with respect to, social issues in the interest of change (see discussion in Scheper-Hughes 1992: 170; 1995: 410–412). There is also the reflection of the anthropologist who uses anthropology to "think on behalf of the world" and act accordingly, as Roy Rappaport (1995: 292) proposes.

Rappaport (1995: 253) outlines a model for a committed and "engaged anthropology," one that critiques and enlightens the members of its own society. This model focuses on the identification of contemporary social disorders, which Rappaport defines as maladaptive and in need of correction. According to Rappaport, "the recognition and definition of social disorders is undertheorized in anthropology" (1995: 261). Although he says that this is not the case in the other social sciences, such as economics, he is critical of economics for neglecting what he calls "the principle of contingency."

The principle of contingency refers to the cross-cultural observation that all social systems (including economic systems) are "contingent on the existence of biological-ecological systems" (Rappaport 1995: 266–267). Rappaport identifies a "common type of disorder" caused by making ultimate values (e.g., the environment) contingent on economic values. Getting values out of order by violating the principle of contingency produces both social and ecological disorders.

By reflecting on and researching potentially destructive, inequitable, or evolutionary trends set in motion by maladaptive social, economic, demographic, and environmental trends, anthropologists may respond to social and cultural processes that are identified as either causing harm or having the potential for doing so. Reflection in this sense might lead to endorsing someone's "moral model of the world" so as to correct disorders. It might also lead to statements about the relationship between global warming, environmental degradation, and evolutionary extinction. Or, it might lead to an immediate response to governmental oversight of critical national issues, such as the social and economic impacts of Hurricane Katrina in the United States. This two-sided approach to the public interest—one staged by citizens, the other by anthropologists—reflects the interactive role of anthropology and the public in which both play a role in constructing the problem and finding solutions.

The many levels of data analysis range from the empirically grounded to the more generally philosophical and abstract, including a consideration of macro-social and meta-cultural processes. Examples of the levels of analysis include (1) treating human social creativity as a field of action (using Bourdieu's sense of the term "field"); (2) grounding contested social issues in the local logic of cultural diversity, neoliberalism, and in regimes of power; (3) critiquing contested social issues by reference to meta-cultural definitions of macro-social guarantees such as found in the constitutional guarantees of any nation; (4) raising issues with respect to generalizable human interests as these are related to the quality of life, the common good, and human and social well-being; and (5) assessing the implications of the current state of the world for the future of the species.

Linking these various levels of analysis is the focus on the interests motivating action. This is a complex subject that can only be touched on here.[3] Generally, interests motivating action range from the particular to the general, from what motivates individuals, groups, and institutions to invest in specific goals to how consensus is reached. The latter may rest on arguments drawing on meta-cultural arguments about normative validity or the principle of contingency. This kind of reflection transcends the consideration of personal or even institutional interests to consider "generalizable interests"—that is, "the interests of a 'general' will achieved in a consensual situation" (Braaten 1991: 32; see also Habermas 1992: 63).

Interests are also located in needs interpretation, whereby one group defines the needs of another (e.g., the need for a home [the homeless public], for food, or for better nutrition). In response to such needs interpretation, publics may be constituted by those who respond to issues of survival and basic human rights (see Fraser 1989: 161–187 for an analysis of the politics of needs interpretation).

The Many Faces of Public Interest Ethnography: Uniting Theory and Action

There is a long ethnographic tradition of anthropologists investing in certain research problems in the interest of public enlightenment and/or social change. Unlike more theoretically oriented ethnography, in which the interest may be purely scholarly, those working in this tradition address public issues by diagnosing ills, investigating disease, addressing inequities, and thinking about cures. One also finds a frequent focus on defamiliarizing the familiar in order to change ways of seeing by evoking public reflection and debate. Based on her Samoan fieldwork, Margaret Mead (1928) presented a view of adolescence that changed the way Americans thought about its dramas. Based on her study of a military community, Catherine Lutz (2002: 9) helps us to understand the social impact of militarism at home. In light of the impact she describes by way of delineating the ethnographic and historical contexts of militarism in Fayetteville, North Carolina, Lutz raises the question of whether there might be another way "when it becomes clearer how few really profit from the old."

Taking a another tack in a different kind of community study, this one located in Queens, New York, Roger Sanjek (1998) places himself in the community of Elmhurst-Cornoa in explicit recognition of the fact that we are all in this together, that what is at stake is "the future of us all," the title he gives to his study of "civic activism" around "quality of life issues." The overarching goal of Sanjek's study is to assess how diverse communities achieve "an integrated body politic" in which community members work together to find common ground in addressing community concerns affecting the quality of life for community members (Sanjek 1998: 2).

Across the world in India, Arjun Appadurai (2002: 22–23) speaks of the "politics of partnership" in his "preliminary analysis of an urban activist movement with global links." The study is of an alliance of housing activists in Mumbai in which very different partners are linked in social action. According to Appadurai, of the various non-state organizations working with the urban poor in Mumbai, "the Alliance has by far the largest constituency, the highest visibility in the eyes of the state, and the most extensive networks in India and elsewhere in the world." The net of social solidarity that this Alliance managed to weave across the social spectrum leads Appadurai to distinguish two broad trends among the many grassroots political movements in the "new global political economy." On the one hand are groups that have opted for armed, militarized solutions to their problems of inclusion, recognition, and participation. On the other are those that have opted for a politics of partnership—partnership, that is, between traditionally opposed groups, such as states, corporations, and workers (Appadurai 2002: 22).

Julia Paley's (2001) provocative ethnography of post-dictatorship Chile provides another example of ethnography in the public interest. This work focuses on the activism of the grassroots health group Paley studied in a poor community in Santiago, Chile. The study is particularly interesting for the way in which Paley uses her ethnography of the transition to democracy to teach the members of this group to reflect on the ways in which the government impinges on their community. She also takes the further step of teaching the members how to use ethnography for gaining the knowledge base to lobby government officials. Paley's close involvement with the health group provides a prime example of how action can influence theory.

In my own work, I launched several ethnographic projects seeking to address anthropology and the public simultaneously. In the first project, I addressed the issue of male dominance, claimed to be universal by some anthropologists (Sanday 1981, 1982) and widespread on North American college campuses through the incidence of acquaintance rape (Sanday 2007b [1990]). The second project addressed the topic of redefining matriarchy as lived and experienced in the Minangkabau villages (Indonesia) where I lived for many years (Sanday 2002). The third project addressed the world view associated with the Wolfe Creek Crater of northwestern Australia, the second largest rimmed meteorite crater in the world, through paintings of the crater by its Aboriginal "traditional owners" (Sanday 2007a).

Campus Sex Culture: One Case Study in Public Interest Anthropology

The first and perhaps the most well known of these examples is my analysis and description of campus sexual culture, explaining the one-in-four statistic characterizing the incidence of acquaintance rape on college campuses. In 1983, I learned from a student of mine that she had been "gang banged" while drunk at a fraternity party. As the case unfolded on campus, two publics vied for attention. The fraternity members boasted about the party, calling the sexual event an "express," referring to the common use of the term "train" for a "gang bang." The public boasting ended when campus feminists and the editor of the campus newspaper decried what happened and called it "rape." In the aftermath, I discovered that similar incidents were being reported on campuses all over the country and that the response by campus administrators was either nonexistent or tepid at best (Sanday 2007b [1990]).

I aired the moral and social issues at stake by providing "I-witness" accounts of fraternity sexual rituals written by participants, which included fraternity brothers as well as female partygoers. The accounts were written to defamiliarize the "boys will be boys" and "she wants it" explanations for "gang bangs" on college campuses. Embedded in the accounts were references to arguments for the validity of nonconsensual sexual practices designed to promote fraternal bonding and social acceptance within the fraternal context. By comparing the graphic descriptions by young women of being drunk and passing out at a fraternity party with the legal definition of rape, I pointed out that the practices were illegal and that administrators who subscribed to the "boys will be boys" discourse were complicit in the rampant sexism I observed on campus. In the years after the book was published, I personally met with or spoke to members of the public by accepting invitations to speak on college campuses and to be interviewed by television, radio, and print reporters.

This project demonstrates the reciprocal relationship between theory and ethnography in which the latter expands the former. The thick description of sexual practices defining fraternity bonding led me to develop the concept of *sexual culture* in direct opposition to the prevailing belief that male sexual aggression is either hormonal or evolutionarily based, hence, universal (Sanday 1997; for the debate, see Sanday 2003 and other articles in Travis 2003 responding to Thornhill and Palmer 2000). The evolutionary argument, while persuasive to some, no longer sways legal thinking, at least in some courts. For example, in January 2003, the California State Supreme Court ruled by a decision of 6–1 that a man is a rapist if he continues to have intercourse with someone who says no, even if she initially consented to sex, but then changed her mind.[4]

The potential for research to influence public action is demonstrated by the interplay between anti-rape activism and engaged scholarship. When I started the project in the early 1980s, few campuses had sexual-assault policies. At the time, the legal definition of rape hung on "earnest," "sufficient," or "utmost resistance." Due to the cooperation between researchers and activists in the intervening period, today most campuses do have sexual-assault policies and there is increasing evidence of a legal commitment to the view that "no means no" and that a rape defense must demonstrate affirmative verbal consent rather than the absence of resistance (Sanday 1997: 265–293).

Conclusion

Drawing from critical theory and the work of a lineage of engaged anthropologists, the multiplicity of issues raised by the conceptual framework outlined in this chapter makes the analysis phase of public interest ethnography (PIE) more multifocal than bifocal. The brief examples of ethnography in the public interest presented here reflect the authors' ethical engagement in critical social issues, and demonstrate the levels of analysis and conceptualization that might be invoked in doing PIE. For example, each focuses on particular publics, explores the interests around which people mobilize for action, inspires reflection about social change, and is concerned with how people find common ground in the interest of working for broader social goals. As such, PIE displays the complex workings of human social creativity. With respect to the written product, PIE aims to communicate to public as well as to academic audiences, either through the writing or the activism associated with the work.

Notes

1. The seminar included three cultural anthropologists (Julia Paley, myself, and Paula Sabloff), one physical anthropologist (Francis Johnston), and several archaeologists who came in for special sessions. Funding came from Ira Harkavy's Center for Community Partnership (see Harkavy et al. 1996). The paper summarizing the seminar's conclusions can be read at *http://www.sas.upenn.edu/anthro/anthro/piapapers*. In the context of the seminar, we addressed many issues: nutrition in West Philadelphia; democracy in Chile and Mongolia; the role of indigenous investment in archaeological projects; museums as a tool for education in cultural diversity; discourse circulation as a vehicle for change. More anthropologists got involved in the discussion in the context of AAA symposia presented in Philadelphia 1998; San Francisco 2000; New Orleans 2002; and, a one-day School of American Research (SAR) workshop in 2003. In these discussions and presentations, Yolanda Moses and James Peacock played a central role, along with Paula Sabloff. Some of the papers associated with the symposia and the SAR workshop can be read at the web page already cited.

2. See especially: (Thesis VIII) "All social life is essentially practical. All mysteries which lead theory to mysticism find their rational solution in human practice and in the comprehension of this practice"; and (Thesis XI) "The philosophers have only interpreted the world, in various ways; the point is to change it." See *www.marxists.org/archive/ marx/works /1845/theses/theses.htm*.

3. For more, see the School of American Research Workshop paper at *http://www.sas.upenn.edu/anthro/anthro/piapapers*.

4. This was reported in the *San Francisco Chronicle*, 12 January 2003, Editorial Section, p. D5. For a similar opinion in the New Jersey Supreme Court in 1992, also see Sanday 1997: 265–266.

References

Appadurai, A. 2002. Deep democracy: Urban governmentality and the horizon of politics. *Public Culture* 14 (1): 21–48.

Benedict, R. 1943. Franz Boas as an ethnologist. In *Franz Boas: 1858–1942. American Anthropologist, Memoir* No. 61, July-September.

Benhabib, S. 1986. *Critique, Norm, and Utopia*. New York: Columbia University Press.

Boas, F. 1969. *Race and Democratic Society*. New York: BIBLO and TANNEN.

Borofsky, R. 2000. Public anthropology: Where to? What next? *Anthropology News* 41 (5): 9–10.

Bourdieu, P. 1998. *Acts of Resistance: Against the Tyranny of the Market*. New York: The New Press.

Bourdieu, P., and Wacquant, L. J. D. 1992. *An Invitation to Reflexive Sociology*. Chicago: University of Chicago Press.

Braaten, J. 1991. *Habermas's Critical Theory of Society*. New York: State University of New York Press.

Calhoun, C. 1995. *Critical Social Theory*. Oxford: Blackwell.

Fraser, N. 1989. *Unruly Practices*. Cambridge: Polity Press.

Geertz, C. 1973. *The Interpretations of Cultures*. New York: Basic Books.

———. 1983. *Local Knowledge: Further Essays in Interpretive Anthropology*. New York: Basic Books.

Habermas, J. 1992. *Moral Consciousness and Communicative Action*. Trans. C. Lenhardt and S. Weber Nicholson. Cambridge, MA: MIT Press.

Harkavy, I., Johnston, F. E., and Puckett, J. L. 1996. The University of Pennsylvania's Center for Community Partnerships as an organizational innovation for advancing action research. *Concepts and Transformation* 1 (1): 15–29.

Lutz, C. 2002. *Homefront: A Military City and the American Twentieth Century*. Boston: Beacon Press.

Mead, M. 1928. *Coming of Age in Samoa*. New York: Blue Ribbon Books.

Paley, J. 2001. *Marketing Democracy: Power and Social Movements in Post-Dictatorship Chile*. Berkeley: University of California Press.

Rappaport, R. 1995. Disorders of our own, in S. Forman (ed.), *Diagnosing America: Anthropology and Public Engagement*. Ann Arbor: University of Michigan Press.

Sanday, P. Reeves (ed.). 1976. *Anthropology and the Public Interest: Fieldwork and Theory*. New York: Academic Press.

———. 1981. *Female Power and Male Dominance: On the Origins of Sexual Inequality*. New York: Cambridge University Press.

———. 1982. The socio-cultural context of rape. *Journal of Social Issues* 35 (4): 5–27.

———. 1997. *A Woman Scorned: Acquaintance Rape on Trial*. Berkeley: University of California Press.

———. 2002. *Women at the Center: Life in a Modern Matriarchy*. Ithaca: Cornell University Press.

———. 2003. Rape-free versus rape-prone: How culture makes a difference, in C. Brown Travis (ed.), *Evolution, Gender, and Rape*, pp. 337–362. Cambridge, MA: MIT Press.

———. 2007a. *Aboriginal Paintings of the Wolfe Creek Crater: Track of the Rainbow Serpent*.

Philadelphia: University of Pennsylvania Museum Press.

———. 2007b [1990]. *Fraternity Gang Rape: Sex, Brotherhood, and Privilege on Campus*. Revised with new introduction and epilogue. New York: NYU Press.

Sanjek, R. 1998. *The Future of Us All: Race and Neighborhood Politics in New York City*. Ithaca: Cornell University Press.

Scheper-Hughes, N. 1992. *Death without Weeping: The Violence of Everyday Life In Brazil*. Berkeley: University of California Press.

———. 1995. The primacy of the ethical: Propositions for a militant anthropology. *Current Anthropology* 36 (3): 409–440.

Thornhill, R., and Palmer, C. T. 2000. *A Natural History of Rape: Biological Bases of Sexual Coercion*. Cambridge, MA: MIT Press.

Travis, C. B. (ed.). 2003. *Evolution, Gender, and Rape*. Cambridge, MA: MIT Press.

37

COMMENTARY:
CULTURAL RESOURCE MANAGEMENT, PUBLIC ARCHAEOLOGY, AND ADVOCACY

Carol McDavid and Fred McGhee

In this essay, we comment upon the challenges of doing a certain type of archaeology in a postcolonial world, and do so from two different perspectives: McGhee is an African-American "CRM" archaeologist working in the private sector, and McDavid is a European-American "public archaeologist" working in the academic/nonprofit sector. Both work within one particularly fraught social and political context: the historical archaeology of African America. McGhee will elaborate on this context in more detail.

Our approach is pragmatic, in the sense that we regard theory, and theorizing, *instrumentally*. That is, theories are tools to think with; they are not goals in themselves (James 1995: 7). Therefore, although we provide references to the key ideas, debates, and literature we find most useful, our use of them is grounded in the realities of everyday archaeological practice. We attempt to avoid armchair theorizing in favor of simply sharing approaches that have worked for us both personally.

This chapter includes a combination of jointly written text (such as this introduction) and individually authored sections. Our original goal was to include some dialogue as well, but for a variety of reasons this was not possible. We have opted, therefore, to say simply that as colleagues (and friends), we do debate the ideas presented here regularly, at great length, with great animation. Our comments are informed by these *ongoing* dialogues, as well as by our individual personal, theoretical, and disciplinary perspectives. Our common interest is to find creative, moral, and practical ways to deal with the intersections between archaeology and the needs and interests of various descendant groups, all of whom claim a different stake in the past and in how the past is used. This chapter offers entry points only: fleshing out the complex ideas touched on will not be possible here, although we do provide numerous references to direct readers to other writing, including our own.

After McDavid defines the two areas of practice addressed here (CRM and "public archaeology"), McGhee discusses CRM practice in more detail, especially with regard to the participatory approaches he finds most useful. McDavid then discusses how one particular theoretical tool, critical race theory, has proved useful in her own public archaeology practice.

Defining Terms

Within Americanist anthropological archaeology, until perhaps the last decade, "public archaeology" was defined as the commercial field of CRM (cultural resource management, or "contract archaeology," described in more detail below). Defining CRM *as* public archaeology derives from the idea that CRM archaeological projects are either funded by the public purse or mandated by public legislation concerning the preservation and stewardship of archaeological resources.

Over the last decade, however, the term "public archaeology" has expanded in meaning. Worldwide, it has evolved into a more general term referring to *any* endeavor in which archaeologists interact with the public, and any research (practical or theoretical) that examines or analyzes the public dimensions of doing archaeology. It has tended, in recent years, to be used alongside or instead of the term "heritage" or "heritage studies," although it is also seen now to be larger than either that *or*

CRM. People who call themselves public archaeologists now work in a number of fields, including, but not limited to, museums, education, new technologies, mass media studies, heritage management, politics and legislation, archaeological ethics, journalism, performance, and tourism—as well as CRM. Public archaeologists are concerned with public perceptions of archaeology, how pasts are created and used, community involvement in archaeology, and the conflict between academic and popular views of the past. Public archaeology research (both qualitative and quantitative) deals with political, social, and economic contexts in which archaeology is undertaken, the attitudes of disempowered and Indigenous peoples toward archaeology, and the educational and public role of the discipline. In short, public archaeology is an arena in which past and present merge, as information about the past is used by contemporary people for contemporary agendas and needs.

McGhee: Strategies for a Postcolonial CRM

Archaeology in the United States is now a practiced profession. About 80 percent of all archaeologists who are employed as such work either in private industry, or as government regulators often overseeing the archaeological work of that private industry.

Neumann and Sanford 2001: 1

The American field that has become known as "cultural resource" or increasingly "heritage" management is largely the outgrowth of the 1966 National Historic Preservation Act (Public Law 89–665; 16 U.S.C. 470 et seq). The act created the National Register of Historic Places, the list of National Historic Landmarks, and the State Historic Preservation Offices, and is perhaps most famous for creating something known under U.S. law as "Section 106 review," which often requires that archaeology be done as part of the development and construction process wherever there is federal involvement. Many states and municipalities have counterpart legislation that mandates surface or subsurface investigation before projects are allowed to proceed. Professional archaeology has become incorporated into the engineering, architecture, and environmental consulting industries and has become an integral discipline in the maintenance and expansion of the physical infrastructure of the United States (Neumann and Sanford 2001: 1). CRM archaeology is therefore a type of "applied anthropology" in the American definition of the term (Ervin 2000: 2), wherein a focus on policy is crucial. Theoretical discussions are rarely part of an applied anthropologist's report to a client; not only are clients unlikely to be interested in theory, but they may find abstraction tedious or incomprehensible (Ervin 2000: 7). Discussions about the applicability of postcolonial theory in the arena where the great majority of American archaeology is actually conducted must bear this fact in mind.

The United States is the only country in the developed world that considers archaeological sites on private land to be private property rather than part of the national heritage (Sebastian 2004: 14). It can be argued that acceptance of this political reality constitutes one of the key points of departure between so-called practicing archaeologists and "public archaeologists," since the legal framework of the Section 106 process does not mandate "public involvement" or "descendant community engagement" in a manner most public archaeologists would find acceptable. It should be noted that archaeology performed in response to statutory mandates has historically also been referred to as "public archaeology," "private-sector archaeology," or "contract archaeology," in a manner similar to the fields of public history, public sociology, and other applied social or natural sciences. While many practitioners have also worked for universities, the idea was (and remains) that this type of public or applied archaeology is performed for, and belongs to, a popular audience, not academics.

Questions of descendant community engagement and empowerment remain central and enduring concerns of postcolonial archaeology. Some have argued that movement toward a postcolonial archaeology necessitates a wholesale rethinking of conceptual frames and archaeological research practices (Nicholas and Hollowell 2007), but such critiques have often tended to be theoretical or "academic" and out of touch with the 80% of archaeologists who have chosen to work outside of the ivory tower and have to confront these questions from a different frame of reference. In keeping with the theme of "implementing postcolonial critique," I have chosen to follow a different line of inquiry. Have descendant communities gained access to interpretive and political power within a CRM context? How are public- and private-sector CRM archaeologists dealing with the challenges posed by Indigenous and public archaeologists? Are there ways of going beyond postcolonial *critique* and deploying strategies "implementing" some of the insights of postcolonial perspectives?

Native American and African American Responses to CRM Archaeology

African Americans and Native Americans have long understood the manner in which scientific racism and colonialism have historically intersected with the law. Both descendant communities have fashioned responses to the Eurocentricity of the American cultural resource management system, although both have crucially *not* sought to overthrow the framework in its entirety but have instead chosen to fight for gains within it instead.

The passage and enactment of the Native American Graves Protection and Repatriation Act of 1990 (NAGPRA) (Public Law 101–601) is probably the most representative example of Indigenous advocacy within existing CRM definitions and institutions. This well-known American law mandates the identification and return of Aboriginal human remains and cultural items to their peoples. More broadly, the law mandates dialogue among archaeologists, historians, and American Indian peoples, and establishes a framework wherein previously excluded Indian perspectives are given legal weight and authority. The legal—and, in some cases, the moral—necessity of tribal consultation has been accepted by most CRM practitioners, and the cultural and religious dimensions of historic "significance" or "effects" are similarly accepted by most CRM archaeologists, albeit often reluctantly.

Legally speaking, NAGPRA can be seen as having been drafted in "moralist mode, with an internal process based on property theory, for rectifying past injustices by using a property rights theory approach as a predicate to its procedural components" (Hutt 2004: 32). Although the law utilizes a "cultural property" framework to classify protected components, American Indian tribes and their advocates are usually quick to point out that NAGPRA's legislative history indicates that the law is primarily a human rights law. As Sherry Hutt notes, "Human rights laws are a blend of property rights and moralist theory that equalizes and enfranchises groups so that they may have access to other laws" (2004: 32).

Depending on who is doing the asking, NAGPRA's record has been mixed. On the positive side, the ownership inventories required by the law have produced the disclosure and repatriation of thousands of previously unidentified human remains and objects. On the downside, some museums and especially federal agencies are far from fully compliant with the law. Not only have mandatory inventories not been completed, but a cottage industry of "pro-science" scholars, some involved in the "Kennewick Man" case, have objected to certain principles contained in the law and work to frustrate efforts to secure repatriation.

The issues are varied, but some of these concerns trace back to NAGPRA's roots in the common law of property. By utilizing this legal theory, NAGPRA's supporters accomplished the goal of achieving the bill's passage, but also created the unfortunate consequence of defining its four categories of protected items as "property." The notion that people can "own" one another, alive or dead, and that disputes over what to do with the remains can become turf battles over who owns them, remains one of the thorniest aspects of NAGPRA practice. Nonetheless, the passage and implementation of NAGPRA can be seen as an explicit effort at decolonizing the shameful legacy of destruction and disrespect perpetrated or countenanced by the American government during the 19th and 20th centuries, as well as before.

African Americans do not benefit from the special legal status enjoyed by federally recognized Indian tribes, and thus activist efforts to confront the colonial legacy of American archaeology have employed different strategies. The focus has largely revolved around battles for interpretive authority and control, as well as the fight to achieve recognition of the contributions made by enslaved Africans and African Americans in building the United States. Crucially, however, black battles for recognition and power are based on the same human rights premises that have marked the Native American struggle (Archaeological Institute of America 2003), especially the fight to ensure recognition of the cultural and religious dimensions of historical "significance" and/or "effects" determinations under the framework of American environmental law.

Nothing throws these issues into greater focus than the fight over the New York City African Burial Ground in the early to mid-1990s. Once the inadequacies of the government's "legally sufficient" Section 106 compliance became better known, the descendant community demanded not only a place at the table but the right to interpret the archaeology and history. This "seizure of intellectual power" (La Roche and Blakey 1997) by community activists and, importantly, their allies in local and state government, led to a more democratic research process and compelled a change of direction from the original research project, which was based on a 12-page research design that "devoted two pages to the site's African or African-American bioarchaeology" and "gave virtually no substantive discussion of New York's black history" (La Roche and Blakey 1997: 86). The new research design gave veto authority to the descendant community, a key component of the AAA Statement of Ethics and the WAC's first Code of Ethics.

The project took a long time to complete and involved considerable resources, and the scientific and governmental racism it had to overcome are a testament to the tenacity of the descendant community's efforts. For instance: "Most of the Euroamerican government officials and their consultants acted without apparent recognition that blacks understood exactly what was being attempted and had effective strategies for surmounting those obstacles. Exclusion, dismissive attitudes, tokenism, and claims of unfairness and "reverse racism" when African Americans seek full access to resources are commonplace interactions with white Americans (La Roche and Blakey 1997: 95).

By almost any measure, the African Burial Ground Project can be judged a success. On April 19, 1993, the site was designated a National Historic Landmark, and on February 27, 2006, President George W. Bush signed a proclamation designating the federal land as the 123rd National Monument. The archaeological, historical, and anthropological research that has been conducted on the site has considerably expanded our understanding of the African and African American experience in America, and has expanded our understanding of the colonial experience in America, particularly in New York City.

Applying Postcolonialism: Community Organizing Approaches to Collaborative Research

In my work, I have found it instructive to bear in mind many of the insights of the noted and legendary community organizer Saul Alinsky (Alinsky 1989a). His insights concerning community organization are useful not only because they intersect with a good deal of postcolonial critique, but also because many of Alinsky's challenging theories form the backbone of much of what is today variously called "advocacy anthropology" (Peterson 1974), "participatory action research" (Ervin 2000: 199–210), or "collaborative research" (Field Museum 2006: 3). A larger-than-life character during his lifetime, whose stock-in-trade was practical strategizing for empowerment rather than academic critique, Alinsky is also worth discussing here because of his credentials as a first-rate social scientist. In addition to conducting pioneering sociological and criminological research with members of Al Capone's gang, Alinsky also studied archaeology at the University of Chicago in the 1920s and 1930s and retained an interest in the subject for the rest of his life. His contributions to theories of human behavior and community empowerment should therefore be taken seriously by the archaeological community.

The understanding that undergirds community organizing is a belief in democracy and in the capacity of relatively uneducated people to represent their own interests effectively. This implies a freedom of choice, a freedom from manipulation (Bullock 1968: 138–139). Also important is recognition of the democratic principle that people ought to have control over decisions that affect them (Rubin and Rubin 1986: 20). The organizer always acts and talks in terms of the experiences and interests of those being organized. So it should be with archaeologists working in disempowered communities. Stated another way, researchers operating under this principle subordinate themselves to what Mack and Blakey (2004: 14) call the "ethical client," not simply the "business client." In practice, this may mean employing anthropological skills and knowledge to represent the needs and priorities of community members from the point of view of the community itself, utilizing language that the community understands. Most importantly, the community "owns" the research; they define the problem, they analyze it, and interpret it. Ideally, they solve it. This democratization of research often produces better-quality research results, fosters goodwill, and respects a community's Indigenous institutions and resources.

The goal is positive social change and community capacity-building. Moving from analysis or critique to policy and empowerment can be challenging for some anthropologists and archaeologists, because skills other than scientific inquiry are required. Good CRM archaeologists understand what it means to subordinate one's advanced education and training to others and are accustomed to working in situations where the research topic or topics are selected by someone else. They are also accustomed to the stakes involved; the research being generated will become the basis for decision-making that in many cases entails significant consequences.

As the ranks of Indigenous archaeologists continues to increase, many of them will surely at some point engage with the archaeological private sector in the United States. I say "engage" and I mean engage, not armchair Monday morning "critique" at a distance. My first bit of unsolicited advice: learn the law. Teach yourself policy. Familiarize yourself with the "profession" that archaeology has now become. Then get to work trying to change the system from inside and outside. Applied work requires allies and advocates (Ervin 1999: 213), and cultivating them from within as well as without is important. In addition, recognize that the perspectives of academia cannot be the perspectives we use to explain our work, because the people we work with do not share such points of view (Ervin 1999: 218). This has been the template followed by the aforementioned minority populations in America, at least up until now.

McDavid Response: Another Approach, Intersecting Goals

Over the past 15 years I have worked with two African-American archaeology projects: the Levi Jordan Plantation Project in Brazoria, Texas, and, recently, the Yates Community Archaeology Project, in Houston, Texas. My work is not done in a CRM setting, but it does take place in the context of Texas historical archaeology, where, as McGhee would agree, antiquities protection is both limited and endangered. Complicating this, in Texas, African-American archaeology tends to be marginalized by the archaeological powers-that-be (Barile 2004). Although recent developments (which McGhee helped to initiate [McGhee 2007]) suggest that change is in the works, the situation is far from resolved.

Within this contested social and political landscape, a postcolonial public archaeology of African America—in the broader sense of public archaeology that I defined above—has to include an understanding of racism and its continued impact on American life today. Archaeologists (academic and otherwise) need to reflect and act upon the ways that race and racism emerge in "everyday" public archaeology practice (with both colleagues and clients) and to find ways to discuss these difficult issues with their publics. Here I suggest that insights from a body of work known as *critical race theory*, and related writing about so-called white privilege, can help to do this.[1]

A large part of my practice is aimed at dismantling the effect of racism on contemporary society. This is an admittedly ideologically driven perspective that does not address policy matters, unlike McGhee's comments above. In a discipline in which objectivity is still valorized, there is perhaps some measure of professional risk in declaring that I am one of "those whose passions drive their questions and methods" (Bergerson 2003: 57). Pragmatist philosophy, which I have discussed elsewhere (McDavid 2000, 2002, 2007, 2008), offers guidance here. The pragmatic move demands that we accept the risk of uncertainty. It maintains that we cannot wait to talk about painful issues until we are certain that it is safe to do so, and it asserts that truths will emerge *within the process of looking for them*. To be engaged in seeking social justice, we cannot afford to be immobilized by fears that we are not being practical, archaeological, academic, sensitive, or correct enough. Time (and, as McGhee rightly points out, *results*) will tell us if our strategies are effective, or if we need to look elsewhere for answers.

Pragmatism also calls for using theories as tools, as mentioned earlier, and critical race theory (CRT) can be one of these tools. Introduced in archaeology by Epperson (2004), CRT, also known as "race-crit," began in the 1970s at the intersection of race and law, but later expanded to include critical race feminism, critical white studies, queer theory, Asian crit, and "lat-crit theory." It represents a wide body of legal and political research, mostly conducted by scholars of color, which critically examines the role of race as a social construct that organizes both everyday and institutional interactions. A major tenet of CRT analysis is to center the study and understanding of racism as something that continues to be tightly knit into the fabric of society: it analyzes how it continues to operate both institutionally and individually, and how it is deeply embedded in all arenas—legal, cultural, and psychological. It is enacted not just through individual acts of prejudice, but, more insidiously, though the everyday realities of white privilege.

By white privilege, I refer to the largely unacknowledged (by white people, that is) advantages and benefits of being white.[2] Whites are *taught* to think of their lives as normative, neutral, and ideal (Thandeka 1999). As described in a now-famous article by Peggy McIntosh, white privilege is the "invisible package of unearned assets which [we] can count on cashing in each day . . . about which [we] were meant to remain oblivious" (McIntosh 1988: 2). Although there are many important and visible examples of how white privilege plays out in societal terms—the fact that white incomes average 10 times more than those of African Americans; the disproportionate criminalization of blacks at every level; and ongoing discrimination in housing, education, and governmental institutions—white privilege is difficult for many whites to acknowledge precisely because it plays out in everyday, commonplace, *seemingly* trite ways. It means, in my own life, not being followed by security guards to see if I am going to shoplift when I go into a fancy store, and *never* being asked to speak for all of the people in my racial group. It means I can worry about racism without seeming to be self-interested, and that I can take a job with an affirmative action employer without having my co-workers suspect I got it because of my race. It means that someone of another color can be prejudiced toward me without this translating to anything I need to survive—because in all likelihood, a slur is as far as it's going to go. Finally, in the context of public archaeology, it means that when I am told about "the founders" of my country, state, or city, most of the time I am hearing about people of my own color—even when people of other colors are part of the story.

One issue raised by race-crits is that of "false empathy," which Delgado (Delgado and Stefancic 2001) points out is the mistake some people make when they believe they can discern the feelings, thoughts, or opinions of another person. This has direct relevance to my work with descendant groups. As a white person, I doubt I can ever truly understand the oppression and racism that my collaborators experience on a daily basis. That is, I cannot rid myself of the protection that white privilege confers, and for me to pretend otherwise would reduce my credibility as we work together for common goals. I tend to agree with white anti-racism scholars Alcoff (1998), Bergerson (2003), and Eichstedt (2001) and also some race-crits (e.g., Delgado and Stefancic 2001) that, in addition to simply doing good re-search (and sharing it with our publics), white scholars should do at least two things: (1) help other whites to acknowledge white privilege, and (2) encourage students and colleagues to find alternate epistemologies that draw as much from "the lived experiences of individuals who have traditionally been marginalized" (Bergerson 2003: 58–60) as they do from traditional scientific methods. A large portion of my own public archaeological practice revolves around this type of effort.

Critical race theory rejects so-called liberal approaches to racism, such as color-blindness, because despite our best intentions, most *people* cannot practice it—we notice one another's color whether we want to or not (McDavid 2007). The CRT critique points out that because color-blindness is *presumed* to fully incorporate racial justice ("justice for all"), it has not allowed American society to develop a concept of justice that takes account of racial difference—or, as Epperson has put it, to "construct an African Diaspora archaeology that is simultaneously race-conscious and anti-essentialist" (Epperson 2004: 105).

To be both race-conscious and anti-essentialist is a tricky maneuver, and not always successful. As mentioned above, CRT demands that we seek the lived experiences of people of color in our work, but doing so in an explicit way is difficult. For example, during a recent meeting of a local history group (dominated by self-defined "progressives"), I suggested that we needed to actively seek more African-American, Hispanic, and Asian members (the group is mostly, though not all, white). Several members bristled at the idea—not because they objected to diversity (the most upset person was Mexican-American), but because they assumed that I meant to implement some sort of "affirmative action" scenario. I dropped it at first, but later pressed the point, attempting to argue that actively recruiting "differently raced" members was not *necessarily* offensive, as long as it was made clear that the *entire person* (including their professional skill) was being recruited, not just their ethnicity. In this case, CRT provided a useful language for inclusion, but this could not offset the more powerful specter of racial quotas. On the other hand, with another group, discussing white privilege with the all-white museum docents of a traditional house museum proved somewhat more successful, and some now use more inclusive language and content in their public tours (McDavid 2007, 2008).

It is important to remember, however, that CRT was developed *by* people of color *for the purposes of* people of color. This begs some cautionary questions: When whites center race in the manner that CRT suggests, does this have the effect of colonizing it to further our own interests? By foregrounding race, and acknowledging whiteness as a race, do we run the risk of foregrounding ourselves? Whites need to take care that our interest in CRT does not deflect the conversation away from CRT's original purpose—to address the issues of people of color.

I should state the obvious while closing: one does not need CRT to embrace diversity and inclusion. For me, it has simply helped to clarify, and seek answers to, several questions. To what extent does our work contribute to or hinder the empowerment of oppressed people? To what extent can this work be used to confront and disrupt white privilege? And finally, to what extent can our study of the history of a people victimized by racism be used to eradicate racism now? Archaeologists who are differently "raced" than I should probably ask themselves the same questions, but their answers will, necessarily, come from a different perspective. It is also true that individual efforts, mine or anyone else's, cannot answer these questions fully. Any postcolonial archaeology must find ways to analyze, confront, and dismantle racism and white privilege: CRT simply provides one more tool to do this.

Conclusion

While we are substantially in agreement about the need for postcolonial awareness in the field of archaeology (public or otherwise), our approaches are different. As an applied anthropologist, McGhee is concerned with policy questions and recognizes that his "real world" clients, and much of the non-archaeological "public," are most interested in "the point," which is to say *outcomes*. This focus on results introduces difficult constraints and makes it incumbent upon archaeological practitioners to advocate strongly for the understanding that *process* and *conduct* matter at least as much as a fetishized focus on "goals." Effective advocacy on this point, however, requires policy knowledge and a realistic understanding of the political and fiscal constraints that characterize modern American governance, as well as a willingness to go beyond academic critique. On the easy end, this could mean advocating for proper archaeological surveys instead of "archaeological monitoring," with explicit Alinsky-informed participatory action research approaches on the "heavier" end.

Questions of representativeness seem to be a mainstay of the archaeological engagement literature (Franklin and McKee 2004: 4; Mack and Blakey 2004:14), with a variety of practitioners making the point that descendant communities are not monolithic and that stakeholders often do not agree (Brandon 2008: 147–149). Alinsky himself raised the question in *Reveille for Radicals*, and his answer is instructive. A 5% participation in any American community is a tremendous demonstration in democracy (Alinsky 1989b: 184). Alinsky's point is not to fixate on the number, but to stress that rank-and-file participation rarely exceeds this level even in mature organizations (e.g., labor unions, political parties) and that the situation is not the dire dilemma that some archaeological observers have made it out to be.

McDavid has no objection to the applied approaches that McGhee suggests, and in fact has adopted several. Her concern here, however, is with one particular issue that emerges while doing the public archaeology of African America—racism. She describes a body of theory, critical race theory, which has proven useful as a tool to think with, and as a tool with which to analyze contemporary behavior in real-world settings. She also advocates a pragmatic philosophical approach that embraces uncertainty and is more experimental: she recognizes that mistakes will be made as she tries to engage with diverse publics about this issue. While she too seeks results, she also knows that her experiments may not work. She does not believe she will see racism and white privilege disappear in her lifetime, but only hopes to see some movement forward, and to include public archaeological work as part of that movement.

What matters, when considering the possibility of a truly *post*colonial archaeology, are not the specific strategies we use, but *how* we use them. On that we agree.

Notes

1. Detailed examples are described in McDavid 2007. See Bell (1992, 1995), Crenshaw et al. (1995), and Delgado and Stefanic (2001) for introductions to CRT writing. For use of CRT in education research (an excellent model for archaeologists), see Bergerson 2003, DeCuir and Dixson 2004; Dixson and Rousseau 2005; Eichstedt 2001; Gorski 2000; Ladson-Billings and Tate 1995; and Lloyd 2004.
2. All of the terms usually used to refer to ethnic groups are problematic (not least because "white" is a color too).

References

Alcoff, L. M. 1998. What should white people do? *Hypatia* 13 (3).

Alinsky, S. D. 1989a [1971]. *Rules for Radicals*. New York: Vintage Books.

———. 1989b [1946]. *Reveille for Radicals*. New York: Vintage Books.

Barile, K. S. 2004. Race, the National Register, and cultural resource management: Creating an historic context for postbellum sites. *Historical Archaeology* 38 (1): 90–100.

Archaeological Institute of America 2003. Return to the African Burial Ground: An interview with physical anthropologist Michael L. Blakey. *Archaeology*, November 20, 2003. Online at www.archaeology.org/online/interviews/blakey/.

Bell, D. A. 1992. *Faces at the Bottom of the Well: The Permanence of Racism*. New York: Basic Books.

———. 1995. Who's afraid of critical race theory? *University of Illinois Law Review*: 893–910.

Bergerson, A. A. 2003. Critical race theory and white racism: Is there room for white scholars in fighting racism in education? *Qualitative Studies in Education* 16 (1): 51–63.

Brandon, J. C. 2008. Disparate diasporas and vindicationist archaeologies: Some comments on excavating America's metaphor. *Historical Archaeology* 42 (2): 147–151.

Bullock P. 1968. Morality and tactics in community organizing, in J. Larner and I. Howe (eds.), *Poverty: Views from the Left*. New York: Wiliam Morrow & Company.

Crenshaw, K., Gotanda, N., Peller, G., and Thomas, K. (eds.). 1995. *Critical Race Theory: The Key Writings That Formed the Movement*. New York: New Press.

DeCuir, J. T., and Dixson, A. D. 2004. "So when it comes out, they aren't that surprised that it is there": Using critical race theory as a tool of analysis of race and racism in education. *Educational Researcher* (June/July): 26–31.

Delgado, R., and Stefancic, J. 2001. *Critical Race Theory: An Introduction*. New York: New York University Press.

Dixson, A. D., and Rousseau, C. K. 2005. And we are still not saved: Critical race theory in education ten years later. *Race, Ethnicity and Education* 8 (March).

Eichstedt, J. L. 2001. Problematic white identities and a search for racial justice. *Sociological Forum* 16 (3): 445–470.

Epperson, T. W. 2004. Critical race theory and the archaeology of the African diaspora. *Historical Archaeology* 38 (1): 101–108.

Ervin, A. M. 1999. *Applied Anthropology: Tools and Perspectives for Contemporary Practice*. Needham Heights, MA: Allyn & Bacon.

The Field Museum. 2006. *Collaborative Research: A Practical Introduction to Participatory Action Research (PAR) for Communities and Scholars*. Chicago: Field Museum.

Franklin, M., and McKee, L. 2004. African diaspora archaeologies: Present insights and expanding discourses. *Historical Archaeology* 38 (1): 1–9.

Gorski, P. 2000. Narrative of whiteness and multicultural education. *Electronic Magazine of Multicultural Education* 2 (1).

Hutt, S. D. 2004. Cultural property law theory: A comparative assessment of contemporary thought, in J. R. Richman and M. P. Forsyth, *Legal Perspectives on Cultural Resources*, pp. 17–36. Walnut Creek, CA: AltaMira Press.

James, W. 1995. What pragmatism means, in G. H. Bird (ed.), *William James: Selected Writings*. London: J. M. Dent and Orion Publishing Group.

King, T. F. 2008. Tom King's CRM Plus. Online blog at *http://crmplus.blogspot.com/*.

Ladson-Billings, G., and Tate, W. F. 1995. Toward a critical race theory of education. *Teaching College Record* 97 (1): 47–68.

La Roche, C., and Blakey, M. 1997. Seizing intellectual power: The dialogue at the New York African Burial Ground. In *In the Realm of Politics: Prospects for Public Participation in African-American Archaeology*, special issue of *Historical Archaeology* 31 (3): 84–106.

Lloyd, K. S. 2004. Teaching the elusive white student: Encouraging white students to think multi-culturally while challenging the myth of whiteness. *AURCO Journal* 10 (Spring): 77–92.

Mack, M. E., and Blakey, M. L. 2004. The New York African Burial Ground Project: Past biases, current dilemmas, and future research opportunities. *Historical Archaeology* 38 (1): 10–17.

McDavid, C. 2000. Archaeology as cultural critique: Pragmatism and the archaeology of a southern United States plantation, in C. Holtorf and H. Karlsson Lindome (eds.), *Philosophy and Archaeological Practice: Perspectives for the 21st Century*. Sweden: Bricoleur Press.

——. 2002. Archaeologies that hurt; descendents that matter: A pragmatic approach to collaboration in the public interpretation of African-American archaeology. *World Archaeology*, special issue "Community Archaeology" 34 (2): 303–314.

——. 2007. Beyond strategy and good intentions: Archaeology, race, and white privilege, in B. Little and P. Shackel (eds.), *An Archaeology of Civic Engagement and Social Justice*.

——. 2008. The public archaeology of African America: A pragmatic model for evaluating approaches, methods and results, in M.-L. Sorensen and J. Carman (eds.), *Making the Means Transparent*. London: Routledge.

McGhee, F. L. 2007. Archaeological politics among and about African-Americans in Texas. Paper read at the Annual Meeting for the Society for American Archaeology, Austin, Texas.

McIntosh, P. 1988. *White Privilege and Male Privilege: A Personal Account of Coming to See Correspondences through Work in Women's Studies*. Wellesley, MA: Center for Research on Women, Wellesley College.

Neumann, T. W., and Sanford, R. M. 2001. *Practicing Archaeology: A Training Manual for Cultural Resources Archaeology*. Walnut Creek, CA: Alta Mira Press.

Nicholas, G., and Hollowell, J. 2007. Ethical challenges to a postcolonial archaeology: The legacy of scientific colonialism, in Y. Hamilakis and P. Duke (eds.), *Archaeology and Capitalism: From Ethics to Politics*. Walnut Creek, CA: Left Coast Press.

Peterson, J., Jr. 1974. Anthropologist as advocate. *Human Organization* 33 (3): 311–318.

Rubin, H. J., and Rubin, I. 1986. *Community Organizing and Development*. New York: Merrill Macmillan International Publishing Group.

Sebastian, L. 2004. Archaeology and the law, in J. R. Richman and M. P. Forsyth (eds.), *Legal Perspectives on Cultural Resources*, pp. 3–16. Walnut Creek, CA: AltaMira Press.

Thandeka. 1999. *Learning to be White: Money, Race and God in America*. New York: Continuum.

38

EPILOGUE: POSTCOLONIALISM AND ARCHAEOLOGY

Uzma Z. Rizvi and Jane Lydon

This handbook is both an intellectual and a political exercise. Situating our critique within contemporary social, political, and economic inequities, this volume locates the intersection of postcolonial critique and archaeology in an effort to reassess historic disparities of knowledge production and evaluation. Indeed, the politics embedded within the production of this volume lead us to address concerns with representation and inclusion, providing some critical self-reflection. Additionally, there are certain theoretical constructs that we wish to highlight as significant future research areas, to show how much of the work presented here lays the foundations for interventions benefiting an archaeology practiced within a contemporary transnational reality.

Postcolonial research in archaeology may unfold in many directions. For example, it has clear implications for work relating to Indigenous archaeologies, in settler communities and colonial regions, specifically in terms of movements for social justice. Questions about the repatriation and restitution of cultural property, and the politics of recuperation, are of importance when contending with the future of ethical practices within archaeology as a whole. The chapters in this volume attest to the significance of a framework, embedded within the postcolonial critique, that shifts the epistemological foundations of archaeological interpretations, methodologies, and practice. In that spirit, each chapter provides new research directions that can be contextually applied within different scenarios. Looking beyond our own world areas, and learning from the histories of both peoples and communities and how they have reinterpreted their own pasts, presents a multifaceted lens through which one can learn about collective—and ruptured—pasts.

Representation and Subjectivity

Realizing the aim of this volume—to include voices from around the world—comes at a price. Not every voice could be heard, and the idea that there might be one narrative that could encapsulate all the perspectives emerging from a region or community is a fallacy. No scholar's subjectivity can be essentialized in this way—that is, implicated in speaking for others within the larger community or region (for more on the politics of representation, see Benavides, this volume, chapter 17). Moreover, in contemporary archaeological practice, the desire to improve the conditions of peoples' lives through work on cultural/social and political/economic empowerment or advocacy places archaeologists, who are often outsiders to the community, in a uniquely constituted location insofar as they become spokespersons within academic discourses for the communities in which, and for which, they work. The delicate exigency of such locations becomes apparent when two possibilities of representation are conflated, as Gayatri Spivak points out, distinguishing between "representation as 'speaking for' as in politics and representation as 're-presentation' as in art or philosophy" (1999: 257). This issue has been explored by feminist scholars such as Linda Alcoff, who has argued that although there may be a confronting "crisis of representation," it is reasonable to assume that ultimately the issue comes down to political efficacy, and thus the ethical ramifications of politically "speaking for" are subsumed within the larger political movement of empowerment for oppressed peoples (1995: 102–112).

The assumption there, of course, is that those in the movement *know* what the "oppressed people" want, need, or even care about. This critique of obviousness (of what certain people want) has been discussed in feminist scholarship and does not require recapitulation here (see, e.g., Ahmed 1998; Chow 1994; Loomba 1998; Mohanty 1991; Spivak 1999); what is relevant to this discussion, however, is an acknowledgment that the issue of representation cannot be subsumed within the rhetoric of intellectuals constructing normative assumptions about which effects and political outcomes are desirable or undesirable. Situating the archaeologist within the postcolonial critique necessarily complicates such representations of subjectivity, and embeds the discourse within a larger ethical and politically progressive framework. Indeed, within this volume, we have intended to complicate the assumptions of "oppression" and "empowerment" and, by extension, the concept of the "native" subject, critically evaluating our field and our theoretical interventions. Such challenges emerge especially clearly from the constructed in-between spaces that are textually represented by the cross-disciplinary chapters in each section of this volume.

The chapter by O. Hugo Benavides (chapter 17) provides a key insight into the discussion about the inclusion of "Native" and, specifically, "Native scholars" in archaeological discourse. In some ways, the overt desire to include Native voices, he argues, instantiates the false dichotomy of Western and Other. This aspiration highlights the non-location of those Native scholars who live in the West and operate within Western academic frameworks. It also suggests that "Natives" were not considered active agents in the production of the archaeological past, as field staff and crew, or as archaeologists at the site (for an example from colonial India, see Lahiri 2005). The focus, then, is not just about including "Natives" into the discourse; it is the recognition that the histories that are produced, in both colonial and postcolonial frameworks, are all parts of the larger web of historical production.

Joost Fontein, in his chapter (chapter 14), refocuses the same lens, elaborating on the location of the Native and Indigenous scholar by illustrating how these new viewpoints challenge the traditional scientific emic/etic distinctions within archaeological scholarship. In Fontein's mind, it is not simply a question of providing alternative histories of the past, but rather one of exploring alternative ways of looking at and understanding the past. This shifts attention from looking for competing representations of the past, toward the ways in which the "authority to represent the past is established and contested," an issue that emerges within the call for Indigenous archaeology, framed as a response to what he calls archaeology's "etic" authority, while simultaneously addressing the "violence" that is perpetuated by archaeology's claim to that ontological location.

In a personal account, Whitney Battle-Baptiste (chapter 29) addresses the violence that is perpetuated by hegemonic archaeological accounts and how it affects individual archaeologists in developing their hidden biases and subjectivities. She peacefully counters it through genealogies and connections, and most significantly, conversations and dialogue. She frames this positive methodology by reclaiming the authority to look at the past and construct a future for historical archaeology—and she does this using the power of *Egun*. In the Yoruba language, *Egun* means "bones"—the bones of ancestors in a metaphorical and spiritual sense, a way to acknowledge the connection between the living and the dead. Her personal journey, beliefs, and gaze powerfully align the concept of *Egun* with "conversation" as a way to heal disparities. She posits a new world view that links all of humanity together: "Without these conversations, we have no connection and are without a genealogy, without an ancestral line, without *Egun*."

This concept of a shared history—a linking of all of our histories as a space within which present discourses can allow for reconciliatory or equitable presents—is an important consideration for a postcolonial archaeology in the future.

Postcolonial Cosmopolitanism

New research under the rubric of "cosmopolitan" archaeology directly addresses this aspiration, linking the ideals of obligation to others and respect for cultural difference to archaeological practice, highlighting the role of ethics and moral responsibility (e.g., Meskell 2009). Scholars across many disciplines have recently drawn upon a reinvigorated notion of "cosmopolitanism" (although it is still a contested term) in the context of globalization, to define new conceptions of political community emerging around the world. As many have noted, enhanced global connectedness is characterized by the dissolution of some boundaries but simultaneously the sharpening of others, as the international circulation of people, media, and economic and cultural capital prompts both homogenization and an increased sense of local distinctiveness. The concept of cosmopolitanism is one means that scholars have used to attempt to explore this process. Some argue for the potential of an ethical stance that entails a commitment to the equal worth and dignity of all human beings, linked to standards of justice that are intended to be applicable to all, while simultaneously retaining an openness to local, different ways of life (Appiah 2006; Cheah 2006). Phenomena such as the participation of Indigenous peoples in international rather than national institutions do not merely challenge the legitimacy of the states' claim to exclusive jurisdiction over territory, but in fact constitute an "emergent cosmopolitanism" (Ivison 2006) that is compatible with universal notions of justice and yet is also rooted in particular, local ways of life. As with other global networks characterized by complex articulations between different orders of practice, including heritage and human rights discourse, debate often focuses on the analytical and concrete tensions between principles of universalism and local difference.

However, in order to imagine a shared past, an equal present or, more specifically, an equal access to the past in the present must be assumed. In an attempt to bring to bear that formulation of equality and a shift in power directionality, cosmopolitan archaeology explores how contemporary heritage practices operate in the present. It is in this space that future discussions must focus. Insofar as Western archaeologists continue to have access to the pasts of developing countries, often at a higher rate and with more expedient results than the archaeologists working within their own communities, the cosmopolitan aspiration may be stifled, no matter how (theoretically) local the basis for the universal may be (see Fiskesjö, this volume, chapter 23; González-Ruibal 2009: 118). These levels of disparity cannot be considered merely within the traditional dichotomies of colonial versus colonized, but must also be examined in the context of colonized and disenfranchised minority communities. Within these groups, there are additional levels of intrinsic inequality, partly based on colonial administrative distinctions (see Voss 2008) and partly on internal histories of inequality that clearly affect discourses about the past (see Breglia 2009). In a contemporary moment, as Benavides (this volume, chapter 17) suggests, this issue is less about cultural difference and more about transnational capital essentializing those differences as a way of reinstating older forms of racial hierarchies. Scholars such as Hugo Benavides, Magnus Fiskesjö, and Alfredo González-Ruibal serve as critical reminders that our own efforts might unintentionally embody the greater global forces at work that reinstate the rhetoric of colonialism (and also see Merry 2003).

Cosmopolitanism can be used to move beyond such dichotomies, including the global/local dichotomy, by claiming that such issues are everyone's concern (Hodder 2009: 184). These global concerns become central for archaeologists, although they are not always so for other disciplines, such as international development (but see Levitt and Merry 2008). Perhaps there is potential for social change if we work in tandem, as Ian Hodder (2009) suggests, with other policy makers or within the framework of human rights, keeping in mind the very well-publicized critique of the wholesale use of such development models within archaeology, as put forth by González-Ruibal (2009). Although an obvious point, we should remember that as part of the critical application of such models, there must be a vernacularization of the conceptual framework, the vocabulary, and the historical context so that it clearly addresses the very local nature of the politics in the region (Levitt and Merry 2009; González-Ruibal 2009).

Shifts in Politics: Indigeneity in a Global Context

A major component of this volume is a focus on Indigenous movements around the world. Yet, the critique of ethnographic representation and the politics of subjectivity have demonstrated that there is no self-evident or natural category of "indigenous" peoples—we create these categories to serve specific political purposes (Jeganathan 2005; Kahn 2005). There are significant reasons, however, why such markers are crucial for some populations, either in helping, or further marginalizing, disenfranchised peoples. In the context of postcolonial struggles for autonomy, essentializing representations of indigeneity have often been used to require peoples to demonstrate the continuity of their connections to place and culture and to meet expectations of "authenticity" and legitimacy. Nonetheless, in former colonies across the globe, Indigenous peoples who once formed a myriad of distinct cultural and linguistic groups now share a history of dispossession and ongoing disadvantage. In this context, intellectual trends that emphasize the mutability and contingency of identity have been perceived as undermining assertions of culture, as Indigenous peoples themselves draw upon such categories to protect their interests and oppose injustice. Where inequities may be reinforced by the logic of the nation-state, within a context of enhanced global interconnectedness Indigenous peoples may now choose to participate in international institutions in preference to national ones, as new categories of global identity are represented by organizations such as the World Archaeological Congress, for example. Such appeals to international norms, together with their Indigenous revaluation, also reveal a relationship between local, state, and global levels "which is pluralist but not state-centric, immanent but also universalist" (Ivison 2006: 121). In addition, Indigenous scholars have argued that conceptions of local culture are changing, shaped by an international context and incorporating a universal notion of human rights without abandoning a sense of local meaning (e.g., Behrendt 2003). The international campaign led by the Mirrar people of the Kakadu region in northern Australia exemplifies this process, to date successfully preventing uranium mining on the Jabiluka mineral lease through appealing to international opinion on the basis of local distinctiveness (Lydon 2009; see also de Costa 2006).

In the future, it seems as though the archaeology of Indigenous peoples must increasingly be conducted by and in collaboration with Indigenous communities. In addition, archaeologists are coming to recognize and engage with culturally distinctive ontologies and epistemologies. As the examples provided in this volume suggest (see especially Part V: Strategies of Practice; also Atalay, this volume, chapter 4), new ways of conceptualizing archaeological questions, designing and implementing methodologies, and presenting results are already in train. Just as a dialogue implies receptivity to our interlocutor and entails a certain open-endedness, it is difficult to predict where such collaborations will lead the discipline of archaeology.

Global Scope of the Postcolonial Critique

This volume provides a robust critique of the development of the discipline of archaeology around the world, having originated in curiosity about the exotic other, as a *modus operandi* for collecting and endowing museums of the West, and in the quest for empirical knowledge. Archaeology was justified and legitimated from the perspective of those on the civilizing mission, who considered the concept of "universal" to exist only in relation to, or because of, the European Enlightenment. In the contemporary world, this has translated to a preference for archaeological materials considered to represent "high culture," values prescribed on materiality by the West, particularly linked to the development of science and democracy and a continued fascination with the exotic other (Bennett 2004; Mitchell 2004).

In an economic context, the antiquities market continues to blossom, and as the free market system continues to assume that everything can be bought or sold, the past continues to be a commodity (Merryman 2000, 2006). This has larger implications for issues about looting, tourism, and tourism's effects on archaeological work with communities (see Bahrani 2003; Brodie and Renfrew 2005; Rizvi 2009). A progressive archaeology must be able to engage in active and critical dialogues within the development world, such as with the International Committee of the Red Cross (ICRC) and other international humanitarian agencies, especially in terms of human rights, issues of migration and assimilation, and the formation of transnational identities. This is not to assume that moving our discussions into the realm of development studies is the best or correct thing to do. But it is one way to further our own understandings of what other forces are at play and how other disciplines are (or are not) taking on shared issues such as contemporary inequalities associated with histories of oppression. As archaeologists, we have a unique link to the ancient and historic world and thus offer an important perspective working with global heritage projects (such as UNESCO). From that vantage point, we can make significant contributions toward challenging the universalizing narratives often expressed by such agencies.

38. Epilogue: Postcolonialism and archaeology

Earlier in this volume, Fiskesjö challenges the very concept of the "universal" in relation to the "Declaration on the Importance and Value of Universal Museums," a statement which, he argues, is a forceful general statement against repatriation. His critique of the "free trade" of cultural objects highlights the hypocrisy of such declarations insofar as they work in favor of the richer, more powerful nation-states at the expense of the former colonial regions. Fiskesjö's focus is on the ways in which these institutions continue to reconstitute themselves by creating such documents and making such statements that provide them with the authority to appear legitimate, ethical, and valid. This desire for relegitimization at the institutional level of the museum covers what is really at stake, which, he argues, is the ideological basis of "Western" identity.

One of the key acknowledgments of this volume is the significance of reconstituting identity, alterity, and forms of subject-hood to account for various stakeholders in the larger web of historical production. In the dialogue between Carol McDavid and Fred McGhee (chapter 37), this issue of subjectivity informs their individual approaches to archaeology and advocacy. They approach the questions of policy and social relations within the context of the United States, rather than on an international level, specifically within the context of race and privilege. Although this particular dialogue is based in the United States, the issue of racism in contemporary societies is one that is, in fact, transnational in its effects and has large-scale ramifications that can be linked to colonial frameworks. In their discussion, McDavid and McGhee approach community involvement and participation from different perspectives, illustrating their standpoints as distinct based on their race and their experiences of being of that race. As an African American, McGhee demonstrates a keener interest in actually seeing change—and being an active part of that change through his research and public work. As a Euro-American, McDavid confronts white privilege head on, and approaches anthropological and archaeological interventions by embracing uncertainty and mistakes that she might make along the way. There is a sense of hope that by continuing to do things in the best faith, something, in time, will change.

It is change that this volume seeks as well. Our contributors have addressed these larger global trajectories of colonialism and how they have affected archaeology, exploring the employment of interdisciplinary methods, comparative frameworks, and new methodologies and practices. In each section, scholars have brought together the postcolonial critique with other approaches within archaeology in order to elucidate the narratives of colonialism and the ways in which we might address and redress the past through restitution, repatriation, and ethics. Methodology informed by ethics asks us to examine ourselves as practitioners in implementing the postcolonial critique. Finally, contributors consider how we deal with issues of alterity and identity in the archaeological record. This collection has explored the significance of methodologies, the changing language/

lexical register that a postcolonial archaeology employs, and the effects on our practice. As a handbook, it encapsulates an anti-colonialist sentiment that stresses individual agency, ethical practice, and a revolutionary spirit. In simple terms (adapted from Mohandas K. Gandhi), we want to be the change we hope to see.

References

Ahmed, S. 1998. *Differences that Matter*. Cambridge: Cambridge University Press.

Alcoff, L. 1995. The problem of speaking for others, in J. Roof and R. Wiegman (eds.), *Who Can Speak: Authority and Critical Identity*. Champaign: University of Illinois Press.

Appiah, K. A. 2006. *Cosmopolitanism: Ethics in a World of Strangers*. New York: Norton and Company.

Bahrani, Z. 2003. Looting and conquest. *The Nation*, May 14, 2003. www.thenation.com/doc/20030526/bahrani (last accessed February 21, 2009).

Behrendt, L. 2003. *Achieving Social Justice*. Annandale: Federation Press.

Bennett, T. 2004. *Pasts beyond Memory: Evolution, Museums, Colonialism*. London and New York: Routledge.

Breglia, L. 2009. "'Walking around like they own the place": Quotidian cosmopolitanism at a Maya and World Heritage archaeological site, in L. Meskell (ed.), *Cosmopolitan Archaeologies*, pp. 205–227. Durham, NC: Duke University Press.

Brodie, N., and Renfrew, C. 2005. Looting and the world's archaeological heritage: The inadequate response. *Annual Review of Anthropology* 34: 343–361.

Cheah, P. 2006. Cosmopolitanism. *Theory, Culture & Society* 23 (2–3): 486–496.

Chow, R. 1994. Where have all the natives gone? in P. Mongia (ed.), *Contemporary Postcolonial Theory: A Reader*. London: Arnold.

de Costa, R. 2006. *A higher authority: Indigenous transnationalism and Australia*. Sydney: University of New South Wales Press.

González-Ruibal, A. 2009. Vernacular cosmopolitanism: An archaeological critique of universalistic reason, in L. Meskell (ed.), *Cosmopolitan Archaeologies*, pp. 113–139. Durham, NC: Duke University Press.

Hodder, I. 2009. Mavili's voice, in L. Meskell (ed.), *Cosmopolitan Archaeologies*, pp. 184–204. Durham, NC: Duke University Press.

——. 2006. Emergent cosmopolitanism: Indigenous peoples and international law, in R. Tinnevelt and G. Verschraegen (eds.), *Between Cosmopolitan Ideals and State Sovereignty*, pp. 120–134. New York: Palgrave.

Jeganathan, P. 2005 Pain, politics, and the epistemological ethics of anthropological disciplinarity, in L. Meskell and P. Pels (eds.), *Embedding Ethics*, pp: 147–168. Wenner-Gren Foundation for Anthropological Research. New York: Berg.

Kahn, J. S. 2005. Anthropology's Malaysian interlocutors: Toward a cosmopolitan ethics of anthropological practice, in L. Meskell and P. Pels (eds.), *Embedding Ethics*, pp. 101–120. Wenner-Gren Foundation for Anthropological Research. New York: Berg.

Lahiri, N. 2005. *Finding Forgotten Cities: How the Indus Civilization was Discovered*. New Delhi: Permanent Black.

Levitt, P., and Merry, S. E. 2009. Unpacking the vernacularization process: The transnational circulation of women's human rights. Paper presented at Stanford Humanities Center, February 2009.

Loomba, A. 1998. *Colonialism/Postcolonialism*. London: Routledge.

Lydon, J. 2009. Young and free: The Australian past in a global future, in L. Meskell (ed.), *Cosmopolitan Archaeologies*, pp. 28–47. Durham, NC: Duke University Press.

Merry, S. E. 2003. Human rights law and the demonization of culture (and anthropology along the way). *Polar: Political and Legal Anthropology Review* 26 (1): 55–77.

Merryman, J. H. 2000. Two ways of thinking about cultural property, in J. H. Merryman (ed.), *Thinking about the Elgin Marbles: Critical Essays on Cultural Property, Art and Law*, pp. 66-91. The Hague and Boston: Kluwer Law International.

Merryman, J. H. (ed.). 2006. *Imperialism, Art and Restitution*. Cambridge: Cambridge University Press.

Meskell, L. (ed.). 2009. *Cosmopolitan Archaeologies*. Durham, NC: Duke University Press.

Mitchell, T. 2004. Orientalism and the exhibitionary order, in D. Preziosi and C. Farago (eds.), *Grasping the World: The Idea of the Museum*. Lund: Humphries.

Mohanty, C. T. 1991. Under Western eyes. Feminist scholarship and colonial discourses, in C. Mohanty, A. Russo and L. Torres (eds.), *Third World Women and the Politics of Feminism*. Bloomington: Indiana University Press.

Rizvi, U. Z. 2009. Selling my heritage to the highest bidder: This is the price of my freedom. Paper for Theoretical Archaeological Group (TAG), Stanford, California.

Spivak, G. 1999. *A Critique of Postcolonial Reason: Toward a History of the Vanishing Present*. Cambridge, MA: Harvard University Press.

Voss, B. 2008. *The Archaeology of Ethnogensis: Race and Sexuality in Colonial San Francisco*. Berkeley: University of California Press.

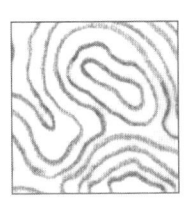

INDEX

Aboriginal Australians, 165, 168, 169; *see also* Australia
acculturation, 147, 149, 151, 155–56, 324, 354, 356–57, 380–81
activist anthropology, 19, 137, 402
Afghanistan, 73, 290
African archaeology, 215, 217, 221, 311–12, 329, 332, 354–55
African diaspora, 141, 185–87, 192–94, 387–88, 489
Afro-Atlantic, 142, 188
AFROMET, 304–08
agency, 45, 62, 147, 151–57, 175, 188–89, 193, 217, 229, 237–38, 368–69, 379–83
Ainu, 81, 94
Algeria, French colonization, 41, 43
alterity, 23, 27, 57, 141, 219, 501
ambivalence, 21, 291
ancient Mediterranean, 40, 136, 354
ancient Phoenicia , 26, 45, 55, 298–300
Anglo-Irish, 201, 203–05
Anishinabe, 68
anti-colonial, literature, 24
anti-colonial, resistance, 18, 316, 502

anti-colonial, nationalism, 311–12
apartheid, Anti-Apartheid Movements, 17, 137, 185, 217, 311, 323, 370, 450–53
Appiah, Kwame Anthony, 292, 305
applied archaeology, 402, 483
appropriation, 35, 39–41, 45, 67, 156, 176, 247, 394, 462, 483
archaeological bureaucracy, 229–31
archaeological cultures, 36, 115, 351–53, 357–60
archaeological methodology, critiques of, 26, 36, 39, 87, 99, 114, 215, 275, 402, 415, 431, 462, 464, 497, 501
Archaeological Survey of India (ASI), 74–75, 77, 143, 227–232
art, 94 –100, 116, 115, 243, 262, 268, 273–74, 285–86, 289–90, 292, 296, 303, 305, 307, 352, 496,
ASI. *See* Archaeological Survey of India.
assimilation policies, 65, 81, 151, 165, 248, 381, 500
Australia, 17, 24, 42, 55, 128, 137, 142, 165–78, 242, 257–64, 267–81, 313, 323, 329–30, 353, 358, 380, 402,

505

413–23, 433, 436, 464, 476, 499; *see also* Aboriginal Australians
authenticity, 84–87, 147, 151, 275, 316, 499
Ayodhya, 143, 230–31

Babri Mosque, Babri Masjid, 143, 230–31
Bangladesh, 73, 76–79
barons, 218
Bhabha, Homi, 21, 23, 25, 316, 430
Bhutan, 73, 76–79
Bicentennial of European settlement, Australia, 142
Black activists, 186, 368
Black loyalists, 191
British colonialism, 41, 44, 54, 73–79, 83, 125, 142, 146, 150, 154, 168–73, 176, 191, 200–08, 215, 280, 353–54
British mandate, 54
buried properties, 96–97

Canada, 62, 137, 146, 191, 207, 268, 275–81, 323, 328, 332, 335
capitalism, 19, 23, 37, 133, 136, 193, 201, 209, 235, 324, 366–69, 376–78, 460, 465
Carthage, city of, 26
censorship, 100, 118–19, 220
Césaire, Aimé , 389
Chakrabarty, Dipesh, 19, 129
Childe, V. Gordon , 41, 353
Civil Rights Movement, 142, 185–87, 394
civil society, 218
Cold War, 82, 84–85, 89, 121, 305
collaboration, collaborative archaeology, collaborative practices, 26, 58, 75, 177, 220, 242, 252–53, 264, 323, 401–02, 405–10, 414–15, 430–31, 434, 438, 439, 446, 500
collections, museum collections, research collections, 26, 67, 70, 83, 96, 97, 100, 104–05, 204, 209, 242, 243, 246–52, 257–64, 285–92, 296–97, 303–07, 316–17, 420, 454
colonial (definitions), 18–23, 39–40
colonial archaeology, 120, 207, 237

colonial discourses, colonial narratives, 18, 20–21, 23, 26, 35, 40–42, 82, 126–27, 141, 145, 152, 193, 215–16, 301, 351, 394, 501
colonial epistemologies, 17, 143, 227
Columbian Quincentennial, USA, 142, 146
Communist, regime, 36, 84, 113, 118–19
cooperation, colonial, 43–45, 88
cosmopolitanism, cosmopolitan archaeologies, 27, 43, 292, 305, 403, 449, 497–98
creolization, 151, 188, 324, 356
critical race theory (CRT), 482, 488–91
CRM. *See* cultural resource management
CRT. *See* critical race theory
cultural affiliation, 66, 249–50, 395, 396
cultural continuity, 152, 338, 352, 354–55, 406
cultural patrimony, 103–04, 242, 249, 257, 259, 260, 261, 263, 406
cultural production, 148, 151
cultural property, 44, 87, 242, 257, 259, 261–64, 285–92, 465, 484, 495
cultural resource management (CRM), 403, 481–91
cultural-ethnic paradigm, 115
culturally Unidentifiable Human Remains, 61, 69, 70, 242, 245, 250
culture history, 55, 202, 360

Declaration on the importance and value of universal museums, 243, 285, 303, 501
decolonization, decolonizing, 18, 23, 37, 42, 51, 56–57, 61–62, 69, 141–42, 145, 149, 186, 192–94, 216, 242, 245, 252–53, 295, 338–39, 401–02, 485
Derrida, Jacques, 135, 317, 338
descendant communities, 23, 137, 145–46, 149, 151, 186, 188, 191–92, 220, 242, 249, 382, 388, 390, 401, 403, 406–09, 421, 431, 433, 446, 481, 483–85, 489, 491
dialectic, dialectical critique, 134, 472
Discourse of Origins, 40–42
disenchantment, 142, 216–22
DNA (deoxyribonucleic acid), 325, 394–97

double colonization, 21
Dutch colonialism, 142, 146, 154, 169, 178, 188, 215

East Asia, 36, 81–90, 93–108, 168, 354, 446
Eastern Europe, 43, 113–21, 330, 352
Egun, 387–90, 497
Egypt, 40, 41, 51, 100, 289, 329, 333, 336, 451
emancipation, 128, 135, 142, 185–94, 203, 237, 368, 370, 473
emic, 52, 243, 311–17, 352, 408–10, 497
Enlightenment (European), 19, 20, 24, 134–35, 285, 290, 315, 475, 500
essentialism, 147, 291, 323, 371; *see also* strategic essentialism
ethics, 26, 27, 149, 230, 241, 285, 304, 413, 435, 446, 454, 482, 485, 497, 501
ethnicity, 115, 151, 156, 192, 274, 323, 379–80, 453, 490
ethnography, 216, 227, 258, 389, 402, 445–54, 471–78
ethnohistory, 359
etic, 243, 311–17, 352, 357, 497
Eurocentrism, 26, 35, 40, 46, 129, 312, 314, 332, 334, 370, 484
European colonialism, 39, 41, 141, 148, 328, 366
European Union, 43, 45, 279, 289
expert witness, 267, 269, 272–73

Fanon, Frantz, 18, 22, 166, 368, 389
federally recognized tribes, 70
fetishism, 305
Foucault, Michel, 20
free black populations, 190
French colonialism, 243, 297
French mandate, 54, 299
funerary objects , 249

Gaelic castles, 142, 200
Gaelic Revival, 199, 202–10
gender, 19–25, 57, 126, 134, 142, 147, 149, 151–56, 237, 278, 323–25, 327–40, 368–69, 389

global market, 209, 238
globalization, 25, 85, 89, 134, 305, 449, 459, 460, 497
Gosden, Chris, 23, 25, 135, 300
governmentality, 230–32, 449
Gramsci, Antonio, 20, 129, 368–69
grand narrative, 85, 89
Great Lakes, Michigan, 36, 62, 66, 146
Greece, 25, 35, 40–41, 74, 100, 306
Guatemala, 359

heritage, 17, 23–25, 35–36, 44, 56–57, 68, 75, 93–105, 136, 149, 150, 153, 166, 176–77, 219, 227–30, 241, 243, 257, 260–64, 267, 269, 271, 275, 277, 280, 288–89, 291, 296, 297, 299–300, 304–08, 311–17, 323, 330, 351, 355, 358, 401–02, 405–10, 413–21, 429–33, 445–54, 460–66, 482–83, 498, 500
heritage, heritage management, 36, 93–95, 99, 103, 177, 230, 314–15, 408, 431, 433, 482
heritage, heritage tourism, 36, 93–105
historical archaeology, 46, 142, 145, 146, 148, 166, 176, 187, 209, 237, 339, 353, 367, 369, 370, 378, 381, 382, 388, 481, 487, 497
HIV/AIDS, 142, 218, 219
Honduras, 307
human remains, 61, 69, 70, 148, 241, 242, 245–53, 257, 262–63, 315–16, 394–97, 451, 484
human rights, 41, 67, 218–19, 245, 249, 472, 475, 484–85, 498–500
hybridity, hybrid, 21, 25–26, 45, 69, 147, 151, 152, 188, 237, 395, 445, 446, 449

ICOMOS/International Committee on Monuments and Sites, 316
identity, 18–21, 23–25, 39–40, 44–45, 55, 103–04, 116, 147, 151, 153–57, 165, 175, 207–08, 216, 220, 242–43, 275, 285, 286, 297–98, 306, 308, 323–25, 336, 339, 351–60, 365–71, 376–82,

388, 393–97, 416, 420, 431, 452–53, 462, 466, 499, 501
imperialism, 17–23, 26, 35, 37, 41, 43, 133, 136, 187, 201, 207, 288, 296, 298–99, 366–67, 430
independence movements, 43, 73–76, 84, 118, 185–87, 190–91, 220, 259, 289, 300–01, 317, 354
India, 20, 73–78, 100, 125–130, 143, 217, 227–32, 354, 476, 497
Indigenous archaeology, 149, 312, 421, 431, 436, 497
Indigenous standpoint theory, 402, 429, 435–41
Indigenous communities, 46, 56, 138, 150, 177, 258–64, 413–22, 429, 432, 434, 440, 449, 500
Intellectual Property Issues in Cultural Heritage Project, 241–43, 257
internationalism, 118, 120, 285–92
Iran, 53, 73, 119, 447
Iraq, 41, 53–58, 291
Ireland, 199–210, 381
Irish archaeology, 142, 199–210
Israel, 53–55, 127

Japan, 36, 81–90, 93–105, 289, 303
Japanese tourism history, 81–90, 93–105
Jomon period, 87
Jordan, 53–58, 460

Kofun period, 84, 87
Kojiki, 84–87

land tenure, archaeology, 106, 268, 275
Latin America, postcolonial theory, 235–38, 405–10
Latin American social archaeology, 237, 405–10
law, 66, 93–99, 107, 148, 153, 219, 242, 245–53, 267–81, 305, 394, 483–85, 488
Lebanon, 53–54, 56, 58
Lebanon, French colonialism, 243, 295–302

liberalism, 23, 259
litigation, 267, 271
local, 36, 56–58, 78, 118, 120, 135, 141–43, 215–22, 288, 291, 298–300, 312–17, 355, 370, 402–03, 405–10, 417–20, 422–23, 438, 446–50, 460, 465, 471–72, 498–500
local collaboration, 220, 405–10, 446
local communities, 58, 219–22, 314, 355, 395, 402, 406–10, 417–18, 420, 447–48, 465
local involvement, 409
looting, 45, 56, 96, 104, 247, 286, 291, 303, 305–306, 461, 500

Maldives, 73, 76–77, 79
Maori, 277, 279–80, 430
marginal, 18, 20, 23, 62, 189, 190, 215, 217, 220, 236, 311, 331, 339, 368, 370, 379–80, 388, 390, 403, 462, 487, 489, 499
marginal histories, 40, 141, 451
maroon settlements, 142, 189
maroons, 189
Marx, Karl, 135, 220, 365, 472
Marxism, 82, 84–85, 88–89, 114–15, 118, 120, 324, 368–371
Marxist perspectives, 36, 85, 88, 365–71
masculinist studies, 22, 334, 338–39
materiality, 24–26, 126, 155, 215, 221, 313–15, 446, 448, 452, 500
Maya peoples, the Maya, 333, 402, 405–08
Maya, archaeology, 336, 406–08
mediation, 86, 142
Meiji, the, 86, 88, 90, 93, 96, 103, 106
Memmi, Albert, 45
Mesoamerica, 333
methodology, 26, 36, 39, 87, 99, 114, 127, 215, 275, 402, 415, 431, 462, 464, 497, 501
Mexico, 146, 191, 303, 333–34, 402, 405, 406, 408–09
Middle Ages, 142, 206

Middle East, 20, 40–41, 51–53, 128, 209, 446
middle-class positionality and professionalization, 134, 192–93, 328, 333
mimicry, 21, 156, 316
modernity, 19, 20, 26, 35, 85, 134–35, 303, 315, 324, 352, 376, 381, 446
Morgan, Lewis Henry, 24
multivocality, 137, 216, 221–22, 324, 339, 402, 431
museum acquisitions, 286, 297, 304, 306–07
museum collections, 26, 67, 70, 105, 243, 247–49, 251–52, 257–64, 285–86, 289, 291, 296–97, 303–07, 316, 420, 454
museums, 26, 40, 53–54, 56, 62, 63, 65, 67, 69, 70, 93, 94, 95–97, 99, 101, 105, 107, 204, 218, 219–20, 228, 236, 242–43, 245, 247–49, 251–53, 258–64, 285–86, 288–91, 295–302, 303–08, 313, 316–17, 360, 420, 446, 450, 454, 462, 464, 466, 478, 482, 484, 490, 500–01

NAGPRA, criticism, 241–42, 245–46
NAGPRA, cultural affiliation, 66, 251–52
NAGPRA, relationship, 61, 70, 290, 394
Napoleon, 35, 51
National Body of Japan, 81, 85–87, 88, 89–90
National Historic Preservation Act of 1966, USA, 483
national identity, 24, 55, 103, 243, 285, 297
National Museum of the American Indian Act (NMAIA), 248–50
National NAGPRA Review Committee, 251–52
nationalism, 19, 24, 35, 36, 43, 54–55, 95, 118, 120, 136, 202, 230, 291, 311–12, 315, 316, 352, 416, 446, 459, 461
nationalist narratives, 55–56
nation-state, role of, 133
Native American , 23, 61–70, 142, 145–57, 187–88, 241–42, 245–53, 287–90, 354, 357, 359, 393–97, 414, 484–86

Native American Graves Protection and Repatriation Act (NAGPRA), 61, 66, 70, 148, 241–42, 245–53, 280, 290, 394, 397, 484–85; *see also* NAGPRA
Native Title, 166, 176, 242, 267–81, 323
Near East, 35, 51–58, 243
Near Eastern archaeology, 51–58
neocolonialism, 19, 36, 45, 73, 77–78, 129, 149, 185, 191
neocolonialist, 120, 194
neoliberal, 44, 56, 450, 474
Nepal, 73, 76–77, 79
New Zealand, 169, 262, 268, 275, 277, 279–80, 288, 323, 380
NGO (nongovernmental organization), 56–58, 218, 238, 448, 449
Nihon-Shoki, 84–87, 107
non-federally recognized tribes, 251
North America, 23, 36, 51, 53–55, 61–70, 145–57, 166, 190–92, 246, 247, 258, 286, 313, 328, 332, 335–36, 339, 354, 393–95, 415
North Korea, 105
Northern Ireland, 199–201, 203–06, 209

objects of cultural patrimony , 242, 249, 257, 259–61, 263, 406
Oceania, 40
Opium War, 81, 82–83, 90
oral testimony, 269, 272
Orient, the, 41, 126–27, 295–96
Orientalism, 20, 126–27, 128, 296
"Other,", the, 26, 35, 39, 41, 43, 192, 311, 430

Pakistan, 73, 75, 77, 79, 227–28
Palestine, 53–54, 58
Parthenon marbles, 286, 306, 308
Partition, 75, 200, 227–28
Peru, 136, 191, 333, 338
Philippines, 269, 275
Phoenician, 26, 45, 55, 298–300
photography, tourist destinations, 100–03

policy, 43, 87, 103, 117–18, 242–43, 257, 258–61, 263–64, 278–79, 286–91, 298, 314, 370, 438, 487–90, 499, 501
politics of the past, 237, 311–15
Portuguese colonization, 43, 74, 188, 215
postcolonial critique, 14, 17–23, 25–26, 82, 128, 165–67, 204, 295, 327, 355–58, 401–504
postcolonial praxis, 358–59
postcolonial, science, 125–32, 227–32
postcolonialism, definitions, 14, 18–23, 199–200
postcolonialism, heterogeneous experiences, 215
postcolonialism, intersections of archaeology, 17–20, 23–27, 43–46, 61–62, 128–29, 133–34, 145–48, 156–57, 185–89, 192–94, 199–201, 205–10, 215–22, 351–52, 388, 482–84, 495–97
postcolonialism, Marxist critiques, 365–71
postfeminist studies, 22
post-Marxism, 368–69
post-medieval, 204–09
postmodernism, 19, 36, 89, 129, 236, 312, 331, 333, 336, 338, 339, 370
postprocessualism, 44, 85, 115, 236, 324, 337, 353
poststructuralism, 19, 311, 333, 402, 430
pre-capitalist societies, 114
preservation legislation, 94–97, 228, 260, 288, 482–83
professionalization, 24, 165, 312
public archaeology, 403, 459–66, 481–91
public interest anthropology, 402, 471–78
public interest ethnography, 475–76

Qing (Ch'ing) dynasty, 81–83, 96
queer studies, 22, 126, 333, 336, 488

racial identities, 353, 375
reparation, 242, 257, 287, 403, 446, 462
repatriation, 14, 68, 70, 241–43, 245–53, 257–64, 286, 288–90, 303–08, 313, 358, 394–97, 402, 407–08, 410, 413–14, 446, 451, 484–85, 495, 501
representation, politics of representation, 20–23, 235–38, 277–80, 311–13, 440, 495–97, 499–500
resistance, 21, 35, 151, 155–56, 170, 171, 175, 188–89, 208–09, 268, 312, 316–17, 324, 357, 370, 380
restitution, 18, 23, 44, 241–322, 446, 495, 501
rock art, 63–65, 67–68, 168, 169, 170, 174–75, 268, 450
romanticism, 133, 134–37, 202
Russia, 96, 106, 113–21. *See also* Soviet Union
Russian colonialism, 36, 113–21, 142, 146, 151, 153–54
Russian empire, 36, 113–21

sacred objects, 148, 241, 249, 261–64, 465
safeguards, 118, 229, 291
Saginaw Chippewa, 62, 68
Said, Edward, 20, 23, 37, 39, 126–29, 166, 201, 216, 220, 295–96, 389
science, 24, 36, 39, 40, 125–29, 136, 143, 227–32, 263, 311, 395, 397, 441, 473, 500
Second World War. *See* World War II
settler colonies, 136, 166–67, 267–80, 323, 432, 495
sexuality, 22, 147, 151, 156, 237, 327–40
Shang period, 83
Showa, the, 88
slave resistance, 188–89
slavery, 120, 142, 185–94, 367–68, 369, 462, 465
South Africa, 17, 136, 185, 217, 280, 323, 334, 370, 445, 449–53
South Asia, 36, 73–79, 227
South Korea, 84–85, 95, 104–05
Soviet Union, 36, 37, 113–21
Spanish colonialism, 141–42, 146–57, 187–91, 339, 357

Spivak, Gayatri, 21, 221, 323, 369, 371, 496
Sri Lanka, 73, 76–79
standpoint theory, 402, 437
State of Israel, 53–55
strategic essentialisms, 291, 323, 371; *see also* essentialism
subaltern, 20–21, 23, 57, 141–42, 185–87, 192–94, 215–17, 220–22, 311, 316, 368, 370
Subaltern Studies Group, 20, 368
subjectivity, 21, 36, 125–29, 228, 231, 337, 381, 496–97, 499, 501
symbolic violence, 217, 286
Syria, 53–55, 58, 300

Taisho, the, 88, 108
Tara, 200, 202
terminology, 149, 150, 199, 329, 353–54, 358, 367, 464
Third World, 77–78, 236, 237
Third World feminisms, 22–23
Tokyo Anthropological Society, 96–97
Torres Strait, 168, 258–64, 402, 413–23, 439
tourism, 36, 55, 93–95, 100–08, 136–37, 155, 304, 323, 406–07, 415, 448, 450–53, 500
tourist images and photography, 100–03
traditional Indigenous knowledge, 62–67, 275, 276, 280, 418, 434–40
traditional owner, 242–43, 258, 272, 280–81, 476
transcultural forms, 19
transnational histories, 25–26, 238, 500–01
tribal archaeology, 68
Trigger, Bruce, 23, 37, 39, 43, 103, 133–34, 135
triple bind, 22
Turkey, 40, 53, 58, 460

UNESCO, 287, 289, 290, 314, 316, 449, 450, 460
United Nations, 17, 137, 280
United States (US), 17, 43–45, 62, 68, 70, 82, 85, 89, 129, 136–37, 146, 148, 152, 185–86, 188, 190–92, 207, 236, 241, 242, 245–53, 260, 263, 268, 275, 277–78, 280, 287–89, 292, 323, 328–35, 337–38, 354, 358, 379, 388, 394, 397, 403, 416, 462, 474, 482–83, 485, 487, 501
universal museums, 243, 285–86, 288–90, 303–07, 501
USSR. *See* Soviet Union

value, 40, 46, 104, 135, 171, 175, 273, 285–86, 297–98, 303–04, 305–06, 308, 312, 314, 317, 352, 409, 447, 453, 459, 472–74, 500
Vietnam, 113
voice, 22–23, 27, 62, 90, 142, 216–17, 220–22, 243, 249, 259, 298, 313, 325, 379, 387, 390, 402, 436–37, 462, 464, 496

Western academy, 23, 435
Wheeler, R.E.M., 75, 229
World Archaeological Congress (WAC), 17–18, 27, 137, 230, 414, 485, 499
World War II, 18–19, 82, 84, 86–89, 113, 115, 120, 136, 286, 353

Yoruba, 387, 497
Yucatán Peninsula, 136
Yucatec Maya, 402, 405–07

Zimbabwe, Great Zimbabwe, 243, 312–17, 329, 354–55

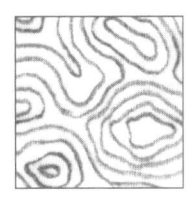

ABOUT THE CONTRIBUTORS

Fernando Armstrong-Fumero is an assistant professor of anthropology at Smith College. He completed a Ph.D. at Stanford University in 2007 and a joint B.A./M.A. at the University of Pennsylvania in 2000. He has conducted ethnographic and historical research in Yucatán since 1997. His research documents how the narratives that rural Maya speakers use to participate in contemporary multicultural politics have their roots in local experiences of earlier social and political institutions, questioning the assumption that local engagements with post–Cold War identity politics are necessarily conditioning the emergence of new, essentialized identities. He also collaborates with Julio Hoil Gutierrez on a community-based heritage project in the community of Xcalakdzonot.

Sonya Atalay is assistant professor of anthropology at Indiana University, an archaeologist with active fieldwork projects in the Middle East and the Great Lakes region of the United States. Her research has two primary aspects. The first relates to community-based participatory research designs, Indigenous forms of heritage management and stewardship, and the ethics of community and public collaboration. Her work in this area involves development of a participatory research program at the Neolithic site of Çatalhöyük, Turkey, and collaborative research with Anishinabe communities in the Great Lakes region of North America. The second research area involves clay and ceramic analysis and an interest in foodways and cooking technologies. As the clay object specialist at Çatalhöyük, Turkey, she has been investigating the production and use of clay cooking devices such as clay balls, hearths, and ovens through laboratory analysis and excavation, as well as through a series of experimental and ethnoarchaeological investigations.

Whitney Battle-Baptiste is an assistant professor of anthropology at the University of Massachusetts-Amherst. She received her Ph.D. in May 2004 from the African Diaspora Graduate Program in Anthropology at the University of Texas at Austin. Her dissertation is titled "A Yard to Sweep: Exploring Race, Gender and the Enslaved Landscape." She is currently working on her first book, which focuses on the intersection of race, gender, and cultural landscapes in historical archaeology. Her work also explores areas of symbolism and expression in African diasporic material culture and gender in the formation of African-American cultural identities. Dr. Battle-Baptiste has taught courses in anthropology and the African diaspora, African-American material and expressive culture, race and the American museum, gender in hip-hop culture, and the archaeology of slavery. Her research interests include black feminist theory, African diaspora archaeology, and African-American expressive and material culture.

Alexander A. Bauer is an assistant professor of anthropology at Queens College, CUNY, having earned his Ph.D. from the University of Pennsylvania. His doctoral research focused on the Bronze Age material from the Sinop Region Archaeological Project, an integrated regional project aimed at exploring the dynamics of interaction and culture change in the Black Sea region from the Neolithic to the present day, on which he now serves as assistant director. This work relates to his larger interest in the interpretation of material culture and social interaction, which is the subject of a forthcoming volume co-edited with Anna Agbe-Davies, *Archaeologies of Trade and Exchange* (Left Coast Press, 2010). Since 2005, he has also served as editor of the *International Journal of Cultural Property*, an interdisciplinary journal on cultural heritage law and policy issues published by Cambridge University Press. Before moving to Queens College, he taught courses on cultural heritage at Princeton University, George Washington University, and the University of Pennsylvania Law School, and he is co-authoring a new text on the subject with Stephen Urice of the University of Miami School of Law.

O. Hugo Benavides is associate professor of anthropology at Fordham University where he also directs the M.A. Program in Humanities and Sciences. His initial archaeological focus provided him an extensive fieldwork practice in Ecuador and two summers at the Roman site of Pompeii. This interest in the politics of the past is present in his first book, *Making Ecuadorian Histories: Four Centuries of Defining Power* (University of Texas Press, 2004). His two latest books, *The Politics of Sentiment: Imagining and Remembering Guayaquil* (UT Press, 2006) and *Drugs, Thugs and Divas: Telenovelas and Narco-Dramas in Latin America* (UT Press, 2008), assess the role of history and popular culture in the production of political hegemony. His articles have appeared in *Latin American Antiquity*, *Social Text*, *Critique of*

Anthropology, Journal of Latin American and Caribbean Anthropology, Arqueología Suramericana, and *ICONOS*. He currently lives with his partner in Brooklyn, New York.

Liam M. Brady is an honorary research fellow at the Centre for Australian Indigenous Studies at Monash University (Australia) and an ARC postdoctoral fellow in the School of Social and Cultural Studies at the University of Western Australia. He recently completed his Ph.D. dissertation on rock art and material culture from the Torres Strait region in far northeastern Australia. He first undertook fieldwork with Torres Strait Islander and Aboriginal communities in 2001 and has since been involved with various research projects elsewhere in Australia and Canada. He is currently continuing his research into the nature and antiquity of occupation in the southwestern Torres Strait islands, and beginning rock art research in southwestern Gulf of Carpentaria, Northern Territory. His main research interests are rock art, interregional interaction, island and coastal archaeology, and archaeology and social identity. In 2006 he was awarded Monash University's Mollie Holman Doctoral Medal for his Ph.D. dissertation.

Ashish Chadha is a lecturer in anthropology, South Asian studies, and film studies at Yale University. He graduated with an M.A. in archaeology from Deccan College, Puné, and a Ph.D. in anthropology from Stanford University. His dissertation research was an ethnographic investigation of Archaeological Survey of India, with a specific emphasis on the epistemic culture of archaeological practices in postcolonial South Asia. His research interest also includes the history of archaeological practices in colonial India.

Dilip K. Chakrabarti, Ph.D., Hon.D.Litt., is emeritus professor of South Asian archaeology at Cambridge University. His recent publications include *The Oxford Companion to Indian Archaeology* (Oxford University Press, 2006), *Archaeological Geography of the Ganga Plain: The Upper Ganga* (Munshiram Manoharla, 2008), and *The Battle for Ancient India, An Essay in the Sociopolitics of Indian Archaeology* (Aryan, 2008). His forthcoming publications include *Between the Yamuna and the Ravi: Archaeological Geography of Haryana and Indian Panjab* and *Globalization of Indian Archaeology and Other Essays*. He was awarded (2007) the S.C. Chakrabarti Memorial Medal of the Asiatic Society of Bengal for his contributions to Indian archaeology, and the Gurudeva Ranade Award (2007) of the Indian Archaeology Society, Delhi, for his book *The Oxford Companion to Indian Archaeology*.

Joe Crouch is a Ph.D. candidate with the Centre for Australian Indigenous Studies, Monash University, Australia. He has practiced partnership archaeology with Indigenous Torres Strait Islander communities for the past seven years, with a focus on the role of their non-residential islands in terms of seascape settlement history.

Sarah Croucher is an assistant professor of anthropology at Wesleyan University,

Connecticut. She is a historical archaeologist, whose research focuses on 18th- and 19th-century Omani colonialism in East Africa. She has directed survey and excavation projects centered on clove plantations on Zanzibar, and at the town of Ujiji in Western Tanzania, with particular interests in how the archaeological data can help to investigate questions of changing identities and the growth of capitalism during this period. Her Ph.D. won the 2008 Society for Historical Archaeology dissertation award, and she is currently revising this for publication, tentatively titled *Capitalism and Cloves*. She is also the co-author, with E. C. Casella, of *The Alderley Sandhills Project: An Archaeology of Community Life in (Post-) Industrial England*, published by Manchester University Press (2010).

Jon Daehnke is a postdoctoral fellow in the humanities at Stanford University. His research interests focus on cultural heritage and the law, public representations of heritage and memory, interactions between descendant communities and anthropologists, and the archaeology of landscapes. He has conducted research throughout the western United States, but focuses on the heritage landscape of the Pacific Northwest of North America. He has published an article on heritage stewardship and the complexities of federal recognition of American Indian nations in the *Journal of Social Archaeology*, and has forthcoming publications on NAGPRA compliance in Hawaii, and on human response to catastrophic changes in landscape. He is currently working on a manuscript that documents and explores the dynamic and contested nature of Indigenous identity, federal recognition, and tangible and intangible heritage on the Columbia River.

Bruno David is QEII Research Fellow at the Programme for Australian Indigenous Archaeology, School of Geography and Environmental Science at Monash University. He is currently researching the archaeology of spiritscapes in Torres Strait and Papua New Guinea (PNG), and the archaeology of long-distance maritime trade networks along the southern coast of PNG. His latest books are the edited *Handbook of Landscape Archaeology* (Left Coast Press, 2008), *Gelam's Homeland* (Queensland Museum, 2008), and *The Social Archaeology of Australian Indigenous Societies* (Aboriginal Studies Press, 2006).

Pavel M. Dolukhanov was born and educated in St. Petersburg, Russia. Until 1990, as a staff member of the Institute of Archaeology, Russian Academy of Sciences, he conducted numerous field projects in various parts of the former USSR. From 1991 until his recent death in December 2009, he was based in the United Kingdom; his latest position was as professor of East European archaeology at Newcastle University. His major publications are *Ecology and Economy in Neolithic Eastern Europe* (Duckworth, 1978), *The Early Slavs:Eastern Europe from the Initial Settlement to the Kievan Rus* (Longman, 1996); and *Sources of Ethnicity* (Evropeiskii Dom, 2000, in Russian).

Magnus Fiskesjö teaches at Cornell University in anthropology and Asian studies, including on global heritage issues. He was educated in his native Sweden, in China, and at the University of Chicago (Ph.D. 2000, jointly in anthropology/archaeology and in East Asian languages and civilizations). In 2000–2005 he was director of the Museum of Far Eastern Antiquities (MFEA) in Stockholm, Sweden, and since then has been a frequent contributor to the global debates over repatriation and collecting. At the MFEA, he reconstructed parts of the museum, including a new permanent display of the museum's founding collections from China's prehistory, and published a bilingual book probing the history and status of these collections (*China before China: Johan Gunnar Andersson, Ding Wenjiang, and the Discovery of China's Prehistory*, co-authored with the Chinese archaeologist Chen Xingcan, 2004). He also studies and writes on the anthropology, politics, and history of inter-ethnic relations in China and Southeast Asia.

Joost Fontein's Ph.D. explored the politics of landscape around the World Heritage site of Great Zimbabwe. It won the ASA UK Audrey Richards Prize in 2004, and a monograph entitled *The Silence of Great Zimbabwe: Contested Landscapes and the Power of Heritage* was published in 2006. He is currently writing a book entitled *Water and Graves: Belonging, Sovereignty and the Political Materiality of Landscape around Lake Mutirikwi in Southern Zimbabwe*, which focuses on the complex reciprocity of material and imaginative aspects of landscape and water in contests over belonging and sovereignty, in the context of land reform and the ongoing reconfiguration of the postcolonial state of Zimbabwe. As a member of the Bones Collective research group at Edinburgh, he is developing a collaborative research project exploring the affective presence and emotive materiality of human remains. After guest-editing a special issue on "The Power of Water," he was appointed editor of the *Journal of Southern African Studies* in 2008. With colleagues at the Centre of African Studies, he is also a founding editor of *Critical African Studies*. He is currently employed as lecturer in social anthropology at Edinburgh.

Alfredo González-Ruibal is a tenured scientist with the Spanish Council for Scientific Research (CSIC). He has been a postdoctoral fellow at Stanford University and an assistant professor of prehistory at the Complutense University of Madrid. Trained as a prehistoric archaeologist, his work focuses now on the archaeology of the contemporary past and ethnoarchaeology. He is interested in modernity, war, repressive technologies, dictatorship, globalization, and colonialism. He has explored colonial phenomena in 1st-millennium B.C. Europe and in 20th-century Africa, using postcolonial theory. His publications have appeared in major international journals, including the *Journal of Social Archaeology*, *Current Anthropology*, and the *Journal of Anthropological Archaeology*. He has carried out fieldwork in Spain, Italy, Brazil, Sudan, and Ethiopia. At present, he does research on the Sudanese-Ethiopian borderland, a long-term project addressing issues of colonialism, conflict, cultural contact, and material culture.

Phil Gordon is the Aboriginal Heritage project officer at the Australian Museum in Sydney. He advises Aboriginal communities on issues such as Aboriginal Museum outreach and repatriation of Aboriginal human remains and other significant cultural property, and provides advice for various government agencies on cultural heritage issues and policy development. He plays an important role in setting up and planning cultural centers and *keeping places*, as well as advising on ongoing training needs.

Michael Green has worked with Indigenous communities in Australia, Papua New Guinea, and New Zealand for over 20 years, beginning with his Ph.D. field research into prehistoric patterns of cranial variation in Papua New Guinea in the latter half of the 1980s. Since that time, he has been responsible for the investigation and repatriation of ancestral Aboriginal skeletal remains, lectured on biological anthropology in the Anthropology Department at the University of Otago, New Zealand, and conducted research into the origins of the Lapita people. He has had management roles in university grants and student administration, and more recently he led a team that was responsible for the delivery of cultural heritage services to some of Victoria's Aboriginal communities. Most recently, he was head of the Indigenous Cultures Department at Museum Victoria, where he led a dedicated team responsible for the care and management of some of Australia's most unique and precious Indigenous objects of material culture. He is currently working as a private consultant, providing a variety of services in biological anthropology, archaeology, Indigenous heritage and museum project management.

Julio Hoil Gutierrez is a graduate student of history at CIESAS Peninsular in Mérida, Yucatán, Mexico. Before beginning to study history, he earned an undergraduate degree in archaeology, with research experience at Dzibilchaltun, Chichén Itzá, and other Mayan sites on the Yucatán Peninsula. A native speaker of Yucatec Maya, he has written several of short stories that have won prizes in major Indigenous-language literature competitions, and he has developed a number of applied writing projects for students in rural communities. His current research interests focus on documenting long-term cultural and social processes through continuities and changes in the everyday material culture of Mayan communities that have taken place from the pre-Hispanic to the postcolonial period. He also collaborates with Fernando Armstrong-Fumero on a community-based heritage project in the community of Xcalakdzonot.

Amy Lonetree (Ho-Chunk) is an assistant professor of American studies at the University of California, Santa Cruz. Her scholarly work focuses on the representation of Native American history and memory in national and tribal museums, and she has conducted research at the Smithsonian's National Museum of the American Indian, the British Museum, the Mille Lacs Indian Museum (a tribal museum in Minnesota), and the Ziibiwing Center for Anishinabe Culture and Lifeways in Michigan. She has published articles based on this research in *Public Historian*, *American*

Indian Quarterly, and *Journal of American History*, and recently completed an edited collection with Amanda J. Cobb, *The National Museum of the American Indian: Critical Conversations* (University of Nebraska Press, 2008). She is currently working on a manuscript that explores the complexities of the changing historical relationship between Indigenous people and museums, and the potential for museums to serve as sites of decolonization.

Ania Loomba is Catharine Bryson Professor of English at the University of Pennsylvania. Her books include *Gender, Race, Renaissance Drama* (Manchester University Press, 1989), *Colonialism/Postcolonialism* (Routledge, 1998), and *Shakespeare, Race, and Colonialism* (Oxford University Press, 2002). Most recently, she has compiled and co-edited *Race in Early Modern England: A Documentary Companion* (Palgrave Macmillan, 2007). She is also co-editor of *Postcolonial Studies and Beyond* (Duke University Press, 2005) and *Postcolonial Shakespeares* (Routledge, 1998).

Gavin Lucas is a lecturer in archaeology with the University of Iceland. His major research interests include the archaeology of the modern world and archaeological theory; recent publications include *Critical Approaches to Fieldwork* (Routledge, 2001), *Archaeologies of the Contemporary Past* (with Victor Buchli, Routledge, 2001), *An Archaeology of Colonial Identity* (Kluwer, 2004), and *The Archaeology of Time* (Routledge, 2005). He has conducted research in Britain, South Africa, and Iceland and is currently investigating a 17th- and 18th-century episcopal manor in the southwest of Iceland.

Jane Lydon is a senior research fellow at the Centre for Australian Indigenous Studies at Monash University, Melbourne, Australia. She has worked as an archaeologist for over 20 years across private, government, and academic spheres. Her books include *Eye Contact: Photographing Indigenous Australians* (Duke University Press, 2005) and *Fantastic Dreaming: The Archaeology of an Aboriginal Mission* (AltaMira, 2009).

Carol McDavid has a master's degree in anthropology from the University of Houston and a Ph.D. in archaeology from the University of Cambridge. Her research focuses on historical archaeology of the African diaspora, and on exploring the intersections between archaeology/history and public agendas/interests (either referred to as "public archaeology" or "archaeological ethnography"). She is currently the executive director of the Community Archaeology Research Institute, Inc., and co-directs Public Archaeology for the Yates Community Archaeology Project, both located in Houston, Texas. For the last 13 years has also served as advisor to and member of the board of directors of the Levi Jordan Plantation Historical Society (information about all projects can be seen online at *www.publicarchaeology.org*). She holds adjunct appointments at the University of Houston and Rice University, is on the boards of directors for The Heritage Society and the Houston History Association, and participates in several other history-based community groups.

Fred McGhee is president of Fred L. McGhee & Associates (*www.flma.org*), an Austin, Texas–based company that is the only African-American owned and operated archaeological consulting company in the United States. He is a historical anthropologist and maritime archaeologist whose work focuses on African diaspora–themed research in Texas, the Caribbean, and the Hawaiian Islands. Between 2001 and 2003, he served as the U.S. Air Force's first archaeologist in Hawai'i, where his base was recognized in 2004 as having the best cultural resource management program in the Department of Defense. His most recent work examines the history and archaeology of the plantation in Trinidad & Tobago and compares it with Hawai'i and elsewhere. He earned his B.S. in linguistics from Northeastern University in Boston and his M.A. and Ph.D. in anthropology from the University of Texas at Austin.

Lynn Meskell is professor of anthropology at Stanford University and is affiliated with the Rock Art Research Institute, University of the Witwatersrand. She has conducted fieldwork in the Middle East, the Mediterranean, and Africa. Her most recent books include *Object Worlds in Ancient Egypt: Material Biographies Past and Present* (Berg, 2004), *Embedding Ethics*, co-edited with Peter Pels (Berg, 2005), and the edited volumes *Archaeologies of Materiality* (Blackwell, 2005) and *Cosmopolitan Archaeologies* (Duke, 2009). She is founding editor of the *Journal of Social Archaeology* (Sage) and of the Material Worlds series (Duke). Her current research examines the constructs of natural and cultural heritage and the related discourses of empowerment around the Kruger National Park, 10 years after democracy in South Africa. This forms the basis of a forthcoming book entitled *The Nature of Culture in the New South Africa*.

Koji Mizoguchi is an associate professor of archaeology at the Graduate School of Social and Cultural Studies, Kyushu University, Japan. His current research interests are in modernity and archaeological discursive formation, and social stratification, changing conceptions of time, and the transformation of self-identity. His previous publications include *An Archaeological History of Japan, 30,000 BC to AD 700* (University of Pennsylvania Press, 2002), and *Archaeology, Society and Identity in Modern Japan* (Cambridge University Press, 2006).

Karega Munene is professor of history at the School of Arts and Sciences, United States International University, Nairobi. He is a former senior staff member at National Museums of Kenya, serving as principal research scientist and head of the Division of Archaeology. He has been involved in a one-year pilot study of heritage issues in Kenya, "Museums and Counter-Museums in the Postcolony," and will be working with Dr. Lotte Hughes on a new project, "Managing Heritage, Building Peace: A Comparative Study of Museums and Memorialisation in Kenya," which has gained funding from the British Academy UK–Africa Partnerships Scheme 2007.

Paul Mullins is associate professor and chair of the Department of Anthropology at Indiana University-Purdue University, Indianapolis. His research focuses on historical archaeology, popular culture, and race and materialism in the urban Midwest. He is the author of *Race and Affluence: An Archaeology of African America and Consumer Culture* (Kluwer, 1999).

Martin Nakata is chair of Australian Indigenous Education and director of Jumbunna Indigenous House of Learning at University of Technology, Sydney, Australia. His primary research interest is in the area of that complex space where Indigenous and non-Indigenous disciplines and knowledge systems converge. He has undertaken research in various areas relating to the inscription of Indigenous people in Western histories and disciplines, in the school, VET and tertiary education sectors, and in knowledge management systems in the library sector. He has presented over 20 plenary and keynote addresses at national and international conferences in various countries, and published over 70 articles on Australian Indigenous people in various academic journals and anthologies, including edited books on *Indigenous Peoples, Racism and the United Nations* (Common Ground Publishing, 2001), *Australian Indigenous Knowledge and Libraries* (Australian Academic and Research Libraries, 2005), and *Anger and Indigenous Men* (Federation Press, 2008). His book *Disciplining the Savages—Savaging the Disciplines* (Aboriginal Studies Press, 2007) relates to topics in this Handbook.

John W. Norder is a member of the Spirit Lake Dakota Nation and faculty in Michigan State University's Department of Anthropology. His studies have focused on past and contemporary North American Indigenous peoples in areas of landscape perception, environmental use, hunter-gatherer ritual and religion, rock art research, and community-based collaborative research on heritage management issues. Recent work has focused on the intersections of social memory and the development of, and interaction with, cultural landscapes, as well as the nature and role of Indigenous people in professional archaeological research and discourse. He has further interests in addressed issues of the repatriation of Native American human remains and the ethics of DNA research among Indigenous communities as a member of the National Congress of American Indians Commission on Repatriation and Burial Sites Protection, the Society for American Archaeology's Committee on Repatriation, and various other professional forums.

Charles E. Orser, Jr., is curator of historical archaeology at the New York State Museum and Distinguished Professor Emeritus at Illinois State University. He has over 30 years of experience in historical archaeology gained on three continents. His principal research interests are in social theory and modern-world archaeology. His most recent field research has been undertaken in Brazil and Ireland. He is the author of, among other books, *Historical Archaeology* (with Brian Fagan; Prentice-Hall, 1997), *A Historical Archaeology of the Modern World* (Plenum, 1996), *The Archaeology of Race and

Racialization in Historic America (University Press of Florida, 2007), and *Unearthing Hidden Ireland: Historical Archaeology at Ballykilcline, County Roscommon* (Wordwell Press, 2006). He is also the founder and editor of the *International Journal of Historical Archaeology*.

Hyung Il Pai is an associate professor at the Department of East Asian Languages and Cultural Studies, University of California, Santa Barbara. She received her Ph.D. from Harvard University's Department of Anthropology where she majored in East Asian archaeology. She has conducted field and archival research in the Republic of Korea and Japan. She has been invited to be a research fellow at Seoul National University, Tokyo National Research Institute of Cultural Properties, Tokyo University Oriental Institute, Kyoto University Department of Archaeology, and the International Research Center for Japanese Studies. Her book *Constructing "Korean Origins": Archaeology, Historiography, and Racial Myth* was published by the Asia Center, Harvard University Press, in 2000. She has published articles on topics ranging from Japanese colonial anthropology/archaeology, to Han dynasty archaeology, state formation, museum studies, and archaeological heritage management, in international journals such as *Antiquity*, *World Archaeology*, *East Asian History*, and *Korean Studies*.

Alistair Paterson is an archaeologist in the School of Social and Cultural Studies at the University of Western Australia whose primary research interest has been the archaeology of culture contact between Indigenous peoples and others. His latest book, *The Lost Legions: Culture Contact in Colonial Australia* (AltaMira, 2007), offers a discussion of the interaction between Australian Aborigines and the first European pastoralists, with comparisons to similar interactions elsewhere around the world. His recent research encompasses historical rock art, sites along coastal Australia related to precolonial and colonial activities, and the colonization of Northwestern Australia. In 2009, he was an Honorary Visiting Fellow at the University of Copenhagen Institut for Tværkulturelle og Regionale Studier.

Tom Patterson is Distinguished Professor of Anthropology at the University of California, Riverside. He conducted archaeological research in Peru during the 1960s; his current research focuses on the historical development of anthropology and archaeology in the political-economic, social, and cultural contexts shaped by nation-states; critical analyses of contemporary trends in social theory; comparative political economy; class and state formation; the intersection of class, race, and gender; theories of change and development, especially the political-economic, social, and cultural changes associated with imperialism and the processes of globalization; and critical investigations of how the realities of past societies are constituted and appropriated into the fabric of everyday life today. His publications include *Karl Marx, Anthropologist* (Berg, 2009) and *Marx's Ghost: Conversations with Archaeologists* (Berg, 2003).

Benjamin Porter is an assistant professor of Near Eastern archaeology in the University of California, Berkeley's Near Eastern Studies Department and a curator of Near Eastern antiquities at the Phoebe A. Hearst Museum of Anthropology. He is co-director of the Dhiban Excavation and Development Project in central Jordan, a community archaeology project. Porter is writing a book about social life in Near Eastern marginal societies.

Louise Ströbeck is finishing her doctoral thesis in archaeology at the Department of Archaeology and Ancient History, Lund University, in Sweden. After studies in, among others, archaeology, history, and feminist and gender studies, she worked as a field archaeologist. Ströbeck returned to the university to pursue studies and research for a Ph.D.; her thesis is titled "Engendering the Roman Iron Age and Society in southeast Scandinavia 0–AD 400." Ströbeck is affiliated with a multi-disciplinary research project in archaeology, historical archaeology, and history of religions, where she has performed much of her research on the former perception of the Roman Iron Age and formulated new perspectives—considering sex, gender, sexuality, and the body—on that time period. She is also member of the Gender Group in archaeology at Lund University, which played a key role in the introduction and elaboration of gender perspectives in the archaeology programs at the university. Furthermore, Ströbeck has taught feminist and gender perspectives in archaeological research, and method and theory in archaeology. Burial archaeology, the Roman Empire and Scandinavia, feminist and gender theories (general, and implementation in archaeology), and world heritage are her main research areas.

Uzma Z. Rizvi is an assistant professor of anthropology and urban studies at Pratt Institute. Since receiving her doctorate from the Department of Anthropology, University of Pennsylvania, in 2007, Rizvi has been faculty fellow and chair for the Initiative on Art, Community Development and Social Change at the Pratt Center (2007–2008) and a postdoctoral fellow in the humanities at Stanford University (2008–2009). *Archaeology and the Postcolonial Critique* (co-edited with M. Liebmann, AltaMira Press, 2008) served as muse for this volume. Her research work in India on community-based archaeology and public interest projects can be read about in "Accounting for Multiple Desires: Decolonizing Methodologies, Archaeology and the Public Interest" (*India Review*, 2006) and in an upcoming manuscript based on her archaeological survey of Northeastern Rajasthan. She is currently completing a catalog manuscript for British Archaeological Reports, *Crafting Capital: Third Millennium BC Copper Arrowheads from Ganeshwar, Rajasthan*.

Peggy Reeves Sanday is professor of anthropology in the Department of Anthropology at the University of Pennsylvania. She is the author of eight books and many articles. Her fields of interest are feminist theory, ethnography, sex and gender, matriarchal studies, and multicultural theory. She is currently working on the development of a paradigm for public interest anthropology which combines on-the-ground practice with theory and change for the 21st century.

Sandra Scham is an archaeologist in the Anthropology Department of the Catholic University of America in Washington, DC. She is the current Washington correspondent for *Archaeology* magazine and the former editor of the journal *Near Eastern Archaeology*. In addition to teaching the archaeology of the ancient Near East at Catholic University, she has also taught at the University of Maryland and Jerusalem University College in Israel. She has done archaeological work in Israel, Jordan, and southeastern Turkey. Between 2001 and 2005, she was the co-director of an Israeli and Palestinian cooperative heritage project funded by the U.S. Department of State—the first such project ever undertaken. From 2008 to 2010 she has been an American Association for the Advancement of Science (AAAS) Science and Technology Policy Fellow in the Asia and Middle East Bureaus of the United States Agency for International Development.

Peter Schmidt is professor of anthropology and former director of the Center for African Studies at the University of Florida. He has held academic posts at Brown University, Makerere University (Uganda), the University of Dar es Salaam, the University of Asmara (Eritrea), and the University of California at Berkeley. He is the author of 8 books and more than 90 articles, chapters, monographs, and films in historical archaeology, African archaeology, ethnoarchaeology, heritage management, and human rights. He has also helped to create new departments of archaeology at the University of Dar es Salaam (1985–1987) and the University of Asmara (1998–1999), where he has also served as dean of the College of Arts and Social Sciences and chief curator of archaeology in the National Museum of Eritrea.

Stephen Silliman is an associate professor of anthropology at the University of Massachusetts Boston and serves as the graduate program director of the Historical Archaeology M.A. Program. His interests include the archaeological study of colonialism, particularly in North America on the east and west coasts; long-term Indigenous histories; social theories of agency, practice, identity, and materiality; postcolonial, community, and collaborative indigenous archaeologies (as demonstrated by his recent book, *Collaborating at the Trowel's Edge: Teaching and Learning in Indigenous Archaeology*, University of Arizona Press, 2008); and the interplay of heritage politics and social justice. He has conducted a collaborative community archaeology project and field school with the Eastern Pequot Tribal Nation in Connecticut since 2003 which is designed to put postcolonial theory into practice.

Theresa A. Singleton is associate professor of anthropology at Syracuse University. She began her study of slavery and plantations in coastal Georgia studying rice plantations. Since that time, she has conducted historical and material-culture research on various aspects of African-American life in United States, contributing to museum exhibitions as well as academic publications. She has written numerous articles and edited two books on the archaeology of African Americans: *The Archaeology of Slavery and Plantation Life* (Academic Press, 1985), and *I, Too, Am America: Archaeological Studies of African-American Life* (University Press of Virginia, 1999). For the past 10 years, she has been undertaking an archaeological study of slavery and plantation life in Cuba, focusing on coffee plantations.

Lina G. Tahan has completed a Ph.D. in archaeology and museum studies from the University of Cambridge, United Kingdom. She is currently a senior research fellow at the Centre for Tourism and Cultural Change at Leeds Metropolitan University and an affiliated scholar at the Department of Archaeology, University of Cambridge. Her research and teaching interests relate to (1) the role of the archaeologist and the museologist in tourism development; (2) the representation issues within Middle Eastern museums' collections, exhibitions and visitors; (3) the history of collections and museum development in Lebanon within the political context; and (4) the role of museums in fostering understanding in divided societies. She is an active member of the International Council of Museums (ICOM), mainly working for promoting museums in the Arab world.

Peter Veth is trained in anthropology/archaeology, with a Ph.D. in Indigenous archaeology. Since 1980 he has worked closely with Indigenous groups on their cultural heritage throughout Australia, Torres Strait, Eastern Indonesia, East Timor, and the remote Pacific. He has particular research interests in the evolution of desert and maritime societies and their different ways of defining domestic and totemic landscapes. He has published 10 volumes on archaeology, first contacts in Australia, maritime archaeology, and art and identity. He has been involved in the preparation of 14 expert witness reports for Native Title in the Federal Court of Australia—the largest of which was Martu—covering some 200,000 square kilometers of the Western Desert. He is interested in how social science and claimant evidence is used in the legal process and how Indigenous culture and justice are portrayed in the media. He is deputy-director of the National Centre for Indigenous Studies at Australia National University (ANU) and holds adjunct chairs at ANU and Charles Darwin University and is a fellow of the Australian Academy of Humanities and Society of Antiquaries at the Australian National University.

green press
INITIATIVE

Left Coast Press is committed to preserving ancient forests and natural resources. We elected to print this title on 30% post consumer recycled paper, processed chlorine free. As a result, for this printing, we have saved:

3 Trees (40' tall and 6-8" diameter)
1 Million BTUs of Total Energy
250 Pounds of Greenhouse Gases
1,205 Gallons of Wastewater
73 Pounds of Solid Waste

Left Coast Press made this paper choice because our printer, Thomson-Shore, Inc., is a member of Green Press Initiative, a nonprofit program dedicated to supporting authors, publishers, and suppliers in their efforts to reduce their use of fiber obtained from endangered forests.

For more information, visit www.greenpressinitiative.org

Environmental impact estimates were made using the Environmental Defense Paper Calculator. For more information visit: www.papercalculator.org.

6777857